HUMAN DEVELOPMENT 97/98

Twenty-Fifth Edition

Editor

Karen L. Freiberg
University of Maryland, Baltimore

Dr. Karen Freiberg has an interdisciplinary educational and employment background in nursing, education, and developmental psychology. She received her B.S. from the State University of New York at Plattsburgh, her M.S. from Cornell University, and her Ph.D. from Syracuse University. She has worked as a school nurse, a pediatric nurse, a public health nurse for the Navajo Indians, an associate project director for a child development clinic, a researcher in several areas of child development, and a university professor. She is the author of an award-winning textbook, *Human Development: A Life-Span Approach,* which is now in its fourth edition. She is currently on the faculty at the University of Maryland, Baltimore County.

Annual Editions
A Library of Information from the Public Press

Dushkin Publishing Group/Brown & Benchmark Publishers
Sluice Dock, Guilford, Connecticut 06437

Visit us on the Internet—http://www.dushkin.com

The Annual Editions Series

ANNUAL EDITIONS is a series of over 65 volumes designed to provide the reader with convenient, low-cost access to a wide range of current, carefully selected articles from some of the most important magazines, newspapers, and journals published today. ANNUAL EDITIONS are updated on an annual basis through a continuous monitoring of over 300 periodical sources. All ANNUAL EDITIONS have a number of features that are designed to make them particularly useful, including topic guides, annotated tables of contents, unit overviews, and indexes. For the teacher using ANNUAL EDITIONS in the classroom, an Instructor's Resource Guide with test questions is available for each volume.

VOLUMES AVAILABLE

Abnormal Psychology
Adolescent Psychology
Africa
Aging
American Foreign Policy
American Government
American History, Pre-Civil War
American History, Post-Civil War
American Public Policy
Anthropology
Archaeology
Biopsychology
Business Ethics
Child Growth and Development
China
Comparative Politics
Computers in Education
Computers in Society
Criminal Justice
Criminology
Developing World
Deviant Behavior
Drugs, Society, and Behavior
Dying, Death, and Bereavement

Early Childhood Education
Economics
Educating Exceptional Children
Education
Educational Psychology
Environment
Geography
Global Issues
Health
Human Development
Human Resources
Human Sexuality
India and South Asia
International Business
Japan and the Pacific Rim
Latin America
Life Management
Macroeconomics
Management
Marketing
Marriage and Family
Mass Media
Microeconomics

Middle East and the
    Islamic World
Multicultural Education
Nutrition
Personal Growth and Behavior
Physical Anthropology
Psychology
Public Administration
Race and Ethnic Relations
Russia, the Eurasian Republics,
    and Central/Eastern Europe
Social Problems
Social Psychology
Sociology
State and Local Government
Urban Society
Western Civilization,
    Pre-Reformation
Western Civilization,
    Post-Reformation
Western Europe
World History, Pre-Modern
World History, Modern
World Politics

Cataloging in Publication Data
Main entry under title: Annual Editions: Human development. 1997/98.
    1. Child study—Periodicals. 2. Socialization—Periodicals. 3. Old age—Periodicals. I. Freiberg, Karen L., comp. II. Title: Human development.
ISBN 0-697-37286-3   155'.05   72-91973   HQ768.A44
ISSN0278-4661

Twenty-Fifth Edition

Cover image © 1996 PhotoDisc, Inc.

Printed in the United States of America

Printed on Recycled Paper

To the Reader

In publishing ANNUAL EDITIONS we recognize the enormous role played by the magazines, newspapers, and journals of the *public press* in providing current, first-rate educational information in a broad spectrum of interest areas. Many of these articles are appropriate for students, researchers, and professionals seeking accurate, current material to help bridge the gap between principles and theories and the real world. These articles, however, become more useful for study when those of lasting value are carefully *collected, organized, indexed,* and *reproduced* in a *low-cost format,* which provides easy and permanent access when the material is needed. That is the role played by ANNUAL EDITIONS. Under the direction of each volume's *academic editor,* who is an expert in the subject area, and with the guidance of an *Advisory Board,* each year we seek to provide in each ANNUAL EDITION a current, well-balanced, carefully selected collection of the best of the public press for your study and enjoyment. We think that you will find this volume useful, and we hope that you will take a moment to let us know what you think.

The popular press discusses human development on a daily basis with a legion of explanations for what might be normal, or abnormal; correct, or incorrect; healthy, or unhealthy. Selecting a few representative articles of good quality is difficult simply due to the magnitude of the product. I am grateful to all the members of my advisory board for helping me cull through the collection and select some of the best articles available for 1997/98.

Annual Editions: Human Development 97/98 is organized according to the absolute time concept of chronos, chronological time, from conception through death. However, the reader should be aware of other relative time concepts: Kairos (God's time); preterition (retrospective time), and futurity (prospective time); transientness (short duration) and diuturnity (long duration); and recurrent time. Human development is more akin to a continuous circle of life than to a line with a discrete beginning and end. Like stars whose light reaches us thousands of years after they expire, our ancestors influence our behaviors long after their deaths. Our hopes for our futures and our children's futures also predestine our developmental milestones: education, initiations, employment, births, weddings, retirements. With an eye to the circle of life, articles have been selected which bridge the gap left by clocked time and discrete ages and stages. Thus, prenatal articles may discuss adult development and late adulthood articles may focus on grandchildren.

As you explore this anthology, you will discover that many articles ask questions that have no answers. As a student, I felt frustrated by such writing. I wanted answers, right answers, right away. Part of the lessons in tolerance that are necessary for maturity are lessons in accepting relativity and acknowledging extenuating circumstances. Life frequently has no right or wrong answers, but rather various alternatives with different consequences. Instead of right versus wrong, a more helpful consideration is "What will bring about the greater good for the greater number?" Controversies promote healthy mental exercise. Different viewpoints should be weighed against societal standards. Different cultural communities should be celebrated for what they offer in creativity and adaptability to changing circumstances. Many selections in this anthology reflect the cultural diversity and the cultural assimilation with which we live today.

The selections for *Annual Editions: Human Development 97/98* have attempted to reflect an ecological view of growth and change. Some articles deal with microsystems such as family, school, and employment. Some deal with exosystems such as television and community. Some writers discuss macrosystems such as economics and government. Most of the compositions deal with mesosystems, those which link systems such as economics, health and nutrition, schools and culture, or heredity and environment. The unique individual's contribution to every system and every system linkage is always paramount.

We hope you will be energized and enriched by the readings in this compendium. Please use the postage-paid article form on the last page to express your opinions. We value your input, and will heed it in future revisions of *Human Development*.

Karen Freiberg

Karen Freiberg, Ph.D.
Editor

Contents

UNIT 1

Genetic and Prenatal Influences on Development

Six selections discuss genetic influences on development, reproductive technology, and the effects of substance abuse on prenatal development.

The concepts in bold italics are developed in the article. For further expansion please refer to the Topic Guide and the Index.

UNIT 2

Development during Infancy and Early Childhood

Seven selections profile the impressive abilities of infants and young children, examine the ways in which children learn, and look at sex differences.

The concepts in bold italics are developed in the article. For further expansion please refer to the Topic Guide and the Index.

UNIT 3

Development during Childhood: Cognition and Schooling

Eight selections examine human development during childhood, paying specific attention to social and emotional development, cognitive and language development, and development problems.

The concepts in bold italics are developed in the article. For further expansion please refer to the Topic Guide and the Index.

UNIT 4

Development during Childhood: Family and Culture

Nine selections discuss the impact of home and culture on childrearing and child development. The topics include parenting styles, family structure, and cultural influences.

UNIT 5

Development during Adolescence and Young Adulthood

Nine selections explore a wide
range of issues and topics
concerning adolescence and
early adulthood.

The concepts in bold italics are developed in the article. For further expansion please refer to the Topic Guide and the Index.

UNIT 6

Development during Middle and Late Adulthood

Eight selections review a variety of biological and psychological aspects of aging, questioning the concept of set life stages.

The concepts in bold italics are developed in the article. For further expansion please refer to the Topic Guide and the Index.

Topic Guide

This topic guide suggests how the selections in this book relate to topics of traditional concern to students and professionals involved with the study of human development. It is useful for locating articles that relate to each other for reading and research. The guide is arranged alphabetically according to topic. Articles may, of course, treat topics that do not appear in the topic guide. In turn, entries in the topic guide do not necessarily constitute a comprehensive listing of all the contents of each selection.

TOPIC AREA	TREATED IN	TOPIC AREA	TREATED IN
Adolescence	31. Adolescence: Whose Hell Is It? 32. Teenage Turning Point 33. Sports Lift Esteem 34. What Is a Bad Kid? 35. HIV Infected Youth Speaks	Divorce	37. Who Stole Fertility? 38. Is There Love after Baby? 39. Saga of Spouse Abuse
Aggression	13. Assertiveness vs. Aggressiveness 23. Fathers' Time 24. Sibling Connections 28. Why Kids Have a Lot to Cry About 30. TV Violence: Myth and Reality 31. Adolescence: Whose Hell Is It? 34. What Is a Bad Kid?	Drug Abuse	4. Role of Lifestyle 5. Cocaine-Exposed Infants 6. Sperm under Siege 31. Adolescence: Whose Hell Is It? 33. Sports Lift Esteem 34. What Is a Bad Kid? 35. HIV Infected Youth Speaks
AIDS	35. HIV Infected Youth Speaks 36. Psychotrends	Early Childhood	10. Case Studies of Environmental Risks 11. Your Child's Brain 12. Changing Demographics 13. Assertiveness vs. Aggressiveness
Child Abuse	26. Lasting Effects of Child Maltreatment 28. Why Kids Have a Lot to Cry About 29. Miracle of Resiliency 35. HIV Infected Youth Speaks	Education/School	12. Changing Demographics 19. Bell, Book, and Scandal 20. Role of Schools 21. Fears in the Classroom 26. Lasting Effects of Child Maltreatment 27. Alienation and the Four Worlds of Childhood 33. Sports Lift Esteem 45. Grandparent Development and Influence
Cognitive Development	8. Amazing Minds of Infants 11. Your Child's Brain 14. It's Magical! It's Malleable! It's . . . Memory 15. DNA-Environment Mix 16. Malnutrition, Poverty, and Intellectual Development 17. Life in Overdrive 20. Role of Schools 21. Fears in the Classroom 23. Fathers' Time 31. Adolescence: Whose Hell Is It? 40. Man's World, Woman's World? 44. Studies Suggest Older Minds Are Stronger than Expected	Emotional Development/ Personality	8. Amazing Minds of Infants 9. Realistic View of Biology and Behavior 11. Your Child's Brain 13. Assertiveness vs. Aggressiveness 15. DNA-Environment Mix 17. Life in Overdrive 22. Your Loving Touch 23. Fathers' Time 24. Sibling Connections 25. Children Who Witness Domestic Violence 26. Lasting Effects of Child Maltreatment 29. Miracle of Resiliency
Creativity	14. It's Magical! It's Malleable! It's . . . Memory 17. Life in Overdrive 42. Midlife Myths	Ethics/Morality	1. Unraveling the Mystery of Life 3. Choosing a Perfect Child 9. Realistic View of Biology and Behavior 32. Teenage Turning Point 39. Saga of Spouse Abuse
Culture	15. DNA-Environment Mix 16. Malnutrition, Poverty, and Intellectual Development 19. Bell, Book, and Scandal 20. Role of Schools 27. Alienation and the Four Worlds of Childhood 28. Why Kids Have a Lot to Cry About 29. Miracle of Resiliency 34. What Is a Bad Kid? 36. Psychotrends 43. Learning to Love Growing Old 45. Grandparent Development and Influence 46. Ageing with Attitude	Family/Parenting	12. Changing Demographics 13. Assertiveness vs. Aggressiveness 20. Role of Schools 22. Your Loving Touch 23. Fathers' Time 24. Sibling Connections 25. Children Who Witness Domestic Violence 26. Lasting Effects of Child Maltreatment 27. Alienation and the Four Worlds of Childhood 29. Miracle of Resiliency 31. Adolescence: Whose Hell Is It?
Depression	31. Adolescence: Whose Hell Is It? 32. Teenage Turning Point 39. Saga of Spouse Abuse		

TOPIC AREA	TREATED IN	TOPIC AREA	TREATED IN
Fertility	3. Choosing a Perfect Child 37. Who Stole Fertility?	**Peers**	13. Assertiveness vs. Aggressiveness 27. Alienation and the Four Worlds of Childhood 31. Adolescence: Whose Hell Is It? 34. What Is a Bad Kid? 42. Midlife Myths
Genetics	1. Unraveling the Mystery of Life 2. Biologists Find Key Genes 3. Choosing a Perfect Child 9. Realistic View of Biology and Behavior 29. Miracle of Resiliency	**Physical Development**	7. How Breast Milk Protects Newborns 10. Case Studies of Environmental Risks 11. Your Child's Brain 15. DNA-Environment Mix 16. Malnutrition, Poverty, and Intellectual Development 19. Bell, Book, and Scandal 31. Adolescence: Whose Hell Is It?
Health	4. Role of Lifestyle 7. How Breast Milk Protects Newborns 10. Case Studies of Environmental Risks 16. Malnutrition, Poverty, and Intellectual Development 28. Why Kids Have a Lot to Cry About 29. Miracle of Resiliency 31. Adolescence: Whose Hell Is It? 35. HIV Infected Youth Speaks 41. Stress: It's Worse than You Think 43. Learning to Love Growing Old 44. Studies Suggest Older Minds Are Stronger than Expected	**Prenatal Development**	2. Biologists Find Key Genes 4. Role of Lifestyle 5. Cocaine-Exposed Infants
		Self-Esteem	6. Sperm under Siege 20. Role of Schools 21. Fears in the Classroom 32. Teenage Turning Point 33. Sports Lift Esteem 37. Who Stole Fertility? 39. Saga of Spouse Abuse 45. Grandparent Development and Influence
Infant Development	5. Cocaine-Exposed Infants 7. How Breast Milk Protects Newborns 8. Amazing Minds of Infants 9. Realistic View of Biology and Behavior 10. Case Studies of Environmental Risks		
Language/ Communication	11. Your Child's Brain 23. Fathers' Time 40. Man's World, Woman's World?	**Sex Differences**	13. Assertiveness vs. Aggressiveness 23. Fathers' Time 32. Teenage Turning Point 36. Psychotrends 40. Man's World, Woman's World?
Late Adulthood	43. Learning to Love Growing Old 44. Studies Suggest Older Minds Are Stronger than Expected 45. Grandparent Development and Influence 46. Ageing with Attitude 47. Solace of Patterns	**Stress**	13. Assertiveness vs. Aggressiveness 28. Why Kids Have a Lot to Cry About 29. Miracle of Resiliency 37. Who Stole Fertility? 41. Stress: It's Worse than You Think 46. Ageing with Attitude
Marriage	36. Psychotrends 38. Is There Love after Baby? 39. Saga of Spouse Abuse 42. Midlife Myths	**Television**	28. Why Kids Have a Lot to Cry About 30. TV Violence: Myth and Reality
Middle Adulthood	40. Man's World, Woman's World? 41. Stress: It's Worse than You Think 42. Midlife Myths	**Teratogens**	4. Role of Lifestyle 5. Cocaine-Exposed Infants 6. Sperm under Siege
Nutrition	4. Role of Lifestyle 7. How Breast Milk Protects Newborns 10. Case Studies of Environmental Risks 16. Malnutrition, Poverty, and Intellectual Development 46. Ageing with Attitude	**Violence/Rape**	25. Children Who Witness Domestic Violence 26. Lasting Effects of Child Maltreatment 28. Why Kids Have a Lot to Cry About 30. TV Violence: Myth and Reality 35. HIV Infected Youth Speaks 39. Saga of Spouse Abuse
Occupation/Work	26. Lasting Effects of Child Maltreatment 27. Alienation and the Four Worlds of Childhood 41. Stress: It's Worse than You Think	**Young Adulthood**	36. Psychotrends 37. Who Stole Fertility? 38. Is There Love after Baby? 39. Saga of Spouse Abuse

Genetic and Prenatal Influences on Development

- Genetic Influences (Articles 1–3)
- Prenatal Influences (Articles 4–6)

The field of genetic knowledge is burgeoning. The human genome (23 pairs of chromosomes with their associated genes) is being mapped in near geometric progression. As the arrangement of gene sites on chromosomes is uncovered, so too are genetic markers (DNA sequences associated with particular traits). This is of vast significance to students of human development! No longer are genes just thought of as important because some carry certain diseases. Genes can be compared to an incredibly complicated computer program. They dictate every aspect of human development: physical structure and formation as well as cognitive, social, and emotional traits.

Human embryology (the study of the first through seventh weeks after conception) and human fetology (the study of the eighth week of pregnancy through birth) have given verification to the idea that behavior precedes birth. The developing embryo/fetus reacts to the internal and external environments provided by the mother and to substances which diffuse through the placental barrier from the mother's body. The embryo reacts to toxins (viruses, antigens) which pass through the umbilical cord. The fetus reacts to an enormous number of other stimuli such as the sounds from the mother's body (digestive rumblings, heart beat) and to her movements, moods, and medicines. How the embryo/fetus reacts (e.g., weakly to strongly; positively to negatively) depends, in large part, on his or her genetic preprogramming. Genes and environment are so inextricably intertwined that the effect of each cannot be studied separately. Prenatal development always has strong genetic influences and vice versa.

The first article included in the genetic section of this unit gives an articulate overview of the history and current research efforts in the science of human genetics. It provides the lay reader with a short dictionary of terms helpful in understanding the descriptions of genome research. It highlights the research being carried out in the Boston, Massachusetts, area but also describes other important studies worldwide. It probes the question "Should we use gene markers to proactively diagnose disease, when the disease is, as yet, incurable?" It also explains why a "Genetic Privacy Act" has been proposed for future legislative action. Prospective parents frequently wonder about genetic screening and what uncovering of deleterious genes will mean to their lives and to the lives of their future offspring.

The second genetic selection answers the difficult question, "How can a single cell, which is replicated into millions of genetically identical cells, become differentiated into a baby? Where do repressor substances, which inhibit most gene messages while allowing one or two genes to direct the cell's action, come from?" This article gives a partially satisfying explanation: Hedgehog morphogenes generate form in each cell and direct structure and function.

Article three addresses the concerns of genetic manipulation. If human behaviors such as alcoholism, homosexuality, and violence are genetically preprogrammed, can the genetic code be altered before birth? Using techniques of in vitro fertilization, can the zygote be diagnosed and treated before implantation or gestation? If genes cannot be altered, could a zygote with a bad diagnosis be destroyed rather than implanted? Is this ethical? Who will make these kinds of decisions and when?

The study of teratology (malformations of the embryo/fetus) and the study of normal prenatal development have historically focused on environmental factors. Until recently, genetic influences on how the embryo/fetus would react to teratogens or nutrients (e.g., weakly to strongly; positively to negatively) was ignored. Today we know that the same environmental factors may influence uniquely developing babies in different ways. Likewise, the age of the developing embryo/fetus makes a difference in the effect of an environmental factor. Keeping individual differences in mind, certain teratogens are dangerous to all unborn babies, and certain nutrients are necessary for all unborn babies.

The first article in the prenatal section of this unit explores the role of the mother's lifestyle in protecting her baby from, or subjecting her baby to, an "at-risk" birth status. At-risk infants are born with low birth weights and immature organ systems which put them in danger of

dying or experiencing delayed or disabled development. The authors discuss not only lifestyle choices but also demographic risks and stress risks, assessment of risk factors, barriers to change, and directions for prevention and intervention. It is an important paper to highlight the need for healthy mothers for healthy babies.

The second prenatal selection is an excellent discussion of the realities and mythologies of cocaine use during pregnancy. Hospitals are experiencing increased numbers of babies born to substance-abusing mothers. These babies should not be written off as helpless, despite at-risk birth status. Their mothers should not be dismissed as hopeless, despite a history of cocaine and/or other substance abuse. Many of the problems of cocaine-exposed infants have been exaggerated. The authors plead with readers to focus on the positive factors in infants' and mothers' lives and to provide protective lifestyle interventions to prevent further problems from developing.

The third article in the prenatal section has been retained from the previous collection because of rave reviews from readers. A mother provides the gestational setting for pregnancy and prenatal development in her uterus. She also provides one half the chromosomes with one half of the genetic materials needed to produce a new human being. Although a father provides the other 50 percent, the contributions of fathers to prenatal growth and change have long been overlooked. Not only do fathers provide one half of the genetic influences on development, but they also indirectly influence the environment that the gestational mother provides. This article discusses the ways in which teratogens can affect developing sperm and shows how important it is for prospective fathers to practice health maintenance and protect themselves from toxins (chemicals, alcohol, tobacco, drugs) for their sperm's sake.

Looking Ahead: Challenge Questions

How much do we know about the human genome? What dilemmas will we face as a human society when the genome is completely mapped?

What are hedgehogs? How have they helped answer the question of diversification of identical cells?

Would you elect to have in vitro fertilization and gene replacement therapy to create a perfect child?

What strategies can reduce the numbers of babies born with low birth weight and at risk of developmental disabilities?

What proactive measures can help cocaine-exposed infants and their cocaine-abusing mothers?

How do sperm contribute to prenatal development?

Unraveling the Mystery of Life

Boston University researchers, in collaboration with other medical science teams, continue to make significant contributions with their discoveries in the field of genetic knowledge.

Mariette DiChristina

Mariette DiChristina (COM '86) *is a senior editor at* Popular Science.

E ACH OF THESE SAMPLES HOLDS A PIECE OF genetic code," says Chris Amemiya, Ph.D., his scarlet and navy paisley tie and khakis poking out from a long white lab coat. In tiny breakers resting atop a black ice bucket like shrimp cocktail, these crucial codes look surprisingly inconsequential—rather like simple tap water.

Yet codes like these have awesome power over human destiny. They determine whether you are tall or short, have blue eyes or brown, curly hair or straight. And more important, they may tell whether you will get sick someday, and from what. There are perhaps 3,000 to 4,000 ailments caused by genetic defects.

In this tidy, well-lit lab, Amemiya, an assistant professor at the Center for Human Genetics at the Boston University School of Medicine, and others are working to help figure out, or characterize, sequences of these genetic codes. Their efforts are just one small part of the impressive ongoing genetic research at the University.

Individually as well as in collaboration with other medical science teams, BU scientists have contributed to many nationally recognized achievements in the complex arena of genetic research. Their work covers the spectrum of discovery—from persevering with pipettes in the lab to number-crunching reams of data with computers to dealing with the human consequences of the search for greater genetic knowledge.

On the world stage, genome research has seen some remarkable advances. So far, some two dozen genes have been linked to human diseases. The past year alone has seen the discovery of a gene commonly implicated in many varieties of cancer, as well as ones for breast cancer, obesity, a form of youth-onset Alzheimer's, even the general site of a gene linked with persistent bed-wetting in children.

Not so long ago, no one even knew what a gene was. Since Gregor Mendel's famous work with peas, scientists have known the importance of heritage. But it wasn't until 1952 that scientists discovered that DNA is the basic stuff of heredity. Short for deoxyribonucleic acid, DNA is a long thread-like molecule that is part of a gene (see "A Genetic Dictionary"). Today we know that DNA acts like a biological computer program some three billion bits long. This program spells out the key instructions for making proteins, the basic building blocks of life. If you could print it out, the entire human genome—the blueprint that makes each of us a unique individual—would fill a thousand 1,000-page telephone books.

The genome is so large and the work to decipher it so painstaking that fewer than 5 percent of these genetic codes have been sequenced. To explain why this is so, many researchers cite the example of the landmark 1989 discovery of the gene for cystic fibrosis. The many independent groups that worked simultaneously on the project often duplicated one another's efforts, and the total cost probably exceeded $120 million.

5,000 Genes a Year

E nter the Human Genome Project. Launched in 1990, the massive, multibillion-dollar project seeks to identify an estimated 50,000 to 100,000 human genes by the year 2005. An international effort involving hundreds of scientists at dozens of universities and medical institutions, the project is supported in the United States by the National Institutes of Health and the Department of Energy.

A pioneer was Charles DeLisi, Ph.D., who initiated the project in the 1980s as a director of the Department of Energy's health and environment research programs. An internationally recognized researcher in molecular structure and function, DeLisi is now professor of biomedical engineering and dean of BU's College of Engineering.

Among those continuing in the wake of DeLisi's efforts are scientists at the BU Center for Advanced Biotechnology, on the Charles River Campus. Charles Cantor, Ph.D., the center's director and a member of the National Academy of Sciences, says a key goal of the researchers is to reduce the tremendous cost and time involved in genetic research.

Shortcuts

To ease the arduous task of sifting through forty-six human chromosomes of marvelous complexity, many scientists seek to create some basic road maps. Cassandra L. Smith, Ph.D., deputy director of the Center for Advanced Biotechnology, is one researcher who focuses on new methods of faster DNA mapping and sequencing.

"The technical problem is that the genome is very large and you can't look at the whole genome at one time with current technology," says Smith. "So we've developed methods of looking at subsets of the genome that are likely to have changes that might cause diseases. When a gene falls into such a region, you already might have a lot of the resources to help pinpoint it."

To explain the point, Smith offers an analogy. Imagine you're looking for a certain house in a city. You could start at any random street and then search block by block. Or you could look at an overall map of the city and get a general idea of where to begin. Having the genetic markers, she says, "is like having a map of the city."

One marking technique is to use restriction enzymes, which chemically clip DNA at places where the enzymes recognize specific base sequences. Eventually gene mappers would like to create a regularly spaced set of markers at close intervals. Using these markers as signposts for genetic "neighborhoods" on the imaginary city map, scientists can then find the important "streets" and "houses." When there are differences around these markers in family members who have a genetic disease — but not in disease-free members — scientists can locate the genetic cause.

This method of gene hunting has produced some notable successes at BU: location of the genes for Waardenburg's syndrome as well as for Huntington's disease.

In 1992 a team led by Clinton T. Baldwin, Ph.D., an associate professor of pediatrics and the director of molecular genetics research at the Center for Human Genetics, found the genetic cause of a form of deafness called Waardenburg's syndrome. Waardenburg's, which is accompanied by pigment disorders of the skin, eyes, and hair, causes about 3 percent of all cases of congenital deafness.

"We determined the [key part of a] DNA sequence of an individual with the disease, compared it to a person without the disease, and found a single base change that resulted in a single amino acid change," explains Baldwin. "This was sufficient to destroy the ability of the protein to function." Using earlier research done on the genetics of mice and fruit flies — which have some genes similar to human genes — also helped the researchers understand the genes involved.

The gene for Huntington's was also located with this search technique. Huntington's is a deadly neurodegenerative disease whose best known victim was folksinger Woodie Guthrie. Unlike Waardenburg's, Huntington's is not a single error. Rather, explains Richard Myers, Ph.D., of the BU Medical Center, it is a "stutter" flaw. There are too many repeats of one tiny bit of code, as if the genetic photocopier went haywire. Myers, who was part of the team that made the 1993 discovery of the Huntington's gene after a decade-long search, says the more copies of this gene a Huntington's patient has, the more severe the symptoms and the earlier the onset of the disease. Continuing in his research, Myers is exploring some puzzling differences in the complexity of nerve cells of Huntington's patients and those without the disease.

Another place scientists look for gene clues is in people whose relationship is even closer than most family members: identical twins. Because identical twins develop from the same fertilized egg, they have the same genetic material.

A GENETIC DICTIONARY

DNA — Two yards of DNA are packed into each one of the 100 trillion cells in your body. A strand of DNA, or deoxyribonucleic acid, is more than 37,000 times thinner than a human hair. The DNA is on twenty-three pairs of chromosomes; you get one set of twenty-three chromosomes from each of your parents.

CHROMOSOME — Each of the forty-six human chromosomes contains the DNA for thousands of individual genes, the chemical units of heredity.

GENE — A gene is a snippet, or sequence, of DNA that holds the recipe for making a specific molecule, usually a protein. These recipes are spelled out in four chemical bases: adenine (A), thymine (T), guanine (G), and cytosine (C). The bases form interlocking pairs; A always pairs with T and G pairs with C. In some cases, genetic defects are caused by the substitution of just one base pair for another.

PROTEIN — Amino acids make up proteins, which are key components of all human organs and chemical activities in your body. Their function depends on their shape, which is determined by the 50,000 to 100,000 genes in the cell nucleus. — MD

Studies of gay men and their twin brothers by psychiatrists Richard Pillard of the BU School of Medicine and J. Michael Bailey of Northeastern University indicate that there is a heredity factor in homosexuality. When one brother is gay, they discovered, there is a far greater likelihood that the identical twin is gay too.

If one twin has a trait that the other doesn't have, this gives scientists a hint about where to look for the specific gene that causes that trait. For example, Cassandra Smith is conducting studies with twins in the search for genes responsible for schizophrenia. "I take identical twins who are discordants — that is, one has and one doesn't have schizophrenia — and compare the DNA to find the differences," she says. By doing so she seeks the triggers for this chronic disease.

A third way to shorten the search for genes is to differentiate between the 3 percent of DNA that creates coding and the 97 percent that is noncoding. Noncoding DNA is called *junk* because no one knows its purpose. "What could this 97 percent be doing?" asks H. Eugene Stanley, Ph.D., professor of physics and director of the Center for Polymer Studies at BU. "One idea is that it's just accumulated during evolution the way junk accumulates in my office," he says with a sweep of his arm taking in stacks of books and piles of paper.

Work by Stanley and colleagues at Boston University and Harvard indicates that the junk may be a language. One language feature in junk—a discovery led by team member S. Martina Ossadnik—is that it has correlations. That is, certain bits of information generally follow certain others—the way *u* follows *q* in English. Taking that a step further, Rosario Mantegna, then a BU graduate student and now a research associate in the physics department, computer-analyzed the junk, applying tests used by linguists. He found "word" repetitions, another common language feature. "Language is a structured thing," adds Stanley. "There is a lot of redundancy: I could leave out a word and you would understand me. A code is the opposite. It is very strict; you cannot make a mistake." Genetic codes do not share these language features.

So what does the junk say? No one is certain. "We can't prove it's a language," stresses Stanley, "but it passes the tests for language."

Once you find a gene for a disease, you can work to develop predictive tests. Richard Myers founded and heads Huntington's testing and counseling at the University. Boston University and Johns Hopkins University, which set up programs simultaneously in 1986, were the first institutions to offer such testing. Today more people have undergone testing for Huntington's than for any other disease that appears in adulthood (see sidebar, "Testing Without Cures").

TESTING WITHOUT CURES

Genetic research will undoubtedly bring unmatched abilities to improve the human condition. But rapidly advancing lab work is leaving society to face some difficult issues. While scientists have found the genetic causes of several diseases and developed predictive tests, treatments remain elusive.

The result, says George Annas, J.D., M.P.H., a professor of health law at the Boston University School of Public Health who has been widely quoted on genome ethics, is that "it gives you scary information that is not terribly useful in your daily life."

Perhaps few have come to know these punishing issues as well as Richard Myers at the BU Medical Center. Myers, whose twenty-year experience with the deadly, incurable Huntington's disease began with his dissertation, participated in the gene's discovery (see main article). At the University, he founded one of the first U.S. testing and counseling programs for Huntington's.

Considering the brutal, relentless progress of Huntington's, Myers speaks of its victims in measured tones tinged with sympathy. "There are plenty of diseases that are pretty nasty. A lot of times you might be better off not knowing how bad it can get," he says. "But for a person to get Huntington's disease, a parent would have had it. They [the children] would have had to watch." Many who come in for counseling choose not to be tested.

Worse, there are fears about twenty-first-century discrimination based on an individual's genetic heritage. For instance, Myers knows of one New England woman in her twenties who was fired from her pharmacy job after her boss discovered that the woman's mother had Huntington's and thus she was vulnerable to developing the disease. Anticipating such cases, the U.S. Equal Opportunity Commission this year concluded that the Americans with Disabilities Act protects healthy people carrying abnormal genes from discrimination.

Annas and two School of Public Health colleagues — Leonard Glantz, J.D., health law professor, and Patricia Roche, J.D., instructor — aim to take that a step further: this spring they proposed legislation to prevent the collection, analysis, and storage of DNA, and disclosure of information derived from such analysis, without the individual's written authorization. The proposed legislation, called the Genetic Privacy Act, was developed over two years under a grant awarded from that portion of the Human Genome Project's budget that goes to ethics research. The act has been introduced in a half-dozen state legislatures, says Annas, who also expects it to be considered as a federal statute.

"Everyone has some bad genes," says Annas. "The problem is these genes are being discovered long before there is any hope for treating these conditions. Nonetheless, there are many opportunities for employers, insurance companies, and others to discriminate on the basis of someone's genetic makeup." — *MD*

While locating a gene doesn't guarantee a cure, it may point the way. Researchers hope to design drugs that can target the cause of an ailment rather than the symptoms. In collaboration with colleagues from other universities and biotechnology companies, Charles Cantor of the Biotechnology Center is working to take advantage of the natural lock-and-key mechanism of a type of protein—a string of amino acids—called streptavidin. One example of a natural lock and key is how antibodies fight infection in your body; the antibody chemically matches the infecting virus and adheres to it—rendering the virus harmless. Streptavidin's lock-and-key binding, however, is a million times stronger than that of antibodies. "You could use this natural mechanism to bring radiation right to the site of a cancerous tumor in a precise way," says Cantor.

Another possible way to treat genetic disease is to correct or replace the altered gene through gene therapy. This involves inserting corrective DNA into human cells to replace flawed genes or to produce proteins that stimulate the body's natural immune system. Such experimental gene therapy to treat Parkinson's disease is just one example of the more than 100 gene-therapy procedures now undergoing testing.

In some cases, too, finding out you are predisposed to a genetic ailment could help you take preventive actions or enable you to get treatment earlier, when it is more likely to be effective. Clinical research will also provide a piece of the genetic puzzle.

A leader in this area is Aubrey Milunsky, M.D., a professor of human genetics, pediatrics, pathology, and obstetrics at BU's School of Medicine and director of the Center for Human Genetics. As head of the human genetics program, Milunsky's landmark work has supported the development of national guidelines for folic acid supplementation to prevent neural tube defects and has focused on prenatal diagnosis and early pregnancy screening for birth defects.

"The power of genetics is that if you have the time and money, you are almost guaranteed to find the gene," says Cassandra Smith. Speaking for many researchers, she adds, "It's just a matter of perseverance."

Biologists Find Key Genes That Shape Patterning of Embryos

A gene named hedgehog directs the development of cells in the limbs and brain.

Natalie Angier

Rare indeed are the scientific findings that make jaws drop and spirits do cartwheels. But the discovery of a class of genes, given the cheeky name hedgehog, has aroused the passions of developmental biologists so vigorously that their normal reserve and skepticism have dissolved, leaving them groping for ever-stronger ways to express the beauty and consequence of what has been divulged.

Three teams of scientists report in the current issue of the journal Cell that they have finally unearthed what developmental scientists have been seeking for the last 25 years, as they studied the implausibly complex sequence of events that allow a single cell, the fertilized egg, to effloresce into a complete animal. They have identified the genes that act on the early embryo to lend it shape and pattern, transforming a nondescript comma of tissue into a vertebrate animal, with limbs and digits, brain and spinal cord, the body shape set from head to heel.

These genes produce so-called morphogens, molecules of celebrated stature that researchers have known must exist but have had tremendous difficulty isolating. The word morphogen means "maker of structure," and the hedgehog proteins are just that. Once switched on inside the

embryo, the molecules sweep slowly across the primordial buds of tissue and begin generating identifiable form, sculpturing arms, hands and fingers on the sides of the embryo, vertebrae and ribs along its midline, a brain within the skull. The morphogen tells the cells it touches where they are situated in the body and what they are destined to become. It gives them their address, their fate, their identity, their purpose in life.

First detected in fruit flies, the hedgehog genes earned their name for their ability, when mutated, to give a fly the bristly appearance of a hedgehog. Their normal function in the fruit fly is to dictate growth, and the latest trio of reports establish that the same genes also dictate structural design in vertebrates.

The papers describe the isolation of hedgehog genes from mice, zebra fish and chickens, three staple organisms of laboratory research, widely separated in evolutionary time.

"This new class of signaling molecules will probably end up being the most important molecules in vertebrate development," said Dr. Clifford J. Tabin, a developmental biologist at Harvard Medical School and the principle author of one of the three reports. When the results on the hedgehog work first became apparent, he said, "I was bouncing off the walls."

Scientists have yet to look for the genes in humans, but they are certain that hedgehog is performing the same role in human embryos as it is in little fish. If this turns out not to be the case, said Dr. Philip W. Ingham, a senior scientist at the Molecular Embryology Laboratory at the Imperial Cancer Research Fund in Oxford, England, and the head investigator on another of the new papers, "I'll resign from science."

And with such a big segment of the puzzle of development now snapped into place, researchers said they can begin filling in the rest of the confounding picture of embryogenesis. They can start to decipher how the hedgehog molecules interact with other essential players known to participate slightly later in development, including the famed Hox genes, also assiduous builders of bodies, which themselves are found across the evolutionary scale.

"This is extraordinary work, it's fantastic, and I wish I'd done it," said Dr. Jim Smith, head of the developmental biology laboratory at the National Institute for Medical Research in London. "When I started working on limb development in 1976, we all knew there had to be something like this, but we didn't necessarily think we'd live to see it."

Dr. Smith, who has written a review of research on the hedgehog genes that will appear in the next issue of Cell, could not contain his enthusiasm. "It's the sort of thing that brings tears to your eyes," he said.

The work is of an exquisitely basic nature, born more of curiosity about nature than of specific clinical goals. But scientists said the findings may prove useful in the quest for better ways to treat head and spinal cord injuries, as well as degenerative diseases of the brain.

"People these days are very interested in molecules that mediate important decisions in the early development of the central nervous system," said Dr. Andrew P. McMahon, a developmental biologist at Harvard University and the principal researcher on the third of the latest papers. "There are a lot of diseases for which one would like to be able to grow new neurons," and understanding the basic signals of nervous system development is one road toward the shimmering Oz of neurological regeneration.

The protein made by the hedgehog gene organizes the fates of neighboring cells.

The hedgehog morphogens also offer relief to developmental biologists who lately had grown dissatisfied with another proffered candidate for the role of omnipotent morphogen: retinoic acid, or vitamin A. In widely publicized reports a few years ago, scientists suggested that retinoic acid could be the long-sought morphogen that sets up a body plan. However, there were sizable gaps in the data and doubts in the minds of many biologists that retinoic acid worked at such a fundamental level in the embryo.

In the new work, the hedgehog genes pass all the litmus tests that vitamin A had failed, displaying with extraordinary precision the properties that scientific theories about morphogens had predicted. It is turned on, or expressed, at pre-cisely the right times of development, and in all the right places. And when scientists manipulate embryos and subtly alter the ways in which hedgehog genes are expressed, they get the sort of macabre developmental mutations they are expecting. For example, they can prompt a growing chick to sprout mirror-image sets of wings simply by inserting active hedgehog genes in the tissue abutting that where the genes are normally expressed.

'Exciting Breakthrough'

With the new results, said Dr. Ingham, "we can forget about retinoic acid" as an architect of the body.

For scientists who work on fruit flies, or Drosophila, the new discoveries prove once again how prescient they were to focus on simple animals as a way of comprehending more complex societies.

"It's a very exciting breakthrough and a vindication of the power of model organisms," said Dr. Matthew P. Scott, a professor of developmental biology and genetics at Stanford University School of Medicine. "Here we have a molecule that was found for its role in determining segmentation in insects, and it's turned out to be extremely important in understanding the most interesting properties of vertebrate growth."

Yet with all the enthusiasm surrounding the new finding, scientists admit they have much to learn. For example, they know that in humans, hedgehog in all likelihood switches on sometime around day 15 of pregnancy, to help shape the central nervous system, and is largely finished with that task by day 28. It comes into play shortly afterward in molding the limbs of the body. However, scientists do not yet have a clue as to what activates hedgehog to get morphogenesis rolling.

Nor do they know much about the hedgehog molecules themselves, what sort of proteins they are and how they manage to communicate with embryonic cells to persuade them to adopt a particular fate. The hedgehog proteins are unlike any detected before, which is both a blessing and a hurdle—a blessing because scientists like novel things and because they knew the molecules they were familiar with were not sufficient to explain the mysteries of development; and a hurdle because they must start from scratch in understanding the molecules. So far, they have found four different hedgehog genes in vertebrate animals, but they suspect there may be more.

The fourth variety, which scientists call Sonic hedgehog, has an illustrious history. Scientists were first inspired to seek morphogens by the seminal research of Dr. John Saunders and others who, in the 1960's and 1970's, painstakingly grafted parts of embryos together to see what resulted. The work yielded a bizarre set of mutant animals with excess or abnormal digits and limbs, but the results were consistent and revealing. Together they indicated that in certain key regions of the primordial embryo, there are what are known as zones of polarizing activity, local headquarters that disseminate essential information about how surrounding cells are supposed to behave.

Scientists' Fantasies Exceeded

"The idea was that these signaling centers sent out a protein that affected neighboring cells and organized their fates," said Dr. Scott.

The signaling protein seems to work in a gradient fashion. By this theory, the protein diffuses from a central zone, getting less concentrated as it spreads. Depending on how much of the informational protein they receive, cells will choose one course of action over another. In the embryonic limb, for example, a heavy dose of the diffusing signal will instruct the cells to prepare to assume the role of a pinkie, while a lighter concentration will inform the cells they are destined to become a thumb.

Neurobiologists also gathered evidence from grafting experiments that a central signaling system helps knead the developing brain into shape. In this case, the zones of information were thought to be located in two embryonic structures, one called the notochord, a stiff rod that serves as the developing creature's temporary backbone, and the other called the floor plate, a bulge of tissue that eventually gives rise to the adult spinal cord. Scientists proposed that the structures jointly secrete a powerful information molecule able to tell surrounding cells whether they are destined to become part of the hind brain, the forebrain, motor nerves or other constituents of the nervous system.

Thus was born the notion of the morphogen, the diffusible conductor of cell fates. Finding it, however, was another matter.

Scientists suspect that the protein stimulates the response of a master gene inside the cells; this potent gene may in turn set off a string of other genes.

Because recent work in fruit flies indicated that the hedgehog gene helps determine the growth of body segments in the larvae, the three research teams thought it worth the effort to seek the vertebrate equivalents of the gene and check whether hedgehog was somehow involved in animal growth.

The results exceeded their fantasies. The Sonic hedgehog molecule proved to be the desperately sought shaper of bodies. It is expressed in the limb at exactly the site known to be the zone of polarizing activity. It is activated exactly where it should be

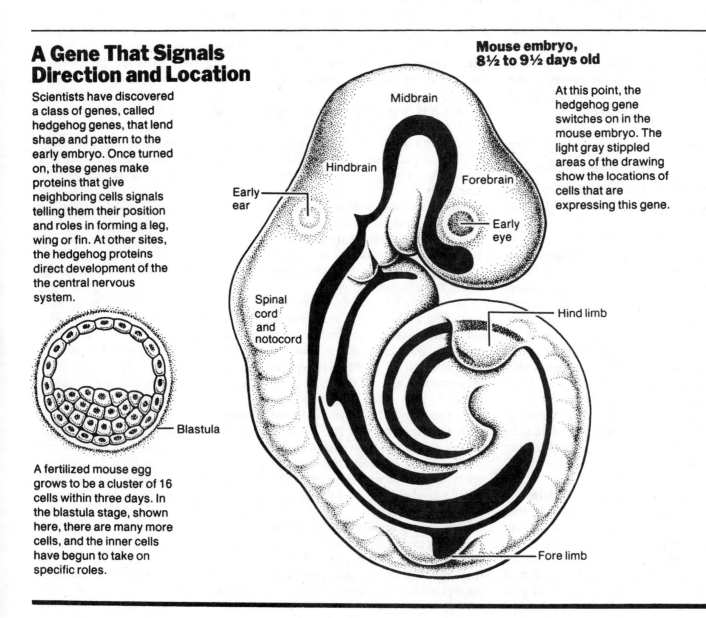

A Gene That Signals Direction and Location

Scientists have discovered a class of genes, called hedgehog genes, that lend shape and pattern to the early embryo. Once turned on, these genes make proteins that give neighboring cells signals telling them their position and roles in forming a leg, wing or fin. At other sites, the hedgehog proteins direct development of the the central nervous system.

A fertilized mouse egg grows to be a cluster of 16 cells within three days. In the blastula stage, shown here, there are many more cells, and the inner cells have begun to take on specific roles.

Blastula

Midbrain

Hindbrain

Early ear

Forebrain

Early eye

Spinal cord and notocord

Hind limb

Fore limb

Mouse embryo, 8½ to 9½ days old

At this point, the hedgehog gene switches on in the mouse embryo. The light gray stippled areas of the drawing show the locations of cells that are expressing this gene.

in the notochord and floor plate in the early central nervous system.

Sonic Hedgehog's Modus Operandi

By manipulating the sonic hedgehog gene alone, the researchers have been able to recapitulate the suite of deformities seen in the older grafting experiments, thus demonstrating they have pinpointed the legendary morphogen.

The scientists have yet to clarify the roles of the three other hedgehog genes they have detected, but these seem more limited in their scope, toiling in specific regions like the sex cells of the body.

The challenge now is to understand the modus operandi of the Sonic hedgehog protein, how it persuades cells to do its bidding as it oozes by them. Scientists suspect that the protein stimulates the response of a master gene inside the cells, perhaps a member of the Hox gene family. That potent gene may in turn set off a string of other genes, which jointly realize the cell's destiny.

Within the early nervous system, the signals arising from the top and from the bottom are involved in formation of specific neurons at specific sites. Neurons at the top are associated with sensory functions, while neurons at the bottom control movement.

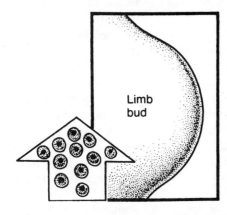

Limb bud

Developing digits

In the limb bud, the positional information from the hedgehog protein makes the cells start defining the arrangement of digits of a future paw.

Sources: Dr. Andrew McMahon, Harvard University; "Molecular Biology of the Cell" (Garland)

Mouse embryo, 14 days old

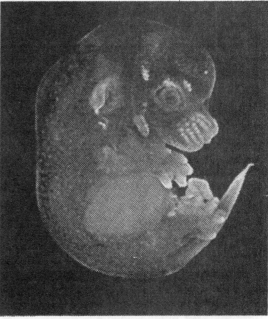

Dr. Bradley R. Smith, Dr. Elwood Lenny, Dr. G. Allan Johnson, Center for In Vivo Microscopy, Duke University Medical Center (N.I.H. National Resource)

Scientists suspect the hedgehog protein stimulates a master gene inside cells that sets off a cascade of other genes. The response to a signal, they think, depends on the local concentration of the hedgehog protein. Biologists expect to find the hedgehog gene in humans, too.

Nancy Sterngold, The New York Times; Illustration by Michael Reingold

Choosing a Perfect Child

Brave new technology is allowing us to look at tiny preembryonic 8-cell clusters and decide which ones are healthy enough to be allowed to develop into babies.

Ricki Lewis

Ricki Lewis is the author of Life, *a college biology text, and has written a human genetics text. She is a genetic counselor and an adjunct assistant professor at SUNY Albany and Miami University, where she has taught human genetics and bioethics courses. She has published hundreds of articles for both laymen and scientists.*

Chloe O'Brien, who celebrates her first birthday this month, is a very wanted child, perhaps more so than most. When she was a mere ball of cells, smaller than the smallest speck of sand, a test determined that she would be free of the cystic fibrosis genes that each of her parents carries. Chloe-to-be, along with another ball of cells (a potential twin), was implanted into her mother's uterus. Only one of the two balls of cells, Chloe-to-be, survived the rigors of prenatal development, and Chloe today is a healthy little girl.

The O'Briens had already had a child who suffered from the stiflingly thick mucus clogging the lungs that is a hallmark of cystic fibrosis, the most common genetic disease among Caucasians. They wanted to spare their future children this fate—but they also wanted to avoid having to end a pregnancy that would yield an affected child.

"Previously, couples had to wait from 9 to 15 weeks [after

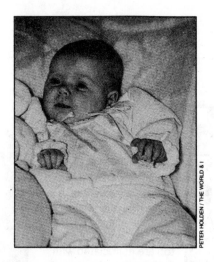

PETER HOLDEN / THE WORLD & I

conception] to find out if their developing baby was affected by a known genetic disease. Now, we can diagnose these inherited diseases within three days after an egg is fertilized in the laboratory, before it is transferred back to the woman," says Mark Hughes of the Baylor College of Medicine in Houston. Hughes, along with John Lesko, also of Baylor, and Alan Handyside, Robert Winston, and Juan Tarin, of Hammersmith Hospital in London, reported the preimplantation diagnosis of cystic fibrosis in September 1992 in the *New England Journal of Medicine.*

The preimplantation genetic diagnosis that confirmed Chloe to be free of the cystic fibrosis gene is built primarily on three existing technologies: in vitro fertil-

ization (IVF); gene amplification, a way to rapidly copy a single gene from a single cell; and gene probing, which detects the gene responsible for the disorder. The latter two interventions are performed on the 8-cell "preembryo."

Few couples have so far had their preembryos examined for genetic problems, and the high costs of the procedure will likely keep the numbers down. However, with the rapid progress being made by the Human Genome Project in identifying genes associated with specific genetic disorders, preembryos in the future may be scrutinized for a wider range of diseases, from rare inherited ailments to the more common heart disease and cancer.

Is a brave new world of mechanized reproduction upon us? To understand how we may someday pick and choose the traits of our children, we must understand the procedures that serve as a backdrop to preimplantation genetic diagnosis.

Prenatal diagnosis—the state of the art

A generation ago, pregnancy was shrouded in secrecy. A woman would discover her expectant state in the second or third month

The biological basis of preimplantation genetic diagnosis is that all the cells of an individual have the same genes.

and announce it in the fourth month, when most risk of miscarriage was past. Today, pregnancy is marked by a series of medical tests providing prenatal peeks into the health of the child-to-be.

The most familiar prenatal test is amniocentesis, a procedure in which a needle is inserted into the amniotic sac cushioning a fetus and a small amount of fluid is withdrawn. The fluid contains a few fetal cells, whose nuclei contain the rod-shaped chromosomes, which consist of the genes. If examination reveals missing or extra chromosomes, the fetus is likely to develop into a baby with a serious syndrome.

Today, amniocentesis is a rite of passage for pregnant women over age 35, because at that age the chance of the fetus having a chromosomal problem about equals the risk of amniocentesis causing miscarriage (1 in 200). (The risk of abnormal fetal chromosomes increases with maternal age.)

The major limitation of amniocentesis is that it is performed in the 16th week of pregnancy. By then the fetus is quite well developed. If a chromosome abnormality is detected, the parents are faced with an agonizing choice: either terminate the pregnancy or prepare for the birth of a physically or mentally challenged child.

An alternative to amniocentesis is chorionic villus sampling (CVS), which also examines fetal chromosomes. This procedure can be performed earlier, usually between weeks 8 and 10. The fetus is far smaller and less well developed, about the size and weight of a paper clip, making the decision to end the pregnancy somewhat easier.

CVS was pioneered in China in the 1970s and became available in the United States only in the mid-1980s. Though the World Health Organization endorsed CVS in 1984, it also suggested

that ways be found to diagnose genetic disease earlier, perhaps before the preembryo implants in the uterus. This occurs on the 6th day after sperm meets egg.

The biological basis of preimplantation genetic diagnosis is that all the cells of an individual have the same genes no matter what the stage of development. In principle, the techniques used to examine the genetic material of cells obtained through amniocentesis or CVS should work for cells obtained at other stages of prenatal development, even at the preembryonic stage.

Screening genes

An individual gene in a preembryo's cell can be identified through a technique invented in 1985, the polymerase chain reaction (PCR).

In PCR an enzyme, DNA polymerase, that is essential to the multiplication of DNA in every cell in the body, selectively multiplies only the DNA from the gene of interest. If that gene is present in the original genetic sample being tested it will be rapidly mass-produced in a test tube. If the gene of interest is not present, then it won't be multiplied by the PCR.

If PCR of a single cell from the 8-cell preembryo results in many copies of the target DNA sequence, then the disease-causing gene is there—as happened to a few of Chloe's potential siblings who were not implanted. If the DNA is not amplified, then the sequence of interest is not there. When the cell from 8-cell Chloe-to-be failed its PCR test, it meant that the 7-cell preembryo could develop into a cystic fibrosis-free baby.

The first experiments using PCR to identify preembryos free of a genetic disease took place in 1989 and 1990 in Hammersmith Hospital. Handyside and his team screened preembryos from couples in which the mothers carried a variety of conditions, called X-linked conditions, that occur mostly in males. X-linked conditions are caused by genes on the X chromosome. Since females have two X chromosomes, and males have one X and one Y chromosome, a male preembryo with a Y chromosome and an X chromosome bearing a disease-causing gene would be destined to have the X-linked condition. By using PCR to amplify a DNA sequence unique to the Y chromosome, Handyside's team could choose a female preembryo that could not inherit the disease carried by the mother. The disorders avoided thanks to early attempts at preimplantation genetic diagnosis include adrenoleukodystrophy, a nervous system degeneration that is lethal in early childhood; Lesch-Nyhan syndrome, in which the profoundly retarded child mutilates himself; and other forms of mental retardation.

In August 1992 Jamie Grifo and colleagues at New York Hospital–Cornell Medical Center reported the first child born in the United States after successful blastomere biopsy and genetic testing to avoid X-linked hemophilia.

Candidates for preimplantation genetic diagnosis

Preimplantation genetic diagnosis is a promising option for couples who know that their children are at a high risk for inheriting a certain disease.

According to the laws of inheritance, parents who both carry the same disorder not on the X chromosome, but on one of the other 22 chromosomes, can conceive children who inherit either two normal genes, or two abnormal genes, or, like the parents, one normal and one abnormal gene. The probability of inheriting two of the same gene, either normal or abnormal, is 1 in 4. The probability of being a carrier like the parents with one normal and one abnormal gene is 1 in 2.

Chloe's parents, for example, each have one disease-causing copy of the cystic fibrosis gene, and one normal copy. Thus there

is a 1 in 4 chance that a child conceived by them will suffer with cystic fibrosis.

The mechanics of preimplantation diagnosis

A human preembryo can be obtained in two ways—it can be flushed out of the uterus after being conceived in the normal manner, in which case it is more than 8 cells, or it can be nurtured from an egg fertilized by a sperm in a laboratory dish, the technique of in vitro fertilization (IVF). The first IVF or "test tube baby," Louise Joy Brown, was born in England in 1978, and has since been followed by thousands of other such children.

IVF is now a fairly routine, if difficult and costly, procedure, with hundreds of facilities providing it in the United States alone, and hundreds of others elsewhere. For the IVF procedure, the woman is given pergonal, a drug that causes the ovary to ripen more than one egg at a

time. Eggs, which appear as small bulges in the ovarian lining, are harvested by inserting a laparoscope, a tiny, illuminated telescopelike device, through an incision made near the woman's navel.

The eggs are placed with sperm donated by the man into a laboratory dish, along with other chemicals that simulate the environment in the woman's body. If all goes well, sperm and egg meet and merge. Extra fertilized eggs are frozen and saved in case they are needed later.

On the third day after fertilization comes the blastomere biopsy. The 8-cell, or 8-blastomere, preembryo is immobilized with a holding pipette (a narrow glass tube). Then a single blastomere is removed from the preembryo by exposing the target cell to a stream of acid and gently prodding it with a second, smaller pipette.

The next step is to thoroughly clean the blastomere, because PCR, the gene amplification part

■ In blastomere biopsy, as shown left to right in the sequence below, the 8-cell preembryo is held by one pipette while another narrower one is used to capture a single blastomere, which is used for genetic testing; the remaining seven cells can continue to develop normally. (Magnification 330x)

COURTESY JUAN COTA / BAYLOR COLLEGE OF MEDICINE

of the process, can give a false genetic diagnosis if even one stray sperm happens to be clinging to the blastomere. When the blastomere is clean, it is broken open by a series of temperature changes to expose and disentangle the DNA. The PCR evaluation is then used to determine if the disease-causing gene is present.

After the blastomere biopsy and PCR, one or two preembryos that have passed the genetic test are implanted into the woman. If pregnancy occurs, human chorionic gonadotropin (hCG), the "pregnancy hormone," appears in the woman's blood and urine by the 14th day. By the fourth week, an ultrasound exam will show a small, oval area in the uterus. This is the sac containing the embryo.

What we can do versus what we should do

At this time, the two biggest drawbacks to preimplantation genetic diagnosis are the low efficiency and high cost of IVF. In 1990, the American Fertility Society surveyed IVF clinics and found a 14 percent "take-home baby rate." However, Yury Verlinsky, director of the Reproductive Genetics Institute of the Illinois Masonic Medical Center in Chicago, and Anver Kuliev, director of the research/cell bank at the same facility, point out that the typical couple seeking IVF has fertility problems and tends to be older, whereas couples seeking IVF as a prelude to preimplantation genetic diagnosis would be younger and more fertile.

The cost is out of reach for many. "The average cost of IVF is $7,000-8,000," says James Douglas of the Trinity Medical Center in Carrollton, Texas. Blastomere biopsy plus PCR can add another $2,000—all for a proce-

"Blastomere biopsy is being performed only at a few IVF centers that are associated with a major medical teaching facility."

dure that may have to be repeated.

Although physicians who perform IVF are excited about the value of preimplantation diagnosis for couples whose offspring are at high risk for genetic disease, they are nevertheless pessimistic about the technology's general utility. This is because once the procedure grows beyond its research stage, it will be prohibitively expensive. And even though there are expectations that automating some of the steps could bring the price down, these developments are on the far horizon.

Also, as Margaret Wallace, assistant professor in the genetics division at the University of Florida in Gainesville, points out, there is the problem of the "slippery slope"—who decides that a disorder is awful enough to intervene to prevent a birth? In 1990, she discovered the gene behind neurofibromatosis (NF1), another common inherited illness. NF1 presents a sticky problem—finding the responsible gene does not indicate how severely an individual may be affected. Manifestations of NF1 can range from a few brown spots on the body to thousands of tumors just beneath the skin.

So far, the diseases detected by preimplantation genetic diagnosis cause extreme suffering to very young children, and the goal is prevention. "But for preimplantation diagnosis of some less devastating disorders, some physicians and insurers might not think it is ethical" to choose

against implanting a diagnosed preembryo, says Wallace.

Another factor that may stifle development of preimplantation genetic diagnosis is that treatments for some genetic disorders are being developed so rapidly that selecting out affected preembryos may become obsolete before the technology can be perfected. "Cystic fibrosis research is moving so quickly that some may say, who cares who is born with it? We can treat them," says Wallace.

For now, preimplantation genetic diagnosis remains highly experimental. "Blastomere biopsy is being performed only at a few IVF centers that are associated with a major medical teaching facility," says Douglas.

However, Verlinsky and Kuliev predict that, once the success stories accumulate and the price drops, preimplantation genetic diagnosis will be offered at a few fetal medicine centers, where teams of embryo experts, molecular biologists, geneticists, and obstetricians will perform genetic tests that will grow ever more numerous as the trek through the human genome nears completion.

Although clearly not yet suitable for the general public, preimplantation genetic diagnosis will allow certain couples to avoid what was once their genetic fate—passing on a disease. And so Chloe O'Brien is today what Louise Joy Brown was to the world 15 years ago—a medical pioneer, after whom many will follow.

The Role of Lifestyle in Preventing Low Birth Weight

Virginia Rall Chomitz
Lilian W.Y. Cheung
Ellice Lieberman

Virginia Rall Chomitz, Ph.D., is project manager of the Eat Well and Keep Moving Project, Department of Nutrition, Harvard School of Public Health.

Lilian W.Y. Cheung, D.Sc., R.D., is a lecturer in the Department of Nutrition and director of the Harvard Nutrition and Fitness Project, Harvard School of Public Health, Department of Nutrition and Center for Health Communication.

Ellice Lieberman, M.D., Dr.PH., is assistant professor in the Department of Obstetrics, Gynecology, and Reproductive Biology, Harvard Medical School and in the Department of Maternal and Child Health, Harvard School of Public Health.

Abstract

Lifestyle behaviors such as cigarette smoking, weight gain during pregnancy, and use of other drugs play an important role in determining fetal growth. The relationship between lifestyle risk factors and low birth weight is complex and is affected by psychosocial, economic, and biological factors. Cigarette smoking is the largest known risk factor for low birth weight. Approximately 20% of all low birth weight could be avoided if women did not smoke during pregnancy. Reducing heavy use of alcohol and other drugs during pregnancy could also reduce the rate of low birth weight births. Pregnancy and the prospect of pregnancy provide an important window of opportunity to improve women's health and the health of children. The adoption before or during pregnancy of more healthful lifestyle behaviors, such as ceasing to smoke, eating an adequate diet and gaining enough weight during pregnancy, and ceasing heavy drug use, can positively affect the long-term health of women and the health of their infants. Detrimental lifestyles can be modified, but successful modification will require large-scale societal changes. In the United States, these societal changes should include a focus on preventive health, family-centered workplace policies, and changes in social norms.

M any of the known risk factors associated with low birth weight, such as socioeconomic status, ethnicity, genetic makeup, and obstetric history, are not within a woman's immediate control. However, there are things that a woman can do to improve her chances of having a normal, healthy child. Lifestyle behaviors, such as cigarette smoking, use of other drugs, and nutrition, play an important role in determining fetal growth. Detrimental habits can be modified, but successful modification requires more than just a dose of individual "self control." Stopping lifelong addictive behaviors is very difficult, and a woman who suffers from them requires support and assistance not only from family members and individuals close to her, but also from the health care system and society.

The relationship between lifestyle risk factors and low birth weight is very complex and is affected by psychosocial, socio- economic, and biological factors. While it is important to describe the independent effects of different behavioral and socio-

This paper is based on Healthy Mothers—Healthy Beginnings, *a paper written with a grant from the CIGNA Foundation and CIGNA Corporation, 1992.*

economic risk factors, we must bear in mind that these factors are not isolated events in women's lives, but are a part of many interrelated complex behaviors and environmental risks. Factors associated with the perinatal health of women and children include demographic factors, medical risks, and maternal behaviors. These risk factors may influence maternal and infant health directly (in terms of physiology) or indirectly (in terms of health behavior). In this article we focus

---

There are things that a woman can do to improve her chances of having a normal, healthy child.

---

primarily on lifestyle behavioral risk factors that are amenable to change and that, if modified before or during pregnancy, can improve the likelihood of the delivery of a full-term healthy infant of appropriate size.

Demographic Factors

Socioeconomic status and race/ethnicity are indicators of complex linkages among environmental events, psychological states, and physiologic factors which may lead to low birth weight or preterm delivery. While we do not fully understand the specific biological pathways responsible, we do know that a woman's social and economic status will influence her general health and access to resources. (See the article by Hughes and Simpson in this journal issue for a detailed analysis of the effects of social factors on low birth weight.) In this section, we review the effects of some demographic indicators.

Socioeconomic Status

Low birth weight and infant mortality are closely related to socioeconomic disadvantage. Socioeconomic status, however, is difficult to measure accurately. Educational attainment, marital status, maternal age, and income are interrelated factors and are often used to approximate socioeconomic status, but no single factor truly measures its underlying influence.

Maternal education, maternal age, and marital status are all reflective of socioeconomic status and predictive of low birth weight. Twenty-four percent of the births in 1989 were to women with less than a high school education.[1] Low educational attainment is associated with higher rates of low birth weight.[2] For example, relative to college graduates, white women with less than a high school education were 50% more likely to have babies with very low birth weight (less than 1,500 grams, or 3 pounds, 5 ounces) and more than twice as likely to have babies with moderately low birth weight (between 1,500 grams and 2,500 grams, or 3 pounds, 5 ounces and 5 pounds, 8 ounces) than were women who graduated from college.[2] Teenage mothers are at greater risk of having a low birth weight baby than are mothers aged 25 to 34.[1] However, it is not clear if the risk of teenage childbearing is due to young maternal age or to the low socioeconomic status that often accompanies teenage pregnancy.

The marital status of the mother also appears to be independently associated with the rate of low birth weight,[2,3] although the relationship appears to vary by maternal age and race. The association of unmarried status with low birth weight is probably strongest for white women over 20 years of age.[2,4] Marital status may also serve as a marker for the "wantedness" of the child, the economic status of the mother, and the social support that the mother has—all of which are factors that may influence the health of the mother and infant.

It has been hypothesized that economic disadvantage may be a risk factor for low birth weight partly because of the high levels of stress and negative life events that are associated with being poor. Both physical stress and fatigue—particularly related to work during pregnancy—and psychological distress have been implicated.[5] In addition, stress and negative life events are associated with health behaviors such as smoking.[6] Social support may act as a moderator or as a buffer from the untoward effects of stressful life experiences and emotional dysfunction.[7]

Race/Ethnicity

The prevalence of low birth weight among white infants is less than half of that for African-American infants (6% and 13%, respectively). This difference reflects a twofold increase of preterm and low birth weight births among African-American mothers.[1] African-American mothers are more likely to have less education, not to be married, and to be younger than white mothers.[1] However, at almost all educational levels and age categories, African-American women have about double the rates of low birth weight as white women.[8] This fact indicates that these demographic differences in education, marital status, and age do not account for the large disparity between African Americans and whites in the incidence of low birth weight.

Among infants of Hispanic origin, who represented approximately 15% of live births in 1989, the rate of low birth weight was relatively low (6.1% overall), particularly given that Hispanic women (except Cuban women) had limited educational attainment and were not as likely as non-Hispanic white women to receive prenatal care early in pregnancy.[1]

However, Hispanics are a very diverse group, and the low birth weight rates vary considerably by national origin. Low birth weight rates range from 9.4% among Puerto Rican mothers to 5.6% among Cuban mothers. Among Asian infants in 1989, the incidence of low birth weight ranged from 5.1% for Chinese births to 7.3% for Filipino births.[1]

It is not known why infants of African-American mothers are twice as likely as all other infants to be born with low birth weights. The etiology of racial disparities in infant mortality and low birth weight is probably multifactorial in nature and is not completely explained by differences in demographics, use of tobacco and other drugs, or medical illnesses.[9] During the primary childbearing years (ages 15 to 29), the general mortality of African-American women exceeds that of white women for virtually every cause of death.

African-American women have higher rates of hypertension, anemia, and low-level lead exposure than other groups,[10] suggesting that the general health status of African-American women may be suboptimal. Infants of African-American foreign-born mothers have lower risks of neonatal mortality than infants of African-American U.S.–born mothers, a relationship that is not seen between foreign- and U.S.–born white women.[11] In addition, racial or ethnic differences in familial structure and social networks may affect morbidity and mortality.[12] More research will be needed to clarify the reasons for these disparities.

Nutrition and Weight Gain

Concerns about nutrition during pregnancy fall into two basic areas, maternal weight gain and nutrient intake, both of which can potentially affect the health of the mother and infant. As with other lifestyle factors, a woman's nutrition and weight gain are closely linked to her socioeconomic status, cigarette smoking, and other health-related behaviors.

Maternal Weight Gain

Maternal weight gain during pregnancy results from a variety of factors, including maternal dietary intake, prepregnancy weight and height, length of gestation, and size of the fetus. The mother's prepregnancy weight and height are, in turn, a consequence of her genetic makeup, past nutritional status, and environmental factors. The relationship between a woman's caloric intake during pregnancy and her infant's birth weight is complex and is moderated through maternal weight gain and other mechanisms during pregnancy.[13,14]

Epidemiologic evidence has demonstrated a nearly linear association between maternal weight gain during pregnancy and birth weight,[15,16] and an inverse relationship to the rate of low birth weight.[16] It comes as no surprise that maternal weight gain during pregnancy is highly correlated with the birth weight of the infant because a large proportion of the weight gain is due to the growth of the fetus itself. Women with total weight gains of 22 pounds (10 kilograms) or less were two to three times more likely to have growth-retarded full-term babies than were women with a gain of more than 22 pounds. Once corrected for the duration

---

It is not known why infants of African-American mothers are twice as likely as all other infants to be born with low birth weights.

---

of pregnancy, the relationship between weight gain and preterm delivery is uncertain.[17,18]

On average, women gain about 30 pounds during pregnancy. Teenage mothers, older mothers, unmarried mothers, and mothers with less than a high school education are most likely to have low or inadequate weight gain during pregnancy. Even after accounting for gestational age and socioeconomic status, African-American mothers gain less weight than white mothers (28 versus 31 pounds).[19] It has been estimated that from 15% to 33% of women gain an inadequate amount of weight (less than 22 pounds) during pregnancy.[13,19] Low weight gain may in part be the result of outdated medical advice and personal beliefs. In one study, one-quarter of the pregnant women believed that they should not gain more than 20 pounds during pregnancy.[20] In addition, belief that a smaller baby is easier to deliver and thus that weight gain and fetal birth weight

---

Smoking during pregnancy has been linked to 20% to 30% of low birth weight births.

---

should be limited influences the amount of weight gained by some women.[21]

While higher maternal weight gain is linked with healthier fetal weight gains, women and clinicians are concerned that women may retain weight after delivery and be at greater risk for obesity. Recent studies have shown that weight retention following delivery increased as weight gain increased, and African-American women retained more weight than white women with comparable weight gains during pregnancy (7.2 versus 1.6 pounds).[22] Thus, weight management programs would be appropriate for some women after delivery, but not during pregnancy.

Diet and Nutrient Intake

During pregnancy, the need for calories and nutrients, such as protein, iron, folate, and the other B vitamins, is increased to meet the demands of the fetus as well as the expansion of maternal tissues that support the fetus. As noted by Nathanielsz in this journal issue, the nutritional needs of the fetus are second only to the needs of the mother's brain. Thus, it is important for a pregnant woman to have a well-balanced, nutritious diet to meet the changing needs of her body and her fetus. Unfortunately, the direct relationship between specific vitamins and minerals and low birth weight is unclear, and controversy exists over the association between maternal hematocrit levels (which is a marker for anemia) and preterm birth.[23–26]

A pregnant woman's current nutritional status is determined by her prepregnant nutritional status, her current intake of nutrients, and her individual physiologi-

cal nutrient requirements. Members of the National Academy of Sciences recently reviewed the available literature on dietary intake of nutrients and minerals among pregnant women. They found that the energy intake (calories) for U.S. women was consistently below recommended levels and that the amount of important vitamins and minerals in their diet was also substantially lower than the recommended daily allowance. On average, intakes of protein, riboflavin, vitamin B-12, niacin, and vitamin C exceeded the recommended daily allowance.[27]

Women at particular risk of nutritional inadequacy during pregnancy may require nutritional counseling. Groups at risk include women voluntarily restricting caloric intake or dieting; pregnant adolescents; women with low income or limited food budgets; women with eating patterns or practices that require balancing food choices, such as strict vegetarians; women with emotional illness; smokers; women with poor knowledge of nutrition due to lack of education or illiteracy; and women with special difficulties in food resource management because of limited physical abilities and poor cooking or budgeting skills.[28]

Lifestyle Choices: Cigarette Smoking, Alcohol, Caffeine, and Illicit Drugs

Cigarette Smoking

Since the 1970s, the Surgeon General has reported that cigarette smoking during pregnancy is linked to fetal growth retardation and to infant mortality.[29] Smoking during pregnancy has been linked to 20% to 30% of low birth weight births and 10% of fetal and infant deaths.[30] Cigarette smoking is unequivocally the largest and most important known modifiable risk factor for low birth weight and infant death.

Approximately 20% to 25% of American women smoke cigarettes during pregnancy.[31,32] White, young, unmarried, and unemployed women, as well as women with fewer than 12 years of education and low socioeconomic status, are more likely to smoke during pregnancy, compared with nonwhite, older, married women with more than 12 years of education and higher socioeconomic status.[27,30,33,34] For example, 35% of mothers with less than a high school education smoke compared with 5% of college graduates.[35]

Smoking retards fetal growth. Birth weight is reduced by 150 to 320 grams (5.3 to 11.4 ounces) in infants born to smokers compared with those born to nonsmokers.[36] It has been consistently reported that, even after controlling other factors, women who smoke are about twice as likely to deliver a low birth weight baby as are women who do not smoke.[37] A dose-response relationship exists between the amount smoked and birth weight: the percent of low birth weight births increases with increasing number of cigarettes smoked during pregnancy. In addition, exposure to environmental cigarette smoke has also been associated with low birth weight.[38] Preterm birth is associated with smoking, but the association is weak compared with the association between low birth weight and smoking.[9,37] Cigarette smoking during pregnancy may account for up to 14% of preterm deliveries.[37]

Studies of women who quit cigarette smoking at almost any point during pregnancy show lower rates of low birth weight. Most fetal growth takes place in the last trimester, so that quitting early in pregnancy can decrease the negative effect of smoking on birth weight.[33] Quitting even as late as the seventh or eighth month has a positive impact on birth weight.[39]

Overall, about one-quarter of women who smoke prior to pregnancy quit upon learning of their pregnancies, and an additional one-third reduce the number of cigarettes they smoke.[33,40] Older women and more educated women are more likely to quit smoking during pregnancy.[41] Light smokers are more likely to quit smoking than heavier smokers. Heavier smokers are likely to reduce the amount they smoke, but are unlikely to quit.[42] Social support appears to be a critical factor in changing smoking behavior.[40]

Even among women who do quit smoking during pregnancy, about a third will relapse before childbirth.[43] In addition, nearly 80% of women who stop smoking during pregnancy relapse within one year after the delivery.[40] These high relapse rates reflect the physiological addictive nature of nicotine. While 57% of the pregnant smokers in one study were able to decrease their intake, 40% "tried and failed" to reduce.[44] Of women who both drank and smoked before pregnancy, fewer women were able to decrease or quit smoking than drinking, despite feelings of social pressure to quit and feelings of guilt at continuing to smoke.[44] The high recidi-

vism rate after childbirth also reflects diminished maternal contact with the health care system as health care provision shifts from obstetrics to pediatrics.[45]

The bulk of evidence shows a clear and consistent association between low birth weight (primarily due to growth retardation, not preterm birth) and infant mortality and smoking during pregnancy. Smoking also impacts on other aspects of the health status of women and infants. Smoking has been linked to long-term effects in infants such as physical, mental, and cognitive impairments.[46,47] The linkages between smoking and illnesses, such as cancer and cardiovascular and respiratory disease, are well known.[48] In addition, research on the effects of passive smoke indicates an increased frequency of respiratory and ear infections among infants and children exposed to this smoke.[33,49]

Alcohol Use

Alcohol use during pregnancy has long been associated with both short- and long-term negative health effects for infants. Alcohol abuse during pregnancy is clearly related to a series of congenital malforma-

tions described as fetal alcohol syndrome. However, the effects of moderate drinking on the fetus are not well established. Alcohol use among women of childbearing age and, specifically, among pregnant women has apparently declined significantly in the past decades.[44] This decreasing trend has generally been confined to more educated and older women. However, there has been little or no change in drinking during pregnancy among smokers, younger women, and women with less than a high school education.[50]

Heavy Drinking During Pregnancy

Numerous studies report an association between chronic alcohol abuse and a series of fetal malformations. Fetal alcohol syndrome is characterized by a pattern of severe birth defects related to alcohol use during pregnancy which include prenatal and postnatal growth retardation, central nervous system disorders, and distinct abnormal craniofacial features.[51] Heavy alcohol consumption has been cited as the leading preventable cause of mental retardation worldwide.[52] It has been estimated that the prevalence of fetal alcohol syndrome is 1 to 3 per 1,000 live births with a significantly increased rate among alco-

---

Heavy alcohol consumption has been cited as the leading preventable cause of mental retardation worldwide.

---

holics of 59 per 1,000 live births. Prenatally alcohol-exposed babies with birth defects who do not meet all required criteria for the syndrome are categorized as having fetal alcohol effects. The prevalence of fetal alcohol effects may be threefold that of fetal alcohol syndrome.[52]

The children of women who continued to drink an average of greater than one drink daily throughout their pregnancies are significantly smaller, shorter, and have smaller head circumferences than infants of control mothers who stop drinking.[53] The risk of low birth weight to women drinking three to five drinks per day was increased twofold over nondrinking mothers and almost threefold for those drinking six or more drinks daily when compared with women who did not drink.[54] A study of French women showed that those who consumed 35 drinks or more a week gave birth to infants that weighed 202 grams (about 7 ounces) less than the infants of women who consumed six or fewer drinks per week.[55]

Moderate Drinking During Pregnancy

While the effects of heavy daily drinking are well documented, the impact of moderate drinking is not as well established. Approximately 40% to 60% of pregnant women consume one drink or less a day. Alcohol use exceeding one drink daily ranges from 3% to 13%. Abstinence levels in pregnant women have been reported to range from 16% to 53%.[50,54,56] Women who consumed less than one alcoholic drink per day had only an 11% increased chance of delivering a growth-retarded infant.[54] Decrements in birth weight from 32 to 225 grams (1.1 to 8 ounces) have been reported for children born to women who drank one to three drinks daily.[55,57] Some studies with long-term follow-up have reported deleterious short-term effects and long-term effects, such as growth, mental, and motor delays, for infants of mothers who drink alcohol during pregnancy.[58,59] However, a number of studies demonstrate insignificant or no effects of "low to moderate" intake on growth at birth[60] and at four and five years of age.[58,61] The role of binge drinking is unknown.

Profile of the Pregnant Drinker

The profile of the pregnant drinker varies by the type of drinking. Any alcohol use during pregnancy is associated with older, white, professional, college-educated women with few previous children. Drinkers are also more likely to be unmarried and to smoke than are nondrinkers.[50] However, heavier alcohol use, in excess of two drinks daily, has been associated with African-American and Hispanic race/ethnicity, less than a high school education, and multiparity. Conversely, women who abstained during pregnancy were more likely to be younger, African-American, and/or of moderate income.[62]

During pregnancy, many woman reduce their drinking[63] with decreases occurring in all types of drinkers.[64] In addition, as pregnancy advances, the proportion of women drinking decreases. In one study, 55% of women drank in the week prior to conception, 50% drank after 32 weeks, and only 20% drank in the last week of their pregnancies.[65]

Many of the studies investigating the relationship of maternal alcohol use to fetal effects suffer from methodologic problems common to substance use research. Most of the studies rely on self-reporting which, because of the stigma attached to alcohol use during pregnancy, may be inaccurate. Studies of drug use also often fail to consider other important factors, such as maternal nutrition, general health, or marijuana use. In addition, the usual dose, frequency of intake, and timing of drinking during pregnancy may result in different consequences, but this information is often lacking.

Caffeine Consumption

Caffeine is one of the most commonly used drugs. At least 52% of people in the United States drink coffee, 29% drink tea, and 58% consume soft drinks.[66] Caffeine is most commonly consumed in beverages such as coffee, tea, and soft drinks; eaten in the form of chocolate; and also taken as part of various prescription and nonprescription drugs. No consistent associations between caffeine and low birth weight or preterm birth have been observed.[67] Most studies have found no association between caffeine use and low birth weight, but some studies report positive yet inconsistent associations.[67] Several studies have found an interaction between caffeine and cigarette smoking, where the adverse effects of caffeine were observed only among smokers. The existence of such an interaction may help to explain the conflicting results.

Illicit Drug Use

In recent years, the rise in use of illegal drugs, particularly prenatal drug and cocaine, or "crack," use has received extensive coverage in the popular press and sparked many investigations. Prenatal cocaine and heroin abuse are clearly associated with adverse birth outcomes. Other factors in a drug addict's lifestyle, including malnutrition, sexually transmitted diseases, and polysubstance abuse, may contribute to an increased risk of adverse pregnancy outcome and often complicate the ability to examine the effects of individual drugs. The effect of marijuana use on the health of women and their infants is not as clear, nor are the effects of the occasional use of cocaine and other drugs.

Several methodologic problems hinder the interpretation and generalizability of much of the research on both the prevalence and effects of prenatal drug exposure. Studies are often based on small, nonrepresentative samples of mothers, and the bulk of the literature regarding illicit drug use relies on self-reporting. It is difficult to elicit valid information about

illegal drug use, and a significant amount of underreporting probably takes place.[68] It is also unclear whether some of the effects of drug use are due to fetal drug exposure or to the generally poorer health and limited prenatal care of many addicted women. Finally, most research has been conducted with low-income urban women who are often in poorer health and under greater stress than their middle-class counterparts. The timing of drug use during the course of pregnancy and the dosage undoubtedly influences the consequences of the actions. However, most studies have been unable to characterize

Prenatal cocaine and heroin abuse are clearly associated with adverse birth outcomes.

accurately the use of drugs in pregnancy. In addition, interactive effects of illicit drugs with alcohol, tobacco, or other drugs have not as yet been adequately examined.

Despite the limitations of the research, a number of studies have shown significant effects of individual illicit substances on women and infants. Elevated rates of fetal growth retardation, perinatal death, and pregnancy and delivery complications—such as abruptio placentae, high blood pressure, and preeclampsia—have been observed among drug-abusing women and their infants.[69–73]

Cocaine Use

Maternal cocaine use has been associated with low birth weight, preterm labor, abruptio placentae, and fetal distress.[68,74,75] Brain damage and genitourinary malformations of the neonate have been reported, as well as fetal hyperthermia, thyroid abnormalities, stroke, and acute cardiac events.[76] Neurobehavioral effects found in neonates born to cocaine-abusing mothers have also been reported. These effects include decreased interactive behavior and poor organizational response to environmental stimuli.[72,74]

Marijuana Use

The effects of prenatal marijuana use on pregnancy and infant outcomes are inconclusive. Children exposed to marijuana *in utero* may be smaller than nonexposed infants.[68] Other reports suggest that pregnant women who smoke marijuana are at higher risk of preterm labor, miscarriage, and stillbirth.[76] However, other studies find no difference between users of marijuana and nonusers in terms of rate of miscarriage, type of presentation at birth, Apgar status, and frequency of complications or major physical anomalies at birth.[77]

Very little is known about the number of women who use drugs while pregnant, their pattern of drug usage during pregnancy, or the intensity of use. The prevalence of illicit drug use among pregnant women has been estimated using state level and hospital-based studies. Based on anonymous urine toxicology analysis combined with self-reporting, the prevalence of drug use among pregnant women has been estimated at 7.5% to 15%.[78,79]

Cocaine use among pregnant women has been estimated at 2.3% to 3.4%.[79,80] Regional and hospital-based data report marijuana use during pregnancy in the range of 3% to 12% and opiate (heroin) use in the range of 2% to 4%.[78,79] Regional data, such as New York City birth certificate data,[81] documented the dramatic increase in cocaine use relative to other drugs during the 1980s.

Figure 1 presents a profile of substance use among one sample of pregnant women.[62] Extrapolation of the data suggests that about half of all pregnant women may completely abstain from cigarette, alcohol, or drug use. However, approximately 14% of pregnant women engage in two or more high-risk behaviors during pregnancy, with about 2.5% of pregnant women, possibly about 100,000 nationwide, combining smoking, drinking, and recreational drug use.

Recent evidence suggests that, for pregnant women who receive treatment for drug abuse before their third trimester, the risks of low birth weight and preterm birth due to cocaine use may be minimized.[82] Little is known about which women quit or reduce drug use and why. In one study, college-educated, employed women were more likely to quit recrea-

Stress is widely cited in the popular literature as a serious risk to mothers and infants, but current research has not characterized its effects.

tional drug use during pregnancy than were teenagers. The cessation rates were similar by racial/ethnic background and household income.[62] In another study, 14% of white women who used marijuana stopped using it upon starting prenatal care, as compared with 6% of African-American women.[83]

Stress, Physical Activity, Employment, Social Support, Violence, and Sexually Transmitted Diseases

As discussed in the previous section on demographic risk factors, physical and psychosocial stress may be associated with low birth weight. Stress is widely cited in the popular literature as a serious risk to mothers and infants, but current research has not characterized its effects. The scientific literature linking stress and anxiety to obstetric outcome has been equivocal, but there is some basis for the notion that maternal emotional distress may be linked to poor reproductive outcome.[84]

Stress

Stress is believed to influence maternal and infant health via changes in neuroendocrine functioning, immune system responses, and health behaviors. Thus, stress may influence pregnancy outcome directly (in terms of physiology) or indirectly (in terms of health behavior). Physiologically, stress has been associated with anxiety and depression.[85] It has been suggested that anxiety may increase metabolic expenditure and may lead to a lower gestational weight gain or to an anxiety-mediated change in catecholamine or hormonal balance which could provoke preterm labor.[37] Maternal psychological stress or emotional distress may interfere with the utilization of prenatal care or co-occur with particular health behaviors such as smoking and alcohol consumption.

However, the many methodological problems in much of the literature on stress and social support limit the extent to which studies can inform and guide policy and research. The studies are often based on small and ungeneralizable samples, and suffer from possible recall biases, poor reliability, and validity of study instruments and confounding. These difficulties arise from the multifactorial nature of stress and social support and from the

Figure 1

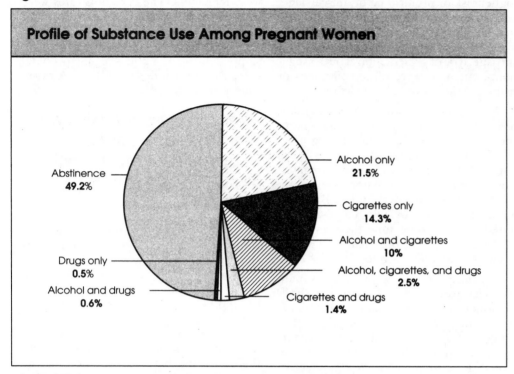

Source: Adapted from Johnson, S.F., McCarter, R.J., and Ferencz, C. Changes in alcohol, cigarette, and recreational drug use during pregnancy: Implications for intervention. *American Journal of Epidemiology* (1987) 126,4:701. Reprinted with permission of the *American Journal of Epidemiology*.

problems inherent in trying to characterize these poorly understood elements of people's lives.

Physical Activity

Concerns about weight gain and health have resulted in a high level of consciousness about weight control. More than one-third of American women participate in some form of regular physical activity.[86] Moderate aerobic exercise during pregnancy appears to have little adverse effect on pregnancy outcomes, and the potential benefits of exercise appear to be considerable.[87] Moderate exercise may be particularly beneficial for women at risk of developing diabetes during pregnancy. Lower levels of blood sugar were observed among diabetic women who were randomly assigned to moderate exercise regimens.[88] Decreases in the discomforts of pregnancy, improved self-esteem, and reduced tensions were reported among women who had participated in moderate physical conditioning programs during pregnancy.[89]

Employment

The majority of American women are employed during pregnancy.[90] Women are employed in a wide range of occupations, which have varying degrees of physical and emotional demands, and varying levels of exposure to employment-related chemicals, radiation, or other toxic substances. Thus, defining a particular "exposure" that characterizes the potential risks of employment has been difficult. In addition, the interrelationship between employment and socioeconomic status is unavoidable. Employed mothers also may accrue positive effects of employment through increased socioeconomic status, better access to medical care, and improved overall lifestyle.[91]

In general, the results of studies evaluating the relationship between employment and low birth weight have been inconclusive.[92] Studies conducted outside the United States have found increased rates of low birth weight and preterm birth among employed women whose jobs required heavy physical labor. However, results of studies conducted in the United States are more mixed and have even demonstrated positive effects of employment. Further advances in this area will be hampered until we are able to better understand the complex relationship among socioeconomic status, employment, stress, and lifestyle.

Domestic Violence

Depending on the population surveyed and the questions asked, the prevalence of battering of pregnant women has been estimated to be 8% to 17%.[93,94] There is some evidence of low birth weight among women who have been abused during pregnancy,[95] possibly due to a physical trauma that initiates abruption, infections, or uterine contractions leading to early onset of labor. In addition, victimization of women may lead to a neglect of chronic medical conditions or to later initiation of prenatal care.[94]

Sexually Transmitted Diseases

Whether or not a woman gets infected with a sexually transmitted disease is highly associated with her sexual behavior and the sexual behavior of her partners. The chance of being infected increases with the number of sexual partners. There is increasing evidence to indicate that various genital infections are associated with low birth weight and preterm delivery.[96] However, the large number of implicated organisms combined with the numerous genital tract sites that they might infect has made the investigation of sexually transmitted diseases and low birth weight very challenging. Aside from the devastating effects on the fetus of untreated syphilis or gonorrhea, few specific organisms or defined genital tract infections have conclusively been shown to be highly correlated with preterm birth or low birth weight.[96] Most of the evidence linking genital organisms or infections to birth outcomes has been inconsistent and has shown only a low to moderate association. Clinical trials of antibiotics aimed at removing the organisms or infections have not consistently improved pregnancy outcomes.[96]

Other maternal infections during pregnancy, such as cytomegalovirus, genitourinary infections, pyelonephritis, and HIV, as well as food- or environmentally-borne infections such as toxoplasmosis and listeriosis, may endanger the health of the mother and fetus.[5,97–99]

Assessing the Impact of Lifestyle Risk Factors on Maternal and Infant Health

In this section, we try to estimate the number of excess low birth weight or small-for-gestational-age babies born due to maternal lifestyle risk factors. As noted earlier, the risk factors for low birth weight described above do not occur as isolated events; rather, they are part of a complex web of social, environmental, and individual factors. To understand the importance of these individual risk factors, we must try to fit them into a framework that represents a realistic picture of what is occurring in women's lives. This task is made more difficult because of our limited knowledge of the many common risk factors and the many potential interactions between factors which would result in a compounding of adverse effects—such as alcohol abuse and heavy cigarette smoking—as well as the role of protective factors.

We started by selecting the risk factors that have a consistent relationship with low birth weight and have been shown to be modifiable. These risk factors are cigarette smoking, alcohol abuse, cocaine abuse, and inadequate weight gain during pregnancy. The data on the prevalence of these factors and the risk incurred were derived from a variety of national and regional studies, and thus the estimates presented reflect the demographic and regional profile of the sample used. The estimates are not the result of a meta-analysis, but are based on published analyses that represent conservative and plausible risk.

We estimated the extra adverse birth outcomes attributed to high-risk lifestyle factors by applying the rate of low birth weight deliveries among cigarette smokers, women with inadequate weight gain, alcohol drinkers, and cocaine users, minus a baseline rate of low birth weight among low-risk women. The effects of reducing stress and exposure to infectious agents cannot be quantified at this time. The numbers we derived are very rough estimates and should be regarded only as order of magnitude estimates.

Prevalence of Lifestyle Risk Factors

From the literature, we extrapolated estimates of the prevalence of high-risk behaviors among pregnant women to the number of live births in the United States in 1989. Some 20% to 25% of pregnant women, or approximately one million, smoked during pregnancy.[32,33] (See Figure 2.) Approximately 15%, or about 600,000 nonobese women, may have an inadequate total weight gain of less than 22 pounds during their pregnancy. More than 40% of women may not completely abstain from alcohol but consume less than one drink per day during pregnancy; about 3%, or 120,000 women, may have one or more drinks per day.[54] Approximately 105,000, or 2.6% of women, may use cocaine around the time of delivery.[79]

Excess Adverse Birth Outcomes

In 1990, there were 4,158,212 births in the United States, and 6.97% (approximately 290,000) of these infants were born low birth weight.[100] It comes as no surprise that reducing cigarette smoking has the largest potential to reduce the incidence of low birth weight. Approximately 48,000 low birth weight births could have been prevented if women had not smoked during pregnancy.

Women who failed to gain adequate weight (less than 22 pounds) by term gave birth to approximately 22,000 extra low birth weight babies who were born at full term. Approximately 14,000 infants a year may be born small for their gestational age due to maternal alcohol consumption, and 10,000 excess low birth weight births could be attributed to prenatal cocaine abuse.

The low birth weight births that are potentially preventable due to smoking, inadequate weight gain, and alcohol use would generally reduce the number of infants who were born too small due to growth retardation but would have little effect on the number of infants born preterm. The lack of a relationship between these risk factors and preterm birth indicates that little improvement in preterm birth rates could be expected with the elimination of these risk factors.

Our estimates of the number of low birth weight births are very rough and may be inaccurate, as these numbers are only as good as our current knowledge of the true relationships between these risk factors and birth outcomes. The number of low birth weight births estimated to be due to each of these factors cannot simply be added together to derive the total number of births that might be prevented by lifestyle changes because these estimates do not take into consideration the interrelationships among the risk factors. For example, a woman who is a heavy smoker and drinker would be counted twice in these calculations.

Directions for Future Research: Identifying Barriers to Change

Women face systemic, psychosocial, biological, or knowledge and attitudinal bar-

Figure 2

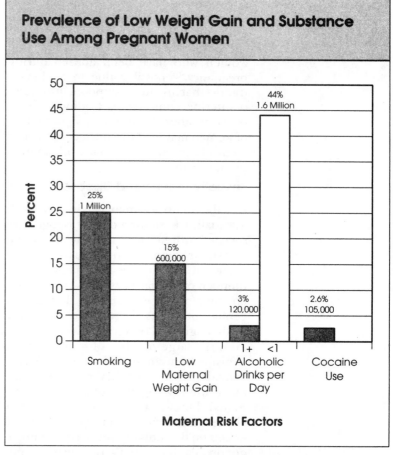

Prevalence of Low Weight Gain and Substance Use Among Pregnant Women

Source: Chomitz, V.R., Cheung, L., and Lieberman, E. *Healthy mothers—Healthy beginnings.* A white paper prepared by the Center for Health Communication, Harvard School of Public Health. Boston: President and Fellows of Harvard College, 1992.

Pregnancy and the prospect of pregnancy provide a window of opportunity to improve a woman's health before pregnancy, during pregnancy, and after the birth of her child.

riers to lifestyle changes. Further research must identify successful strategies for influencing behaviors. Figure 3 illustrates the complexity and interrelationship of common barriers to improving prenatal care and nutritional status, and for modifying smoking, drinking, and drug use.

Although some individuals within an economically depressed or stressful situation may be involved in adverse lifestyle behaviors, most women are not. It is therefore important not only to conduct research with those individuals who have less healthy lifestyles, but also to profile and learn from those who, given similar environmental pressures, do not engage in

Figure 3

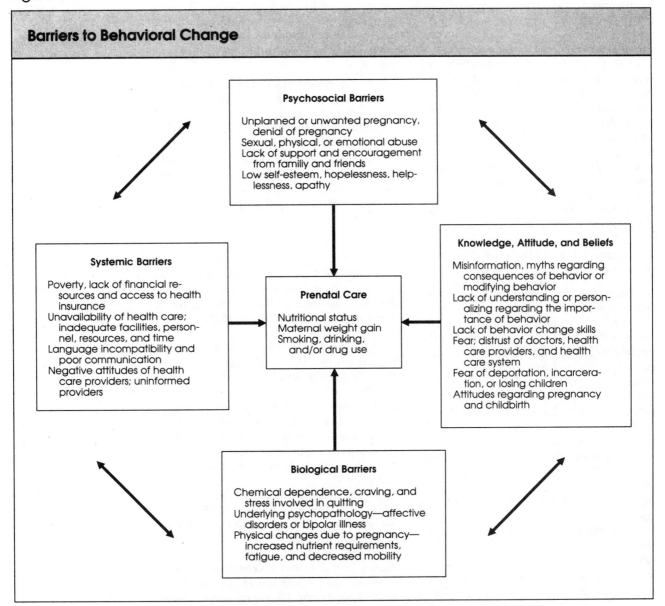

Barriers to Behavioral Change

Psychosocial Barriers

Unplanned or unwanted pregnancy, denial of pregnancy
Sexual, physical, or emotional abuse
Lack of support and encouragement from family and friends
Low self-esteem, hopelessness, helplessness, apathy

Systemic Barriers

Poverty, lack of financial resources and access to health insurance
Unavailability of health care; inadequate facilities, personnel, resources, and time
Language incompatibility and poor communication
Negative attitudes of health care providers; uninformed providers

Prenatal Care

Nutritional status
Maternal weight gain
Smoking, drinking, and/or drug use

Knowledge, Attitude, and Beliefs

Misinformation, myths regarding consequences of behavior or modifying behavior
Lack of understanding or personalizing regarding the importance of behavior
Lack of behavior change skills
Fear; distrust of doctors, health care providers, and health care system
Fear of deportation, incarceration, or losing children
Attitudes regarding pregnancy and childbirth

Biological Barriers

Chemical dependence, craving, and stress involved in quitting
Underlying psychopathology—affective disorders or bipolar illness
Physical changes due to pregnancy—increased nutrient requirements, fatigue, and decreased mobility

Source: Center for Health Communication, Harvard School of Public Health.

high-risk behaviors or who have been able to change; that is, we must discover the protective strategies or resilience among individuals who are not engaged in adverse lifestyle behaviors, and apply the lessons learned to intervention programs.

Directions for Prevention/Intervention

Pregnancy and the prospect of pregnancy provide a window of opportunity to improve a woman's health before pregnancy, during pregnancy, and after the birth of her child. Pregnancy provides an opportunity for increased contact with the health care system and is associated with a heightened concern regarding health. More-

over, healthier mothers are more likely to provide more healthful beginnings for their children.

The adoption of healthful lifestyle behaviors before or during pregnancy, such as ceasing to smoke cigarettes, eating foods that supply adequate nutrition and produce an appropriate pregnancy weight gain, ceasing or reducing alcohol consumption, and ceasing illicit drug use, can also positively affect the long-term health of women, future pregnancy outcomes, and the health of children.

The health of the family, in general, may also be improved through household dietary changes and the reduction of environmental risks such as secondhand smoke. However, it must be reiterated that behaviors should not be isolated from the environment (society, community, and family) that fosters and supports them, and thus a change in the elements within the environment will facilitate an individual's ability to change his or her behavior. Despite the importance of maternal behavior modification to the health of mothers, infants, and families, it is important to recognize that there are systemic, biological, psychosocial, and belief and attitudinal barriers to behavioral change which women also must overcome. Expecting women simply to change or modify their behavior without support and attention from the health care system, society, and influential people in their lives is unrealistic and may help to foster the belief that women are solely to blame for undesirable behaviors.

Barriers to successful intervention will not be overcome in the short term and will require both system-level reform and individual efforts. Many women who smoke, engage in high-risk behaviors, eat poorly, or lack access to health care also live surrounded by poverty and violence, and go without adequate housing or employment. Under such circumstances, living a healthful lifestyle may not be a priority compared with day-to-day survival.

Overcoming these social circumstances will require increased access and availability to quality health care, as well as other affiliated resources and facilities such as child care, social services, law enforcement services, affordable and quality food, transportation, and maternity provisions during employment.

Finding ways to improve maternal and infant health and decrease the low birth weight rate is difficult, at least in part because the known causes of low birth weight are multifactorial, and much of the etiology remains unknown. The independent effects of economic disadvantage and inadequate health care coverage on maternal and infant health are difficult to isolate. In addition, medical risk factors that are identified and managed either before or during pregnancy can positively influence the health of women and their infants. Thus, linking women to continuous health care early in pregnancy or, ideally, before conception is a high priority for intervention.

Health promotion efforts aimed at improving infant health must do so by improving women's health. Improving women's health before, during, and after pregnancy is the key to reducing the human and economic costs associated with infant mortality and morbidity. To improve both women's and infants' health, efforts must target long-term, societal elements that involve policy or legislative changes.

These efforts should include an emphasis on preventive health care services, family-oriented work site options, changes in social norms, and individual behavior modification.

Strategies that can reduce the burden of low birth weight do exist. The public and private sectors must work together to define, develop, and implement these strategies.

Notes

1. National Center for Health Statistics. *Advance report of final natality statistics, 1991.* Monthly Vital Statistics Report, Vol. 42, No. 3, Suppl. Hyattsville, MD: Public Health Service, September 9, 1993.

2. Kleinman, J., and Kessel, S. Racial differences in low birthweight: Trends and risk factors. *New England Journal of Medicine* (1987) 317,12:749–53.

3. Ahmed, F. Unmarried mothers as a high-risk group for adverse pregnancy outcomes. *Journal of Community Health* (1990) 15,1:35–44.

4. Bennett, T. Marital status and infant health outcomes. *Social Science Medicine* (1992) 35,9:1179–87.

5. Institute of Medicine, Committee to Study the Prevention of Low Birthweight. *Preventing low birthweight.* Washington, DC: National Academy Press, 1985.

6. McCormick, M. C., Brooks-Gunn, J., Shorter, T., et al. Factors associated with smoking in low income pregnant women: Relationship to birthweight, stressful life events, social support, health behaviors, and mental distress. *Journal of Clinical Epidemiology* (1990) 43:441–48.

7. Brooks-Gunn, J. Support and stress during pregnancy: What do they tell us about low birthweight? In *Advances in the prevention of low birthweight: An international symposium.* H. Berendes, S. Kessel, and S. Yaffe, eds. Washington, DC: National Center for Education in Maternal and Child Health, 1991, pp. 39–60.

8. Collins, Jr., J. W., and David, R. J. The differential effect of traditional risk factors on infant birthweight among blacks and whites in Chicago. *American Journal of Public Health* (1990) 80,6:679.

9. Shiono, P., Klebanoff, M., and Rhoads, G. Smoking and drinking during pregnancy. *Journal of the American Medical Association* (1986) 255:82–84.

10. Geronimus, A. T., and Bound, J. Black/white differences in women's reproductive-related

health status: Evidence from vital statistics. *Demography* (1990) 27,3:457–66.

11. Kleinman, J., Fingerhut, L. A., and Prager K. Differences in infant mortality by race, nativity status, and other maternal characteristics. *American Journal of Diseases of Children* (1991) 145:194–99.

12. Moss, N. Demographic and behavioral sciences five year research plan. Draft. Bethesda, MD: National Institute of Child Health and Human Development, 1991.

13. Scholl, T., Hediger, J., Khoo, C., et al. Maternal weight gain, diet and infant birth weight: Correlations during adolescent pregnancy. *Journal of Clinical Epidemiology* (1991) 44:423–28.

14. Susser, M. Maternal weight gain, infant birth weight, and diet: Causal sequences. *American Journal of Clinical Nutrition* (1991) 53,6:1384–96.

15. Kleinman, J. *Maternal weight gain during pregnancy: Determinants and consequences.* Working Paper No. 33. Hyattsville, MD: National Center for Health Statistics, 1990.

16. Luke, B., Dickinson, C., and Petrie, R. H. Intrauterine growth: Correlations of maternal nutritional status and rate of gestational weight gain. *European Journal of Obstetrics, Gynecology, and Reproductive Biology* (1981) 12:113–21.

17. Kramer, M. S., McLean, F. H., Eason, E. L., and Usher, R. H. Maternal nutrition and spontaneous preterm birth. *American Journal of Epidemiology* (1992) 136:574–83.

18. Kramer, M. S., Coates, A. L., Michoud, M., and Hamilton, E. F. Maternal nutrition and idiopathic preterm labor. *Pediatric Research* (1994) 35,4:277A.

19. National Center for Health Statistics. *Advance report of maternal and infant health data from the birth certificate, 1990.* Monthly Vital Statistics Report, Vol. 42, No. 2, Suppl. Hyattsville, MD: Public Health Service, July 8, 1993.

20. Carruth, B. R., and Skinner, J. D. Practitioners beware: Regional differences in beliefs about nutrition during pregnancy. *Journal of American Dietetic Association* (1991) 91,4:435–40.

21. Chez, R. Weight gain during pregnancy. *American Journal of Public Health* (1986) 76:1390–91.

22. Keppel, K. G., and Taffel, S. M. Pregnancy-related weight gain and retention: Implications of the 1990 Institute of Medicine Guidelines. *American Journal of Public Health* (1993) 83:1100–1103.

23. Klein, L. Premature birth and maternal prenatal anemia. *American Journal of Obstetrics and Gynecology* (1962) 83,5:588–90.

24. Klebanoff, M. A., Shiono, P. H., Selby, J. V., et al. Anemia and spontaneous preterm birth. *American Journal of Obstetrics and Gynecology* (1991) 164:59–63.

25. Lieberman, E., Ryan, K., Monson, R. R., and Schoenbaum, S. C. Association of maternal hematocrit with premature labor. *American Journal of Obstetrics and Gynecology* (1988) 159:107–14.

26. Klebanoff, J., and Shiono, P. H. Facts and artifacts about anemia and preterm birth. *Journal of the American Medical Association* (1989) 262:511–15.

27. Institute of Medicine, Subcommittee on Nutritional Status and Weight Gain During Pregnancy. *Nutrition during pregnancy.* Washington, DC: National Academy Press, 1990.

28. Dwyer, J. Impact of maternal nutrition on infant health. *Medical Times* (1983) 111:30–38.

29. U.S. Department of Health, Education, and Welfare. *The health consequences of smoking.* DHEW/HSM 73-8704. Washington, DC: DHEW, 1973.

30. Kleinman, J., and Madans, J. H. The effects of maternal smoking, physical stature, and educational attainment on the incidence of low birth weight. *American Journal of Epidemiology* (1985) 121:832–55.

31. National Center for Health Statistics. *Advance report of new data from the 1989 birth certificate, 1989: Final data from the National Center for Health Statistics.* Monthly Vital Statistics Report, Vol. 40, No. 12. Hyattsville, MD: Public Health Service, April 15, 1992.

32. National Center for Health Statistics. *Advance report of final mortality statistics, 1989: Final data from the National Center for Health Statistics.* Monthly Vital Statistics Report, Vol. 40, No. 8, Suppl. 2. Hyattsville, MD: Public Health Service, January 7, 1992.

33. U.S. Department of Health and Human Services. *The health benefits of smoking cessation: A report of the Surgeon General.* DHHS/CDC 90-8416. Washington, DC: DHHS, 1990.

34. Cardoza, L. D., Gibb, D. M. F., Studd, J. W. W., and Cooper, D. J. Social and obstetric features associated with smoking in pregnancy. *British Journal of Obstetrics and Gynecology* (1982) 89:622–27.

35. See note no. 32, National Center for Health Statistics, for mortality statistics in 1989.

36. Butler, N., Goldstein, H., and Ross, E. Cigarette smoking in pregnancy: Its influence on birth weight and perinatal mortality. *British Medical Journal* (1972) 2:127–30.

37. Kramer, M. S. Determinants of low birth weight: Methodological assessment and meta-analysis. *Bulletin of the World Health Organization* (1987) 65:663–737.

38. Martin, T., and Bracken, M. Association of low birth weight with passive smoke exposure in pregnancy. *American Journal of Epidemiology* (1986) 124:633–42.

39. Rush, D., and Cassano, P. Relationship of cigarette smoking and social class to birth weight and perinatal mortality among all births in Britain, 5–11 April 1970. *Journal of Epidemiology and Community Health* (1983) 37: 249–55.

40. Wilner, S., Secker-Walker, R. H., Flynn, B. S., et al. How to help the pregnant woman stop smoking. In *Smoking and reproductive health*. M. J. Rosenberg, ed. Littleton, MA: PSG Publishing, 1987, pp. 215–22.

41. Fingerhut, L. A., Kleinman, J. C., and Kendrick, J. S. Smoking before, during, and after pregnancy. *American Journal of Public Health* (1990) 80:541–44.

42. Waterson, E. J., and Murray-Lyon, I. M. Drinking and smoking patterns amongst women attending an antenatal clinic—II. During pregnancy. *Alcohol and Alcoholism* (1989) 24,2:163–73.

43. Windsor, R. *The handbook to plan, implement and evaluate smoking cessation programs for pregnant women*. White Plains, NY: March of Dimes Birth Defects Foundation, 1990.

44. Condon, J. T., and Hilton, C. A. A comparison of smoking and drinking behaviors in pregnant women: Who abstains and why. *Medical Journal of Australia* (1988) 148:381–85.

45. Burns, D., and Pierce, J. P. *Tobacco use in California 1990–1991*. Sacramento: California Department of Health Services, 1992.

46. Brandt. E. N. Smoking and reproductive health. In *Smoking and reproductive health*. M. J. Rosenberg, ed. Littleton, MA: PSG Publishing, 1987, pp 1–3.

47. Weitzman, M., Gortmaker, S., Walker, D. K., and Sobol, A. Maternal smoking and childhood asthma. *Pediatrics* (1990) 85: 505–11.

48. U.S. Department of Health and Human Services. *Reducing the health consequences of smoking: A report of the Surgeon General.* DHHS/CDC 89-8411. Rockville, MD: DHHS, 1989.

49. Samet, J. M., Lewit, E. M., and Warner, K. E. Involuntary smoking and children's health. *The Future of Children.* (Winter 1994) 4,3:94–114.

50. Serdula, M., Williamson, D., Kendrick, J., et al. Trends in alcohol consumption by pregnant women. *Journal of the American Medical Association* (1991) 265:876–79.

51. Ouellette, E. M., Rosett, H. L., Rosman, N. P., and Weiner, L. Adverse effects on offspring of maternal alcohol abuse during pregnancy. *New England Journal of Medicine* (1977) 297,10:528–30.

52. Abel, E. L., and Sokol, R. J. Incidence of fetal alcohol syndrome and economic impact of FAS-related anomalies. *Drug and Alcohol Dependence* (1987) 19:51–70.

53. Day, N. L., Jasperse, D., Richardson, G., et al. Prenatal exposure to alcohol: Effect on infant growth and morphologic characteristics. *Pediatrics* (1989) 84,3:536–41.

54. Mills, J. L., Graubard, B. I., Harley, E. E., et al. Maternal alcohol consumption and birth weight: How much drinking during pregnancy is safe? *Journal of the American Medical Association* (1984) 252,14:1875–79.

55. Larroque, B., Kaminski, M., Lelong, N., et al. Effects on birth weight of alcohol and caffeine consumption during pregnancy. *American Journal of Epidemiology* (1993) 137:941–50.

56. Halmesmaki, E., Raivio, K., and Ylikorkala, O. Patterns of alcohol consumption during pregnancy. *Obstetrics and Gynecology* (1987) 69:594–97.

57. Little, R., Asker, R. L., Sampson, P. D., and Renwick, J. H. Fetal growth and moderate drinking in early pregnancy. *American Journal of Epidemiology* (1986) 123,2:270–78.

58. Streissguth, A. P., Bookstein, F. L., Sampson, P. D., and Barr, H. M. Neurobehavioral effects of prenatal alcohol: Part III. PLS analyses of neuropsychologic tests. *Neurotoxicology and Teratology* (1989) 11,5:493–507.

59. Streissguth, A. P., Barr, H. M., and Sampson, P. D. Moderate prenatal alcohol exposure: Effects on child IQ and learning problems at age 7 ½ years. *Alcoholism, Clinical and Experimental Research* (1990) 14,5:662–69.

60. Walpole, I., Zubrick, S., and Pontre, J. Is there a fetal effect with low to moderate alcohol use before or during pregnancy? *Journal of Epidemiology and Community Health* (1990) 44,4:297–301.

61. Ernhart, C. B., Sokol. R. J., Ager, J. W., et al. Alcohol-related birth defects: Assessing the risk. *Annals of the New York Academy of Sciences* (1989) 562:159–72.

62. Johnson, S. F., McCarter, R. J., and Ferencz, C. Changes in alcohol, cigarette, and recreational drug use during pregnancy: Implications for intervention. *American Journal of Epidemiology* (1987) 126,4:695–702.

63. Little, R. Schultz, F., and Mandell, W. Alcohol consumption during pregnancy. *Journal of Studies on Alcohol* (1976) 37:375–79.

64. Russell, M. Drinking and pregnancy: A review of current research. *New York State Journal of Medicine* (1983) 8:1218–21.

65. See note no. 56, Halmesmaki, Raivio, and Ylikorkala, for more information about alcohol consumption patterns during pregnancy.

66. Lecos, C. Caffeine jitters: Some safety questions remain. *FDA Consumer* (December 1987/January 1988) 21:22.

67. Shiono, P. H., and Klebanoff, M. A. Invited commentary: Caffeine and birth outcomes. *American Journal of Epidemiology* (1993) 137:951–54.

68. Zuckerman, B., Frank, D. A., Hingson, R., et al. Effects of maternal marijuana and cocaine use on fetal growth. *New England Journal of Medicine* (1989) 320:762–68.

69. Zelson, C., Rubio, E., and Wasserman, E. Neonatal narcotic addiction: 10 year observation. *Pediatrics* (1971) 48,2:178–89.

70. Fricker, H., and Segal, S. Narcotic addiction, pregnancy, and the newborn. *American Journal of Diseases of Children* (1978) 132:360–66.

71. Lifschitz, M., Wilson, G., Smith, E., et al.

Fetal and postnatal growth of children born to narcotic-dependent women. *Journal of Pediatrics* (1983) 102:686–91.

72. Robins, L. N., and Mills, J. L., Krulewitch, C., and Herman, A. A. Effects of in utero exposure to street drugs. *American Journal of Public Health* (December 1993) 83,12:S9.

73. Oleske, J. Experiences with 118 infants born to narcotic-using mothers. *Clinical Pediatrics* (1977) 16:418–23.

74. Dattel, B. J. Substance abuse in pregnancy. *Seminars in Perinatology* (1990) 14,2:179–87.

75. Bateman, D. A., Ng, S. K. C., Hansen, C. A., and Heagarty, M. C. The effects of intrauterine cocaine exposure in newborns. *American Journal of Public Health* (1993) 83,2:190–93.

76. Office for Substance Abuse Prevention. *Alcohol and other drugs can harm an unborn baby: Fact sheet and resource list.* Rockville, MD: National Clearinghouse for Alcohol and Drug Information, 1989, pp 1–19.

77. Fried, P. A., and Makin, J. E. Neonatal behavioral correlates of prenatal exposure to marijuana, cigarettes and alcohol in a low risk population. *Neurotoxicology and Teratology* (1986) 9:1–7.

78. Chasnoff, I. J., Landress, H. J., and Barrett, M. E. The prevalence of illicit-drug or alcohol use during pregnancy and discrepancies in mandatory reporting in Pinellas County, Florida. *New England Journal of Medicine* (1990) 322:1202–6.

79. Centers for Disease Control and Prevention. Statewide prevalence of illicit drug use by pregnant women—Rhode Island. *Morbidity and Mortality Weekly Report* (1990) 39,14:225–27.

80. Handler, A., Kistin, N., Davis, F., and Ferré, C. Cocaine use during pregnancy: Perinatal outcomes. *American Journal of Epidemiology* (1991) 133:818–25.

81. Zeitel, L., Bauer, T. A., and Brooks, P. *Infants at risk: Solutions within our reach.* New York: Greater New York March of Dimes/United Hospital Fund of New York, 1991.

82. U.S. General Accounting Office. *Drug abuse: The crack cocaine epidemic: Health consequences and treatment.* HRD-91-55FS. Washington, DC: GAO, 1991.

83. McCaul, M. E., Svikis, D. S., and Feng, T. Pregnancy and addiction: Outcomes and interventions. *Maryland Medical Journal* (1991) 40:995–1001.

84. Newberger, E. H., Barkan, S. E., Lieberman, E. S., et al. Abuse of pregnant women and adverse birth outcome: Current knowledge and implications for practice. *Journal of the American Medical Association* (1992) 267,17:2370–72.

85. McAnarney, E. R., and Stevens-Simon, C. Maternal psychological stress/depression and low birth weight. *American Journal of Diseases of Children* (1990) 144:789–92.

86. Katch, F. I., and McArdle, W. E. *Introduction to nutrition, exercise and health.* 4th ed. Philadelphia: Lea and Febiger, 1993.

87. Dewey, K. G., and McCrory, M. A. Effects of dieting and physical activity on pregnancy and lactation. *American Journal of Clinical Nutrition* (1994) 59:446S–53S.

88. Jovanovic-Peterson, L., Durak, E. P., and Peterson, C. M. Randomized trial of diet versus diet plus cardiovascular conditioning on glucose levels in gestational diabetes. *American Journal of Obstetrics and Gynecology* (1989) 161:415–19.

89. Hall, D. C., and Kaufmann, D. A. Effects of aerobic and strength conditioning on pregnancy outcomes. *American Journal of Obstetrics and Gynecology* (1987) 157:1199–1203.

90. U.S. Bureau of the Census. *Work and family patterns of American women.* Current Population Reports, Series P-23, No. 165. Washington, DC: U.S. Government Printing Office, 1990.

91. Poerksen, A., and Petitti, D. B. Employment and low birth weight in black women. *Social Science and Medicine* (1991) 33:1281–96.

92. Simpson, J. L., Are physical activity and employment related to preterm birth and low birth weight? *American Journal of Obstetrics and Gynecology* (1993) 168:1231–38.

93. Helton, A. S., McFarlane, J., and Anderson, E. T. Battered and pregnant: A prevalence study. *American Journal of Public Health* (1987) 77,10:1337–39.

94. McFarlane, J., Parker, B., Soeken, K., and Bullock, L. Assessing for abuse during pregnancy: Severity and frequency of injuries and associated entry into prenatal care. *Journal of the American Medical Association* (1992) 267,23:3176–78.

95. Bullock, L. F., and McFarlane, J. The birthweight/battering connection. *American Journal of Nursing* (September 1989):1153–55.

96. Gibbs, R. S., Romero, R., Hillier, S. L., et al. A review of premature birth and subclinical infection. *American Journal of Obstetrics and Gynecology* (1992) 166:1515–28.

97. Carroll, J. C. Chlamydia trachomatis during pregnancy: To screen or not to screen? *Canadian Family Physician* (1993) 39:97–102.

98. Kramer, M. S. The etiology and prevention of low birthweight: Current knowledge and priorities for future research. In *Advances in the prevention of low birthweight: An international symposium.* H. Berendes, S. Kessel, and S. Yaffe, eds. Washington, DC: National Center for Education in Maternal and Child Health, 1991, pp. 25–39.

99. Zygmunt, D. J. Toxoplasma gondii. *Infection Control and Hospital Epidemiology* (1990) 11,4:207–11.

100. Wegman, M. E. Annual summary of vital statistics—1992. *Pediatrics* (1993) 92,6:743–54.

Cocaine-Exposed Infants:
Myths and Misunderstandings

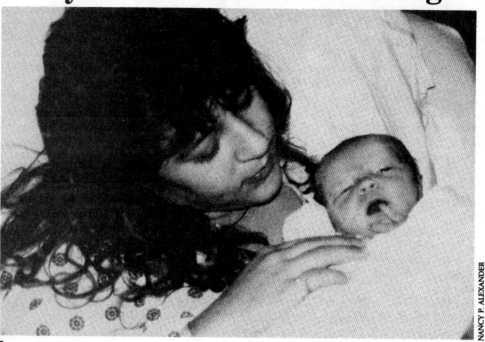

NANCY P. ALEXANDER

Barbara J. Myers
Heather Carmichael Olson
Karol Kaltenbach

Barbara J. Myers, Virginia Commonwealth University, Richmond, VA; Heather Carmichael Olson, University of Seattle, Seattle, WA; Karol Kaltenbach, Jefferson Medical College, Thomas Jefferson University, Philadelphia, PA

Note: All three authors are supported in whole or in part by grants from the National Institute of Drug Abuse which support research and treatment of substance-using mothers and their infants.

What do we really know about cocaine-exposed babies? Are they terribly damaged from birth with disabilities that will affect them all their lives? Is cocaine a teratogen that affects the development of limbs, organs, brains, and emotions? Or is this picture a distortion of the small amount of available research findings? New research findings are emerging almost every day. It is hard to know what to think, for what we knew yesterday is changed in today's press, and what we read today is most likely already out of date. *The simple truth at this point is that we do not yet know what the effects are of prenatal cocaine exposure.*

What does the media publish?

The popular press has covered this emotional topic frequently for a public which is deeply concerned for the welfare of these children. In the effort to spread information widely, the media tend to present a simple, brief, and dramatic picture. This may be an effective way to motivate people into action, but a careful eye is needed to watch for oversimplification, especially since it is common in the media to present individual worst-case stories and then draw broad generalizations.

Most of the media presentations have been decidedly negative in their accounts of drug-exposed infants. Titles of articles sound an alarm before the story begins. Some capitalize on fears about crack cocaine: "Crack Comes to the Nursery" (*Time,* Sept. 19, 1988); "Crack in the Cradle" (*Discover,* Sept. 1989). Others point to an alleged addiction which the babies are born with (a hypothesis no longer supported by most studies of cocaine-exposed infants): "Cocaine Babies: Hooked at Birth" (*Newsweek,* July 28, 1986); "I Gave Birth to an Addicted Baby" (*Good Housekeeping,* April, 1990); "Kids Who Can't Say No" (*Readers's Digest,* February, 1991). Some articles stigmatize these children. *The Washington Post* referred to cocaine-exposed babies as a "bio-underclass," a "potential human plague almost too horrible to imagine" (Sept. 17, 1989).

Magazines and newspapers often begin their articles with heart-wrenching accounts of a single baby who is severely affected, presumably as a result of drug exposure. Those of us who work with infants with disabilities will recognize early signs of trouble and feel a sympathetic connection with the infants and what they face. We should be aware, though, of exaggerations. For example, "Guillermo, a newborn at Broward General Medical Center in Ft. Lauderdale, has spent his whole short life crying. He is jittery and goes into spasms when he is touched. His eyes don't focus. He can't stick out his tongue, or suck. Born a week ago to a cocaine addict, Guillermo is described by his doctors as an addict himself" (*Newsweek*, July 28, 1986). (*A baby who has spent his whole life crying? Does that seem accurate? Is this story really a typical one? Does this account stigmatize Guillermo?*) Or consider the account of an infant named Robert: "Most of the babies at Highland General Hospital in Oakland, California, are asleep at this hour. But little Robert, brought in by his mother, has been awake for days. He cries inconsolably, and his tiny limbs jerk and jitter constantly. Periodically, his hands fly back to the sides of his head and his large, dark eyes freeze wide in startled terror . . . . At birth, the infant plunged into a nightmarish withdrawal from drugs used by his mother" (*Readers Digest*, February, 1991). (*Is it possible for an infant to be awake for days? Is he seeing nightmares, or are his hands moving up in a simple Moro reflex?*)

In addition to watching out for oversimplification and exaggerations, readers of these articles should remember that study of drug effects is very complex. A first question to ask is how probable it is that disabilities, if and when they are found, are a result of the cocaine exposure. Certainly many babies who are born with disabilities were never exposed to drugs; often, the cause for the problem is never known. When cocaine-exposed infants show disabling conditions, we cannot be certain that prenatal cocaine was responsible. Cocaine-exposed infants, like any other infants, may have parents with previously undetected recessive genetic abnormalities. Their mothers may have avoided prenatal care to escape detection of their drug dependence, and so a variety of obstetrical complications and other health problems might have been left untreated. The mothers may have eaten poorly during the pregnancy and not taken their prenatal vitamins. Most cocaine-using mothers are polydrug users: They drink alcohol, or smoke cigarettes, or use marijuana, or use a variety of prescription or street drugs, cut with a variety of substances. And substance-using women, like any other group of women, can have babies with problems whose cause is unknown. Given this complicated course of prenatal history, it is premature to link every problem shown by a cocaine-exposed infant to the cocaine. Cocaine may indeed have played a role in an infant's problem, but cocaine is just one of the risks, known and unknown, to which these babies were exposed.

Many articles in the media focus on the long-term effects of cocaine exposure. At times it seems that articles are discussing events that have been well documented. Yet studies of cocaine-exposed infants have not followed these children past age three or four, and most studies are of newborn infants. In *The New York Times* (Sept. 17, 1989), for example, we read, ". . . studies suggest that without help, the children of addicted mothers may be unable to develop into adults with basic employment skills and unable

to form close human relationships. " (*Adults without basic employment skills? And unable to form close human relationships? These assertions cannot come from anyone's data, as nobody has followed children that far.*) On the same day, *The Washington Post* noted, "Already, a few [cocaine-exposed children] are turning up in first- and second-grade classrooms around the country, wreaking havoc on themselves and others. Severe emotional damage and even physical deformities not so readily apparent today may mushroom in the near future. The children's irritability and anger—along with their need for love and understanding—will surely grow." (*This article appeared before the group of cocaine-exposed children were old enough to enter school. Why are irritability and anger expected outcomes? Why should there be problems tomorrow—"emotional damage and physical deformities"—which are not apparent today?*) An education journal written for popular use also predicts the future for children exposed to cocaine: "In the typical classroom environment . . . cocaine-exposed children tend to react in one of two ways. They withdraw completely, or they become wild and difficult to control" (*The Education Digest*, May, 1990). (*One must read this article carefully to pick up that the author is talking about her own predictions of the future.*) We need to be careful not to create ideas to fill the gaps in our knowledge, especially when we have strong feelings about the topic and want to know the answers now.

What does the research show?

In contrast to these disturbing popular accounts, available research on drug-exposed infants shows a mix of findings: In some studies, especially those published early on, cocaine-exposed infants were found to be different from (and "worse" than) comparison infants. But many studies detect no differences between cocaine-exposed and non-exposed infants, and that is important to know. These "no difference" studies are not readily published in professional journals or noted in the press. Indeed, Koren et al. (1989) documented that research studies which found that substance-exposed infants were *not* different from non-exposed infants were significantly more likely to be rejected for presentation at scientific meetings than were studies which found the substance-exposed infants *to* be different.

Two current research review articles give in-depth and readable examinations of the many research articles published through 1991 (Neuspiel & Hamel, 1991; Myers, Britt, Lodder, Kendall, & Williams-Petersen, in press). Both articles agree that the only finding which seems substantiated across many well-controlled studies is that babies who are prenatally exposed to cocaine are at risk for being younger and smaller at birth: This includes lower birth weight, birth length, head circumference, and gestational age. Cocaine-exposed babies were more likely to have shorter gestation (and thus to be premature); some were also found to be small for gestational age (SGA). Prematurity, SGA, and low birth weight are all risk factors for a variety of poor outcomes, whether or not cocaine has played a role. Thus, when cocaine-exposed children who were born too early or too small have problems, it is difficult to untangle what is the direct, and the indirect, cause. Certainly, cocaine plays at least an indirect causal role in this instance. Even though cocaine exposure places an infant at higher *risk* for prematurity and low birth weight, many exposed infants are born full-term and at appropriate weight. In fact, *the large majority of exposed infants are not premature and not low birth weight,* especially in programs which offer good prenatal care and nutrition education.

For many areas of infant development, one study shows infants exposed to cocaine to be different from comparison infants, while the next study finds no difference. We find this for areas as disparate as incidence of stillbirths, SIDS, anomalies of various organ systems, neurological abnormalities, newborn behavior as measured by the NBAS (Neonatal Behavioral Assessment Scale), social-emotional functioning, and parenting practices.

Why do scientists arrive at such different answers to straightforward questions? As researchers, we point to the methodological problems which accompany this difficult area of study. Although research design questions may seem boring and technical, they are at the heart of our difficulty in answering the complex questions posed by prenatal substance exposure.

Methodological problems in studying prenatal substance exposure

The answers we get about any research question depend in large part on how the research study is structured and conducted. The "ideal" for research is to conduct a true experimental study, with participants randomly assigned to one of several conditions. But random assignment to drug use or nonuse is obviously impossible and unethical. Some "less than perfect" methods are a necessity right from the start. Still, there are steps that can be taken to improve the validity and reliability of research in this area.

A first area of concern is who are the subjects in the study. Consider the following case: A 30-year-old white paralegal started using cocaine in the late 1970's because she thought it wasn't addictive. Concerned about her weight, she wanted to get high on fewer calories than alcohol supplied. Now a successful lawyer, she attends 12-step meetings at lunchtime and is in recovery. Although cocaine is used by people of all social classes and ethnic groups, this middle-class lawyer would not end up as a subject in a typical research project. There are currently *no* published studies of middle- and upper-class cocaine-using mothers and their infants. Rather, low-income women and their infants make up the study populations. This means that conditions of poverty get mixed up with effects of cocaine exposure. In addition, studies often use groups of women who are enrolled in ongoing drug treatment and recovery programs. These mothers are the healthiest, most stable, and most self-aware of low-income drug-using women. Thus we miss out on knowing about both upper-income women and the less motivated of the lower-income women—the

two groups which are probably the "best" and the "worst" of the substance-using population in terms of health, stability, and personal resources. We cannot study babies whose mothers do not want to be studied or for whom no active research study is available.

Researchers have also learned that ascertaining drug use is a very challenging task. Drug users often deny their drug involvement (indeed, "denial" is one of the signs that the individual is in trouble with drugs or alcohol). In some states, admission of drug use is enough to prompt criminal proceedings, so denial may keep a mother out of jail or keep her children from being taken from her. Urine toxicology identifies traces of the drug or its metabolites from use only in the past 2-3 days, and so many users plan ahead and abstain prior to scheduled clinic appointments. Thus, many studies undoubtedly report data from a few drug users mixed in with the non-users. Even when drug use is admitted or discovered, it is difficult to establish the frequency, quantity, quality, type, and timing of substances used. Dose-effect relationships in the human fetus are nearly impossible to establish. Polydrug use, including opiates, marijuana, alcohol, nicotine and prescription drugs, is probably the most common pattern, yet this makes the job of untangling effects even more challenging. We know that smoking significantly reduces birth weight, and that alcohol is a teratogen. It is rare to find a woman who used cocaine during her pregnancy who did not also drink, smoke, or use other drugs; rarer still would be such a woman who also ate well, had good prenatal care, and had a stable and supportive home life. There are a thousand and one individual patterns, which underscores the need to treat each woman and her baby as a unique and individual dyad.

Should the professional who examines a baby know that drug exposure has taken place? While this knowledge may be valuable clinically, it can influence findings in a research study, and so the ideal is to have examiners who are blind to exposure status. Many studies fail to keep examiners blind, and so there is a threat of the examiners' expectations affecting findings. This implies that non-exposed infants are being studied at the same time and in the same setting. Many times there is no comparison group, or the comparison group is different on a number of factors other than cocaine exposure. Comparison groups need to be drawn from the same community as the cocaine-using sample, so that differences which really come from local customs, social class, health practices, and ethnicity are not unknowingly confused with the effects of the cocaine exposure.

After the baby is born and goes home, the caregiving environment becomes critically important. What is a cocaine-user's home environment like? It is no doubt a widely diverse picture, from suburban subdivisions to crowded apartments to shelters for the homeless, but our research at this point offers little information. From a research perspective, it is important not to confound results which stem from prenatal chemical exposure with results which come from how a baby is raised. This area is critical, but we know very little about how the caretaking environment(s) of substance-exposed infants impact their development.

Research with families in which substances are abused is expensive and difficult to do. Even the most well-seasoned and devoted team of researchers can become overwhelmed with both the scientific problems and the personal drain that this work presents. Cocaine-using mothers are a diverse group, and this diversity sometimes includes situations of extreme poverty, unstable lifestyles, and personal danger. Any critical assessment of research in this field should compliment those individuals who are doing the best they know how in a difficult situation.

Continued research in the area of perinatal substance exposure is needed, especially research which is well-designed and carefully conducted. The National Institute of Drug Abuse is currently funding such research. Twenty programs (referred to as the "Perinatal 20") are participating in treatment-research demonstrations involving adult and adolescent pregnant and postpartum women and their children. These sites are working together to share ideas and techniques in an effort to provide sound answers to some of the questions about substance-exposed children and which treatment models are the most effective in producing favorable outcomes for both mother and child.

What is our model of cocaine effects?

With our current state of knowledge, most researchers in this area now view this group of children using a risk model, not a deficit model. That is, we recognize the various risks—biological, environmental, interpersonal—which individuals are subject to, and we also recognize the many strengths and protective factors which individuals may have available. Whether a risk factor such as cocaine exposure shows an impact upon a child's health or behavior depends on the complex interplay of all the risk factors and protective factors. Cocaine exposure is no doubt a biological risk factor, and many prenatally-exposed infants will have other risk factors at work as well. Certainly there are a great many such children whose prenatal care was inadequate, whose lives are chaotic, whose neighborhoods are dangerous, whose diets are terrible, and whose parents are emotionally unavailable to them. But most children also have some protective factors which can soften and relieve the stressors. These might include their general good health, easy temperament, a loving grandparent, a safe and appropriately stimulating home, a mother who loves and cherishes her child, or a community which provides adequate health and intervention services. Whether an individual child shows negative effects of cocaine exposure depends on the complex and ever-changing interactions among all the risk factors and protective factors in the child's life. This model is a graceful one that embraces each of us—every baby, every child, every adult. Not only is it philosophically satisfying, it also is supported by the data. Assessments of children which take into account a great many biological,

environmental, and personal factors, and the ongoing changes in these forces, provide a more accurate prediction of child outcome than do static measures of isolated variables.

What can professionals who work with infants and young children do in the meantime? We cannot wait until all of the research is documented, because large numbers of infants prenatally exposed to drugs are born every day and some may be referred to us for evaluation or services. Here are some suggestions:

(1) Accept that the full picture is not yet known about substance-exposed babies.

(2) Remember the diversity of substance-using families, and be sensitive to the individual mother and her baby.

(3) Resist believing the stereotypes and participating in the stigmatization of drug abusers. Truly accept that it could be you, it could be your sister.

(4) Work from a risk and protective factors model, not a deficit model. Identify the positive factors in infants' and mothers' lives, as well as the problems.

(5) Think in terms of polydrug exposure, not just cocaine exposure. Be especially aware of alcohol effects and cigarette smoking.

(6) From what we know so far, the supports and interventions that substance-exposed infants need are no different from what other babies need. The interventions you offer need to be sensitive to the family's culture, but you will not need a special set of materials and activities for these babies.

(7) Chemical dependence adds new dimensions to what the family needs. As infant interventionists, we need to expand our own training to include knowledge and experience in the course of addiction and recovery. We need to become partners in our communities with agencies that provide substance abuse treatment if we are to be effective advocates for the infants and families we serve.

References

Koren, G. Shear, H., Graham, K., & Einarson, T. (1989). Bias against the null hypothesis: The reproductive hazards of cocaine. *The Lancet, 2, No. 8677*, 1440-1442.

Mayes, L. C., Granger, R. H., Bornstein, M. H., & Zuckerman, B. (Jan. 15, 1992). The problem of prenatal cocaine exposure: A rush to judgment. *Journal of the American Medical Association, 267* (No. 3), 406-408.

Myers, B. J., Britt, G. C., Lodder, D. E., Kendall, K. A., & Williams-Petersen, M. G. (In press). Cocaine exposure and infant development: A review of the literature. *Journal of Child and Family Studies.*

Neuspiel, D. R., & Hamel, S. C. (1991). Cocaine and infant behavior. *Journal of Developmental and Behavioral Pediatrics, 12*, 55-64.

Zuckerman, B. , & Frank, D. (1992). "Crack Kids": Not broken. *Pediatrics, 89* (no. 2), 337-339.

SPERM UNDER SIEGE

MORE THAN WE EVER GUESSED, HAVING A HEALTHY BABY MAY DEPEND ON DAD

Anne Merewood

IT DIDN'T MAKE SENSE. Kate Malone's* first pregnancy had gone so smoothly. Yet when she and her husband Paul* tried to have a second child, their efforts were plagued by disaster. For two years, Kate couldn't become pregnant. Then she suffered an ectopic pregnancy, in which the embryo began to grow in one of her fallopian tubes and had to be surgically removed. Her next pregnancy heralded more heartache—it ended in miscarriage at four months and tests revealed that the fetus was genetically abnormal. Within months, she became pregnant and miscarried yet again. By this point, some four years after their troubles began, the couple had adopted a son; baffled and demoralized by the string of apparent bad luck, they gave up trying to have another child. "We had been to the top doctors in the country and no one could find a reason for the infertility or the miscarriages," says Kate.

Soon, however, thanks to a newspaper article she read, Kate uncovered what she now considers the likely cause of the couple's reproductive woes. When it all started, Paul had just been hired by a manufacturing company that used a chemical called paradichlorobenzene, which derives from benzene, a known carcinogen. The article discussed the potential effects of exposure to chemicals, including benzene, on a man's sperm. Kate remembered hearing that two other men in Paul's small office were also suffering from inexplicable infertility. Both of their wives had gone through three miscarriages as well. Kate had always considered their similar misfortunes to be a tragic coincidence. Now she became convinced that the chemical (which has not yet been studied for its effects on reproduction) had blighted the three men's sperm.

Paul had found a new job in a chemical-free workplace, so the couple decided to try once more to have a baby. Kate conceived immediately—and last August gave birth to a healthy boy. The Malones are now arranging for the National Institute for Occupational Safety and Health (NIOSH), the

*These names have been changed.

federal agency that assesses work-related health hazards for the public, to inspect Paul's former job site. "Our aim isn't to sue the company, but to help people who are still there," says Kate.

The Malones' suspicions about sperm damage echo the concerns of an increasing number of researchers. These scientists are challenging the double standard that leads women to overhaul their lives before a pregnancy—avoiding stress, cigarettes and champagne—while men are left confident that their lifestyle has little bearing on their fertility or their future child's health. Growing evidence suggests that sperm is both more fragile and potentially more dangerous than previously thought. "There seems to have been both a scientific resistance, and a resistance based on cultural preconceptions, to accepting these new ideas," says Gladys Friedler, Ph.D, an associate professor of psychiatry and pharmacology at Boston University School of Medicine.

But as more and more research is completed, sperm may finally be stripped of its macho image. For example, in one startling review of data on nearly 15,000 newborns, scientists at the University of North Carolina in Chapel Hill concluded that a father's drinking and smoking habits, and even his age, can increase his child's risk of birth defects—ranging from cleft palates to *hydrocephalus*, an abnormal accumulation of spinal fluid in the brain. Other new and equally worrisome studies have linked higher-than-normal rates of stillbirth, premature delivery and low birthweight (which predisposes a baby to medical and developmental problems) to fathers who faced on-the-job exposure to certain chemicals. In fact, one study found that a baby was more likely to be harmed if the father rather than the mother worked in an unsafe environment in the months before conception.

The surprising news of sperm's delicate nature may shift the balance of responsibility for a newborn's wellbeing. The research may also have social and economic implications far beyond the concerns of couples planning a family. In recent years a growing number of companies have sought

From *Health*, April 1991, pp. 53-57, 76-77. © 1991 by Anne Merewood. Reprinted by permission.

to ban women of childbearing age from jobs that entail exposure to hazardous substances. The idea is to protect the women's future children from defects—and the companies themselves from lawsuits. Already, the "fetal protection policy" of one Milwaukee-based company has prompted female employees to file a sex discrimination suit that is now before the U.S. Supreme Court. Conversely, if the new research on sperm is borne out, men whose future plans include fatherhood may go to court to *insist* on protection from hazards. Faced with potential lawsuits from so many individuals, companies may be forced to ensure that workplaces are safe for *all* employees.

SPERM UND DRANG

At the center of all this controversy are the microscopic products of the male reproductive system. Sperm (officially, spermatozoa) are manufactured by *spermatagonia,* special cells in the testes that are constantly stimulated by the male hormone testosterone. Once formed, a sperm continues to mature as it travels for some 80 days through the *epididymis* (a microscopic network of tubes behind the testicle) to the "waiting area" around the prostate gland, where it is expelled in the next ejaculation.

A normal sperm contains 23 chromosomes—the threadlike strands that house DNA, the molecular foundation of genetic material. While a woman is born with all the eggs she will ever produce, a man creates millions of sperm every day from puberty onwards. This awesome productivity is also what makes sperm so fragile. If a single sperm's DNA is damaged, the result may be a mutation that distorts the genetic information it carries. "Because of the constant turnover of sperm, mutations caused by the environment can arise more frequently in men than in women," says David A. Savitz, Ph.D., an associate professor of epidemiology and chief researcher of the North Carolina review.

If a damaged sperm fertilizes the egg, the consequences can be devastating. "Such sperm can lead to spontaneous abortions, malformations, and functional or behavioral abnormalities," says Marvin Legator, Ph.D., director of environmental toxicology at the department of preventative medicine at the University of Texas in Galveston. And in some cases, sperm may be too badly harmed even to penetrate an egg, leading to mysterious infertility.

Though the findings on sperm's vulnerability are certainly dramatic, researchers emphasize that they are also preliminary. "We have only a very vague notion of how exposure might affect fetal development, and the whole area of research is at a very early stage of investigation," says Savitz. Indeed, questions still far outnumber answers. For starters, there is no hard evidence that a chemical damages an infant by adversely affecting the father's sperm. A man who comes in contact with dangerous substances might harm the baby by exposing his partner indirectly—for example, through contaminated clothing. Another theory holds that the harmful pollutants may be carried in the seminal fluid that buoys sperm. But more researchers are becoming convinced that chemicals can inflict their silent damage directly on the sperm itself.

THE CHEMICAL CONNECTION

The most well-known—and most controversial—evidence that chemicals can harm sperm comes from research on U.S. veterans of the Vietnam war who were exposed to the herbicide Agent Orange (dioxin), used by the U.S. military to destroy foliage that hid enemy forces. A number of veterans believe the chemical is responsible for birth defects in their children. The latest study on the issue, published last year by the Harvard School of Public Health, found that Vietnam vets had almost twice the risk of other men of fathering infants with one or more major malformations. But a number of previous studies found conflicting results, and because so little is known about how paternal exposure could translate into birth defects, the veterans have been unsuccessful in their lawsuits against the government.

Scientific uncertainty also dogs investigations into other potentially hazardous chemicals and contaminants. "There seem to be windows of vulnerability for sperm: Certain chemicals may be harmful only at a certain period during sperm production," explains Donald Mattison, M.D., dean of the School of Public Health at the University of Pittsburgh. There isn't enough specific data to make definitive lists of "danger chemicals." Still, a quick scan of the research shows that particular substances often crop up as likely troublemakers. Chief among them: lead, benzene, paint solvents, vinyl chloride, carbon disulphide, the pesticide DBCP, anesthetic gases and radiation. Not surprisingly, occupations that involve contact with these substances also figure heavily in studies of sperm damage. For example, men employed in the paper, wood, chemical, drug and paint industries may have a greater chance of siring stillborn children. And increased leukemia rates have been detected among children whose fathers are medical workers, aircraft or auto mechanics, or who are exposed regularly to paint or radiation. In fact, a study of workers at Britain's Sellafield nuclear power plant in West Cambria found a sixfold leukemia risk among children whose fathers were exposed to the plant's highest radiation levels (about 9 percent of all employees).

Workers in "high-risk" industries should not panic, says Savitz. "The credibility of the studies is limited because we have no firm evidence that certain exposures cause certain birth defects." Yet it makes sense to be watchful for warning signs. For example, if pollution levels are high enough to cause skin irritations, thyroid trouble, or breathing problems, the reproductive system might also be at risk. Another danger signal is a clustered outbreak of male infertility or of a particular disease: It was local concern about high levels of childhood leukemia, for instance, that sparked the investigation at the Sellafield nuclear plant.

The rise in industrial "fetal protection policies" is

adding even more controversy to the issue of occupational hazards to sperm. In 1984, employees brought a class-action suit against Milwaukee-based Johnson Controls, the nation's largest manufacturer of car batteries, after the company restricted women "capable of bearing children" from holding jobs in factory areas where lead exceeded a specific level. The suit—which the Supreme Court is scheduled to rule on this spring—focuses on the obstacles the policy creates for women's career advancement. Johnson Controls defends its regulation by pointing to "overwhelming" evidence that a mother's exposure to lead can harm the fetus.

In effect, the company's rule may be a case of reverse discrimination against men. Males continue to work in areas banned to women despite growing evidence that lead may not be safe for sperm either. In several studies over the past 10 years, paternal exposure to lead (and radiation) has been connected to Wilms' tumor, a type of kidney cancer in children. In another recent study, University of Maryland toxicologist Ellen Silbergeld, Ph.D., exposed male rats to lead amounts equivalent to levels below the current occupational safety standards for humans. The rats were then mated with females who had not been exposed at all. Result: The offspring showed clear defects in brain development.

Johnson Controls claims that evidence linking fetal problems to a father's contact with lead is insufficient. But further research into chemicals' effects on sperm may eventually force companies to reduce pollution levels, since *both* sexes can hardly be banned from the factory floor. Says Mattison: "The workplace should be safe for everyone who wants to work there, men and women alike!"

FATHER TIME

Whatever his occupation, a man's age may play an unexpected role in his reproductive health. When researchers at the University of Calgary and the Alberta Children's Hospital in Canada examined sperm samples taken from 30 healthy men aged 20 to 52, they found that the older men had a higher percentage of sperm with structurally abnormal chromosomes. Specifically, only 2 to 3 percent of the sperm from men between ages 20 and 34 were genetically abnormal, while the figure jumped to 7 percent in men 35 to 44 and to almost 14 percent in those 45 and over. "The findings are logical," says Renée Martin, Ph.D., the professor of pediatrics who led the study. "The cells that create sperm are constantly dividing from puberty onwards, and every time they divide they are subject to error."

Such mistakes are more likely to result in miscarriages than in unhealthy babies. "When part of a chromosome is missing or broken, the embryo is more likely to abort as a miscarriage [than to carry to term]," Martin says. Yet her findings may help explain why Savitz's North Carolina study noted a doubled rate of birth defects like cleft palate and hydrocephalus in children whose fathers were over 35 at the time of conception, no matter what the mothers' age.

Currently, there are no tests available to pre-identify sperm likely to cause genetic defects. "Unfortunately there's nothing offered, because [the research] is all so new," says Martin. But tests such as amniocentesis, alpha fetoprotein (AFP) and chorionic villi sampling (CVS) can ferret out some fetal genetic defects that are linked to Mom *or* Dad. Amniocentesis, for example, is routinely recommended for all pregnant women over 35 because with age a woman increases her risk of producing a Down's syndrome baby, characterized by mental retardation and physical abnormalities.

With respect to Down's syndrome, Martin's study provided some good news for older men: It confirmed previous findings that a man's risk of fathering a child afflicted with the syndrome actually drops with age. Some popular textbooks still warn that men over 55 have a high chance of fathering Down's syndrome babies. "That information is outdated," Martin insists. "We now know that for certain."

THE SINS OF THE FATHERS?

For all the hidden dangers facing a man's reproductive system, the most common hazards may be the ones most under his control.

Smoking. Tobacco addicts take note: Smoke gets in your sperm. Cigarettes can reduce fertility by lowering sperm count—the number of individual sperm released in a single ejaculation. "More than half a pack a day can cause sperm density to drop by 20 percent," says Machelle Seibel, M.D., director of the Faulkner Centre for Reproductive Medicine in Boston. One Danish study found that for each pack of cigarettes a father tended to smoke daily (assuming the mother didn't smoke at all), his infant's birthweight fell 4.2 ounces below average. Savitz has found that male smokers double their chances of fathering infants with abnormalities like hydrocephalus, *Bell's palsy* (paralysis of the facial nerve), and mouth cysts. In Savitz's most recent study, children whose fathers smoked around the time of conception were 20 percent more likely to develop brain cancer, lymphoma and leukemia than were children whose fathers did not smoke (the results still held regardless of whether the mother had a tobacco habit).

This is scary news—and not particularly helpful: Savitz's studies didn't record how frequently the fathers lit up, and no research at all suggests why the links appeared. Researchers can't even say for sure that defective sperm was to blame. The babies may instead have been victims of passive smoking—affected by Dad's tobacco while in the womb or shortly after birth.

Drinking. Mothers-to-be are routinely cautioned against sipping any alcohol while pregnant. Now studies suggest that the father's drinking habits just before conception may also pose a danger. So far, research hasn't discovered why alcohol has an adverse effect on sperm, but it does suggest that further investigation is needed. For starters, one study of laboratory rats linked heavy alcohol use with infertility because the liquor lowered testosterone levels. Another study, from the University of Washington in Seattle, discovered that newborn babies whose fathers drank at least two glasses of wine or two bottles of beer per day weighed an average of 3 ounces less than babies whose fathers were only occasional sippers—even when all other factors were considered.

Illicit Drugs. Many experts believe that a man's frequent use of substances such as marijuana and cocaine may also result in an unhealthy fetus, but studies that could document such findings have yet to be conducted. However, preliminary research has linked marijuana to infertility. And recent tests at the Yale Infertility Clinic found that long-term cocaine use led to both very low sperm counts and a greater number of sperm with motion problems.

WHAT A DAD CAN DO

The best news about sperm troubles is that many of the risk factors can be easily prevented. Because the body overhauls sperm supplies every 90 days, it only takes a season to get a fresh start on creating a healthy baby. Most experts advise that men wait for three months after quitting smoking, cutting out drug use or abstaining from alcohol before trying to sire a child.

Men who fear they are exposed to work chemicals that may compromise the health of future children can contact NIOSH. (Write to the Division of Standards Development and Technology Transfer, Technical Information Branch, 4676 Columbia Parkway, Mailstop C-19, Cincinnati, OH 45226. Or call [800] 356-4674.) NIOSH keeps files on hazardous chemicals and their effects, and can arrange for a local inspection of the workplace. Because it is primarily a research institution, NIOSH is most useful for investigating chemicals that haven't been studied previously for sperm effects (which is why

the Malones approached NIOSH with their concerns about paradichlorobenzene). For better-known pollutants, it's best to ask the federal Occupational Safety and Health Administration (OSHA) to inspect the job site (OSHA has regional offices in most U.S. cities).

There is also advice for men who are concerned over exposure to radiation during medical treatment. Direct radiation to the area around the testes can spur infertility by halting sperm production for more than three years. According to a recent study, it can also triple the number of abnormal sperm the testes produce. Men who know they will be exposed to testicular radiation for medical reasons should consider "banking" sperm before the treatment, for later use in artificial insemination. Most hospitals use lead shields during radiation therapy, but for routine X-rays, even dental X-rays, protection might not be offered automatically. If it's not offered, patients should be sure to request it. "The risks are really, really low, but to be absolutely safe, patients—male or female—should *always* ask for a lead apron to protect their reproductive organs," stresses Martin.

Though the study of sperm health is still in its infancy, it is already clear that a man's reproductive system needs to be treated with respect and caution. Women do not carry the full responsibility for bearing a healthy infant. "The focus should be on both parents—not on 'blaming' either the mother or the father, but on accepting that each plays a role," says Friedler.

Mattison agrees: "Until recently, when a woman had a miscarriage, she would be told it was because she had a 'blighted ovum' [egg]. We never heard anything about a 'blighted sperm.' This new data suggests that both may be responsible. That is not unreasonable," he concludes, "given that it takes both an egg and a sperm to create a baby!"

Development during Infancy and Early Childhood

- Infancy (Articles 7–10)
- Early Childhood (Articles 11–13)

Newborns seem to do little besides eat, sleep, and eliminate. This is exactly what nature intended for them to do to maximize development. Newborns are quite well developed in some areas, and incredibly deficient in other areas. Babies' brains, for example, already have their full complement of neurons (worker cells). The neuroglia (supportive cells) are almost completely developed and will reach their final numbers by age one. In contrast, babies' legs and feet are tiny, weak, and barely functional. Looking at newborns from another perspective, however, makes their brains seem somewhat less superior. The neurons and neuroglia present at birth must last a lifetime. Neurons cannot replace themselves by mitosis after birth. If they die, the brain's number of neurons remains forever diminished. By contrast, the cells of the baby's legs and feet (skin, fat, muscles, bones, blood vessels) are able to replace themselves by mitosis indefinitely. Their numbers will continue to grow through early adulthood, then their quantity and quality can be retained through old age.

In order to protect the brain and nervous system of the newborn, as well as encourage growth and development of other vital systems, the eat, sleep, and elimination functions are critical. All three functions are enhanced by human breast milk. The first article included in this unit of *Human Development* gives scientific explanations of why human milk is so much better for babies than milk derived from soy, or taken from cows, goats, or sheep. Human milk aids digestion, stimulates the gut, prevents infection, selectively kills harmful bacteria while leaving good bacteria alone, strengthens the baby's immune response, stimulates growth and development and, by extension, allows for sounder sleep. The author, a Canadian pediatrician who has worked in Central and South America as well as New Zealand and Africa, brings cross-cultural knowledge to his invocation on the benefits of breast milk.

The developing brain in infancy is a truly fascinating organ. At birth, it is poorly organized. The lower (primitive) brain parts (brain stem, pons, medulla, cerebellum) are well enough developed to allow the infant to live. The lower brain directs vital organ systems (heart, lungs, kidneys, etc.). The higher (advanced) brain parts (cerebral hemispheres) have all their neurons, but the nerve cells and cell processes (axon, dendrites) are small, underdeveloped, and unorganized. During infancy, these higher (cerebral) nerve cells (which allow the baby to think, reason, and remember) grow at astronomical rates. They develop multiple dendritic connections, migrate to permanent locations in the hemispheres, develop myelin sheathing (insulation), and conduct all kinds of messages. Piaget, the father of cognitive psychology, wrote that all brain activity in the newborn was reflexive, based on instincts for survival. Now researchers are discovering that fetuses can learn and newborns can think as well as learn. The second article in this unit addresses some of the newest research in the area of infant cognition. Amazingly enough, the authors contend that infants develop not only memory, but also math, language, and physics abilities. New research also suggests that intervention strategies can improve the ways in which infants emote and process information.

The third article included in this unit invokes more attention to the development of social and emotional behaviors in infancy, as opposed to physical and cognitive development. The author, Jerome Kagan, is a Harvard professor with a worldwide reputation as an expert in socioemotional aspects of development. In this article, he contends that neither environmental explanations of human behavior (popular in the 1960s and 70s) nor biological explanations of traits (popular today) are sufficient to explain temperament. He sees a danger in excusing antisocial behaviors and unrestrained emotions as due to inheritance. He stresses the need for socialization practices which focus on moral obligations to be civil and responsible.

The "Case Studies" included in the infancy section round out the message of nature-nurture interactive effects. The article presents information about three chemical contaminants prevalent in our environment which are very harmful to some babies, harmful to most children, and relatively harmless to adults. Risk is related not only to age, but to health, inherited factors, and exposure factors. This type of information is still sparse but needs to be researched more carefully for our children's future protection.

The selections about toddlers and preschoolers which are included in this anthology continue the trend of looking at development physically, cognitively, and socioemotionally. Each of the articles, while focusing on one topic, views the whole child across all three domains considering both hereditary and environmental factors.

"Your Child's Brain" continues the discussion of the rapid myelinization of neurons and their migration to per-

manent locations in the brain during early childhood. The author contends that extra experience in the pursuit of an area of knowledge (e.g., math, language, music) can trigger more neurons to be sent to the area of the cerebral hemisphere involved in acquiring, storing, and retrieving that kind of information. This accommodation is a clear-cut example of nature-nurture interaction.

The article on changing demographics focuses on cognitive development as it relates to early childhood education programs. The author asserts that we are experiencing a child care revolution. Single parenting and two-wage earner families have made the need for excellence in early childhood education critical. The possibility of public funding to ensure quality control is discussed.

The concluding article in this unit addresses one of the biggest questions in the socialization of young children. Do we want them to be aggressive, submissive, or assertive? What is self-assertion? How can teaching self-assertiveness skills to preschoolers improve socioemotional development?

Looking Ahead: Challenge Questions

How can a human mother's milk actively enhance her newborn's growth and development?

What are the intellectual potentials of babies?

Is infant reactivity and temperamental style a factor in the development of personal and social skills?

What environmental substances are safe for adults but potentially poisonous for infants and young children?

How can environmental exposure and exercise help form the brain's circuitry for areas such as music and math?

In what ways might young children's cognitive development be stimulated by early childhood education programs?

Why should personal and social skills training include lessons on assertiveness in early childhood?

How Breast Milk Protects Newborns

Some of the molecules and cells in human milk actively help infants stave off infection

Jack Newman

Doctors have long known that infants who are breast-fed contract fewer infections than do those who are given formula. Until fairly recently, most physicians presumed that breast-fed children fared better simply because milk supplied directly from the breast is free of bacteria. Formula, which must often be mixed with water and placed in bottles, can become contaminated easily. Yet even infants who receive sterilized formula suffer from more meningitis and infection of the gut, ear, respiratory tract and urinary tract than do breast-fed youngsters.

The reason, it turns out, is that mother's milk actively helps newborns avoid disease in a variety of ways. Such assistance is particularly beneficial during the first few months of life, when an infant often cannot mount an effective immune response against foreign organisms. And although it is not the norm in most industrial cultures, UNICEF and the World Health Organization both advise breast-feeding to "two years and beyond." Indeed, a child's immune response does not reach its full strength until age five or so.

All human babies receive some coverage in advance of birth. During pregnancy, the mother passes antibodies to her fetus through the placenta. These proteins circulate in the infant's blood for weeks to months after birth, neutralizing microbes or marking them for destruction by phagocytes—immune cells that consume and break down bacteria, viruses and cellular debris. But breast-fed infants gain extra protection from antibodies, other proteins and immune cells in human milk.

Once ingested, these molecules and cells help to prevent microorganisms from penetrating the body's tissues. Some of the molecules bind to microbes in the hollow space (lumen) of the gastrointestinal tract. In this way, they block microbes from attaching to and crossing through the mucosa—the layer of cells, also known as the epithelium, that lines the digestive tract and other body cavities. Other molecules lessen the supply of particular minerals and vitamins that harmful bacteria need to survive in the digestive tract. Certain immune cells in human milk are phagocytes that attack microbes directly. Another set produces chemicals that invigorate the infant's own immune response.

Breast Milk Antibodies

Antibodies, which are also called immunoglobulins, take five basic forms, denoted as IgG, IgA, IgM, IgD and IgE. All have been found in human milk, but by far the most abundant type is IgA, specifically the form known as secretory IgA, which is found in great amounts throughout the

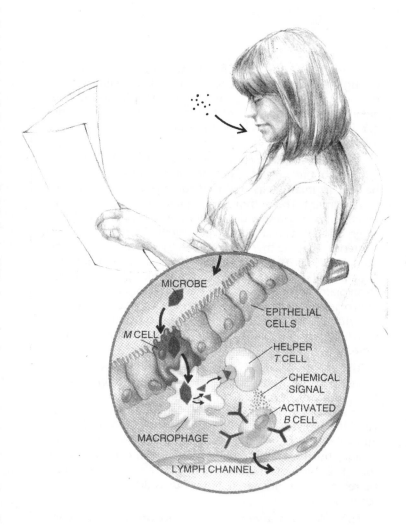

AFTER INGESTING A MICROBE (*left*), a new mother manufactures antibody molecules termed secretory IgA that enter breast milk (*center*) and help to protect the breast-fed baby from pathogens in its environment (*right*). More specifically, a microbe is taken up by the mother's *M* cells (*inset at left*)—specialized cells in the epithelial lining of the digestive tract—

gut and respiratory system of adults. These antibodies consist of two joined IgA molecules and a so-called secretory component that seems to shield the antibody molecules from being degraded by the gastric acid and digestive enzymes in the stomach and intestines. Infants who are bottle-fed have few means for battling ingested pathogens until they begin making secretory IgA on their own, often several weeks or even months after birth.

The secretory IgA molecules passed to the suckling child are helpful in ways that go beyond their ability to bind to microorganisms and keep them away from the body's tissues. First, the collection of antibodies transmitted to an infant is highly targeted against pathogens in that child's immediate surroundings. The mother synthesizes antibodies when she ingests, inhales or otherwise comes in contact with a disease-causing agent. Each antibody she makes is specific to that agent; that is, it binds to a single protein, or antigen, on the agent and will not waste time attacking irrelevant substances. Because the mother makes antibodies only to pathogens in her environment, the baby receives the protection it most needs—against the infectious agents it is most likely to encounter in the first weeks of life.

Second, the antibodies delivered to the infant ignore useful bacteria normally found in the gut. This flora serves to crowd out the growth of harmful organisms, thus providing another measure of resistance. Researchers do not yet know how the mother's immune system knows to make antibodies against only pathogenic and not normal bacteria, but whatever the process may be, it favors the establishment of "good bacteria" in a baby's gut.

Secretory IgA molecules further keep an infant from harm in that, unlike most other antibodies, they ward off disease without causing inflammation—a process in which various chemicals destroy microbes but potentially hurt healthy tissue. In an infant's developing gut, the mucosal membrane is extremely delicate, and an excess of these

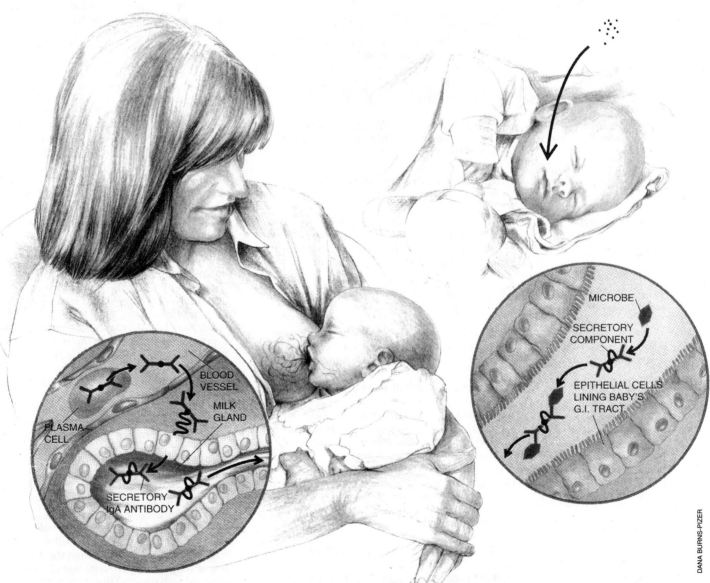

and passed to immune cells known as macrophages. The macrophages break down the pathogen and display fragments of it (antigens) to other immune cells called helper *T* lymphocytes, which secrete chemicals that activate still other immune cells, *B* lymphocytes. The *B* cells, in turn, mature into so-called plasma cells that travel to epithelial tissues in the breast and release antibodies (*inset at center*). Some of these molecules enter the milk and are swallowed by the baby. In the infant's digestive tract (*inset at right*), the antibodies, which are protected from breakdown by a so-called secretory component, prevent microorganisms from penetrating the baby's gut.

DANA BURNS-PIZER

Immune Benefits of Breast Milk at a Glance

Component	Action
White Blood Cells	
B lymphocytes	Give rise to antibodies targeted against specific microbes.
Macrophages	Kill microbes outright in the baby's gut, produce lysozyme and activate other components of the immune system.
Neutrophils	May act as phagocytes, injesting bacteria in baby's digestive system.
T lymphocytes	Kill infected cells directly or send out chemical messages to mobilize other defenses. They proliferate in the presence of organisms that cause serious illness in infants. They also manufacture compounds that can strengthen a child's own immune response.
Molecules	
Antibodies of secretory IgA class	Bind to microbes in baby's digestive tract and thereby prevent them from passing through walls of the gut into body's tissues.
B_{12} binding protein	Reduces amount of vitamin B_{12}, which bacteria need in order to grow.
Bifidus factor	Promotes growth of *Lactobacillus bifidus*, a harmless bacterium, in baby's gut. Growth of such nonpathogenic bacteria helps to crowd out dangerous varieties.
Fatty acids	Disrupt membranes surrounding certain viruses and destroy them.
Fibronectin	Increases antimicrobial activity of macrophages; helps to repair tissues that have been damaged by immune reactions in baby's gut.
Gamma-interferon	Enhances antimicrobial activity of immune cells.
Hormones and growth factors	Stimulate baby's digestive tract to mature more quickly. Once the initially "leaky" membranes lining the gut mature, infants become less vulnerable to microorganisms.
Lactoferrin	Binds to iron, a mineral many bacteria need to survive. By reducing the available amount of iron, lactoferrin thwarts growth of pathogenic bacteria.
Lysozyme	Kills bacteria by disrupting their cell walls.
Mucins	Adhere to bacteria and viruses, thus keeping such microorganisms from attaching to mucosal surfaces.
Oligosaccharides	Bind to microorganisms and bar them from attaching to mucosal surfaces.

chemicals can do considerable damage.

Interestingly, secretory IgA can probably protect mucosal surfaces other than those in the gut. In many countries, particularly in the Middle East, western South America and northern Africa, women put milk in their infants' eyes to treat infections there. I do not know if this remedy has ever been tested scientifically, but there are theoretical reasons to believe it would work. It probably does work at least some of the time, or the practice would have died out.

An Abundance of Helpful Molecules

Several molecules in human milk besides secretory IgA prevent microbes from attaching to mucosal surfaces. Oligosaccharides, which are simple chains of sugars, often contain domains that resemble the binding sites through which bacteria gain entry into the cells lining the intestinal tract. Thus, these sugars can intercept bacteria, forming harmless complexes that the baby excretes. In addition, human milk contains large molecules called mucins that include a great deal of protein and carbohydrate. They, too, are capable of adhering to bacteria and viruses and eliminating them from the body.

The molecules in milk have other valuable functions as well. Each molecule of a protein called lactoferrin, for example, can bind to two atoms of iron. Because many pathogenic bacteria thrive on iron, lactoferrin halts their spread by making iron unavailable. It is especially effective at stalling the proliferation of organisms that often cause serious illness in infants, including *Staphylococcus aureus*. Lactoferrin also disrupts the process by which bacteria digest carbohydrates, further limiting their growth. Similarly, B_{12} binding protein, as its name suggests, deprives microorganisms of vitamin B_{12}.

Bifidus factor, one of the oldest known disease-resistance factors in human milk, promotes the growth of a beneficial organism named *Lactobacillus bifidus*. Free fatty acids present in milk can damage the membranes of enveloped viruses, such as the chicken pox virus, which are packets of genetic material encased in protein shells. Interferon, found particularly in colostrum—the scant, sometimes yellowish milk a mother produces during the first few days after birth—also has strong antiviral activity. And fibronectin, present in large quantities in colostrum, can make certain phagocytes more aggressive so that they will ingest microbes even when the microbes have not been tagged by an antibody. Like secretory IgA, fibronectin minimizes inflammation; it also seems to aid in repairing tissue damaged by inflammation.

Cellular Defenses

As is true of defensive molecules, immune cells are abundant in human milk. They consist of white blood cells, or leukocytes, that fight infection themselves and activate other defense mechanisms. The most impressive amount is found in colostrum. Most of the cells are neutrophils, a type of phagocyte that normally circulates in the bloodstream. Some evidence suggests that neutrophils continue to act as phagocytes in the infant's gut. Yet they are less aggressive than blood neutrophils and virtually disappear from breast milk six weeks after birth. So perhaps they serve some other function, such as protecting the breast from infection.

The next most common milk leukocyte is the macrophage, which is phagocytic like neutrophils and performs a number of other protective functions. Macrophages make up some 40 percent of all the leukocytes in colostrum. They are far more active than milk neutrophils, and recent experiments suggest that they are more motile than are their counterparts in blood. Aside from being phagocytic, the macrophages in breast milk manufacture lysozyme, increasing its amount in the infant's gastrointestinal tract. Lysozyme is an enzyme that destroys bacteria by disrupting their cell walls.

In addition, macrophages in the digestive tract can rally lymphocytes into action against invaders. Lymphocytes constitute the remaining 10 percent of white cells in the milk. About 20 percent of these cells are B lymphocytes, which give rise to antibodies; the rest

SINGLE IgA UNIT

SECRETORY COMPONENT

J CHAIN

ANTIGEN BINDING DOMAIN

DANA BURNS-PIZER; SOURCE: JIRI MESTECKY

SECRETORY IgA ANTIBODY, depicted schematically, consists of two IgA molecules "glued" together by a protein fragment known as the J chain. The secretory element (*stripes*) wraps around the joined molecules. The ellipses represent functional domains. Each of the four arms in such antibodies contains an antigen binding domain.

are *T* lymphocytes, which kill infected cells directly or send out chemical messages that mobilize still other components of the immune system. Milk lymphocytes seem to behave differently from blood lymphocytes. Those in milk, for example, proliferate in the presence of *Escherichia coli,* a bacterium that can cause life-threatening illness in babies, but they are far less responsive than blood lymphocytes to agents posing less threat to infants. Milk lymphocytes also manufacture several chemicals—including gamma-interferon, migration inhibition factor and monocyte chemotactic factor—that can strengthen an infant's own immune response.

Added Benefits

Several studies indicate that some factors in human milk may induce an infant's immune system to mature more quickly than it would were the child fed artificially. For example, breast-fed babies produce higher levels of antibodies in response to immunizations.

Also, certain hormones in milk (such as cortisol) and smaller proteins (including epidermal growth factor, nerve growth factor, insulin-like growth factor and somatomedin C) act to close up the leaky mucosal lining of the newborn, making it relatively impermeable to unwanted pathogens and other potentially harmful agents. Indeed, animal studies have demonstrated that postnatal development of the intestine occurs faster in animals fed their mother's milk. And animals that also receive colostrum, containing the highest concentrations of epidermal growth factor, mature even more rapidly.

Other unknown compounds in human milk must stimulate a baby's own production of secretory IgA, lactoferrin and lysozyme. All three molecules are found in larger amounts in the urine of breast-fed babies than in that of bottle-fed babies. Yet breast-fed babies cannot absorb these molecules from human milk into their gut. It would appear that the molecules must be produced in the mucosa of the youngsters' urinary tract. In other words, it seems that breast-feeding induces local immunity in the urinary tract.

In support of this notion, recent clinical studies have demonstrated that the breast-fed infant has a lower risk of acquiring urinary tract infections. Finally, some evidence also suggests that an unknown factor in human milk may cause breast-fed infants to produce more fibronectin on their own than do bottle-fed babies.

All things considered, breast milk is truly a fascinating fluid that supplies infants with far more than nutrition. It protects them against infection until they can protect themselves.

The Author

JACK NEWMAN founded the breast-feeding clinic at the Hospital for Sick Children in Toronto in 1984 and serves as its director. He has more recently established similar clinics at Doctors Hospital and St. Michael's Hospital, both in Toronto. Newman received his medical degree in 1970 from the University of Toronto, where he is now an assistant professor. He completed his postgraduate training in New Zealand and Canada. As a consultant for UNICEF, he has worked with pediatricians in Africa. He has also practiced in New Zealand and in Central and South America.

Further Reading

MUCOSAL IMMUNITY: THE IMMUNOLOGY OF BREAST MILK. H. B. Slade and S. A. Schwartz in *Journal of Allergy and Clinical Immunology,* Vol. 80, No. 3, pages 348–356; September 1987.

IMMUNOLOGY OF MILK AND THE NEONATE. Edited by J. Mestecky et al. Plenum Press, 1991.

BREASTFEEDING AND HEALTH IN THE 1980'S: A GLOBAL EPIDEMIOLOGIC REVIEW. Allan S. Cunningham in *Journal of Pediatrics,* Vol. 118, No. 5, pages 659–666; May 1991.

THE IMMUNE SYSTEM OF HUMAN MILK: ANTIMICROBIAL, ANTIINFLAMMATORY AND IMMUNOMODULATING PROPERTIES. A. S. Goldman in *Pediatric Infectious Disease Journal,* Vol. 12, No. 8, pages 664–671; August 1993.

HOST-RESISTANCE FACTORS AND IMMUNOLOGIC SIGNIFICANCE OF HUMAN MILK. In *Breastfeeding: A Guide for the Medical Profession,* by Ruth A. Lawrence. Mosby Year Book, 1994.

The Amazing Minds of Infants

Looking here, looking there, babies are like little scientists, constantly exploring the world around them, with innate abilities we're just beginning to understand.

Text by **Lisa Grunwald**
Reporting by **Jeff Goldberg**

Additional reporting: **Stacey Bernstein, Anne Hollister**

A light comes on. Shapes and colors appear. Some of the colors and shapes start moving. Some of the colors and shapes make noise. Some of the noises are voices. One is a mother's. Sometimes she sings. Sometimes she says things. Sometimes she leaves. What can an infant make of the world? In the blur of perception and chaos of feeling, what does a baby know?

Most parents, observing infancy, are like travelers searching for famous sites: first tooth, first step, first word, first illness, first shoes, first full night of sleep. Most subtle, and most profound of all, is the first time the clouds of infancy part to reveal the little light of a human intelligence.

For many parents, that revelation may be the moment when they see their baby's first smile. For others, it may be the moment when they watch their child show an actual

---

At three months, babies can learn—and remember for weeks—visual sequences and simple mechanical tasks.

---

preference—for a lullaby, perhaps, or a stuffed animal. But new evidence is emerging to show that even before those moments, babies already have wonderfully active minds.

Of course, they're not exactly chatty in their first year of life, so what—and how—babies truly think may always remain a mystery. But using a variety of ingenious techniques that interpret how infants watch and move, students of child development are discovering a host of unsuspected skills. From a rudimentary understanding of math to a sense of the past and the future, from precocious language ability to an innate understanding of physical laws, children one year and younger know a lot more than they're saying.

MEMORY

Does an infant remember anything? Penelope Leach, that slightly scolding doyenne of the child development field, warns in *Babyhood* that a six- to eight-month-old "cannot hold in his mind a picture of his mother, nor of where she is." And traditionally psychologists have assumed that infants cannot store memories until, like adults, they have the language skills needed to form and retrieve them. But new research suggests that babies as young as three months may be taking quite accurate mental notes.

Babies show an unexpected ability to remember surprisingly intricate details.

Rick Yarian/photo

In his lab at the University of Denver, psychologist Marshall Haith has spent much of the past four years putting infants into large black boxes where they lie and look up at TV screens. The program they see is a Haith invention: a sequence of colorful objects appearing on different sides of the monitor. Using an infrared camera linked to a computer, Haith follows the babies' eye movements and has found that after only five tries the babies can anticipate where the next object will appear. With a little more practice, they can foresee a four-step sequence. And up to two weeks later, most can still predict it. Says Haith: "The babies are not just looking. They're analyzing, creating little hypotheses."

Similar findings by Carolyn Rovee-Collier, a psychologist at Rutgers University, suggest that infants can remember surprisingly intricate details. In a typical experiment, she places a baby in a crib beneath an elaborate mobile, ties one of the baby's ankles to it with a satin ribbon, then observes as the baby kicks and—often gleefully—makes it move. When, weeks later, the baby's feet are left untied and the mobile is returned to the crib, the baby will try to kick again, presumably recalling the palmy days of kicking the last time. But if the mobile's elements are changed even slightly, the baby will remain unmoved—and unmoving. "When we change things," explains Rovee-Collier, "it wipes out the memory. But as soon as we bring back what had become familiar and expected, the memory comes right back. What we've learned from this is that even at two and a half months, an infant's memory is very developed, very specific and incredibly detailed."

Rachel Clifton, a psychologist at the University of Massachusetts, says that an infant's experience at six months can be remembered a full two years later. Clifton stumbled upon her findings while researching motor and hearing skills. Three years ago she placed 16 six-month-olds in a pitch-dark room with objects that made different sounds. Using infrared cameras like Haith's, she observed how and when the infants reached for the objects. Later, realizing she had created a unique situation that couldn't have been duplicated in real life, she wondered if the babies would remember their experience. Two years after the original experiment, collaborating with psychologist Nancy Myers, she brought the same 16 children back to the lab, along with a control group of 16 other two-and-a-half-year-olds. Amazingly, the experimental group showed the behavior they had at six months, reaching for objects and showing no fear. Fewer control-group toddlers reached for the objects, and many of them cried.

Says Myers: "For so long, we didn't think that infants could rep-

---

At five months, babies have the raw ability to add.

---

resent in their memories the events that were going on around them, but put them back in a similar situation, as we did, and you can make the memory accessible."

MATH

At least a few parental eyebrows—and undoubtedly some expectations—were raised by this recent headline in *The New York Times:* "Study Finds Babies at 5 Months Grasp Simple Mathematics." The story, which reported on the findings of Karen Wynn, a psychologist at the University of Arizona, explained that infants as young as five months had been found to exhibit "a rudimentary ability to add and subtract."

Wynn, who published her research in the renowned scientific journal *Nature,* had based her experiments on a widely observed phenomenon: Infants look longer at things that are unexpected to them, thereby revealing what they do expect, or know. Wynn enacted addition and subtraction equations for babies using Mickey Mouse dolls. In a typical example, she had the babies watch as she placed a doll on a puppet stage, hid it behind a screen, then placed a second doll behind the screen (to represent one plus one). When she removed the screen to reveal three, not two, Mickey Mouse dolls, the infants stared longer at such incorrect outcomes than they had at correct ones. Wynn believes that babies' numerical understanding is "an innate mechanism, somehow built into the biological structure."

Her findings have been met with enthusiasm in the field—not least from Mark Strauss at the University of Pittsburgh, who a decade ago found that somewhat older babies could distinguish at a glance the difference between one, two, three and four balls—nearly as many objects as adults can decipher without counting. Says Strauss: "Five-month-olds are clearly thinking about quantities and applying numerical concepts to their world."

Wynn's conclusions have also inspired skepticism among some researchers who believe her results may reflect infants' ability to perceive things but not necessarily an ability to know what they're perceiving. Wynn herself warns parents not to leap to any conclu-

sions, and certainly not to start tossing algebra texts into their children's cribs. Still, she insists: "A lot more is happening in infants' minds than we've tended to give them credit for."

LANGUAGE

In an old stand-up routine, Robin Williams used to describe his son's dawning ability as a mimic of words—particularly those of the deeply embarrassing four-letter variety. Most parents decide they can no longer speak with complete freedom when their children start talking. Yet current research on language might prompt some to start censoring themselves even earlier.

At six months, babies recognize their native tongue.

At Seattle's University of Washington, psychologist Patricia Kuhl has shown that long before infants actually begin to learn words, they can sort through a jumble of spoken sounds in search of the ones that have meaning. From birth to four months, according to Kuhl, babies are "universal linguists" capable of distinguishing each of the 150 sounds that make up all human speech. But by just six months, they have begun the metamorphosis into specialists who recognize the speech sounds of their native tongue.

In Kuhl's experiment babies listened as a tape-recorded voice repeated vowel and consonant combinations. Each time the sounds changed—from "ah" to "oooh," for example—a toy bear in a box

was lit up and danced. The babies quickly learned to look at the bear when they heard sounds that were new to them. Studying Swedish and American six-month-olds, Kuhl found they ignored subtle variations in pronunciation of their own language's sounds—for instance, the different ways two people might pronounce "ee"—but they heard similar variations in a foreign language as separate sounds. The implication? Six-month-olds can already discern the sounds they will later need for speech. Says Kuhl: "There's nothing external in these six-month-olds that would provide you with a clue that something like this is going on."

By eight to nine months, comprehension is more visible, with babies looking at a ball when their mothers say "ball," for example. According to psychologist Donna Thal at the University of California, San Diego, it is still impossible to gauge just how many words babies understand at this point, but her recent studies of slightly older children indicate that comprehension may exceed expression by a factor as high as a hundred to one. Thal's studies show that although some babies are slow in starting to talk, comprehension appears to be equal between the late talkers and early ones.

PHYSICS

No, no one is claiming that an eight-month-old can compute the trajectory of a moon around a planet. But at Cornell University, psychologist Elizabeth Spelke is finding that babies as young as four months have a rudimentary knowledge of the way the world works—or should work.

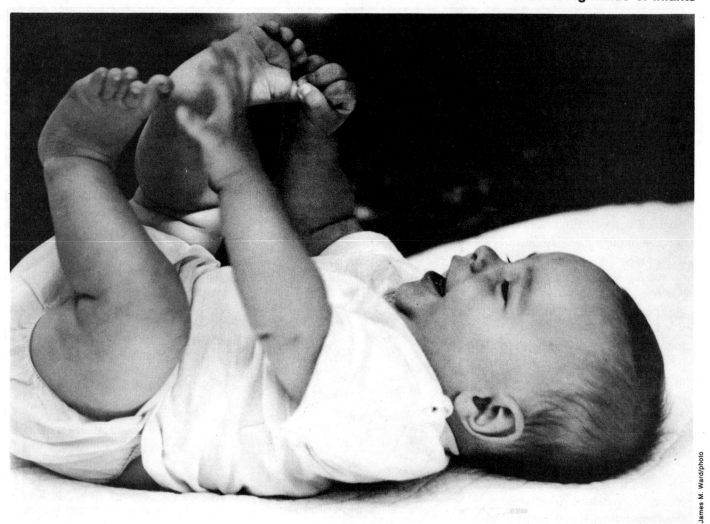

Babies learn how physical objects behave by moving their body parts.

Babies have a built-in sense of how objects behave.

Spelke sets her young subjects up before a puppet stage, where she shows them a series of unexpected actions: a ball seems to roll through a solid barrier, another seems to leap between two platforms, a third seems to hang in midair. Like Karen Wynn with her math experiments, Spelke measures the babies' looking time and has recorded longer intervals for unexpected actions than for expected ones. Again like Wynn, Spelke be-

lieves that babies must have some "core" knowledge—in this case, about the way physical objects behave. Says Spelke: "At an age when infants are not able to talk about objects, move around objects, reach for and manipulate objects, or even see objects with high resolution, they appear to recognize where a moving object is when it has left their view and make inferences about where it should be when it comes into sight again."

The notion of an infant's possessing any innate mechanism—other than reflexes like sucking that fade with time—would have shocked the shoes off the pioneers of child development research, who believed, as some still do, that

what we know can be learned only through experience. But the belief in biologically programmed core knowledge lies at the heart of the current research—not only with math and physics but with other cognitive skills as well. Indeed, Carnegie Mellon's Mark Johnson believes that the ability of infants to recognize the human face is not learned, as previously thought, but is present at birth. Studying infants, some only 10 minutes old, Johnson has observed a marked preference for pictures of faces to pictures of blank ovals or faces with scrambled features. He believes that we are born with a "template" of the human face that aids our survival by helping us recognize our meal ticket.

EMOTIONS: THE SHY AND THE LIVELY

A growing number of researchers believe early temperament may indicate later troubles.

One thing that infants are *not* good at is hiding what they feel. Fear, glee, rage, affection: Long before babies start talking, emotions tumble out of them in gestures, tears and belly laughs. But measuring infant temperament—finding a way to quantify its traits—has always been harder than measuring skills.

Around the country, researchers are now combining questionnaires filled in by parents, home visits by trained observers, and newly devised lab tests to explore the mystery of temperamenat. Concentrating on babies older than eight months (the age at which the full range of infant emotions has emerged), investigators have designed more than 50 experimental situations to provoke emotions from fear to sadness, from interest to pleasure. Most children's reactions fall within an average range on such tests. But there are babies on either extreme, and psychologist Nathan Fox at the University of Maryland has begun to explore their responses. Putting his babies in electroencephalogram (EEG) helmets, he has found that particularly inhibited babies show a distinctive brain-wave pattern, which others believe may predict later emotional problems, including depression. Although some scientists agree that early behavior can predict later temperament, other researchers argue that enduring character traits are the exception, not the rule. For psychiatrist Stanley Greenspan of Bethesda, Md., the ability of infants to change is an article of faith. Specializing in babies as young as three months, Greenspan says he can treat what he calls the garden-variety problems of sleep disorders, tan-

Long before babies begin talking, emotions are graphically expressed in their gestures and facial expressions.

trums and anger in a few sessions. (Don't imagine tiny couches for infant patients; although the babies are closely observed, it's the parents who often get treatment.) For more severe problems, such as suspected learning disorders, he recommends more intensive early intervention—often involving a team of therapists—and has found that this can make a huge difference: "Babies who were very scared, shy and inhibited can completely change and become very assertive, outgoing and confident over a number of months."

The University of Washington's Mary Rothbart has compared infants in Japan, the Netherlands and the U.S. and notes that northern European mothers are most prone to ignore their babies' fussiness with a stiff-upper-lip approach. When tested at one year by having their mothers leave a room, the Dutch babies are the most distressed and ignore their mothers upon their return. Psychologists call this response an "insecure attachment relationship," and some regard it as an early warning of later anxiety disorders. Says Rothbart: "In the process of soothing a baby, you're helping to teach it to shift its attention away from negative sensations. Adults with anxiety disorders may never have learned to do this." Tellingly, when Dutch mothers were instructed to soothe and play with their fussy babies, the follow-up sessions showed positive results. "With intervention," concludes Rothbart, "you can turn things around."

TAKING INFANTS SERIOUSLY

The ultimate question becomes, should education begin at three months?

One question that might leap to the minds of parents newly informed of their infants' skills is a simple one: So what? What does it mean if children really have these unexpected abilities?

Pointing to the findings on memory that she has published with partner Rachel Clifton, Nancy Myers suggests that if memories of the babies' experience allowed them to be unafraid in the pitch-black room, then exposing children to a wide variety of events and places may make them more accepting of similar situations later on. "I don't want to say that mothers should make an extreme effort to stimulate their babies," Myers says, "but taking a baby to different places, allowing him to see and smell different things, is an important means of establishing familiarity. It will allow the baby to feel freer in the future."

But what about other kinds of skills: Should infants' innate abilities with language or math be consciously nurtured and pushed along?

In Philadelphia, instructors at the Institutes for the Achievement of Human Potential have been coaching parents since 1963 to teach their babies to read from birth. Touting "genetic potential," their program recommends that parents write out on cards everything from "nose" to "kiss" to "Mommy." The new findings about infants' skills have hardly gone unnoticed at the Institutes, where director Janet Doman says: "For the past thirty years, we've been saying that children can learn at very early ages. It's nice to know that science is finally validating what we've known all along."

Yet many of the scientists performing the experiments question the value of such intensive efforts. Says Rutgers's Carolyn Rovee-Collier: "Most of us agree that an infant could be taught to recognize letters and numbers. But the problem is that parents who do these kinds of programs start investing a lot in their infants and become very bound up in their success. It puts great strain on the infants and the parents."

University of Denver psychologist Marshall Haith agrees: "Babies are born prepared to take on the world. We've got to get away from the feeling that we've got this wonderful brain sitting there and we've got to keep pumping information into it. Nature wouldn't have done anything so stupid."

To most researchers, the moral of the story seems to be: Respect your baby, but don't go nuts. "Don't waste your child's fun months," says Karen Wynn, who says her findings about math "should be viewed as no more than a new insight for parents who have young children." Says the University of Pittsburgh's Mark Strauss: "Ideally, we can tell parents a lot more about subtle things they can watch happening in their infants, and that will make watching and getting involved more fun."

The Realistic View of Biology and Behavior

Jerome Kagan

Jerome Kagan is professor of psychology at Harvard University. He is the author of Galen's Prophecy: Temperament in Human Nature (*BasicBooks, 1994*).

Although families with more than one child know that each infant brings into the world a distinctive mood and manner, during most of this century Americans have resisted the idea that biology might form at least part of the foundation of some personality traits. The strength of American skepticism is odd, because generations of previous commentators on human nature, beginning with the ancient Greeks, acknowledged that each person's physiology made a small contribution to his or her energy, emotional adaptability, and style of interaction with others.

The source of American resistance, though, is the laudable, egalitarian hope that benevolent home and school experiences can overcome individual biological variations and create a society of relative equals. Because that hope sustains liberal legislation, many people—including scholars—believe that it is dangerous to challenge it, no matter how mildly.

However, the evidence for physiology's influence on some behavior is sufficient to overcome any hesitation to discuss openly the nature of biologically based predispositions. Research in many laboratories, including my own, reveals that many people inherit a physiology that can affect, for example, a proneness to be melancholic or sanguine. At the same time, we must not become so enamored of such discoveries that we forget biology's real limits.

The campaign to suppress discussion of biology grew strong during the opening decades of this century. Politically liberal scholars, joined by journalists of like mind, wished to mute the arguments of conservatives who argued for halting immigration from Eastern Europe on the ground that the immigrants had genetic flaws. The liberals were helped by Ivan Pavlov's discovery of conditioning, in the early 1900's, in a St. Petersburg laboratory. If a dog could be taught to salivate at a sound, surely a child could be taught anything, was the message John Watson, America's first behaviorist, brought to American parents after World War I. That bold claim was congruent with Sigmund Freud's creative hypothesis that family experiences in the early years could create or prevent a future neurosis.

By the late 1920's, the broad acceptance of inherited temperamental traits, which had lasted for two millennia, had been banished, its demise speeded by our society's need to believe in the power of social experience.

As the discipline of psychology—born in Europe during the last quarter of the 19th century—became recognized at American colleges and universities, many faculty members began to emphasize the influence of social experience on behavior. This approach became easier to defend after Hitler proposed the repugnant philosophy that Aryans were superior to other people.

After World War II, social science in America also became more positivistic, demanding objective evidence for all theoretical statements. Neuroscience was still young in the late 1940's and was unable to supply evidence that could explain, for example, how a particular physiological profile might be the foundation of an anxious or an angry mood.

> *"Hundreds of studies of the way families influence growing children had not produced the powerful generalizations that had been anticipated a half century earlier."*

By the 1970's, however, the historical context had again changed. Hundreds of studies of the way families influence growing children had not produced the powerful generalizations that had been anticipated a half century earlier. Equally important,

 From *The Chronicle of Higher Education*, October 5, 1994, p. A64. © 1994 by Jerome Kagan. Reprinted by permission of the author.

engineers and scientists had invented ingenious ways to study the brain. Suddenly it became possible to speculate about how a particular neurochemistry could produce excessive anxiety, sadness, or anger. Scientists who put forward such explanations were not treated as intellectual terrorists for suggesting, for example, that a woman with panic attacks might have inherited a neurochemistry that rendered her especially vulnerable to a sudden, inexplicable sharp rise in heart rate, a feeling of suffocation, and a surge of fear.

But I believe that some psychiatrists and neuroscientists are moving too quickly toward a biological determinism that is as extreme as the earlier loyalty of some psychologists to an environmental explanation of behavior. Fortunately, a majority of scientists recognize that no human psychological profile is a product of genes alone. To rephrase a graceful sentence by the philosopher W. V. O. Quine, every behavior can be likened to a pale gray fabric composed of black threads, for biology, and white threads, for experience, but it is not possible to detect any purely black threads nor any white ones.

Support for this more complex, but realistic, view of the relation between brain and behavior is found in the fact that if one member of a pair of identical twins develops schizophrenia, the odds are less than 50 per cent that the other twin will come down with the same psychosis. Because inherited biological propensities do not affect all psychological outcomes equally, the proper strategy is to ask which psychological characteristics are most, and which least, vulnerable to biological forces. Serious depression belongs to the former category, while preference for a seaside holiday belongs to the latter.

At the moment, two psychological categories, which can be observed clearly in children, appear to be heavily influenced by biology. Between 15 per cent and 20 per cent of a large group of healthy infants we studied, who were born into secure homes, were found to have inherited a tendency to be unusually aroused and distressed by new, unexpected events. When they were observed in our laboratory at four months of age, they thrashed their limbs and cried when they saw colorful, moving mobiles or heard tape recordings of human speech. About two-thirds of these easily aroused infants, whom we call "high reactive," became extremely shy, fearful, subdued toddlers. Based on other data, we estimate that about one-half of this group of toddlers will become quiet, introverted adolescents. Not all of the high-reactive infants will become introverted, however, because their life experiences lead them to develop differently.

A second, larger group of infants—about 35 per cent of the children we studied—are the opposite of the high-reactive, shy children. These infants are relaxed and rarely cry when they experience new events. Two-thirds of this group become sociable, relatively fearless young children. Stressful events, however, can produce a fearful or shy manner in such children, even though they began life with a minimally excitable temperament.

Support for a biological contribution to the development of these two types of children comes from the fact that the two groups differ in many aspects of their physiological functioning, as well as in their body build. The fearful children show larger increases in heart rate and blood pressure when they are challenged—signs of a more reactive sympathetic nervous system. They have a higher prevalence of the allergies that produce hay fever and hives (and, surprisingly, possess narrower faces). Studies of identical and fraternal twins support the belief that each of these temperamental types is influenced, in part, by heredity.

Hippocrates and Galen of Pergamon would not have been surprised by these discoveries. Many Americans, however, will be troubled, because they will misinterpret the evidence as implying an exaggerated biological influence on behavior. Some social scientists will also resist acknowledging the contribution of brain chemistry and physiology to behavior because they will worry that, if they let the camel's nose under the tent, the animal will soon be inside, forcing all the residents to leave.

All the more reason that we who study the relationship of biology to behavior must make clear that psychological phenomena, like a fearful or a fearless style of behavior, cannot be reduced completely to a person's biology: The child's life history influences the adult's psychological profile. Because the course of that life history is unknown when children are very young, we cannot at that time select the very small proportion of the 5 per cent to 10 per cent of children whose temperaments dispose them to be fearless, impulsive, and aggressive who will go on to develop an asocial or criminal personality. It would be unethical, for example, to tell parents that their 3-year-old son is at serious risk for delinquent behavior.

Similar arguments can be made about predicting which children will develop panic attacks, depression, or schizophrenia. A small group of children are at risk for each of these disorders because of the physiology they inherit, but we are unable at the present time to say which of the children will eventually develop a particular disorder—because we do not know what vicissitudes life will hold for them.

Perhaps future discoveries will supply the information that will make such predictions accurate enough to warrant benevolent intervention early in the child's life. We will have to wait and see whether that promise can be fulfilled.

A more subtle implication of the research on temperament involves people's willingness to take responsibility for their own actions. I trust that most Americans still believe in the notion of free will—that we can decide what action we will take or not take—and that each of us has a moral obligation to be civil and responsible, even when we wake up feeling blue, angry, or anxious. Our culture still insists that we should pull up our socks and act responsibly, even if that posture comes at some emotional price.

The danger in the new romance with biology is that many people will begin to award temperament too strong a voice, deciding, for example, to be permissive and accepting of friends who lose their tempers too easily. Each of us does inherit a temperamental bias for one or more characteristics, but we also inherit the human capacity for restraint. Most of the time, humans are able to control the behavior that their temperament presses upon them, if they choose to do so. The new research on temperament and biology should not be used to excuse asocial behavior. Rather, the purpose of the inquiry is to help us understand the bases for the extraordinary variation in human motivation, mood, and social behavior.

We would do well to remember that although the poet-philosopher Lucretius believed in temperamental variation he was also convinced that the "lingering traces of inborn temperament that cannot be eliminated by philosophy are so slight that there is nothing to prevent men from leading a life worthy of the gods."

Case Studies of Environmental Risks to Children

Lynn R. Goldman

Abstract

Doing a better job of protecting children from environmental hazards requires having more and better information about both children's susceptibility and their exposure to toxic substances. There are many critical gaps in knowledge of this issue. This article presents several examples specifically related to children's exposure to pesticides which illustrate environmental risks for children. The cases examined include the risk posed to children by the use of the insecticide aldicarb on bananas, and reported illnesses in children caused by the use of the insecticide diazinon in the home and by the use of interior house paint containing mercury. The cases presented illustrate how regulatory agencies, parents, health care providers, and others who come into contact with children on a regular basis all have roles to play in filling in the information gaps regarding children's exposure to environmental hazards and the deleterious effects of these exposures.

Lynn R. Goldman, M.D., M.P.H., is a pediatrician and an epidemiologist, and is the assistant administrator for the Office of Prevention, Pesticides, and Toxic Substances of the U.S. Environmental Protection Agency, Washington, DC.

As discussed by Bearer in this journal issue, children are more susceptible to the deleterious effects of many environmental exposures than adults. Much current knowledge about the effects of environmental hazards on children comes from experience. We have learned from major environmental disasters, such as the Love Canal experience, which showed what can go wrong when an elementary school is built directly over a hazardous waste disposal site, and from other cases of exposures to chemicals whose effects are not obvious for decades, such as vaginal cancer following exposure *in utero* to diethylstilbestrol (DES).[1] Each discovery of a new deleterious effect adds to the urgency of understanding and responding to the consequences for children of environmental hazards. Environmental legislation of the 1970s and 1980s, which responded to public concern about evidence of a pattern of environmental destruction in America, created a network of laws and regulations to protect the environment. These statutes—including the Clean Air and Water acts, Toxic Substances Control Act, Resource Conservation and Recovery Act, Safe Drinking Water Act, and Comprehensive Environmental Response, Compensation, and Liability Act

(Superfund law), along with state laws and programs—have helped to benefit public health and protect the environment. But more can be done, particularly to safeguard children from environmental risks. Recognizing that children are not simply "little adults" is key to making environmental policy more responsive to children's needs.

Doing a better job of assessing risks for children requires more information about both their susceptibility and their exposure to toxic substances. Too many critical gaps in existing data persist. Although developing the needed information is a complex matter, scientists in government, academia, and elsewhere have succeeded in filling some of the gaps, and research currently under way needs continued support. At the same time, however, incorporating existing information into the assessment of children's risks must become a priority.

Although children typically face environmental risks from a variety of sources, this article presents a series of examples specifically related to pesticides to illustrate environmental risk issues involving children. These cases, drawn from government reporting systems and clinical observation of children, highlight the importance of taking the special status of children into consideration when developing environmental policy.

Government Reporting Systems

One mechanism that can identify the potential effects of environmental chemicals on children is the reporting required of chemical manufacturers by the federal government. One part of that reporting takes place when the manufacturer is seeking government approval for a product. For a pesticide to gain approval for use, manufacturers are required to follow formal testing procedures to show that the product works as intended and does not present an unreasonable risk to humans or the environment. Tolerances, or legal limits, for the amount of a pesticide which is permitted to be present in food are determined from the information gained during this process.[2] This federal reporting system identified circumstances under which aldicarb, a widely used pesticide, posed a special hazard for children.

Aldicarb

Aldicarb is an insecticide that has been used since the 1970s on fruits, nuts, potatoes, and various other vegetables and recently came under increased scrutiny for potential risk to children.[3,4] Aldicarb is systemic; that is, it is taken up by the roots of a plant and ends up in the plant itself, and

therefore, cannot be removed by simply washing or peeling fruits and vegetables. Aldicarb acts by inhibiting acetylcholinesterase, the enzyme necessary for the proper transmission of nerve impulses. Chemicals that inhibit cholinesterase can be very toxic to humans. Aldicarb belongs to the class of cholinesterase inhibitors called carbamates. They can cause a number of effects, including diarrhea, blurred vision, vomiting, and changes in the function of the central nervous system.

In 1991, the manufacturer of aldicarb notified the Environmental Protection Agency (EPA) of some unexpected aldicarb residues in bananas. Generally, the residues were below the established tolerance when the bananas were blended together.[5] However, when the bananas were analyzed one at a time, some of these bananas were found to have "hot" levels of aldicarb that were up to 10 times more than the legal limit. Therefore, more than the safety threshold for a whole day's exposure could occur in a single serving if certain individuals happened to eat one of the "hot" bananas.

After these data were reported, the U.S. Food and Drug Administration (FDA) checked aldicarb levels in bananas as they were used for different purposes. Processed bananas used for baby food were found to have very low aldicarb levels, probably because the baby foods are made by blending large numbers of bananas. Therefore, children who ate their bananas in that form were relatively safe from high levels of exposure to aldicarb. However, children who ate pieces of bananas or entire individual bananas were more at risk. The levels of aldicarb in some individual bananas were not only well above the legal limit but potentially high enough to make a child acutely ill. EPA's dietary risk assessment found that, for the "hottest" bananas, the allowable daily limit of aldicarb would be exceeded by an adult's eating more than one-eighth of a banana and by a child's eating more than one bite of a banana. Even for bananas at the legal limit, just one-third of a banana would be an excess for a toddler and one-seventh of a banana would be above the allowable daily intake for an infant.

This increased risk of exposure for children to high levels of pesticide residue on food is compounded by the typical child's diet. In general, children's diets are less varied than those of adults. As a consequence, they eat larger volumes of certain foods per pound of body weight than adults do. A toddler's eating one banana (a fairly common occurrence) is roughly equivalent to an adult's eating five bananas, on a body-weight basis. For this reason, children were at greater risk of high levels of exposure to aldicarb than adults.

Based on this information, the manufacturer voluntarily agreed to stop the sale of aldicarb for use on bananas. The registration of aldicarb for bananas has since been canceled. The company also agreed to reduce the amount of aldicarb recommended for use on citrus fruits, but it is still used on some crops.[6] The pesticide is currently undergoing special review for groundwater concerns.

This case study is particularly disturbing in light of the fact that FDA tests about 40 food samples each day for a limited number of pesticides.[7] Because of this limited sampling and the large number of pesticides used, there are many pesticides for which the EPA never tests, and therefore, their prevalence in the food supply is

unknown.[8] Aldicarb is one pesticide for which a specific risk has been identified, but the potential for many more such risks to go undetected is real.

Clinician Diagnosis and Reporting

Environmental risks to children are sometimes discovered by clinicians when treating children with unusual health problems. The following section discusses two examples of environmental effects upon children which were diagnosed by physicians alert to the effects of changes in the environment upon their patients.

Diazinon

The first example involves an infant in Oregon diagnosed with chronic diazinon poisoning.[9] In December 1989, a routine physical examination at age 12 weeks found that the child had excessive muscle tone in her legs—her leg muscles had increased resistance to stretching (hypertonicity). A month later, when symptoms did not improve, the pediatrician consult-

The levels of aldicarb in some individual bananas were not only well above the legal limit but potentially high enough to make a child acutely ill.

ed a specialist, who examined the infant. At this examination, the hypertonicity was also occurring in her arms and hands, and the consultant suspected that the child had a mild case of cerebral palsy. Treatment and physical therapy for cerebral palsy were begun.

Several months later, the child's parents informed the physician that the home had been sprayed with an insecticide a month prior to the first examination. An unlicensed applicator had sprayed the home, including the entire area and furniture of some rooms, with the insecticide diazinon. This type of application was a misuse of the pesticide; the diazinon product should be applied only to cracks, crevices, and small areas. The clinician reported the exposure to the state Pesticide

Analytical and Response Center, which began an investigation. Diazinon residues in the home were evaluated, and urine samples were taken from the child and adults in the home for testing for the metabolites of diazinon. Unexpectedly high levels of residues were found in the home, and the child's urine sample showed levels of metabolites of diazinon (alkylphosphate) comparable to levels found in farmworkers who work with this pesticide. The adults' alkylphosphate levels were too low to be detected by the testing. For the child's sake, the family was advised to leave the home. Six weeks after being removed from the home environment, the child no longer exhibited hypertonicity symptoms, and all cerebral palsy treatment was discontinued.

The infant in this case was more vulnerable to diazinon than the adults for several reasons. Because the pesticide was sprayed over entire floor surfaces, it is likely that the child was exposed partly by contact with the floor. Children's contact with the floor is typically more extensive than that of adults because of their height and means of getting around. In addition, infants take in more air for their size than adults and breathe more rapidly, so the airborne particles of diazinon which came from the initial application and from disturbances of the floor surfaces (such as by vacuuming) would be more concentrated in the child's body. Moreover, studies have found that young animals are more susceptible to organophosphate chemicals like diazinon than are older animals, and the existence of a parallel phenomenon in humans is quite possible. [10,11]

The unusual feature in this case is that the clinician made the connection between the spraying of the insecticide and the child's problems, even in the absence of effects on the adults in the home and when a different diagnosis had already been proposed and accepted. The clinician also promptly reported the exposure and set in motion laboratory procedures to identify diazinon in the home and to test for metabolites in the child. Even though the child's symptoms were not necessarily the same as those of an adult with similar exposure,[12] the cause of the symptoms was identified and the child was removed from the harmful home environment. Under other circumstances, this child might have gone on to have chronic neurological damage from the exposure, and no one would have known why.

This example also shows that, through the use of home and garden pesticides, parents can inadvertently expose their children to much heavier levels of pesticides than they would normally be exposed to in food, water, or air. Despite good intentions, without knowledge of the potential effects of pesticides on their children, parents themselves may be the largest factor contributing to the exposure of their children. Educating parents about the effects of pesticides on children is one important method of decreasing children's exposure.

Mercury

The second example concerns chronic mercury toxicity in a child.[13] In this 1989 case, a four-year-old child from Michigan presented in a clinician's office with sweating, itching, headaches, difficulty in walking, gingivitis, hypertension, and red discoloration of the palms and the soles of the feet—all symptoms of mercury poisoning. The physician had knowledge of mercury poisoning cases from the earlier part of this century. At that time, medicines and teething powders containing mercury were commonly prescribed for young children. Children who were exposed to large amounts of mercury developed a condition called acrodynia (which means "painful extremities") weeks or months after exposure. The symptoms of acrodynia include irritability, red discoloration of the hands and feet, pain in joints, heavy sweating, muscle weakness, and difficulty standing or walking. Despite the severity of the effects, it was not until the 1940s that the cause was determined to be mercury poisoning and the use of mercury in medicines for young children was banned. Today it is possible to treat acrodynia, but many physicians are unaware of its existence because it is so rare. This physician, because of his experience, suspected mercury poisoning as the cause of the child's symptoms and began to search for a source of exposure.

The physician reported the symptoms and his suspicion of acrodynia to the Department of Public Health, which found that the mercury exposure came from the painting of the interior of the child's home with latex paint just ten days before the child became ill. At one time, biocides containing mercury were added to about one-fourth of interior latex paints in low concentrations to extend the shelf life of the paint and in higher concentrations to make paints mildew resistant. The paint the family used contained a mercury biocide. After the house was painted, the family slept with the air conditioning system on and the windows closed. The mercury in the paint vaporized, and the child and his family breathed it in. When tested, all members of the family had elevated mercury urine levels; however, only the child was symptomatic. He was hospitalized for four months and received treatments to increase the amount of mercury excreted from the body. After treatment, almost all of the symptoms disappeared, and he could walk again.

There are several reasons the child was more vulnerable to mercury inhalation than the adults in this case. As in the diazinon case, children's higher rate of respiration causes them to take in a greater amount of both air and its contaminants relative to their size than adults (see the article by Bearer in this journal issue). Mercury vapor is also heavier than air, so the area in a room that has the greatest concentration of mercury will be near the floor, where small children play.[14]

Since 1990, the mercury compound involved has been banned for use in house paints, but this case raises the question of whether there have been a number of instances of similar exposure of children in the recent past that went unrecognized. It also raises a more global question. Chemicals such as mercury were used for many years before their effects became

---

Chemicals such as mercury were used for many years before their effects became known and their use was banned. How many chemicals currently in use are having other, unknown effects on children?

---

known and their use was banned. How many chemicals currently in use are hav-

ing other, unknown effects on children? According to the EPA, an estimated three million children each year may have been exposed to mercury through latex paint manufactured before the ban took effect.[15] If three million children were exposed to mercury through paint alone, the number exposed to other harmful chemicals in a variety of forms is likely to be much greater.

Multiple Exposures

In addition to exposures from single sources, such as the cases presented here, many children may experience multiple chemical exposures, which are even more difficult to identify and evaluate. Pesticides alone could account for several exposures to an individual child. Suppose, for example, that a child's home is treated with a pesticide, and others are used to treat the child's school for pests. Still other pesticides are in the food the child eats. Over a single day, a child may be exposed to pesticides from many sources, as well as numerous other environmental contaminants.

Illnesses resulting from these multiple exposures are difficult to diagnose and treat for two major reasons. First, several classes of pesticides, such as the organophosphates and carbamates, contain specific chemicals that act in the same way in the body. If a child has an illness caused by a combination of similarly acting chemicals, the source of the contamination causing a particular illness may not be clear. In addition, the effects of exposure to multiple toxins are not well understood, particularly when the chemicals have different modes of action. It is simply not known whether these chemicals inhibit each other or if they are additive or synergistic, multiplying one another's potential effects on children. Given the large number of chemicals many children are exposed to daily, the task of sorting out the effects of multiple exposures is daunting and has not yet been accomplished. Because of this lack of knowledge, regulations on maximum exposure levels generally have not taken the effects of multiple exposures into account but, instead, treat each exposure as if it occurred in isolation.[16]

Given the large number of chemicals many children are exposed to daily, the task of sorting out the effects of multiple exposures is daunting and has not yet been accomplished.

Conclusion

Much is still unknown about the effects of environmental chemical exposures on people, and on infants and children in particular. Filling the information gaps on effects and exposures is essential, but achieving that goal will take time, focused effort, and support for research dedicated to this end. The cases presented here illustrate that, in addition to regulatory agencies, parents, physicians, and others who come in contact with children on a regular basis all have roles to play. Among clinicians, increased alertness to environmental toxicity when making a diagnosis can be a direct route to identifying environmental causes of disease. Parents can help by identifying, and protecting children from, environmental exposures and by advising physicians involved in treating a child's health problem about possible exposures. Regulators and others who are responsible for environmental safety will have to be particularly sensitive to the increased vulnerability of children, in setting research agendas and regulatory policy and in sharing critical information on risks to children with those who are directly responsible for protecting children.

Notes

1. Schardein, J. L. Hormones and hormonal antagonists. *Chemically induced birth defects.* New York: Marcel Dekker, 1993, pp. 271–84.

2. According to the Food and Drug Administration, pesticide tolerances for food "reflect a very conservative margin of safety—normally more than 100 to 1,000 times lower than the level that caused 'no effect' in test animals." Farley, D. Setting safe limits on pesticide residues. *FDA Consumer* (October 1988) 6–7.

3. National Academy of Sciences, National Research Council. *Pesticides in the diets of infants and children.* Washington, DC: National Academy Press, 1993, p. 246.

4. Jehl, D. Pesticide may peril children when used on bananas and potatoes, EPA study says. *Los Angeles Times,* March 2, 1989, at sec. 1, pp. 11.

5. See note no. 3, National Academy of Sciences, pp. 289–96.

6. Sugarman, C. Small amount of tainted bananas found. *Washington Post.* June 5, 1991, at A14.

7. Farley, D. Setting safe limits on pesticide residues. *FDA Consumer* (October 1988) 11.

8. According to the EPA, there are 860 pesticides currently registered in the United States. U.S. Environmental Protection Agency. *Quantities of pesticides used in the United States.* Information sheet. Washington, DC: 1994. If an FDA test detects "more than 100 different pesticides" in a single sample, there are many that are not monitored. Farley, D. Setting safe limits on pesticide residues. *FDA Consumer* (October 1988) 10.

9. Wagner, S. L., and Orwick, D. L. Chronic organophosphate exposure associated with transient hypertonia in an infant. *Pediatrics* (1994) 94, 1:94–97.

10. Gupta, R. C., Rech, R. H., Lovell, K. L., et al. Brain cholinergic, behavioral, and morphological development in rats exposed in utero to methylparathion. *Toxicology and Applied Pharmacology* (1985) 77:405–13.

11. Mendoza, C. E., and Shields, J. B. Effects on esterases and comparisons of I_{50} and LD_{50} values of malathion in suckling rats. *Bulletin of Environmental Contamination and Toxicology* (1977) 17:9–15.

12. Zwiener, R. J., and Ginsburg, C. M. Organophosphate and carbamate poisoning in infants and children. *Pediatrics* (1988) 81:121–26.

13. Blondell, J. M., and Knott, S. M. Risk analysis for phenylmercuric acetate in indoor latex house paint. In *Pesticides in urban environments: Fate and significance.* K. D. Racke and A. R. Leslie, eds. Washington, DC: American Chemical Society, 1993.

14. Guzelian, P. S., Henry, C. J., and Olin S. S. *Similarities and differences between children and adults.* Washington, DC: International Life Sciences Institute Press, 1992, p. 206.

15. U.S. Environmental Protection Agency. *Environmental fact sheet: Mercury biocides in paint, voluntary cancellation, voluntary deletion, and amended registration.* Washington, DC: July 1990. Cited in *Pesticides in urban environments: Fate and significance.* K. D. Racke and A. R. Leslie, eds. Washington, DC: American Chemical Society, 1993, p. 315.

16. See note no. 3, National Academy of Sciences, p. 297.

A baby's brain is a work in progress, trillions of neurons waiting to be wired into a mind. The experiences of childhood, pioneering research shows, help form the brain's circuits—for music and math, language and emotion.

Your Child's Brain

Sharon Begley

YOU HOLD YOUR NEWBORN SO his sky-blue eyes are just inches from the brightly patterned wallpaper. *ZZZt:* a neuron from his retina makes an electrical connection with one in his brain's visual cortex. You gently touch his palm with a clothespin; he grasps it, drops it, and you return it to him with soft words and a smile. *Crackle:* neurons from his hand strengthen their connection to those in his sensory-motor cortex. He cries in the night; you feed him, holding his gaze because nature has seen to it that the distance from a parent's crooked elbow to his eyes exactly matches the distance at which a baby focuses. *Zap:* neurons in the brain's amygdala send pulses of electricity through the circuits that control emotion. You hold him on your lap and talk . . . and neurons from his ears start hard-wiring connections to the auditory cortex.

And you thought you were just playing with your kid.

When a baby comes into the world her brain is a jumble of neurons, all waiting to be woven into the intricate tapestry of the mind. Some of the neurons have already been hard-wired, by the genes in the fertilized egg, into circuits that command breathing or control heartbeat, regulate body temperature or produce reflexes. But trillions upon trillions more are like the Pentium chips in a computer before the factory preloads the software. They are pure and of almost infinite potential, unprogrammed circuits that might one day compose rap songs and do calculus, erupt in fury and melt in ecstasy. If the neurons are used, they become integrated into the circuitry of the brain by connecting to other neurons; if they are not used, they may die. It is the experiences of childhood, determining which neurons are used, that wire the circuits of the brain as surely as a programmer at a keyboard reconfigures the circuits in a computer. Which keys are typed—which experiences a child has—determines whether the child grows up to be intelligent or dull, fearful or self-assured, articulate or tongue-tied. Early experiences are so powerful, says pediatric neurobiologist Harry Chungani of Wayne State University, that "they can completely change the way a person turns out."

By adulthood the brain is crisscrossed with more than 100 billion neurons, each reaching out to thousands of others so that, all told, the brain has more than 100 trillion connections. It is those connections—more than the number of galaxies in the known universe—that give the brain its unrivaled powers. The traditional view was that the wiring diagram is predetermined, like one for a new house, by the genes in the fertilized egg. Unfortunately, even though half the genes—50,000—are involved in the central nervous system in some way, there are not enough of them to specify the brain's incomparably complex wiring. That leaves another possibility: genes might determine only the brain's main circuits, with something else shaping the trillions of finer connections. That something else is the environment, the myriad messages that the brain receives from the outside world. According to the emerging paradigm, "there are two broad stages of brain wiring," says developmental neurobiologist Carla Shatz of the University of California, Berkeley: "an early period, when experience is not required, and a later one, when it is."

Yet, once wired, there are limits to the brain's ability to create itself. Time limits. Called "critical periods," they are windows of opportunity that nature flings open, starting before birth, and them slams shut, one by one, with every additional candle on the child's birthday cake. In the experiments that gave birth to this paradigm in the 1970s, Torsten Wiesel and David Hubel found that sewing shut one eye of a newborn kitten rewired its brain: so few neurons connected from the shut eye to the visual cortex that the animal was blind even after its eye was reopened.

The Logical Brain

SKILL: Math and logic

LEARNING WINDOW: Birth to 4 years

WHAT WE KNOW: Circuits for math reside in the brain's cortex, near those for music. Toddlers taught simple concepts, like one and many, do better in math. Music lessons may help develop spatial skills.

WHAT WE CAN DO ABOUT IT: Play counting games with a toddler. Have him set the table to learn one-to-one relationships—one plate, one fork per person. And, to hedge your bets, turn on a Mozart CD.

Such rewiring did not occur in adult cats whose eyes were shut. Conclusion: there is a short, early period when circuits connect the retina to the visual cortex. When brain regions mature dictates how long they stay malleable. Sensory areas mature in early childhood; the emotional limbic system is wired by puberty; the frontal lobes—seat of understanding—develop at least through the age of 16.

The implications of this new understanding are at once promising and disturbing. They suggest that, with the right input at the right time, almost anything is possible. But they imply, too, that if you miss the window you're playing with a handicap. They offer an explanation of why the gains a toddler makes in Head Start are so often evanescent: this intensive instruction begins too late to fundamentally rewire the brain. And they make clear the mistake of postponing instruction in a second language (see box, "Why Do Schools Flunk Biology?"). As Chugani asks, "What idiot decreed that foreign-language instruction not begin until high school?"

Neurobiologists are still at the dawn of understanding exactly which kinds of experiences, or sensory input, wire the brain in which ways. They know a great deal about the circuit for vision. It has a neuron-growth spurt at the age of 2 to 4 months, which corresponds to when babies start to really notice the world, and peaks at 8 months, when each neuron is connected to an astonishing 15,000 other neurons. A baby whose eyes are clouded by cataracts from birth will, despite cataract-removal surgery at the age of 2, be forever blind. For other systems, researchers know what happens, but not—at the level of neurons and molecules—how. They nevertheless remain confident that cognitive abilities work much like sensory ones, for the brain is parsimonious in how it conducts its affairs: a mechanism that works fine for wiring vision is not likely to be abandoned when it comes to circuits for music. "Connections are not forming willy-nilly," says Dale Purves of Duke University, "but are promoted by activity."

Language: Before there are words, in the world of a newborn, there are sounds. In English they are phonemes such as sharp ba's and da's, drawn-out ee's and ll's and sibilant sss's. In Japanese they are different—barked *hi's*, merged rr/ll's. When a child hears a phoneme over and over, neurons from his ear stimulate the formation of dedicated connections in his brain's auditory cortex. This "perceptual map," explains Patricia Kuhl of the University of Washington, reflects the apparent distance—and thus the similarity—between sounds. So in English-speakers, neurons in the auditory cortex that respond to "ra" lie far from those that respond to "la." But for Japanese, where the sounds are nearly identical, neurons that respond to "ra" are practically intertwined, like L.A. freeway spaghetti, with those for "la." As a result, a Japanese-speaker will have trouble distinguishing the two sounds.

Researchers find evidence of these tendencies across many languages. By 6 months of age, Kuhl reports, infants in English-speaking homes already have different auditory maps (as shown by electrical measurements that identify which neurons respond to different sounds) from those in Swedish-speaking homes. Children are functionally deaf to sounds absent from their native tongue. The map is completed by the first birthday. "By 12 months," says Kuhl, "infants have lost the ability to discriminate sounds that are not significant in their language. And their babbling has acquired the sound of their language."

Kuhl's findings help explain why learning a second language after, rather than with, the first is so difficult. "The perceptual map of the first language constrains the learning of a second," she says. In other words, the circuits are already wired for Spanish, and the remaining undedicated neurons have lost their ability to form basic new connections for, say, Greek. A child taught a second language after the age of 10 or so is unlikely ever to speak it like a native. Kuhl's work also suggests why related languages such as Spanish and French are easier to learn than unrelated ones: more of the existing circuits can do double duty.

With this basic circuitry established, a baby is primed to turn sounds into words. The more words a child hears, the faster she learns language, according to psychiatrist Janellen Huttenlocher of the University of Chicago. Infants whose mothers spoke to them a lot knew 131 more words at 20 months than did babies of more taciturn, or less involved, mothers; at 24 months, the gap had widened to 295 words. (Presumably the findings would also apply to a father if he were the primary caregiver.) It didn't matter which words the mother used—monosyllables seemed to work. The sound of words, it seems, builds up neural circuitry that can then absorb more words, much as creating a computer file allows the user to fill it with prose. "There is a huge vocabulary to be acquired," says Huttenlocher, "and it can only be acquired through repeated exposure to words."

Music: Last October researchers at the University of Konstanz in Germany reported that exposure to music rewires neural

The Language Brain

SKILL: Language

LEARNING WINDOW: Birth to 10 years

WHAT WE KNOW: Circuits in the auditory cortex, representing the sounds that form words, are wired by the age of 1. The more words a child hears by 2, the larger her vocabulary will grow. Hearing problems can impair the ability to match sounds to letters.

WHAT WE CAN DO ABOUT IT: Talk to your child—a lot. If you want her to master a second language, introduce it by the age of 10. Protect hearing by treating ear infections promptly.

circuits. In the brains of nine string players examined with magnetic resonance imaging, the amount of somatosensory cortex dedicated to the thumb and fifth finger of the left hand—the fingering digits—was significantly larger than in nonplayers. How long the players practiced each day did not affect the cortical map. But the age at which they had been introduced to their muse did: the younger the child when she took up an instrument, the more cortex she devoted to playing it.

Like other circuits formed early in life, the ones for music endure. Wayne State's Chugani played the guitar as a child, then gave it up. A few years ago he started taking piano lessons with his young daughter. She learned easily, but he couldn't get his fingers to follow his wishes. Yet when Chugani recently picked up a guitar, he found to his delight that "the songs are still there," much like the muscle memory for riding a bicycle.

Math and logic: At UC Irvine, Gordon Shaw suspected that all higher-order thinking is characterized by similar patterns of neuron firing. "If you're working with little kids," says Shaw, "you're not going to teach them higher mathematics or chess. But they are interested in and can process music." So Shaw and Frances Rauscher gave 19 preschoolers piano or singing lessons. After eight months, the researchers found, the children "dramatically improved in spatial reasoning," compared with children given no music lessons, as shown in their ability to work mazes, draw geometric figures and copy patterns of two-color blocks. The mechanism behind the "Mozart effect" remains murky, but Shaw suspects that when children exercise cortical neurons by listening to classical music, they are also strengthening circuits used for mathematics. Music, says the UC team, "excites the inherent brain patterns and enhances their use in complex reasoning tasks."

The Musical Brain

SKILL: Music

LEARNING WINDOW: 3 to 10 years

WHAT WE KNOW: String players have a larger area of their sensory cortex dedicated to the fingering digits on their left hand. Few concert-level performers begin playing later than the age of 10. It is much harder to learn an instrument as an adult.

WHAT WE CAN DO ABOUT IT: Sing songs with children. Play structured, melodic music. If a child shows any musical aptitude or interest, get an instrument into her hand early.

Emotions: The trunk lines for the circuits controlling emotion are laid down before birth. Then parents take over. Perhaps the strongest influence is what psychiatrist Daniel Stern calls attunement—whether caregivers "play back a child's inner feelings." If a baby's squeal of delight at a puppy is met with a smile and hug, if her excitement at seeing a plane overhead is mirrored, circuits for these emotions are reinforced. Apparently, the brain uses the same pathways to generate an emotion as to respond to one. So if an emotion is reciprocated, the electrical and chemical signals that produced it are reinforced. But if emotions are repeatedly met with indifference or a clashing response—Baby is proud of building a skyscraper out of Mom's best pots, and Mom is terminally annoyed—those circuits become confused and fail to strengthen. The key here is "repeatedly": one dismissive harrumph will not scar a child for life. It's the pattern that counts, and it can be very powerful: in one of Stern's studies, a baby whose mother never matched her level of excitement became extremely passive, unable to feel excitement or joy.

Experience can also wire the brain's "calm down" circuit, as Daniel Goleman describes in his best-selling "Emotional Intelligence." One father gently soothes his crying infant, another drops him into his crib; one mother hugs the toddler who just skinned her knee, another screams "It's your own stupid fault!" The first responses are attuned to the child's distress; the others are wildly out of emotional sync. Between 10 and 18 months, a cluster of cells in the rational prefrontal cortex is busy hooking up to the emotion regions. The circuit seems to grow into a control switch, able to calm agitation by infusing reason into emotion. Perhaps parental soothing trains this circuit, strengthening the neural connections that form it, so that the child learns how to calm herself down. This all happens so early that the effects of nurture can be misperceived as innate nature.

Stress and constant threats also rewire emotion circuits. These circuits are centered on the amygdala, a little almond-shaped structure deep in the brain whose job is to scan incoming sights and sounds for emotional content. According to a wiring diagram worked out by Joseph LeDoux of New York University, impulses from eye and ear reach the amygdala before they get to the rational, thoughtful neocortex. If a sight, sound or experience has proved painful before—Dad's drunken arrival home was followed by a beating—then the amygdala floods the circuits with neurochemicals before the higher brain knows what's happening. The more often this pathway is used, the easier it is to trigger: the mere memory of Dad may induce fear. Since the circuits can stay excited for days, the brain remains on high alert. In this state, says neuroscientist Bruce Perry of Baylor College of Medicine, more circuits attend to nonverbal cues—facial expressions, angry noises—that warn of impending danger. As a result, the cortex falls behind in development and has trouble assimilating complex information such as language.

Movement: Fetal movements begin at 7 weeks and peak between the 15th and 17th weeks. That is when regions of the brain controlling movement start to wire up. The critical period lasts a while: it takes up to two years for cells in the cerebellum, which controls posture and movement, to form functional circuits. "A lot of organization takes place using information gleaned from when the child moves about in the world," says William Greenough of the University of Illinois. "If you restrict activity you inhibit the formation of synaptic connections in the cerebellum." The child's initially spastic movements send a signal to the brain's motor cortex; the more the arm, for instance, moves, the stronger the circuit, and the better the brain will become at moving the arm intentionally and fluidly. The window lasts only a few years: a child immobilized in a body cast until the age of 4 will learn to walk eventually, but never smoothly.

THERE ARE MANY MORE CIRCUITS to discover, and many more environmental influences to pin down. Still, neuro labs are filled with an unmistakable air of optimism these days. It stems from a growing understanding of how, at the level of nerve cells and molecules, the brain's circuits form. In the beginning, the brain-to-be consists of only a few advance scouts breaking trail: within a week of conception they march out of the embryo's "neural tube," a cylinder of cells extending from head to tail. Multiplying as they go (the brain adds an astonishing 250,000 neurons per minute during gestation), the neurons clump into the brain stem which commands heartbeat and breathing, build the little cerebellum at the back of the head which controls posture and movement, and form the grooved and rumpled cortex wherein thought and perception originate. The neural cells are so small, and the distance so great, that a neuron striking out for what will be the prefrontal cortex migrates a distance equivalent to a human's walking from New York to California, says developmental neurobiologist Mary Beth Hatten of Rockefeller University.

Only when they reach their destinations do these cells become true neurons. They grow a fiber called an axon that carries electrical signals. The axon might reach only to a neuron next door, or it might wend its way clear across to the other side of the brain. It is the axonal connections that form the brain's circuits. Genes determine the main highways along which axons travel to make their connection. But to reach particular target cells, axons follow chemical cues strewn along their path. Some of these chemicals attract: this way to the motor cortex! Some repel: no, *that* way to the olfactory cortex. By the fifth month of gestation most axons have reached their general destination. But like the prettiest girl in the bar, target cells attract way more suitors—axons—than they can accommodate.

How does the wiring get sorted out? The baby neurons fire electrical pulses once a minute, in a fit of what Berkeley's Shatz calls auto-dialing. If cells fire together, the target cells "ring" together. The target cells then release a flood of chemicals, called trophic factors, that strengthen the incipient connections. Active neurons respond better to trophic factors than inactive ones, Barbara Barres of Stanford University reported in October. So neurons that are quiet when others throb lose their grip on the target cell. "Cells that fire together wire together," says Shatz.

The same basic process continues after birth. Now, it is not an auto-dialer that sends signals, but stimuli from the senses. In experiments with rats, Illinois's Greenough found that animals raised with playmates and toys and other stimuli grow 25 percent more synapses than rats deprived of such stimuli.

Rats are not children, but all evidence suggests that the same rules of brain development hold. For decades Head Start has fallen short of the high hopes invested in it: the children's IQ gains fade after about three years. Craig Ramey of the University of Alabama suspected the culprit was timing: Head Start enrolls 2-, 3- and 4- year-olds. So in 1972 he launched the Abecedarian Project. Children from 20 poor families were assigned to one of four groups: intensive early education in a day-care center from about 4 months to age 8, from 4 months to 5 years, from 5 to 8

Why Do Schools Flunk Biology?

LYNNELL HANCOCK

BIOLOGY IS A STAPLE AT MOST American high schools. Yet when it comes to the biology of the students themselves—how their brains develop and retain knowledge—school officials would rather not pay attention to the lessons. Can first graders handle French? What time should school start? Should music be cut? Biologists have some important evidence to offer. But not only are they ignored, their findings are often turned upside down.

Force of habit rules the hallways and classrooms. Neither brain science nor education research has been able to free the majority of America's schools from their 19th-century roots. If more administrators were tuned into brain research, scientists argue, not only would schedules change, but subjects such as foreign language and geometry would be offered to much younger children. Music and gym would be daily requirements. Lectures, work sheets and rote memorization would be replaced by hands-on materials, drama and project work. And teachers would pay greater attention to children's emotional connections to subjects. "We do more education research than anyone else in the world," says Frank Vellutino, a professor of educational psychology at State University of New York at Albany, "and we ignore more as well."

Plato once said that music "is a more potent instrument than any other for education." Now scientists know why. Music, they believe, trains the brain for higher forms of thinking. Researchers at the University of California, Irvine, studied the power of music by observing two groups of preschoolers. One group took piano lessons and sang daily in chorus. The other did not. After eight months the musical 3-year-olds were expert puzzlemasters, scoring 80 percent higher than their playmates did in spatial intelligence—the ability to visualize the world accurately.

This skill later translates into complex math and engineering skills. "Early music training can enhance a child's ability to reason," says Irvine physicist Gordon Shaw. Yet music education is often the first "frill" to be cut when school budgets shrink. Schools on average have only one music teacher for every 500 children, according to the National Commission on Music Education.

Then there's gym—another expendable hour by most school standards. Only 36 percent of schoolchildren today are required to partic-

The Windows of Opportunity

PRENATAL	BIRTH	1 YEAR OLD	2 YEARS	3 YEARS
Motor development				
Emotional control				
Vision				
Social attachment				
Vocabulary				
Second language				
	Math/logic			
				Music

ipate in daily physical education. Yet researchers now know that exercise is good not only for the heart. It also juices up the brain, feeding it nutrients in the form of glucose and increasing nerve connections—all of which make it easier for kids of all ages to learn. Neuroscientist William Greenough confirmed this by watching rats at his University of Illinois at Urbana-Champaign lab. One group did nothing. A second exercised on an automatic treadmill. A third was set loose in a Barnum & Bailey obstacle course requiring the rats to perform acrobatic feats. These "supersmart" rats grew "an enormous amount of gray matter" compared with their sedentary partners, says Greenough.

Of course, children don't ordinarily run such gantlets; still, Greenough believes, the results are significant. Numerous studies, he says, show that children who exercise regularly do better in school.

The implication for schools goes beyond simple exercise. Children also need to be more physically active in the classroom, not sitting quietly in their seats memorizing subtraction tables. Knowledge is retained longer if children connect not only aurally but emotionally and physically to the material, says University of Oregon education professor Robert Sylwester in "A Celebration of Neurons."

Good teachers know that lecturing on the American Revolution is far less effective than acting out a battle. Angles and dimensions are better understood if children chuck their work sheets and build a complex model to scale. The smell of the glue enters memory through one sensory system, the touch of the wood blocks another, the sight of the finished model still another. The brain then creates a multidimensional mental model of the experience—one easier to retrieve. "Explaining a smell," says Sylwester, "is not as good as actually smelling it."

Scientists argue that children are capable of far more at younger ages than schools generally realize. People obviously continue learning their whole lives, but the optimum "windows of opportunity for learning" last until about the age of 10 or 12, says Harry Chugani of Wayne State University's Children's Hospital of Michigan. Chugani determined this by measuring the brain's consumption of its chief energy source, glucose. (The more glucose it uses, the more active the brain.) Children's brains, he observes, gobble up glucose at twice the adult rate from the age of 4 to puberty. So young brains are as primed as they'll ever be to process new information. Complex subjects such as trigonometry or foreign language shouldn't wait for puberty to be introduced. In fact, Chugani says, it's far easier for an elementary-school child to hear and process a second language—and even speak it without an accent. Yet most U.S. districts wait until junior high to introduce Spanish or French— after the "windows" are closed.

Reform could begin at the beginning. Many sleep researchers now believe that most teens' biological clocks are set later than those of their fellow humans. But high school starts at 7:30 a.m., usually to accommodate bus schedules. The result can be wasted class time for whole groups of kids. Making matters worse, many kids have trouble readjusting their natural sleep rhythm. Dr. Richard Allen of Johns Hopkins University found that teens went to sleep at the same time whether they had to be at school by 7:30 a.m. or 9:30 a.m. The later-to-rise teens not only get more sleep, he says; they also get better grades. The obvious solution would be to start school later when kids hit puberty. But at school, there's what's obvious, and then there's tradition.

Why is this body of research rarely used in most American classrooms? Not many administrators or school-board members know it exists, says Linda Darling-Hammond, professor of education at Columbia University's Teachers College. In most states, neither teachers nor administrators are required to know much about how children learn in order to be certified. What's worse, she says, decisions to cut music or gym are often made by noneducators, whose concerns are more often monetary than educational. "Our school system was invented in the late 1800s, and little has changed," she says. "Can you imagine if the medical profession ran this way?"

With PAT WINGERT *and* MARY HAGER *in Washington*

Circuits in different regions of the brain mature at different times. As a result, different circuits are most sensitive to life's experiences at different ages. Give your children the stimulation they need when they need it, and anything's possible. Stumble, and all bets are off.

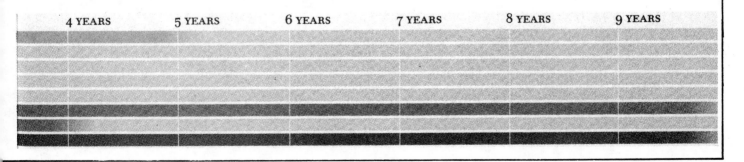

| 4 YEARS | 5 YEARS | 6 YEARS | 7 YEARS | 8 YEARS | 9 YEARS |

2. DEVELOPMENT: During Early Childhood

years, or none at all. What does it mean to "educate" a 4-month-old? Nothing fancy: blocks, beads, talking to him, playing games such as peek-a-boo. As outlined in the book "Learningames,"* each of the 200-odd activities was designed to enhance cognitive, language, social or motor development. In a recent paper, Ramey and Frances Campbell of the University of North Carolina report that children enrolled in Abecedarian as preschoolers still scored higher in math and reading at the age of 15 than untreated children. The children still retained an average IQ edge of 4.6 points. The earlier the children were enrolled, the more enduring the gain. And intervention after age 5 conferred no IQ or academic benefit.

All of which raises a troubling question. If the windows of the mind close, for the most part, before we're out of elementary school, is all hope lost for children whose parents did not have them count beads to stimulate their math circuits, or babble to them to build their language loops? At one level, no: the brain retains the ability to learn throughout life, as witness anyone who was befuddled by Greek in college only to master it during retirement. But on a deeper level the news is sobering. Chil-dren whose neural circuits are not stimulated before kindergarten are never going to be what they could have been. "You want to say that it is never too late," says Joseph Sparling, who designed the Abecedarian curriculum. "But there seems to be something very special about the early years."

And yet . . . there is new evidence that certain kinds of intervention can reach even the older brain and, like a microscopic screwdriver, rewire broken circuits. In January, scientists led by Paula Tallal of Rutgers University and Michael Merzenich of UC San Francisco described a study of children who have "language-based learning disabilities"—reading problems. LLD affects 7 million children in the United States. Tallal has long argued that LLD arises from a child's inability to distinguish short, staccato sounds—such as "d" and "b." Normally, it takes neurons in the auditory cortex something like .015 second to respond to a signal from the ear, calm down and get ready to respond to the next sound; in LLD children, it takes five to 10 times as long. (Merzenich speculates that the defect might be the result of chronic middle-ear infections in infancy: the brain never "hears" sounds clearly and so fails to draw a sharp auditory map.) Short sounds such as "b" and "d" go by too fast—.04 second—to process. Unable to associate sounds with letters, the children develop reading problems.

The scientists drilled the 5- to 10-year-olds three hours a day with computer-produced sound that draws out short consonants, like an LP played too slow. The result: LLD children who were one to three years behind in language ability improved by a full two years after only four weeks. The improvement has lasted. The training, Merzenich suspect, redrew the wiring diagram in the children's auditory cortex to process fast sounds. Their reading problems vanished like the sounds of the letters that, before, they never heard.

Such neural rehab may be the ultimate payoff of the discovery that the experiences of life are etched in the bumps and squiggles of the brain. For now, it is enough to know that we are born with a world of potential—potential that will be realized only if it is tapped. And that is challenge enough.

With MARY HAGER

Joseph Sparling and Isabelle Lewis (226 pages. Walker. $8.95).

Changing Demographics: Past and Future Demands for Early Childhood Programs

Donald J. Hernandez

Abstract

Donald J. Hernandez, Ph.D., is chief of the Marriage and Family Statistics Branch of the U.S. Bureau of the Census.

This article provides a historical analysis of how demographic changes in the organization of American family life from the mid-1800s to the present have shaped the demand for programs to complement the efforts of families to educate and care for their children. The author asserts that the United States is in the midst of a second child care revolution. The first occurred in the late 1800s, when families left farming to enable fathers to take jobs in urban areas and when compulsory free public schooling was established for children age six and above. The second has developed over the past 55 years as the proportion of children under six living in families with two wage earners or a single working parent has escalated and propelled more and more young children into the early childhood care and education programs discussed throughout this journal issue.

Looking to the future, the author sees indications that the demand for early childhood care and education programs will continue to grow while the needs of the children to be served will become increasingly diverse. To meet these dual pressures, the author argues that public funding for early childhood programs—like funding for public schools—is justified by the value such programs have for the broader society.

Today's children are the adults—the parents, workers, and citizens—of tomorrow. Yet while they learn and develop the abilities they will need later in life, children depend almost entirely upon adults to meet their needs and to make decisions on their behalf. Key among those are decisions about the roles parents and children will take on both inside and outside the home. This article takes a historical look at how changing patterns of employment among parents have been linked to changes in children's attendance at school and out-of-home child care programs like those discussed throughout this issue.

During the past 150 years, the family economy was revolutionized twice, as fathers and then mothers left the home to spend much of the day away

From *The Future of Children*, Winter 1995, pp. 145-160. © 1995 by the Center for the Future of Children of the David and Lucile Packard Foundation,, 300 Second Street, Suite 102, Los Altos, CA 94022, 415-917-7114. Reprinted by permission.

at jobs as family breadwinners. With these changes, with instability in fathers' work, and with increasing divorce and out-of-wedlock childbearing, never during the past half century were a majority of children born into "Ozzie and Harriet" families in which the father worked full time year round, the mother was a full-time homemaker, and all of the children were born after the parents' only marriage. Corresponding revolutions in child care occurred, as children age six and over, and then younger children, began to spend increasing amounts of time in school or in the care of someone other than their parents.

This article reviews each of these revolutions to clarify the factors that lie behind the growing demand for out-of-home programs to serve preschool-age children, drawing on census and survey data charting a wide array of family and economic changes from the mid-1800s to the present.[1] It addresses the following questions:

1. To what extent have young children experienced a decline in parental time potentially available for their care?

2. How have increasing employment among mothers and the rise in one-parent families contributed to the decline in parental availability to care for children at home?

3. What major demographic and family trends are responsible for increasing employment of mothers and for one-parent family living?

4. How may demographic trends influence the demand for child care during the coming decades?

5. What lessons from the first child care revolution—compulsory public schooling—can guide child care policy today?

The focus on historical changes as experienced by children provides a unique vantage point for understanding the child care revolution young children are now experiencing and for speculating about what the future may hold.

The Decline in Parental Availability for Child Care

The daily experiences young children have at home, in school, or in child care depend in important ways on the composition of their families. In the middle of the twentieth century, most children under the age of six lived in breadwinner-homemaker families, that is, in two-parent families where the father worked outside the home to support the family, and the mother could care for the children at home because she was not in the paid labor force. In 1940, 87% of young children (throughout this article, the term "young children" refers to children under the age of six) had a nonemployed parent who could provide full-time care. By 1989, however, the same could be said of only 48% of children under six.

This dramatic decline resulted from the growing prevalence of dual-earner families and one-parent families with an employed head. As Figure 1 shows, between 1940 and 1989, the percentage of young children living in dual-earner families (that is, two-parent families with both parents in the labor force) increased sevenfold, from 5% to 38%. During the same period, the proportion of children living with a lone parent who worked increased fivefold, from 2% to 13%. In about half the families, the parents worked full time; in the others, one or both parents worked part time. Together, the trends toward dual-earner households and one-parent families increased by 43 percent-

Figure 1

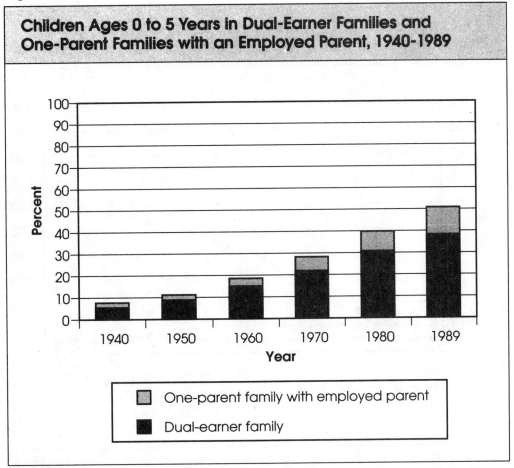

Children Ages 0 to 5 Years in Dual-Earner Families and One-Parent Families with an Employed Parent, 1940-1989

One-parent family with employed parent
Dual-earner family

Source: Hernandez, D. J. *America's Children: Resources from family, government, and the economy.* New York: Russell Sage Foundation, 1993, Table 5.2. Reprinted by permission of the Russell Sage Foundation.

age points the proportion of young children who did not have a parent at home who could provide full-time care. From 1940 to 1989, the percentage of children under six who needed alternative child care arrangements rose from 8% to 51%.

About three-fourths of the increased demand for child care was accounted for by dual-earner families, and the remaining one-fourth stemmed from one-parent families with working parents. Because the growing demand for child care for preschool-age children is rooted in the new prevalence of dual-earner families and one-parent employed families, an understanding of what the future may hold must rest upon an examination of the earlier historical changes that led to these transformations in the family lives of children.

The Revolutionary Increase in Mothers' Employment

The proportion of young children with employed mothers jumped from about 7%

in 1940 to 43% in 1980. Since then it increased again to 51% in 1990, but no further change had occurred as of 1993.[2] The explanation for much of this increase in mothers' employment after 1940 can be found in earlier historic changes that occurred in fathers' work and family residence, in family size, and in children's school attendance and educational attainment. Each of those factors paved the way for the growing participation of mothers in the paid labor force.

Fathers' Increasing Nonfarm Work

For hundreds of years, agriculture and the two-parent farm family were the primary forms of economic production and family organization in Western countries. On the family farm, economic production, parenting, and child care were combined as parents and children worked together to support themselves. This life pattern changed with the Industrial Revolution, however. Families moved to urban areas, and

Figure 2

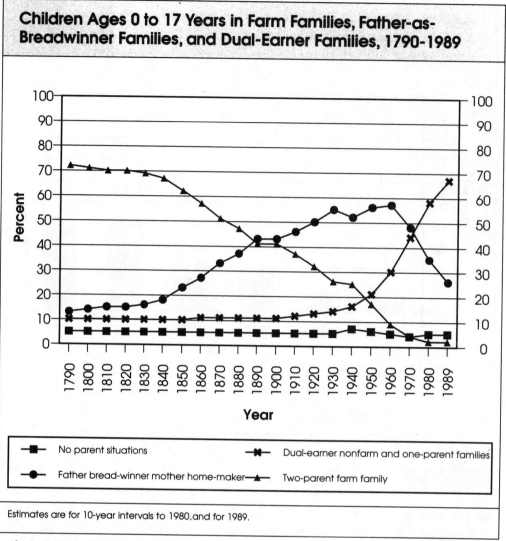

Children Ages 0 to 17 Years in Farm Families, Father-as-Breadwinner Families, and Dual-Earner Families, 1790-1989

Estimates are for 10-year intervals to 1980, and for 1989.

Source: Hernandez, D. J. *America's Children: Resources from family, government, and the economy.* New York: Russell Sage Foundation, 1993, p. 103. Reprinted by permission of the Russell Sage Foundation.

childhood was transformed in unprecedented ways. Fathers in urban families spent much of the day away from home working at jobs to earn the income required to support their families, while mothers remained at home to care for their children and to perform other household chores.

The shift away from farming, when it occurred, was very rapid. Figure 2 provides a historical view of the likelihood that children would live in each of four basic family types between 1790 and the present. Between 1830 and 1930, the proportion of children living in two-parent farm families dropped from about 70% to only 30%, while the proportion living in nonfarm families with breadwinner fathers and homemaker mothers jumped from 15% to 55%.

The shift from farming to urban occupations enabled many families to improve their relative economic status because comparatively favorable economic opportunities existed in urban areas. Urban jobs generated incomes higher than many people could earn through farming, and, given the precarious economic situations faced by many rural families, even poorly paid or dangerous jobs in urban areas were attractive.

Falling Family Size

The massive migration to urban areas was accompanied by a dramatic decline in family size. Figure 3 depicts the number of siblings in typical families from 1865 to the present. Among children born in 1865, 82% lived in families with five or more children, but only 30% of those born in 1930 had such

Figure 3

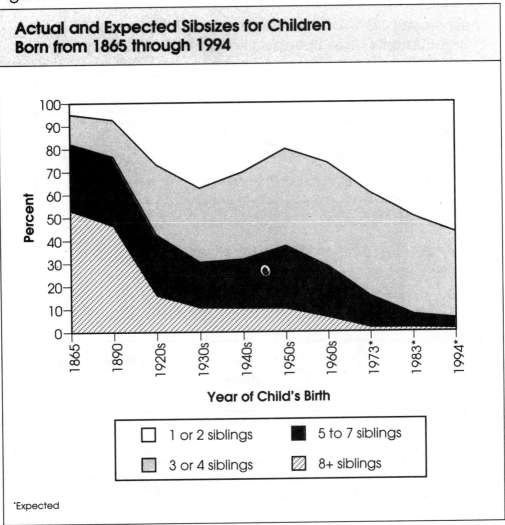

Actual and Expected Sibsizes for Children Born from 1865 through 1994

Year of Child's Birth

Legend:
- ☐ 1 or 2 siblings
- ■ 5 to 7 siblings
- ▨ 3 or 4 siblings
- ▨ 8+ siblings

*Expected

Source: Hernandez, D. J. *America's Children: Resources from family, government, and the economy.* New York: Russell Sage Foundation, 1993, p. 34. Reprinted by permission of the Russell Sage Foundation.

large families. The median number of siblings in a typical family dropped from more than seven siblings to only two or three.

Parents may have restricted themselves to a small number of children for reasons of household economics. Moving from the farm to urban areas meant that housing, food, clothing, and other necessities had to be paid for with cash, so the costs of supporting additional children became increasingly apparent. Also, as economic growth led to increases in the quality and quantity of available consumer products and services, expected consumption standards rose. Individuals had to spend more money simply to maintain the standard of living they considered normal, and their rising expectations also increased the costs of supporting each additional child at a "normal" level.

Meanwhile, the economic contribution that children could make to their parents and families was sharply reduced by the passage of laws restricting child labor. More and more parents limited their families to a comparatively small number of children, ensuring that available family income could be spread less thinly and that the family's expected standard of living could be maintained.

Increasing Schooling and Educational Attainments

A third revolutionary change in children's lives resulted from the enormous increase in school enrollment and educational attainments that took place between 1870 and 1940. As farming was overshadowed by an industrial economy in which fathers worked for pay at jobs located away from home, the

Figure 4

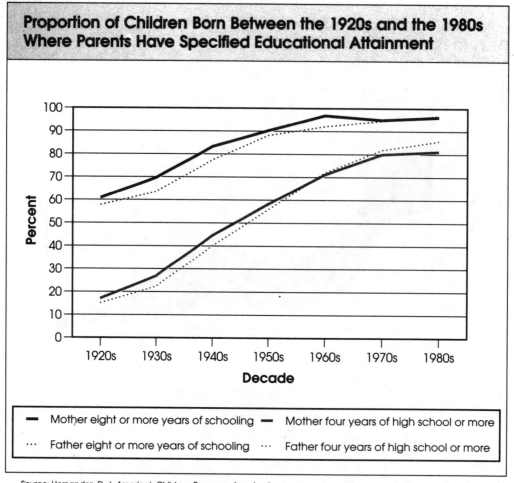

Proportion of Children Born Between the 1920s and the 1980s Where Parents Have Specified Educational Attainment

Legend:
— Mother eight or more years of schooling   ▬ Mother four years of high school or more
··· Father eight or more years of schooling   ··· Father four years of high school or more

Source: Hernandez, D. J. *America's Children: Resources from family, government, and the economy.* New York: Russell Sage Foundation, 1993, p. 197. Reprinted by permission of the Russell Sage Foundation.

economic role of children also changed with the enactment of compulsory school attendance and child labor laws. School enrollment rates jumped sharply. In 1870, about 50% of children 5 through 19 years old were enrolled in school. By 1940, 95% of children 7 through 13 years old were enrolled, as were 79% of children 14 through 17. The length of the school year also increased over that period. The number of days that enrolled students spent in school doubled from 21% to 42% of the total days in the year, or 59% of the nonweekend days. This represented a dramatic change in how children who were six or over spent much of their waking time.

Why did parents send their children to school in greater numbers and for longer periods? There are several plausible explanations. School enrollments increased during the period when laws limiting child labor were passed. Labor unions sought these laws

to ensure that jobs would be available for adults (mainly fathers), while the child welfare movement sought them to protect children from unsafe and unfair working conditions. Compulsory education laws supported by the same movements led to universal schooling that was mandated and paid for by local governments.

In addition, as time passed, higher educational attainments were needed to obtain jobs with higher incomes and greater prestige. Hence, parents encouraged their children's educational attainments as a path to achieving economic success in adulthood. Because the children of today are the parents of tomorrow, this enormous increase in schooling led to significant later increases in the education levels of parents. For example, as Figure 4 shows, only 15% of children born in 1920 had fathers who had completed four years of high school, compared with 39% of those born in 1940. Levels of education among mothers increased as well. By 1940, fully 44% of young children had mothers with four years of high school education. Today, more than 80% of adolescents have parents who completed at least four years of high school.

Explaining the Increasing Employment of Mothers

How did the historic shifts toward nonfarm work, urban residence, smaller families, and increased educational attainments that took place between the Industrial Revolution and about 1940 lead to increased employment by mothers? One explanation focuses on efforts parents made to maintain, improve, or regain their economic standing relative to other families.

Until about 1940, three major avenues were open to parents who wanted to improve their economic standing. First, they could move off the farm to allow the husband to work in a better-paid job in the growing urban-industrial economy. Second, they could limit themselves to a smaller number of children so that available family income could be spread less thinly. Third, they could increase their educational attainments so as to be qualified to enter well-paid occupations. By 1940, however, most families had already taken these steps. Only 23% of Americans still lived on farms; 70% of parents had only one or two dependent children in the home; and adults beyond age 25 often found it difficult or impractical to pursue additional schooling. Consequently, for many parents, these historical avenues for improving their economic standing had run their course.

A fourth major avenue to increasing family income emerged between 1940 and 1960, namely, paid work by wives and mothers. The traditional supply of female nonfarm labor—unmarried women—was limited, while the war effort and the economic boom created an escalating demand for additional female workers.[3] Meanwhile, mothers also were becoming more available and qualified for work outside the home. By 1940, the enrollment of children over six in school had released mothers with school-age children from child care responsibilities for about two-thirds of a full-time workday, and for about two-thirds

of a full-time work year. In addition, many women were highly educated because compulsory, free schooling applied to girls as well as boys and the educational attainments of women had increased along with those of men. By 1940, young women were more likely than young men to graduate from high school, and they were about two-thirds as likely to graduate from college.

Paid work for mothers was becoming increasingly attractive both as an economic advantage in a competitive, consumption-oriented society and as a hedge against possible economic disaster. Families with two earners could jump ahead economically of many families with only a single earner.[4] Moreover, a woman of 24 could look forward to about 40 years during which she could work for pay to help support her family. Additional motivations that drew many wives and mothers into the labor force included the personal nonfinancial rewards of working, the opportunity to be productively involved with other

---

By 1993, about 24% of young children lived in mother-child families; in about half those families, the parent worked.

---

adults, and career satisfactions for those who entered a high-prestige occupation. In addition, the historic rise in divorce (discussed below) made paid work attractive to mothers who feared they might lose most or all of their husband's income through divorce.

Economic insecurity among families in which the fathers faced low wages or joblessness made mothers' work virtually essential. Many families experienced economic insecurity and need when widespread unemployment prevailed during the Great Depression. In 1940, 40% of children lived with fathers who did not work full time year round. While this proportion declined after the Great Depression, it has continued at high levels. Throughout the past 50 years, at least one-fifth of children have lived with fathers who, during any given year, experienced part-time work or joblessness. This has been a powerful incentive for many mothers to work for pay.

Figure 5

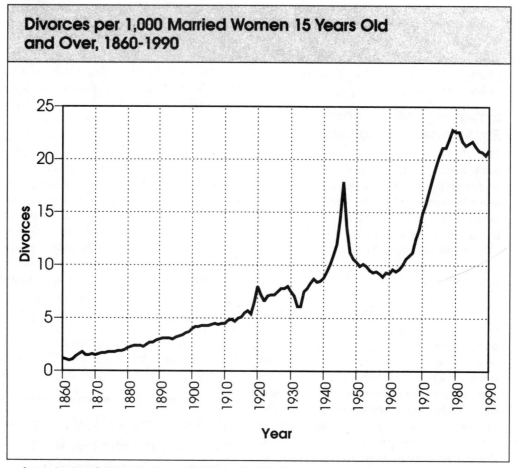

Divorces per 1,000 Married Women 15 Years Old and Over, 1860-1990

Source: Jacobson, P. H. *American Marraige and Divorce.* New York: Rinehart, 1950; U. S. National Center for Health Statistics. *Advance report of final divorce statistics, 1988.* vol. 39, no. 12, supplement 2. Washington, DC: USNCHS, 1991.

The Rising Number of Mother-Only Families

In addition to increasing employment among mothers, a second reason for the decline in parental availability to provide full-time child care lies in the new prevalence of one-parent, working-parent families that became evident after 1960, 20 years after the rise in dual-earner families began. Most one-parent families are mother-child families, created through separation, divorce, or out-of-wedlock childbearing. By 1993, about 24% of young children lived in mother-child families (another 4% lived with their fathers only). In about half those families, the parent worked: 12% of young children lived with a lone working mother, and an added 3% lived with a lone working father. A number of earlier changes in family life help explain these revolutionary changes in family structure.

High Rates of Divorce

As Figure 5 shows, a remarkably steady rise in rates of divorce is evident between the 1860s and the 1960s, resulting in an eight-fold increase during the century. (See also the Spring 1994 issue of *The Future of Children,* which focused on Children and Divorce).[5] One way of explaining this long-term increase focuses on the role the family plays as an economic unit. On preindustrial farms, fathers and mothers had to work together to sustain the family, but with a nonfarm job, the father could depend on his own work alone for his income. He could leave his family but keep his income. And, at the same time as urban employment weakened the economic interdependence of husbands and wives, by moving to urban areas families also left behind the rural small-town social controls that once censured divorce.

In addition, recent research suggests that the economic insecurity and need that result from erratic or limited employment prospects for men can also increase hostility between husbands and wives, decrease marital quality, and increase the risk of divorce.[6-8] In fact, during each of the three economic recessions that occurred between 1970 and 1982, the proportion of mother-only families increased substantially more than during the preceding nonrecessionary period. Those recessions can account for about 30% of the overall increase in mother-child families between 1968 and 1988 or for about 50% of the increase in families headed by separated or divorced mothers.[1]

Stresses on Black Families

Between 1940 and 1960, black children experienced much larger increases than white children in the proportion who lived in a mother-child family with a divorced or separated mother. The factors that led to increased separation and divorce were similar among whites and among blacks—movement off the farm and exposure to economic insecurity. Those forces affected black families with special intensity, however. The proportion of blacks living on farms dropped precipitously during the 20-year period between 1940 and 1960. In 1940, 44% of black children lived on farms, while by 1960, this figure had plummeted to only 11%. This startling drop and the extraordinary economic pressures and hardships faced by black families may account for the fact that a much higher proportion of black children than white children came to live in mother-child families.[1]

In addition, especially since 1970, black children have experienced extremely large increases in the proportion who live with a never-married mother. One explanation for this difference is offered by William Julius Wilson, who points out that unemployment among young males makes marriage less likely and so contributes to the rate of births that occur out of wedlock.[9] Calculations using survey data show that in 1955 there was little difference in rates of joblessness for young black and young white men. However, by 1976–1989, white men 16 to 24 years old were 15 to 25 percentage points more likely to be employed than were black men of the same ages.[1] The large and rapid drop in the ability of black men in the main family-building ages to secure employment and provide significant support to a family appears to have depressed marriage rates. Many young black women may be reluctant to initiate a marriage that would likely be temporary and unrewarding, instead choosing to bear children out of wedlock.

Summary

In short, the growing reliance of American families on nonparental child care is rooted in several historical changes. First was the revolutionary increase in mothers' labor force participation that occurred during the past half-century. By 1940, many mothers were potentially available for work, and mothers' work had become the only major avenue available to most couples over age 25 who sought to improve their relative social and economic status. Parents had earlier limited themselves to smaller families and moved off the farm so that fathers could work at better-paid jobs in urban areas. Increasing rates of school attendance by children six years old and over freed many mothers from the need to stay home, and, over time, public schooling increased the educational attainments of young women and made them better qualified as employees. After 1940, not only was there an increasing economic demand for married women to enter the labor force, they also faced the need to work and experienced the attractions of work.

By 1989 about 40% of preschoolers spent considerable time in the care of someone other than their parents while the parents worked.

In addition, the proportion of young children living in one-parent, working-parent families has increased substantially since 1960. Underlying this increase are sharply rising rates of divorce and out-of-wedlock childbearing. The incomes of working women helped to weaken the economic interdependence between husbands and wives, setting the stage for a historic rise in rates of separation and divorce. The experience of economic insecurity associated with fathers' part-time work, joblessness, or difficulties finding employment also made marriage less attractive and less sustainable for many families.

The consequence of all these trends is the fact that today most children live either in dual-earner families in which both parents work at jobs away from home or in one-parent families. As a result, a growing proportion of children under six need care by people other than their parents for a significant portion of the day.

Demographic Trends: Implications for Child Care

The family and economic circumstances in which children live have important implications for the development of early childhood programs. By 1989, although about 12% of children lived in dual-earner families in which the parents worked different hours or days and could personally care for their children, about 40% of preschoolers spent considerable time in the care of someone other than their parents while the parents worked. If mothers' labor force participation continues to rise, the demand for nonparental child care will rise with it.

Continued Growth in the Demand for Child Care

The revolutionary increase in mothers' labor force participation during the past half-century led to enormous increases in nonparental care of young children. Looking to the future, between 1992 and 2005, the labor force participation rate for women between the ages of 25 and 54 is projected to increase from 75% to 83%.[10] Continued increases in rates of employment among women are likely to lead to a further decline in the availability of mothers who can be home to provide full-time care for their children.

The rising prevalence of one-parent families also is likely to continue. The divorce rate reached a peak in 1979 and declined slightly thereafter, but the graph in Figure 5 shows that the divorce rate remains extremely high by historical standards. Meanwhile, the proportion of births occurring out of wedlock continues to increase at a steady pace. If this trend persists, the proportion of children in one-parent families with working parents will rise even further.

Some families headed by single mothers with limited labor force participation have been able to rely financially on public assistance through the Aid to Families with Dependent Children (AFDC) program.

Most current welfare reform proposals, however, aim to increase labor force participation among AFDC recipients. If such reforms are enacted and if they successfully increase employment rates, there will be a corresponding increase in the need for nonparental child care for children of these mothers.[11]

As a result of all these demographic and policy changes, the need for nonparental child care for children in one-parent, working-parent families is likely to continue to rise.

Characteristics of the Children Who Will Need Child Care

This article has focused thus far on how family and economic change is increasing the demand for nonparental child care. But the changing family life of children can also influence the nature and content of the care that children will need. Ongoing demographic trends suggest that, in the coming decades, early childhood programs will be serving a population of children which is increasingly diverse in economic resources, racial and ethnic background, and family structure.

Increasing Economic Inequality

Economic well-being can be viewed in terms of absolute levels of family income or in terms of relative economic standing compared with other families. Economists from Adam Smith to John Kenneth Galbraith have argued that poverty must be defined in

---

The proportion of children under age 18 who are white is projected to decline steadily and rapidly, from 69% in 1990 to only 50% in 2030.

---

terms of contemporary standards of living.[12] In Galbraith's words, ". . . people are poverty-stricken when their income, even if adequate for survival, falls markedly behind that of the community."

In an absolute sense, real income levels and living standards rose dramatically between 1940 and 1973, as median family income more than doubled, although it has changed comparatively little since then. Since 1959, however, economic expansion

Figure 6

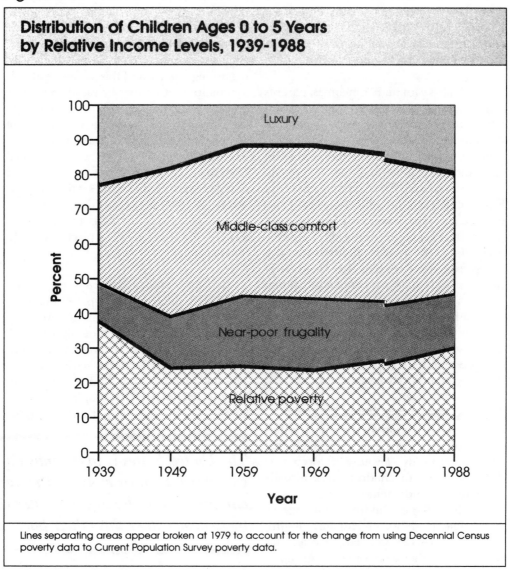

Distribution of Children Ages 0 to 5 Years by Relative Income Levels, 1939-1988

Lines separating areas appear broken at 1979 to account for the change from using Decennial Census poverty data to Current Population Survey poverty data.

Source: Hernandez, D. J. *America's Children: Resources from family, government, and the economy.* New York: Russell Sage Foundation, 1993, p. 260. Reprinted by permission of the Russell Sage Foundation.

has done little to reduce the uneven distribution of income across families, and since 1969, economic inequality has increased. To examine the income distribution, families can be classified as living in relative poverty, near-poor frugality, middle-class comfort, or luxury, based on income thresholds set at 50%, 75%, and 150% of median family income in specific years and adjusted for family size.[1]

Figure 6 is a graph showing the distribution of children into these income categories from 1939 to 1988. This measure shows that the proportion of young children from birth to five years living in relative poverty dropped from a high of 38% after the Great Depression to remain at less than 25% from 1949 through 1979, before it jumped to 30% in 1988 and 33% in 1993. Another 15% of children in 1988 and 1993 lived in near-poor frugality. At the opposite extreme, the proportion of young children in families with luxury level incomes declined from 23% in 1939 to about 12% in the 1950s, before increasing to 20% in 1988 and to 23% in 1993. The years from 1969 to 1993 saw a significant decline in middle-class comfort, as more and more children lived at the extremes of luxury and poverty.

In other words, the past 25 years—when the demand for nonparental child care was growing fastest—also brought a substantial expansion in economic inequality among families. As a result, the quantitative increases in the total need for nonparental care during the past quarter-century have been accompanied by increased qualitative differences in the educational needs of the children who enter child care.

In families with higher incomes, parents can usually afford to provide resources and educational experiences that foster the development of their children, while children from poor homes rely more on child care and preschool programs to provide those experiences.[13] As a result, children from families at different income levels may enter child care situations with different needs. In recognition of the unmet developmental needs of many children who live in poverty, for example, the Head Start program adds to its preschool educational activities a comprehensive set of nutritional, health, and social services that are not typically offered to children from more advantaged families.[14] Research, policies, and programs that explicitly address these differences are sorely needed.

Growing Racial and Ethnic Diversity

Race and ethnic origin define another dimension along which it seems likely that educational needs of young children may differ.[15] American children were already quite racially and ethnically diverse as of 1990, when 69% of children under age 18 were white (and not of Hispanic origin), 15% were black, 12% were Hispanic, and 4% were from another racial or ethnic group.

Immigration and differential birthrates across ethnic groups will likely increase that diversity in the coming years. Looking to the future, Figure 7 shows that the proportion of children under age 18 who are white is projected to decline steadily and rapidly, from 69% in 1990 to only 50% in 2030. Conversely, the proportion of all children who are Hispanic or who are black or of another nonwhite race is expected to climb from 31% to 50%.

Poverty, language barriers, and cultural isolation are important factors that influence many nonwhite or Hispanic children, who may have educational needs (and related social needs) that differ from those of white children. As a result, these projections highlight an increasing need to understand these differences through research and to plan new child care policies and programs appropriate to a diverse population of children.[16]

Diverse Family Living Arrangements

Children also vary greatly in their family living arrangements, and this is true separately for children within specific racial and ethnic groups. Even among children under age one, historical data show that, in 1940, 7% of white infants and 25% of black infants lived in a one-parent family or were separated from their parents. By 1980, these rates had doubled to 13% for whites and 54% for blacks. In 1993, the proportion of children under age six with one parent in the home was 21% for whites, 66% for blacks, and 34% for Hispanics.

Recent evidence indicates that, compared with children in two-parent families, children in one-parent families have higher risks of dropping out of high school, bearing children as teenagers, and not being employed by their early twenties. The low incomes and sudden declines in income experienced by children in these families are the most important reason for

The United States is in the midst of a child care revolution, as more and more young children under the age of six are cared for by someone other than their parents.

their disadvantaged outcomes, although research suggests that other differences in family life also play a significant role.[17] Children in one-parent families are therefore likely to have educational needs that differ from children in two-parent families and that should be understood and addressed.

Summary

In short, the United States is in the midst of a child care revolution, as more and more young children under the age of six are cared for by someone other than their parents. Broad demographic trends as well as efforts to reform the welfare system are likely to increase rates of labor force participation by mothers with young children, further expanding the demand for nonparental child care. At the same time, the diversity in the characteristics and needs of the nation's

Figure 7

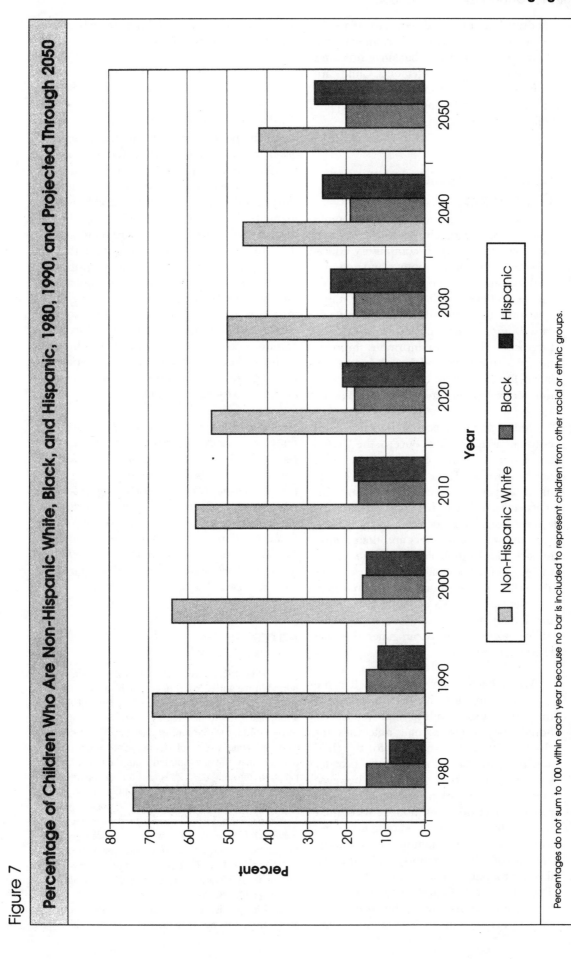

Percentage of Children Who Are Non-Hispanic White, Black, and Hispanic, 1980, 1990, and Projected Through 2050

Percentages do not sum to 100 within each year because no bar is included to represent children from other racial or ethnic groups.

Source: U.S. Bureau of the Census. *U.S. Population Estimates by Age, Sex, and Hispanic Origin: 1980-1991*. Current Population Reports, Series P-25, No. 1095. Washington, DC: U.S. Government Printing Office, 1993; U.S. Bureau of the Census. *Population Projections of the United States, by Age, Sex, Race, and Hispanic Origin: 1993-2050*. Current Population Reports, Series P-25, No. 1104. Washington, DC: U.S. Government Printing Office, 1993.

children has also increased, particularly in terms of their economic circumstances, their racial and ethnic backgrounds, and their family living arrangements. Child care policies and programs must be designed to respond to the differing needs of the many children who use them.

Lessons to Guide Child Care Policy

The first child care revolution began more than 100 years ago, and it affected children over age five. Through compulsory education laws, government both mandated and paid for universal schooling for all children age six and over. As time passed, the upper age limit for compulsory schooling was raised, and public funding for schooling increased. This led to enormous improvements in the skills and knowledge of the labor force, thereby contributing to economic development and rising real incomes.

Today, as global economic competition becomes an increasing concern, the United States is in the midst of a second child care revolution, one affecting children under age six whose parent or parents work. From this perspective, one can see child care as valuable or essential to society at large. It facilitates the work of mothers and their contribution both to their family income and to the economy. The quality of child care may also influence the future international competitiveness of the U.S. economy by fostering the development of productive workers who will support the baby boom generation as it reaches retirement.

When high-quality child care, like the preschool programs that are the subject of this journal issue, leads to improved educational and developmental outcomes for children, it has value not only for the child and the parents, but also for the broader society. Child care is expensive, however. Overall, families with a preschool child who pay for child care devote about 10% of their incomes to child care, but this figure ranges from only 6% for families with annual incomes of $50,000 or more to 23% for families with annual incomes under $15,000.[18] The relative cost of child care as an expense associated with having a job is quite high for low-income families. The question then arises: Should the cost of that care be borne mainly or solely by parents?

The first child care revolution was mandated and paid for by government as a social good in the public interest. Today, evolving economic conditions effectively require that an increasing proportion of mothers work, and proposed welfare reforms will mandate that other mothers of young children find employment to support their families. In this context, it is important that new research inform the public policy debate about the kinds, the costs, and the quality of child care available to the youngest members of American society. Research about the value of child care to children, parents, and society at large may also help inform policy debate about the appropriate role of government in fostering and funding quality care for American children.

The author is indebted to Arthur J. Norton for institutional leadership, scholarly counsel, and personal enthusiasm and encouragement which created an indispensable and nurturing home in the U. S. Bureau of the Census for writing the book which provides the foundation for this article. Thanks are due also to Edith Reeves and Catherine O'Brien for statistical support, and to Stephanie Kennedy for secretarial support. The author bears sole responsibility for the results and opinions presented here.

NOTES

1. This article draws especially on research reported in the author's recent book which used census and survey data for 1940, 1950, 1960, 1970, 1980, and 1989 to develop the first-ever statistics using children as the unit of analysis. These data chart a wide array of family and economic changes that affected children from the Great Depression through the 1980s. Additional analyses of previously published data extend the investigation back an additional 150 years. Hernandez, D. J. *America's children: Resources from government, family, and the economy.* New York: Russell Sage Foundation, 1993. This research was also reported in Hernandez, D. J. Children's changing access to resources: A historical perspective. *Social Policy Report* (1993) 8,1:1–23.

2. The precise estimate of 6% to 8% is obtained from note no. 1, Hernandez, *America's chil-*

dren, Table 5.2. The estimates for 1980, 1990, and 1993 were provided by the U.S. Bureau of Labor Statistics, Howard Hayghe.

3. Oppenheimer, V. K. *The female labor force in the United States.* Population Monograph Series, No. 5. Berkeley, CA: Institute of International Studies, University of California Press, 1970.

4. Oppenheimer, V. K. *Work and family.* New York: Academic Press, 1982.

5. *The Future of Children* (Spring 1994) 5,1.

6. Conger, R. D., Elder, G. H., Jr., Lorenz, F. O., et al. Linking economic hardship to marital quality and instability. *Journal of Marriage and the Family* (1990) 52:643–56.

7. Conger, R. D., Elder, G. H., Jr., with Lorenz, F. O., Simons, R. L., and Whitbeck, L. B. *Families in troubled times: Adapting to change in rural America.* New York: Aldine de Gruyter, 1994.

8. Liker, J. K., and Elder, G. H., Jr. Economic hardship and marital relations in the 1930s. *American Sociological Review* (1983)48:343–59.

9. Wilson, W. J. *The truly disadvantaged: The inner city, the underclass, and public policy.* Chicago: University of Chicago Press, 1987.

10. U.S. Department of Labor, Bureau of Labor Statistics. Bulletin 2452. Washington, DC: U.S. Government Printing Office, April 1994, Table A-1.

11. Another important goal of many welfare reform proposals is to reduce out-of-wedlock childbearing, but available evidence suggests that the effect of welfare on out-of-wedlock childbearing is small. For a discussion of the extent to which welfare programs have contributed to the increase in mother-only families, see note no. 1, Hernandez, *America's children* pp. 291–300.

12. Adam Smith was cited in U.S. Congress. *Alternative measures of poverty.* Staff study prepared for the Joint Economic Committee. Washington, DC, October 18, 1994, p. 10. The quote from Galbraith can be found in Galbraith, J. K. *The affluent society.* Boston: Houghton, Mifflin, 1958, pp. 323–24.

13. For recent studies on the effects for children of poverty and economic inequality, see papers from the Consequences of Growing Up Poor conference, held February 2–3, 1995, at the National Academy of Sciences, organized by the National Institute of Child Health and Development (NICHD) Family and Child Well-Being Network, the Russell Sage Foundation, and the National Academy of Sciences Board on Children and Families.

14. U.S. General Accounting Office. *Early childhood centers: services to prepare children for school often limited.* GAO/HEHS-95–21. Washington, DC: U.S. GAO, March 1995.

15. For additional discussions of child indicators pertaining to race, ethnicity, and educational needs, see Lewit, E. M. and Baker, L. G. Race and ethnicity—changes for children. *The Future of Children* (Winter 1994) 4,3:134–44.

16. Phillips, D., and Crowell, N. A., eds. *Cultural diversity and early education.* Washington, DC: National Academy Press, 1994.

17. McLanahan, S., and Sandefur, G. *Growing up with a single parent: What hurts, what helps.* Cambridge, MA: Harvard University Press, 1994.

18. Hofferth, S. L., Brayfield, A., Deich, S., and Holcomb, P. *National Child Care Survey,* 1990. Washington, DC: Urban Institute Press, 1991.

Assertiveness vs. Aggressiveness

What's the Difference?

Robert H. Deluty

Robert H. Deluty is the Director of the Clinical Psychology Doctoral Program at UMBC. He and his wife of 12 years, Barbara, live in Ellicott City with their children, Laura (7) and David (3).

"Why is my son so aggressive?" "Why won't my daughter stand up for herself?" "Why do my children punch, kick, and scream whenever they are frustrated or angered?" Mental health professionals are routinely asked such questions by concerned parents. Although the questions are simple and straightforward, often the answers are not. Children act aggressively, assertively, or submissively for a wide variety of reasons; generally, a combination of factors underlies how a particular child will behave in any given situation. These factors include how the child sizes up the situation, what response alternatives she can think of, and what she expects will be the consequences of each response alternative.

The assertive child expresses herself openly and directly while respecting the rights and feelings of others. For example, in response to being teased about her new haircut, Sally says calmly, assertively, "Please top teasing me. You wouldn't like it if I made fun of you. I really like the way my hair looks." If assertiveness entails both self-expression and the non-violation of others' rights, then unassertiveness can take one of two forms: aggressiveness or submissiveness. Aggressive children express their thoughts and feelings openly, but they do so coercively and at other people's expense. Submissive children take into account the feelings, power, and authority of others, but deny (or do not stand up for) their own rights and feelings.

For some aggressive children and for some submissive children, the thought of acting assertively simply never occurs to them. These children see their options as limited to "fight" or "flight"; for example, Tommy may think that when he is ridiculed, his only options are to punch, pinch, bite, scream, or spit ("fight" responses), or to run away, cry, hide, or sulk ("flight" responses). In Tommy's world of black and white options, shades of gray (i.e., assertive solutions) are nowhere to be found.

Other aggressive and submissive children, however, can conceive of assertive alternatives, but choose not to exhibit such behavior because they believe that aggressive or submissive acts will yield greater benefits and/or fewer costs than assertive behaviors. For example, James may physically threaten or verbally abuse his classmates because it results in their giving him their lunch money and doing his homework; as far as James is concerned, aggression "pays." In contrast, Patty may exhibit much submissive behavior because she believes submissive acts are kinder and more "ladylike" than aggressive or assertive responses; she may fear that assertive expression will result in unpleasant confrontation and diminished popularity (e.g., "If I let them know how I feel, they may get mad at me and no longer want to play with me"). Clearly, the consequences (real or imagined) that a child associates with particular behaviors have a powerful influence on the actions he/she chooses.

Parents play a critical role in shaping aggressive and prosocial behavior in their children. Boys (who consistently manifest more physical and verbal aggression than girls) tend to be given more freedom that girls to express aggression toward their parents and their peers; in contrast, girls receive relatively more praise for being "good" and are more often threatened with withdrawal of parental love for "bad" behavior. Non-aggressive boys have been shown by psychology researchers to be far more likely than aggressive males to have had parents who placed high demands on them to be "polite" and "responsible."

Although much behavior is shaped into new patterns by direct rewards (e.g., parental compliments) or punishments (e.g., withdrawal of privileges), social behaviors like aggressiveness or assertiveness are acquired largely through the process of imitation or modeling. A crucial determinant of a child's aggressiveness, assertiveness, and submissiveness is the interpersonal behavior exhibited by the parents, teachers, and peers who serve as models in the child's environment. Parents who rant, scream, and slam doors when things don't go their way typically do not have far to look when searching for the principal causes of their children's aggressiveness.

When teaching children how to be assertive, parents must pay careful attention to both the verbal and nonverbal components of assertiveness. Parents need to attend to not only what the child is saying, but how he/she is saying it. An assertive verbalization (e.g., "Please turn down the stereo. It's hurting my ears.") may be undone by a whiny, unsteady voice and poor eye contact. Furthermore, children need to be taught how to be assertive not only in the face of conflict (e.g., in response to frustration, aggression, or ridicule), but also under pleasurable circumstances. Learning how to give or to accept a compliment, or how to express agreement with others' opinions is at least as important as learning how to stand up for oneself in conflictual situations.

It is also important for children to understand that assertive behavior is not always the most adaptive means of handling conflict. Indeed, under certain circumstances, assertiveness would be counter-indicated. If a child is in the process of being physically attacked by a group of older, stronger kids, assertive expression ("Guys, it makes me angry when I'm punched and kicked") would likely be quite unproductive. In some situations, submissively complying with an unreasonable request could strengthen a friendship or advance an important long-range goal. Thus, children need to be advised not only how to express themselves assertively, but also when (and when not) to do so.

Approximately 2000 years ago, the great sage, Hillel, posed the following questions: "If I am not for myself, who will be for me? And if I am only for myself, what am I? And if not now—when?" Some of the most important lessons we can teach our children involve how to balance self-expression and self-interest with concern for others and appreciation of others' rights and feelings. And when should parents teach these lessons? As Hillel asked, "If not now—when?"

Development during Childhood: Cognition and Schooling

- Cognition (Articles 14–17)
- Schooling (Articles 18–21)

Cognition is the mental process of knowing. It includes aspects such as awareness, perception, reasoning, and judgment. Intelligence is the capacity to acquire and apply knowledge. It is usually assumed that intelligence can be measured. The ratio of tested mental age to chronological age is expressed as an intelligence quotient (IQ). For years, school children have been classified and tracked educationally by IQ scores. This practice has been both obsequiously praised and venomously opposed. The links between IQ scores and school achievement are positive, but no significant correlations exist between IQ scores and life success. Many kinds of achievement which require superb cognitive processes (awareness, perception, reasoning, judgment) cannot be measured with intelligence tests, or with achievement tests. Consider, for example, the motor coordination and kinesthetic abilities of a baseball player such as Cal Ripken, Jr. A Harvard psychologist, Howard Gardner, has suggested that there are at least seven different kinds of intelligences. These include the body movement skills of athletes and dancers, a musical type, and linguistic, logical-mathematical, spatial, self-understanding, and social understanding types. The 1990s have been host to a spate of research about the last two types of intelligences: self-understanding and social understanding. Some psychologists have suggested that measuring one's emotional quotient (EQ) might make more sense than measuring one's intelligence quotient (IQ). The typical tests of intelligence only measure achievement and abilities in the logical-mathematical, and to some extent spatial, and linguistic areas of intelligence.

Jean Piaget, the Swiss founder of cognitive psychology, was involved in the creation of the world's first intelligence test, the Simon-Binet Test. He became disillusioned with trying to quantify how much children knew at chronological ages. He was much more intrigued with what they did not know, what they knew incorrectly, and how they came to know the world in the ways in which they knew it. He started a Centre for Genetic Epistemology in Geneva, Switzerland, and began to study the nature, extent, and validity of children's knowledge. He discovered qualitative, rather than quantitative, differences in cognitive processes over the life span. Infants know the world through their senses and their motor responses. After language develops, toddlers and preschoolers know the world through their language/symbolic perspectives. Piaget likened early childhood cognitive processes to bad thought, or thought akin to daydreams. By school age, children know things in concrete terms which allow them to number, seriate, classify, conserve, think backwards and forwards, and think about themselves thinking (metacognition). They are able to use reason. However, Piaget believed that children do not acquire the cognitive processes necessary to think abstractly and use clear, consistent, logical patterns of thought until early adolescence.

Contemporary cognitive researchers are refining Piaget's theories. They are discovering that children acquire many abilities earlier than Piaget postulated. In the first article in this unit, Jill Neimark discusses the extraordinary intricacy of a child's cognitive processes. An event may be processed at several levels and in several areas of the brain. For example, a part of an event may be stored unconsciously, a part of it may be stored in a content area, and another part of it may be stored in an emotional area. Piaget's belief that early childhood cognitive processes are akin to daydreams may be due to a young child's inability to consolidate memory traces from multiple areas. However, new research on cognition suggests that older children and adults may consolidate false memory traces along with those which are true. Jill Neimark's exposition on memory attempts to explain malleable, lost, and recovered memories as well as the physiology known about information coding, storage, and retrieval.

The second article in this unit questions the idea that the capacity to acquire and apply knowledge is predominantly genetically predetermined. Most cognitive research indicates that genes do provide a potential for cognitive abilities. However, the environment in which a person grows and develops can inhibit learning, or, more positively, be able to bring the genetic potential to its maximum fruition. The third article deals with some aspects of the environment which may inhibit cognitive potential. Mentation is influenced by nutrition in more ways and in different ways than previously assumed. The authors dis-

on by frontal lobe differences may inhibit some reasoning and judgment. If children with ADHD are labeled less intelligent, they may have little incentive to learn and perform to their maximum genetic potentialities.

The first two articles in the schooling subsection of this unit address the issues of defining and testing intelligence for purposes of school placement and educational programming. How important is self-understanding and social understanding? Should schools teach empathy? Is emotional control the true yardstick of human intellectual potential? Politicians play with the rhetoric about what our children should and should not learn in school. "Bell, Book and Scandal" gives an historic overview of IQ testing and the use of IQ tests to differentiate children by achievement in the logical-mathematical type of intelligence. To what extent is this placement practice discriminating against other children with high motivation and potential to achieve but different types of intelligences? The last two articles in the schooling section deal with very real problems of educating children in our schools. How do we help children with fearful behaviors?

Can we foster the courage to achieve? How do we sustain the benefits of early childhood education programs in public primary schools? Can it be done?

Looking Ahead: Challenge Questions

How are memories encoded, stored, and retrieved?

How can parents and teachers help children maximize their genetic learning potential?

What are the links between nutrition and mental performance?

Is attention deficit a different cognitive style rather than a "disorder"? Explain.

In whay ways are emotions another measure of human intelligence?

Why is *The Bell Curve* so controversial? Is it a scandalous idea?

How does fear interfere with school mastery and success?

How can public schools sustain the benefits which children receive in early childhood education programs?

cuss new research on the links between undernutrition and brain functioning. They also consider ways in which poverty may exacerbate the effects of poor diet. The fourth article presents some aspects of a genetic/biological predetermined brain functioning which may influence the capacity to acquire and apply knowledge. Children (and adults) with attention deficit hyperactive disorder (ADHD) may have frontal lobes circuitry different from non-ADHD affected persons. This may give them certain advantages: creativity, spontaneity, effervescence. However, their short attention spans and impulsivity brought

It's Magical! It's Malleable! It's . . . Memory

So complex and evanescent is memory, our best metaphors fall short, bogged down in materialism. Yet through the creative blending and reblending of experience and emotion, memory builds that about us which often seems most solid—our sense of self. We remember, therefore we are.

Jill Neimark

We never know exactly why certain subjects—like certain people—claim us, and do not let us go. Elizabeth Loftus is a research psychologist who has devoted her life to the study of memory, its mystery and malleability. Of late, she has gained ingenious experiments, which have shown repeatedly that about 25 percent of individuals can be easily induced to remember events that never happened to them—false memories that feel absolutely real.

So it was something of a shock when, at a family gathering, an uncle informed the then 44-year-old Loftus that 30 years earlier, when her mother had drowned, she had been the one to discover the body in the pool. Loftus believed she had never seen her mother's dead body; in fact, she remembered little about the death itself.

Almost immediately after her uncle's revelation, "the memories began to drift back," she recalls in her recent book, *The Myth of Repressed Memory* (St. Martin), "like the crisp, piney smoke from evening camp fires. My mother, dressed in her nightgown, was floating face down. . . . I started screaming. I remembered the police cars, their lights flashing. For three days my memory expanded and swelled.

"Then, early one morning, my brother called to tell me that my uncle had made a mistake. Now he remembered (and other relatives confirmed) that Aunt Pearl found my mother's body." Suddenly Loftus understood firsthand what she had been studying for decades. "My own experiment had inadvertently been performed on me! I was left with a sense of wonder at the inherent credulity of even my skeptical mind."

Memory has become a lightning rod of late. This has been a time of fascinating, grisly stories—of recovered memories of satanic cults, butchered babies, and incest that have spawned church scandals, lawsuits, suicides, splintered families, murders, and endless fodder for talk shows. Three major books on the fallibility of memory were reviewed on the front page of the *New York Times Book Review* last spring, and three more were published this fall. The essential nature of memory, which ought by rights to be a scientific debate, has so galvanized the culture that laws have actually been revoked and repealed over it; in Illinois, for example, a law that bars people over 30 from filing lawsuits based on remembered abuse was repealed in 1992, and is now being reinstated.

Memory's ambiguities and paradoxes seem to have suddenly claimed us as they have claimed researchers for decades. This fascination cannot be explained away by the human need to memorialize the past—a need that expresses itself beautifully and indelibly in monuments like the Vietnam memorial or the AIDS quilt, and in projects like Steven Spielberg's ongoing documentary of holocaust survivors.

Memory is the likelihood that, among a vast tangle of neurons, the pathway of connections an experience forges in the brain can be reactivated again. It is the ability to repeat a performance—albeit with mistakes.

It's as if we've awakened, at the turn of the millennium, and realized that memory is the bedrock of the self—and that it may be perpetually shifting and terrifically malleable. That image of memory, whose river runs into tabloids and traumas, seems both terrifying and baptismal. If we can repress life-shaping events (such as sexual or physical abuse), or actually invent memories of events that never happened (from UFO abductions to rapes and murders), memory carries a power that promises to utterly reshape the self.

And so it's exciting news that in the past few years, scientists have begun to piece together a picture of memory that is stunning in its specifics:

• Sophisticated PET (positron emission tomography) scans can record the actual firing of the neurons that hold the pictures of our lives, and observe memory move like a current across the brain while it sleeps or wakes.

• How and where the brain lays down and consolidates memory—that is, makes it permanent—is yielding to understanding. As one researcher states, we are seeing "an explosion of knowledge about what parts of the brain are doing what."

• Hormones that help engrave the narrative of our lives into our cells have now been identified.

• Certain drugs block or enhance memory, and they may hold the key to preventing disorders as wide-ranging as Alzheimer's disease and posttraumatic stress disorder (PTSD).

• The well-known "fight-or-flight" response to stress can sear "indelible" memories into the brain.

• Memory is not a single entity residing in a single place. It is the likelihood that the pathway of neurons and connections an experience forges in the brain can be reactivated again. It involves multiple systems in the brain. The emotion associated with a memory, for example, is stored in a different place than the content of the memory itself.

• Some memories occur in a primitive part of the brain, unknown to conscious perception. That part functions "below" the senses, as it were. That is why individuals with brain damage can sometimes learn and remember—without knowing they do so.

• There is a growing understanding that an infant's early experience of emotional attachment can direct the nature and durability of childhood memories and the way they are stored in the brain.

Memory, it turns out, is both far more complex and more primitive than we knew. Ancient parts of the brain can record memory before it even reaches our senses—our sight and hearing, for instance. At the same time, "there are between 200 and 400 billion neurons in the brain and each neuron has about 10,000 connections," notes psychiatrist Daniel Siegel, M.D. "The parallel processing involved in memory is so complex we can't even begin to think how it works."

The one thing that we can say for certain is this: If memory is the bedrock of the self, then even though that self may seem coherent and unchanging, it is built on shifting sands.

13 WAYS OF LOOKING AT THE BRAIN

Moments after being removed from the skull, the brain begins to collapse into a jellylike mass. And yet this wet aspic of tissue contains a fantastic archeology of glands, organs, and lobes, all of which have their own specialized jobs. Much of this archeology is devoted to the complex tasks of memory.

But just what is memory? According to Nobel Prize-winning neuroscientist Gerald Edelman, Ph.D., author of *Bright Air, Brilliant Fire* (Basic Books), memory is the ability to repeat a performance—with mistakes. Without memory, life itself would never have evolved. The genetic code must be able to repeat itself in DNA and RNA; an immune cell must be able to remember an antigen and repeat a highly specific defense next time they meet; a neuron in the brain must be able to send the same signal each time you encounter (for example) a lion escaped from the local zoo. Every living system must be able to remember; but what is most dangerous and wonderful about memory is that it must occasionally make errors. It must be wrong. Mere repetition might explain the way a crystal grows but not the way a brain works. Memory classifies and adapts to our environment. That adaptation requires flexibility. The very ability to make mistakes is precious.

Now you can bravely step into the hall of mirrors that is memory. And though our words to describe this evanescent process are still crude and oversimplistic, here are a few tools to travel with:

Memory can be implicit or explicit. Implicit memory is involved in learning habits—such as riding a bicycle or driving a car. It does not require "conscious" awareness, which is why you can sometimes be lost in thought as you drive and find you've driven home without realizing it. Explicit memory is conscious, and is sometimes called declarative. One form of declarative memory is autobiographical memory—our ability to tell the story of our life in the context of time.

We often talk of memory storage and retrieval, as if memory were filed in a honeycomb of compartments, but these words are really only metaphors. If memory is the reactivation of a weblike network of neurons that were first activated when an event occurred, each time that network is stimulated the memory is strengthened, or consolidated. Storage, retrieval, consolidation—how comforting and solid they sound; but in fact they consist of electrical charges leaping among a vast tangle of neurons.

In truth, even the simplest memory stimulates complex neural networks at several different sites in the brain. The content (what happened) and meaning (how it felt) of an event are laid down in separate parts of the brain. In fact, research at Yale University by Patricia Goldman-Rakic, Ph.D., has shown that neurons themselves are specialized for different types of memories—features, patterns, location, direction. "The coding is so specific that it can be mapped to different areas . . . in the prefrontal region."

What is activating these myriad connections? We still don't know. Gerald Edelman calls this mystery "the homunculus crisis." Who is thinking? Is memory remembering us? "The intricacy and numerosity of brain connections are extraordinary," writes Edelman. "The layers and loops between them are dynamic, they continually change."

Yet the center holds. The master regulator of memory, the hub at the center of the wheel, is a little seahorse-shaped organ called the hippocampus. Like the rest of the brain, it is lateralized; it exists in both the right and left hemispheres. Without it, we learn and remember nothing—in fact, we are lost to ourselves.

THE SEAHORSE AND THE SELF

"He's 33 years old, and he never remembers that his father is dead. Every time he rediscovers this fact he goes through the whole grieving process again," Mark Gluck, Ph.D., a professor at the Center for Molecular and Behavioral Neuroscience at Rutgers University, says of M.P., a young man who lost his memory after a stroke six years ago. Gluck has been studying M.P. for several years. After his stroke, M.P. forgot that on that very morning he had proposed marriage to his girlfriend. "He can store no new information in his long-term memory. If you tell him a phone number and ask him to repeat it, he will; but if you change the subject and then ask him the number, he can't remember. M.P. is going to be living in the present for the rest of his life. He has lost the essential ability of the self to evolve."

M.P. is uncannily similar to one of the most remarkable and intensively studied patients of all time, a man called H.M., who lost his memory after undergoing brain surgery to treat epilepsy. This type of memory loss, called anterograde amnesia, stops time. It usually results from damage to the hippocampus, which normally processes, discards, or dispatches information by sending signals to other parts of the brain.

"The hippocampus is critical for learning," says Gluck, "and it's also one of the most volatile, unstable parts of the brain—one of the first parts damaged if oxygen is cut off. Think of it as a highly maneuverable kayak; it has to immediately capture a whole range of information about an event and needs the ability to go rapidly through many changes. We think the hippocampus serves as a filter, learning new associations and deciding what is important and what to ignore or compress. That's why it's critical for learning." The hippocampus is, in a sense, a collating machine, sorting and then sending various packets of information to other parts of the brain.

One of the most exciting advances in neuroscience may lie ahead as researchers begin to actually model the living brain on the computer—creating a new era of artificial intelligence called neural networks. Gluck and researchers at New York University have begun to model the hippocampus, creating "lesions" and watching what happens—in the hope that they can develop specialized tests that will identify Alzheimer's in its early stages, as well as develop machinery that can learn the way a brain does. Thus far their predictions about its role have been borne out—in fact, Gluck is developing applications for the military so that hippocampal-like computers can learn the early signals of engine malfunctions and sound the alarm long before a breakdown.

The hippocampus does not store memories permanently. It is a way station, though a supremely important one. Like a football player in the heat of the game, it passes the ball to other parts of the brain. This takes minutes, or maybe even hours, according to James McGaugh, Ph.D., of the University of California at Irvine. At that point, memories can still be lost.

They need to be consolidated; the network of neurons responsible for a memory needs to be strengthened through repeated stimuli, until the memory exists independent of the hippocampus, a process known as long-term potentiation (LTP).

Once again, a word picture of this process is extremely crude. In actuality, Edelman points out, "the circuits of the brain look like no others we have seen before. The neurons have treelike arbors that overlap in myriad ways. Their signaling is like the vast aggregate of interactive events in a jungle."

No one is certain how long it takes to fully consolidate a memory. Days? Weeks? Perhaps it takes even years until the linkages of networks are so deeply engraved that the memory becomes almost crystallized—easy to recall, detailed and clear. Individuals like M.P. seem to lose several years of memory just prior to hippocampal damage; so do Alzheimer's patients, who usually suffer hippocampal damage as their brains begin to malfunction, and who recall their childhood days with fine-etched clarity but find the present blurred.

A MAGIC RHYTHM OF MEMORY?

Just how and when do memories become permanent? Scientists now have direct evidence of what they have long suspected—that consolidation of memories, or LTP, takes place during sleep or during deeply relaxed states. It is then that brain waves slow to a rhythm known as "theta," and perhaps, according to McGaugh, the brain releases chemicals that enhance storage.

In an ingenious experiment reported in the journal *Science* last July, researchers planted electrodes in different cells in rats' hippocampi, and watched each cell fire as the animals explored different parts of a box. After returning to their cages, the rats slept. And during sleep the very same cells fired.

There seems to be a specific brain rhythm dedicated to LTP. "It's the magic rhythm of theta! The theta rhythm is the natural, indigenous rhythm of the hippocampus," exclaims neuroscientist Gary Lynch, Ph.D., of the University of California at Irvine. Lynch is known for his inspiring, if slightly mad, brilliance. His laboratory found that LTP is strongest when stimulation is delivered to the hippocampus in a frequency that corresponds to the slow rhythms of theta, of deep relaxation. Research by James McGaugh seems to confirm this: the more theta waves that appear in an animal's EEG (electroencephalogram), the more it remembers.

No wonder, then, that recent experiments show sleep improves memory in humans—and specifically, the sleep associated with dreaming, REM (rapid eye movement) sleep. In Canada, students who slept after cramming for an exam retained more information than those who pulled an all-nighter. In Israel, researchers Avi Karni and Dov Sagi at the Weizmann Institute found that interrupting REM sleep 60 times in a night completely blocked learning; interrupting non-REM sleep just as often did not. These findings give scientific punch to "superlearning" methods like that of Bulgarian psychiatrist Georgi Lozanov, which utilizes deep relaxation through diaphragmatic breathing and music, combined with rhythmic bursts of information.

THE HAUNTED BRAIN

What happens when memory goes awry? It seems that some memories are so deeply engraved in the brain that they haunt an individual as if he were a character in an Edgar Allen Poe story. How, asks Roger Pittman, M.D., coordinator of research and development at the Manchester (New Hampshire) Veterans Administration Medical Center and associate professor at Harvard Medical School, does the traumatic event "carve its canyons and basins of memory into the living brain?"

'We believe that the brain takes advantage of hormones and chemicals, released during stress and powerful emotions, to regulate the strength of memory.' We owe our very lives to this; a dangerous event needs to be recalled.

In any kind of emotionally arousing experience, the brain takes advantage of the fight-or-flight reaction, which floods cells with two powerful stress hormones, adrenaline and nor-adrenaline. "We believe that the brain takes advantage of the chemicals released during stress and powerful emotions," says James McGaugh, "to regulate the strength of storage of the memory." These stress hormones stimulate the heart to pump faster and the muscles to tense; they also act on neurons in the brain. A memory associated with emotionally charged information gets seared into the brain. We owe our very lives to this: a dangerous, threatening, or exciting event needs to be recalled well so that we may take precautions when meeting similar danger again.

Scientists are now beginning to understand just how emotional memory works and why it is so powerful. According to Joseph Ledoux, Ph.D., of the Center for Neural Science at New York University, the hormones associated with strong emotion stimulate the amygdala, an almond-shaped organ in the brain's cortex.

It's long been known that when rats are subjected to the sound of a tone and a shock, they soon learn to respond fearfully to the tone alone. The shocker is that when the auditory cortex—the part of the brain that receives sound—is completely destroyed, the rats are still able to learn the exact same fear response. How can a rat learn to be afraid of a sound it cannot hear?

The tone, it appears, is carried directly back to the amygdala, as well as to the auditory cortex. Destroy the amygdala, and even a rat with perfect hearing will never learn to be afraid of the sound. As neurologist Richard Restak, M.D., notes, this "implies that much of our brain's emotional processing occurs unconsciously. The amygdala may process many of our unconscious fear responses." This explains in part why phobias are so difficult to treat by psychotherapy. The brain's memory for emotional experiences is an enduring one.

But the ability of the brain to utilize stress hormones can go badly awry—and a memory can become not simply permanent but intrusive and relentless. "Suppose somebody shoots you and years later you're still waking up in a cold sweat with nightmares," says McGaugh. "The hormonal regulation of memory, when pushed to an extreme in a traumatic situation, may make memories virtually indelible."

Such memories seem so powerful that even an innocuous stimulus can arouse them. Roger Pittman compares the inescapable memories of PTSD, where flashbacks to a nightmarish trauma intrude relentlessly on daily life, to a black hole, "a place in space-time that has such high gravity that even light cannot pass by without being drawn into it."

So with ordinary associations and memories in PTSD: "As all roads lead to Rome, all the patient's thoughts lead to the trauma. A war veteran can't look at his wife's nude body without recalling with revulsion the naked bodies he saw in a burial pit in Vietnam, can't stand the sight of children's dolls because their eyes remind him of the staring eyes of the war dead."

The tragic twist is that, Pittman believes, each time a memory floods in again, the same stress hormones are released, running the same neural paths of that particular memory and binding the victim ever tighter in the noose of the past. Yet in response to the stress of recalling trauma, the body releases a flood of calming opiates. These neurochemicals, which help us meet the immediate demands of stress and trauma, might create a kind of unfortunate biochemical reward for the traumatic memory. "This whole question of an appetitive component to trauma is really fascinating and as yet unexplored," notes Pittman. "It may explain the intrusive, repeating nature of these memories. Maybe, however horrible the trauma, there's something rewarding in the brain chemicals released."

A solution, then, to treating the kind of PTSD we see in war veterans and victims of rape and child abuse, might lie in blocking the action of some of these stress hormones. And perhaps a key to enhancing ordinary learning is to create a judicious amount of stress—excitement, surprise, even a healthy dose of fear (like the kind one may feel before cramming for a demanding final exam).

A landmark study recently reported by James McGaugh and Larry Cahill, in *Nature,* indicates that any emotion, even ordinary emotion, is linked to learning. They gave two groups of college students a drug that blocks the effects of adrenaline and noradrenaline, then showed the students a series of 12 slides that depicted scenes such as a boy crossing the street with his mother or visiting a man at a hospital. A control group was told an ordinary story (son and mother visit the boy's surgeon father) that corresponded to some of the slides. The experimental group heard a story of disaster (boy is hit by car; a surgeon attempts to reattach his severed feet).

Two weeks later, the volunteers were given a surprise memory test. Students who heard the ordinary story recalled all 12 slides poorly. The second group, however, recalled significantly better the slides associated with the story of disaster.

Then, in an ingenious twist, McGaugh and Cahill repeated the experiment with new volunteers. Just before the slide show, the experimental group was given a beta blocker—a drug that acts on nerve cells to block the effect of stress hormones. Two weeks later they could not be distinguished from the control group. They similarly remembered all 12 slides poorly.

The implications of this elegant experiment are far reaching. "Let's suppose," postulates McGaugh, "that a plane crashes near Pittsburgh and you're hired to pick out the body parts. If we give you a beta blocker, we impair your 'emotional' memory, the memory for the trauma, without impairing your normal memory."

Pittman looks forward in the next decade to drugs that not only block PTSD but help ameliorate it. "There seems to be a window of opportunity, up to six hours or so in rats in any case, before memories are consolidated." During that time effective drugs, such as beta blockers, might be administered.

MEMORY LOST AND REGAINED

The stories are legendary. Elizabeth Loftus has found ordinary memory to be so malleable that she can prompt volunteers to "remember nonexistent broken glass and tape recorders; to think of a clean-shaven man as having a mustache, of straight hair as curly, of hammers as screwdrivers, to place a barn in a bucolic scene that contained no buildings at all, to believe in characters who never existed and events that never happened."

Sometimes the memories become so seemingly fantastical that they lead to court cases and ruined lives. "I testified in a case recently in a small town in the state of Washington," Loftus recalls, "where the memories went from, 'Daddy made me play with his penis in the shower' to 'Daddy made me stick my fist up the anus of a horse,' and they were bringing in a veterinarian to talk about just what a horse would do in that circumstance. The father is ill and will be spending close to $100,000 to defend himself."

Nobody is quite sure how memories might be lost to us and then later retrieved—so-called repression. Whatever it is, it is a different process than traumatic amnesia, a well-known phenomenon where a particular horrendous event is forgotten because it was never consolidated in long-term memory in the first place. Such is the amnesia of an accident victim who loses consciousness after injury. Repressed memory, on the other hand, is alleged to involve repeated traumas.

According to UCLA's Daniel Siegel, both amnesia and repression may be due to a malfunction of the hippocampus. In order to recall an explicit memory, and to be able to depict it in words and pictures, the hippocampus must process it first. Perhaps, postulates Siegel, the work of the hippocampus is disrupted during trauma—while other components of memory carry on. We know, for example, that primitive responses like fear or excitement stimulate the amygdala directly; learning can occur without our "knowing" it.

If explicit memory is impaired—you forget what happened to you—but implicit memory is intact, you may still be profoundly influenced by an experience. Siegel thinks that some individuals remove conscious attention during repeated trauma, say from an unbearable event like repeated rapes. In the parlance of the mind trade, they "dissociate."

While his theory may explain repressed memory plausibly, it doesn't suggest how the memory emerges decades later, explicit and intrusive. And it doesn't answer the contention of many researchers that such repression is probably rare, and that the wave of repressed memories we are hearing about today may be due to invention.

It turns out that it's relatively easy to confuse imagery with perception. The work of Stephen Kossyln, Ph.D., a psychologist at Harvard University and author of *Image and Brain* (MIT press), has shown that the exact same centers in the brain are activated by both imagination and perception. "PET studies have shown that, when subjects close their eyes and form visual images, the same areas are activated as if they were actually seeing." The strength of the imagined "signal" (or image) is about half that of a real one. Other research shows that the source of a memory—the time, place, or way the memory began—is the first part to fade. After all, the source of a memory is fragile.

If we concentrate on generating images that then get recorded in the web of neurons as if they were real, we might actually convince ourselves that confabulations are true. (This might also explain how some individuals who lie about an event eventually convince themselves, through repeated lying, that the lie is true.)

The fragility of source memory explains why, in a famous experiment by psychologist John Neisser, John Dean's testimony about Richard Nixon was shown to be both incredibly accurate and hugely inaccurate. "His initial testimony was so impressive that people called him a human tape recorder," recalls psychologist Charles Thompson, Ph.D. "Neisser then compared the actual tapes to his testimony, and found that if you really looked at the specifics, who said what and when, Dean was wrong all over the place. But if you just looked at his general sense of what was going on in the meetings he was right on target. His confusion was about the source." In general, supposes Thompson, this is how memory works. We have an accurate sense of the core truth of an event, but we can easily get the details wrong.

'It's easy to confuse memory with experience. The exact same brain centers are activated by imagination and perception.'

"Memory is more reconstructive than reproductive. As time passes, details are lost. We did a study where we asked people to keep a daily diary for up to a year and a half, and later asked them questions about recorded events. The memory of the core event and its content stayed at a high level of about 70 percent, while the peripheral details dropped quickly."

CAN MEMORY CREATE THE SELF?

From Freud on down, it was believed that memories from infancy or early childhood were repressed and somehow inaccessible—but that their clues, like the bits of bread dropped by Hansel and Gretel in the forest, could be found in dreams or in the pathology of waking life. Now we know better. It's that the brain systems that support declarative memory develop late—two or three years into life.

If we don't actually lay down any memories of our first few years, how can they shape our later life? An intriguing answer can be pieced together from findings by far-flung researchers.

Daniel Siegel plows the field of childhood memory and attachment theory. He finds that memory is profoundly affected in children whose mothers had rejected or avoided them. "We don't know why this happens, but at 10 years old, these children have a unique paucity in the content of their spontaneous autobiographical narratives." As adults, they do not recall childhood family experiences.

It may be that memory storage is impaired in the case of childhood trauma. Or it may be, Siegel suggests, that avoidant parents don't "talk to children about their experiences and memories. Those children don't have much practice in autobiographical narrative. Not only are their memories weak or nonexistent, the sense of self is not as rich. As a psychotherapist, I try to teach people to tell stories about their lives. It helps them develop a richer sense of self."

As far as the biology of the brain goes, this may be no different than training an 18-year-old boy to distinguish between whales and submarines; if the hippocampus is continually fed a stimulus, it will allocate more of the brain's capacities to recording and recognizing that stimulus. In the case of autobiographical narrative, however, what emerges is magical and necessary: the self.

That is almost like saying memory creates the self, and in a sense it does. But memory is also created and recreated by the self. The synergy between the two is like two sticks rubbed together in a forest, creating fire. "We now have a new paradigm of memory," notes Loftus, "where memories are understood as creative blendings of fact and fiction, where images are alchemized by experience and emotion into memories."

"I think it's safe to say we make meaning out of life, and the meaning-making process is shaped by who we are as self," says Siegel. Yet that self is shaped by the nature of memory. "It's this endless feedback loop which maintains itself and allows us to come alive."

When we think of our lives, we become storytellers—heroes of our own narrative, a tale that illumines that precious and mysterious "self" at the center. That "I am" cannot be quantified or conveyed precisely and yet it feels absolute. As Christopher Isherwood wrote long ago in *The Berlin Stories,* "I am a camera." Yet, as the science is showing us, there is no single camera—or if there is, it is more like the impressionist, constantly shifting camera of *Last Year at Marienbad.* Memory is malleable—and so are we.

DNA-environment mix forms intellectual fate

People may not be able to exceed their genetic potential, but environmental factors may determine whether that potential is reached.

Beth Azar

Monitor *staff*

Those who believe in destiny think each person's lot in life is determined at conception: Whatever happens is programmed from the start. With so much discussion in the media of genetics and "nature" as opposed to nurture, is "destiny" just an antiquated word for DNA?

Most researchers agree that a combination of biology and environment contribute to behavioral traits. But just what proportion of each is vigorously debated, especially in the area of intelligence.

Some psychologists believe heredity is the dominant influence on intelligence. They base that view on research that concentrates on variations among people in general cognitive ability, or IQ. Others believe such research overemphasizes the concept of IQ and gives too much credit to genetics.

Twins and IQ scores

Most agree that an inadequate environment will decrease an individual's or a population's intelligence, said intelligence researcher Thomas Bouchard, PhD, of the University of Minnesota. However, "when individuals are under reasonably good circumstances . . . much of the variation [in IQ] among them is genetic," said Bouchard, who directs the Minnesota Center for Twin and Adoption Research. As with variations in height—which are considered close to 95 percent genetic—once envi-

ronment is equalized, the only reason for differences in IQ can be biology, said Bouchard.

Researchers estimate that from 40 percent to 80 percent of differences in IQ score are due to inheritance. The higher estimate comes from large studies of identical twins separated at birth. Because identical twins share all the same genes, any truly inherited trait should correlate perfectly. Any trait due to environment should have no more than chance correlation.

Therefore, correlations for identical twins reared in separate environments should give a good estimate of heritability of that trait. In Bouchard's sample of between 42 and 48 pairs of identical twins reared apart (numbers varied between studies), he found very

high rates of correlation for IQ. From his results, he estimates that IQ is between 75 percent and 80 percent heritable. Such data suggest that environment accounts for as little as 20 percent of scores on intelligence tests.

Environmental influences

Certainly "part of the functioning of

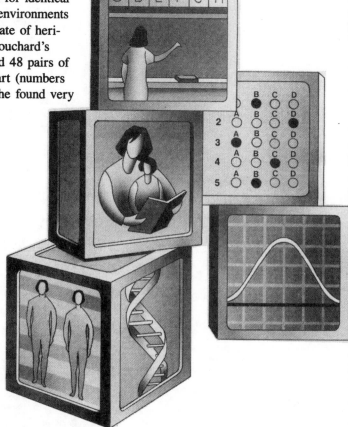

the brain is determined by environmental factors," said Douglas Detterman, PhD, an intelligence researcher at Case Western Reserve University. However it's difficult to say which factors and how big of an effect they have. Few environmental variables have been found that account for a substantial portion of the variation in intelligence, he said.

Factors such as poor nutrition, lead poisoning, poor health care and head injuries have been linked to low IQ scores. But none has been found to account for more than a few percent of the variation in scores, agree researchers.

"Understanding how the environment affects intelligence is the most difficult of all to study," though it's important, said Detterman. He thinks the effect of environment is multifaceted, and it will be extremely complex to find out how all the variables relate, he said.

Socioeconomic status is the one factor that has been strongly linked to IQ. Poverty predicts low IQ in study after study, but it's difficult to determine causation. Most researchers presume that poverty—associated with risk factors such as poor home environment, poor schools and lack of access to special programs—causes a drop in intellectual attainment. But some, such as Richard Herrnstein, PhD, and Charles Murray, PhD, in their recent book, *The Bell Curve,* propose that low IQ may be responsible for low socioeconomic status.

A loaded concept

Researchers shouldn't overestimate the role of inheritance, according to Stephen Ceci, PhD, of Cornell University.

"Every important aspect [of behavior] has a role for biology and a role for ecology," he said. The two are "inextricably intertwined," he added.

Heritability is "an extremely environmentally loaded concept," he said. People may have a certain genetic potential that can't be exceeded, but a conducive environment is what makes an organism "much more able to bring [that potential] to fruition," he said.

Indeed, IQ measures the level of intelligence that the environment has allowed a person to reach, believes Edward Zigler, PhD, director of the Bush Center for Child Development and Social Policy at Yale University and one of the founders of the national Head Start program.

His research on intelligence and learning shows that IQ measures three things: cognitive ability, achievement (accumulated knowledge based on personal experience, such as a definition for the word regatta) and motivational factors, he said. The more traditional view of IQ tests posits that they measure cognitive ability alone.

Cognitive ability, he admits, is "probably the least open to changes," Zigler said. He estimates that approximately 50 percent of cognitive ability is influenced by genetics, which leaves at least 50 percent up to environment, he said. Achievement is somewhat related to cognitive ability, said Zigler, but it is even more affected by environment.

Motivation is almost totally influenced by one's environment, said Zigler. Children learn to be unmotivated; children growing up in poor environments have little incentive to answer test questions, let alone to perform well, he said.

So environment has a larger influ-

ence than genetics in the three combined aspects of IQ, said Zigler. Getting children to use their genetically determined intelligence optimally is the way to improve achievement, he said.

Zigler's research points out what he calls reaction range. Any one person has a maximum and a minimum IQ score that he or she can reach. Environment predicts how optimally one reaches that maximum or how close to the minimum one scores. Environment can account for as many as 25 IQ points, said Zigler.

Preschool programs such as Head Start apply this premise by trying to improve children's overall environments through educational day-care, family programming, nutritional programming and health care.

Contrary to claims of some researchers and the media, the goal of Head Start was never to raise IQ, said Zigler. That became the perceived goal because the first evaluations of the program focused on IQ scores, he said.

Over the past 30 years Zigler has tried to change that perception to one of social competence, he said. This includes producing children who remain in the correct grade for their age, who stay out of special education, who graduate from high school and who don't become pregnant in their teens.

Such programs capitalize on abilities that are underutilized by tapping "a child's motivational system," Zigler said.

IQ aside, "the environment has to be good enough to provide the resources to nurture individual strengths," said Ceci.

Malnutrition, Poverty and Intellectual Development

Research into childhood nutrition reveals that a poor diet influences mental development in more ways than expected. Other aspects of poverty exacerbate the effects.

J. Larry Brown and Ernesto Pollitt

J. LARRY BROWN and ERNESTO POLLITT have collaborated for several years on the policy implications of childhood nutrition. Brown, director of the Center on Hunger, Poverty and Nutrition Policy at Tufts University, is also professor of nutrition and health policy at the School of Nutrition Science and Policy and at the School of Medicine. Pollitt is professor of human development in the department of pediatrics at the School of Medicine at the University of California, Davis, and is also a member of the Program of International Nutrition.

The prevalence of malnutrition in children is staggering. Globally, nearly 195 million children younger than five years are undernourished. Malnutrition is most obvious in the developing countries, where the condition often takes severe forms; images of emaciated bodies in famine-struck or war-torn regions are tragically familiar. Yet milder forms are more common, especially in developed nations. Indeed, in 1992 an estimated 12 million American children consumed diets that were significantly below the recommended allowances of nutrients established by the National Academy of Sciences.

Undernutrition triggers an array of health problems in children, many of which can become chronic. It can lead to extreme weight loss, stunted growth, weakened resistance to infection and, in the worst cases, early death. The effects can be particularly devastating in the first few years of life, when the body is growing rapidly and the need for calories and nutrients is greatest.

Inadequate nutrition can also disrupt cognition—although in different ways than were previously assumed. At one time, underfeeding in childhood was thought to hinder mental development solely by producing permanent, structural damage to the brain. More recent work, however, indicates that malnutrition can impair the intellect by other means as well. Furthermore, even in cases where the brain's hardware is damaged, some of the injury may be reversible. These new findings have important implications for policies aimed at bolstering achievement among underprivileged children.

Scientists first investigated the link between malnutrition and mental performance early in this century, but the subject did not attract serious attention until decades later. In the 1960s increasing evidence of undernutrition in industrial nations, including the U.S., along with continuing concern about severe malnutrition in developing countries, prompted researchers to examine the lasting effects of food deprivation. A number of studies in Latin America, Africa and the U.S. reported that on intelligence tests children with a history of malnutrition attained lower scores than children of similar social and economic status who were properly nourished. These surveys had various experimental limitations that made them inconclusive, but later research has firmly established that undernutrition in early life can limit long-term intellectual development.

Worry over Brain Damage

For many years, scientists considered the connection between nutrition and intellectual development to be straightforward. They assumed that poor nutrition was primarily a worry from conception to age two, when the brain grows to roughly 80 percent of its adult size. In this critical period, any degree of malnutrition was thought to halt the normal development of the brain and thereby to inflict severe, lasting damage.

Gradually, though, investigators recognized that the main-effect model, as we have termed this view, was too simplistic. For instance, the emphasis on

Effects of Poverty and Malnutrition: The Guatemalan Project

In a project carried out by the Institute of Nutrition of Central America and Panama, children and young adults in Guatemala who had received nutritional supplements in infancy were studied to assess the influence of early diet and poverty on later intellectual development. Subjects, including the boys at the right, were given a battery of cognitive tests. Individuals who regularly consumed a highly nutritious supplement called Atole before the age of two performed at about the same level on most tests, such as tests of vocabulary skills, regardless of economic status (*bottom left*). But the performance of those given a less nutritious supplement called Fresco varied with poverty level. Evidently, good nutrition early in life can help counteract the destructive effects of poverty on intellectual development. Among individuals who had more than two years of formal education, those who consumed Atole scored significantly higher than those who received Fresco (*bottom right*)—an indication that poor nutrition in infancy can subsequently undermine the benefits of schooling. —*E.P.*

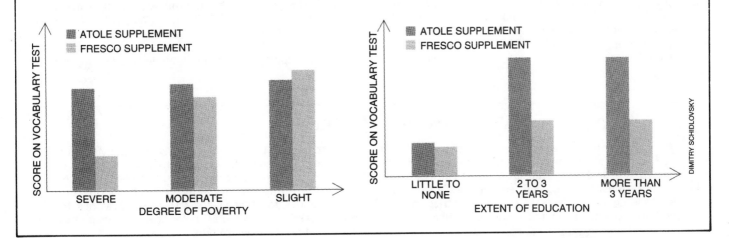

the first two years of life proved somewhat misguided. Brain growth in that period is not always terminated irreversibly in undernourished children. Rather it may be put on hold temporarily; if diet improves by age three or so, growth of the brain may continue at close to a normal pace. Conversely, injury to the brain can occur even when a child suffers malnutrition after the first two years of life—a sign that providing adequate nutrition throughout childhood is important to cognitive development. Focusing exclusively on the first two years of life is thus inadequate.

Furthermore, although severe underfeeding in infancy can certainly lead to irreparable cognitive deficits, as the main-effect model predicts, the model cannot fully account for intellectual impairment stemming from more moderate malnutrition. This flaw became apparent in the 1960s, when researchers showed that mildly undernourished children from middle- or upper-income families (whose nutrient deficits stemmed from medical conditions) did not suffer the same intellectual troubles as did mildly underfed children in impoverished communities. If poor nutrition impaired cognition only by structurally altering the brain, the two groups should have performed alike. Something

else had to be at work as well. In other words, factors such as income, education and other aspects of the environment could apparently protect children against the harmful effects of a poor diet or could exacerbate the insult of malnutrition.

No Energy to Learn

In the 1970s research by David A. Levitsky and Richard H. Barnes of Cornell University helped to clarify how malnutrition might hinder cognitive development in ways other than injuring the brain. Levitsky and Barnes studied rodents to examine the effects of malnutrition. Levitsky concluded that the malnourished animals performed less well on tests of mental ability, such as maze running, not because they suffered brain damage but mostly because, lacking energy, they essentially withdrew from contact with their peers and the objects in their environment. In addition, mothers coddled the less mobile infants, further hindering their growth and independence.

By extrapolation, the findings implied that cognitive disability in undernourished children might stem in part from reduced interaction with other people and with their surroundings. This fun-

damental shift in understanding produced increased optimism about the prospects for remediation; if decreased social interaction was partly at fault for cognitive impairment, then social and intellectual remediation could presumably help make up for deficits in the youngsters' experiences.

Although the new ideas were compelling, scientists did not have much human evidence to buttress the changing views. A recent study by one of us (Pollitt) and several collaborators adds strong support to the notion that malnutrition affects intellectual development in part by compromising many different aspects of a child's development. The research also provides added insight into how poor diet and economic adversities during childhood combine to impede intellectual functioning later in life. Pollitt's collaborators included Reynaldo Martorell of Emory University, Kathleen S. Gorman of the University of Vermont, Patrice L. Engle of California Polytechnic State University and Juan A. Rivera of the Institute of Nutrition of Central America and Panama.

The project was an extensive follow-up of Guatemalan children who were studied by other scientists many years earlier. In 1969 the Institute of Nutrition of Central America and Panama, with the help of various U.S. government agencies and private foundations, began a massive effort to examine the value of nutritional supplements in preventing the health problems of malnutrition. For eight years, residents of four villages in Guatemala received one of two nutritional supplements. When this phase of the study was being planned, researchers felt that protein was the most important nutrient missing from diets in developing countries. Therefore, project workers looked specifically at how children would respond to added protein in their diets. The mothers and children in two of the villages received a high-protein supplement called Atole (the Guatemalan name for a hot maize

gruel). Inhabitants of the other two villages—who constituted the control group—received Fresco, a sweet, fruit-flavored drink, which contained no protein. Both supplements provided vitamins and minerals as well as calories; Fresco provided a third the calories of Atole.

When the study began, all pregnant women, and all children under the age of seven in the villages, were invited to participate. During the course of the study, children under seven who moved into the villages and women who became pregnant were also asked to join the project. More than 2,000 children and mothers participated between 1969 and 1977. Regular medical exams of the children revealed that both supple-

ments improved the health of the participants, but Atole performed more impressively. For instance, in all four villages, the rate of infant mortality decreased. But in the villages that received Atole, infant mortality decreased 69 percent, whereas in villages receiving Fresco, the rate went down by just 24 percent. Also, only Atole improved growth rates in children under three.

Gains in Guatemala

In the follow-up study, carried out in 1988 and 1989, Pollitt and his colleagues visited the villages to assess how these early nutritional supplements affected intellectual development over

Avoiding Malnutrition

Opinions on what constitutes malnutrition—and recommendations for avoiding the problem—have been refined over time. Early studies considered lack of protein to be the most troubling deficiency in the diets of underfed children, especially in developing countries. Ingested protein is broken down into amino acids, which are then

DIETARY requirements for children can be met by eating several servings a day from each of five food categories.

recycled to build the specific proteins needed by the individual at any given time. Proteins form many structural elements of the body and carry out most cellular processes. By the 1970s, though, investigators had begun to worry about calories, too. When faced with a lack of calories, the body breaks down amino acids for energy instead of using them to make new proteins.

In more recent years, nutrition research has emphasized that shortages of vitamins and minerals—particularly vitamin A, iodine and iron—contribute to significant health problems. Vitamin A is important for good vision, bone growth, tooth development and resistance to infection. Iodine, which tends to be scarce in developing countries, is needed for proper operation of the central nervous system. Iron is a constituent of hemoglobin, which transports oxygen to tissues. Iron also helps the body fight infections; levels of the mineral are low in diets of many poor children in the U.S. Hence, most investigators now believe malnutrition is best avoided by a diet that supplies enough protein, calories, vitamins and minerals to ensure normal growth. Some standard guidelines for optimal nutrition in children are listed below.   —J.L.B.

FOOD CATEGORY	SERVINGS PER DAY	SERVING SIZE*		
		AGE 1 TO 3 YEARS	4 TO 6 YEARS	7 TO 10 YEARS
WHOLE-GRAIN OR ENRICHED BREADS, CEREALS, RICE, PASTA	6 OR MORE	1/2 SLICE BREAD OR 1/4 CUP RICE OR NOODLES	1 SLICE BREAD OR 1/2 CUP RICE OR NOODLES	1 TO 2 SLICES BREAD OR 1/2 TO 1 CUP RICE OR NOODLES
VEGETABLES	3 OR MORE	2 TO 4 TBSP OR 1/2 CUP JUICE	1/4 TO 1/2 CUP OR 1/2 CUP JUICE	1/2 TO 3/4 CUP OR 1/2 CUP JUICE
FRUITS	2 OR MORE	2 TO 4 TBSP OR 1/2 CUP JUICE	1/4 TO 1/2 CUP OR 1/2 CUP JUICE	1/2 TO 3/4 CUP OR 1/2 CUP JUICE
LEAN MEATS, FISH, POULTRY, EGGS, NUTS, BEANS	2 OR MORE	1 TO 2 OZ	1 TO 2 OZ	2 TO 3 OZ
MILK AND CHEESE	3 TO 4	1/2 TO 3/4 CUP MILK OR 1/2 TO 3/4 OZ CHEESE	3/4 CUP MILK OR 3/4 OZ CHEESE	3/4 TO 1 CUP MILK OR 3/4 TO 1 OZ CHEESE

Data from "Growth and Nutrient Requirements of Children." P. M. Queen and R. R. Henry in Pediatric Nutrition, edited by R. J. Grand et al. Butterworth, 1987

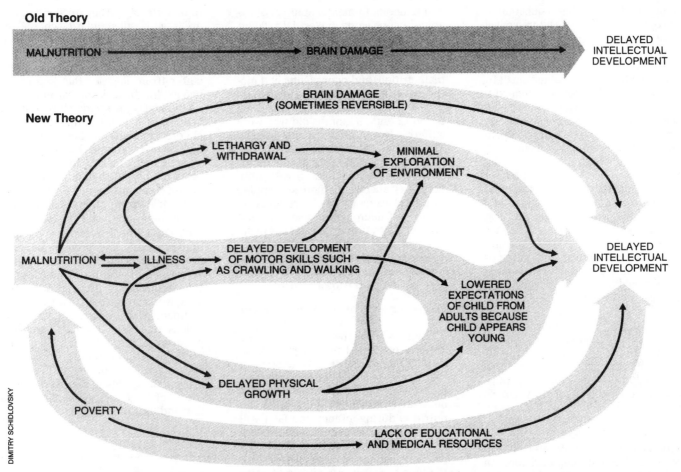

Old Theory

MALNUTRITION → BRAIN DAMAGE → DELAYED INTELLECTUAL DEVELOPMENT

New Theory

BRAIN DAMAGE (SOMETIMES REVERSIBLE)

LETHARGY AND WITHDRAWAL

MINIMAL EXPLORATION OF ENVIRONMENT

MALNUTRITION ↔ ILLNESS

DELAYED DEVELOPMENT OF MOTOR SKILLS SUCH AS CRAWLING AND WALKING

LOWERED EXPECTATIONS OF CHILD FROM ADULTS BECAUSE CHILD APPEARS YOUNG

DELAYED INTELLECTUAL DEVELOPMENT

DELAYED PHYSICAL GROWTH

POVERTY

LACK OF EDUCATIONAL AND MEDICAL RESOURCES

DIMITRY SCHIDLOVSKY

MALNUTRITION HINDERS COGNITIVE ABILITIES through several interacting routes, according to recent research. Early models of malnutrition considered cognitive deficiencies to result only from damage to the brain (*top*). Now scientists also believe (*bottom*) that malnutrition alters intellectual development by interfering with overall health as well as the child's energy level, rate of motor development and rate of growth. In addition, low economic status can exacerbate all these factors, placing impoverished children at particular risk for cognitive impairment later in life.

the long term. More than 70 percent of the original participants—by then, ranging in age from 11 to 27 years old—agreed to take part in the follow-up. In particular, the team's analysis concentrated on the group of roughly 600 people who were exposed to Atole or Fresco both prenatally and for at least two years after birth. These adolescents and young adults took literacy, vocabulary and reading comprehension tests, a general knowledge exam, an arithmetic test and a standard nonverbal intelligence test. The researchers then determined how education and economic status (measured by house quality, father's occupation and mother's education) correlated with test scores.

The subjects who received Atole in early life performed significantly better on most tests of cognition than those who received Fresco. The strongest effects of Atole were observed among those at the low end of the social and economic ladder: these children performed as well as the more privileged

children in their villages [*see box, Effects of Poverty and Malnutrition: The Guatemalan Project*]. Atole thus served as a kind of social equalizer, helping children from low-income families achieve at the same level as their slightly more economically advantaged peers within the village. But the children of this study all lived in extreme poverty and did not perform at the same level as, say, a child from a middle-class household in a more prosperous area of Guatemala. Hence, adequate nutrition by itself could not fully compensate for the negative effects of poverty on intellectual growth.

In addition, Atole appeared to have increased the advantage of education. With every additional year of schooling, the differences in achievement between the adolescents who received Atole and those who consumed Fresco increased. This result indicates that poor nutrition can essentially negate some typical benefits of education. In separate

but related studies, Pollitt and his collaborators, working in Peru, and Sally Grantham-McGregor of the University of the West Indies, working in Jamaica, have demonstrated that learning capabilities are affected by how recently one has eaten. So breakfast every day before school is indeed important, particularly among children at risk for undernutrition.

The better long-term effects in the Atole group can largely be explained by the differences in the children's motor skills, physical growth, and social and emotional development. The youngsters who received Fresco in their early life suffered more physical disadvantages—a slower rate of growth and a slower rate of recovery from infection, for example—compared with those who received Atole. Because development was hindered, these children also learned to crawl and walk slightly later on average than the infants who received Atole. Pollitt and his colleagues speculate that for the infants who took Fresco, this limitation delayed the acquisition of the cognitive skills that children develop when they explore their social and physical environment.

Furthermore, because these undernourished toddlers remained small for their age, adults might have tended to treat them as if they were younger than their actual age. Such a response would very likely slow cognitive development, if the toddlers were not challenged—to talk, for instance—in the same way that other children their age were. Children who consumed Atole, in contrast, avoided malnutrition, grew up faster and were presumably exposed to more challenges in their social environment. Of course, the results do not rule out the possibility that the Fresco recipients may have suffered some degree of brain damage that impeded their later functioning. The findings, however, imply that additional factors, such as the child's social environment, played a major role as well.

The results in Guatemala are also consistent with the prevailing understanding of the interactions between poor nutrition, poverty and education. Nutritional supplements combat the effects of poverty, but only somewhat. A well-nourished child may be better able to explore the environment, but an impoverished community may offer little to investigate. And although schools can provide much of the stimulation children need, early malnutrition can undermine the overall value of education. Most important, this study demonstrates that poor nutrition in early childhood can continue to hinder intellectual performance into adulthood.

Because the early planners of the Guatemalan study chose to examine protein, these results emphasize protein's importance to intellectual growth. The supplements also included calories, vitamins and minerals; consequently, their role should be taken into account, but the arrangement of this particular study makes isolating the effects difficult.

Other work links essential vitamins and minerals to mental ability. For example, in one study in West Java, Pollitt and his colleagues showed a close association between iron-deficiency anemia (the most common consequence of malnutrition) and poor mental and motor skills in children. The researchers gave iron supplements to babies between 12 and 18 months old who were suffering from iron-deficiency anemia. The mineral significantly improved the infants' scores on mental and motor skills tests. Sadly, children with iron-deficiency anemia are more susceptible to lead poisoning, which produces its own set of neurological disorders that interfere with proper cognition. Consequently, poor children face a double jeopardy: they are more likely to be anemic and more likely to live where lead poisoning is widespread.

Correcting and Preventing Impairment

Studies such as the one in Guatemala have prompted many scholars, including one of us (Brown), to suggest that when the social and economic aspects of a child's environment cannot be easily changed, providing adequate nutrition during infancy and later will at least lessen the cognitive deficits engendered by poverty. Nutritional supplements cannot by themselves reverse the long-term adverse effects of earlier undernutrition, however. The ideal would be to provide additional support, such as tutoring, opportunities to develop new social skills and guidance from an involved parent or another concerned adult. Recent studies have shown that enriched education programs for children in economically impoverished communities can often ameliorate some of the problems associated with previous malnutrition.

To have the best chance at being useful, such intervention should be comprehensive and sustained. Most undernourished children face persistent challenges that can exacerbate the effects of underfeeding. They frequently live in areas with substandard schools and with little or no medical care. Their parents are often unemployed or work for very low wages. And the children may suffer from illnesses that sap energy needed for the tasks of learning.

On balance, it seems clear that prevention of malnutrition among young children remains the best policy—not only on moral grounds but on economic ones as well. The U.S., for example, invests billions of dollars in education, yet much of this money goes to waste when children appear at the school door intellectually crippled from undernutrition. The immediate expense of nutrition programs and broader interventions should be considered a critical investment in the future. Malnutrition alters educational preparedness and, later, workforce productivity, making it an unacceptable risk for its victims as well as for a nation's strength and competitiveness. Steps taken today to combat malnutrition and its intellectual effects can go a long way toward improving the quality of life—and productivity—of large segments of a population and thus of society as a whole.

Further Reading

NUTRITION AND BEHAVIOR. Edited by Janina R. Galler. Plenum Press, 1984.

THE EFFECTS OF IMPROVED NUTRITION IN EARLY CHILDHOOD: THE INSTITUTE OF CENTRAL AMERICA AND PANAMA (IN-CAP) FOLLOW-UP STUDY. Edited by Reynaldo Martorell and Nevin S. Scrimshaw. Supplement to *Journal of Nutrition*, Vol. 125, No. 4S; April 1995.

THE RELATIONSHIP BETWEEN UNDERNUTRITION AND BEHAVIORAL DEVELOPMENT IN CHILDREN. Edited by Ernesto Pollitt. *Supplement to Journal of Nutrition*, Vol. 125, No. 8S; August 1995.

LIFE IN OVERDRIVE

Doctors say huge numbers of kids and adults have attention deficit disorder. Is it for real?

CLAUDIA WALLIS

USTY NASH, AN ANGELIC-looking blond child of seven, awoke at 5 one recent morning in his Chicago home and proceeded to throw a fit. He wailed. He kicked. Every muscle in his 50-lb. body flew in furious motion. Finally, after about 30 minutes, Dusty pulled himself together sufficiently to head downstairs for breakfast. While his mother bustled about the kitchen, the hyperkinetic child pulled a box of Kix cereal from the cupboard and sat on a chair.

But sitting still was not in the cards this morning. After grabbing some cereal with his hands, he began kicking the box, scattering little round corn puffs across the room. Next he turned his attention to the TV set, or rather, the table supporting it. The table was covered with a checkerboard Con-Tact paper, and Dusty began peeling it off. Then he became intrigued with the spilled cereal and started stomping it to bits. At this point his mother interceded. In a firm but calm voice she told her son to get the stand-up dust pan and broom and clean up the mess. Dusty got out the dust pan but forgot the rest of the order. Within seconds he was dismantling the plastic dust pan, piece by piece. His next project: grabbing three rolls of toilet paper from the bathroom and unraveling them around the house.

It was only 7:30, and his mother Kyle Nash, who teaches a medical-school course on death and dying, was already feeling half dead from exhaustion. Dusty was to see his doctors that day at 4, and they had asked her not to give the boy the drug he usually takes to control his hyperactivity and attention problems, a condition known as attention deficit hyperactivity disorder (ADHD). It was going to be a very long day without help from Ritalin.

Karenne Bloomgarden remembers such days all too well. The peppy, 43-year-old entrepreneur and gym teacher was a disaster as a child growing up in New Jersey. "I did very poorly in school," she recalls. Her teachers and parents were constantly on her case for rowdy behavior. "They just felt I was being bad—too loud, too physical, too everything." A rebellious tomboy with few friends, she saw a psychologist at age 10, "but nobody came up with a diagnosis." As a teenager she began prescribing her own medication: marijuana, Valium and, later, cocaine.

The athletic Bloomgarden managed to get into college, but she admits that she cheated her way to a diploma. "I would study and study, and I wouldn't remember a thing. I really felt it was my fault." After graduating, she did fine in physically active jobs but was flustered with administrative work. Then, four years ago, a doctor put a label on her troubles: ADHD. "It's been such a weight off my shoulders," says Bloomgarden, who takes both the stimulant Ritalin and the antidepressant Zoloft to improve her concentration. "I had 38 years of thinking I was a bad person. Now I'm rewriting the tapes of who I thought I was to who I really am."

Fifteen years ago, no one had ever heard of attention deficit hyperactivity disorder. Today it is the most common behavioral disorder in American children, the subject of thousands of studies and symposiums and no small degree of controversy. Experts on ADHD say it afflicts as many as 3½ million American youngsters, or up to 5% of those under 18. It is two to three times as likely to be diagnosed in boys as in girls. The disorder has replaced what used to be popularly called "hyperactivity," and it includes a broader collection of symptoms. ADHD has three main hallmarks: extreme distractibility, an almost reckless impulsiveness and, in some but not all cases, a knee-jiggling, toe-tapping hyperactivity that makes sitting still all but impossible. (Without hyperactivity, the disorder is called attention deficit disorder, or ADD.)

For children with ADHD, a ticking clock or sounds and sights caught through a window can drown out a teacher's voice, although an intriguing project can absorb them for hours. Such children act before thinking; they blurt out answers in class. They enrage peers with an inability to wait their turn or play by the rules. These are the kids no one wants at a birthday party.

Ten years ago, doctors believed that the symptoms of ADHD faded with maturity. Now it is one of the fastest-growing diagnostic categories for adults. One-third to two-thirds of ADHD kids continue to have symptoms as adults, says psychiatrist Paul Wender, director of the adult ADHD clinic at the University of Utah School of Medicine. Many adults respond to the diagnosis with relief—a sense that "at last my problem has a name and it's not my fault." As more people are diagnosed, the use of Ritalin (or its generic equivalent, methylphenidate), the drug of choice for ADHD, has surged: prescriptions are up more than 390% in just four years.

As the numbers have grown, ADHD awareness has become an industry, a passion, an almost messianic movement. An advocacy and support group called CHADD (Children and Adults with Attention Deficit Disorders) has exploded from its founding in 1987 to 28,000 members in 48 states. Information bulletin boards and support groups for adults have sprung up on CompuServe, Prodigy and America Online. Numerous popular books have been published on the subject. There are summer camps designed to help ADHD kids, videos and children's books with titles like *Jumpin' Johnny Get Back to Work!* and, of course, therapists, tutors and workshops offering their services to the increasingly self-aware ADHD community.

IT IS A COMMUNITY THAT VIEWS ITSELF with some pride. Popular books and lectures about ADHD often point out positive aspects of the condition. Adults see themselves as creative; their impulsiveness can be viewed as spontaneity; hyperactivity gives them enormous energy and drive; even their distractibility has the virtue of making them alert to changes in the environment. "Kids with ADHD are wild, funny, effervescent. They have a love of life. The rest of us sometimes envy them," says psychologist Russell Barkley of the University of Massachusetts Medical Center. "ADHD adults," he notes, "can be incredibly successful. Sometimes being impulsive means being decisive." Many ADHD adults gravitate into creative fields or work that provides an outlet for emotions, says Barkley. "In our clinic we saw an adult poet who couldn't write poetry when she was on Ritalin. ADHD people make good salespeople. They're lousy at desk jobs."

In an attempt to promote the positive side of ADHD, some CHADD chapters circulate lists of illustrious figures who, they contend, probably suffered from the disorder: the messy and disorganized Ben Franklin, the wildly impulsive and distractible Winston Churchill. For reasons that are less clear, these lists also include folks like Socrates, Isaac Newton, Leonardo da Vinci—almost any genius of note. (At least two doctors interviewed for this story suggested that the sometimes scattered Bill Clinton belongs on the list.)

However creative they may be, people with ADHD don't function particularly well in standard schools and typical office jobs. Increasingly, parents and lobby groups are demanding that accommodations be made. About half the kids diagnosed with ADHD receive help from special-education teachers in their schools, in some cases because they also have other learning disabilities. Where schools have failed to provide services, parents have sometimes sued. In one notable case that went to the U.S. Supreme Court last year, parents argued—successfully—that since the public school denied their child special education, the district must pay for her to attend private school. Another accommodation requested with increasing frequency: permission to take college-entrance exams without a time limit. Part of what motivates parents to fight for special services is frightening research showing that without proper care, kids with ADHD have an extremely high risk not only of failing at school but also of becoming drug abusers, alcoholics and lawbreakers.

Adults with ADHD are beginning to seek special treatment. Under the 1990 Americans with Disabilities Act, they can insist upon help in the workplace. Usually the interventions are quite modest: an office door or white-noise machine to reduce distractions, or longer deadlines on assignments. Another legal trend that concerns even ADHD advocates: the disorder is being raised as a defense in criminal cases. Psychologist Barkley says he knows of 55 such instances in the U.S., all in the past 10 years. ADHD was cited as a mitigating factor by the attorney for Michael Fay, the 19-year-old American who was charged with vandalism and caned in Singapore.

Many of those who treat ADHD see the recognition of the problem as a humane breakthrough: finally we will stop blaming kids for behavior they cannot control. But some are worried that the disorder is being embraced with too much gusto. "A lot of people are jumping on the bandwagon," complains psychologist Mark Stein, director of a special ADHD clinic at the University of Chicago. "Parents are putting pressure on health professionals to make the diagnosis." The allure of ADHD is that it is "a label of forgiveness," says Robert Reid, an assistant professor in the department of special education at the University of Nebraska in Lincoln. "The kid's problems are not his parents' fault, not the teacher's fault, not the kid's fault. It's better to say this kid has ADHD than to say this kid drives everybody up the wall." For adults, the diagnosis may provide an excuse for personal or professional failures, observes Richard Bromfield, a psychologist at Harvard Medical School. "Some people like to say, 'The biological devil made me do it.'"

A DISORDER WITH A PAST Other than the name itself, there is nothing new about this suddenly ubiquitous disorder. The world has always had its share of obstreperous kids, and it has generally treated them as behavior problems rather than patients. Most of the world still does so: European nations like France and England report one-tenth the U.S. rate of ADHD. In Japan the disorder has barely been studied.

The medical record on ADHD is said to have begun in 1902, when British pediatrician George Still published an account of 20 children in his practice who were "passionate," defiant, spiteful and lacking "inhibitory volition." Still made the then radical suggestion that bad parenting was not to blame; instead he suspected a subtle brain injury. This theory gained greater credence in the years following the 1917-18 epidemic of viral encephalitis, when doctors observed that the infection left some children with impaired attention, memory and control over their impulses. In the 1940s and '50s, the same constellation of symptoms was called minimal brain damage and, later, minimal brain dysfunction. In 1937 a Rhode Island pediatrician reported that giving stimulants called amphetamines to children with these symptoms had the unexpected effect of calming them down. By the mid-1970s, Ritalin had become the most prescribed drug for what was eventually termed, in 1987, attention deficit hyperactivity disorder.

Nobody fully understands how Ritalin and other stimulants work, nor do doctors have a very precise picture of the physiology of ADHD. Researchers generally suspect a defect in the frontal lobes of the brain, which regulate behavior. This region is rich in the neurotransmitters dopamine and norepinephrine, which are influenced by drugs like Ritalin. But the lack of a more specific explanation has led some psychologists to question whether ADHD is truly a disorder at all or merely a set of characteristics that tend to cluster together. Just because something responds to a drug doesn't mean it is a sickness.

ADHD researchers counter the skeptics by pointing to a growing body of biological clues. For instance, several studies have found that people with ADHD have decreased blood flow and lower levels of electrical activity in the frontal lobes than normal adults and children. In 1990 Dr. Alan Zametkin at the National Institute of Mental Health found that in PET scans, adults with ADD showed slightly lower rates of metabolism in areas of the brain's cortex known to be involved in the control of attention, impulses and motor activity.

Zametkin's study was hailed as the long-awaited proof of the biological basis of ADD, though Zametkin himself is quite cautious. A newer study used another tool—magnetic resonance imaging—to compare the brains of 18 ADHD boys with those of other children and found several "very subtle" but "striking" anatomical differences, says co-author Judith Rapoport, chief of the child psychiatry branch at NIMH. Says Zametkin: "I'm absolutely convinced that this disorder has a biological basis, but just what it is we cannot yet say."

WHAT RESEARCHERS DO say with great certainty is that the condition is inherited. External factors such as birth injuries and maternal alcohol or tobacco consumption may play a role in less than 10% of cases. Suspicions that a diet high in sugar might cause hyperactivity have been discounted. But the influence of genes is unmistakable. Barkley estimates that 40% of adhd kids have a parent who has the trait and 35% have a sibling with the problem; if the sibling is an identical twin, the chances rise to between 80% and 92%.

Interest in the genetics of ADHD is enormous. In Australia a vast trial involving 3,400 pairs of twins between the ages of 4 and 12 is examining the incidence of ADHD and other behavioral difficulties. At NIMH,

Zametkin's group is recruiting 200 families who have at least two members with ADHD. The hope: to identify genes for the disorder. It is worth noting, though, that even if such genes are found, this may not settle the debate about ADHD. After all, it is just as likely that researchers will someday discover a gene for a hot temper, which also runs in families. But that doesn't mean that having a short fuse is a disease requiring medical intervention.

TRICKY DIAGNOSIS In the absence of any biological test, diagnosing ADHD is a rather inexact proposition. In most cases, it is a teacher who initiates the process by informing parents that their child is daydreaming in class, failing to complete assignments or driving everyone crazy with thoughtless behavior. "The problem is that the parent then goes to the family doctor, who writes a prescription for Ritalin and doesn't stop to think of the other possibilities," says child psychiatrist Larry Silver of Georgetown University Medical Center. To make a careful diagnosis, Silver argues, one must eliminate other explanations for the symptoms.

The most common cause, he points out, is anxiety. A child who is worried about a problem at home or some other matter "can look hyperactive and distractible." Depression can also cause ADHD-like behavior. "A third cause is another form of neurological dysfunction, like a learning disorder," says Silver. "The child starts doodling because he didn't understand the teacher's instructions." All this is made more complicated by the fact that some kids—and adults—with ADHD also suffer from depression and other problems. To distinguish these symptoms from ADHD, doctors usually rely on interviews with parents and teachers, behavior-ratings scales and psychological tests, which can cost from $500 to $3,000, depending on the thoroughness of the testing. Insurance coverage is spotty.

Among the most important clues doctors look for is whether the child's problems can be linked to some specific experience or time or whether they have been present almost from birth. "You don't suddenly get ADD," says Wade Horn, a child psychologist and former executive director of CHADD. Taking a careful history is therefore vital.

For kids who are hyperactive, the pattern is unmistakable, says Dr. Bruce Roseman, a pediatric neurologist with several offices in the New York City area, who has ADHD himself. "You say to the mother, 'What kind of personality did the child have as a baby? Was he active, alert? Was he colicky?' She'll say, 'He wouldn't stop—waaah, waaah, waaah!' You ask, 'When did he start to walk?' One mother said to me, 'Walk? My son didn't walk. He got his pilot's license at one year of age. His feet haven't touched the ground since.' You ask, 'Mrs. Smith, how about the terrible twos?' She'll start to cry, 'You mean the terrible twos, threes, fours, the awful fives, the horrendous sixes, the God-awful eights, the divorced nines, the I-want-to-die tens!' "

Diagnosing those with ADD without hyperactivity can be trickier. Such kids are often described as daydreamers, space cases. They are not disruptive or antsy. But, says Roseman, "they sit in front of a book and for 45 minutes, nothing happens." Many girls with ADD fit this model; they are often misunderstood or overlooked.

Christy Rade, who will be entering the ninth grade in West Des Moines, Iowa, is fairly typical. Before she was diagnosed with ADD in the third grade, Christy's teacher described her to her parents as a "dizzy blond and a space cadet." "Teachers used to get fed up with me," recalls Christy, who now takes Ritalin and gets some extra support from her teachers. "Everyone thought I was purposely not paying attention." According to her mother Julie Doy, people at Christy's school were familiar with hyperactivity but not ADD. "She didn't have behavior problems. She was the kind of kid who could fall through the cracks, and did."

Most experts say ADHD is a lifelong condition but by late adolescence many people can compensate for their impulsiveness and disorganization. They may channel hyperactivity into sports. In other cases, the symptoms still wreak havoc, says UCLA psychiatrist Walid Shekim. "Patients cannot settle on a career. They cannot keep a job. They procrastinate a lot. They are the kind of people who would tell their boss to take this job and shove it before they've found another job."

Doctors diagnose adults with methods similar to those used with children. Patients are sometimes asked to dig up old report cards for clues to their childhood behavior—an essential indicator. Many adults seek help only after one of their children is diagnosed. Such was the case with Chuck Pearson of Birmingham, Michigan, who was diagnosed three years ago, at 54. Pearson had struggled for decades in what might be the worst possible career for someone with ADD: accounting. In the first 12 years of his marriage, he was fired from 15 jobs. "I was frightened," says Zoe, his wife of 35 years. "We had two small children, a mortgage. Bill collectors were calling perpetually. We almost lost the house." Chuck admits he had trouble focusing on details, completing tasks and judging how long an assignment would take. He was so distracted behind the wheel that he lost his license for a year after getting 14 traffic tickets. Unwittingly, Pearson began medicating himself: "In my mid-30s, I would drink 30 to 40 cups of coffee a day. The caffeine helped." After he was diagnosed, the Pearsons founded the Adult Attention Deficit Foundation, a clearinghouse for information about ADD; he hopes to spare others some of his own regret: "I had a deep and abiding sadness over the life I could have given my family if I had been treated effectively."

PERSONALITY OR PATHOLOGY? While Chuck Pearson's problems were extreme, many if not all adults have trouble at times sticking with boring tasks, setting priorities and keeping their minds on what they are doing. The furious pace of society, the strain on families, the lack of community support can make anyone feel beset by ADD. "I personally think we are living in a society that is so out of control that we say, 'Give me a stimulant so I can cope.'" says Charlotte Tomaino, a clinical neuropsychologist in White Plains, New York. As word of ADHD spreads, swarms of adults are seeking the diagnosis as an explanation for their troubles. "So many really have symptoms that began in adulthood and reflected depression or other problems," says psychiatrist Silver. In their best-selling new book, *Driven to Distraction*, Edward Hallowell and John Ratey suggest that American life is "ADD-ogenic": "American society tends to create ADD-like symptoms in us all. The fast pace. The sound bite. The quick cuts. The TV remote-control clicker. It is important to keep this in mind, or you may start thinking that everybody you know has ADD."

And that is the conundrum. How do you draw the line between a spontaneous, high-energy person who is feeling overwhelmed by the details of life and someone afflicted with a neurological disorder? Where is the boundary between personality and pathology? Even an expert in the field like the University of Chicago's Mark Stein admits, "We need to find more precise ways of diagnosing it than just saying you have these symptoms." Barkley also concedes the vagueness. The traits that constitute ADHD "are personality characteristics," he agrees. But it becomes pathology, he says, when the traits are so extreme that they interfere with people's lives.

THE RISKS There is no question that ADHD can disrupt lives. Kids with the disorder frequently have few friends. Their parents may be ostracized by neighbors and relatives, who blame them for failing to control the child. "I've got criticism of my parenting skills from strangers," says the mother of a hyperactive boy in New Jersey. "When you're out in public, you're always on guard. Whenever I'd hear a child cry, I'd turn to see if it was because of Jeremy."

School can be a shattering experience for such kids. Frequently reprimanded and

HAIL TO THE HYPERACTIVE HUNTER

Why is attention deficit hyperactivity disorder so common? Is there an evolutionary reason why these traits are found in as many as 1 in 20 American youngsters? Such questions have prompted intriguing speculation. Harvard psychiatrist John Ratey finds no mystery in the prevalence of ADHD in the U.S. It is a nation of immigrants who, he notes, "risked it all and left their homelands." Characteristics like impulsiveness, high energy and risk taking are therefore highly represented in the U.S. gene pool. "We have more Nobel laureates and more criminals than anywhere else in the world. We have more people who absolutely push the envelope."

But why would ADHD have evolved in the first place? perhaps, like the sickle-cell trait, which can help thwart malaria, attention deficit confers an advantage in certain circumstances. In *Attention Deficit Disorder: A Different Perception*, author Thom Hartmann has laid out a controversial but appealing theory that the characteristics known today as ADHD were vitally important in early hunting societies. They became a mixed blessing only when human societies turned agrarian, Hartmann suggests. "If you are walking in the night and see a little flash, distractibility would be a tremendous asset. Snap decision making, which we call impulsiveness, is a survival skill if you are a hunter." For a farmer, however, such traits can be disastrous. "If this is the perfect day to plant the crops, you can't suddenly decided to wander off into the woods."

Modern society, Hartmann contends, generally favors the farmer mentality, rewarding those who develop plans, meet deadlines and plod through schedules. But there's still a place for hunters, says the author, who counts himself as one: they can be found in large numbers among entrepreneurs, police detectives, emergency-room personnel, race-care drivers and, of course, those who stalk the high-stakes jungle known as Wall Street.

of arrest histories. And yet, despite decades of research, no one is certain exactly what the optimal intervention should be.

TREATMENT The best-known therapy for ADHD remains stimulant drugs. Though Ritalin is the most popular choice, some patients do better with Dexedrine or Cylert or even certain antidepressants. About 70% of kids respond to stimulants. In the correct dosage, these uppers surprisingly "make people slow down," says Swanson. "They make you focus your attention and apply more effort to whatever you're supposed to do." Ritalin kicks in within 30 minutes to an hour after being taken, but its effects last only about three hours. Most kids take a dose at breakfast and another at lunchtime to get them through a school day.

When drug therapy works, says Utah's Wender, "it is one of the most dramatic effects in psychiatry." Roseman tells how one first-grader came into his office after trying Ritalin and announced, "I know how it works." "You do?" asked the doctor. "Yes," the child replied. "It cleaned out my ears. Now I can hear the teacher." A third-grader told Roseman that Ritalin had enabled him to play basketball. "Now when I get the ball, I turn around, I go down to the end of the room, and if I look up, there's a net there. I never used to see the net, because there was too much screaming."

For adults, the results can be just as striking. "Helen," a 43-year-old mother of three in northern Virginia, began taking the drug after being diagnosed with ADD in 1983. "The very first day, I noticed a difference," she marvels. For the first time ever, "I was able to sit down and listen to what my husband had done at work. Shortly after, I was able to sit in bed and read while my husband watched TV."

Given such outcomes, doctors can be tempted to throw a little Ritalin at any problem. Some even use it as a diagnostic tool, believing—wrongly—that if the child's concentration improves with Ritalin, then

tuned out, they lose any sense of self-worth and fall ever further behind in their work. More than a quarter are held back a grade; about a third fail to graduate from high school. ADHD kids are also prone to accidents, says neurologist Roseman. "These are the kids I'm going to see in the emergency room this summer. They rode their bicycle right into the street and didn't look. They jumped off the deck and forgot it was high."

But the psychological injuries are often greater. By ages five to seven, says Barkley, half to two-thirds are hostile and defiant. By ages 10 to 12, they run the risk of developing what psychologists call "conduct disorder"—lying, stealing, running away from home and ultimately getting into trouble

with the law. As adults, says Barkley, 25% to 30% will experience substance-abuse problems, mostly with depressants like marijuana and alcohol. One study of hyperactive boys found that 40% had been arrested at least once by age 18—and these were kids who had been treated with stimulant medication; among those who had been treated with the drug plus other measures, the rate was 20%—still very high.

It is an article of faith among ADHD researchers that the right interventions can prevent such dreadful outcomes. "If you can have an impact with these kids, you can change whether they go to jail or to Harvard Law School," says psychologist James Swanson at the University of California at Irvine, who co-authored the study

---

DO YOU HAVE ATTENTION DEFICIT?

If eight or more of the following statements accurately describe your child or yourself as a child, particularly before age 7, there may be reason to suspect ADHD. A definitive diagnosis requires further examination.

1. Often fidgets or squirms in seat.

2. Has difficulty remaining seated.

3. Is easily distracted.

4. Has difficulty awaiting turn in groups.

5. Often blurts out answers to questions.

6. Has difficulty following instructions.

7. Has difficulty sustaining attention to tasks.

8. Often shifts from one

uncompleted activity to another.

9. Has difficulty playing quietly.

10. Often talks excessively.

11. Often interrupts or intrudes on others.

12. Often does not seem to listen.

13. Often loses things necessary for tasks.

14. Often engages in physically dangerous activities without considering consequences.

Source: *The ADHD Rating Scale: Normative Data, Reliability, and Validity.*

he or she must have ADD. In fact, you don't have to have an attention problem to get a boost from Ritalin. By the late 1980s, overprescription became a big issue, raised in large measure by the Church of Scientology, which opposes psychiatry in general and launched a vigorous campaign against Ritalin. After a brief decline fostered by the scare, the drug is now hot once again. Swanson has heard of some classrooms where 20% to 30% of the boys are on Ritalin. "That's just ridiculous!" he says.

Ritalin use varies from state to state, town to town, depending largely on the attitude of the doctors and local schools. Idaho is the No. 1 consumer of the drug. A study of Ritalin consumption in Michigan, which ranks just behind Idaho, found that use ranged from less than 1% of boys in one county to as high as 10% in another, with no correlation to affluence.

Patients who are taking Ritalin must be closely monitored, since the drug can cause loss of appetite, insomnia and occasionally tics. Doctors often recommend "drug holidays" during school vacations. Medication is frequently combined with other treatments, including psychotherapy, special education and cognitive training, although the benefits of such expensive measures are unclear. "We really haven't known which treatment to use for which child and how to combine treatments," says Dr. Peter Jensen, chief of NIMH's Child and Adolescent Disorders Research Branch. His group has embarked on a study involving 600 children in six cities. By 1998 they hope to have learned how medication alone compares to medication with psychological intervention and other approaches.

BEYOND DRUGS A rough consensus has emerged among ADHD specialists that whether or not drugs are used, it is best to teach kids—often through behavior modification—how to gain more control over their impulses and restless energy. Also recommended is training in the fine art of being organized: establishing a predictable schedule of activities, learning to use a date book, assigning a location for possessions at school and at home. This takes considerable effort on the part of teachers and parents as well as the kids themselves. Praise, most agree, is vitally important.

Within the classroom "some simple, practical things work well," says Reid. Let hyperactive kids move around. Give them stand-up desks, for instance. "I've seen kids who from the chest up were very diligently working on a math problem, but from the chest down, they're dancing like Fred Astaire." To minimize distractions, ADHD kids should sit very close to the teacher and be permitted to take important tests in a quiet area. "Unfortunately," Reid observes, "not many teachers are trained in

behavior management. It is a historic shortfall in American education."

In Irvine, California, James Swanson has tried to create the ideal setting for teaching kids with ADHD. The Child Development Center, an elementary school that serves 45 kids with the disorder, is a kind of experiment in progress. The emphasis is on behavior modification: throughout the day students earn points—and are relentlessly cheered on—for good behavior. High scorers are rewarded with special privileges at the end of the day, but each morning kids start afresh with another shot at the rewards. Special classes also drill in social skills: sharing, being a good sport, ignoring annoyances rather than striking out in anger. Only 35% of the kids at the center are on stimulant drugs, less than half the national rate for ADHD kids.

Elsewhere around the country, enterprising parents have struggled to find their own answers to attention deficit. Bonnie and Neil Fell of Skokie, Illinois, have three sons, all of whom have been diagnosed with ADD. They have "required more structure and consistency than other kids," says Bonnie. "We had to break down activities into clear time slots." To help their sons, who take Ritalin, the Fells have employed tutors, psychotherapists and a speech and language specialist. None of this comes cheap: they estimate their current annual ADD-related expenses at $15,000. "Our goal is to get them through school with their self-esteem intact," says Bonnie.

The efforts seem to be paying off. Dan, the eldest at 15, has become an outgoing A student, a wrestling star and a writer for the school paper. "ADD gives you energy and creativity," he says. "I've learned to cope. I've become strong." On the other hand, he is acutely aware of his disability. "What people don't realize is that I have to work harder than everyone else. I start studying for finals a month before other people do."

COPING Adults can also train themselves to compensate for ADHD. Therapists working with them typically emphasize organizational skills, time management, stress reduction and ways to monitor their own distractibility and stay focused.

IN HER OFFICE IN WHITE PLAINS, Tomaino has a miniature Zen garden, a meditative sculpture and all sorts of other items to help tense patients relax. Since many people with ADHD also have learning disabilities, she tests each patient and then often uses computer programs to strengthen weak areas. But most important is helping people define their goals and take orderly steps to reach them. Whether working with a stockbroker or a homemaker, she says, "I teach adults basic

rewards and goals. For instance, you can't go out to lunch until you've cleaned the kitchen."

Tomaino tells of one very hyperactive and articulate young man who got all the way through college without incident, thanks in good measure to a large and tolerant extended family. Then he flunked out of law school three times. Diagnosed with ADHD, the patient took stock of his goals and decided to enter the family restaurant business, where, Tomaino says, he is a raging success. "ADHD was a deficit if he wanted to be a lawyer, but it's an advantage in the restaurant business. He gets to go around to meet and greet."

For neurologist Roseman, the same thing is true. With 11 offices in four states, he is perpetually on the go. "I'm at rest in motion," says the doctor. "I surround myself with partners who provide the structure. My practice allows me to be creative." Roseman has accountants to do the bookkeeping. He starts his day at 6:30 with a hike and doesn't slow down until midnight. "Thank God for my ADD," he says. But, he admits, "had I listened to all the negative things that people said when I was growing up, I'd probably be digging ditches in Idaho."

LESSONS Whether ADHD is a brain disorder or simply a personality type, the degree to which it is a handicap depends not only on the severity of the traits but also on one's environment. The right school, job or home situation can make all the difference. The lessons of ADHD are truisms. All kids do not learn in the same way. Nor are all adults suitable for the same line of work.

Unfortunately, American society seems to have evolved into a one-size-fits-all system. Schools can resemble factories: put the kids on the assembly line, plug in the right components and send 'em out the door. Everyone is supposed to go to college; there is virtually no other route to success. In other times and in other places, there have been alternatives: apprenticeships, settling a new land, starting a business out of the garage, going to sea. In a conformist society, it becomes necessary to medicate some people to make them fit in.

This is not to deny that some people genuinely need Ritalin, just as others need tranquilizers or insulin. But surely an epidemic of attention deficit disorder is a warning to us all. Children need individual supervision. Many of them need more structure than the average helter-skelter household provides. They need a more consistent approach to discipline and schools that tailor teaching to their individual learning styles. Adults too could use a society that's more flexible in its expectations, more accommodating to differences. Most of all, we all need to slow down. And pay attention. —*With reporting by* **Hannah Bloch/New York, Wendy Cole/Chicago and James Willwerth/Irvine**

The EQ Factor

New brain research suggests that emotions, not IQ, may be the true measure of human intelligence

NANCY GIBBS

I
T TURNS OUT THAT A SCIENTIST can see the future by watching four-year-olds interact with a marshmallow. The researcher invites the children, one by one, into a plain room and begins the gentle torment. You can have this marshmallow right now, he says. But if you wait while I run an errand, you can have two marshmallows when I get back. And then he leaves.

Some children grab for the treat the minute he's out the door. Some last a few minutes before they give in. But others are determined to wait. They cover their eyes; they put their heads down; they sing to themselves; they try to play games or even fall asleep. When the researcher returns, he gives these children their hard-earned marshmallows. And then, science waits for them to grow up.

By the time the children reach high school, something remarkable has happened. A survey of the children's parents and teachers found that those who as four-year-olds had the fortitude to hold out for the second marshmallow generally grew up to be better adjusted, more popular, adventurous, confident and dependable teenagers. The children who gave in to temptation early on were more likely to be lonely, easily frustrated and stubborn. They buckled under stress and shied away from challenges. And when some of the students in the two groups took the Scholastic Aptitude Test, the kids who had held out longer scored an average of 210 points higher.

When we think of brilliance we see Einstein, deep-eyed, woolly haired, a thinking machine with skin and mismatched socks. High achievers, we imagine, were wired for greatness from birth. But then you have to wonder why, over time, natural talent seems to ignite in some people and dim in others. This is where the marshmallows come in. It seems that the ability to delay gratification is a master skill, a triumph of the reasoning brain over the impulsive one. It is a sign, in short, of emotional intelligence. And it doesn't show up on an IQ test.

For most of this century, scientists have worshipped the hardware of the brain and the software of the mind; the messy powers of the heart were left to the poets. But cognitive theory could simply not explain the questions we wonder about most: why some people just seem to have a gift for living well; why the smartest kid in the class will probably not end up the richest; why we like some people virtually on sight and distrust others; why some people remain buoyant in the face of troubles that would sink a less resilient soul. What qualities of the mind or spirit, in short, determine who succeeds?

The phrase "emotional intelligence" was coined by Yale psychologist Peter Salovey and the University of New Hampshire's John Mayer five years ago to describe qualities like understanding one's own feelings, empathy for the feelings of others and "the regulation of emotion in a way that enhances living." Their notion is about to bound into the national conversation, handily shortened to EQ, thanks to a new book, *Emotional Intelligence* (Bantam; $23.95) by Daniel Goleman. Goleman, a Harvard psychology Ph.D. and a New York *Times* science writer with a gift for making even the chewiest scientific theories digestible to lay readers, has brought together a decade's worth of behavioral research into how the mind processes feelings. His goal, he announces on the cover, is to redefine what it means to be smart. His thesis: when it comes to predicting people's success, brainpower as measured by IQ and standardized achievement tests may actually matter less than the qualities of mind once thought of as "character" before the word began to sound quaint.

At first glance, there would seem to be little that's new here to any close reader of fortune cookies. There may be no less original idea than the notion that our hearts hold dominion over our heads. "I was so angry," we say, "I couldn't think straight." Neither is it surprising that "people skills" are useful, which amounts to saying, it's good to be nice. "It's so true it's trivial," says Dr. Paul McHugh, director of psychiatry at Johns Hopkins University School of Medicine. But if it were that simple, the book would not be quite so interesting or its implications so controversial.

This is no abstract investigation. Goleman is looking for antidotes to restore "civility to our streets and caring to our communal life." He sees practical applications everywhere for how companies should decide whom to hire, how couples can increase the odds that their marriages will last, how parents should raise their children and how schools should teach them. When street gangs substitute for families and schoolyard insults end in stabbings, when more than half of marriages end in divorce, when the majority of the children murdered in this country are killed by parents and stepparents, many of whom say they were trying to discipline the child for behavior like blocking the TV or crying too much, it suggests a demand for remedial emotional education. While children are still young, Goleman argues, there is a "neurological window of opportunity" since the brain's prefrontal circuitry, which regulates how we act on what we feel, probably does not mature until mid-adolescence.

And it is here the arguments will break out. Goleman's highly popularized conclusions, says McHugh, "will chill any veteran scholar of psychotherapy and any neuroscientist who worries about how his research may come to be applied." While many researchers in this relatively new field are glad to see emotional issues finally taken seriously, they fear that a notion as handy as EQ invites misuse. Goleman admits the danger of suggesting that you can assign a numerical yardstick to a person's character as well as his intellect; Goleman never even uses the phrase EQ in his book. But he (begrudgingly) approved an "unscientific" EQ test in *USA Today* with choices like "I am aware of even subtle feelings as I have them," and "I can sense the pulse of a group or relationship and state unspoken feelings."

"You don't want to take an average of your emotional skill," argues Harvard psychology professor Jerome Kagan, a pioneer in child-development research. "That's what's wrong with the concept of intelligence for mental skills too. Some people handle anger well but can't handle fear. Some people can't take joy. So each emotion has to be viewed differently."

EQ is not the opposite of IQ. Some people are blessed with a lot of both, some with little of either. What researchers have been trying to understand is how they complement each other; how one's ability to handle stress, for instance, affects the ability to concentrate and put intelligence to use. Among the ingredients for success, researchers now generally agree that IQ counts for about 20%; the rest depends on everything from class to luck to the neural pathways that have developed in the brain over millions of years of human evolution.

It is actually the neuroscientists and evolutionists who do the best job of explaining the reasons behind the most unreasonable behavior. In the past decade or so, scientists have learned enough about the brain to make judgments about where emotion comes from and why we need it. Primitive emotional responses held the keys to survival: fear drives the blood into the large muscles, making it easier to run; surprise triggers the eyebrows to rise, allowing the eyes to widen their view and gather more information about an unexpected event. Disgust wrinkles up the face and closes the nostrils to keep out foul smells.

Emotional life grows out of an area of the brain called the limbic system, specifically the amygdala, whence come delight and disgust and fear and anger. Millions of years ago, the neocortex was added on, enabling humans to plan, learn and remember. Lust grows from the limbic system; love, from the neocortex. Animals like reptiles that have no neocortex cannot experience anything like maternal love; this is why baby snakes have to hide to avoid being eaten by their parents. Humans, with their capacity for love, will protect their offspring, allowing the brains of the young time to develop. The more connections between limbic system and the neocortex, the more emotional responses are possible.

It was scientists like Joseph LeDoux of New York University who uncovered these cerebral pathways. LeDoux's parents owned a meat market. As a boy in Louisiana, he first learned about his future specialty by cutting up cows' brains for sweetbreads. "I found them the most interesting part of the cow's anatomy," he recalls. "They were visually pleasing—lots of folds, convolutions and patterns. The cerebellum was more interesting to look at than steak." The butchers' son became a neuroscientist, and it was he who discovered the short circuit in the brain that lets emotions drive action before the intellect gets a chance to intervene.

A hiker on a mountain path, for example, sees a long, curved shape in the grass out of the corner of his eye. He leaps out of the way before he realizes it is only a stick that looks like a snake. Then he calms down; his cortex gets the message a few milliseconds after his amygdala and "regulates" its primitive response.

Without these emotional reflexes, rarely conscious but often terribly powerful, we would scarcely be able to function. "Most decisions we make have a vast number of possible outcomes, and any attempt to analyze all of them would never end," says University of Iowa neurologist Antonio Damasio, author of *Descartes' Error: Emotion, Reason and the Human Brain.* "I'd ask you to lunch tomorrow, and when the appointed time arrived, you'd still be thinking about whether you should come." What tips the balance, Damasio contends, is our unconscious assigning of emotional values to some of those choices. Whether we experience a somatic response—a gut feeling of dread or a giddy sense of elation—emotions are helping to limit the field in any choice we have to make. If the prospect of lunch with a neurologist is unnerving or distasteful, Damasio suggests, the invitee will conveniently remember a previous engagement.

When Damasio worked with patients in whom the connection between emotional brain and neocortex had been severed because of damage to the brain, he discovered how central that hidden pathway is to how we live our lives. People who had lost that linkage were just as smart and quick to reason, but their lives often fell apart nonetheless. They could not make decisions because they didn't know how they felt about their choices. They couldn't react to warnings or anger in other people. If they made a mistake, like a bad investment, they felt no regret or shame and so were bound to repeat it.

If there is a cornerstone to emotional intelligence on which most other emotional skills depend, it is a sense of self-awareness, of being smart about what we feel. A person whose day starts badly at home may be grouchy all day at work without quite knowing why. Once an emotional response comes into awareness—or, physiologically, is processed through the neocortex—the chances of handling it appropriately improve. Scientists refer to "metamood," the ability to pull back and recognize that "what I'm feeling is anger," or sorrow, or shame.

Metamood is a difficult skill because emotions so often appear in disguise. A person in mourning may know he is sad, but he may not recognize that he is also angry at the person for dying—because this seems somehow inappropriate. A parent who yells at the child who ran into the street is expressing anger at disobedience, but the degree of anger may owe more to the fear the parent feels at what could have happened.

In Goleman's analysis, self-awareness is perhaps the most crucial ability because it allows us to exercise some self-control. The idea is not to repress feeling (the reaction that has made psychoanalysts rich) but rather to do what Aristotle considered the hard work of the will. "Anyone can become angry—that is easy," he wrote in the *Nicomachean Ethics.* "But to be angry with the right person, to the right degree, at the right time, for the right purpose, and in the right way—that is not easy."

Some impulses seem to be easier to control than others. Anger, not surprisingly, is one of the hardest, perhaps because of its evolutionary value in priming people to action. Researchers believe anger usually arises out of a sense of being trespassed against—the belief that one is being robbed of what is rightfully his. The body's first response is a surge of energy, the release of a cascade of neurotransmitters called catecholamines. If a person is already aroused or under stress, the threshold for release is lower, which helps explain why people's tempers shorten during a hard day.

Scientists are not only discovering where anger comes from; they are also exposing myths about how best to handle it. Popular wisdom argues for "letting it all hang out" and having a good cathartic rant. But Goleman cites studies showing that dwelling on anger actually increases its power; the body needs a chance to process the adrenaline through exercise, relaxation techniques, a well-timed intervention or even the old admonition to count to 10.

Anxiety serves a similar useful purpose, so long as it doesn't spin out of control. Worrying is a rehearsal for danger; the act of fretting focuses the mind on a problem so it can search efficiently for solutions. The danger comes when worrying blocks thinking, becoming an end in itself or a path to resignation instead of perseverance. Over-worrying about failing increases the likelihood of failure; a salesman so concerned about his falling sales that he can't bring himself to pick up the phone guarantees that his sales will fall even further.

But why are some people better able to "snap out of it" and get on with the task at hand? Again, given sufficient self-awareness, people develop coping mechanisms. Sadness and discouragement, for instance, are "low arousal" states, and the dispirited salesman who goes out for a run is triggering a high arousal state that is incompatible with staying blue. Relaxation works better for high-energy moods like anger or anxiety. Either way, the idea is to shift to a state of arousal that breaks the destructive cycle of the dominant mood.

The idea of being able to predict which salesmen are most likely to prosper was not an abstraction for Metropolitan Life, which in the mid-'80s was hiring 5,000 salespeople a year and training them at a cost of more than $30,000 each. Half quit the first year, and four out of five within four years. The reason: selling life insurance involves having the door slammed in your face over and over again. Was it possible to identify which people would be better at handling frustration and take each refusal as a challenge rather than a setback?

The head of the company approached psychologist Martin Seligman at the University of Pennsylvania and invited him to test some of his theories about the importance of optimism in people's success. When optimists fail, he has found, they attribute the failure to something they can change, not some innate weakness that they are helpless to overcome. And that confidence in their power to effect change is self-reinforcing. Seligman tracked 15,000 new workers who had taken two tests. One was the company's regular screening exam, the other Seligman's test measuring their levels of optimism.

One Way to Test Your EQ

UNLIKE IQ, WHICH IS GAUGED BY THE FAMOUS STANFORD-Binet tests, EQ does not lend itself to any single numerical measure. Nor should it, say experts. Emotional intelligence is by definition a complex, multifaceted quality representing such intangibles as self-awareness, empathy, persistence and social deftness.

Some aspects of emotional intelligence, however, can be quantified. Optimism, for example, is a handy measure of a person's self-worth. According to Martin Seligman, a University of Pennsylvania psychologist, how people respond to setbacks—optimistically or pessimistically—is a fairly accurate indicator of how well they will succeed in school, in sports and in certain kinds of work. To test his theory, Seligman devised a questionnaire to screen insurance salesmen at MetLife.

In Seligman's test, job applicants were asked to imagine a hypothetical event and then choose the response (A or B) that most closely resembled their own. Some samples from his questionnaire:

You forget your spouse's (boyfriend's/girlfriend's) birthday.
A. I'm not good at remembering birthdays.
B. I was preoccupied with other things.

You owe the library $10 for an overdue book.
A. When I am really involved in what I am reading, I often forget when it's due.
B. I was so involved in writing the report, I forgot to return the book.

You lose your temper with a friend.
A. He or she is always nagging me.
B. He or she was in a hostile mood.

You are penalized for returning your income-tax forms late.
A. I always put off doing my taxes.
B. I was lazy about getting my taxes done this year.

You've been feeling run-down.
A. I never get a chance to relax.
B. I was exceptionally busy this week.

A friend says something that hurts your feelings.
A. She always blurts things out without thinking of others.
B. My friend was in a bad mood and took it out on me.

You fall down a great deal while skiing.
A. Skiing is difficult.
B. The trails were icy.

You gain weight over the holidays, and you can't lose it.
A. Diets don't work in the long run.
B. The diet I tried didn't work.

Seligman found that those insurance salesmen who answered with more B's than A's were better able to overcome bad sales days, recovered more easily from rejection and were less likely to quit. People with an optimistic view of life tend to treat obstacles and setbacks as temporary (and therefore surmountable). Pessimists take them personally; what others see as fleeting, localized impediments, they view as pervasive and permanent.

The most dramatic proof of his theory, says Seligman, came at the 1988 Olympic Games in Seoul, South Korea, after U.S. swimmer Matt Biondi turned in two disappointing performances in his first two races. Before the Games, Biondi had been favored to win seven golds—as Mark Spitz had done 16 years earlier. After those first two races, most commentators thought Biondi would be unable to recover from his setback. Not Seligman. He had given some members of the U.S swim team a version of his optimism test before the races; it showed that Biondi possessed an extraordinarily upbeat attitude. Rather than losing heart after turning in a bad time, as others might, Biondi tended to respond by swimming even faster. Sure enough, Biondi bounced right back, winning five gold medals in the next five races.
—*By Alice Park*

Among the new hires was a group who flunked the screening test but scored as "superoptimists" on Seligman's exam. And sure enough, they did the best of all; they outsold the pessimists in the regular group by 21% in the first year and 57% in the second. For years after that, passing Seligman's test was one way to get hired as a MetLife salesperson.

Perhaps the most visible emotional skills, the ones we recognize most readily, are the "people skills" like empathy, graciousness, the ability to read a social situation. Researchers believe that about 90% of emotional communication is nonverbal. Harvard psychologist Robert Rosenthal developed the PONS test (Profile of Nonverbal Sensitivity) to measure people's ability to read emotional cues. He shows subjects a film of a young woman expressing feelings—anger, love, jealousy, gratitude, seduction—edited so that one or another nonverbal cue is blanked out. In some instances the face is visible but not the body, or the woman's eyes are hidden, so that viewers have to judge the feeling by subtle cues. Once again, people with higher PONS scores tend to be more successful in their work and relationships; children who score well are more popular and successful in school, even then their IQs are quite average.

Like other emotional skills, empathy is an innate quality that can be shaped by experience. Infants as young as three months old exhibit empathy when they get upset at the sound of another baby crying. Even very young children learn by imitation; by watching how others act when they see someone in distress, these children acquire a repertoire of sensitive responses. If, on the other hand, the feelings they begin to express are not recognized and reinforced by the adults around them, they not only cease to express those feelings but they also become less able to recognize them in themselves or others.

Empathy too can be seen as a survival skill. Bert Cohler, a University of Chicago psychologist, and Fran Stott, dean of the Erikson Institute for Advanced Study in Child Development in Chicago, have found that children from psychically damaged families frequently become hypervigilant, developing an intense attunement to their parents' moods. One child they studied, Nicholas, had a horrible habit of approaching other kids in his nursery-school class as if he were going to kiss them, then would bite them instead. The scientists went back to study videos of Nicholas at 20 months interacting with his psychotic mother and found that she had responded to his every expression of anger or independence with compulsive kisses. The researchers dubbed them "kisses of death," and their true significance was obvious to Nicholas, who arched his back in horror at

Square Pegs in the Oval Office?

IF A HIGH DEGREE OF EMOTIONAL INTELLIGENCE IS A PREREQUISITE FOR OUTstanding achievement, there ought to be no better place to find it than in the White House. It turns out, however, that not every man who reached the pinnacle of American leadership was a gleaming example of self-awareness, empathy, impulse control and all the other qualities that mark an elevated EQ.

Oliver Wendell Holmes, who knew intelligence when he saw it, judged Franklin Roosevelt "a second-class intellect, but a first-class temperament." Born and educated as an aristocrat, F.D.R. had polio and needed a wheelchair for most of his adult life. Yet, far from becoming a self-pitying wretch, he developed an unbridled optimism that served him and the country well during the Depression and World War II—this despite, or because of, what Princeton professor Fred Greenstein calls Roosevelt's "tendency toward deviousness and duplicity."

Even a first-class temperament, however, is not a sure predictor of a successful presidency. According to Duke University political scientist James David Barber, the most perfect blend of intellect and warmth of personality in a Chief Executive was the brilliant Thomas Jefferson, who "knew the importance of communication and empathy. He never lost the common touch." Richard Ellis, a professor of politics at Oregon's Willamette University who is skeptical of the whole EQ theory, cites two 19th century Presidents who did not fit the mold. "Martin Van Buren was well adjusted, balanced, empathetic and persuasive, but he was not very successful," says Ellis. "Andrew Jackson was less well adjusted, less balanced, less empathetic and was terrible at controlling his own impulses, but he transformed the presidency."

Lyndon Johnson as Senate majority leader was a brilliant practitioner of the art of political persuasion, yet failed utterly to transfer that gift to the White House. In fact, says Princeton's Greenstein, L. B. J. and Richard Nixon would be labeled "worst cases" on any EQ scale of Presidents. Each was touched with political genius, yet each met with disaster. "To some extent," says Greenstein, "this is a function of the extreme aspects of their psyches; they are the political versions of Van Gogh, who does unbelievable paintings and then cuts off his ear."

History professor William Leuchtenburg of the University of North Carolina at Chapel Hill suggests that the 20th century Presidents with perhaps the highest IQs—Wilson, Hoover and Carter—also had the most trouble connecting with their constituents. Woodrow Wilson, he says, "was very high strung [and] arrogant; he was not willing to strike any middle ground. Herbert Hoover was so locked into certain ideas that you could never convince him otherwise. Jimmy Carter is probably the most puzzling of the three. He didn't have a deficiency of temperament; in fact, he was too temperate. There was an excessive rationalization about Carter's approach."

That was never a problem for John Kennedy and Ronald Reagan. Nobody ever accused them of intellectual genius, yet both radiated qualities of leadership with an infectious confidence and openheartedness that endeared them to the nation. Whether President Clinton will be so endeared remains a puzzle. That he is a Rhodes scholar makes him certifiably brainy, but his emotional intelligence is shaky. He obviously has the knack for establishing rapport with people, but he often appears so eager to please that he looks weak. "As for controlling his impulses," says Willamette's Ellis, "Clinton is terrible." —By Jesse Birnbaum.
Reported by James Carney/Washington and Lisa H. Towle/Raleigh

her approaching lips—and passed his own rage on to his classmates years later.

Empathy also acts as a buffer to cruelty, and it is a quality conspicuously lacking in child molesters and psychopaths. Goleman cites some chilling research into brutality by Robert Hare, a psychologist at the University of British Columbia. Hare found that psychopaths, when hooked up to

electrodes and told they are going to receive a shock, show none of the visceral responses that fear of pain typically triggers: rapid heartbeat, sweating and so on. How could the threat of punishment deter such people from committing crimes?

It is easy to draw the obvious lesson from these test results. How much happier would we be, how much more successful as individuals and civil as a society, if we were more alert to the importance of emotional intelligence and more adept at teaching it? From kindergartens to business schools to corporations across the country, people are taking seriously the idea that a little more time spent on the "touchy-feely" skills so often derided may in fact pay rich dividends.

In the corporate world, according to personnel executives, IQ gets you hired, but EQ gets you promoted. Goleman likes to tell of a manager at AT&T's Bell Labs, a think tank for brilliant engineers in New Jersey, who was asked to rank his top performers. They weren't the ones with the highest IQs; they were the ones whose E-mail got answered. Those workers who were good collaborators and networkers and popular with colleagues were more likely to get the cooperation they needed to reach their goals than the socially awkward, lone-wolf geniuses.

When David Campbell and others at the Center for Creative Leadership studied "derailed executives," the rising stars who flamed out, the researchers found that these executives failed most often because of "an interpersonal flaw" rather than a technical inability. Interviews with top executives in the U.S. and Europe turned up nine so-called fatal flaws, many of them classic emotional failings, such as "poor working relations," being "authoritarian" or "too ambitious" and having "conflict with upper management."

At the center's executive-leadership seminars across the country, managers come to get emotionally retooled. "This isn't sensitivity training or Sunday-supplement stuff," says Campbell. "One thing they know when they get through is what other people think of them." And the executives have an incentive to listen. Says Karen Boylston, director of the center's team-leadership group: "Customers are telling businesses, 'I don't care if every member of your staff graduated with honors from Harvard, Stanford and Wharton. I will take my business and go where I am understood and treated with respect.'"

Nowhere is the discussion of emotional intelligence more pressing than in schools, where both the stakes and the opportunities seem greatest. Instead of con-

stant crisis intervention, or declarations of war on drug abuse or teen pregnancy or violence, it is time, Goleman argues, for preventive medicine. "Five years ago, teachers didn't want to think about this," says principal Roberta Kirshbaum of P.S. 75 in New York City. "But when kids are getting killed in high school, we have to deal with it." Five years ago, Kirshbaum's school adopted an emotional literacy program, designed to help children learn to manage anger, frustration, loneliness. Since then, fights at lunchtime have decreased from two or three a day to almost none.

Educators can point to all sorts of data to support this new direction. Students who are depressed or angry literally cannot learn. Children who have trouble being accepted by their classmates are 2 to 8 times as likely to drop out. An inability to distinguish distressing feelings or handle frustration has been linked to eating disorders in girls.

Many school administrators are completely rethinking the weight they have been giving to traditional lessons and standardized tests. Peter Relic, president of the National Association of Independent Schools, would like to junk the SAT completely. "Yes, it may cost a heck of a lot more money to assess someone's EQ rather than using a machine-scored test to measure IQ," he says. "But if we don't, then we're saying that a test score is more important to us than who a child is as a human being. That means an immense loss in terms of human potential because we've defined success too narrowly."

This warm embrace by educators has left some scientists in a bind. On one hand, says Yale psychologist Salovey, "I love the idea that we want to teach people a richer understanding of their emotional life, to help them achieve their goals." But, he adds, "what I would oppose is training conformity to social expectations." The danger is that any campaign to hone emotional skills in children will end up teaching that there is a "right" emotional response for any given situation—laugh at parades, cry at funerals, sit still at church. "You can teach self-control," says Dr. Alvin Poussaint, professor of psychiatry at Harvard Medical School. "You can teach that it's better to talk out your anger and not use violence. But is it good emotional intelligence not to challenge authority?"

SOME PSYCHOLOGISTS GO further and challenge the very idea that emotional skills can or should be taught in any kind of formal, classroom way. Goleman's premise that children can be trained to analyze their feelings strikes Johns Hopkins' McHugh as an effort to reinvent the encounter group: "I consider that an abominable idea, an idea we have seen with adults. That failed, and now he wants to try it with children? Good grief!" He cites the description in Goleman's book of an experimental program at the Nueva Learning Center in San Francisco. In one scene, two fifth-grade boys start to argue over the rules of an exercise, and the teacher breaks in to ask them to talk about what they're feeling. "I appreciate the way you're being assertive in talking with Tucker," she says to one student. "You're not attacking." This strikes McHugh as pure folly. "The author is presuming that someone has the key to the right emotions to be taught to children. We don't even know the right emotions to be taught to adults. Do you really think a child of eight or nine really understands the difference between aggressiveness and assertiveness?"

The problem may be that there is an ingredient missing. Emotional skills, like intellectual ones, are morally neutral. Just as a genius could use his intellect either to cure cancer or engineer a deadly virus, someone with great empathic insight could use it to inspire colleagues or exploit them. Without a moral compass to guide people in how to employ their gifts, emotional intelligence can be used for good or evil. Columbia University psychologist Walter Mischel, who invented the marshmallow test and others like it, observes that the knack for delaying gratification that makes a child one marshmallow richer can help him become a better citizen or—just as easily—an even more brilliant criminal.

Given the passionate arguments that are raging over the state of moral instruction in this country, it is no wonder Goleman chose to focus more on neutral emotional skills than on the values that should govern their use. That's another book—and another debate. —*Reported by Sharon E. Epperson and Lawrence Mondi/New York, James L. Graff/Chicago and Lisa H. Towle/Raleigh*

Bell, book and scandal

For more than a century intelligence testing has been a field rich in disputed evidence and questionable conclusions. "The Bell Curve", by Charles Murray and Richard Herrnstein, has ensured it will remain so

THERE is plenty of room for debate about which was the most amusing book of 1994, or which the best written. But nobody can seriously quibble about which was the most controversial. "The Bell Curve: Intelligence and Class Structure in American Life", an 845-page tome by Charles Murray and Richard Herrnstein*, has reignited a debate that is likely to rage on for years yet, consuming reputations and research grants as it goes.

"The Bell Curve" is an ambitious attempt to resuscitate IQ ("intelligence quotient") testing, one of the most controversial ideas in recent intellectual history; and to use that idea to explain some of the more unpalatable features of modern America. Mr Murray, a sociologist, and Herrnstein, a psychologist who died shortly before the book's publication, argue that individuals differ substantially in their "cognitive abilities"; that these differences are inherited as much as acquired; and that intelligence is distributed in the population along a normal distribution curve—the bell curve of the book's title—with a few geniuses at the top, a mass of ordinary Joes in the middle and a minority of dullards at the bottom (see chart).

Then, into this relatively innocuous cocktail, Messrs Murray and Herrnstein mix two explosive arguments. The first is that different races do not perform equally in the IQ stakes—that, in America, Asians score, on average, slightly above the norm, and blacks, on average, substantially below it. The second is that America is calcifying into impermeable castes. The bright are inter-marrying, spawning bright offspring and bagging well-paid jobs; and the dull are doomed to teenage pregnancy, welfare dependency, drugs and crime.

For the past three months it has been almost impossible to pick up an American newspaper or tune into an American television station without learning more about Mr Murray's views. Dozens of academics are hard at work rebutting (they would say refuting) his arguments. Thanks to the controversy, "The Bell Curve" has sold more than a quarter of a million copies.

Undoubtedly, Mr Murray has been lucky in his timing. Left-wingers point out that Americans have seldom been so disillu-

* The Free Press. New York, 1994

sioned with welfare policy: the voters are turning not just to Republicans, but to Republicans who are arguing seriously about the merits of state orphanages and of compulsory adoption. Mr Murray's arguments answer to a feeling that social policies may have failed not because they were incompetently designed or inadequately funded, but because they are incompatible with certain "facts" of human nature.

Right-wingers retort that it is liberals' addiction to "affirmative action" that has supplied Mr Murray with much of his material. Affirmative action has institutionalised the idea that different ethnic groups have different cognitive abilities: "race norming", now *de rigueur* in academia, means that a black can perform significantly less well than, say, an Asian, and still beat him into a university. It has also resulted in America's having a compilation of statistics about race unequalled outside South Africa.

Differently weird

The regularity with which discussion of IQ testing turns into an argument that ethnic groups differ in their innate abilities, with blacks at the bottom of the cognitive pile, has done more than anything else to make theorists and practitioners of IQ testing into figures of academic notoriety reviled everywhere from Haight-Ashbury to Holland Park. The early 1970s saw a furious argument about "Jensenism", named after Arthur Jensen, a psychologist at the University of California, Berkeley, who published an article arguing, among other things, that the average black had a lower IQ than the average white. William Shockley, also known as a co-inventor of the transistor, drew the anti-Jensenists' fire by saying that blacks' and whites' brains were "differently wired".

But, even if it could be extricated from arguments about ethnic differences, IQ testing would remain controversial. One reason is that few people like the idea that inequality might be inevitable, the result of natural laws rather than particular circumstances (and the more so, perhaps, when economic inequalities seem likely to widen as labour markets put an ever-higher premium on intelligence). The implication is that egalitarian policies are self-defeating: the more inherited prejudices are broken down, the more society resolves into intellectual castes.

A second reason for controversy is that IQ testers are all too prone to the fatal conceit of thinking that their discipline equips them to know what is best for their fellow men. To most parents the idea that a man with a book of tests and a clipboard can divine what is best for their children is an intolerable presumption (who can know a child as well as its parents?) and an insupportable invasion of liberty (surely people should be free to choose the best school for their children?). Nor has the IQ testers' image been helped by their having often been asked—as in England in the days of the 11-plus school entry examination—to help make already contentious decisions.

A third reason IQ testers excite concern is that they seem to make a fetish of intelligence. Many people feel instinctively that intelligence is only one of the qualities that make for success in life—that looks, luck and charm also play their part; they also like to feel that intelligence is less important than what they call "character", which can turn even a dull person into a useful citizen.

But the thing which, in the end, really frightens people about IQ testing is its message of genetic Calvinism: that IQ both determines one's destiny, and is dictated by one's genes. This flies in the face of the liberal notion that we are each responsible for fashioning our own fate. It also upsets two beliefs held particularly firmly in America: that anybody can win out, provided they have "the right stuff"; and that everybody should be given as many educational chances as possible, rather than sorted out and classified at the earliest possible opportunity. (Thus "Forrest Gump", a film that appeared shortly before publication of "The Bell Curve", enjoyed great popularity and critical acclaim for its portrayal of a well-meaning simpleton who won all America's glittering prizes.)

Hunting down Sir Humphrey

How, then, did so widely distrusted a discipline originate? To answer that question means a trip to a rather unexpected place, the Whitehall of the mid-19th century. Traditionally, jobs in the British civil service had been handed out on the basis of family connections, in a sort of affirmative-action programme for upper-class twits. But as Britain developed a world-beating economy and a world-spanning empire, reformers argued that preferment should go to the most intelligent candidates, their identity to be discovered by competitive examinations.

This innovation proved so successful that policy-makers applied the same principle to the universities and schools. Their aim was to construct an educational system capable of discovering real ability wherever it occurred, and of matching that ability with the appropriate opportunities.

Ironically, it was children at the other end of the ability scale who inspired the first IQ tests as such. The introduction of compulsory schooling for the masses confronted teachers with the full variety of human abilities, and obliged them to distinguish between the lazy and the congenitally dull. Most investigators contented themselves

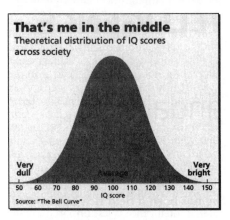

That's me in the middle
Theoretical distribution of IQ scores across society

Very dull | Average | Very bright
50 60 70 80 90 100 110 120 130 140 150
IQ score
Source: "The Bell Curve"

with measuring children's heads. But in 1905 Alfred Binet, a French psychologist, came up with the idea of assigning an age level to a variety of simple intellectual operations, determined by the earliest age at which the average child could perform them, and ranking children both against their peers and against a normal development curve. Binet's idea was refined soon afterwards by introducing the arithmetical device of dividing mental age by chronological age and multiplying by 100.

Two English psychologists turned intelligence testing into a sort of scientific movement. The first was Francis Galton, a rich and well connected man (Charles Darwin was a cousin) who devoted his life to the nascent sciences of statistics and genetics. His motto was "wherever you can, count", and he measured everything from the distended buttocks of Hottentot women (with a theodolite) to the distribution of "pulchritude" in the British Isles. He compiled family trees of everybody from Cambridge wranglers to West Country wrestlers to prove his belief that "characteristics cling to families" and "ability goes by descent."

Combining his two passions, Galton speculated that abilities in the British population were distributed along a "bell curve", with the upper classes at the top and an underclass at the bottom. He was so worried

that those at the bottom of the curve were outbreeding those at the top that he spent most of his fortune bankrolling another "science", eugenics.

Galton's mission was completed by a retired soldier, Charles Spearman. Deciding that the results of certain tests correlated with each other to a remarkable degree, Spearman concluded, in a seminal article published in 1904, that all mental abilities were manifestations of a single general ability, which he called "g": all individuals inherited a fixed quantity of mental energy, which infused every intellectual act they performed and determined what they were capable of in life. The right tests could capture how much "g" each individual possessed and express it as a single number.

Intelligence testing went on to enjoy decades of growing popularity. The American army used it on recruits in the first world war, employing more than 300 psychologists, and other armies followed. Schools used tests to help in streaming or selecting their pupils. Bureaucrats and businessmen used them to identify talented recruits. Tests were thought indispensable for discovering and diagnosing learning problems.

Only in the 1960s did opinion turn sharply against the IQ testers. Educationalists accused them of allowing an obsession with classification to blind them to the full range of human abilities. Sociologists (and sociologically minded psychologists) argued that intellectual differences owed more to social circumstances than to genes. In Britain, disillusionment with IQ tests hastened the introduction of comprehensive schools. In the United States, schools abandoned the use of IQ tests to classify children. In 1978 a district court in San Francisco even ruled unconstitutional the use of IQ tests to place children in classes for the backward if the use of such tests meant that the classes contained a "grossly disproportionate" number of black children.

Dropping clangers
"The Bell Curve" thus represents an attempt to rehabilitate an idea that had fallen into two or three decades of disfavour. But have Messrs Murray and Herrnstein got their science right?

So far, the debate on "The Bell Curve" has been billed as if it were psychometrists (mind-measurers) versus the rest. In fact, IQ testers divide among themselves on all sorts of key issues, from the structure of the mind to the reliability of tests; moreover, Messrs Murray and Herrnstein occupy a rather eccentric position among psychometrists. They are unabashed supporters of Charles Spearman, believing that intelligence is a unitary quality expressible in a single number, such that people who are good at one thing will also be good at others. Yet this is one of the most hotly disputed topics within psychometry. A British pioneer, Godfrey

Thomson, argued that the correlations which so excited Spearman might be explained by the laws of chance. He concluded that the mind had no fixed structure and that intelligence tests gave little more than a hint of a person's mental powers.

Among other psychologists, L.L. Thurstone argued for the existence of dozens of different types of mental abilities, such as mathematical, verbal and visio-spatial abilities. Liam Hudson has found IQ tests to reward a particular type of "convergent" thinker. Howard Gardner thinks there are many sorts of "intelligence".

Synaptitude
IQ testers have clashed and go on clashing over less arcane issues too. They endorse widely different estimates of the heritability of IQ, ranging from 40% to 80%. They squabble about the accuracy of IQ tests: some argue that such tests are nothing more than estimates that need to be repeated frequently and to be supplemented by personal interviews (and indeed, observably, children can learn, or be taught, to raise their IQ scores). Some of the most illustrious psychometrists are even starting to argue that IQ tests should be replaced by physical tests to measure the speed of reactions, the production of glucose in the brain, the speed of neural transmission and even the size of the brain.

Psychometrists disagree, too, about the validity of generalising about groups in the way that Murray and Herrnstein do. It is widely accepted that differences within groups may reflect hereditary factors; but differences between groups are susceptible to other explanations (just as people in one place may be taller on average than people in another place, for example, but for reasons of nutrition, not genetics).

Oddly, Messrs Murray and Herrnstein have chosen to dispute (or ignore) one of the few arguments on which other psychometrists agree: that children do not necessarily have the same IQ as their parents. "The Bell Curve" argues that society is fixing itself into impermeable castes. But psychometry is a theory of social mobility, not social stasis. It tries to explain why bright people often have dull children and dull people often have bright children. Sex ensures that genes are re-sorted in each generation.

In fact, it is hereditarianism's sworn enemy, environmentalism, which is really a theory of social stasis: if the rich and educated can pass on their advantages to their children undisturbed by the dance of the chromosomes, then social mobility will always be something of a freak. Messrs Murray and Herrnstein are, perhaps, environmentalists in hereditarian clothing.

Politically, "The Bell Curve" has reinforced the impression that IQ testers are anti-welfare conservatives. Some are. But IQ tests have been invoked in defence of a wide variety of political positions, respectable and otherwise. American psychologists have popped up to support abominations such as compulsory sterilisation and ethnically sensitive immigration laws. Others have been socialists, keen on upward mobility, child-centred education and generous provision for the backward. In Britain between the wars Labour Party intellectuals such as R.H. Tawney argued for IQ testing as a way to ensure educational opportunities were allocated on the basis of innate ability rather than family connections; psychologists such as Cyril Burt have been passionate supporters of nursery-school education and better treatment of backward children. (The fusty T.S. Eliot, on the other hand, thought IQ tests were a plot to promote social mobility and debase education. A particularly crusty Cambridge don, Edward Welbourne, denounced them as "devices invented by Jews for the advancement of Jews.")

Too clever by half

What makes the IQ debate particularly frustrating is that both sides have long been addicted to exaggeration. The earliest IQ testers were guilty of hubris when they argued that they had invented an infallible technique for measuring mental abilities and distributing educational and occupational opportunities. As if that was not bad enough, they exacerbated their error by claiming that their method contributed to economic efficiency (by making the best use of human resources) and personal happiness (by ensuring that people were given jobs suited to their abilities).

The enemies of IQ testing were also guilty of terrible exaggeration when they accused testers of shoring up capitalism, perpetuating inequality, and justifying sexism, racism, even fascism. In fact, the IQ testers were never anywhere near as influential as they, or their opponents, imagined.

IQ theory played no part in persuading the American Congress to pass the Immigration Restriction Act of 1924; British grammar schools used IQ tests only to supplement other, more traditional selection procedures, such as scholastic examinations and interviews; Hitler and Mussolini had no time for IQ tests that were liable to contradict their own racial prejudices.

What the IQ debate needs now is a dash of cold water. Opponents of testing should forget their over-heated rhetoric about legitimising capitalism and racism. Supporters should fold up their more grandiose blueprints for building the meritocracy, and limit themselves to helping with practical problems. They should point out that IQ tests are useful ways of identifying and diagnosing mental deficiency, just so long as they are administered along with other diagnostic tools by a trained psychologist. They should add that IQ tests can also be useful in helping to allocate places in oversubscribed schools; that, indeed, they are less class-biased than scholastic tests (which favour the well-taught) or personal interviews (which favour the well-brought up). It is a pity that Charles Murray and Richard Herrnstein have chosen to douse the debate not with cold water but with petrol.

The Role of Schools in Sustaining Early Childhood Program Benefits

Doris R. Entwisle

Doris R. Entwisle, Ph.D., is professor of sociology and engineering science in the Department of Sociology at Johns Hopkins University.

Abstract

A number of articles in this journal issue have documented effects of early childhood programs on children's cognitive abilities, achievement, and social adjustment as they mature to become schoolchildren, adolescents, and young adults. This article carefully considers the role that school experiences play in transmitting and sustaining the cognitive gains made by children in preschool.

The author discusses the process of schooling in the early elementary grades, focusing on how children's achievement is influenced by the expectations of parents and teachers, and by school practices such as assignment to within-class ability groups, retention in grade, and placement in special education. Because attending preschool boosts children's performance, even temporarily, it can ease their transition into first grade and reduce their exposure to negative tracking by the school and to low expectations on the part of their parents and teachers. The link between preschool and first grade is key to understanding and explaining the long-term effects of preschool.

This article examines the role played by elementary schools in sustaining the benefits of early childhood programs, and proposes new ways of thinking about the links between preschool experience and the early years of elementary school. Surprisingly little is known about the process of schooling in the first, second, and third grades, let alone how preschooling interacts with it.

Studies of how children respond to preschool programs indicate that preschooling has only transient effects on children's intelligence quotient (IQ) and cognitive achievement but, nevertheless, is associated with greater success in school. Children who attend preschool are less often retained in grade and placed in special education, and they more often graduate from high school.[1] While these findings are widely reported, little effort has gone into explaining them. How do the early effects of preschool alter the later experiences children have in their families and school classrooms?

From *The Future of Children,* Winter 1995, pp. 133-144. © 1995 by the Center for the Future of Children of the David and Lucile Packard Foundation, 300 Second Street, Suite 102, Los Altos, CA 94022, 415-917-7114. Reprinted by permission.

This article focuses on the process of early schooling, and it identifies several factors in the family and the elementary school that influence children's success in school and that could play a part in sustaining the performance of disadvantaged youngsters who have attended preschool. Simply put, because children from disadvantaged backgrounds are especially likely to suffer setbacks during the first grade, preschool programs that boost their performance during the critical transition into school may protect them from school tracking practices such as retention in grade, and may prevent parents and teachers from developing low expectations of the children's performance.

Conceptualizing how the primary grades mediate the long-term effects of preschools requires a life course paradigm that focuses attention on the social contexts in which individuals develop, the substantial influence that individuals have in producing their own development, and the importance of life transitions (such as school entry) as critical periods in development.[2] Preschool may change children directly by building their skills or bolstering their abilities, and it may also affect them indirectly by changing the beliefs or expectations of the people who surround the children. In addition, children are full-fledged players who shape their own schooling. For instance, children who do their homework contribute to their own cognitive growth, and those who enter school with the socioemotional maturity that teachers expect are positioned to benefit from the opportunities for growth offered them in first grade.

Life course transitions introduce individuals into new social contexts, reconfiguring their roles, changing their notions about themselves, and forcing them to learn to function in new institutional contexts. In making the transition from home to full-time schooling, for example, children must construct a self-image as a student, discover the norms and mores of the school, learn how to get along with new peers and authority figures, and map strategies for mastering the necessary skills. In the new environment, they develop different patterns of learning and different patterns of reliance on significant others to support that learning. Because these patterns tend to persist and can place boundaries on later attainment, it is important to consider the ways in which attending preschool helps children make a successful transition into first grade.

The Effects of Preschool on Cognitive and School Outcomes

The most robust data bearing on long-term effects of preschooling come from a report by researchers who pooled follow-up data gathered on about 11 preschool programs.[1,3] These programs, which randomly assigned children to preschooling or to a control group, had a number of short-term influences on children's intellectual performance and their socioemotional functioning. The attention of researchers and the public focused particularly on the ability of the programs to boost IQ test scores by about five points. However, these IQ gains faded two or three years after the children entered public school. There were, however, two solidly established longer-term effects on children and two effects on parents. Preschooled children were less often referred for special education and retained in grade through the end of high school. As for parents, mothers of the preschooled children were more satisfied with their children's school performance than were other mothers. The mothers of preschooled children also held consistently higher occupational aspirations than their children held for themselves, while other mothers' aspirations showed no consistent patterns.

Effects of preschooling also seemed to persist in the adaptation of the students upon leaving high school.[4,5] A separate evaluation based on three studies that followed 192 youngsters through adolescence[6] found that preschooled youngsters were more likely to graduate from high school, and 66% of the students who had no retentions and graduated from high school were employed, compared with 41% of the others.

Most research evaluating the effects of preschools, even when it has been longitudinal, has focused on the individual child as the target of the intervention. The evaluation reports sketch in the nature of the children's preschool experiences, but there is little information about the educational practices used in the schools the children attended from first grade onward or about the educational opportunities provided to them in elementary classrooms. The tacit presumption that underlies these evaluations is that, if preschooling changes youngsters, then they will do better henceforth, but exactly why they should do better is left open.

Explaining Preschool Effects

Some reviewers have speculated about mechanisms that could turn short-term preschool benefits into long-term success and adaptation. For example, one review of studies showing long-term benefits from preschool suggests that attention should be focused not so much on variables like IQ which are designed to measure permanent changes in the child's psychological functioning but, instead, on short-term improvements that could change the child's ability to function in school.[7] Indeed, the pattern of outcomes found in the longitudinal evaluations of preschooling suggests that the positive long-term effects came about mainly because preschooled children had different experiences in elementary school.

This article examines two paths by which the short-term effects of preschool on children could change the social context of school entry and, thereby, affect children's academic success. One path is by enhancing children's cognitive abilities

in a way that eases the transition into school and reduces the likelihood that they will be tracked into low ability groups, placed in special education, or retained in grade. Another path is by inducing both parents and teachers to have positive expectations for the child's performance and so to encourage and support the child's academic efforts. Before examining how these paths may transmit the effects of preschool programs, the general nature of children's early school experience and research on parent, teacher, and peer influences will be briefly reviewed.

The Nature of Early Schooling

Doing better in the early grades is important for long-term success because the early grades in school constitute a "critical period" for children's adjustment as students.[8] Entering school changes children's social environments at a time when their capabilities are also changing. Moreover, children's experiences during this period often have lasting consequences. The reputations they earn during the first few years of school can help or hinder them for many years to come.

School Entry as a Critical Period

Entering school places the child in a social context that is different from the one experienced at home or even in preschool. In many preschools, parents have influence over the program, and caregivers may feel they report to parents. When children begin first grade, however, not only are they no

---

The reputations children earn during the first few years of school can help or hinder them for many years to come.

---

longer wholly dependent on the family, but the family virtually relinquishes control over them during school hours to first grade teachers who, as professionals, often resist attempts by parents to exert control. Also, in first grade, children's work begins to be seriously evaluated in a comparative framework by teachers and classmates. The conventions of the school, with its achievement

© Loren Santow/Impact Visuals

orientation, its expectation that children will stay on task and work independently without close monitoring, its insistence on punctuality, and its evaluation of children in terms of what they can do instead of who they are, all can be daunting to children.

The beginning school transition coincides with some key cognitive changes within children. The onset of formal schooling occurs at about the same time children move from preoperational to operational modes of thinking. Around age six, many children seeing liquid poured from a fat, short container into a tall, thin container will think, after the transfer, that the tall container holds more liquid. In the next couple of years, though, their cognitive capacities change, and they can understand why the width of the container as well as its height must be considered. Similar changes affect children's understanding of language, as they become able to think of how words can replace one another in sentences. That is, when asked the first word they think of after you say "went," they say "go"; and to "heavily," they respond "lightly." In the first few years of school, these and other rapidly developing cognitive capacities enable children to take enormous strides in understanding the world around them. In fact, one researcher estimates that children's learning rate in first grade is about 10 times what it is in high school.[9] It

is no accident that in the United States and other countries, the transition into full-time schooling coincides with this spurt in cognitive growth.

Also prominent among the psychological characteristics of six- to eight-year-old children is their receptiveness to the school experience. Most elementary students are very much in tune with the goals of the school. They are learning about important everyday activities—how to make change, select lunch, tell time, or read signs—that help them get along in the world. The curriculum, therefore, makes sense to them and to their parents. There is considerable evidence that children's liking for school tends to decline as they go through school, as does their academic self-image.[10] Making a good adaptation in the first few grades, therefore, can lead to considerable differences in the amounts children learn over their school careers, especially since the basic skills covered in the early years provide a crucial foundation for later learning.

Perhaps the most important way that entry into school serves as a critical period, in terms of the topic of this article, is that children are sorted and categorized over the first year or two of school in ways that can launch them into achievement trajectories. They construct their self-images as students, and school personnel begin keeping written dossiers that shadow them through high school and beyond. In addition, beginning in the first grade, schools stratify children along a continuum of academic achievement and potential, and sort them into different groups for instruction. Administrative sorting arrangements in elementary schools include assignment to ability groups within the classroom, referral to special education, and retention in grade. Although they are not usually labeled this way, these sorting arrangements are effectively tracks (a term more commonly used in reference to instruction in high school). They serve as a form of educational stratification that has gone largely unresearched.

School Tracking Practices

Ability Grouping

One form of administrative sorting in early primary school is the use of within-class ability grouping, a practice until lately universal: in first grade, more than 90% of elementary schools use such ability groups for reading.[11] The aim of creating ability groups is to reduce heterogeneity, to enable teachers to target their instruction to children's competence. Three or four groups are most typical, but as few as two groups and as many as five groups are found.[12] Because the groups are constructed within each classroom, a given child's placement is influenced more by how able the teacher perceives him or her to be relative to classmates than by any absolute measure of ability in reading. An average student in a classroom of very bright peers will fall in a low reading group while the same student in a classroom of children with educational difficulties might be assigned to the top group. Once the child has been assigned to a group, however, real consequences begin to follow. Placement in reading groups effectively determines the amount and type of instruction children receive;[13,14] it influences group process (interruptions and disruptions);[15,16] and it affects how children are viewed by parents and teachers.[17]

Research shows that children in higher groups are taught more words,[18] so it is hardly surprising that children in higher groups make greater progress in reading. Even more to the point, teaching style varies by ability group even when children are reading from the same basal reader.[19] Children in low groups are encouraged to read word

by word while teachers provide clues for decoding isolated words. This instructional style does not give beginning readers much chance to apply their knowledge of spoken language. In high groups, by contrast, clauses, expressive intonation, and supposed emotional states of characters are brought to children's attention. Needless to say, it is much more exciting to tell or hear a story where the characters are "human" than to hear one where each word is stumbled over and maybe revised. Reading group rank also determines the ranges within which teachers assign marks.[20] Children in low ability groups in high-ability classrooms often get lower marks than other children of the same tested ability who are in low-ability classrooms. First graders are strongly influenced by the marks they receive, so marks can directly encourage (or discourage) their learning. For these and other reasons, placements in low-ability groups tend to have effects in the later grades of elementary school.[17]

Retention

Another key way that children are sorted in first grade is by retention. School systems often retain students for another year to expose them to the same material a second time, yet these students usually are not favored with special curricula designed to remedy their particular difficulties. Although repeating a grade may help students master

---

More than 90% of elementary schools use ability groups for reading to reduce heterogeneity and to enable teachers to target their instruction to children's competence.

---

basic skills, students thus held back are separated from their age-mates and may acquire a variety of pejorative labels. National data on retention are not available, but one study found that about 50% of males and 40% of females in poverty level households, where the head is a high school dropout, are "behind" in school at least one year.[21] In a random sample of Baltimore children selected in 1982 (see Box 1 for a description of the Beginning School Study), more than 16% were held back at the end of first grade, and another 8% were held back in their second year.[10]

Box 1

The Beginning School Study

The Beginning School Study provides a strong research base for discovering how social structural factors (minority/majority status, gender, socioeconomic background) and the immediate social context (parents, teachers, peers) help or hinder children's cognitive development as they make the transition to full-time schooling.

The study is based on a two-stage random sample of 825 children who entered first grade in 20 Baltimore public elementary schools in 1982. The schools were chosen so as to reflect the racial/ethnic and economic diversity represented in the city school system. Children were selected at random from all the first grade classrooms, with 51 different classes represented. The education level of the students' parents averaged slightly below high school; about 55% of the students were African American. The research team gathered data from school records on several occasions, from parents, teachers, and from many direct interviews with the students themselves.

The following table (based on 585 students with complete data) shows the proportion of first graders who were placed in low ability groups, retained, or referred for special education.

Children experiencing low placements (585 total)

Lowest reading group in the fall	28%
Lowest reading group in the spring	22%
Retained to repeat first grade	14%
Designated for special education	7%

Of the children touched by these experiences (203 total)

One low placement only	35%
Multiple low placements	65%

Source: Entwisle, D.R., and Alexander, K.L. Entry into school: The beginning school transition and educational stratification in the United States. *Annual Review of Sociology* (1993)19:401–23.

Special Education Placement

Special education placement is less common than retention in first grade but still far from rare. Since the passage of Public Law 94-142 in 1975, practices in special education have changed, and the number receiving special education services rose to 4.8 million children 3 to 21 years of age in 1990–91.[22] Most special education is provided to children in regular classrooms by offering pull-out services (68% of special education children were served in this way in 1985–86). In Baltimore, referral to special education is a sorting practice that becomes common in second grade and later. In the Baltimore study, 13% of children were in special education by the end of their second school year, in addition to the 24% who had been retained by then.[23]

Thus, administrative tracking of one kind or another touches a great many young children, and for many it begins when their school careers begin. There is also considerable overlap in children's placements. In the Baltimore study, for example, 85% of the children who repeated first grade also were in low reading groups or were receiving special education services.[23] As noted, retention is much more common in first grade than later, and it seems that, if retention is not effective in getting children up to satisfactory performance levels, special education often is the next step taken.

Expectations of Significant Others

A separate line of research deals with long-term effects of the expectations of significant others (teachers and parents) on children's school performance, another route by which social contexts could transmit effects of preschool. Several studies have found that, if parents believe their children are smarter than other children, their children tend to do better than other children[24,25]—a relationship that appears to be stronger in middle-class than in working-class families. In fact, parents' beliefs about children's ability can predict children's school performance better than children's actual ability, as measured by standardized tests.[26] Several other studies show that parents' expectations early in school can produce long-term effects in children's performance.[27,28]

Parents' favorable beliefs about children in the first few grades could be associated with improved achievement in two ways. Their effects may be direct and continuous: parents' positive beliefs may persist, affecting children's achievement year by year. But there also may be important indirect effects that act over time. If parents believe their first grade children will do well, and this belief translates into better marks or achievement scores for children in first grade, then those children may continue to achieve at higher levels. High marks in first grade set a standard for subsequent marks and raise expectations for success, contributing positively to later performance.[3] When a child does better in first grade, the learning itself also helps to improve performance in the next and later grades.

Similarly, long-term teacher effects could come either directly or indirectly. Direct effects occur when teachers prompt a superior performance from some students in elementary school. Studies show that children for whom teachers hold high expectations are held to stricter standards, are called upon more frequently, and are more often pressed for answers in class.[29] These demands promote more learning in the early grades and help children establish high achievement levels. Indirect effects come about when the teacher influences the first grader's own attitudes toward achievement, which are then carried forward within the child. Several studies by different research teams found long-term effects of first, second, and third grade teachers' expectations on performance in high school and beyond which were best explained by such indirect routes.[27,28,30,31] These findings suggest that children's achievement responds for a long time to the social influences the children experienced during the critical first few years of school.

How Preschool Effects Can Be Transmitted

As noted in the beginning of this article, the most widely publicized effect of preschool is the beneficial but transient boosting of IQ test scores by about five points. Because these IQ gains faded after only two or three years, however, early evaluations dismissed their importance. When follow-up evaluations showed reduced rates of retention in grade and placement in special education, early childhood researchers were challenged to explain how the preschooled children's early cognitive gains could lead to these important school outcomes. The analysis provided in this article of how the transition into school and the process of early schooling affect children suggests several ways that preschool experience might influence children's elementary school careers.

Easing the Transition to First Grade

First, finding elevated IQs in first grade signals that preschooling can ease the transition into first grade. The positive effects of preschool are more cognitive than social: preschooled children's IQs, marks, and achievement test scores were higher. Studies have shown that, like preschool, attending kindergarten for a

Children for whom teachers hold high expectations are held to stricter standards, are called on more frequently, and are more often pressed for answers in class.

full day rather than part day significantly increases children's scores on standardized tests, especially among minority group members. It is the cognitive advantage from these early experiences that helps children do better in first grade, not their having learned to be better behaved.[32] Recent research on school readiness shows that kindergarten teachers give relatively little weight to socialization, or deportment, as an aspect of school readiness. Only 42% of teachers in a national study rated the child's ability to sit still and pay attention as "essential" or "very important" to readiness.[33]

Preventing Placement in Low Tracks

Second, the modest IQ gains and higher achievement scores that preschool children received during the early grades could reduce the likelihood of retention in grade and placement in special education. These kinds of early administrative sorting were not assessed in the preschool follow-up literature. However, most decisions to hold

---

At seventh grade, 14% of preschooled versus 35% of children who did not attend preschool had been retained or placed in special education.

---

children back are made in the early grades, and retention rates are universally highest in first grade.[10] In many elementary schools that enroll disadvantaged children (children like those in the preschool programs that were rigorously evaluated), even a temporary increase in test scores in first grade could prevent retention. Because retention puts children on a separate track from their promoted classmates and many retained children later enter special education, even a relatively small elevation in children's IQ test scores in the first couple of grades could be critical for their long-term prospects.

Although there is no published evidence on reading group assignments for the youngsters included in the studies examined by the Consortium of Longitudinal Studies,[1,3] the children who attended preschool received higher test scores, and that would place them in higher groups in many schools. If so, preschooled youngsters would have been able to take advantage of the additional learning opportunities offered in higher ability groups—since their IQs were temporarily elevated—and many probably did well enough to avoid damaging administrative placements. At seventh grade, 14% of preschooled versus 35% of children who did not attend preschool had been retained or placed in special education.[34]

Raising the Expectations Held by Significant Others

A third explanation for the superior long-term achievement of preschooled children focuses on the expectations that important people around them held for their success. The preschoolers might have achieved more because they were "defined" as good students by virtue of their higher reading group placement and, perhaps, because their having attended preschool raised others' expectations for them. This effect has not been documented in evaluations of preschool programs, despite speculations that such processes might be at work.[35]

Further insights come from a recent study involving disadvantaged youngsters in Chicago public schools.[36,37] Using data for about 1,500 disadvantaged African-American youngsters, this study links experience in preschool programs to later school outcomes. Children's social contexts played a role in transmitting preschool effects: (1) preschooling changed the character of the setting in which later learning took place because children with preschool experience and higher achievement levels attended kindergarten together, and (2) preschooling promoted higher levels of parent involvement in school when children were in first grade. These differences were directly related to preschooled children's reading and math achievement in kindergarten and first grade, and also to their socioemotional maturity at the end of first grade, as rated by teachers on items such as "Came to my class ready to learn" and the like. These data show that preschooling affected parents and peers in ways that changed the social context of children's first grade experience, and these contextual changes helped the children overcome the disadvantage of their family backgrounds.

Providing the Support of Peers

Finally, the importance of peer links over the transition between preschooling and kindergarten is further clarified by researchers who study children's peer play.[38] They report that children who were "cooperative players" in preschool were seen as more sociable by kindergarten teachers and were better liked by their classmates. Furthermore, the longer children had attended preschool, the less anxious they were and the better was their attendance in kindergarten. No widely known evaluations of structured preschool programs have examined the effects on children of entering school in a stable peer group, although research on older children suggests that being with a group of familiar peers could ease the stress of the transition into first grade for preschooled children.[39]

Conclusion

This examination of research on preschool and the process of schooling in the primary grades suggests that the link between preschool and the first grade may be key to understanding preschool effects. The evidence shows that even a temporary cognitive boost enables children from disadvantaged backgrounds to make a successful transition into school, and it appears to be the school's response to the preschooled children that produced the lasting benefits. These children may have been easier for the first grade teacher to teach, their parents may have been more impressed by their abilities, or they may have found the transition into school less jarring. In any event, processes of schooling must play a crucial but little-understood part in the preschool story.

The Process of Early Schooling

From a policy standpoint, the most important questions about early schooling relate to schools because it is much more feasible to change schools than it is to try to change families. Although research on high schools indicates that the administrative features of schools (like library size or teachers' years of experience) matter little compared with the characteristics of pupils in those schools, the same may not be as true of grade schools. To recommend changes, however, we need to know much more about the process of early schooling. For example, more research is needed on school tracking in the early grades and how it interacts with preschooling. In most past research, effects of retention, special education, and ability grouping have been studied in isolation, but children's experience is not isolated. The retained child often ends up in special education, and the child in the lowest reading group is often retained. Studies that are limited to one dimension of early tracking risk misconstruing the source of children's difficulties, and they cannot show how consequences compound across dimensions of tracking or how tracking interacts with preschool experience in working to the advantage of some children and the disadvantage of others.

The Generalizability of Preschool Effects

It will also be important to extend research on preschool effects to include larger, more diverse samples. The bulk of prior research on preschool effects has involved disadvantaged African-American children. An exception is the recent analysis of nationally representative data that evaluated the effects of Head Start for both white and African-American children. White children showed positive and persistent effects from their participation in Head Start, including less likelihood of retention, but only transient effects and no difference in retention rates emerged for African-American children.[40] While this difference may reflect methodological problems (the children were not randomly assigned to attend preschool), it is possible that Head Start programs for African-American children placed less emphasis on academic achievement or that white children's grade school milieux differed from those of African-American children.

To clarify findings like these, additional longitudinal research is needed that spans ethnic and socioeconomic groups. With a few exceptions,[24,25,36,40] there is little longitudinal research on large samples in the first three grades. Additional insights may also come from national education surveys now being planned that will cover preschoolers as well as elementary school youngsters. Research using large, diverse samples is

The most important questions about early schooling relate to schools because it is much more feasible to change schools than it is to try to change families.

needed to disentangle school from community effects, home from school effects, and family configuration from economic effects. Recent research on achievement in the first two grades shows that differences in economic resources of families matter more for children's performance than do ethnicity or school composition.[41,42] Likewise, the economic resources a second parent provides account for much of the academic advantage of children who reside in two-parent families.[43,44]

Who Attends Preschool Programs?

Although the benefits of preschool are most evident among children from poor, minority backgrounds, those groups are not the most likely to attend preschool programs. As of 1991, 40% of white children, about 31% of African-American children, and 21% of Hispanic three- to four-year-olds were enrolled in prekindergartens.[45] Children from homes with incomes in the highest quartile are more than twice as likely to attend prekindergarten programs as are children whose families are in the lowest quartile (52% versus 22%). However, when income and similar factors are controlled, African-American children are more likely than other children to be enrolled in a center-based program.[46] By contrast, differences in attendance between children of mothers with more or less education appear consistently across income categories. These findings suggest that efforts will be needed to draw children in teen-mother and like families into preschool programs so as to increase their success in school.

Mounting evidence testifies to the powerful effects that early schooling can have on children's life chances and ultimate well-being, in part because educational stratification begins in earnest during these years. Providing preschool programs to help children negotiate the first grade transition can yield large returns, especially for children from economically disadvantaged families. More research is needed to determine how best to structure these programs and make them more accessible to disadvantaged children.

Notes

1. Consortium of Longitudinal Studies, ed. *As the twig is bent...lasting effects of preschool programs* . Hillsdale, NJ: Erlbaum, 1983.

2. Lazar, I., and Darlington, R. Lasting effects of early education: A report from the Consortium for Longitudinal Studies. *Monographs of the Society for Research in Child Development* (1982) 47, no. 2-3.

3. Entwisle, D. R. Schools and the adolescent. In *At the threshold*. S. S. Feldman and G. R. Elliott, eds. Cambridge, MA: Harvard University Press, 1990.

4. Berreuta-Clement, J. R., Schweinhart, L. J., Barnett, W. S., et al. *Changed lives: The effect of the Perry Preschool Program on youths through age 19*. Monograph of the High/Scope Educational Research Foundation. Ypsilanti, MI: High/Scope Press, 1984.

5. Neiman, R. H., and Gaithright, J. F. *The long-term effects of ESEA Title I preschool and all-day kindergarten: An eight year follow-up*. Cincinnati, OH: Cincinnati Public Schools, 1981.

6. See note no. 1, Consortium of Longitudinal Studies, p. 43.

7. Woodhead, M. When psychology informs public policy: The case of early childhood intervention. *American Psychologist* (1988) 43: 443-54.

8. Entwisle, D. R., and Alexander, K. L. Early schooling as a "critical period" phenomenon. In *Sociology of education and socialization*. K. Namboodiri and R. G. Corwin, eds. Greenwich, CT: JAI Press, 1989, pp. 27-55.

9. Jencks, C. How much do high school students learn? *Sociology of Education* (1985) 58:128-53.

10. Alexander, K. L., Entwisle, D. R., and Dauber S. L. *On the success of failure: A reassessment of the effects of retention in the primary grades*. Cambridge, MA: Cambridge University Press, 1994.

11. McPartland, J. M., Coldiron, J. R., and Braddock, J. H. *School structures and classroom practices in elementary, middle and secondary schools*. Report No. 14. Baltimore, MD: Johns Hopkins University, Center for Research on Elementary and Middle Schools, 1987.

12. Hallinan, M. T., and Sörensen, A. B. The formation and stability of instructional groups. *American Sociological Review* (1983) 48:838-51.

13. Barr, R., and Dreeben, R. *How schools work*. Chicago: University of Chicago Press, 1983.

14. Bossert, S. T., Barnett, B. G., and Filby, N. N. Grouping and instructional organization. In *The social context of instruction: Group organization and group process*. P. L. Peterson, L. C. Wilkinson, and M. Hallinan, eds. New York: Academic Press, 1984.

15. Eder, D. Ability grouping as a self-fulfilling prophecy: A micro-analysis of teacher-student interaction. *Sociology of Education* (1981) 54:151-62.

16. Felmlee, D., and Eder, D. Contextual effects in the classroom: The impact of ability group on student attention. *Sociology of Education* (1983) 56:77-87.

17. Pallas, A. M., Entwisle, D. R., Alexander, K. L., and Stluka, M. F. Ability-group effects: Instructional, social or institutional? *Sociology of Education* (1994) 67:27-46.

18. Gamoran, A. The effects of stratification in secondary schools: Synthesis of survey and ethnographic research. *Review of Educational Research* (1986) 57:415-35.

19. Collins, J. Differential instruction in

reading groups. In *The social construction of literacy.* J. Cook-Gumperz, ed. Cambridge, England: Cambridge University Press, 1986.

20. Reuman, D. A. How social comparison mediates the relation between ability-grouping practices and students' achievement expectancies in mathematics. *Journal of Educational psychology* (1989) 88:178–89.

21. Bianchi, S. M. Children's progress through school: A research note. *Sociology of Education* (1984) 57:184–92.

22. Viadero, D. Report finds record jump in special-education enrollment. *Education Week,* August 5, 1992, p. 19.

23. Entwisle, D. R., and Alexander, K. L. Entry into schools: The beginning school transition and educational stratification in the United States. In *Annual Review of Sociology,* Vol. 19, pp. 401–23. Palo Alto, CA: Annual Reviews, 1993.

24. Entwisle, D. R., and Hayduk, L. A. *Early schooling.* Baltimore, MD: John Hopkins Press, 1982.

@9/10 = 25. Alexander, K. L., and Entwisle, D. R. Achievement in the first two years of school: Patterns and processes. *Monographs of the Society for Research in Child Development.* Serial No. 218 (1988) 53,2.

26. Parsons, J. E., Adler, T. F., and Kaczala, C. M. Socialization of achievement attitudes and beliefs: Parental influences. *Child development* (1982) 53:322–39.

27. Entwisle, D. R., and Hayduk, L. A. Lasting effects of elementary school. *Sociology of Education* (1988) 61:147–59.

28. Hess, R. D., Holloway, S. D., Dickson, W. P., and Price, G. G. Maternal variables as predictors of children's school readiness and later achievement in vocabulary and mathematics in sixth grade. *Child Development* (1984) 55:1902–12.

29. Brophy, J. E., and Good, T. L. *Teacher-student relationships: Causes and consequences.* New York: Holt, Rinehart, and Winston, 1974.

30. Pedersen, E., Faucher, T. A., and Eaton, W. W. A new perspective on the effects of first-grade teachers on children's subsequent adult status. *Harvard Educational Review* (1978) 48:1–31.

31. Stevenson, H. W., and Newman, R. S. Long-term prediction of achievement and attitudes in mathematics and reading. *Child Development* (1986) 56:646–59.

32. Entwisle, D. R., Alexander, K. L., Cadigan, D., and Pallas, A. M. Kindergarten experience: Cognitive effects or socialization. *American Educational Research Journal* (1987) 24: 337–64.

33. West, J., Hanusken, E., and Collins, M. *Readiness for kindergarten: Parent and teacher beliefs.* Washington, DC: Office of Educational Research and Improvement, 1993.

34. See note no.. 1, Consortium of Longitudinal Studies, p. 433.

35. Lazar, I. Discussion and implications of the findings. In *As the twig is bent...lasting effects of preschool programs.* Consortium of Longitudinal Studies. Hillsdale, NJ: Erlbaum, 1983, p. 463.

36. Reynolds, A. J. A structural model of first-grade outcomes for an urban, low socioeconomic status, minority population. *Journal of Educational Psychology* (1989) 81:594–603.

37. Reynolds, A. J. Effects of a preschool plus follow-on intervention for children at risk. *Developmental Psychology* (1994) 30:787–804.

38. Ladd, G. W., and Price, J. M. Predicting children's social and school adjustment following the transition from preschool to kindergarten. *Child Development* (1987) 58:1168–89.

39. Felner, R. D., Ginter, M., and Primavera, J. Primary prevention during school transitions: Social support and environmental structure. *American Journal of Community Psychology* (1982) 10:277–90.

40. Currie, J., and Duncan, T. Does Head Start make a difference? *American Economic Review* (1995) 85,3:341–64.

41. Entwisle, D. R., and Alexander, K. L. Summer setback: Race, poverty, school composition, and mathematics achievement in the first two years of school. *American Sociological Review* (1992) 57:72–84.

42. Entwisle, D. R., and Alexander, K. L. Winter setback: School racial composition and learning to read. *American Sociological Review* (1994) 59:446–60.

43. Entwisle, D. R., and Alexander, K. L. A parent's economic shadow: Family structure versus family resources as influences on early school achievement. *Journal of Marriage and the Family* (1995) 57:399–409.

44. McLanahan, S. S., and Sandefur, G. *Growing up with a single parent: What hurts, what helps.* Cambridge, MA: Harvard University Press, 1994.

45. U.S. Department of Education. *The condition of education.* Washington, DC: National Center for Education Statistics, 1994.

46. U.S. Department of Education. *Access to early childhood programs for children at risk.* Washington, DC: National Center for Education Statistics. In *Annual Review of Sociology,* Vol. 19, pp. 401–23. Palo Alto, CA: Annual Reviews, 1993.

Fears in the Classroom:
Psychological Issues and Pedagogical Implications

Robert H. Deluty and Joseph L. DeVitis

N othing is terrible except fear itself.
—*Francis Bacon (1623)*

The authors explore common clinical childhood fears and offer suggestions for balancing treatment with input from psychologists, teachers, and parents.

For children, fear can be an adaptive response in many contexts. Children's fears are common and usually transitory, and their onset and course may be viewed as part of a normal developmental process. The mere appearance of fear is, therefore, not a sign of psychopathology and, indeed, often is a necessary concomitant of normal development.[1] On other occasions, however, fear may deter development and impinge on mastery, growth, and success. The present article will examine three types of fear or anxiety disorders that may manifest themselves in the classroom: Separation Anxiety Disorder, Social Phobia, and Generalized Anxiety Disorder. The diagnostic features of each disorder will be discussed, as will various psychological treatment models and pedagogical strategies for these problem behaviors.

Separation Anxiety Disorder

Robert H. Deluty is Associate Professor of Psychology and the Director of the Clinical Psychology Doctoral Program at the University of Maryland Baltimore County, Baltimore, Maryland. Joseph L. DeVitis is Professor of Education and Human Development at the State University of New York at Binghamton. He is past president of the American Educational Studies Association and the Council of Learned Societies in Education.

Solitude lies at the lowest depth of the human condition. Man is the only being who feels himself to be alone and the only one who is searching for the Other.

—*Octavio Paz (1950)*

The essential feature of Separation Anxiety Disorder is excessive anxiety involving separation from one's home or from persons to whom one is attached. This fear goes beyond what would be expected given the individual's developmental level, lasts for a period of at least four weeks, begins before eighteen years of age, and causes significant distress or impairment in social, academic, or other important areas of functioning.[2]

Children with this disorder may become extremely homesick and miserable when away from home. They often yearn to return home and are

This article originally appeared in *Educational Horizons* quarterly journal, Spring 1996, pp. 108-113. © 1996 by Phi Lambda Theta, international honor society and professional association in education, Bloomington, IN 47407-6626. Reprinted by permission.

preoccupied with reunion fantasies. When separated from their attachment figures, such children typically have intrusive thoughts involving accidents or illnesses that will befall the attachment figures or themselves (e.g., kidnapping, automobile accidents, attacks by monsters). Concerns about death and dying are common, and fears of being lost and never being reunited with parents are often experienced.[3]

Children who suffer from Separation Anxiety Disorder may refuse to go to school, leading to academic difficulties and social avoidance. If forced to separate, such children may become extremely upset or angry, and may occasionally attack (physically or verbally) the person who is demanding separation. Children with this disorder are frequently portrayed as demanding, clinging, and in need of constant attention.[4] Their excessive demands at school often become a source of teacher and peer frustration, resulting in resentment, ridicule, and conflict within the classroom.

Social Phobia

Fear is the main source of superstition, and one of the main sources of cruelty. To conquer fear is the beginning of wisdom.
—Bertrand Russell (1950)

The cardinal feature of Social Phobia (or Social Anxiety Disorder) is a marked, persistent fear of social or performance situations in which embarrassment may occur. Exposure to such situations nearly always elicits an immediate anxiety response. Although socially phobic adolescents and adults typically recognize that their fear is excessive or unreasonable, this is frequently not the case with children. Most often, socially phobic individuals avoid social or performance situations, although on occasion, they will endure such situations with substantial dread.[5]

Children with Social Phobia often evince crying, tantrums, freezing, clinging or remaining close to a familiar person, and inhibited interactions (even to the point of mutism). They may appear exceedingly timid in unfamiliar social contexts, avoid contact with others, refuse to join group play, remain on the periphery of social activities, or try to stay close to familiar, "safe" adults. Often associated with such social fears are a decline in academic performance and refusal to attend school.[6]

In feared situations, socially phobic children are concerned that they will embarrass themselves and worry that peers and adults will view them as anxious, weak, weird, or stupid. In the classroom, they may fear public speaking, convinced that others will notice their trembling voice or hands; or they may suffer intense anxiety when conversing with others, fearing they will appear inarticulate. Some children will avoid eating, drinking, or writing in public due to fear of being embarrassed by having classmates or teachers see their hands shake, or out of concern that they may spill, drop, or break something. Socially phobic children nearly always experience somatic and cognitive symptoms of anxiety, including palpitations, tremors, sweating, blushing, muscle tension, confusion, diarrhea, and gastrointestinal discomfort.[7]

Generalized Anxiety Disorder

What was at one time called "overanxious disorder" (a childhood syndrome) is now considered to be the childhood version of Generalized Anxiety Disorder (GAD). For children and adolescents, this disorder typically takes the form of anticipatory performance anxiety.[8] The child with GAD perpetually asks himself such questions as, Will I pass the test? Will I be picked when we choose up sides for softball? Will I make errors if I do get to play? Will I embarrass myself when it's my turn in the spelling bee? As these concerns suggest, such children generally have grave doubts about their own capabilities, doubts that result in their constantly seeking approval and reassurance.

The chronic worrying and self-doubt of these youngsters tend to breed failure. Because it strips behavior of its spontaneity, anticipatory anxiety often fosters the very problems that were anticipated. Petrified that they will fail the midterm or not receive a Valentine's Day card

---

Anxious when working, guilty if shirking.
Fearing heightened expectations when work is commendable,
Dreading disapproving gazes for efforts lamentable.
And should perfection be achieved, comfort is painfully brief,
For a fall from grace is awaited, stifling hope of lasting relief.

—Robert H. Deluty (1995)

---

from a classmate, children with GAD run a greater risk of failing and being excluded. These failures and disappointments typically lead to even more anxiety and even more failure.[9]

Cognitive-Behavioral Treatment Approaches

Clinical researchers and practitioners have often drawn from the adult anxiety literature in designing treatments for children. Six cognitive-behavioral treatment strategies have proved effective in reducing children's anxiety: (1) relaxation training; (2) cognitive restructuring; (3) problem solving; (4) contingent reinforcement; (5) modeling; and (6) imaginal and "in vivo" exposure.[10]

In relaxation training, the body's major muscle groups are progressively relaxed through systematic tension-releasing exercises. By tensing and relaxing different muscle groups, the child learns to perceive sensations of somatic tension and to use these sensations as stimuli to relax.[11]

Cognitive restructuring is often a critical strategy in the treatment of anxiety. Counselors or teachers work with the child to (1) reduce or remove characteristic misinterpretations of environmental events; (2) challenge faulty logic or irrational self-statements; and (3) gradually and systematically construct a frame of reference that includes adaptive coping strategies.[12]

Cognitive-behavioral treatment of anxiety often involves training in problem solving. D'Zurilla and Goldfried[13] have outlined a five-stage problem-solving sequence: (1) the person prepares for the solution of the problem; (2) the problem is defined and formulated and the major goals are described; (3) the person generates alternative solutions and the process of decision making occurs; (4) as soon as a decision is made, it is implemented; and (5) the success of the person's choice is verified.

According to operant theory, reinforcement occurs when an event following a response increases the probability that the response will reoccur. Contingent reinforcement has succeeded in modifying widely varied behaviors, including school phobic behavior.[14]

Modeling is yet another important cognitive-behavioral strategy for reducing anxiety. Nonfearful responses are enacted in fear-producing contexts, thereby demonstrating adaptive responses to the fear-inducing stimuli; consequently, fears may be reduced and appropriate behaviors acquired. In addition, the child is instructed to imitate the model and provided consistent feedback and reinforcement for per-

formance that approximates that of the model.[15]

"Exposure" involves placing the person in the fear-eliciting situation, either imaginally or "in vivo," until he or she "acclimatizes.[16] Fear reduction is linked to the extent to which the person can discriminate between threatening and nonthreatening stimuli. Very careful planning of exposure is essential so that the procedure is not so unpleasant that it actually strengthens the fear.

In applying cognitive-behavioral treatment approaches, Edward S. Shapiro recommends that school psychologists assess "broad bands of behavior" in order to gain information about the student's problem from the teacher's perspective. As the primary referral source, the teacher is interviewed "to identify specific antecedents, consequences, and parameters surrounding problem behaviors." Shapiro also encourages a close collaboration between the teacher and the clinician so that the former becomes a fuller partner in intervention, and thus feels ownership in the actual evaluation and implementation of psychological and pedagogical strategies for reducing the student's fears.[17]

Indeed, the classroom teacher can play an important role in identifying and analyzing whether discrete events in the pupil's life are sufficiently worrisome to warrant intervention. If the latter is necessary, the teacher can observe behavior over time and make appropriate changes in her helping techniques. Blom, Cheney, and Snoddy suggest that teachers follow a stress-intervention model that includes the following features: an initial teacher appraisal (i.e., information gathering to scrutinize the effects of specific stress and fear); an assessment of the student's behavioral indicators or reactions to the stressors; and a background check on the student's current psychological status. The teacher can then monitor the student's concrete behaviors and the impact of reactive interventions on

her own part. Depending on the need for further treatment, the in-

Indeed, the classroom teacher can play an important role in identifying and analyzing whether discrete events in the pupil's life are sufficiently worrisome to warrant intervention.

tervention may be continued, modified, or discontinued.[18]

The determination of whether the student's behavioral response to fear merits intervention can indeed be problematic. Blom et al. argue that intervention should be considered "when there is a change in the child's behavior or some atypical behavior that is either excessively severe or overly minimal in relation to the response expected." Conversely, apparently fearful responses that are fleeting, non-intense, or appropriate for the stressor involved would likely not require active intervention.[19]

Adlerian Treatment Approaches

Rudolf Dreikurs, the principal successor to Alfred Adler, also developed a treatment model that may be useful for teachers who

Rather than criticizing the child's fearful behavior or school failures, the teacher should provide sufficient encouragement to foster courage in the student.

come in contact with fearful pupils. Dreikurs postulated that some children believe there is little opportunity to find a place for themselves in the classroom environment. As a consequence, they begin to display feelings of inadequacy. Other children who are routinely unsuccessful in school may become discouraged over time. Since they come to expect failure, they become excessively passive, seldom engage in classroom activities, and instead concentrate on avoiding embarrassing or humiliating experiences. Their fear is a natural reaction to a faulty and restrictive goal pattern that they construct out of their school circumstances. Adlerian psychologists insist that teachers need to help such students identify, understand, and change those misdirected goals of behavior.

For example, the teacher might ask the fearful child, "Could it be that you want to be left alone because you are afraid to fail?" In such classroom interaction, it is vital that both the teacher and classmates offer encouragement to the pupil who sees herself as unsuccessful in her schoolwork. In addition, the teacher should maximize that child's opportunities for success by structuring appropriate activities and giving her manageable tasks that will likely lead to success.[20]

Adlerian clinicians advise teachers to learn the motivations (intentions) of their pupils so that "mistaken behavior" can be pinpointed at its source and modified in more "socially useful" directions.[21] Dreikurs applied the principle of "natural and logical consequences" as a learning device to permit the child to experience the results of her behavior in the classroom and to evaluate her actions accordingly. This intentional judgment can be important in changing the fearful child's erroneous view of the world. As Adler himself asserted:

It is a significant fact that what determines the development of

the child is neither his own intrinsic ability nor the objective environment, but the interpretation that the child happens to make of the external reality and of his relations to it.[22]

According to Dreikurs, "Fear implies the assumption that we are unable to control a situation. And when we are afraid that we cannot do something, we paralyze ourselves so that we can't." In a real sense, fear serves the irrational purpose of sapping the child's courage, placing her in a position to win attention, but also relegating her to an emotional state of inferiority and inadequacy.[23]

The instilling of courage and mastery is critical in Adlerian pedagogy. Rather than criticizing the child's fearful behavior or school failures, the teacher should provide sufficient encouragement to foster courage in the student. In so doing, she may well be laying the foundation for the kind of attitudinal change that will presage mastery of basic skills and higher forms of cognitive development.

Psychodynamic Treatment Approaches

Clinicians and teachers grounded in the psychodynamic, or psychoanalytic, tradition tend to stress the roles of exploration, fantasy, and play in their application of treatment modalities. Particularly in the cases of fear and anxiety, it is crucial to permit the pupil to express her feelings in an environment of relative freedom and security.

Anna Freud and D.W. Winnicott, for example, emphasized the significance of imaginative kinds of play. Through careful observation of the child at play, teachers can better understand her defenses against fear, stress, and anxiety. Play also affords students an opportunity to assimilate fantasy and reality to the point that fear-inducing events can become less frightening. Psychoanalytic education would allow the child's past developmental roots to be naturally embedded in her present and future life, ideally permitting her to meld the world of fantasy into the experience of reality. It might prove helpful, for instance, for the teacher to allow the fearful child to bring a comforting play object to school, or to surround her with empathetic classmates who will make her feel appreciated in a classroom that is warm and inviting rather than restrictive and hostile.[24]

Psychoanalytic and psychodynamic practitioners have encouraged parents and teachers to bear in mind that, in general, fears which are apparently groundless to adults are very real to the child. If parents [and teachers] recognize a child's thought processes and capabilities at each stage and deal with him accordingly, the child will gradually work his way through his childhood fears.[25]

Too-precipitous overexposure to life's realities (including fear-laden events) may disarm the child, leaving her unprotected and defenseless. At the same time, her fantasy world has already been inhabited by ghosts and goblins—precursors of the unsafe later life that will have to be faced and dealt with in head-on fashion.

British educator Geoffrey Yarlott captures the essence of psychodynamic pedagogy in relation to the child's fears in a succinct and apt manner:

[The child] alternates between wanting to experiment, to predict and control events for himself and desiring to be protected from intolerable degrees of stress and anxiety. Perceptive teaching consists in helping the child to reconcile his alternating needs—in preserving a balance between that degree of anxiety or tension which is desirable, and that which may become unbearable or abnormal if not effectively dispelled.[26]

Postscript

In their poignant narrative, *Vivienne: The Life and Suicide of an Adolescent Girl*, John E. Mack and Holly Hickler depict how psychologists and teachers can collaborate as helping professionals in school situations that are indeed desperate and mind-numbing. Fears in the classroom may well precipitate cries for help from both the student and the teacher. How can professional psychologists and teachers work toward the common goal of eradicating fear and providing for a classroom atmosphere that nurtures warmth, safety, and self-expression? Mack and Hickler offer a fitting endnote to the often perplexing, but increasingly necessary, responsibilities shared by psychologists and teachers:

The distinction between the [teacher and the psychologist] is entirely proper. In some ways, teachers represent reality and daily partnership. A teacher may see as "lazy" what a psychologist would label "paralyzed." A teacher could respond to "hostility" where a psychologist would see "depression." Young people need to know both aspects of themselves: the effect of their behavior and, when it is troubling, the emotional logic that causes it. Perhaps these two functions cannot be blended in one person, but it is safe to say that the two viewpoints ought to come closer together and that teachers should make new relationships with counselors.[27]

1. Philip C. Kendall, Tamar Ellsas Chansky, Michael Friedman, Ray Kim, Elizabeth Kortlander, Frances M. Sessa, and Lynne Siqueland, "Treating Anxiety Disorders in Children and Adolescents," in *Child and Adolescent Therapy: Cognitive-Behavioral Procedures*, ed. Philip C. Kendall (New York: Guilford, 1991).
2. American Psychiatric Association, *Diagnostic and Statistical Manual of Mental Disorders*, 4th ed. (Washington, D.C.: Author, 1994), 110.
3. Lauren B. Alloy, Joan Acocella, and Richard R. Bootzin, *Abnormal Psychology: Current Perspectives*, 7th ed. (New York: McGraw-Hill, 1996).
4. American Psychiatric Association, DSM-IV, 111.
5. Ibid., 411.
6. Ibid., 413-414.
7. Ibid., 412.
8. Alloy et al., *Abnormal Psychology*.
9. Andrew R. Eisen and L.B. Engler, "Chronic Anxiety," in *Clinical Handbook of Anxiety Disorders in Children and Adolescents*, ed. Andrew R. Eisen, Christopher A. Kearney, and Charles E. Schaefer (Northvale, N.J.: Aronson, 1995).
10. Kendall et al., "Treating Anxiety Disorders in Children and Adolescents."
11. Neville J. King, David I. Hamilton, and Thomas H. Ollendick, *Children's Phobias: A Behavioral Perspective* (Chichester, England: Wiley, 1988).
12. Kendall et al., "Treating Anxiety Disorders in Children and Adolescents."
13. Thomas J. D'Zurilla and Marvin R. Goldfried, "'Problem-Solving and Behavior Modification," *Journal of Abnormal Psychology* 78 (1971): 107-126.
14. Kendall et al., "Treating Anxiety Disorders in Children and Adolescents."
15. Ibid.
16. Isaac M. Marks, *Fears, Phobias, and Rituals: Panic, Anxiety, and Their Disorders* (New York: Oxford University Press, 1987).
17. Edward S. Shapiro, *Behavioral Assessment in School Psychology* (Hillsdale, N.J.: Erlbaum, 1987), 124, 15.
18. Gaston E. Blom, Bruce D. Cheney, and James E. Snoddy, *Stress in Childhood: An Intervention Model for Teachers and Other Professionals* (New York: Teachers College Press, 1986), 17-24.
19. Ibid., 74-75.
20. Rudolf Dreikurs, Bernice Bronia Grunwald, and Floy C. Pepper, *Maintaining Sanity in the Classroom: Illustrated Teaching Techniques* (New York: Harper and Row, 1971), 17-20.
21. Rudolf Dreikurs with Vicki Soltz, *Children: The Challenge* (New York: Hawthorne, 1964), 57-67.
22. Alfred Adler, *The Education of Children* (New York: Greenberg, 1930), 96.
23. Dreikurs, *Children: The Challenge*, 216, 221.
24. Anna Freud, *Normality and Pathology in Childhood* (New York: International Universities Press, 1965); and D.W. Winnicott, *Playing and Reality* (New York: Basic Books, 1971).
25. Mary Forman Rice and Charles H. Flatter, *Help Me Learn: A Handbook for Teaching Children from Birth to Third Grade* (Englewood Cliffs, N.J.: Prentice-Hall, 1979), 211.
26. Geoffrey Yarlott, *Education and Children's Emotions: An Introduction* (London: Weidenfeld and Nicolson, 1972), 63.
27. John E. Mack and Holly Hickler, *Vivienne: The Life and Suicide of an Adolescent Girl* (Boston: Little, Brown, 1981), 225.

Development during Childhood: Family and Culture

- Family (Articles 22–26)
- Culture (Articles 27–30)

Is there a set of family values that is superior to another set of family values? Is there a culture that has more correct answers than another culture? It is often assumed by the lay person that children's behaviors and personalities have a direct correlation with the behaviors and personalities of the person or persons who provided their socialization during infancy and childhood. Are you a mirror image of the person or persons who raised you? Why or why not? How many of their behaviors do you reflect?

During childhood, one's family values get compared to, and tested against, the values of one's school, community, and culture. Peers, schoolmates, teachers, neighbors, extracurricular activity leaders, religious leaders, even shopkeepers play increasingly important roles. Culture influences the growing developing child not only through the people with whom the child has one-on-one interaction, but also through holidays, styles of dress, music, television, movies, slang, games played, parents' jobs, transportation, and exposure to sex, drugs, and violence. The ecological theorist, Urie Bronfenbrenner, calls these exosystem and macrosystem influences. The developing personality of a child has multiple interwoven influences: from genetic potentialities through family values and socialization practices through community and cultural pressures for behaviors.

The first article in this unit addresses the issue of family affection. Family responsiveness with plenty of tender loving care and communication is essential to the healthy social and emotional development of a school-age child. A working mother, a working father, a single, poor, adoptive, divorced, or even homeless parent can be a good parent when he or she attends to the child's need for loving support. Many overly simplistic generalizations have been made about families being "at-risk" of dysfunction due to such things as poverty or cultural background. A school-age child is not necessarily in danger of becoming disturbed if the mother or father is poor, absent, divorced, unemployed, or from a minority culture. Some children (called dandelion children) seem to thrive despite multiple stressors and family and cultural adversities. Other children seem to wilt with life handed to them on the proverbial "silver platter." Hardiness in children is enhanced by loving and touching, by adequate health, safety, and nutrition, and by discipline, democracy, and togetherness. Resilient children can develop in any economic, political, racial, religious, or social group.

The second article in this unit appeals to partnerships in parenting: fathers plus mothers. Fathers have been relegated to "second banana" position, often viewed as breadwinners and disciplinarians. School-age children need parents who are both responsive and demanding. Discipline is crucial to a healthy personality. However, mothers as well as fathers need to be disciplinarians, and fathers as well as mothers need to provide tender, loving, and responsive caregiving. The authors are both fathers who have important things to say about their roles in their children's lives.

The third article in this section adds another dimension to family responsiveness and demandingness. Siblings are very important agents of socialization with each other. Much has been written about sibling rivalry. Less has been said about positive sibling connections. This selection gives sibling relationships credence and attention, and addresses their impact for better and for worse.

The fourth and fifth articles in the family section present the opposite dimensions of loving responsiveness and caring discipline. One presents some of the long-term consequences on school-age children of witnessing physical abuse between their parents. The second, retained from previous editions because of reader accolades, speaks to the long-term consequences on children of being physically abused themselves. Violence begets violence. Children who witness violence, or have it perpetrated against themselves, are at risk of many types of dysfunctional behavior later in life. They can benefit from counseling intervention.

The articles in this section address cultural issues. The first begins with the classic analysis of the four worlds of childhood (family, peers, school, and work) by the world-renowned ecological theorist, Urie Bronfenbrenner. To be cut off from any of these systems is to be culturally alienated. The second article is also a classic exposition on childhood culture by the prolific writer and cognitive psychologist, David Elkind. Both of these essays have been retained because of their importance and their continued usefulness to readers.

School-age children base right and wrong on criteria such as the approval of others, relationship maintenance, social order maintenance, and respect for authority. When adult role models condone an environment that includes violence, drugs, and sexual promiscuity, children come to think of these behaviors as socially and morally acceptable. Some children experience a great deal of stress trying to figure out why what they hear and see all around them is labeled wrong by some parents, teachers, peers, and religious leaders. Is a loved adult's opinion more important than the majority opinion? What is the opinion of the greater society in a rapidly changing culture? What mores continue to exert pressure? What social climate should be maintained? The third article in this section gives a partial answer to the questions posed by Professors Bronfenbrenner and Elkind about how to cope in a confusing culture, and that is that one loving, caring adult can make a difference. An attentive parent or mentor can be a stabilizing element in a child's life. In addition, as Dr. Bronfenbrenner pointed out, communities and schools can provide support and care for children who feel alienated.

Peer pressures, including sibling pressures, increase as children grow older. Parental pressures are usually paramount for decisions about school, religious participation, community participation, and major time allocation issues. Peer pressures are usually paramount for decisions about self in dress, slang usage, choice of music, free-time leisure activities, and television viewing. The last article in this section deals with the question of television as a pervasive influence on the psyche of the school-age child. The reality is that the average child spends more time in front of a television set than in a school classroom. Despite early psychological studies which suggested that the effect of television might be cathartic (a relief of tension and anxiety by bringing repressed feelings and fears to consciousness), current research explicitly demonstrates that children learn violent behaviors from television and practice them in their real worlds.

Looking Ahead: Challenge Questions

In what ways does tender, loving touch impact on a child's development and personality?

How important are fathers in the lives of their children?

How important are siblings in each other's lives?

What happens to children who witness domestic violence?

What happens to children who experience child abuse?

In what ways do children feel alienated from any of the four "worlds" of childhood?

What is there in today's culture that causes insecurity and stress?

Who can help a child develop resiliency?

What are the myths and what is the reality about viewing televised violence?

Your Loving Touch

The hugs, cuddles, and kisses you give your children will benefit them throughout their lives.

Janice T. Gibson, Ed.D.

Janice T. Gibson, Ed.D., is a contributing editor of *Parents* Magazine.

Like most mothers, I remember vividly the births of my two children, Robin and Mark. Each time I cuddled my newborn children in my arms—snuggling them gently against my skin and caressing them with my hands and lips—I felt peace and an extraordinarily personal happiness. For each child, born four years apart, it took only an instant for me to fall in love! My joy made me want to continue cuddling and, in the process, strengthened a learned need to hug. Years later, when Mark was in fourth grade, I would hide behind the kitchen door and nab him for a hug when he came home from school. (He always put up with me, except in front of his friends.) And when Robin dressed for the prom, I zipped her gown, patted her on the shoulders, and wrapped my arms around her before she left with her date.

The power of touch.

Affectionate physical contact is meaningful at all age levels. Everyone needs affection, especially when frightened, insecure, or overtired. But particularly for children who cannot yet talk or understand words, cuddling and other forms of affectionate touch convey strong nonverbal messages and serve as important means of communication. When your baby is tired and snuggles in your arms, the gentle body-to-body contact relaxes him and communicates, "You're special. I love you."

Cuddling teaches infants about their environment and the people in it. They explore by touching with their fingers and tongue. Since touching is a reciprocal act, by cuddling your child you teach him to cuddle back. And by responding to his actions, you teach your baby to feel good about himself.

As your child grows older and snuggles with you after a frightening experience, a gentle hug that says "You are safe" will relieve him of his anxiety and help him to feel secure. If during a tantrum he lets you pick him up and hold him on your lap, he will be able to calm down and gain control of his emotions. Furthermore, your affectionate touch can help if your child misbehaves. If he hits his baby brother, for example, you can hold him on your lap as you tell him, "Hitting your brother is not okay." These words, together with the affectionate actions, tell him that although his behavior is not acceptable, you still love him. And when your child exhibits positive behavior, by praising him with a hug and a kiss or an enthusiastic high five, you will convey the message "I'm proud of you."

Why touch is so important.

Physical affection is crucial to a child's development. First of all, parents form strong affectional ties to their children by cuddling and touching them. Gary Johnson, of Delavan, Wisconsin, recalls how he felt after the birth of his first child, Jake: "I got to hold him in my arms for the first twenty minutes of his life. From those first moments together, I never felt strange with him. He was this little helpless creature who needed to be held, cuddled, and protected."

Whether an attachment such as the one Gary describes occurs immediately or over time, it increases the probability that parents will respond to their children's needs. Later, this strong attachment increases the child's psychological well-being.

For babies whose parents don't respond to their signals for close bodily contact, the result is what Mary Ainsworth, Ph.D., professor of psychology emeritus at the University of Virginia, in Charlottesville, has termed "anxious avoidance attachment." She and her colleagues found that babies whose mothers seldom pick them up to comfort them, and who rebuff their attempts to snuggle and cuddle, eventually learn to mask their emotions. When these babies are anxious and upset and most want their mother, they will avoid her so as not to risk being rejected again. "These babies often become adults who don't trust people and find it difficult to form close attachments," remarks Ainsworth. Thus the cycle becomes vicious and self-perpetuating.

The results of a recently completed 36-year study further demonstrate that the effects of parental affection are lifelong. In 1951 a team of psychologists from Harvard University, in Cambridge, Massachusetts, studied 379 five-year-olds in Boston. They asked the children's mothers about their own and their husband's child-rearing practices, including how the mothers responded when their child cried and whether they played with him; whether the father hugged and kissed the child when he came home from work; and whether he spent free time with the child. The researchers found that kindergartners whose parents were warm and affectionate and cuddled them frequently were happier, played better, and had fewer feeding, behavior, and bed-wetting problems than did their peers raised by colder and more reserved parents.

In a 1987 follow-up study involving 76 of the original subjects, researchers found that as adults, those who were raised by warm, nurturing parents tended to have longer, happier marriages and better relationships with close friends than did adult peers whose early child rearing was not so warm. According to psychologist Carol Franz, Ph.D., one of the study's researchers, "Affectionate touching was always associated with a lot of warmth. The more warmth parents exhibited, the more socially adjusted their child was at midlife."

Cuddling barriers.

Most parents provide what their babies need and want. Holding, carrying, rocking, and caressing are part of child rearing in most societies. Infant massage, in which babies are systematically touched and stroked in caring ways, is practiced throughout the world. In some countries, such as India, mothers massage with scented oils. And in China, moms not only massage their youngsters but also use acupuncture to relax them.

But in contrast with people from other countries, Americans, in general, aren't "touchy." In my own cross-cultural studies of child rearing, I've found that although mothers and fathers in the United States are basically as affectionate as other parents, they tend to refrain from physical expressions of love. Although a baby's need for constant physical attention is obvious, the need is less obvious for older children and adults. Consequently, as U.S. children grow older, touching becomes less a part of parent-child interaction.

Some parents are uncomfortable behaving affectionately because they are afraid that it will spoil their children. Far from spoiling children, however, it teaches them to trust you and to view the world as a safe place to explore. Youngsters whose parents pick them up and hug them when they are hurt, frightened, or insecure develop feelings of security that make it easier for them to do things on their own.

Although there has been a lot of talk about how much more involved dads are today, many fathers still have a problem touching their children affectionately. Ronald Levant, Ed.D., former director of Boston University's Fatherhood Project and coauthor of *Between Father and Child* (Penguin), explains that today's generation of men have been raised to be like their fathers, who were the family breadwinners, and as a result they have grown up to be stoic. "As boys, they did not learn the basic psychological skills that girls did—such as self-awareness and empathy—which are necessary to nurture and care for children."

Furthermore, when dads do give their children affection, they tend to give more hugs and kisses to their daughters than to their sons. Why? Some fathers think that cuddling is not masculine and that too much physical affection will turn boys into "sissies." One dad admitted that when his wife was pregnant with their first child, he secretly hoped for a girl. "My father was not a very tactile person. We mostly shook hands. So I was concerned that if I had a son, I'd be too reserved. I was afraid to touch a son." Levant assures, however, that boys who are cuddled by their dads will not become "sissies" but will learn to be nurturing themselves. And more good news: The fathers of this generation are recognizing that they missed affection from their dads and, says Levant, are "breaking the old molds" of masculine reserve.

Some women also feel uncomfortable kissing and hugging their children because their parents weren't comfortable showing affection. One mother says that on the surface, her parents were warm and loving and she was well taken care of, "but I was rarely touched, hugged, or kissed." She wasn't comfortable cuddling with her children until she went into therapy and talked about her feelings. Now, she says, "I don't even think about it anymore. Hugging comes very naturally."

The high rate of divorce today, and the large number of single-parent homes in which the head of the household must work outside the home, also make it more difficult for some parents to provide the physical affection that their children may want or need at any given time. The recent concern raised by the specter of child abuse hasn't made it easier either. Highly publicized cases of purported sexual abuse of children by caregivers or estranged parents make some adults afraid that cuddling and touching may be construed as sexual and harmful. So what can be done? Although it is critical to protect children from sexual abuse, it is equally important to show all children that they are loved and needed. Children need healthy affection, and parents need to find ways to provide it.

Some parents are uncomfortable behaving affectionately with their children because they are afraid it will spoil them. On the contrary, it will help them develop feelings of security.

There are 1,001 ways to demonstrate affection, and not everyone needs to do it the same way. Parents who aren't comfortable giving their children big hugs and kisses shouldn't feel obliged to do so. Patting on the hand or back—or giving a squeeze—plus some loving words, can convey affection if it is done in a meaningful way.

Cuddling comfort.

Like some parents, some children are uncomfortable about being held closely, not because they don't want affection, but because they are uncomfortable feeling physically constrained. For such children, you can stroke their shoulders or back gently, give them lots of kisses, or tickle them gently so that they don't feel entrapped. Eventually they may even like to be cuddled. Gary Johnson's four-year-old daughter, Hallie, and one-year-old son, Nate, weren't as cuddly from the beginning with their father as was their older brother, Jake. But now Hallie is "Daddy's little girl and a permanent fixture on my lap." And Nate has just recently started to want Gary to cuddle him. "It's a real thrill to me to have him reach out for a hug from Dad," he says.

If you work outside the home and are away for most of the day, be sure that your caregiver supplies all the physical love your child needs. The Johnsons were concerned about leaving their kids in somebody else's care. "Becky and I believe that kids need plenty of physical love and affection, and we were afraid that someone else might not give them enough," says Gary. So they searched carefully. "We were fortunate to find a warm, loving, and wonderful caregiver. We can tell the kids are happy."

When peers become important to your child, he may start to shun your affections, particularly if his friends are present. Statements of rejection, such as "Yuck, Mom, don't kiss me" and "Leave my hair alone," do sting, but they signal that your child is growing up and striving for independence. Because he still needs your affection, you might try hugging him at bedtime when his friends aren't around.

As boys and girls reach puberty, touching becomes charged with sexual meaning, making it hard for many adolescents even to acknowledge the desire to touch or be touched in non-sexual ways. Parents should respect their teens' discomfort. When a hug may be too threatening, you can still express your love with a squeeze of the hand or a pat on the back.

If you are divorced, your child needs love from both you and your ex-spouse, even more than before the separation. So, if possible, work together with your ex-spouse to help your child to understand that both of you care. Sometimes boys raised in fatherless households, interpreting the loss of their father as making them the "man of the house," decide that permitting their mother to hug or kiss them makes them less manly. Mothers should respect these feelings but should not stop showing affection: A hug at bedtime or a lingering pat on the arm while going over homework will do wonders.

A recent experience underscored the message for me that even in adulthood, we still need, and benefit from, touch. It was while my now adult children and I were mourning their father's death. We stood silently for some minutes in a circle, our arms around one another, holding on tightly. The feel of our bodies touching consoled us and gave us strength. It convinced us, in a very concrete way, that we would be able to get on with our lives.

Fathers' Time

Their style is vastly different, but dads can no longer be looked on as second bananas in the parenting biz. New studies show fathers are crucial for the emotional and intellectual growth of their kids, influencing how they ultimately turn out. Writer/father PAUL ROBERTS reports on the importance of being a papa. Actor/father BILL MOSELEY's dispatches reveal what it's like on the front lines.

Paul Roberts

PAUL ROBERTS is a Seattle-based freelance writer. Actor BILL MOSELEY interviewed Timothy Leary for *PT* in 1995.

This was supposed to be the Golden Era of Paternity. After decades of domestic aloofness, men came charging into parenthood with an almost religious enthusiasm. We attended Lamaze classes and crowded into birthing rooms. We mastered diapering, spent more time at home with the kids, and wallowed in the flood of "papa" literature unleashed by Bill Cosby's 1986 best-seller Fatherhood.

Yet for all our fervor, the paternal revolution has had a slightly hollow ring. It's not simply the relentless accounts of fatherhood's dark side—the abuse, the neglect, the abandonment—that make us so self-conscious. Rather, it's the fact that for all our earnest sensitivity, we can't escape questions of our psychological necessity: What is it, precisely, that fathers do? What critical difference do we make in the lives of our children?

Think about it. The modern mother, no matter how many nontraditional duties she assumes, is still seen as the family's primary nurturer and emotional guardian. It's in her genes. It's in her soul. But mainstream Western society accords no corresponding position to the modern father. Aside from chromosomes and feeling somewhat responsible for household income, there's no similarly celebrated deep link between father and child, no widely recognized "paternal instinct." Margaret Mead's quip that fathers are "a biological necessity but

Diary of a Dad

I love this time. Jane Moseley puts her hunter mare through its paces. Time slows to a trot, works up to a canter, drops to a lazy walk.

She announces she won't wear her riding hat. I insist she must. She refuses, would rather not ride. I can't believe she'd give up The Most Important Thing in her Life over this. Fine, don't ride. This triggers an outpouring of vitriol. I pay attention, but don't take it personally. Thirty minutes later she's holding my hand as we walk down Melrose.

a social accident" may be a little harsh. But it does capture the second-banana status that many fathers have when it comes to taking their measure as parents.

Happily, a new wave of research is likely to substantially boost that standing. Over the last decade, researchers like Jay Belsky, Ph.D., at Pennsylvania State University, and Ross Parke, Ph.D., of the University of California/Riverside Center for Family Studies, have been mapping out the psychology of the father-child bond, detailing how it functions and how it differs—sometimes substantially—from the bond between mother and child. What emerges from their work is the beginning of a truly modern concept of paternity, one in which old assumptions are overturned or, at the very least, cast in a radically different light. Far from Mead's "social accident," fatherhood turns out to be a complex and unique phenomenon with huge consequences for the emotional and intellectual growth of children.

Key to this new idea of fatherhood is a premise so mundane that most of us take it for granted: fathers parent differently than mothers do. They play with their children more. Their interactions tend to be more physical and less intimate, with more of a reliance on humor and excitement. While such distinctions may hardly seem revelatory, they can mean a world of difference to kids. A father's more playful interactive style, for example, turns out to be critical in teaching a child emotional self-control. Likewise, father-child interactions appear to be central to the development of a child's ability to maintain strong, fulfilling social relationships later in life. But it's not simply a matter of paternal behavior differing from maternal methods. The fabric of the father-child bond is also different. Studies show that fathers with low self-esteem have a greater negative impact in their children than do mothers who don't like themselves. In addition, the father-child bond seems to be more fragile—and therefore more easily severed—during periods of strife between parents.

Amid this welter of findings two things are clear. First, given our rapidly evolving conceptions of "father" and "family", fatherhood in the 1990s is probably tougher, psychologically, than at any other time in recent history. Plainly put, there are precious few positive role models to guide today's papas. Yet at the same time, the absence of any guidance holds hidden promise. Given the new information on fatherhood, the potential for a rich and deeply rewarding paternal experience is significantly greater today than even a generation ago. "The possibilities for fathering have never been better," Belsky says. "Culturally speaking, there is so much more that fathers are 'allowed' to do."

Our Forefathers

The surge of interest in fatherhood has a distinctly modern feel, as if after thousands of years of unquestioned maternal preeminence, men are just now discovering and asserting their parental prerogatives. But in fact, this unquestioned maternal dominance is itself a relatively recent development. Up until the mid-1700s, when most fathers worked in or near the home and took a much greater hand in child rearing, Western culture regarded them and not mothers as the more competent parent—and ultimately held them more responsible for how their children turned out. Not only were books and manuals on parenting written chiefly for men, according to R. L. Griswold, author of *Fatherhood in America*, men were routinely awarded custody of their kids in cases of divorce.

With the Industrial Revolution, however, more fathers began working outside their homes and thus were effectively removed from domestic life. As Vicky Phares, Ph.D., assistant professor of psychology at the University of South Florida, wrote in *Fathers and Developmental Psychopathology*, industrialization ushered in the "feminization of the domestic sphere and the marginalization of fathers' involvement with their children." By the mid-1800s, Phares notes, "child-rearing manuals were geared toward mothers, and this trend

After Jane and I had a snack, she wanted to box. So we waltzed around for 20 minutes, floating like a butterfly (me), stinging like a bee (Jane). I've taught her the rudiments of pugilism: how to make a fist (don't wrap your fingers around your thumb); how she should always stand sideways to her opponent, watching the hands not the eyes, etc. After a few fun-filled injury-free rounds, I came to my senses and ended our play.

Jane is an only child, so I figure it's my job to play with her as a brother or provide her with a sibling—playing with her is easier!

continued for the most part until the mid 1970s."

The implication here—that parental roles have largely been defined by economics—is still a subject of cultural debate. Less arguable, however, is the fact that by the turn of the twentieth century, both science and society saw the psychology of parenting largely as the psychology of motherhood. Not only were mothers somehow more "naturally" inclined to parent, they were also genetically better prepared for the task. Indeed, in 1916, Phares notes, one prominent investigator went so far as to "prove" the existence of the maternal instinct—and the lack of paternal equivalent—largely based on the notion that "few fathers were naturally skilled at taking care of infants."

Granted, bogus scientific claims were plentiful in those times. But even Freud, who believed fathers figured heavily in children's development of conscience and sexual identity, dismissed the idea that they had any impact until well past a child's third year. And even then, many psychologists argued, these paternal contributions consisted primarily of providing income, discipline, and a masculine role model, along with periodic injections of what might be called "real world" experience—that is, things that took place outside the home. "The classical psychological view held that a father's 'job' was to expand his children's horizon beyond the bosom of the family and the mother-child relationship," Belsky observes. "Mothers preserved and protected children from discomfort. But fathers imposed a realistic, the world-is-tough perspective."

By the 1920s, the classic "mother-centric" view was showing its cracks. Not only did subsequent empirical studies find little hard evidence of any unique maternal instinct but, as Phares points out, the phenomenon of "mother-blaming"—that is, blaming mothers for all the emotional and behavioral problems of their children—prodded some researchers (and, no doubt, a good many mothers) to ask whether fathers might share some of the responsibility.

By the 1950s, science began to recognize that there was some paternal impact on early childhood—even if it was only in the negative context of divorce or the extended absence of a father. Psychologist Michael Lamb, Ph.D., research director at the National Institute for Child Health and Human Development in Bethesda, Maryland, explains: "The assumption was that by comparing the behavior and personalities of children raised with and without fathers, one could—essentially by a process of subtraction—estimate what sort of influence fathers typically had."

Wʜᴀᴛ Dᴀᴅs Dᴏ

It wasn't until the feminist movement of the 1970s that researchers thought to ask whether dads could be as nurturing as moms. To everyone's astonishment, the answer was yes.

Actually, that was half the answer. Subsequent inquiries showed that while fathers could be as nurturing as mothers, they tended to leave such duties to moms. Hardly news to millions of overworked women, this finding was crucial. For the first time, researchers began systematically studying how and why male and female parenting strategies diverged, and more to the point, what those differences meant for children.

Although the total fatherhood experience runs from conception on, research has focused most keenly on the first few years of the parent-child relationship. It's here that children are most open to parental influence; they function primarily as receivers, consuming not only huge quantities of nourishment and comfort but stimuli as well. For decades, investigators have understood that infants not only enjoy taking in such rudimentary knowledge but absolutely require it for intellectual, physical, and especially emotional growth.

Without such constant interaction, argues W. Andrew Collins, Ph.D., of the University of Minnesota's Institute for Child Development, infants might never fully develop a sense of comfort and security. As important, they might not develop a sense of being connected to—and thus having some degree of control over—the world around them. "The key ingredient is a 'contingent responsiveness,' " says Collins, "where infants learn their actions will elicit certain reliable responses from others."

It's also during this crucial period that one of the most fundamental differences between male and female parenting styles takes place. Work by several psychiatrists, including San Diego's Martin Greenberg, M.D., and Kyle Pruett, M.D., a professor of psychiatry at the Yale Child Study Center, suggests that while new mothers are inclined to relate to their infants in a more soothing, loving, and serious way, new fathers "hold their children differently and have a different kind of patience and frustration cycle than mothers," Pruett observes.

I crave adult company, but I don't have a baby-sitter for tonight. So I'm trying to lug Jane all the way to Santa Monica to see Wing Chun, a kung-fu movie she says she doesn't want to see. Oh, no you don't, kid, it's my time now, and we're going to Santa Monica. Of course, Jane winds up loving the movie. Later that night we watch a video of Captains Courageous. I am reminded of all the songs that the two of us have made up over the past several years: "Feed Lot," "Ain't No Bridge," "Don't Drink the Water," "When the Vulture Swoops," etc. (Lyrics upon request).

Why it is fathers behave this way isn't entirely clear. (And when fathers are primary caregivers, they are likely to display many of the so-called maternal traits.) Some studies suggest these gender differences are part of a larger male preference for stimulating, novel activities that arises from neurobiological differences in the way stimuli and pleasure are linked in male and female brains, and likely a result of genetics. Individuals high in the sensation-seeking trait are far more likely to engage in new and exciting pastimes. Though not all guys qualify as sensation seekers, the trait is far more common in men—particularly young ones—than it is in women, and might help explain why any young fathers start off having a parenting style that's stimulating for them as well as their child.

Tʜᴇ Dᴀᴅᴅʏ Dʏɴᴀᴍɪᴄ

Whatever its origins, this more playful, jocular approach carries major consequences for developing children. Where the "average" mother cushions her baby against irritating stimulation, the "average" father heaps it on, consistently producing a broader range of arousal. The resulting ups and downs force children to "stretch," emotionally and physically.

This emotion-stretching dynamic becomes more pronounced as father-child relationships enter into their second and third years. When playing, fathers tend to be more physical with their toddlers—wrestling, playing tag, and so on—while mothers emphasize verbal exchanges and interacting with objects, like toys. In nearly all instances, says Lamb, fathers are much more likely "to get children worked up, negatively or positively, with fear as well as delight, forcing them to learn to regulate their feelings."

In a sense, then, fathers push children to cope with the world outside the mother-child bond, as classical theory argued. But more than this, fathering behavior also seems to make children develop a more complex set of interactive skills, what Parke calls "emotional communication" skills.

First, children learn how to "read" their father's emotions via his facial expressions, tone of voice, and other nonverbal cues, and respond accordingly. Is Daddy really going to chase me down and gobble me up, or is he joking? Did I really hurt Daddy by poking him in the eye? Is Daddy in the mood to play, or is he tired?

Second, children learn how to clearly communicate their own emotions to others. One common example is the child who by crying lets her daddy know that he's playing too roughly or is scaring her. Kids also learn to indicate when interactions aren't stimulating enough; they'll show they've lost interest by not responding or wandering off.

Finally, children learn how to "listen" to their own emotional state. For instance, a child soon learns that if he becomes too "worked up" and begins to cry, he may in effect drive his play partner away.

The consequences of such emotional mastery are far-reaching. By successfully coping with stimulating, emotionally stretching interactions, children learn that they can indeed ef-

Made Jane cry—down on her for not helping me put away the groceries, make dinner. She wanted to play Super Mario Bros. (So did I.) She called me an idiot. I yelled at her about not pulling her oar—sounded just like my dad—and sent her to her room. I kept her in there for a few minutes, felt bad, knocked on the door, and sat on her bed and apologized for losing my temper. "You hurt my feelings," she sniffed.

CREATING A NEW PATRIARCHY

Even the most dedicated dads quickly discover that the road to modern fatherhood is strewn with obstacles. Positive role models are in short supply and personal experiences are usually no help. Jerrold Lee Shapiro, Ph.D., professor of psychology at Santa Clara University, says understanding your relationship with your own father is the first step. If not, you're bound to automatically and unconciously replicate things from your childhood.

Here are several strategies both parents can use to strengthen the father-child bond.

◆ Start early. While involvement doesn't always equal intimacy, fathers who immerse themselves in all aspects of parenting from birth on are more likely to be closer to their children. Take part in as many prenatal activities as possible and schedule at least a week away from work after the baby is born to practice parenting skills and overcome anxieties about handling the baby.

◆ Create "fathering space": Schedule times and activities in which you take care of your newborn entirely on your own. The traditional practice of deferring to mothers as "experts" gives new fathers few chances to hone their parenting skills, bolster their confidence, and build solid bonds with baby.

Sue Dickinson, M.S.W., a marriage and family therapist in Cle Elum, Washington, suggests persuading mom to go out of the house so you can have the experience of being *the* parent. Martin Greenberg, M.D., recommends bundling your baby in a chest pack and going for walks. The feeling of a baby's body—together with his or her warmth and smell—is captivating.

◆ Articulate feelings. Although fatherhood is routinely described as "the most wonderful experience" a man can have, new fathers may feel anxious, fearful, and frustrated. They may also be jealous of the time their wives spend with the baby and of their wives' "natural" parenting skills. These feelings may only make it harder for you to

wholeheartedly participate in parenting and create distance between you and your child. New fathers need to identify such feelings and discuss them with their wives.

◆ Mind the details. Tune in to your children and avoid relying on mom to "read" what your baby wants.

◆ Respect diversity. Accept your partner's parenting style without criticizing. Mothers often regard fathers' more boisterous style as too harsh or insensitive. But such criticism can derail a dad's desire for involvement. "Just because he's doing something you wouldn't do doesn't make it wrong," says Jay Belsky, Ph.D. Mothers have to temper their need to protect and remember dads offer things moms don't.

◆ Be realistic. Fathers who want to adopt a more hands-on approach than they themselves experienced are often frustrated when kids don't immediately respond. But children accustomed to having mom as the primary caregiver simply cannot adapt to "sudden" paternal involvement overnight. Above all, parenting requires patience.

fect change both on internal matters (their feelings) and in the outside world (their father's actions). In that regard, links have been found between the quality of father-child interactions and a child's later development of certain life skills, including an ability to manage frustration, a willingness to explore new things and activities, and persistence in problem solving.

As important as learning to regulate the emotional intensity of their interactions is children's ability to master the larger interactive process, the give and take that makes up social communication. "Kids who learn how to decode and encode emotions early on will be better off later when it comes to any social encounter," Parke says.

Such benefits have been intensely studied in the area of sibling relationships. Work by Belsky and Brenda Volling, Ph.D., an assistant professor of psychology at the University of Michigan, suggests that the emotion-management "lessons" learned by children from their fathers during play are applied later in interactions with siblings—and ultimately with people outside the family—and lead to more cooperation and less fighting. The press release announcing Belsky and Volling's research quipped, "If Adam had been a better father, things might have turned out differently for Cain and Abel."

Such findings come with plenty of caveats. A mother's more comforting manner is just as crucial to her children, helping them foster, among other things, a critical sense of security and self-confidence. Indeed, a mere preference for stimulating activities does not a good father make; obviously, the quality of father-child interactions is important. Successful fathers both monitor and modulate their play, maintaining a level of stimulation that keeps children engaged without making them feel like they've been pushed too far. This requires complete engagement—something many of today's busy fathers find difficult to manage. "What often happens is fathers don't pay attention to the cues their kids are sending," Belsky says. "A kid is crying 'uncle' and his father doesn't hear it."

Of course, fathers aren't the only parent who can teach these coping skills. Mothers physically play with their kids and, depending on the dynamics and history of the family, may also be the ones providing more of a "paternal" influence—teaching coping skills through play. Yet this "stretching" role typically falls to fathers because men gravitate toward less intimate, more physical interactions. And, as Reed

Anna's sleeping over. Earlier in the evening, Jane was on the floor of her bedroom looking up my shorts, laughing, saying she saw my penis. Later, I spy Jane and Anna holding up our cat Jackson. Must be a penis hunt, little-girl style. It's already in full swing and they're seven and eight!

In addition to being cook, chauffeur, maid, and spiritual protector, I am also Sex Authority! Two years ago, I explained, in a general way, the birds and the bees to Jane, correcting the misinformation she'd been given by her good friend Olivia.

Larson, Ph.D., a psychologist at the University of Illinois-Champagne, observes, "when dads stop having fun interacting with their kids, they're more likely than mothers to exit."

Whether these differences are genetic, cultural, or, more likely, a combination of the two, is still hotly debated. But the fact remains that in terms of time spent with children, fathers typically spend more of it playing with their kids than mothers do—a difference that from very early on, children pick up on. Studies show that during stressful situations, one-year-old and 18-month-old babies more often turn to their primary caretaker—in most families, mom—for help. By contrast, when researchers measured so-called affiliative behaviors like smelling and vocalizing, during their first two years, babies showed a preference for their fathers. Just as dramatic, almost as soon as a child can crawl or walk, he or she will typically seek out dad for play and mom for comfort and other needs.

DOWNSIDE OF THE DADDY TRACK

On the face of it, fathers would seem to enjoy considerable advantages over mothers during their children's first years. Not only do they do less of the dirty work, but it's almost as if they've been anointed to handle the fun art of parenting. Yet as time goes on this situation changes dramatically. While a mother's more intimate, need-related approach to parenting generally continues to cement her bond with her children, a father's more playful and stimulating style steadily loses its appeal. By the age of eight or nine, a child may already be angry at his father's teasing, or bored or annoyed by his I'm-gonna-gitcha style.

This discrepancy often becomes quite pronounced as children reach adolescence. Research suggests that preteens and teens of both sexes continue to rely on their mothers for intimacy and needs, and increasingly view her as the favored parent for topics requiring sensitivity and trust. By contrast, Parke says, the joking, playful style that serves fathers so well during children's first years may begin to alienate teens, giving them the impression that their father doesn't take their thoughts and needs seriously.

Adding to this tension is the father's traditional role as the dispenser of discipline and firmness. It's hypothesized that fathers' less intimate interactive style may make it easier—although not more pleasant—for them to play the "heavy." In any case, adolescents come to see their fathers as the harsher, more distant parent. This feeling may increase teenagers' tendency to interact more often and intimately with their mothers, which in turn only heightens the sense of estrangement and tension between fathers and their kids.

As to whether fathers' possibly not being at home as much as mothers makes it easier or more difficult for them to be the disciplinarian, Parke says there are too many other factors involved to make such a determination. He does note, however, that many mothers faced with unruly kids still employ the threat, "Wait 'til your father gets home."

Clearly, the distance between fathers and adolescent children is not solely as result of fathers' playfulness earlier on. A central function of adolescence is a child's gradual movement toward emotional and physical autonomy from both parents. But studies suggest this movement is most directly and forcefully spurred by fathers' less intimate ways.

Does a father's parenting style during adolescence produce more closeness between father and child? The answer is probably no, says Parke. But if the question is, does a father's style serve a launching, independence-gaining function, the answer is probably yes. "Mothers' continued nurturance maintains a child's connectedness to the family, while fathers encourage differentiation," Parke says. In fact, according to a recent survey of adolescents by Israeli researchers Shmuel Shulman, Ph.D., and Moshe Klein, Ph.D., most perceived their fathers as being the primary source of support for their teenage autonomy.

Such notions will undoubtedly strike some as disturbingly regressive, as if researchers have simply found new, complex ways to justify outdated stereotypes of paternal behavior. For as any sensitive observer knows, the totality of fatherhood goes well beyond a tendency toward stimulating interactions and away from intimacy. Nonetheless, this does appear to be a central component of fathering behavior and may help explain why some seemingly antiquated modes of fathering persist. Despite evolution in gender roles, Belsky says, fathers are still more likely to provide less sensitivity, require kids to adjust to 'tough' realities, and perhaps be less understanding and empathetic.

Yet if the father-child bond truly serves as a mechanism for preparing children for the external world, the bond itself seems remarkably sensitive, even vulnerable, to that world. External variables, such as a father's relationships beyond his family—and in particular his experience in the workplace—appear to be linked to both the kinds of fathering behavior he exhibits and the success he achieves with it. Some of these links are obvious. Few would be surprised to learn that fathers with high-stress jobs are apt to be more distant from their kids or use harsher, physical discipline when dealing with youthful infractions.

Other links between a man's external world and the way he fathers are more subtle. According to Parke, there are significant and intriguing fathering differences between men whose jobs involve a great degree of independence and those who are heavily managed. Fathers with workplace autonomy tend to expect and encourage more independence in their children. Moreover, they generally place grater emphasis on a child's intent when assessing misbehavior, and aren't inclined toward physical discipline. By contrast, men in highly supervised jobs with little autonomy are more likely to value and expect conformity from their kids. They're also more likely to consider the consequences of their children's misbehavior when meting out punishment, and discipline them physically.

This so-called spillover effect is hardly mysterious. We would expect parents whose jobs reward them for creativity, independence, and intent to value those qualities, and to emphasize them in their interactions with their children. Not that men have a monopoly on job spillover. A mother whose job is stressful probably isn't able to parent at one hundred percent either.

Dads Who Disconnect

Other factors may also have a greater impact on the father-child bond than on the bond between mother and child. "If things aren't going well in a marriage," says Lamb, "it's more likely to have a negative impact on a father's relationship with his child. " This is surely due in part to a child's history of intimacy with his or her mother. But Lamb also speculates that fathers simply find it easier to "disconnect" from their kids during times of conflict.

Speculations like these raise the specter of some genetic explanation. If fathers are inclined to relate to their children in a less intimate way, they may naturally be less capable of building and maintaining strong parent-child bonds. Yet while Lamb and Parke acknowledge some degree of innate, gender-related parenting differences, they place far more emphasis on cultural or learned factors.

Jane's legs hurt tonight; she calls them growing pains. I got mad, then simmered down (when my fear subsided), gave her Tylenol after she brushed her teeth. Read her a chapter from Great Expectations.

When Jane's sick, her mother takes such good care of her with medicines, doctors. I was raised Christian Scientist, taught that sickness and injury are illusions that should be healed with prayer and proper thinking. I'm just getting over my anger, my fear of disease, doctors, medicine.

Lately, I've felt a little more thin-skinned with Jane. I think it dates back to around the time of her Christmas break. Jane's not as cuddly, pliable, obedient as she was before. Rather, she's more headstrong, defiant, sometimes openly mocking of me, my authority.

I guess she's becoming independent, setting her own boundaries. Yipes! Thankfully, Lucinda explained this. I figured Jane was going through a bad patch, or maybe her friends or mother were encouraging her to resist my fine parenting! Instead, it's my parenting that's helped foster her confidence.

Bill Moseley

Of these, the most important may be the parenting models today's men and women have from their own childhoods—models that very likely ran along traditional lines, and most significantly indicated mothering was mandatory and fathering far more discretionary. A mother may be angry and depressed. Lamb says, "but parenting has to be done and the buck stops with her, whereas dads have traditionally been given leeway."

It's changing, of course. New legal sanctions, such as those against deadbeat dads, coupled with a rising sense—not just among conservatives—of fathers' familial obligations, are making it tougher for men to simply walk away physically or emotionally. Today men getting divorced are likely to fight for primary or joint custody of their kids. We may even reach a point where one parent isn't deemed mandatory and the other "allowed" to drop back.

Bringing the Revolution Home

Researchers say the more compelling changes in fathering are, or ought to be, taking place not just on a social level but on a personal one. One of the simplest steps is refiguring the division of parental duties: mom takes on some of the play master role, while dad does more of the need-based parenting—everything from changing diapers to ferrying the kids to dance lessons. By doing more of the "mandatory" parenting, Parke says, fathers will encourage their kids to see them not simply as a playmate, but as a comfort provider too.

No one's advocating a complete role reversal, or suggesting a complete shift is possible. Parke says men have difficulty "giving up their robust interactive styles, even when they are the parent staying at home." Instead, families should take advantage of the difference between men's and women's parenting approaches. Since fathers' boisterous antics seem to help prepare children for life outside the family, mothers shouldn't cancel this out by intervening or being overly protective.

At the same time, a more androgynous approach has its advantages. Children will be less inclined to mark one parent for fun and the other for comfort. For fathers this might mean more opportunities to deal with emotional ups and downs and develop the empathy and emotional depth.

Of course, fathers will experience difficulties making this shift. Yet the potential rewards are huge. Not only will we give our children more progressive examples of parenting—examples that will be crucial when they raise their own children—but we'll greatly enhance our own parenting experiences.

Fatherhood may be more confusing and open-ended than ever before, but the possibilities—for those willing to take the risks—are endless. "In the theater of modern family life," says Belsky, "there are just many more parts that fathers can play."

Sibling connections

That most vital but overlooked of relationships

Laura M. Markowitz

The Family Therapy Networker

We agonize over ups and downs with our parents, spouses, and children, but mostly ignore one of our first and most primal bonds—our relationships with our brothers and sisters.

Whether as adults we find those relationships harmonious, acrimonious, or somewhere in between, we discount them at our peril. For the sibling bond is powerful, providing us with connection, validation, and belonging like no other.

Brothers and sisters push buttons you'd forgotten you had, never forget old humiliations and painful nicknames, never let you grow up. They share your obscure, ancient memories of car trips and long-dead pets, know just what you mean about Mom and Dad, and can make you laugh so hard you cry.

To understand the potent cocktail of anger, love, competitiveness, and protectiveness that is the sibling bond is ultimately to come closer to understanding ourselves. Not that understanding always leads to trouble-free friendship. Indeed, achieving tension-free kinship with a sibling is probably impossible, since ambivalence seems to be the most natural state of the relationship. But coming to know why no one else can make you feel more empathy, anger, or delight than those earliest companions provides a useful insight. May it also lead to a closer bond.

At first, the case appeared to have nothing at all to do with siblings. Alice, a 40-year-old journalist and single mother, came in with her only child, 18-year-old Becky, who had threatened to run away form home because "my mom is like a prison warden." Becky told the therapist, Syracuse University doctoral student Tracy Laszloffy, that she would go live with her Aunt Tess, who had told her she was always welcome. This was her trump card, and it had the desired effect: Her mother's eyes narrowed in anger. "I always knew she'd do something like this to get even with me," said Alice.

"Why do you think Becky wants to get even with you?" the therapist asked.

"Not Becky," explained Alice. "Tess! My older sister always hated me and has never let me forget that when I was born, she had to take care of me.

For there is
no friend like a
sister
In calm or
stormy weather;
To cheer one on
the tedious way,
To fetch one if
one goes astray,
To lift one if one
totters down,
To strengthen
whilst one
stands.
—Christina
Rossetti

She's always making me pay for that. Now she wants to steal my daughter away!"

Laszloffy helped Alice and Becky find a compromise for their most pressing problems—Becky's demand to be allowed to go to unsupervised parties and Alice's insistence that Becky get better grades. Despite Becky's description of her mother as harsh, it became evident that Alice vacillated between the conflicting roles of parent and peer. Laszloffy felt that the real work for this family needed to happen elsewhere. She decided that including Tess in a session might be the key, and her hunch was confirmed when Alice flinched at the suggestion. "Why her? She already knows I'm a screwup." She agreed, however, for Becky's sake.

From the first moment the sisters walked in—Tess a matronly 50-year-old woman in sensible shoes, and Alice looking fashionable in a mini-skirt—it was clear their relationship organized the way they thought about themselves. The sisters immediately began to compare themselves to each other: "She was always the creative one," said Tess. "I never had any real talent, except for making pot roast."

"Yeah, but you were also the good daughter, the one everyone approved of," countered Alice. Tess bristled. Was Alice mocking her for being a stay-at-home mom and housewife?

"I feel judged by Alice constantly," Tess said. "I have arguments with her in my head while I'm vacuuming about who has it better, me or her." She admitted that she did sometimes have regrets about her life, but said she never felt comfortable letting down her guard with her sister.

"I guess I feel threatened when Tess isn't her usual confident and bossy self," Alice said. "It's like a balance we have. One of us is the caretaker, one of us is the. . . . Well, I'm used to being the one who needs taking care of. I'm not sure I'd know what to do if she needed my advice, or help."

The next session began with the sisters reporting on a lunch that week that had ended with a big fight over their memories of their mother. Tess had recalled her as a cold, disengaged woman wrapped up in her own problems; Alice remembered her as being affectionate to the point of being stifling. Laszloffy explained that no siblings grow up in the same family—the emotional, economic, and even physical circumstances of the family are distinct for each child, and the parents often respond differently to each. Tess looked irritated, unused to relinquishing her right, as eldest, to define the way things were. Alice said she felt guilty that she had gotten the "nice" mother while Tess had gotten the "mean" one.

"So why did you run away from home, if Mom was so loving and caring?" Tess asked her sister, referring to the year when 18-year-old

Alice dropped out of high school three weeks before graduation and moved to California.

"To get away from her! She was *too* loving; it was suffocating me!" Alice said, frustrated that her sister needed to be told the obvious.

Tess's mouth dropped open. "I thought you ran away because you were mad at me for leaving you at home with Mom when I got married and had kids of my own."

"No! In fact, I was trying to get out of your hair so you wouldn't have to keep taking care of me, because I knew you hated that—and hated me because of it," Alice choked on the last words, tears welling up.

"I never hated you," Tess said softly. "What ever gave you that idea?"

Alice blew her nose. "I'll never forget the time when I was 5, you were 15, and you were supposed to take me to the playground. You

The parent-child bond has been under the microscope, yet sibling connections have been largely ignored.

yelled at Mom that you hated me and wanted to go out with your friends. Then you left." Alice, with her tear-streaked face and forlorn expression, looked like the abandoned little girl she was describing.

Tess had no memory of the incident Alice was talking about. Of course there had been moments she resented having to take care of her baby sister, but most of the time she loved and cherished Alice. "Why do you think I rushed ahead to have babies of my own?" Tess asked her. "Because you had been the best thing in my life, and I wanted to have kids just like you." For the first time in 35 years, Alice could hear the love in her sister's voice.

"I've wanted to be close to you for a long time, but you kept pushing me away," said Tess. "I could never figure out what I had done to make you hate me—hate me so much that you don't even want Becky to visit me." Now Tess was crying too.

"Why didn't we ever talk about this stuff before?" Alice wondered. "We've wasted so much time being mad at things that never really happened the way we thought they did."

Big sisters are the crab grass in the lawn of life.
—Charles Schulz

We are family—I got all my sisters with me.
—Sister Sledge

Lord, confound this surly sister, Blight her brow with blotch and blister, Cramp her larynx, lung and liver, In her guts a galling give her.
—John Millington Synge

They also had spent a lot of time frozen in roles that no longer fit them as adults. In therapy, Alice learned that she could be more of an adult with and parent to Becky without turning into her sister. Tess began to accept that she wasn't as stuck in her life as she imagined. As if they were unfolding a map and seeing a multitude of possible roads to take, each of the sisters could now see herself as more than simply the other's road not taken.

Clearly, the sibling relationship was the pivotal factor in this case, yet there was little in her training to lead Laszloffy—or most family therapists—to consider siblings as a point of leverage. Mental health practitioners have spent a century putting the parent-child bond and marital relationship under the microscope, yet sibling connections have been largely ignored. "My pet peeve with the field is that when we say 'family of origin,' most of us really mean parent-child relationships, which is a very limited and linear view of family that derives from our rigidly hierarchical way of seeing the world," says Ken Hardy, professor of family therapy at Syracuse University.

Laszloffy's case is striking because the intensity between the siblings lay close to the surface. Most of us respond to our brothers and sisters with subtler rumblings, having long ago learned to bury powerful emotions in order to survive years of living with them—resentment at having been an easy target of a sibling's anger; longing for closeness masked by habitual guardedness; hidden desires for attention, approval, vindication. As adults, we still may wish our siblings would apologize for past hurts, abandonments, humiliations; we still may feel responsible for them, afraid for them, stuck with them.

Normally articulate and insightful people grow tongue-tied when it comes to describing their relationships with their siblings. Writers of books about siblings struggle to manufacture encompass-

Only children

Is it really so bad to grow up without sibs?

AT 14 I LEARNED A LESSON THAT MOST KIDS master well before their age hits double digits. When a boy who'd taunted me all through junior high asked me to sign his yearbook, I thought it was a trick—I knew he hated me; he'd been my tormentor for years. So of course I refused. To my surprise, his genuinely quizzical look told me that the request had been sincere.

It was an understandable mistake on my part, though. Most of the kids I knew had learned how to tease and be teased much earlier in life than I finally did. That's because they all had something I lacked: siblings.

As the only child in my family, I grew up with no one to make faces at me, slam me against the wall, steal my hair ribbon, or frighten me with rubber bugs. My parents may have had a bad day now and then, but hey, they never hid my math book or called me "bunnyface." How was I to know that most kids deal with such treatment every day of their lives?

This lack of sibling savvy made me more sensitive than most of my peers, and maybe I didn't roll with the punches as easily as they did. But those appear to be about the worst effects the absence of brothers and sisters had on me. Otherwise, I grew up happy, made friends, did well in college, and married a great guy (who also happens to be an only child).

So what about the pervasive idea that all children without siblings are selfish, lonely, and spoiled? Well, according to nearly everyone who studies these things, the stereotypical attention-grabbing, foot-stamping, tantrum-throwing only child resides mainly in our collective imagination.

"Being an only child accounts for no more than about 2 percent of the variants affecting personality and behavior," says Toni Falbo, a professor of sociology and educational psychology at the University of Texas at Austin. "The other 98 percent are determined by a host of more important factors: social class, gender, education, quality of parenting, and family members' physical and psychological health."

After reviewing almost 150 published studies and conducting her own research on the subject, Falbo—who's the country's leading authority on only children—has concluded that onlies are generally just as happy and well-adjusted as kids with siblings. What's more, the differences that do exist are frequently to the onlies' advantage. Only children tend to get slightly better grades, be more ambitious, earn more advanced acing theories about our connection to these people after we no longer have to wear their hand-me-downs, share a bedroom, or put up with their teasing. But there are no givens for what kind of relationships emerge between adult siblings. Some grow up to be one another's closest friends; others become like distant acquaintances, sharing nothing of their adult lives. Some continue to use their siblings as a compass point for measuring who they have become. Some consider each other ancient enemies to avoid, while others casually drift apart without concern. For every "truth" about siblings, the exact opposite also may be correct. Most of us are still trying to figure out who these familiar strangers are to us.

In the beginning we orbit our parents like planets vying for the position closest to the sun. They are the primary source of light, warmth, and love, but we have to compete with omnipresent siblings who at times eclipse us, collide with us, and even, at odd moments,

awkwardly love us. In myth and literature, the bond between siblings is portrayed as far more ambivalent than the attachment between parents and children, dramatized in extremes of enmity and loyalty. In the Bible, the relationship between the first brothers, Cain and Abel, ended in fratricide. Joseph's brothers sold him into slavery in Egypt. In *King Lear,* Cordelia's older sisters outmaneuvered her to get their father's kingdom and delighted in her banishment. Still, Hansel took hold of Gretel's hand in the forest and promised to protect her; Joseph forgave his brothers and saved them during a deadly famine.

The seeds of enmity between siblings may be planted early: The introduction of a new child into the family is often experienced as an irretrievable loss by the older child. The trauma of being displaced by a younger sibling can turn into rage, envy, even hatred of the usurper. The earliest impulses to commit murder are felt in the young child who has been dethroned as centerpiece of the family. Therapists report cases in which older siblings tried to drown their younger

ademic degrees, and display greater self-esteem.

Then why the negative stereotype? Perhaps it's because most people don't have much firsthand experience with only children, who have traditionally been in short supply. A decade ago, just 10 percent of American women had had a single child by the end of their childbearing years. These days, however, that number has jumped to an all-time high of 17 percent—which means that one in six women will be the mother of an only child.

Despite their increasing numbers, Falbo notes that typecasting of only children persists. "The truth," she says, laughing, "is that last-born kids often act more spoiled than onlies do."

Perhaps the sharpest concern many one-child parents feel is that their kids will be lonely. "I did worry at first," admits Anita Daucunas of

Boulder, Colorado, who has a 5-year-old daugher. "But Jennifer is in school all day with other kids, and when she gets home she goes right out to play with the neighborhood children."

At the same time, onlies are often more comfortable playing by themselves. Sandra Lee Steadham of Dallas says that her daughter, 9-year-old Zoe, is outgoing but also enjoys spending time on her own. "For Zoe," she explains, "being alone isn't the same as being lonely."

Like any other type of family, single-child households do have trouble spots. For one thing, the parents of an only child have a tendency to be overly attentive, says Murray Kappelman, a professor of pediatrics and psychiatry at the University of Maryland. Too much concern about the child's health, for example, can encourage hypochondria. Performance

expectations that are too rigorous can create a heightened need for approval, and an overabundance of material rewards can give the child a bad case of the I wants.

"But those tendencies exist with most firstborns," Kappelman emphasizes, "not just with onlies." The fact is that *any* family size creates its own set of problems. There is no perfect number of children.

—*Katy Koontz*
Special Report

Excerpted with permission from Special Report *(March/April 1993). Subscriptions: $15/yr. (6 issues) from Special Report, Box 2191, Knoxville, TN 37901.*

brothers and sisters, or "helped" them have accidents near sharp objects or open windows.

Freud codified the notion of sibling rivalry, which was already widely accepted, saying it was natural that the introduction of a new sibling into a family would stir up envy, aggression, and competitiveness in the other siblings. But normalizing sibling rivalry created an expectation that brothers and sisters were destined to feel lifelong antagonism, resent one another's accomplishments, and envy one another's talents and privileges. Until recently, the phenomenon was believed to be so self-evident that no one bothered to challenge it. But are aggression and envy really the overarching emotions siblings have for one another? Recent feminist theorists suggest that Freud's theory was tainted by male bias. Siblings may not always be locked in mortal combat; interdependence and companionship are as much a part of siblinghood as competition and antagonism, says Laura Roberto, family therapy professor at Eastern Virginia Medical School. "Until we began to see how female development is also forged in affiliation and relationship, we tended to ignore these facets of the sibling bond." Feminists point to the lifelong friendship between many sisters who, increasingly outliving their male relations, may spend the last years of their lives together. This feminist challenge has given us a new lens for regarding both female and male sibling relationships, suggests family therapist Michael Kahn, co-author of *The Sibling Bond*. "Women are more interested in horizontal ties," says Kahn, "and are asking new kinds of questions like, 'What is lost when one sibling wins at another's expense?'"

Other critics point out that sibling rivalry isn't a primary force among siblings in other cultures; in some African societies, for example, one's greatest support, both material and emotional, comes not from one's parents but from one's siblings. Not all families in our society operate exclusively from Eurocentric values of individualism, points out Ken Hardy. For example, as a response to racism, African-American parents, brothers, and sisters often pour all their resources and energy into one child, who carries the family torch like a bright beacon into the institutions of mainstream success. "It is not uncommon to see an African-American family in which one brother is a surgeon or lawyer while the other siblings are locked into menial jobs or struggling with unemployment," he says. "The one who made it sends back money and helps the others, repays the debt."

To look only at the negative feelings of siblinghood is to forget how important we are to one another, how in a sense our siblings are as responsible for creating us as our parents are. All planets, though drawn to the sun, exert a pull on one another, shaping one another's course. "I

was the coddled one; he the witness of coddling," wrote novelist Vladimir Nabokov about his older brother, describing the natural complementarity that exists among siblings.

Our siblings are peers who share not only the same family, but also the same history and culture, not to mention a sizable chunk of our genetic material. Even among those with a significant age difference, siblings' personal histories intertwine so that there is no escaping a mutual influence. During a family therapy session, two adult sisters and their brother talk about how they were influenced by one another. "I learned to be the family entertainer because you and Mom were always fighting," says the brother to his older sister. "I hated the yelling, so I would try to make you both laugh. I still do that whenever I'm around conflict—try to defuse it."

"I think I wouldn't have been such a rebel if you two hadn't been such goody-goodies," says the younger sister. "You still compete with each other, like who's more successful or whose kids are the smartest. Since I was never in the running, I tried to do things neither of you did. Using a lot of drugs was a way to feel like I had something over both of you, like I was more mature or cool."

"I always felt so responsible for you two," says the older sister. "Mom would yell at me if you guys made a mess or got in a fight. I grew up believing that everyone else's problems come first, because other people are younger, smaller, more needy, or whatever. In my marriage, I kept on doing the same thing, putting his needs first because it was what I knew. And having kids just replicated what it was like to be the oldest sister. Since the divorce, I've been trying to figure out who takes care of me."

W hat exactly does it mean to be the product not only of one's parents, but also of one's siblings? How does it happen? The most elaborate theory of siblinghood concerns birth order. Although Freud said that "a child's position in the sequence of brothers and sisters is of very great significance for the course of his later life," the main work in the area of birth order has been done by Austrian-born family therapist Walter Toman, author of *Family Constellation: Its Effects on Personality and Social Behaviour*. Toman's basic assertion is that the order of one's birth determines certain personality characteristics that shape the choices we make and the likelihood of our success and even how we think about ourselves. Toman developed profiles of sibling positions, including only children, saying, for example, that older siblings tend to take on more responsibility and to be somewhat overcontrolling while only children are inclined to be loners, and women who are not fond of children tend to be youngest siblings.

I was the older brother. And when I was growing up I didn't like all those brothers and sisters. No kid likes to be the oldest. . . . But when they turn to you for help—what can you do? They kept me so busy caring for them that I had no time to become a junkie or an alcoholic.
—James Baldwin

The younger brother hath the more wit.
—English proverb

All happy families resemble one another, but each unhappy family is unhappy in its own way.
—Leo Tolstoy

146

But even without a highly schematized birth order theory about siblings, practitioners have described siblinghood as the first social laboratory, where we learn how to be a peer. Even when the fights make us cry, we are growing a thicker skin, which we need later on as adults; we learn that life doesn't always seem fair; we learn how to forgive. "After listening to my brother and sister hurl insults at each other one day, I was surprised to see them playing together the next morning as if nothing had happened," says a 40-year-old man. "It was a revelation to me that you could hate someone one day and forget about it the next."

It is possible that in siblinghood we experience more intensity of emotion than in any other relationship that follows. Our worlds are shoulder to shoulder, and our vulnerabilities are laid bare. "I've never loved or hated as intensely as I love and hate my brothers," says a 36-year-old youngest brother of six boys. With our siblings, we test the limits of tolerance and forgiveness more than we do in any other relationship. As long as the family provides an appropriate container for the intensity, siblings can benefit from the lessons.

Unless something goes dramatically wrong, as in sibling incest or sibling illness or death, our relationships with our brothers and sisters rarely take center stage in the therapy room. But increasingly, family therapists are discovering what a gold mine of information and support siblings can be. As inheritors of the same multigenerational legacy, albeit with different views of the family stories, they can often make a unique contribution to therapy. One family therapist was having a hard time with an 8-year-old boy who had set himself on fire twice because he believed his father hated him. The father was a large, impassive man who never looked at his son and spoke to him only when he had to. Hoping for some clue about why the father was so inaccessible, the therapist invited the father's younger brother to a session.

After the therapist outlined the situation, the younger brother turned to his nephew and asked him to wait in the next room. Then he said to his brother, the boy's father, "I remember right before Mom left him, Dad used to tell everyone you were someone else's bastard." The older brother looked numb, but the therapist sighed with relief. He finally understood what was going on under the surface of this family. His own father's rejection of him had left this father feeling confused about what fathers were supposed to say to sons. "He loved his child, but regarded his own silence as a way of protecting his son from the possibly abusive things that might come out of his mouth in anger," says the therapist. What the man was only dimly aware of himself, his brother had been able to put his finger on immediately.

Family therapy also can help people get out of constraining roles with their siblings. Family-of-origin specialist Murray Bowen years ago described how he dramatically disentangled himself from a lifetime of emotional triangles with his siblings. He believed the family's ongoing emotional process was responsible for the legacy that Walter Toman attributed to birth order. Accordingly, Bowen reasoned that one ought to be able to go back and change the family's emotional process, which created and sustained sibling roles.

One Bowen-trained therapist treated a couple who were fighting about the husband's intrusive family. Lisa was fed up with hearing about her in-laws' problems and wanted Henry to separate himself from their incessant dramas. She was upset that he had loaned his irresponsible younger sister money and had become caught up in the ongoing fight between his older brother and their father. The constant phone calls from Henry's family were driving her crazy. When she drew their family diagram, the therapist says, "a million things seemed to jump out at me," particularly the multigenerational patterns of enmeshment in Henry's family and cutoffs in Lisa's, but the overwhelming fact was the contrast in the couple's birth positions: Henry was a middle child, Lisa an only child.

As an only child, Lisa was used to being the center of attention and didn't like competing with her brother- and sister-in-law. As a middle child, Henry was the family caretaker and peacekeeper, but he wasn't sure he wanted to keep the role. "If I wasn't in the middle of their lives, maybe I'd have more of a life of my own," he said.

The therapist coached Henry on how to develop more independence from his family. "The next time my brother called to complain about Dad, I told him I was sure he could work it out and changed the subject to football," says Henry. His sister called to cry over her latest investment flop, hinting that she needed another loan. "I told her she had a lot of experience pulling herself out of holes, and I was sure she would find a way to do it again," Henry recalls.

The therapist suggested that Lisa could help Henry remember that he was entitled to be the center of attention sometimes, too. During the next family gathering, Henry and Lisa both deliberately steered the conversation to Henry's latest project at work. "It was a surprise to realize that no one in my family knew much about me," says Henry. Changing his behavior shifted his relationship with his siblings, who became "much more respectful of my boundaries," almost timidly asking if it was all right to call, spending more time listening to Henry instead of talking at him.

Our word *cad* originally meant a younger brother.
—Bergen Evans

A brother is born for adversity.
—*Proverbs 17:17*

Some uninformed newspapers printed: "Mrs. C.L. Lane, Sister of the Famous Comedian Will Rogers." They were greatly misinformed. It's the other way around. I am the brother of Mrs. C.L. Lane, the friend of humanity. . . . It was the proudest moment of my life that I was her brother.
—Will Rogers, after the funeral of his sister Maud

One of the most wrenching issues that brings siblings to family therapy occurs at midlife, when they face the failing health of parents and need to make long-term decisions about their

In siblinghood we may experience more intense emotions than in any other relationship that follows.

care. It's extremely difficult for a family to have to acknowledge the demise of its elders, evoking buried fears of death and abandonment. Often, the grown children don't feel ready for the changing of the guard. "I look in the mirror and see an older, white-haired man, but inside I still feel 25 and way too young to become the older generation," says one therapist, whose elderly father recently came to live with him. "I look at his shrunken body and I can't help feeling repulsed. He used to be a strapping, handsome guy. Now the chronic pain from arthritis doesn't let him sleep. I have to feed him by hand as if he were a baby. It's very sad, and very surreal." Is this what will happen to us, siblings wonder?

Not only does the individual's relationship with the parent change dramatically as the older generation loses its authority, but the need to collaborate closely with a sibling, sometimes after 40 years of mutual alienation, can revive feelings of insecurity, competitiveness, and resentment. In the face of huge existential issues like death, some adult siblings find it is easier to fall back on picking on one another, feeding the illusion that they will be children forever instead of accepting terminal adulthood.

Boston family therapist David Treadway worked with three siblings in their 60s—an eminent jurist, a history professor, and a successful businesswoman. They were not interested in talking about the past, but needed a facilitator to help them come to an agreement about their aging mother.

"They didn't acknowledge that their struggle had anything to do with their childhood roles, but the roots of the conflict surfaced within the first 10 minutes," says Treadway. They found that they could not come to any agreement without first understanding the curse of each one's sibling position. After this exercise, they could begin the hard work of real negotiation and compromise.

In some families, a parent's death removes the force that holds siblings in their habitual

orbits. The question then becomes, Will the brothers and sisters drift apart, finally dissolving the tenuous threads of connection? Most of the time siblings find the pull among them is strong enough to draw them into a new configuration. In a family of two brothers and two sisters, after the parents died no one came forward at first to organize family gatherings during the holidays. After spending the first Thanksgiving of their lives apart, they set up a rotation so they would each plan one holiday a year.

When adult siblings maintain their connection in later life, the relationship takes on a special importance because, as veterans of multiple losses—deaths, divorce, children moving away—they realize that no one else alive can remember the way it was when they were children. The parents' deaths may even open up a space for siblings to know each other for the first time without competitive friction. "I never really thought, 'Would I like this person if he were not my brother?'" says a 56-year-old therapist. "After our parents were gone, I found myself calling him up, and he'd call me. We enjoy each other's company now. It's comfortable in a way I don't feel with anyone else because we've known each other forever." It can be a sweet and unexpected discovery to realize that the people with whom one feels the most affinity and closeness after a lifetime of struggle or emotional distance are our own siblings.

M any of us take our siblings for granted. They simply are, as unavoidable as gravity. Even as adults, we may not have devoted much thought to figuring out how they fit into our lives and how they shaped us. There's something in us that resists giving our sibling relationships the credence and attention they deserve. Cherishing our adult autonomy and freedom, we strive to bury our childish vulnerabilities and reinvent ourselves, but our sibs get in the way.

The boy who was teased by the neighborhood kids and grows up to be a confident, successful businessman doesn't want to remember those days of hot tears and humiliation. He may feel uneasy in the presence of the older sister who remembers all too clearly a time he'd rather forget. In a sense, our siblings don't let us put the past behind us. "Every time I see you, I try to be open to the idea that you are a different person than the one I used to know," one brother told his sister. "But it's hard, because I know you so well."

In this knowledge is, perhaps, the paradox of the sibling relationship. Siblings are the living remnant of our past, a buffer against the loss of our own history, the deepest, oldest memories of us. But in these memories lies a terrible power:

I worry about people who get born nowadays because they get born into such tiny families—sometimes into no family at all. When you're the only pea in the pod, your parents are likely to get you confused with the Hope Diamond.
—Russell Baker

Relations are simply a tedious pack of people, who haven't got the remotest knowledge of how to live, nor the smallest instinct about when to die.
—Oscar Wilde

Our siblings hold up a mirror before us, forcing us to look at an image of ourselves that may be either comforting or devastating, perhaps evoking self-acceptance and pride, perhaps shame and humiliation.

There is a fateful perpetuity about sibling relationships: Our brothers and sisters will always be our contemporaries; we can't ever quite leave them. However convenient it would be, we can't consign them to irrelevancy. No wonder that when sibling relationships are bad, they leave deep, irreparable scars of bitterness, betrayal, and rage. No wonder that when they are good, they are a source of profound satisfaction, one of the best and most fulfilling of human ties. Whether our siblings are thorns in our side or balm for our wounds, they are fellow travelers who have witnessed our journey, living bridges between who we once were and who we have become.

Children Who Witness Domestic Violence: The Invisible Victims

Joy D. Osofsky

Children need to be safe and secure at home to develop a positive sense of self necessary to their growing into healthy, productive, caring adults; children need to be safe in their communities to be able to explore and develop relationships with other people; and children need to be safe at school in order to successfully learn.

—Position Statement on Violence in the Lives of Children
(National Association for the Education of Young Children, 1993)

As the incidence of violence in the United States has soared in recent years, so concern has grown about its effects on children. Children are being exposed to violence at an alarming rate—either as direct victims or as witnesses to it. The Children's Defense Fund points out that homicide is now the third leading cause of death among elementary school children (Kochanek & Hudson, 1995). And countless other children whom we never hear about are witness daily to widespread violence in their homes and in their neighborhoods. These latter are the *invisible victims*, the focus of this report.

Background

A Theoretical Framework

A systems approach—i.e., an approach encompassing not just the child but all the interlocking layers that link the child and society—offers a useful theoretical framework for conceptualizing the effects of violence on children. This approach can also inform the prevention and intervention strategies aimed at addressing the problem. We have found in our research that working with people and agencies in the community can effect changes in the system that stand to help children and families traumatized by violence. We have also found that a developmental perspective, including psychoanalytic and social learning principles, provides a helpful background for shaping the skills and techniques needed to counsel children and educate parents, teachers, police, and others about violence.

A developmental approach emphasizes the emergence of trust and empathy as crucial sensitivities. In *Childhood and Society*, Erik Erikson (1963) held that the development of trust is the initial step in forming healthy relationships.

From *Social Policy Report*, Vol. 9, No. 3, 1995, pp. 1-16. © 1995 by the Society for Research in Child Development. Reprinted by permission.

Trust develops early and is primarily contingent on the infant's relationship with his or her caregiver. If this first psychosocial stage of trust building is successfully resolved, the infant will learn to trust others, which will then help with later relationship building. Mistrust, in contrast, can result from a single trauma or from chronic environmental stress. If parents are emotionally unavailable, for instance, or are inconsistent, continually negative, or abusive, the infant or child may fail to develop basic trust (Egeland & Erickson, 1987). In light of this theoretical perspective, one must ask how growing up in a neighborhood rife with poverty, drugs, and violence and in a home marked by instability and violence may interfere with a child's developing trust. For far too many children, those very relationships on which the development of trust and trusting relationships are built may be limited or changeable.

Social learning theory also informs our understanding of the origins of violent behavior. Children learn and imitate what they see and experience. Considerable evidence indicates that children who are exposed to domestic violence, as well as to violence in their community, are at much higher risk of becoming both perpetrators and victims of violence (Bell, 1995). Imitation and modeling appear to play significant roles in this process.

Exposure to Community Violence

Although exposure to community violence is not the focus of this report, it is instructive to consider the literature on its effects. More is known about it, and it may differ from exposure to domestic violence in important ways (Bell & Jenkins, 1993; Garbarino, 1992; Marans & Cohen, 1993; Pynoos, 1993; Osofsky, 1995; Richters, 1993).

Much of the increase in violence in the United States, which has doubled since the 1950s, has been among adolescents and young adults, ages 15 to 24 years. While homicides decreased slightly in 1995, many criminologists

believe this reflects a demographic trend in the adolescent and young-adult population. A recent report estimated that the number of teenagers in the population is expected to increase substantially in the next 6 to 8 years, and that the crime rate will also rise as a consequence (Blumstein, 1995).

Children are being exposed to violence at high rates in many inner-city neighborhoods. In a survey of sixth, eighth, and tenth graders in New Haven in 1992, 40% reported witnessing at least one violent crime in the past year (Marans & Cohen, 1993). Very few of the children escaped some exposure to violence, and almost all of the eighth-grade respondents knew someone who had been killed. In Los Angeles it was estimated that children witness approximately 10% to 20% of the homicides committed in that city (Pynoos & Eth, 1986). In a study of African American children living in a Chicago neighborhood, one-third of the school-aged children had witnessed a homicide and two-thirds had witnessed a serious assault (Bell & Jenkins, 1991). Yet another study showed that children's social and emotional adjustment in the classroom was related to their exposure to community violence. However, the children's adjustment was also positively related to the presence of social support in their lives, regardless of the level of violence in the community or amount of exposure (Hill, 1995).

Two other studies have documented that children are victims of and witnesses to significant amounts of violence. The first (Richters & Martinez, 1993) collected interviews of 165 mothers of children ages 6 to 10 living in a low-income neighborhood in Washington, DC. The second (Osofsky, Wewers, Hann, & Fick, 1993), in an attempt to gather similar data in New Orleans, included interviews with 53 African American mothers of children ages 9 to 12 in a low-income neighborhood, which police statistics showed to have higher violence rates than the Washington neighborhood. Fifty-one percent of the New Orleans fifth graders and 32% of the Washington, DC, children reported being victims of violence; 91% of the New Orleans children and 72% of those in Washington had witnessed some type of violence. Both studies also found a significant relationship between children's reported exposure to community violence and intrafamily conflict as measured by the Conflict Tactics Scale (Straus, 1979).

While few studies make the distinction between domestic and community violence, the Richters and Martinez (1993) and Osofsky et al. (1993) studies highlight the importance of including measures of both to determine how being raised in a violent home versus a violent neighborhood may, separately or in combination, affect children. Some evidence suggests (see the sections below: "A Special Case" (p. 4) and "Protective factors" (p. 6) that witnessing domestic-level violence may have more dire effects.

Exposure to Domestic Violence

While much less is known about children's witnessing of domestic violence, we do know that many homicides and incidents of severe violence occur in the home. It has been estimated that 25% to 30% of American women are beaten at least once in the course of intimate relationships (Pagelow, 1984). Nationwide surveys show that nearly one-eighth of husbands in the U.S. commit one or more acts of physical violence against their wives each year, and one-fifth to one-third of all women are assaulted by a partner or ex-partner during their lifetime (Frieze & Browne, 1989; Straus & Gelles, 1990). Over half the calls for police assistance in many communities are for domestic disturbances. How much of this violence occurs in the presence of children is unknown, which is why they are considered *invisible victims*. As Judge Cindy Lederman of Miami has poignantly described, unlike most people who can escape violence by simply switching off the TV, some children cannot turn off the real-life violence in their lives (personal communication, November, 1995).

It has been estimated that at least 3.3 mil-

lion children witness physical and verbal spousal abuse each year, including a range of behaviors from insults and hitting to fatal assaults with guns and knives (Jaffee, Wolfe, & Wilson, 1990). In homes where domestic violence occurs, children are physically abused and neglected at a rate 15 times higher than the national average (Senate Judiciary Committee Hearing 101-939 [as cited in Massachusetts Coalition, 1995]). Several studies have found that in 60% to 75% of families where a woman is battered, children are also battered (Bowker, 1988; McKibben, DeVos, & Newberger, 1989; Straus, Gelles, & Steinmetz, 1980). Although some excellent work is beginning to emerge (e.g., McCloskey, Figueredo, & Koss, 1995; Zuckerman, Augustyn, Groves, & Parker, 1995), relatively little research has focused on the effects of domestic violence on children, and public policy initiatives have been almost nonexistent in this crucial area.

What Do We Know about the Effects of Violence Exposure?

Children's Behavioral and Psychological Responses at Different Ages

Very young children. Although very young children may be partially protected from exposure to a traumatic incident because they do not fully appreciate the potential danger (Drell, Siegel, & Gaensbauer, 1993; Pynoos, 1993), it is important that we not ignore or de-emphasize their reactions to violence. Numerous studies have documented that even young children are likely to exhibit emotional distress, immature behavior, somatic complaints, and regressions in toileting and language (Bell, 1995; Drell et al., 1993; Jaffe et al., 1990; Margolin, 1995; Osofsky & Fenichel, 1995; Pynoos, 1993; Scheeringa & Zeanah, 1994). Recent reports have even noted the presence of symptoms very similar to post-traumatic stress disorder in adults, including repeated reexperiencing of the traumatic event,

Then comes the spectral recognition that the past is never really gone. *What we learn as children speaks through us indefinitely, often in dramatic fashion. Wife-battering may be just such a thing"* (present author's emphasis). The editorial goes on to tell a story of a recent incident about a young man who had been jailed for pistol whipping his wife. Women were property, according to his religious tradition, and he considered wife-beating his right. He was continuing an old family theme. The article went on to note that when he was a child, his own father went to jail for badly beating a woman. The young man's grandfather had also been a public batterer, a habit he may have learned the way his sons did. One concludes that violence is handed down and essentially woven into the social fabric. Thus, "the fist that breaks and smashes travels through time, destroying more lives and bodies as it goes" (Staples, 1995). At this point, the field lacks objective data supporting the idea of intergenerational transmission of family violence, but evidence from both clinical and personal experience provides important leads to the systematic study of this phenomenon.

What Is the Status of Research on Domestic Violence Exposure?

Further Studies Needed

Most of the research on domestic violence exposure to date is descriptive, consisting of studies like those cited in this report that have documented the behavioral and psychological symptoms associated with exposure. But it is generally agreed that more work is needed (Groves & Zuckerman, in press; Margolin, 1995; Osofsky, 1995; Zuckerman et al., 1995): studies, for example, that would sharpen the conceptualization of violence exposure in general, and domestic violence exposure in particular, investigate possible causal mechanisms at different developmental stages, identify possible protective factors, and evaluate different approaches to intervention.

Conceptualization. Response to violence exposure, as a construct, needs further definition. For instance, although children's symptoms are likened to those associated with post-traumatic stress disorder (Augustyn et al., 1995; Burman & Allen-Meares, 1994; Osofsky, Cohen, et al., 1995; Pynoos, 1993; Richters & Martinez, 1993), "we have not fully conceptualized the impact of exposure to violence on children compared with other groups such as veterans of the Korean and Vietnam Wars" (Bell in Atnafou, 1995, p. 8).

Causal mechanisms. A series of experimental studies have investigated children's response to parental anger, with interesting results (Cummings, Hennessy, Rabideau, & Cicchetti, 1994; Cummings & Zahn-Waxler, 1992). It was shown that even expressions of anger between parents negatively affect children's emotions and behavior. Children exposed to more anger showed increased negative behaviors and affect, and exposure led to more aggressive responses in boys and more withdrawal in girls. Such studies can provide important clues to the study of violence exposure in real-world settings.

Descriptive studies have established that children's response to violence changes with increasing age. What is needed now are more precise demonstrations of the interaction of exposure to domestic violence with development, e.g., with changes in cognitive or socioemotional capacities.

Protective factors. Is exposure to domestic violence universally devastating, or do some children fare better than others? Growing interest in the study of resiliency—the process of surmounting adversity—may be helpful in exploring protective factors that mitigate the effects of violence exposure (Garmezy, 1993; Hawkins, 1995; Zimmerman, 1994). As mentioned earlier, the presence of social support appears to be an important protective factor for children exposed to community violence (Hill, 1995). A recent study of consequences of domestic violence, however, found that while it had been hypothesized that a positive relationship between parent and child might buffer children, this was not borne out (McCloskey et al., 1995).

Interventions. Early referral of the child to clinical services may well be one example of a protective factor against the worst ravages of violence exposure, but little research has been conducted in this area. In one study of 28 child witnesses (aged 1½ to 14 years) from 14 families in which the father killed the mother, delays in referrals for treatment for the children ranged from 2 weeks to 11 years (Black & Kaplan, 1988). In another study, delays ranged from 1 month to several years, with those children whose referral came after a year often showing a more serious diagnostic picture (Eth & Pynoos, 1994). Our clinical experience has been consistent with these reports; we have observed delays in referral, few preventive intervention programs, and children frequently receiving treatment only after serious behavior problems have been identified.

Problems of Methodology

While laboratory studies afford greater control, they cannot duplicate real-life circumstances, and therefore special care must be taken in generalizing from the findings of experimental studies. On the other hand, studies in real-life settings—especially of a phenomenon like domestic violence exposure, which cannot be manipulated—are plagued with a variety of methodological problems.

Much of what we know about domestic violence has been obtained from interviews of parents or sometimes older children living in shelters (Jouriles & O'Leary, 1985; Margolin, 1995; O'Brien, John, Margolin, & Erel, 1994). More often than not, violence exposure is just one of multiple traumas experienced by the child, so that findings on exposure per se are confounded. Most of such children, for example, have just undergone significant loss; they may be living in a new situation with a traumatized parent or with other traumatized children and parents.

Problems with the accuracy of reports of family violence must also be taken into account. Agreement between parents about whether or not violence has occurred tends to be low, and reliability drops even lower when parents are asked if their child has been a witness (Jouriles & O'Leary, 1985; Margolin, 1987; O'Brien et al., 1994).

Interrater agreement between children and parents about whether the child has witnessed domestic violence is also low. Children who are living in families where violence has been documented can often give detailed reports about the violence that their parents assumed went unnoticed (Jaffe et al., 1990; Rosenberg, 1987). Parents tend to underestimate the extent to which their children have been witness to domestic violence—which may not be surprising. Children, out of fear, may try to be unseen while observing; and parents, wishing that their children were not exposed, may be reluctant to acknowledge it. When older children, who tend to be more reliable reporters, are questioned, they are likely to report higher levels of exposure than do parents. To determine the effects on children, more reliable data are needed on both actual exposure and children's perceptions of family violence (Grych, Seid, & Fincham, 1992; Margolin, 1995; O'Brien et al., 1994).

How Can Communities Help the Invisible Victims of Violence Exposure?

Law Enforcement

Beyond the violence perpetrated by people children love and trust, what additional impact do authority figures, such as police officers or protective service workers, have when they come into the home to investigate or defuse a domestic dispute? What does it mean, for instance, for a young child to see his or her father being treated harshly or taken away? What happens when children feel they cannot make their mother safe?

While much has been written about the

role of protective services, the response of police, who so often are the first to arrive on the scene, has received much less attention. Yet education and preventive intervention programs involving the police are greatly needed (see Bell, 1995; Bell in Atnafou, 1995; Bell & Jenkins, 1991; Eth & Pynoos, 1994; Garbarino, 1992; Groves & Zuckerman, in press; Lewis, Osofsky, & Fick, 1995; Marans & Cohen, 1993; Osofsky, 1995; Osofsky & Fenichel, 1994; Perry, Pollard, Blakley, Baker, & Vigilante, 1995; Pynoos, 1993).

In an effort to develop a better system of referrals for children exposed to violence and to stimulate community-based intervention programs, my colleagues and I have been involved in a collaborative effort with the local police in New Orleans; similar efforts are underway in New Haven, Boston, and Los Angeles. These programs involve educating police officers about the effects of violence on children and providing mental health consultation and services for the children and their families. Although these programs share a similar philosophy, each is tailored to the needs of the particular city, based on level of violence and availability of resources and support systems. Intervention programs with the police tend to address both community and domestic violence, making it difficult to separate effects by setting.

In New Orleans. We have developed a program model in one of the two police districts with the highest level of violence in the city. It provides an educational component for new recruits in the police academy and patrol and ranking officers in the districts on the effects of violence on children. Also provided is a 24-hour mental health crisis referral and consultation service for children in collaboration with other community agencies. Through the program, we are supporting the development of greater understanding between the police and the children and families who live in high-violence areas of the city.

As part of the program, we carried out a needs assessment related to violence, including domestic violence and neighborhood safety, with 353 police officers, 250 elementary school children, 60 parents, and 68 teachers (Fick, Osofsky, & Lewis, in press; Lewis et al., 1995). Because the police have frequently reported that adolescents from such locations are quite explicit in stating and showing their mistrust of the police, the findings of the study were somewhat unexpected. The children's responses were more positive than either their parents or the police expected. The majority, ages 8 to 12, reported that they trusted police officers as the first people they would go to if they were lost or needed help. We are now gathering empirical data to investigate if and when the level of trust shifts and what factors may influence changes over the course of development (Osofsky, Fick, et al., 1995).

The police respondents showed strong beliefs about domestic violence. Overwhelmingly, law enforcement officers in this study reported that domestic disputes are the most dangerous, unpredictable situations they face in the community. And many officers reported believing that women are just as problematic as men in this situation (Jenkins, Seydlitz, Osofsky, Fisk, & Lewis, 1995; Lewis et al., 1995). They reported that learning more about family dynamics, children's development, and conflict resolution strategies has helped them feel more comfortable and supported when they have to intervene. Having available an emergency crisis and referral service, staffed by familiar professionals, has given them greater security.

The findings from this developmentally grounded study have been useful in our intervention work with the police and the community. Parents and police have been able to discuss and deal with issues concerning trust and mistrust—both how to improve relationships and how to strengthen children's positive attitudes. With increased education on alternative ways to respond, the police may have the opportunity to develop more proactive and helpful strategies for interacting with the community and dealing with children who witness domestic disputes. As funding becomes available, with the encouragement of the police department, we plan to expand the training throughout the city.

What effects the project may have on referrals is yet to be determined. We plan to assess referral patterns and then consequences, e.g., child and family adjustment following referral.

In New Haven. The Yale Child Study Center Program on Child Development and Community Policing is one of the first programs to link the police with the mental health community (Marans & Cohen, 1993). Started in New Haven in the early 1990s, this collaborative program facilitates the response of mental health professionals and police to children and families exposed to violence. It attempts to change police officers' orientation in their interactions with children toward optimizing their role as providers of a sense of security and positive authority and as models to be emulated. The three major components of the program are (1) training of all incoming police recruits about principles of child and adolescent development; (2) clinical fellowships for veteran officers who have field supervisory roles; and (3) a 24-hour consultation service for officers responding to calls in which children are either the direct victims or witnesses of violence.

The Yale program is designed to increase the effectiveness of the outreach force of police officers who have the most immediate and sustained contact with families touched by community violence. This expanded role of police officers focuses their attention on the child's experience of violence and on the caregiver's capacity to attend to his or her child's needs. Because the city is smaller, the relative level of violence lower, and the community and mental health resources more available (compared with Boston, Los Angeles, and New Orleans), the team has been able to implement the program throughout the city.

In Boston. The Massachusetts attorney general's office has sponsored an initiative in Boston that builds on the city's community policing efforts; the initiative is targeted at the community with the second highest level of violence in the city. The collaboration includes police, the district attorney's office, the courts, community business leaders, youth agencies, community health centers, and a hospital. With so many agencies and systems working together, neighborhood crime is responded to more broadly. Criminal justice professionals are linked with child health and mental health professionals who hold seminars for the police on child development and mental health issues. Child mental health specialists and court professionals also collaborate, especially in domestic violence cases. This initiative follows the earlier establishment at Boston City Hospital of the Child Witness to Violence Project, which developed in response to the urgent need to help children and families who witness violence (Groves & Zuckerman, in press). One of every 10 children attending the Pediatric Primary Care Clinic at this inner-city hospital has witnessed a shooting or stabbing before the age of 6, half of these in their homes and half on the street (Taylor, Zuckerman, Harik, & Groves, 1994). More detail on this program and its focus on the "silent victims" of violence follows in the section on health and mental health care.

In Los Angeles. Researchers have been working with the Inglewood police department in establishing a Community Policing Agency (Pynoos, in press). The goals of this community policing effort are somewhat different from the other programs described thus far. The Inglewood chief of police decided to station some of the community-based police officers at the elementary schools as a way of promoting a relationship between the officers and neighborhood children who were to become involved in a school-based intervention program. The officers assigned to the schools are given training in child development and mental health and are encouraged to interact with the children in two main areas: The first is as part of a regular psychotherapy group where the child can learn more about the officer's action or inaction with regard to child's traumatic experience. The second is as part of a crisis intervention module in which the children and the police, along with a clinician, discuss concerns about exposure to violent incidents, fears of retaliation, feelings of revenge, confidentiality issues with the police, etc. These interactions build a different type of relationship between children and police officers that can lead to more effective prevention and intervention efforts for children exposed to violence.

Health Care and Mental Health Care Systems

Helpers in the health and mental health fields have important roles to play with children exposed to violence. Yet they may not always fully appreciate the distress of children who witness domestic violence and may, therefore, miss the opportunity to provide needed help. In a paper addressed to pediatricians, Wolfe and Korsch (1994) point out that exposure to domestic conflict and violence can affect how children learn to relate to others, how they develop their self-concepts and self-control, and how they interact with dating and marital partners in the future. Thus, what needs to be recognized by mental health and other health care providers is that it is not just diagnosable outcomes that are important, but also the broader range of social and behavioral outcomes resulting from violence exposure.

Along with their work at Boston City Hospital with law enforcement and the judicial system, Zuckerman et al. (1995) emphasize that because the scars of children who witness violence are invisible, because these are "silent victims," pediatricians and other primary care clinicians must be consciously alert, even in regular office visits, to the possibility of exposure and victimization and be proactive in providing help. They suggest a pattern of nonintrusive inquiry that can be used by the pediatrician or nurse as a tool for uncovering problems that can then be addressed by the physician or handled through referral to a mental health professional—in those situations of extreme trauma or when post-traumatic or depressive symptoms are present.

A range of counseling and treatment options are relevant for mental health professionals, including 24-hour crisis intervention, brief counseling for children and families, parental guidance, longer-term therapy, and follow-up. Because the treatment of traumatized children and families can be particularly distressing and taxing for the mental health professionals, working as a team or with colleagues can be especially helpful. Creating a safe environment, which can be difficult to accomplish, is the sine qua non for successful treatment of trauma cases (Pynoos, 1993; Zeanah, 1994). Systems changes are aided by individual efforts to promote better community-based services and health and mental health care for children and families. Initiatives in these areas are crucial for effective violence prevention efforts.

Public Policy Initiatives for Children Living with Domestic Violence

The problem of children's exposure to violence is well recognized by both the research and policymaking communities. And many different groups, including the American Psychological Association (1993), the Children's Defense Fund (1994), the Carnegie Corporation of New York (1994), the National Research Council (1993), and Zero to Three/National Center for Clinical Infant Programs (Osofsky & Fenichel, 1994), have recommended policy initiatives to address the problem and its solution.

In 1993 the National Research Council's Commission on Behavioral and Social Sciences and Education and the Institute of Medicine established the Board on Children and Families. The following year the newly formed Board on Children and Families convened the Committee on the Assessment of Family Violence Interventions to examine the state of knowledge about efforts to treat, control, and prevent different forms of family violence. Over the course of 30 months, the 18-member committee has been meeting, taking part in site visits, and organizing workshops to develop findings and recommendations. Interim workshop reports will be published, and the final report is expected in fall 1996. The objectives of the committee are

- to document the costs of family violence interventions to public- and private-sector services;
- to synthesize the relevant research literature and develop a conceptual framework for clarifying what is known about risk and protective factors associated with family violence;
- to characterize what is known about selected interventions in dealing with family violence;
- to identify policy and program elements that appear to improve or inhibit the development of effective responses to family violence; and
- to provide a set of criteria and principles that can guide the development of future evaluation of family violence intervention programs.

This work is being sponsored by the Carnegie Corporation of New York and six federal agencies in the U.S. Department of Health and Human Services and the U.S. Department of Justice.

In 1987 the American Psychological Association established the Public Interest Directorate to support and promote members' efforts to apply the study of psychology to the advancement of human welfare. The Public Interest Directorate has taken several initiatives regarding the effects of violence on children and youth. APA's press published a volume, *Reason to Hope: A Psychosocial Perspective on Violence and Youth*, based on work of the Commission on Violence and Youth (Eron et al., 1994). APA President Ronald Fox appointed a 10-member Task Force on Violence and the Family as part of the 1994-95 focus on families. The task force was directed to summarize a broad range of research on the psychological aspects of family violence, its inci-

dence, the scope of the problem, its causes, the risk factors, and interventions. The group's primary goal is to increase public awareness of family violence and to explore what role psychology can play in ameliorating it. The task force report is scheduled for release in December 1995. Finally, the Public Interest Initiatives Office of APA, in collaboration with the American Academy of Pediatrics, has completed a public education brochure, *Raising Children to Resist Violence: What You Can Do*, for parents and others who care for children. The work of the American Psychological Association on children and youth violence is very informative both in terms of how violence affects children and possible directions for public policy initiatives.[1]

In order to prevent and alleviate the effects of witnessing domestic violence on children, it is recommended (see Osofsky, 1995[2]) that we band together

. . . to launch a national campaign to change attitudes toward domestic violence.

Policymakers, media leaders, child development specialists, and citizens at-large must work together to change the image of violence, in general, and domestic violence, in particular, from something we view as acceptable, even admirable, to something disdained. The media, with their glamorizing of violence, have a crucial role to play in reshaping this image. But to the extent the media reflect societal values, the responsibility for change falls to all of us.

. . . to foster prevention and intervention approaches that build on family and community strengths.

Children, families, and communities bring a variety of strengths to combat domestic violence. They require support, but the most effective strategies seek to empower local forces, such as neighborhood schools and church groups, and encourage self-determining efforts with family and community.

. . . to provide education to parents, educators, law enforcement officials, and health and mental health professionals (1) about the effects of children's witnessing of domestic violence, and (2) about alternative approaches to resolving conflict.

All individuals who come into contact with children, including those working in day-care centers, schools, law enforcement agencies, and parenting education groups, should be well-informed about all aspects of domestic and other violence exposure and children, from its precursors to its detection and treatment, and also be versed in alternative conflict resolution strategies.

. . . to promote research that will (1) expand our understanding of domestic violence expo- **sure and (2) contribute to the development of prevention and intervention strategies.**

Although we have considerable understanding of some aspects of violence exposure, more research and program evaluation are needed to fill in the knowledge gaps in this field and to assist in planning more effective interventions that can both reduce domestic violence and aid its innocent victims.

Notes

[1]For more information, contact the Public Interest Directorate, (202) 336–6050.
[2]These recommendations relate specifically to domestic violence. They are drawn from an earlier set of recommendations that address societal violence more broadly (Osofsky, 1995).

References

American Bar Association. (1994). *Report to the President: The impact of domestic violence on children.* Chicago: Author.

American Psychological Association Commission on Violence and Youth. (1993). *Violence and youth: Psychology's response* (vol.1). Washington, DC: Author.

Atnafou, R. (1995). Children as witnesses to community violence. *Options* (newsletter of the Adolescent Violence Resource Center, Educational Development Center, Inc.), 2, 7–11.

Augustyn, M., Parker, S., Groves, B. M., & Zuckerman, B. (1995). Children who witness violence. *Contemporary Pediatrics, 12,* 35–57.

Bell, C. (1995, January 6). Exposure to violence distresses children and may lead to their becoming violent. *Psychiatric News,* pp. 6–8, 15.

Bell, C., & Jenkins, E. J. (1991). Traumatic stress and children. *Journal of Health Care for the Poor and Underserved, 2,* 175–185.

Bell, C., & Jenkins, E. (1993). Community violence and children on Chicago's Southside. *Psychiatry, 56,* 46-54.

Black, D., & Kaplan, T. (1988). Father kills mother: Issues and problems encountered by a child psychiatric team. *British Journal of Psychiatry, 153,* 624–630.

Blumstein, A. (August, 1995). Why the deadly nexus? *National Institute of Justice Journal,* No. 229, 2–9.

Bowker, L. H. (1988). On the relationship between wife beating and child abuse. In K. Yllo & M. Bograd (Eds.), *Feminist perspec-*

tives on wife abuse. Newbury Park, CA: Sage Publications.

Burman, S., & Allen-Meares, P. (1994). Neglected victims of murder: Children witness to parental homicide. *Social Work, 39,* 28–34.

Carnegie Corporation of New York. (1994). *Starting points: Meeting the needs of our youngest children*. New York: Author.

Children's Defense Fund. (1994, October). *Children's Defense Fund and religious leaders launch crusade to protect children against violence* (press release). Washington, DC: Author.

Cummings, E. M., Hennessy, K., Rabideau, G., & Cicchetti, D. (1994). Responses of physically abused boys to interadult anger involving their mothers. *Development and Psychopathology, 6,* 31–41.

Cummings, E. M., & Zahn-Waxler, C. (1992). Emotions and the socialization of aggression: Adults' angry behavior and children's arousal and aggression. In A. Fraczek & H. Zumley (Eds.), *Socialization and Aggression* (pp. 61–84). New York: Springer-Verlag.

Drell, M., Siegel, C., & Gaensbauer, T. (1993). Post traumatic stress disorders. In C. Zeanah (Ed.), *Handbook of infant mental health* (pp. 291–304). New York: Guilford Press.

Egeland, B., & Erickson, N. F., (1987). Psychologically unavailable caregiving. In M. R. Brassard, R. Germain, & S. N. Hart (Eds.), *Psychological maltreatment of children and youth* (pp. 110–120). New York: Pergamon Press

Erikson, E. (1963). *Childhood and society* (2nd ed.). New York: Norton.

Eron, L. D., Gentry, J. H., & Schlegel, P. (Eds.). (1994). *Reason to hope: A psychosocial perspective on violence and youth*. Washington, DC: American Psychological Association.

Eth, S., & Pynoos, R. (1994). Children who witness the homicide of a parent. *Psychiatry, 57,* 287–306.

Fantuzzo, J., DePaola, L., Lambert, L., & Martino, T. (1991). Effects of interparental violence on the psychological adjustment and competencies of young children. *Journal of Consulting and Clinical Psychology, 59,* 258–265.

Fick, A. C., Osofsky, J. D., & Lewis, M. L. (in press). Police and parents' preceptions and understanding of violence. In J. D. Osofsky (Ed.), *Children and youth violence: Searching for solutions*. New York: Guilford Press.

Frieze, I. H., & Browne, A. (1989). Violence in marriage. In L. Ohlin & M. Tonry (Eds.), *Family violence* (pp. 163–218). Chicago: University of Chicago Press.

Garbarino, J. (1992). *Children in danger: Coping with the consequences of community violence.* San Francisco: Jossey–Bass Publishers.

Garmezy, N. (1993). Children in poverty: Resilience despite risk. In D. Reiss, J. E. Richters, M. Radke–Yarrow, & D. Scharf (Eds.), *Children and violence* (pp. 127–136). New York: Guilford Press.

Groves, B., & Zuckerman, B. (in press). Interventions with parents and community caregivers. In J. D. Osofsky (Ed.), *Children and youth violence: Searching for solutions.* New York: Guilford Press.

Groves, B., Zuckerman, B., Marans, S., & Cohen, D. (1993). Silent victims: Children who witness violence. *Journal of the American Medical Association, 269,* 262–264.

Grych, J. H., Seid, M., & Fincham, R. D. (1992). Assessing marital conflict from the child's perspective: The children's perception of interparental conflict scale. *Child Development, 63,* 558–572.

Hawkins, J. D. (1995). Controlling crime before it happens: Risk-focused prevention. *National Institute of Justice Journal, 229,* 10–18.

Hill, H. (1995, April). *Community violence and the social and emotional adjustment of African American children*. Poster presented at the biennial meeting of the Society for Research in Child Development, Indianapolis, IN.

Hughes, H. M. (1988). Psychological and behavioral correlates of family violence in child witnesses and victims. *American Journal of Orthopsychiatry, 58*, 77–90.

Hurley, D. J., & Jaffe, P. (1990). Children's observations of violence: II. Clinical implications for children's mental health professionals. *Canadian Journal of Psychiatry, 35*, 471–476.

Jaffe, P. G., Wolfe, D. A., & Wilson, S. K. (1990). *Children of battered women.* Newbury Park, CA: Sage.

Jaffe, P. G., Wolfe, D. A., Wilson, S. K., & Zak, L. (1986). Similarities in behavioral and social maladjustment among child victims and witnesses to family violence. *American Journal of Orthopsychiatry, 56*, 142–146.

Jenkins, P., Seydlitz, R., Osofsky, J. D., Fick, A. C., & Lewis, M. L. (1995, April). *Police perceptions of domestic violence.* Paper presented at the biennial meeting of the Society for Research in Child Development, Indianapolis, IN.

Jenkins, E., & Thompson, B. (1986). *Children talk about violence: Preliminary findings from a survey of black elementary children.* Paper presented at the Nineteenth Annual Convention of the Association of Black Psychologists, Oakland, CA.

Jouriles, E. N., & O'Leary, K. D. (1985). Interspousal reliability of reports of marital violence. *Journal of Consulting and Clinical Psychology, 53*, 419–421.

Kashani, J., Daniel, A. E., Dandoy, A. C., & Holcomb, W. R. (1992). Family violence: Impact on children. *Journal of the American Academy of Child and Adolescent Psychiatry, 31*, 181–182.

Kochanek, K. D., & Hudson, B. L. (1995). *Advance report of final mortality statistics, 1992* (Monthly Vital Statistics Report, 43, 6, suppl.). Hyattsville, MD: National Center for Health Statistics.

Lewis, M. L., Osofsky, J. D., & Fick, A. C. (1995, April). *The New Orleans Violence and Children Intervention Project: Development of a police education curriculum on the effects of violence on children.* Poster presented at the biennial meeting of the Society for Research in Child Development, Indianapolis, IN.

Marans, S., & Cohen, D. (1993). Children and inner-city violence: Strategies for intervention. In L. Leavitt & N. Fox (Eds.), *Psychological effects of war and violence on children* (pp. 281–302). Hillsdale, NJ: Erlbaum.

Margolin, G. (1987). The multiple forms of aggressiveness between marital partners: How do we identify them? *Journal of Marriage and Family Therapy, 13*, 77–84.

Margolin, G. (1995, January). *The effects of domestic violence on children.* Paper presented at the Conference on Violence against Children in the Family and Community, Los Angeles.

Massachusetts Coalition of Battered Women Service Groups. (1995, December). *Children of domestic violence* (working report of the Children's Working Group). Boston: Author.

McCloskey, L. A., Figueredo, A. J., & Koss, M. P. (1995). The effects of systemic family violence on children's mental health. *Child Development, 66*, 1239–1261.

McKibben, L., DeVos, E. & Newberger, E. (1989). Victimization of mothers of abused children: A controlled study. *Pediatrics, 84*, 531–535.

National Association for the Education of Young Children, Position Statement on Violence in the Lives of Young Children. (1993, September). *Young Children*, 81-84.

National Research Council. (1993). *Understanding child abuse and neglect.* Washington, DC: National Academy Press.

O'Brien, M., John, R. S., Margolin, G., & Erel, O. (1994). Reliability and diagnostic efficacy of parents' reports regarding children's exposure to marital aggression. *Violence and Victims, 9*, 45–62.

Osofsky, J. D. (1995). The effects of violence exposure on young children. *American Psychologist, 50*, 782–788.

Osofsky, J. D., Cohen, G., & Drell, M. (1995). The effects of trauma on young children: A case of 2-year-old twins. *International Journal of Psychoanalysis, 76,* 595–607.

Osofsky, J. D., & Fenichel, E. (Eds.). (1994). *Hurt, healing, and hope: Caring for infants and toddlers in violent environments.* Arlington, VA: Zero to Three/National Center for Clinical Infant Programs.

Osofsky, J. D., Fick, A. C., Flowers, A. L., & Lewis, M. L. (1995, April). *Trust in children living with violence.* Poster presented at the biennial meeting of the Society for Research in Child Development, Indianapolis, IN.

Osofsky, J. D., Wewers, S., Hann, D., & Fick, A. C. (1993). Chronic community violence: What is happening to our children? *Psychiatry, 56,* 36–45.

Pagelow, M. D. (1984). *Family violence.* New York: Praeger.

Parsons, E. R. (1994). Inner city children of trauma: Urban violence traumatic stress syndrome (U-VTS) and therapists' responses. In J. Wilson & J. Lindy (Eds.), *Countertransference in the treatment of post-traumatic stress disorder* (pp. 151–178). New York: Guilford Press.

Perry, B., Pollard, R. A., Blakley, T. L., Baker, W. L., & Vigilante, D. (1995). Childhood trauma, the neurobiology of adaptation and "use-dependent" development of the brain: How states become traits. *Infant Mental Health Journal, 16,* 271-291.

Prothrow-Stith, D. (1991). *Deadly consequences.* New York: Harper-Collins.

Pynoos, R. S. (1993). Traumatic stress and developmental psychopathology in children and adolescents. In J. M. Oldham, M. B. Riba, & A. Tasman (Eds.), *American Psychiatric Press Review of Psychiatry,* vol. 12 (pp. 205-238). Washington, DC: American Psychiatric Press.

Pynoos, R. S. (in press). Trauma/grief focused group psychotherapy in an elementary school-based violence prevention intervention program. In J. D. Osofsky (Ed.), *Children and youth violence: Searching for solutions.* New York: Guilford Press.

Pynoos, R. S., & Eth, S. (1986). Witness to violence: The child interview. *Journal of the American Academy of Child and Adolescent Psychiatry, 25,* 306–319.

Richters, J. E. (1993). Community violence and children's development: Toward a research agenda for the 1990's. In D. Reiss, J. E. Richters, M. Radke-Yarrow, & D. Scharf, (Eds.), *Children and violence* (pp. 3–6). New York: Guilford Press.

Richters, J. E., & Martinez, P. (1993). The NIMH Community Violence Project: Children as victims of and witnesses to violence. In D. Reiss, J. E. Richters, M. Radke–Yarrow, & D. Scharf, (Eds.), *Children and violence* (pp. 7–21). New York: Guilford Press.

Rosenberg, M. S. (1987). The children of battered women: The effects of witnessing violence on their social problem-solving abilities. *Behavior Therapist, 4,* 85– 89.

Scheeringa, M., & Zeanah, C. (1994). Two approaches to the diagnosis of posttraumatic stress disorder in infancy and early childhood. *American Academy of Child and Adolescent Psychiatry, 34,* 191–200.

Shakoor, B., & Chalmers, D. (1991). Co-victimization of African American children who witness violence and the theoretical implications of its effect on their cognitive, emotional, and behavioral development. *Journal of the National Medical Association, 83,* 233-238.

Staples, B. (1995, February 12). Learning how to batter women: Wife-beating as "inherited" behavior. *New York Times,* A14.

Straus, M. A. (1979). Measuring intrafamilial conflict and violence: The Conflict Tactics Scales. *Journal of Marriage and Family, 41,* 75–88.

Straus, M. A., & Gelles, R. J. (1990). How violent are American families? Estimates from the National Violence Survey and other studies. In M. A. Straus & R. J. Gelles (Eds.), *Physical violence in American families* (pp. 95–112). New Brunswick, NJ: Transaction.

Straus, M. A., Gelles, R. J., & Steinmetz, S. (1980). *Behind closed doors.* New York: Anchor.

Taylor, L., Zuckerman, B., Harik, V., Groves, B. M. (1994). Witnessing violence by young children and their mothers. *Journal of Developmental and Behavioral Pediatrics, 15,* 120.

Wolfe, D., Jaffe, P., Wilson, S., & Zak, L. (1985). Children of battered women: The relation between child behavior, family violence, and maternal stress. *Journal of Consulting and Clinical Psychology, 53,* 657-665.

Wolfe, D. A., & Korsch, B. (1994). Witnessing domestic violence during childhood and adolescence: Implications for pediatric practice. *Pediatrics, 94,* 594–599.

Zeanah, C. H. (1994). The assessment and treatment of infants and toddlers exposed to violence. In J. D. Osofsky & E. Fenichel (Eds.), *Caring for infants and toddlers in violent environments: Hurt, healing, and hope* (pp. 29–37). Arlington, VA: Zero to Three/National Center for Clinical Infant Programs.

Zimmerman, M. A. (1994). Resiliency research: Implications for schools and policy. *Social Policy Report, 8*(4), 1–18.

Zuckerman, B., Augustyn, M., Groves, B. M., Parker, S. (1995). Silent victims revisited: The special case of domestic violence. *Pediatrics, 96,* 511–513.

About the Author

Joy D. Osofsky, Ph.D., is professor of pediatrics and psychiatry at Louisiana State University Medical Center in New Orleans and adjunct professor of psychology at University of New Orleans. She is coeditor of *Hurt, Healing and Hope: Caring for Infants and Toddlers in Violent Environments* and is editing another book, *Children and Youth Violence: Searching for Solutions.* She is on the National Research Council Committee on the Assessment of Family Violence Interventions and also co-chairs the Louisiana Violence Prevention Task Force. She is promoting an initiative within SRCD concerned with children's exposure to violence.

Acknowledgments

I want to express special appreciation to Nancy Thomas for her untiring efforts and her consistent availability and support during the preparation of this report. Support for the author's work reported in this paper has been provided by the Entergy Corporation, Institute of Mental Hygiene, the Booth-Bricker Fund, the Brown Foundation, the Greater New Orleans Foundation, the Frost Foundation, Bell South Mobility, the Jones Family Foundation, and anonymous donors.

THE LASTING EFFECTS OF CHILD MALTREATMENT

Raymond H. Starr, Jr.

Raymond H. Starr, Jr., is a developmental psychologist on the faculty of the University of Maryland, Baltimore County. He has been conducting research with maltreated children and their families for more than sixteen years and was also a founder and first president of the National Down Syndrome Congress.

Every day, the media contain examples of increasingly extreme cases of child abuse and neglect and their consequences. The cases have a blurring sameness. Take, for example, the fourteen-year-old crack addict who lives on the streets by selling his body. A reporter befriends him and writes a vivid account of the beatings the boy received from his father. There is the pedophile who is on death row for mutilating and murdering a four-year-old girl. His record shows a sixth-grade teacher threatened to rape and kill him if he told anyone what the teacher had done to him. There is the fifteen-year-old girl who felt that her parents didn't love her. So she found love on the streets and had a baby she later abandoned in a trash barrel. And there are the prostitutes on a talk show who tell how the men their mothers had trusted sexually abused them as children. These and hundreds more examples assault us and lead us to believe that abused children become problem adolescents and adults.

Are these incidents the whole story? Case examples are dramatic, but have you ever wondered how such maltreatment changes the course of a child's life? In this sound-bite era, most of us rarely stop to think about this important question. We seldom ask why trauma should play such an important role in shaping the course of a child's life.

To examine these questions, we need to understand what psychologists know about the course of lives and how they study them—the subject of the field of life-span developmental psychology.

LIFE-SPAN DEVELOPMENT

Understanding why people behave the way they do is a complex topic that has puzzled philosophers, theologians, and scientists. The course of life is so complex that we tend to focus on critical incidents and key events. Most of us can remember a teacher who played an important role in our own development, but we have to consider that other teachers may have been important. If his seventh-grade civics teacher, Ms. Jones, is the person Bill says showed him the drama of the law, leading him to become a lawyer, does this mean that his sixth-grade English teacher, Ms. Hazelton, played no role in his career choice? An outside observer might say that Ms. Hazelton was the key person because she had a debate club and Bill was the most able debater in his class.

Case descriptions fascinate us, but it is hard to divine the reasons for life courses from such examples. It is for this reason that scientists studying human behavior prefer to use prospective studies. By following people from a certain age, we can obtain direct evidence about the life course and factors that influence it. However, most of our information comes from retrospective studies in which people are asked what has happened to them in the past and how it relates to their present functioning.

Life-span developmental theory seeks to explain the way life events have influenced individual development. Of necessity, such explanations are complex; lives themselves are complex. They are built on a biological foundation, shaped by genetic characteristics, structured by immediate events, and indirectly influenced by happenings that are external to the family. As if this were not complex enough, contemporary theory holds that our interpretation of each event is dependent on the prior interactions of all these factors.

Hank's reaction to the loss of his wife to cancer will differ from George's reaction to his wife's death from a similar cancer. Many factors can contribute to these differing reactions. Hank may have grown up with two parents who were loving and attentive, while George may never have known his father. He may have had a mother who was so depressed that from the time he was two, he had lived in a series of foster homes, never knowing a secure, loving, consistent parent.

MALTREATED CHILDREN AS ADULTS

Research has shown that there is a direct relation between a child's exposure to negative emotional, social, and environmental events and the presence of problems during adulthood. Psychiatrist Michael Rutter compared young women who were removed from strife-filled homes and who later came back to live with their parents to women from more harmonious homes.[1] The women from discordant homes were more likely to become pregnant as teens, were less skilled in parenting their children, and had unhappy marriages to men who also had psychological and social problems. Adversity begat adversity.

Do the above examples and theoretical views mean that abused and neglected children will, with great certainty, become adults with problems? Research on this issue has focused on three questions: First, do maltreated children grow up to

tween 25 percent and 35 percent.[2] Thus, it is far from certain that an abused child will grow up to be an abusive parent. Physical abuse should be seen as a risk factor for becoming an abusive adult, not as a certainty. Many abusive adults were never abused when they were children.

Researchers have also taken a broader approach by examining the cycle of family violence. Sociologist Murray Straus surveyed a randomly selected national sample of families about the extent of violence between family members.[3] Members of the

as a training ground for later child abuse.

To summarize, this evidence suggests that maltreatment during childhood is but one of many factors that lead to a person's becoming an abusive parent. Being abused as a child is a risk marker for later parenting problems and not a cause of such difficulties. It accounts for, at most, less than a third of all cases of physical abuse. Research suggests that a number of other factors, such as stress and social isolation, also play a role as causes of child abuse.[4]

Research has shown that there is a direct relation between a child's exposure to negative emotional, social, and environmental events and the presence of problems during adulthood.

---

maltreat their children? Second, are yesterday's maltreated children today's criminals? Third, are there more general effects of abuse and neglect on later psychological and social functioning? A number of research studies have examined these questions.

The cycle of maltreatment. It makes logical sense that we tend to raise our own children as we ourselves were raised. Different theoretical views of personality development suggest that this should be the case. Psychoanalytic theorists think that intergenerational transmission of parenting styles is unconscious. Others, such as learning theorists, agree that transmission occurs but differ about the mechanism. Learning parenting skills from our parents is the key mode by which child-rearing practices are transmitted from one generation to the next, according to members of the latter group of theorists.

Research suggests that the correspondence between being maltreated as a child and becoming a maltreating adult is far from the one-to-one relationship that has been proposed. Studies have focused on physical abuse; data are not available for either sexual abuse or neglect. In one recent review, the authors conclude that the rate of intergenerational transmission of physical abuse is be-

surveyed families were asked about experiences of violence when they were children and how much husband-wife and parent-child violence there had been in the family in the prior year.

Straus concluded that slightly fewer than 20 percent of parents whose mothers had been violent toward them more than once a year during childhood were abusive toward their own child. The child abuse rate for parents with less violent mothers was less than 12 percent. Having or not having a violent father was less strongly related to whether or not fathers grew up to be abusive toward their own children. Interestingly, the amount of intergenerational transmission was higher if a parent was physically punished by his or her opposite-sex parent.

Straus also found that the abusive adults in his study did not have to have been abused in childhood to become abusive adults. A violent home environment can lead a nonabused child to become an abusive adult. Boys who saw their fathers hit their mothers were 38 percent more likely to grow up to be abusive than were boys who never saw their father hit their mother (13.3 vs. 9.7 percent). Similarly, mothers who saw their mothers hit their fathers were 42 percent more likely to become abusive mothers (24.4 vs. 17.2 percent). Straus views seeing parents fight

Maltreatment and later criminality. Later criminal behavior is one of the most commonly discussed consequences of child abuse. Research on this subject has examined the consequences of both physical abuse and sexual abuse. Maltreatment has been linked to both juvenile delinquency and adult criminality.

It is difficult to do research on this topic. Furthermore, the results of studies must be carefully interpreted to avoid overstating the connection between maltreatment and criminality. For example, researchers often combine samples of abused and neglected children, making it hard to determine the exact effects of specific forms of maltreatment.

Two types of study have typically been done. Retrospective studies examine the family backgrounds of criminals and find the extent to which they were maltreated as children. It is obvious that the validity of the results of such studies may be compromised by the criminals' distortion of or lack of memory concerning childhood experiences. Prospective studies, in which a sample of children is selected and followed through childhood and into adolescence or adulthood, are generally seen as a more valid research strategy. Such studies are expensive and time-consuming to do.

One review of nine studies concluded that from 8 to 26 percent of delinquent youths studied retrospectively had been abused as children.[5] The rate for prospective studies was always found to be less than 20 percent. In one of the best studies, Joan McCord analyzed case records for more than 250 boys, almost 50 percent of whom had been abused by a parent.[6] Data were also collected when the men were in middle age. McCord found that 39 percent of the abused boys had been convicted of a crime as juveniles, adults, or at both ages, compared to 23 percent of a sample of 101 men who, as boys, had been classified as loved by their parents. The crime rate for both sets of boys is higher than would be expected because McCord's sample lived in deteriorated, urban areas where both crime and abuse are common.

Researchers have also examined the relationship between abuse and later violent criminality. Research results suggest that there is a weak relationship between abuse and later violence. For example, in one study, 16 percent of a group of abused children were later arrested —but not necessarily convicted—as suspects in violent criminal cases.[7] This was twice the arrest rate for nonabused adolescents and adults. Neglected children were also more likely to experience such arrests. These data are higher than would be the case in the general population because the samples contained a disproportionately high percentage of subjects from low-income backgrounds.

The connection between childhood sexual abuse and the commission of sex crimes in adolescence and adulthood is less clear. Most of the small number of studies that have been done have relied upon self-reports of childhood molestation made by convicted perpetrators. Their results show considerable variation in the frequency with which childhood victimization is reported. Incidence figures range from a low of 19 percent to a high of 57 percent. However, we should look at such data with suspicion. In an interesting study, perpetrators of sex crimes against children were much less likely to report that they had been sexually abused during their own childhood when they knew that the truthfulness of their answers would be validated by a polygraph examination and that lies were likely to result in being sent to jail.[8] Thus, people arrested for child sexual abuse commonly lie, claiming that they were abusing children because they themselves had been victims of sexual abuse as children.

To summarize, there is a link between childhood abuse and later criminality. Although some studies lead to a conclusion that this relationship is simple, others suggest that it is really quite complex. The latter view is probably correct.

The case of neglect is an example of this complexity. Widom, in her study discussed above, found that 12 percent of adolescents and adults arrested for violent offenses were neglected as children and 7 percent experienced both abuse and neglect (compared to 8 percent of her nonmaltreated control adolescents and adults).

Psychoanalytic theorists think that intergenerational transmission of parenting styles is unconscious.

These data raise an interesting question: Why is neglect, typically considered to be a nonviolent offense, linked to later criminality? Poverty seems to be the mediating factor. Neglect is more common among impoverished families. Poor families experience high levels of frustration, known to be a common cause of aggression. Similarly, we know that lower-class families are, in general, more violent.[9] For these reasons, all the forms of maltreatment we have considered make it somewhat more likely that a maltreated child will grow up to commit criminal acts.

Maltreatment in context. Research suggests that maltreatment during childhood has far-reaching consequences. These are best seen as the results of a failure to meet the emotional needs of the developing child. Indeed, in many cases, the trust the child places in the parent is betrayed by the parent.

This betrayal has been linked to many and varied consequences. The greatest amount of research has focused on the long-term effects of sexual abuse. Studies have looked at samples that are representative of the normal population and also at groups of adults who are seeking psychotherapy because of emotional problems. The most valid findings come from the former type of study. One review of research concluded that almost 90 percent of studies found some lasting effect of sexual abuse.[10]

Sexual abuse has been linked to a wide variety of psychological disturbances. These include depression, low self-esteem, psychosis, anxiety, sleep problems, alcohol and drug abuse, and sexual dysfunction (including a predisposition to revictimization during adulthood). As was true for the research reviewed in the preceding two sections of this article, any particular problem is present in only a minority of adult survivors of childhood sexual victimization.

We know less about the long-term effects of physical abuse. Most of the limited amount of available research has used data obtained from clinical samples. Such studies have two problems. First, they rely on retrospective adult reports concerning events that happened during childhood. Second, the use of such samples results in an overestimate of the extent to which physical abuse has long-term consequences. Compared with a random sample of the general population, clinical samples contain individuals who are already identified as having emotional difficulties, regardless of whether or not they have been abused.

Researchers in one study found that more than 40 percent of inpatients being treated in a psychiatric hospital had been sexually or physically abused as children, usually by a family member.[11] Also, the abuse was typically chronic rather than a onetime occurrence. The abused patients were almost 50 percent more likely to have tried to commit suicide, were 25 percent more likely to have been violent toward others, and were 15 percent more likely to have had some involvement with the criminal justice system than were other patients at the same hospital who had not experienced childhood maltreatment.

Much research remains to be done in this area. We know little about the long-term consequences of particular forms of abuse. The best that we can say is that many victims of physical and sexual abuse experience psychological trauma lasting into adulthood.

The lack of universal consequences. The above analysis suggests that many victims of childhood maltreatment do *not* have significant problems functioning as adults. Researchers are only beginning to ask why many adult victims apparently have escaped unsullied. Factors that mediate and soften the influence of abuse and neglect are called buffers.

The search for buffers is a difficult one. Many of the negative outcomes that have been discussed in the preceding sections may be the result of a number of factors other than maltreatment itself. For example, abused children commonly have behavior problems that are similar to those that have been reported in children raised by drug addicts or adults suffering from major psychological disturbances. Abused children do not exhibit any problems that can be attributed only to abuse. A given behavior problem can have many causes.

One view of the way in which buffers act to limit the extent to which physical abuse is perpetuated across succeeding generations has been proposed by David Wolfe.[12] He believes that there is a three-part process involving the parent, the child, and the relationships between

ating factors that work at this level include normal developmental changes in child behavior, parental attendance at child management classes, and the development of parental ability to cope with the child's escalating annoying actions. Finally, additional compensatory factors work to limit the ongoing use of aggression as a solution to parenting problems.

The amount of intergenerational transmission was higher if a parent was physically punished by his or her opposite-sex parent.

Parents may realize that researchers are indeed correct when they say that physical punishment is an ineffective way of changing child behavior. In addition, children may respond positively to parental use of nonaggressive disciplinary procedures and, at a broader level, society or individuals in the parents' circle of friends may inhibit the use of physical punishment by making their disapproval known. Parents who were abused as children are therefore less likely to abuse their own children if any or all of these mediating factors are present.

Research suggests that the factors

One study compared parents who broke the cycle of abuse to those who did not.[13] Mothers who were not abusive had larger, more supportive social networks. Support included help with child care and financial assistance during times of crisis. Mothers who did not continue the abusive cycle also were more in touch with their own abuse as children and expressed doubts about their parenting ability. This awareness made them more able to relive and discuss their own negative childhood experiences.

To summarize, investigators have gone beyond just looking at the negative consequences of childhood maltreatment. They are devoting increasing attention to determining what factors in a child's environment may inoculate the child against the effects of maltreatment. While research is starting to provide us with information concerning some of these mediating influences, much more work needs to be done before we can specify the most important mediators and know how they exert their influences.

Physical abuse should be seen as a risk factor for becoming an abusive adult, not as a certainty.

CONCLUSIONS

We know much about the intergenerational transmission of childhood physical and sexual abuse. Research suggests that abused children are (1) at an increased risk of either repeating the acts they experienced with their own children or, in the case of sexual abuse, with both their own and with unrelated children; (2) more likely to be involved with the criminal justice system as adolescents or adults; and (3) likely to suffer long-lasting emotional effects of abuse even if they do not abuse their own children or commit criminal acts.

This does not mean that abused chil-

the two. In the first stage, factors predisposing a parent to child abuse (including stress and a willingness to be aggressive toward the child) are buffered by such factors as social support and an income adequate for the purchase of child-care services. Next, Wolfe notes that children often do things that annoy parents and create crises that may lead to abuse because the parent is unprepared to handle the child's provocative behavior. Amelior-

mentioned by Wolfe and other influences all can work to buffer the adult effects of childhood maltreatment. These include knowing a nurturing, loving adult who provides social support, intellectually restructuring the maltreatment so that it is not seen so negatively, being altruistic and giving to others what one did not get as a child, having good skills for coping with stressful events, and getting psychotherapy.

People arrested for child sexual abuse commonly lie, claiming that they were abusing children because they themselves had been victims of sexual abuse as children.

dren invariably grow up to be adults with problems. Many adults escape the negative legacy of abuse. They grow up to be normal, contributing members of society. Their escape from maltreatment is usually related to the presence of factors that buffer the effects of the physical blows and verbal barbs.

The knowledge base underlying these conclusions is of varied quality. We know more about the relationship of physical and sexual abuse to adult abusiveness and criminality, less about long-term psychological problems and buffering factors, and almost nothing about the relationship of neglect to any of these outcomes. Almost no research has been done on neglect, a situation leading to a discussion of the reasons behind our "neglect of neglect."[14] Our ignorance is all the more surprising when we consider that neglect is the most common form of reported maltreatment.

The issues involved are complex. We can no longer see the development of children from a view examining such simple cause-effect relationships as exemplified by the proposal that abused children grow up to be abusive adults. Contemporary de-

velopmental psychology recognizes that many interacting forces work together to shape development. Children exist in a context that contains their own status as biological beings, their parents and the background they bring to the task of child-rearing, the many and varied environments such as work and school that exert both direct and indirect influences on family members, and the overall societal acceptance of violence.

Advances in research methods allow us to evaluate the interrelationships of all the above factors to arrive at a coherent view of the course of development. Appropriate studies are difficult to plan and expensive to conduct. Without such research, the best that we can do is to continue performing small studies that give us glimpses of particular elements of the picture that we call the life course.

Research is necessary if we are to develop and evaluate the effectiveness of child maltreatment prevention and treatment programs. Our existing knowledge base provides hints that are used by program planners and psychotherapists to find families where there is a high risk of

maltreatment and to intervene early. But when such hints are all we have to guide us in working to break the cycle of maltreatment, there continues to be risk of intergenerational perpetuation.

1. Michael Rutter, "Intergenerational Continuities and Discontinuities in Serious Parenting Difficulties," in *Child Maltreatment: Theory and Research on the Causes and Consequences of Child Abuse and Neglect*, ed., Dante Cicchetti and Vicki Carlson (New York: Cambridge University Press, 1989), 317–348.

2. Joan Kaufman and Edward Zigler, "Do Abused Children Become Abusive Adults?" *American Journal of Orthopsychiatry* 57 (April 1987): 186–192.

3. Murray A. Straus, "Family Patterns and Child Abuse in a Nationally Representative American Sample," *Child Abuse and Neglect* 3 (1979): 213–225.

4. Raymond H. Starr, Jr., "Physical Abuse of Children," in *Handbook of Family Violence* ed. Vincent B. Van Hasselt, et al. (New York: Plenum Press, 1988): 119–155.

5. Cathy Spatz Widom, "Does Violence Beget Violence? A Critical Examination of the Literature," *Psychological Bulletin* 106 (1989): 3–28.

6. Joan McCord, "A Forty-year Perspective on Effects of Child Abuse and Neglect," *Child Abuse and Neglect* 7 (1983): 265–270. Joan McCord, "Parental Aggressiveness and Physical Punishment in Long-term Perspective," in *Family Abuse and Its Consequences*, ed. Gerald T. Hotaling, et al. (Newbury Park, Calif.: Sage Publishing, 1988): 91–98.

7. Cathy Spatz Widom, "The Cycle of Violence," *Science*, 14 April 1989.

8. Jan Hindman, "Research Disputes Assumptions about Child Molesters," *National District Attorneys' Association Bulletin* 7 (July/August 1988): 1.

9. Murray A. Straus, Richard J. Gelles, and Suzanne K. Steinmetz, *Behind Closed Doors: Violence in the American Family* (New York: Anchor Press, 1980).

10. David Finkelhor and Angela Browne, "Assessing the Long-term Impact of Child Sexual Abuse: A Review and Conceptualization," in *Family Abuse and Its Consequences*, ed. Gerald T. Hotaling, et al.: 270–284.

11. Elaine (Hilberman) Carmen, Patricia Perri Rieker, and Trudy Mills, "Victims of Violence and Psychiatric Illness," *American Journal of Psychiatry* 141 (March 1984): 378–383.

12. David A. Wolfe, *Child Abuse: Implications for Child Development and Psychopathology* (Newbury Park, Calif.: Sage Publishing, 1987).

13. Rosemary S. Hunter and Nancy Kilstrom, "Breaking the Cycle in Abusive Families," 136 (1979): 1320–22.

14. Isabel Wolock and Bernard Horowitz, "Child Maltreatment as a Social Problem: The Neglect of Neglect," *American Journal of Orthopsychiatry* 54 (1984); 530–543.

ALIENATION

AND THE FOUR WORLDS OF CHILDHOOD

The forces that produce youthful alienation are growing in strength and scope, says Mr. Bronfenbrenner. And the best way to counteract alienation is through the creation of connections or links throughout our culture. The schools can build such links.

Urie Bronfenbrenner

Urie Bronfenbrenner is Jacob Gould Shurman Professor of Human Development and Family Studies and of Psychology at Cornell University, Ithaca, N.Y.

To be alienated is to lack a sense of belonging, to feel cut off from family, friends, school, or work—the four worlds of childhood.

At some point in the process of growing up, many of us have probably felt cut off from one or another of these worlds, but usually not for long and not from more than one world at a time. If things weren't going well in school, we usually still had family, friends, or some activity to turn to. But if, over an extended period, a young person feels unwanted or insecure in several of these worlds simultaneously or if the worlds are at war with one another, trouble may lie ahead.

What makes a young person feel that he or she doesn't belong? Individual differences in personality can certainly be one cause, but, especially in recent years, scientists who study human behavior and development have identified an equal (if not even more powerful) factor: the circumstances in which a young person lives.

Many readers may feel that they recognize the families depicted in the vignettes that are to follow. This is so because they reflect the way we tend to look at families today: namely, that we see parents as being good or not-so-good without fully tak-

ing into account the circumstances in their lives.

Take Charles and Philip, for example. Both are seventh-graders who live in a middle-class suburb of a large U.S. city. In many ways their surroundings seem similar; yet, in terms of the risk of alienation, they live in rather different worlds. See if you can spot the important differences.

CHARLES

The oldest of three children, Charles is amiable, outgoing, and responsible. Both of his parents have full-time jobs outside the home. They've been able to arrange their working hours, however, so that at least one of them is at home when the children return from school. If for some reason they can't be home, they have an arrangement with a neighbor, an elderly woman who lives alone. They can phone her and ask her to look after the children until they arrive. The children have grown so fond of this woman that she is like another grandparent—a nice situation for them, since their real grandparents live far away.

Homework time is one of the most important parts of the day for Charles and his younger brother and sister. Charles's parents help the children with their homework if they need it, but most of the time they just make sure that the children have a period of peace and quiet—without TV—in which to do their work. The children are allowed to watch television one hour each

night—but only after they have completed their homework. Since Charles is doing well in school, homework isn't much of an issue, however.

Sometimes Charles helps his mother or father prepare dinner, a job that everyone in the family shares and enjoys. Those family members who don't cook on a given evening are responsible for cleaning up.

Charles also shares his butterfly collection with his family. He started the collection when he first began learning about butterflies during a fourth-grade science project. The whole family enjoys picnicking and hunting butterflies together, and Charles occasionally asks his father to help him mount and catalogue his trophies.

Charles is a bit of a loner. He's not a very good athlete, and this makes him somewhat self-conscious. But he does have one very close friend, a boy in his class who lives just down the block. The two boys have been good friends for years.

Charles is a good-looking, warm, happy young man. Now that he's beginning to be interested in girls, he's gratified to find that the interest is returned.

PHILIP

Philip is 12 and lives with his mother, father, and 6-year-old brother. Both of his parents work in the city, commuting more than an hour each way. Pandemonium strikes every weekday morning as

From *Phi Delta Kappan*, February 1986, pp. 430-436. © 1986 by Phi Delta Kappa, Inc. Reprinted by permission of the author and *Phi Delta Kappan*.

the entire family prepares to leave for school and work.

Philip is on his own from the time school is dismissed until just before dinner, when his parents return after stopping to pick up his little brother at a nearby day-care home. At one time, Philip took care of his little brother after school, but he resented having to do so. That arrangement ended one day when Philip took his brother out to play and the little boy wandered off and got lost. Philip didn't even notice for several hours that his brother was missing. He felt guilty at first about not having done a better job. But not having to mind his brother freed him to hang out with his friends or to watch television, his two major after-school activities.

The pace of their life is so demanding that Philip's parents spend their weekends just trying to relax. Their favorite weekend schedule calls for watching a ball game on television and then having a cookout in the back yard. Philip's mother resigned herself long ago to a messy house; pizza, TV dinners, or fast foods are all she can manage in the way of meals on most nights. Philip's father has made it clear that she can do whatever she wants in managing the house, as long as she doesn't try to involve him in the effort. After a hard day's work, he's too tired to be interested in housekeeping.

Philip knows that getting a good education is important; his parents have stressed that. But he just can't seem to concentrate in school. He'd much rather fool around with his friends. The thing that he and his friends like to do best is to ride the bus downtown and go to a movie, where they can show off, make noise, and make one another laugh.

Sometimes they smoke a little marijuana during the movie. One young man in Philip's social group was arrested once for having marijuana in his jacket pocket. He was trying to sell it on the street so that he could buy food. Philip thinks his friend was stupid to get caught. If you're smart, he believes, you don't let that happen. He's glad that his parents never found out about the incident.

Once, he brought two of his friends home during the weekend. His parents told him later that they didn't like the kind of people he was hanging around with. Now Philip goes out of his way to keep his friends and his parents apart.

THE FAMILY UNDER PRESSURE

In many ways the worlds of both

Institutions that play important roles in human development are rapidly being eroded, mainly through benign neglect.

teenagers are similar, even typical. Both live in families that have been significantly affected by one of the most important developments in American family life in the postwar years: the employment of both parents outside the home. Their mothers share this status with 64% of all married women in the U.S. who have school-age children. Fifty percent of mothers of preschool children and 46% of mothers with infants under the age of 3 work outside the home. For single-parent families, the rates are even higher: 53% of all mothers in single-parent households who have infants under age 3 work outside the home, as do 69% of all single mothers who have school-age children.[1]

These statistics have profound implications for families — sometimes for better, sometimes for worse. The determining factor is how well a given family can cope with the "havoc in the home" that two jobs can create. For, unlike most other industrialized nations, the U.S. has yet to introduce the kinds of policies and practices that make work life and family life compatible.

It is all too easy for family life in the U.S. to become hectic and stressful, as both parents try to coordinate the disparate demands of family and jobs in a world in which everyone has to be transported at least twice a day in a variety of directions. Under these circumstances, meal preparation, child care, shopping, and cleaning — the most basic tasks in a family — become major challenges. Dealing with these challenges may sometimes take precedence over the family's equally important child-rearing, educational, and nurturing roles.

But that is not the main danger. What

threatens the well-being of children and young people the most is that the external havoc can become internal, first for parents and then for their children. And that is exactly the sequence in which the psychological havoc of families under stress usually moves.

Recent studies indicate that conditions at work constitute one of the major sources of stress for American families.[2] Stress at work carries over to the home, where it affects first the relationship of parents to each other. Marital conflict then disturbs the parent/child relationship. Indeed, as long as tensions at work do not impair the relationship between the parents, the children are not likely to be affected. In other words, the influence of parental employment on children is indirect, operating through its effect on the parents.

That this influence is indirect does not make it any less potent, however. Once the parent/child relationship is seriously disturbed, children begin to feel insecure — and a door to the world of alienation has been opened. That door can open to children at any age, from preschool to high school and beyond.

My reference to the world of school is not accidental, for it is in that world that the next step toward alienation is likely to be taken. Children who feel rootless or caught in conflict at home find it difficult to pay attention in school. Once they begin to miss out on learning, they feel lost in the classroom, and they begin to seek acceptance elsewhere. Like Philip, they often find acceptance in a group of peers with similar histories who, having no welcoming place to go and nothing challenging to do, look for excitement on the streets.

OTHER INFLUENCES

In contemporary American society the growth of two-wage-earner families is not the only — or even the most serious — social change requiring accommodation through public policy and practice in order to avoid the risks of alienation. Other social changes include lengthy trips to and from work; the loss of the extended family, the close neighborhood, and other support systems previously available to families; and the omnipresent threat of television and other media to the family's traditional role as the primary transmitter of culture and values. Along with most families today, the families of Charles and Philip are experiencing the unraveling and disintegration of social institutions that in the past were central to the health and well-being of children and their parents.

Notice that both Charles and Philip come from two-parent, middle-class families. This is still the norm in the U.S. Thus neither family has to contend with two changes now taking place in U.S. society that have profound implications for the future of American families and the well-being of the next generation. The first of these changes is the increasing number of single-parent families. Although the divorce rate in the U.S. has been leveling off of late, this decrease has been more than compensated for by a rise in the number of unwed mothers, especially teenagers. Studies of the children brought up in single-parent families indicate that they are at greater risk of alienation than their counterparts from two-parent families. However, their vulnerability appears to have its roots not in the single-parent family structure as such, but in the treatment of single parents by U.S. society.[3]

In this nation, single parenthood is almost synonymous with poverty. And the growing gap between poor families and the rest of us is today the most powerful and destructive force producing alienation in the lives of millions of young people in America. In recent years, we have witnessed what the U.S. Census Bureau calls "the largest decline in family income in the post-World War II period." According to the latest Census, 25% of all children under age 6 now live in families whose incomes place them below the poverty line.

COUNTERING THE RISKS

Despite the similar stresses on their families, the risks of alienation for Charles and Philip are not the same. Clearly, Charles's parents have made a deliberate effort to create a variety of arrangements and practices that work against alienation. They have probably not done so as part of a deliberate program of "alienation prevention" — parents don't usually think in those terms. They're just being good parents. They spend time with their children and take an active interest in what their children are thinking, doing, and learning. They control their television set instead of letting it control them. They've found support systems to back them up when they're not available.

Without being aware of it, Charles's parents are employing a principle that the great Russian educator Makarenko employed in his extraordinarily successful programs for the reform of wayward adolescents in the 1920s: "The maximum of support with the maximum of challenge."[4] Families that produce effective, competent children often follow this principle, whether they're aware of it or not. They neither maintain strict control nor allow their children total freedom. They're always opening doors — and then giving their children a gentle but firm shove to encourage them to move on and grow. This combination of support and challenge is essential, if children are to avoid alienation and develop into capable young adults.

From a longitudinal study of youthful alienation and delinquency that is now considered a classic, Finnish psychologist Lea Pulkkinen arrived at a conclusion strikingly similar to Makarenko's. She found "guidance" — a combination of love and direction — to be a critical predictor of healthy development in youngsters.[5]

No such pattern is apparent in Philip's family. Unlike Charles's parents, Philip's parents neither recognize nor respond to the challenges they face. They have dispensed with the simple amenities of family self-discipline in favor of whatever is easiest. They may not be indifferent to their children, but the demands of their jobs leave them with little energy to be actively involved in their children's lives. (Note that Charles's parents have work schedules that are flexible enough to allow one of them to be at home most afternoons. In this regard, Philip's family is much more the norm, however. One of the most constructive steps that employers could take to strengthen families would be to enact clear policies making such flexibility possible.)

But perhaps the clearest danger signal in Philip's life is his dependence on his peer group. Pulkkinen found heavy reliance on peers to be one of the strongest predictors of problem behavior in adolescence and young adulthood. From a developmental viewpoint, adolescence is a time of challenge — a period in which young people seek activities that will serve as outlets for their energy, imagination, and longings. If healthy and constructive challenges are not available to them, they will find their challenges in such peer-group-related behaviors as poor school performance, aggressiveness or social withdrawal (sometimes both), school absenteeism or dropping out, smoking, drinking, early and promiscuous sexual activity, teenage parenthood, drugs, and juvenile delinquency.

This pattern has now been identified in a number of modern industrial societies, including the U.S., England, West Germany, Finland, and Australia. The pattern is both predictable from the circumstances of a child's early family life and predictive of life experiences still to come, e.g., difficulties in establishing relationships with the opposite sex, marital discord, divorce, economic failure, criminality.

If the roots of alienation are to be found in disorganized families living in disorganized environments, its bitter fruits are to be seen in these patterns of disrupted development. This is not a harvest that our nation can easily afford. Is it a price that other modern societies are paying, as well?

A CROSS-NATIONAL PERSPECTIVE

The available answers to that question will not make Americans feel better about what is occurring in the U.S. In our society, the forces that produce youthful alienation are growing in strength and scope. Families, schools, and other institutions that play important roles in human development are rapidly being eroded, *mainly through benign neglect*. Unlike the citizens of other modern nations, we Americans have simply not been willing to make the necessary effort to forestall the alienation of our young people.

As part of a new experiment in higher education at Cornell University, I have been teaching a multidisciplinary course for the past few years titled "Human Development in Post-Industrial Societies." One of the things we have done in that course is to gather comparative data from several nations, including France, Canada, Japan, Australia, Germany, England, and the U.S. One student summarized our findings succinctly: "With respect to families, schools, children, and youth, such countries as France, Japan, Canada, and Australia have more in common with each other than the United States has with any of them." For example:

• The U.S. has by far the highest rate of teenage pregnancy of any industrialized nation — twice the rate of its nearest competitor, England.
• The U.S. divorce rate is the highest in the world — nearly double that of its nearest competitor, Sweden.
• The U.S. is the only industrialized society in which nearly one-fourth of all infants and preschool children live in families whose incomes fall below the

poverty line. These children lack such basics as adequate health care.

• The U.S. has fewer support systems for individuals in all age groups, including adolescence. The U.S. also has the highest incidence of alcohol and drug abuse among adolescents of any country in the world.[6]

All these problems are part of the unraveling of the social fabric that has been going on since World War II. These problems are not unique to the U.S., but in many cases they are more pronounced here than elsewhere.

WHAT COMMUNITIES CAN DO

The more we learn about alienation and its effects in contemporary postindustrial societies, the stronger are the imperatives to counteract it. If the essence of alienation is disconnectedness, then the best way to counteract alienation is through the creation of connections or links.

For the well-being of children and adolescents, the most important links must be those between the home, the peer group, and the school. A recent study in West Germany effectively demonstrated how important this basic triangle can be. The study examined student achievement and social behavior in 20 schools. For all the schools, the researchers developed measures of the links between the home, the peer group, and the school. Controlling for social class and other variables, the researchers found that they were able to predict children's behavior from the number of such links they found. Students who had no links were alienated. They were not doing well in school, and they exhibited a variety of behavioral problems. By contrast, students who had such links were doing well and were growing up to be responsible citizens.[7]

In addition to creating links within the basic triangle of home, peer group, and school, we need to consider two other structures in today's society that affect the lives of young people: the world of work (for both parents and children) and the community, which provides an overarching context for all the other worlds of childhood.

Philip's family is one example of how the world of work can contribute to alienation. The U.S. lags far behind other industrialized nations in providing child-care services and other benefits designed to promote the well-being of children and their families. Among the most needed benefits are maternity and paternity leaves, flex-time, job-sharing

C aring is surely an essential aspect of education in a free society; yet we have almost completely neglected it.

arrangements, and personal leaves for parents when their children are ill. These benefits are a matter of course in many of the nations with which the U.S. is generally compared.

In contemporary American society, however, the parents' world of work is not the only world that both policy and practice ought to be accommodating. There is also the children's world of work. According to the most recent figures available, 50% of all high school students now work part-time — sometimes as much as 40 to 50 hours per week. This fact poses a major problem for the schools. Under such circumstances, how can teachers assign homework with any expectation that it will be completed?

The problem is further complicated by the kind of work that most young people are doing. For many years, a number of social scientists — myself included — advocated more work opportunities for adolescents. We argued that such experiences would provide valuable contact with adult models and thereby further the development of responsibility and general maturity. However, from their studies of U.S. high school students who are employed, Ellen Greenberger and Lawrence Steinberg conclude that most of the jobs held by these youngsters are highly routinized and afford little opportunity for contact with adults. The largest employers of teenagers in the U.S. are fast-food restaurants. Greenberger and Steinberg argue that, instead of providing maturing experiences, such settings give adolescents even greater exposure to the values and lifestyles of their peer group. And the adolescent peer group tends to emphasize immediate gratification and consumerism.[8]

Finally, in order to counteract the

mounting forces of alienation in U.S. society, we must establish a working alliance between the private sector and the public one (at both the local level and the national level) to forge links between the major institutions in U.S. society and to re-create a sense of community. Examples from other countries abound:

• Switzerland has a law that no institution for the care of the elderly can be established unless it is adjacent to and shares facilities with a day-care center, a school, or some other kind of institution serving children.

• In many public places throughout Australia, the Department of Social Security has displayed a poster that states, in 16 languages: "If you need an interpreter, call this number." The department maintains a network of interpreters who are available 16 hours a day, seven days a week. They can help callers get in touch with a doctor, an ambulance, a fire brigade, or the police; they can also help callers with practical or personal problems.

• In the USSR, factories, offices, and places of business customarily "adopt" groups of children, e.g., a day-care center, a class of schoolchildren, or a children's ward in a hospital. The employees visit the children, take them on outings, and invite them to visit their place of work.

We Americans can offer a few good examples of alliances between the public and private sectors, as well. For example, in Flint, Michigan, some years ago, Mildred Smith developed a community program to improve school performance among low-income minority pupils. About a thousand children were involved. The program required no change in the regular school curriculum; its principal focus was on building links between home and school. This was accomplished in a variety of ways.

• A core group of low-income parents went from door to door, telling their neighbors that the school needed their help.

• Parents were asked to keep younger children out of the way so that the older children could complete their homework.

• Schoolchildren were given tags to wear at home that said, "May I read to you?"

• Students in the high school business program typed and duplicated teaching materials, thus freeing teachers to work directly with the children.

• Working parents visited school classrooms to talk about their jobs and about how their own schooling now helped them in their work.

WHAT SCHOOLS CAN DO

As the program in Flint demonstrates, the school is in the best position of all U.S. institutions to initiate and strengthen links that support children and adolescents. This is so for several reasons. First, one of the major — but often unrecognized — responsibilities of the school is to enable young people to move from the secluded and supportive environment of the home into responsible and productive citizenship. Yet, as the studies we conducted at Cornell revealed, most other modern nations are ahead of the U.S. in this area.

In these other nations, schools are not merely — or even primarily — places where the basics are taught. Both in purpose and in practice, they function instead as settings in which young people learn "citizenship": what it means to be a member of the society, how to behave toward others, what one's responsibilities are to the community and to the nation.

I do not mean to imply that such learnings do not occur in American schools. But when they occur, it is mostly by accident and not because of thoughtful planning and careful effort. What form might such an effort take? I will present here some ideas that are too new to have stood the test of time but that may be worth trying.

Creating an American classroom. This is a simple idea. Teachers could encourage their students to learn about schools (and, especially, about individual classrooms) in such modern industrialized societies as France, Japan, Canada, West Germany, the Soviet Union, and Australia. The children could acquire such information in a variety of ways: from reading, from films, from the firsthand reports of children and adults who have attended school abroad, from exchanging letters and materials with students and their teachers in other countries. Through such exposure, American students would become aware of how attending school in other countries is both similar to and different from attending school in the U.S.

But the main learning experience would come from asking students to consider what kinds of things *should* be happening — or not happening — in American classrooms, given our nation's values and ideals. For example, how should children relate to one another and to their teachers, if they are doing things in an *American* way? If a student's idea seems to make sense, the American tradition of pragmatism makes the next step obvious: try the idea to see if it works.

The curriculum for caring. This effort also has roots in our values as a nation. Its goal is to make caring an essential part of the school curriculum. However, students would not simply learn about caring; they would actually engage in it. Children would be asked to spend time with and to care for younger children, the elderly, the sick, and the lonely. Caring institutions, such as day-care centers, could be located adjacent to or even within the schools. But it would be important for young caregivers to learn about the environment in which their charges live and the other people with whom their charges interact each day. For example, older children who took responsibility for younger ones would become acquainted with the younger children's parents and living arrangements by escorting them home from school.

Just as many schools now train superb drum corps, they could also train "caring corps" — groups of young men and women who would be on call to handle a variety of emergencies. If a parent fell suddenly ill, these students could come into the home to care for the children, prepare meals, run errands, and serve as an effective source of support for their fellow human beings. Caring is surely an essential aspect of education in a free society; yet we have almost completely neglected it.

Mentors for the young. A mentor is someone with a skill that he or she wishes to teach to a younger person. To be a true mentor, the older person must be willing to take the time and to make the commitment that such teaching requires.

We don't make much use of mentors in U.S. society, and we don't give much recognition or encouragement to individuals who play this important role. As a result, many U.S. children have few significant and committed adults in their lives. Most often, their mentors are their own parents, perhaps a teacher or two, a coach, or — more rarely — a relative, a neighbor, or an older classmate. However, in a diverse society such as ours, with its strong tradition of volunteerism, potential mentors abound. The schools need to seek them out and match them with young people who will respond positively to their particular knowledge and skills.

The school is the institution best suited to take the initiative in this task, because the school is the only place in which all children gather every day. It is also the only institution that has the right (and the responsibility) to turn to the community for help in an activity that represents the noblest kind of education: the building of character in the young.

There is yet another reason why schools should take a leading role in rebuilding links among the four worlds of childhood: schools have the most to gain. In the recent reports bemoaning the state of American education, a recurring theme has been the anomie and chaos that pervade many U.S. schools, to the detriment of effective teaching and learning. Clearly, we are in danger of allowing our schools to become academies of alienation.

In taking the initiative to rebuild links among the four worlds of childhood, U.S. schools will be taking necessary action to combat the destructive forces of alienation — first, within their own walls, and thereafter, in the life experience and future development of new generations of Americans.

1. Urie Bronfenbrenner, "New Worlds for Families," paper presented at the Boston Children's Museum, 4 May 1984.
2. Urie Bronfenbrenner, "The Ecology of the Family as a Context for Human Development," *Developmental Psychology*, in press.
3. Mavis Heatherington, "Children of Divorce," in R. Henderson, ed., *Parent-Child Interaction* (New York: Academic Press, 1981).
4. A.S. Makarenko, *The Collective Family: A Handbook for Russian Parents* (New York: Doubleday, 1967).
5. Lea Pulkkinen, "Self-Control and Continuity from Childhood to Adolescence," in Paul Baltes and Orville G. Brim, eds., *Life-Span Development and Behavior*, Vol. 4 (New York: Academic Press, 1982), pp. 64-102.
6. S.B. Kamerman, *Parenting in an Unresponsive Society* (New York: Free Press, 1980); S.B. Kamerman and A.J. Kahn, *Social Services in International Perspective* (Washington, D.C.: U.S. Department of Health, Education, and Welfare, n.d.); and Lloyd Johnston, Jerald Bachman, and Patrick O'Malley, *Use of Licit and Illicit Drugs by America's High School Students — 1975-84* (Washington, D.C.: U.S. Government Printing Office, 1985).
7. Kurt Aurin, personal communication, 1985.
8. Ellen Greenberger and Lawrence Steinberg, *The Work of Growing Up* (New York: Basic Books, forthcoming).

WAAAH!..

Why kids have a lot to cry about

David Elkind, Ph.D.

David Elkind, Ph.D., professor of child study at Tufts University, is the author of more than 400 articles. He is perhaps best known for his books The Hurried Child; All Grown Up and No Place to Go *and* Ties That Stress: Childrearing in a Postmodern Society. *He is an active consultant to government agencies, private foundations, clinics, and mental-health centers.*

"MOMMY," THE FIVE-YEAR-OLD GIRL asked her mother, "why don't you get divorced again?" Her thrice-married mother was taken aback and said in return, "Honey, why in the world should I do that?" To which her daughter replied, "Well, I haven't seen you in love for such a long time."

This young girl perceives family life and the adult world in a very different way than did her counterpart less than half a century ago. Likewise, the mother perceives her daughter quite differently than did a mother raising a child in the 1940s. Although this mother was surprised at her daughter's question, she was not surprised at her understanding of divorce, nor at her familiarity with the symptoms of romance.

As this anecdote suggests, there has been a remarkable transformation over the last 50 years in our children's perceptions of us, and in our perceptions of our children. These altered perceptions are a very small part of a much larger tectonic shift in our society in general and in our families in particular. This shift is nothing less than a transformation of the basic framework, or paradigm, within which we think about and thus perceive our world. To understand the changes in the family, the perceptions of family members, and of parenting that have been brought about, we first have to look at this broader "paradigm shift" and what it has meant for family sentiments, values, and perceptions.

FROM MODERN TO POSTMODERN

Without fully realizing it perhaps, we have been transported into the postmodern era. Although this era has been called "postindustrial" and, alternatively, "information age," neither of these phrases is broad enough to encompass the breadth and depth of the changes that have occurred. The terms modern and postmodern, in contrast, encompass all aspects of society and speak to the changes in science, philosophy, architecture, literature, and the arts—as well as in industry and technology—that have marked our society since mid-century.

THE MODERN AND THE NUCLEAR FAMILY

The modern era, which began with the Renaissance and spanned the Industrial Revolution, was based upon three related assumptions. One was the idea of *human progress*—the notion that the natural direction of human and societal development is toward a more equitable, peaceful, and harmonious world in which every individual would be entitled to life, liberty, and the pursuit of happiness. A second assumption is *universality*. There were, it was taken as given, universal laws of nature of art, science, economics, and so on that transcended time and culture. The third basic assumption was that of *regularity*—the belief that the world is an orderly place, that animals and plants, geological layers and chemical elements could be classified in an orderly hierarchy. As Einstein put it, "God does not play dice with the universe!"

These assumptions gave a unique character and distinctiveness to modern life. Modern science, literature, architecture, philosophy, and industry all embodied these premises. And they were enshrined in the Modern Family as well. The modern nuclear family, for example, was seen as the end result of a progressive evolution of family forms. Two parents, two or three children, one parent working and one staying home to rear the children and maintain the home was thought to be the ideal family form toward which all prior, "primitive" forms were merely preliminary stages.

SENTIMENTS OF THE NUCLEAR FAMILY
The Modern Family was shaped by three sentiments that also reflected the underlying assumptions of modernity. One of these was Romantic Love. In premodern times, couples married by familial and community dictates. Considerations of property and social position were paramount. This community influence declined in the modern era, and couples increasingly came to choose one another on the basis of mutual attraction. This attraction became idealized into the notion that "Some enchanted evening, you will meet a stranger" for whom you and only you were destined ("You were meant for me, I was meant for you"), and that couples would stay together for the rest of their lives, happily "foreveraftering."

A second sentiment of the Modern Family was that of Maternal Love—the idea that women have a maternal "instinct" and a need to care for children, particularly when they are small. The idea of a maternal instinct was a thoroughly modern invention that emerged only after modern medicine and nutrition reduced infant mortality. In premodern times, infant mortality was so high that the young were not even named until they were two years old and stood a good chance of surviving. It was also not uncommon for urban parents to have their infants "wet-nursed" in the country. Often these

infants died because the wet-nurse fed her own child before she fed the stranger, and there was little nourishment left. Such practices could hardly be engaged in by a mother with a "maternal instinct."

The third sentiment of the Modern Family was Domesticity, a belief that relationships within the family are always more powerful and binding than are those outside it. The family was, as Christopher Lasch wrote, "a haven in a heartless world." As a haven, the nuclear family shielded and protected its members from the evils and temptations of the outside world. This sentiment also extended to the family's religious, ethnic, and social-class affiliations. Those individuals who shared these affiliations were to be preferred, as friends and spouses, over those with different affiliations.

PARENTING THE INNOCENT
The modern perceptions of parenting, children, and teenagers grew out of these family sentiments. Modern parents, for example, were seen as intuitively or instinctively knowledgeable about child-rearing. Professional help was needed only to encourage parents to do "what comes naturally." In keeping with this view of parenting was the perception of children as innocent and in need of parental nurturance and protection. Teenagers, in turn, were seen as immature and requiring adult guidance and direction. Adolescence, regarded as the age of preparation for adulthood, brought with it the inevitable "storm and stress," as young people broke from the tight nuclear family bonds and became socially and financially independent.

These modern perceptions of parenting and of children and youth were reinforced by the social mirror of the media, the law and the health professions. Motion pictures such as the Andy Hardy series (starring Mickey Rooney) depicted a teenage boy getting into youthful scrapes at school and with friends from which he was extricated by his guardian the judge, played by Harlan Stone. Fiction similarly portrayed teenagers as immature young people struggling to find themselves. Mark Twain's Huck Finn was an early version of the modern immature adolescent, while J. D. Salinger's Holden Caulfield is a modern version.

Modern laws, such as the child-labor laws and compulsory-education statutes were enacted to protect both children and

adolescents. And the health professions attributed the mental-health problems of children and youth to conflicts arising from the tight emotional bonds of the nuclear family.

POSTMODERNITY AND THE POSTMODERN FAMILY
The postmodern view has largely grown out of the failure of modern assumptions about progress, universality, and regularity. Many of the events of this century have made the idea of progress difficult to maintain. Germany, one of the most educationally, scientifically, and culturally advanced countries of the world, engaged in the most heinous genocide. Modern science gave birth to the atomic bomb that was dropped on Hiroshima and Nagasaki. Environmental degradation, pollution, population explosions, and widespread famine can hardly be reconciled with the notion of progress.

Secondly, the belief in universal principles has been challenged as the "grand" theories of the modern era—such as those of Marx, Darwin, and Freud—are now recognized as limited by the social and historical contexts in which they were elaborated. Modern theorists believed that they could transcend social-historical boundaries; the postmodern worker recognizes that he or she is constrained by the particular discourse of narrative in play at the time. Likewise, the search for abiding ethical, moral, and religious universals is giving way to a recognition that there are many different ethics, moralities, and religions, each of which has a claim to legitimacy.

Finally, the belief in regularity has given way to a recognition of the importance of irregularity, indeterminacy, chaos, and fuzzy logic. There is much in nature, such as the weather, that remains unpredictable—not because it is perverse, but only because the weather is affected by non-regular events. Sure regularity appears, but irregularity is now seen as a genuine phenomenon in its own right. It is no longer seen, as it was in the modern era, as the result of some failure to discover an underlying regularity.

In place of these modern assumptions, a new, postmodern paradigm with its own basic premises has been invented. The assumption of progress, to illustrate, has given way to the presumption of *difference*. There are many different forms and types of progress, and not all progressions are necessarily for the better. Likewise, the belief in universals has moved aside for the belief in *particulars*. Different phenomena may have different rules and principles that are not necessarily generalizable. For example, a particular family or a particular class of children is a non-replicable event that can never be exactly duplicated and to which universal principles do not apply. Finally, the assumption of regularity moved aside to make room for the principle of *irregularity*. The world is not as orderly and as logically organized as we had imagined.

As the societal paradigm has shifted, so has the structure of the family. The ideal nuclear family, thought to be the product of progressive social evolution, has given way to what might be called the *Permeable Family* of the postmodern era. The Permeable Family encompasses many different family forms: traditional or nuclear, two-parent working, single-parent, blended, adopted child, test-tube, surrogate mother, and co-parent families. Each of these is valuable and a potentially successful family form.

The family is permeable in other ways as well. It is no longer isolated from the larger community. Thanks to personal computers, fax and answering machines, the workplace has moved into the homeplace. The homeplace, in turn, thanks to childcare facilities in office buildings and factories, has moved into the workplace. The home is also permeated by television, which brings the outside world into the living room and bedrooms. And an ever-expanding number of TV shows (*Oprah, Donahue, Geraldo, and Sally Jessy Raphael*), all detailing the variety of family problems, brings the living room and the bedroom into the outside world.

Quite different sentiments animate the postmodern Permeable Family than animated the modern nuclear family. The transformation of family sentiments came about in a variety of ways, from the civil-rights movement, the women's movement, changes in media, and laws that were part of the postmodern revolution. Because there is a constant interaction between the family and the larger society, it is impossible to say whether changes in the family were brought about by changes in society or vice versa. Things moved in both directions.

For a number of reasons, the Modern Family sentiment of Romantic Love has been transformed in the Postmodern era into the sentiment of *Consensual Love*. In contrast to the idealism and perfectionism of Romantic Love, consensual love is realistic and practical. It recognizes the legitimacy of premarital relations and is not premised on long-term commitment. Consensual Love is an agreement or contract between the partners; as an agreement it can be broken. The difference between Romantic Love and Consensual Love is summed up in the prenuptial agreement, which acknowledges the possible rupture of a marriage—before the marriage actually occurs. The current emphasis upon safe sex is likewise a symptom of consensual, not romantic, love.

The Modern Family sentiment of maternal love has yielded to other changes. Today, more than 50 percent of women are in the workforce, and some 60 percent of these women have children under the age of six. These figures make it clear that non-maternal and non-parental figures are now playing a major role in child-rearing. As part of this revision of child-rearing responsibilities, a new sentiment has emerged that might be called *shared parenting*. What this sentiment entails is the understanding that not only mothers, but fathers and professional caregivers are a necessary part of the child-rearing process. Child-rearing and childcare are no longer looked upon as the sole or primary responsibility of the mother.

The permeability of the Postmodern Family has also largely done away with the Modern Family sentiment of domesticity. The family can no longer protect individuals from the pressures of the outside world. Indeed, the impulse of the Permeable Family is to move in the other direction. Permeable Families tend to thrust children and teenagers forward to deal with realities of the outside world at ever earlier ages. This has resulted in what I have called the "hurrying" of children to grow up fast. Much of the hurrying of children and youth is a well-intentioned effort on the part of parents to help prepare children and youth for the onrush of information, challenges, and temptations coming at them through the now-permeable boundaries of family life.

POSTMODERN PARENTS OF KIDS WITHOUT INNOCENCE

These new, postmodern sentiments have given rise to new perceptions of parenting, of children, and of adolescents. Now that parenting is an activity shared with non-parental figures, we no longer regard it as an instinct that emerges once we have become parents; it is now regarded as a matter of learned *technique*.

Postmodern parents understand that doing "what comes naturally" may not be good for children. There are ways to say things to children that are less stressful than others. There are ways of disciplining that do not damage the child's sense of self esteem. The problem for parents today is to choose from the hundreds of books and other media sources bombarding them with advice on child-rearing. As one mother said to me, "I've read your books and they sound okay, but what if you're wrong?"

With respect to children, the perception of childhood innocence has given way to the perception of childhood competence. Now that children are living in Permeable Families with—thanks to television—a steady diet of overt violence, sexuality, substance abuse, and environmental degradation, we can no longer assume they are innocent. Rather, perhaps to cover our own inability to control what our children are seeing, we perceive them as competent to deal with all of this material. Indeed, we get so caught up in this perception of competence that we teach four- and five-year-olds about AIDS and child abuse and provide "toys" that simulate pregnancy or the dismemberment that accidents can cause unbuckled-up occupants. And the media reinforce this competence perception with films such as *Look Who's Talking* and *Home Alone*.

If children are seen as competent, teenagers can no longer be seen as immature. Rather they are now seen as sophisticated in the ways of the world, knowledgeable about sex, drugs, crime, and much more. This is a convenient fiction for parents suffering a time-famine. Such parents can take the perception of teenage sophistication as a rationale to abrogate their responsibility to provide young people with limits, guidance, and supervision. Increasingly, teenagers are on their own. Even junior and senior high schools no longer provide the social programs and clubs they once did.

This new perception of teenagers is also reflected in the social mirror of media, school and law. Postmodern films like *Risky Business* (in which teenager runs a bordello in the parents' home) and *Angel* (demure high school student by day, avenging hooker by night) are a far cry from the Andy Hardy films. Postmodern TV sitcoms such as *Married with Children* and *Roseanne* present images of teenage sophistication hardly reconcilable with the teenagers portrayed in modern

TV shows such as *My Three Sons* or *Ozzie and Harriet*. Postmodern legal thinking is concerned with protecting the *rights* of children and teenagers, rather than protecting children themselves. Children and teenagers can now sue their parents for divorce, visitation rights, and for remaining in the United States when the family travels overseas.

REALITY IS HERE TO STAY

The postmodern perceptions of children as competent and of teenagers as sophisticated did not grow out of any injustices nor harm visited upon children and youth. Rather they grew out of a golden era for young people that lasted from the end of the last century to the middle of this one. Society as a whole was geared to regard children as innocent and teenagers as immature, and sought to protect children and gradually inculcate teenagers into the ways of the world.

In contrast, the perceptions of childhood competence and teenage sophistication have had detrimental effects upon children and youth. Indeed, these perceptions have placed children and teenagers under inordinate stress. And it shows. On every measure that we have, children and adolescents are doing less well today than they did a quarter century ago, when the new postmodern perceptions were coming into play. While it would be unwise to attribute all of these negative effects to changed perceptions alone—economics and government policy clearly played a role—it is also true that government policy and economics are affected by the way young people are perceived.

The statistics speak for themselves. There has been a 50-percent increase in obesity in children and youth over the past two decades. We lose some ten thousand teenagers a year in substance-related accidents, not including injured and maimed. One in four teenagers drinks to excess every two weeks, and we have two million alcoholic teenagers.

Teenage girls in America get pregnant at the rate of one million per year, twice the rate of the next Western country, England. Suicide has tripled among teenagers in the last 20 years, and between five and six thousand teenagers take their own lives each year. It is estimated that one out of four teenage girls manifests at least one symptom of an eating disorder, most commonly severe dieting. The 14- to 19-year-old age group has the second-highest homicide rate of any age group.

These are frightening statistics. Yet they are not necessarily an indictment of the postmodern world, nor of our changed perceptions of children and youth. We have gone through enormous social changes in a very brief period of time. No other society on Earth changes, or can change, as rapidly as we do. That is both our strength and our weakness. It has made us, and will keep us, the leading industrial nation in the world because we are more flexible than any other society, including Japan.

But rapid social change is a catastrophe for children and youth, who require stability and security for healthy growth and development. Fortunately, we are now moving toward a more stable society. A whole generation of parents was caught in the transition between Modern and Postmodern Family sentiments; among them, divorce, open marriage, and remarriage became at least as commonplace as the permanent nuclear family. The current generation of parents have, however, grown up with the new family sentiments and are not as conflicted as their own parents were.

As a result, we are slowly moving back to a more realistic perception of both children and teenagers, as well as toward a family structure that is supportive of all family members. We are moving towards what might be called the *Vital Family*. In the Vital Family, the modern value of togetherness is given equal weight with the Postmodern Family value of autonomy. Children are seen as *growing into competence* and as still needing the help and support of parents. Likewise, teenagers are increasingly seen as *maturing into sophistication*, and able to benefit from adult guidance, limits, and direction.

These new perceptions pop up in the media. Increasingly, newspapers and magazines feature articles on the negative effects pressures for early achievement have upon children. We are also beginning to see articles about the negative effects the demands for sophistication place upon teenagers. A number of recent TV shows (such as *Beverly Hills 90210*) have begun to portray children and youth as sophisticated, but also as responsible and accepting of adult guidance and supervision. There is still much too much gratuitous sex and violence, but at least there are signs of greater responsibility and recognition that children and adolescents may not really be prepared for everything we would like to throw at them.

After 10 years of traveling and lecturing all over the country, I have an impression that the American family is alive and well. It has changed dramatically, and we are still accommodating to the changes. And, as always happens, children and youths are more harmed by change than are adults. But our basic value system remains intact. We do have a strong Judeo-Christian heritage; we believe in hard work, democracy, and autonomy. But our sense of social and parental responsibility, however, was temporarily deadened by the pace of social change. Now that we are getting comfortable in our new Permeable Family sentiments and perceptions, we are once again becoming concerned with those who are young and those who are less fortunate.

As human beings we all have a need to become the best that we can be. But we also have a need to love and to be loved, to care and to be cared for. The Modern Family spoke to our need to belong at the expense, particularly for women, of the need to become.

The Permeable Family, in contrast, celebrates the need to become at the expense of the need to belong, and this has been particularly hard on children and youth. Now we are moving towards a Vital Family that ensures both our need to become and our need to belong. We are not there yet, but the good news is, we are on our way.

the MIRACLE OF RESILIENCY

DAVID GELMAN

There are sharp differences in the way children bear up under stress

A prominent child psychiatrist, E. James Anthony, once proposed this analogy: there are three dolls, one made of glass, the second of plastic, the third of steel. Struck with a hammer, the glass doll shatters; the plastic doll is scarred. But the steel doll proves invulnerable, reacting only with a metallic ping.

In life, no one is unbreakable. But child-health specialists know there are sharp differences in the way children bear up under stress. In the aftermath of divorce or physical abuse, for instance, some are apt to become nervous and withdrawn; some may be illness-prone and slow to develop. But there are also so-called resilient children who shrug off the hammer blows and go on to highly productive lives. The same small miracle of resiliency has been found under even the most harrowing conditions—in Cambodian refugee camps, in crack-ridden Chicago housing projects. Doctors repeatedly encounter the phenomenon: the one child in a large, benighted brood of five or six who seems able to take adversity in stride. "There are kids in families from very adverse situations who really do beautifully, and seem to rise to the top of their potential, even with everything else working against them," says Dr. W. Thomas Boyce, director of the division of behavioral and developmental pediatrics at the University of California, San Francisco. "Nothing touches them; they thrive no matter what."

Something, clearly, has gone right with these children, but what? Researchers habitually have come at the issue the other way around. The preponderance of the literature has to do with why children fail, fall ill, turn delinquent. Only recently, doctors realized they were neglecting the equally important question of why some children *don't* get sick. Instead of working backward from failure, they decided, there might be as much or more to be learned from studying the secrets of success. In the course of looking at such "risk factors" as poverty, physical impairment or abusive parents, they gradually became aware that there were also "protective factors" that served as buffers against the risks. If those could be identified, the reasoning went, they might help develop interventions that could change the destiny of more vulnerable children.

At the same time, the recognition that many children have these built-in defenses has plunged resiliency research into political controversy. "There is a danger among certain groups who advocate nonfederal involvement in assistance to children," says Duke University professor Neil Boothby, a child psychologist who has studied children in war zones. "They use it to blame people who don't move out of poverty. Internationally, the whole notion of resiliency has been used as an excuse not to do anything."

The quest to identify protective factors has produced an eager burst of studies in the past 10 or 15 years, with new publications tumbling off the presses every month. Although the studies so far offer no startling insights, they are providing fresh perspectives on how nature and nurture intertwine in childhood development. One of the prime protective factors, for example, is a matter of genetic luck of the draw: a child born with an easygoing disposition invariably handles stress better than one with a nervous, overreactive temperament. But even highly reactive children can acquire resilience if they have a consistent, stabilizing element in their young lives—something like an attentive parent or mentor.

The most dramatic evidence on that score comes not from humans but from their more

From *Newsweek*, Special Edition, Summer 1991, pp. 44-47. © 1991 by Newsweek, Inc. All rights reserved. Reprinted by permission.

researchable cousins, the apes. In one five-year-long study, primate researcher Stephen Suomi has shown that by putting infant monkeys in the care of supportive mothers, he could virtually turn their lives around. Suomi, who heads the Laboratory of Comparative Ethology at the National Institute of Child Health and Human Development, has been comparing "vulnerable" and "invulnerable" monkeys to see if there are useful nurturing approaches to be learned. Differences of temperament can be spotted in monkeys before they're a week old. Like their human counterparts, vulnerable monkey infants show measurable increases in heart rate and stress-hormone production in response to threat situations. "You see a fairly consistent pattern of physiological arousal, and also major behavioral differences," says Suomi. "Parallel patterns have been found in human-developmental labs, so we feel we're looking at the same phenomena."

Left alone in a regular troop, these high-strung infants grow up to be marginal figures in their troops. But by putting them in the care of particularly loving, attentive foster mothers within their first four days of life, Suomi turns the timid monkeys into social lions. Within two months, they become bold and outgoing. Males in the species Suomi has been working with normally leave their native troop at puberty and eventually work their way into a new troop. The nervous, vulnerable individuals usually are the last to leave home. But after being "cross-fostered" to loving mothers, they develop enough confidence so that they're first to leave.

Once on their own, monkeys have complicated (but somehow familiar) patterns of alliances. Their status often depends on whom they know and to whom they're related. In squabbles, they quickly generate support among friends and family members. The cross-fostered monkeys grow very adept at recruiting that kind of support. It's a knack they somehow get through interaction with their foster mothers, in which they evidently pick up coping styles as well as information. "It's essentially a social-learning phenomenon," says Suomi. "I would argue that's what's going on at the human level, too. Evidently, you can learn styles in addition to specific information."

In the long run, the vulnerable infants not only were turned around to normality, they often rose to the top of their hierarchies; they became community leaders. Boyce notes there are significant "commonalities" between Suomi's findings and studies of vulnerable children. "The implications are that vulnerable children, if placed in the right social environment, might become extraordinarily productive and competent adult individuals," he says.

Children, of course, can't be fostered off to new parents or social conditions as readily as monkeys. Most resiliency research is based on children who have not had such interventions in their lives. Nevertheless, some of the findings are revealing. One of the definitive studies was conducted by Emmy E. Werner, a professor of human development at the University of California, Davis, and Ruth S. Smith, a clinical psychologist on the Hawaiian island of Kauai. Together, they followed 698 children, all descendants of Kauaiian plantation workers, from their birth (in 1955) up to their early 30s. About half the children grew up in poverty; one in six had physical or intellectual handicaps diagnosed between birth and age 2. Of the 225 designated as high risk, two thirds had developed serious learning or behavior problems within their first decade of life. By 18 they had delinquency records, mental-health problems or teenage pregnancies. "Yet one out of three," Werner and Smith noted, "grew into competent young adults who loved well, worked well, played well and expected well."

Some of the protective factors the two psychologists identified underscore the nature-nurture connection. Like other researchers, they found that children who started out with robust, sunny personalities were often twice lucky: not only were they better equipped to cope with life to begin with, but their winning ways made them immediately lovable. In effect, the "nicer" the children, the more readily they won affection—both nature and nurture smiled upon them. There were also other important resiliency factors, including self-esteem and a strong sense of identity. Boyce says he encounters some children who even at 2 or 3 have a sense of "presence" and independence that seem to prefigure success. "It's as if these kids have had the 'Who am I' questions answered for them," he says.

One of the more intriguing findings of the Kauai research was that resilient children were likely to have characteristics of both sexes. Boys and girls in the study tended to be outgoing and autonomous, in the male fashion, but also nurturant and emotionally sensitive, like females. "It's a little similar to what we find in creative children," observes Werner. Some other key factors were inherent in the children's surroundings rather than their personalities. It helped to have a readily available support network of grandparents, neighbors or relatives. Others note that for children anywhere, it doesn't hurt at all to be born to well-off parents. "The advantage of middle-class life is there's a safety net," says Arnold Sameroff, a developmental psychologist at Brown University's Bradley Hospital. "If you screw up, there's someone to bail you out."

In most cases, resilient children have "clusters" of protective factors, not just one or two. But the sine qua non, according to Werner, is a "basic, trusting relationship" with an adult. In all the clusters in the Kauai study, "there is not one that didn't include that one good relationship, whether with a parent, grandparent, older sibling, teacher or mentor—someone consistent enough in that person's life to say, 'You count,' and that sort of begins to radiate other support in their lives." Even children of abusive or schizophrenic parents may prove resilient if they have had at least one caring adult looking out for them—someone, as Tom Boyce says, "who serves as a kind of beacon presence in their lives."

Such relationships do the most good when they are lasting. There is no lasting guarantee for resiliency itself, which is subject to change, de-

Researchers can spot differences of temperament in monkeys before they're a week old

pending on what sort of ups and downs people encounter. Children's ability to cope often improves naturally as they develop and gain experience, although it may decline after a setback in school or at home. Werner notes that around half the vulnerable children in the Kauai study had shaken off their previous problems by the time they reached their late 20s or early 30s. "In the long-term view, more people come through in spite of circumstances. There is an amazing amount of recovery, if you don't focus on one particular time when things are falling apart."

Ironically, this "self-righting" tendency has made the resiliency issue something of a political football. Conservatives have seized on the research to bolster their case against further social spending. "It's the politics of 'It's all within the kid'," says Lisbeth Schorr, a lecturer in social medicine at Harvard Medical School whose book, "Within Our Reach: Breaking the Cycle of Disadvantage," has had a wide impact in the field. "The conservative argument against interventions like Operation Head Start and family-support programs is that if these inner-city kids and families just showed a little grit they would pull themselves up by their own bootstraps. But people working on resilience are aware that when it comes to environments like the inner city, it really doesn't make a lot of sense to talk about what's intrinsic to the kids, because the environment is so overwhelming."

So overwhelming, indeed, that some researchers voice serious doubts over how much change can be brought about in multiple-risk children. Brown's Sameroff, who has been dealing with poor inner-city black and white families in Rochester, N.Y., says the experience has left him "more realistic" about what is possible. "Interventions are important if we can target one or two things wrong with a child. So you provide psychotherapy or extra help in the classroom, then there's a lot better chance." But the children he deals with usually have much more than that going against them—not only poverty but large families, absent fathers, drug-ridden neighborhoods and so on. "We find the more risk factors the worse the outcome," says Sameroff. "With eight or nine, *nobody* does well. For the majority of these children, it's going to involve changing the whole circumstance in which they are raised."

Others are expressing their own reservations, as the first rush of enthusiasm in resiliency research cools somewhat. "A lot of the early intervention procedures that don't follow through have been oversold," says Emmy Werner. "Not every-

one benefited equally from such programs as Head Start." Yet, according to child-development specialists, only a third of high-risk children are able to pull through relatively unaided by such interventions. Says Werner: "At least the high-risk children should be guaranteed basic health and social programs."

Interestingly, when Suomi separates his vulnerable monkeys from their foster mothers at 7 months—around the same time that mothers in the wild go off to breed, leaving their young behind—the genes reassert themselves, and the monkeys revert to fearful behavior. According to Suomi, they do recover again when the mothers return and their new coping skills seem to stay with them. Yet their experience underscores the frailty of change. Boyce, an admirer of Suomi's work, acknowledges that the question of how lasting the effects of early interventions are remains open. But, he adds, programs like Head Start continue to reverberate as much as 15 years later, with reportedly higher school-completion rates and lower rates of delinquency and teen pregnancies.

Boyce recalls that years ago, when he was at the University of North Carolina, he dealt with an 8-year-old child from an impoverished, rural black family, who had been abandoned by his mother. The boy also had "prune-belly syndrome," an anomaly of the abdominal musculature that left him with significant kidney and urinary problems, requiring extensive surgery. But he also had two doting grandparents who had raised him from infancy. They showered him with love and unfailingly accompanied him on his hospital visits. Despite his physical problems and loss of a mother, the boy managed to perform "superbly" in school. By the age of 10, when Boyce last saw him, he was "thriving."

Children may not be as manageable or resilient as laboratory monkeys. If anything, they are more susceptible in the early years. But with the right help at the right time, they can overcome almost anything. "Extreme adversity can have devastating effects on development," says psychologist Ann Masten, who did some of the groundbreaking work in the resiliency field with her University of Minnesota colleague Norman Garmezy. "But our species has an enormous capacity for recovery. Children living in a hostile caregiving environment have great difficulty, but a lot of ability to recover to better functioning if they're given a chance. That's a very important message from the resiliency literature." Unfortunately, the message may not be getting through to the people who can provide that chance.

> There are kids from adverse situations who do beautifully and seem to rise to their potential

TV VIOLENCE
Myth and Reality

MARY A. HEPBURN

Mary A. Hepburn is professor of social science education and head of the Citizen Education Division at the Carl Vinson Institute of Government, University of Georgia, Athens.

With an average national TV viewing time of 7¼ hours daily, the prevalence of violence in broadcasts is a serious concern. Television programming in the United States is considered the most violent in advanced industrialized nations. Violence is common in TV entertainment—the dramas that portray stories about crime, psychotic murderers, police cases, emergency services, international terrorism, and war. The dramas are played out in highly realistic scenes of violent attacks accompanied by music and other sounds that churn up emotions.

As the realism and gore in the screen images of TV entertainment have intensified, local news cameras have also increasingly focused directly on the bloody violence done to individuals in drive-by shootings, gang attacks, and domestic beatings. Why must these visual details be presented in the news? Why does a typical television evening include so many beatings, shootings, stabbings, and rapes in dramas designed for "entertainment"?

Producers of programming ascertain that scenes of violent action with accompanying fear-striking music can be counted on to hold viewers' attention, keep them awake and watching, and make them less likely to switch channels. The purpose is to gain and maintain a large number of viewers—the factor that appeals to advertisers. The generations of younger adults who have grown up with daily viewing of violence in entertainment are considered to be "hooked." A program has more commercial value if it can hold more viewers, and programmers attempt to ensure high viewer attention with doses of violent action in the program. How does all of this violence affect young people?

The Results of Research

Several decades ago, a few psychologists hypothesized that viewing violence in the unreal television world would have a cathartic effect and thus reduce the chances of violent behavior in the real world. But other psychologists began to doubt this notion when their research with children revealed that much action on the TV screen is perceived as real by children. Huesmann and Eron (1986), who studied the effects of media violence on 758 youngsters in grades 1 through 3, found that children's behavior was influenced by television, especially if the youngsters were heavy viewers of violent programming. Television violence, according to the researchers, provided a script for the children to act out aggressive behavior in relationships with others. The most aggressive youngsters strongly identified with aggressive characters in the TV story, had aggressive fantasies, and expressed the attitude that violent programs portrayed life as it is. These children were also likely to perform poorly in school and often were unpopular with their peers.

Huesmann and Eron state that television is not the *only* variable involved, but their many years of research have left them with no doubt that heavy exposure to media violence is a highly influential factor in children and later in their adult lives (see also Institute for Social Research 1994 and medical research by Zuckerman and Zuckerman 1985 and by Holroyd 1985).

Research in the field of public communications also supports the conclusion that exposure to television violence contributes to increased rates of aggression and violent behavior. Centerwall (1989, 1993) analyzed crime data in areas of the world with and without television and, in addition, made comparisons in areas before and after the introduction of TV. His studies determined that homicide rates doubled in ten to fifteen years after TV was introduced for the first time into specified areas of the United States and Canada. Observing that violent television programming exerts its aggressive effects primarily on children, Centerwall noted that the ten- to fifteen-year lag time can be expected before homicide rates increase. Acknowledging that other factors besides TV do have some influence on the quantity of violent crimes, Centerwall's careful statistical analysis indicated, nevertheless, that when the negative effects of TV were removed, quantitative evidence showed "there would be 10,000 fewer homicides, 70,000 fewer rapes, and 700,000 fewer injurious assaults" (1993, 64).

Centerwall (1993) has also brought to light important research literature that has been little known among social scientists and educators concerned about television violence. In the late sixties, as a result of public hearings and a national report implying that exposure to TV increases physical aggression, the large television networks decided to commission their own research projects. NBC appointed a team of four researchers, three of whom were NBC employees, to observe more than two thousand school children up to three years to determine if watching television programs increased their physical aggressiveness. NBC reported no effect. Centerwall points out, however, that every independent researcher who has analyzed the same data finds an increase in levels of physical aggression.

In the study commissioned by the ABC network, a team at Temple University surveyed young male felons who

From *Social Education*, September 1995, pp. 309-311. © 1995 by the National Council for the Social Studies. Reprinted by permission.

had been imprisoned for violent crimes. Results of these interviews showed that 22 to 34 percent of the young felons, especially those who were the most violent, said they had consciously imitated crime techniques learned from television programs. It was learned that, as children, felons in the study had watched an average of six hours of TV per day, about twice as much as children in the general population at that time. Research results were published privately by ABC and not released to the general public or to scientists (Centerwall 1993, 65).

CBS commissioned a study to be conducted in London and ultimately published in England (Belson 1978). In the study, 1,565 teenaged boys were studied for behavioral effects of viewing violent television programs, many of which were imported from the United States. The study (Belson 1978) revealed that those who watched above average hours of TV violence before adolescence committed a 49 percent higher rate of serious acts of violence than did boys who had viewed below average quantities of violence. The final report was "very strongly supportive of the hypothesis that high exposure to television violence increases the degree to which boys engage in serious violence" (Belson 1978, 15).

Five types of TV programming were most powerful in triggering violent behavior in the boys in the London study: (1) TV plays or films in which violence is demonstrated in close personal relationships; (2) programs where violence was not necessary to the plot but just added for its own sake; (3) fictional violence of a very realistic kind; (4) violent "Westerns"; and (5) programs that present violence as being for a good cause. In summarizing the implications of the study, the research director made it clear that the results also applied to boys in U.S. cities with the same kind of violence in TV programming (ibid. 528).

For about fifteen years, these studies have received little attention. Each was either filed away or distributed to a very limited audience—not to the general public, the research community, or the press. Today, that seems eerily similar to the fate of tobacco company research on the ill effects of smoking, the results of which were also disseminated only to a small

select group. The Commission on Violence and Youth of the American Psychological Association recently communicated the above-mentioned and other supporting research to its members. It concluded that evidence clearly reveals that viewing and hearing high levels of violence on television, day after day, were correlated with increased acceptance of aggression and more aggressive behavior. The commission noted that the highest level of consumption of television violence is by those most vulnerable to the effects, those who receive no moderating or mediating of what is seen on the screen. (Slaby 1994, Institute for Social Research 1994; see also Holroyd 1985; Zuckerman and Zuckerman 1985).

This information is of great significance to social studies educators. Yet it is only in the last two years that the network-funded studies of the seventies and eighties have been gaining some attention in journals that reach educational professionals. In January 1994, an article in the *Chronicle of Higher Education* pointed up the huge "education gap" that exists between the effects of television violence that have been conclusively documented by psychological and medical researchers and what the general public knows. According to the article, "Until recently, researchers' voices have been drowned out in the din of denial and disinformation coming from executives of the television and movie industries, whose self-serving defense of violent programming has prevailed" (Slaby 1994).

TV industry spokespersons argue that violent programs are a mere reflection of the society, and that any effort to modify programming would interfere with First Amendment guarantees of freedom of the press. Others claim to be giving the public "what they want" and take no responsibility for the effects on viewers. Another response from the networks is that parents or families must take the responsibility for preventing viewing of violent programs. In none of these defenses are the networks willing to recognize research information that shows that an appetite for violence has been stimulated by the glorification of violence and a daily diet of violent programs broadcast into every home in America.

History and Social Science Content

The issue of the influence of electronic media on the American life-style is of direct concern to social studies (Hepburn 1990). The curriculum must include study of the influence of the media. Students should be aware of how persistent viewing of violent acts and violent language and music can motivate violent behavior. A number of suggestions for media-related student activities accompany this article.

Although readings about the influence of media are hard to find in school textbooks, at last, magazines, newspapers, public television, and CNN have begun to examine the role of the mass media in the decline of civility and the loss of community. Commercial television networks have been compared with individuals who seek only their own profit, lack respect for others, and feel no sense of public trust. Are these fair conclusions? Social studies can pick up the debate.

Could a media-literate public demand and get better news presentation and more depth in the discussion of alternative social and economic policies? Is there a parallel between the decades in which the public lacked information about the lethal effects of cigarette smoking and the two decades in which the public has been unaware of the effects of heavy doses of television violence on youngsters? Can the reduction of violence in mass media be accomplished by means of increased citizen knowledge and action? Are First Amendment rights of the broadcast industry threatened by public pressures? Will television and radio respond to public discourse and a changed perception of the public market? These are social studies issues of interest to students.

From many passive hours in front of television, what life roles are instilled in viewers, especially more impressionable young viewers? From TV and radio, what values and visions of family life, leadership, friendship, personal relationships, heroism, and public responsibility are absorbed from the images and voices they see and hear? A discussion of role models, of both the norms and realities, can greatly stimulate the awareness and interest of young citizens. This is the stuff of social studies.

Student Activities to Develop Critical Media Skills

1. Our Favorite Programs. Take a poll of students in your class to find out what their favorite weekday prime time (8-11 p.m.) programs are, and also their favorite programs on Saturday and Sunday. Favorite programs can be summarized by type (e.g., movies, cartoons, police dramas) on a poster for a later study of contents. If each student has a notebook for the study of mass media, the results of this poll could be the first entry.

2. What's on the Air? Assign each student a different TV channel (include local, regular network, public TV, and pay cable network channels), and ask each to use TV listings in newspapers or magazines to determine how many minutes on a specified day are designated for (1) young children's entertainment, (2) special programs for teenagers, (3) public affairs information and discussion programs, (4) adult entertainment programs (dramas, sitcoms, quiz shows, science fiction, detective series, love stories), (5) religious programs, and (6) cooking and household repair programs.

3. What Are the Rules and Obligations? The airwaves are publicly owned. Licensing and oversight of the use of the airwaves is conducted by the Federal Communications Commission (FCC). To obtain guidelines and legal explanation of the responsibilities of all broadcasters to consider community needs and interests in their programming, write or call the FCC, 1919 M Street, NW, Washington, DC 20554; phone 202-418-0200. Reference books and government books in the school library will help clarify the legal framework for radio and television broadcasting.

4. How Much Violence Is in Our Entertainment? Discuss the kinds of violent acts and language in television programs and movies to prepare students to monitor "violence" in TV programs. From the list of "favorite programs" (no. 1 above), prepare slips of paper with program titles, so students can randomly draw a program title and plan to monitor the program for violent action, language, or threats. Students should take notes on the name, time, station, and advertisers for each program, and describe the violence discussed or shown in the program. This monitoring activity can be extended to other programs over a weekend or over several evenings. Students can invite their parents to join them in noting how much violence is depicted, suggested, or threatened.

Following a period of collecting data, student groups can share their findings: Which programs contained the most violence? Is violence common in prime time programs and/or at other times? On cable? On regular network channels? On public channels? Which advertisers support programs with heavy violence? Finally, prepare a class summary listing of the most violent and least violent programs.

5. How Does TV Violence Affect Us? Discussion: Using notes from program monitoring and recollections or videotape of violent scenes, analyze the images, sounds, and dialogue that hold the viewer's attention. Which are the most frightening, hard to forget, or likely to give people nightmares? Why are some viewers fascinated by scenes of beating, killing, and hurting people? Would these scenes and sounds encourage similar behavior by young viewers? Why or why not?

6. How Do Music and Sounds Affect Our Emotions? To further analyze the contents and affects of violent programming, have students return to a selected program that is usually violent and scary. Have them experiment with turning down the sound in dramatic scenes without dialogue. Ask them to observe how pulsating, eerie, pounding music and sounds of howling wind, roaring cars, squealing cats, and other noises can arouse excitement or fear. In turn, they can observe programs where soothing music, laughing children, and cheerful sounds help to make the viewer feel at ease.

7. Why Would Advertisers Select Programs with Violence? Discuss with students the fascination that violence and fast action have for some viewer groups, including youngsters, uncritical adults, and less educated individuals. Discuss how people can be mesmerized and fascinated by images of violent conflict, especially if they watch violence daily and begin to see it as a way of life. (References to writings by psychologists and sociologists in the article above will lead you to books and readings about the appeal of violent scenes and the high vulnerability of certain groups of people.) Students can reflect on how advertisers look for programs with large numbers of viewers. In turn, discuss how critical viewers might influence advertisers to select better quality programs for their ads.

8. TV Consumer Power. Discuss the power potential of viewers to select quality programs. Students can learn about "market share" and Nielsen ratings from magazines and newspapers. A local TV station or radio station manager can explain how "market share" affects program selection.

Sources

Belson, W. A. *Television Violence and the Adolescent Boy.* Westmead, England: Saxon House, 1978.

Bowen, Wally. "Media Violence." *Education Week* (March 16, 1994): 60ff.

Centerwall, B. S. "Exposure to Television as a Cause of Violence." In *Public Communication and Behavior.* volume 2, edited by G. Comstock. San Diego: Academic Press, 1989.

_____. "Television and Violent Crime." *The Public Interest* 3 (1993): 56-71.

Gamson, W. A., D. Croteau, W. Hoynes, and T. Sasson. "Media Images and the Social Construction of Reality." *Annual Review of Sociology* 18 (1992): 373-93.

Hepburn, M. A. "Americans Glued to the Tube: Mass Media, Information, and Social Studies." *Social Education* 54, no. 4 (April/May 1990): 233-237.

Holroyd, H. J. "Children, Adolescents, and Television." *American Journal of Diseases in Children* 139, no. 6 (1985): 549-550.

Huesmann, L. R., and L. D. Eron. "The Development of Aggression in American Children as a Consequence of Television Violence Viewing." In *Television and the Aggressive Child: A Cross-National Comparison,* edited by L. R. Huesmann and L. D. Eron. Hillsdale, New Jersey: Erlbaum Associates, 1986.

Institute for Social Research. "Televised Violence and Kids: A Public Health Problem?" *ISR Newsletter* 18 (1994): 1.

National Association of Broadcasters. *America's Watching–Public Attitudes Toward Television 1993.* New York: The Network Television Association and the National Association of Broadcasters.

Nielsen Media Research. *1992-1993 Report on Television.* New York: A.C. Nielsen Co., 1993.

Postman, N. *The Disappearance of Childhood.* New York: Delacorte Press, 1982.

Roper Organization. *Public Attitudes Toward Television and Other Media in a Time of Change.* New York: Television Information Office, 1985.

Slaby, R. G. "Combating Television Violence." *The Chronicle of Higher Education* 40, no. 18 (January 5, 1994): B1-2.

Zuckerman, D. M., and B. S. Zuckerman. "Television's Impact on Children." *Pediatrics* 75, no. 2 (1985): 233-240.

Development during Adolescence and Young Adulthood

- Adolescence (Articles 31–35)
- Young Adulthood (Articles 36–39)

The concept of adolescence, the period of time between the onset of puberty and maturity, was invented by an American psychologist, G. Stanley Hall, at the turn of the twentieth century. Prior to that it was typical for young men to begin working in middle childhood (there were no child labor laws) and for young women to become wives and mothers as soon as they were fertile and/or spoken for. The beginning of adolescence today is often marked by the desire to be independent of parental control as much as by the beginning of sexual maturation. The end of adolescence, which at the turn of the century coincided with the age of legal maturity (usually 16 or 18 depending on local laws), has now been extended upwards. Although legal maturity is now usually age 18 (vote, enlist in the Armed Services, own property, marry without permission), the social norm is to consider persons in their late teens as adolescents, not adults. Even college students, or students in post-degree programs (e.g., graduate schools, medical schools, law schools) are usually not considered "mature" until they have reached their final or desired educational attainments. "Maturity" is usually reserved for those who have achieved full independence as adults.

As adolescence has been extended, so too has young adulthood. One hundred years ago, life expectancy did not extend too far beyond menopause for women and retirement for men. Chronic and/or debilitating illnesses made people in their sixties feel old. Today life expectancy has been extended into the mid-seventies, and it is not unusual for persons to live for 100 years. Improved health care, diet, exercise, and a safer food and water supply have allowed persons in their sixties and seventies to enjoy vigorous good health. One hundred years ago, young adulthood ended when children reached puberty. Parents of teenagers were middle-aged between 35 and 55. With the passage of the Social Security Act in 1935, the end of middle-age and the beginning of old age was redefined as age 65. Today retirement is usually postponed until age 70, which has again redefined the line between middle age and old age. Later marriages and delayed child-bearing have, concurrently, redefined the line between young adulthood and middle age. Many people today do not appreciate or agree to the label "middle-aged" until they are closer to 50.

Adolescence, by anyone's description, is a time of accelerated growth and change. A child becomes an adult through a series of profound physical changes, including becoming sexually reproductive. Accompanying the physical and physiological alterations in the child's body are stupendous changes in emotions, in cognitions, and in a desire for social freedoms. The first article included in this section is an excellent description of some of the repercussions of the transformation from child to adult. Virginia Rutter asks and answers the question "Whose Hell Is It?" She provides several quotes from teenagers about their worries: parents, school, peers, guns, gangs, drugs, AIDS. She discusses, in turn, parents' worries: adolescents, jobs, peers, guns, gangs, drugs, AIDS. She advises parents to continue parenting through these turbulent years.

The second and third articles in the adolescence section of this unit deal with self-esteem. Why do so many females lose self-esteem in adolescence? What can be done to help them retain positive feelings about themselves? The author of the second article cites several research findings that help answer these questions. The author of the third article suggests that involvement in something as basic as athletics can boost both self-esteem and achievement motivation.

The fourth article in the adolescence section of this compendium looks at cross-cultural views of adolescent behaviors. The behaviors most frequently associated with a "bad kid" were lack of self-control (American), acts against society (Chinese), and disruptions of interpersonal harmony (Japanese). Do these responses reflect different cultural values? What do they mean for a world with increased multicultural interactions?

The last article in the adolescence section is an essay by an HIV infected youth. It will have an emotional impact on all readers. It deals with many topics: child abuse, rape, drug abuse, and AIDS. It depicts a slice of the all-too-real life of one adolescent turned young adult. The author pleads for support and health care for persons like himself.

Erik Erikson, the personal-social personality theorist, marked the passage from adolescence to young adulthood by a change in the nuclear conflicts of the two life stages. Adolescents struggle to answer the question "Who am I?" Young adults struggle to answer questions about their commitments to partnerships and intimate relationships. They struggle to find a place within the existing social order where they can feel propinquity rather than isolation. In the 1960s Erikson wrote that some females resolve both their conflicts of identity and intimacy by living vicariously through their husbands. He did not comment, however, on whether or not some males resolve their conflicts of identity and intimacy by living vicariously through their wives. He felt that true intimacy was difficult to achieve if the person seeking it had not first become a trusting, autonomous, self-initiating, industrious, and self-knowledgeable human being. Role confusion and isolation were what Erikson predicted for adolescents and young adults who remain immature.

The first article in the young adult section of this unit deals with the problems inherent in developing a mature, self-identified, intimate orientation toward life in the 1990s. The author discusses what he calls "psychotrends" (e.g., greater sexual equality, a new masculinity, diversity of sexual expression, a more forgiving religious attitude, expanding sexual entertainment) and the impact that these trends are having on relationships. He also scrutinizes divorce rates, cohabitation, single-parenting, childless families, interracial families, same-sex families, and multiadult households as trends which are affecting the way young adults resolve their crisis of intimacy versus isolation.

The second young adulthood article asks "Who Stole Fertility?" It considers the impact of reproductive technology on the lives of young couples. The third young adulthood article asks "Is There Love after Baby?" It considers the impact of children on marriages. It reviews some of the research on marital unhappiness, separation, and divorce after childbirth. It also gives suggestions for rebalancing relationships and reducing the stressors of early family life. The last selection included in this section addresses the issue of spousal abuse. The author is a lawyer who has been on the receiving end of a fist. The manuscript communicates not only why abused persons stay in abusive relationships but also takes notice of what legal and societal changes are necessary to protect victims and reduce domestic violence.

Looking Ahead: Challenge Questions

Why is adolescence difficult for both parents and kids?

Describe the sex differences in self-esteem in adolescence.

How do sports lift self-esteem?

Describe some cultural differences in what is considered "bad" behavior?

What can we offer adolescents who are HIV positive?

Where are psychotrends taking young adults?

Who stole fertility?

Discuss the research on marital concord after babies are born.

What can be done to reduce spousal abuse?

Adolescence
Whose Hell Is It?

The image of teenagers as menacing and rebellious is a big fiction that's boomeranging on kids. We've mythologized adolescence to conceal a startling fact: It is indeed a difficult and turbulent time—for parents. The trouble is, kids look like adults much sooner than ever before. Kids wind up feeling abandoned—and angry at the loss of their safety net. If we haven't got adolescence exactly figured out yet, there's some consolation in the fact that it's a brand-new phenomenon in human history.

Virginia Rutter

I recently spent the weekend with a friend's 13-year-old son. In contrast to the tiny tots most of my friends have, Matthew seemed much more like an adult. The time spent with him wasn't so much like baby-sitting; it was like having company. It was impressive to see how self-sufficient he was. Simple matters struck me: he didn't need someone to go to the bathroom with him at the movies; he could help himself to ice cream; he was actually interested in following the O. J. Simpson story, and we discussed it.

He was polite, thoughtful, and interesting. While the intensive caretaking necessary for smaller children has its own rewards (I suppose), Matthew's contrasting autonomy was pleasant to me. And so I imagined it would be for parents of adolescents. But then, I am not a parent. And most parents report not feeling pleasant about their adolescents.

The weekend reminded me of how easy it is to think of these youngsters as adults. Compared to an eight-year-old, an adolescent is a lot like an adult. Can't reason like an adult, but doesn't think like a child anymore, either. Some parents are tempted to cut 'em loose rather than adjust to the new status of their teenager. Others fail to observe their

adolescent's new adultlike status, and continue monitoring them as closely as a child. But it's obvious that adolescents aren't miniature adults. They are individuals on their way to adulthood; their brains and bodies—to say nothing of their sexuality—stretching uneasily toward maturity.

A couple of teachers are my heroes. My history teacher is great because he listens to what everybody has to say and never judges.
—Chelsea, 14, Bakersfield, California

Yet the sight of kids reaching for some form of adult status commonly evokes contempt rather than curiosity. Negative feelings about teenagers have a strong grip on American culture in general, and on surprising numbers of parents in particular. It's not uncommon for parents to anticipate their child's adolescence with fear and trepidation even before they've gotten out of diapers. They expect a war at home.

"It becomes a self-fulfilling prophesy that adolescence is seen as this bizarre, otherworldly period of development, complete with a battleground set for World War III," says Tina Wagers, Psy.D., a psychologist who treats teens and their families at Kaiser Permanente Medical Center in Denver.

We were all once 13, but it seems we can no longer imagine what kind of parenting a 13-year-old needs. Perhaps it's gotten worse with all the outside opportunities for trouble kids have—gangs, guns, drugs. Families used to extend their turf into their children's schools, friends, and athletic activities. But kids now inhabit unknown territory, and it is scary for parents. "I think this fear and lack of understanding makes some parents more likely to back off and neglect teenagers," reports Wagers. "There is an expectation that you can't influence them anyhow."

This skeptical, sometimes hostile view of teens, however, was countered by my experience with Matthew. I found him hardly a "teenager from hell." Like most teens, Matthew prefers to be with his own friends more than with family or other grown-ups. He's not good with time, and music, basketball, and girls are more central to him than achievement, responsibility, and family. (Despite his tastes, he does very well in school.) At home there is more conflict than there has been in the past, though not less love and commitment to his mom, with whom he lives in eastern Washington.

The story of Matthew falls in line with new research on adolescents, and it's causing psychologists to totally revise conventional wisdom on the subject. According to psychologist Laurence Steinberg, Ph.D., of Temple University, the majority of adolescents are not contentious, unpleasant, heartless creatures. They do not hate their parents—although they do fight with them (but not as much as you might think). "In scrutinizing interviews with adolescents and their families, I reaffirmed that adolescence is a relatively peaceful time in the house." Kids report continued high levels of respect for their parents, whether single, divorced, or together, and regardless of economic background.

When fighting does occur, it's in families with younger teenagers, and it has to do at least in part with their burgeoning cognitive abilities. Newly able to grasp abstract ideas, they can become absorbed in pursuing hypocrisy or questioning authority. In time, they learn to deploy relativistic and critical thinking more selectively.

NOT A DISEASE

If adolescents aren't the incorrigibles we think—then what to make of the endless stream of news reports of teen sexism, harassment, drug abuse, depression, delinquency, gangs, guns, and suicide?

Any way you measure it, teens today are in deep trouble. They face increasing rates of depression (now at 20 percent), suicide (12 percent have considered it, 5 percent attempted), substance abuse (20 percent of high school seniors), delinquency (1.5 million juvenile arrests—about 1 percent of teens—in 1992), early sexual activity (29 percent have had sexual relations by age 15), and even an increased rate of health problems (20 percent have conditions that will hamper their health as adults). And kids' problems appear to be getting worse.

How to reconcile the two parts of the story: adolescents aren't so bad, but a growing number are jeopardizing their future through destructive behavior? Though we look upon teenagers as time bombs set to self-destruct at puberty, in fact the problems teens face are not

encoded in their genes. Their natural development, including a surge of hormonal activity during the first few years of adolescence, may make them a little more depressed or aggressive—but how we treat them has much more to do with teenagers' lives today. From the look of it, we aren't treating them very well.

A CRISIS OF ADULTS

If what goes on in adolescence happens largely in the kids, what goes wrong with adolescence happens primarily in the parents. "It wasn't until I turned to the parents' interviews that I really got a sense that something unusual was going on," reports Steinberg of his ongoing studies of over 200 adolescents and their families. As he details in his recent book, *Crossing Paths: How Your Child's Adolescence Triggers Your Own Crisis* (Simon & Schuster), Steinberg finds that adolescence sets off a crisis for parents.

Teenagers say that parents are not understanding and I don't think it is always that way.
—Gabriel, 16, Albuquerque, New Mexico

Parents do not have positive feelings during the time their kids go through adolescence, and it isn't simply because they expect their kids to be bad (although that's part of it). Scientists have studied the behavior and emotions of parents as well as their adolescent children, and found that when children reach puberty, parents experience tremendous changes in themselves. What's more, they shift their attitudes toward their children. It isn't just the kids who are distressed. Parents are too. Consider the following:

- Marital satisfaction, which typically declines over the course of marriage, reaches its all-time low when the oldest child reaches adolescence. Married parents of adolescents have an average of seven minutes alone with each other every day. For the marriages that don't pass the point of no return during their kids' teen years, there is actually an increase in satisfaction after the kids complete adolescence.

- Happily married parents have more positive interactions with their kids than unhappy parents. In single-parent families, parental happiness also influences their response to adolescence.

- In a surprising finding, the marital satisfaction of fathers is directly affected by how actively their adolescents are dating. Especially when sons are busy dating, fathers report a marked decline in interest in their wives. Dads aren't lusting for the girls Johnny brings home, they just miss what now seem like their own good old days.

Adults want kids to learn to take care of themselves. Kids need guides and advice. That is how you help people mature—not by leaving them alone.
—Michelle, 16, Clackamas, Oregon

- In family discussions, parents become increasingly negative toward their adolescents—there's more criticism, whining, frustration, anger, and defensiveness expressed verbally or in grimaces. While the kids are always more negative than their parents (it comes with increasing cognitive ability, in part), the parents are actually increasing the amount of negativity toward their children at a higher rate.

- Working mothers don't spend less time at home with their teenagers than nonworking moms do, but they do risk higher levels of burnout, because they continue to cover the lioness' share of work at home. On the other hand, a mother's employment makes her less vulnerable to the ups and downs of parenting an adolescent. Maternal employment also benefits kids, especially teen daughters, who report higher levels of self-esteem.

- Despite their fulfillment, mothers' self-esteem is actually lower while they are with their adolescents than when they are not. After all, a mother's authority is constantly being challenged, and she is being shunted to the margins of her child's universe.

- Teenagers turn increasingly to their friends, a distancing maneuver that

189

feels like an emotional divorce to parents. Since mothers are generally more emotionally engaged with their children than are fathers, the separation can feel most painful to them. In fact, mothers typically report looking forward to the departure of their kids after high school. After the kids leave, mothers' emotional state improves.

- Fathers emotional states follow a different course. Fathers have more difficulty launching their adolescents, mostly because they feel regret about the time they didn't spend with them. Fathers have more difficulty dealing with their kids growing into adolescence and adulthood; they can't get used to the idea that they no longer have a little playmate who is going to do what daddy wants to do.

Add it all up and you get a bona fide midlife crisis in some parents, according to Steinberg. All along we've thought that a midlife crisis happens to some adults around the age of 40. But it turns out that midlife crisis has nothing to do with the age of the adult—and everything to do with the age of the oldest child in a family. It is set off by the entry of a family's first-born into adolescence.

Once the oldest child hits adolescence, parents are catapulted into a process of life review. "Where have I been, where am I now, where am I going?" These questions gnaw at parents who observe their children at the brink of adulthood.

It hits hardest the parent who is the same sex as the adolescent. Mothers and daughters actually have more difficulty than fathers and sons. In either case, the children tend to serve as a mirror of their younger lost selves, and bear the brunt of parents' regrets as parents distance themselves.

Steinberg tracks the psychological unrest associated with midlife crisis in parents:

- The onset of puberty is unavoidable evidence that their child is growing up.
- Along with puberty comes a child's burgeoning sexuality. For parents, this can raise doubts about their own attractiveness, their current sex life, as well as regrets or nostalgia for their teenage sexual experiences.
- The kids' new independence can make parents feel powerless. For fathers in particular this can remind them of the powerlessness they feel in the office if their careers have hit a plateau.
- Teens also become less concerned with their parents' approval. Their peer group approval becomes more important. This hits mothers of daughters quite hard, especially single mothers, whose relationship to their daughters most resembles a friendship.
- Finally, de-idealization—kids' often blunt criticism of their parents—is a strong predictor of decline in parental mental health. Parents who used to be the ultimate expert to their kids are now reduced to debating partner for kids who have developed a new cognitive skill called relativism.

A clear picture begins to emerge: parents of a teenager feel depressed about their own life or their own marriage; feel the loss of their child; feel jealous, rejected, and confused about their child's new sexually mature looks, bad moods, withdrawal into privacy at home, and increasing involvement with friends. The kid is tied up in her (or his) own problems and wonders what planet mom and dad are on.

EMOTIONAL DIVORCE

The sad consequence is that parents who experience a midlife crisis begin avoiding their adolescent. Although a small proportion of parents are holding on to their teens too closely—usually they come from traditional families and have fundamentalist religious beliefs—more parents are backing off. The catch is that these teenagers want their parents' guidance. But more and more they just aren't getting it.

Some parents back away not out of their own inner confusion but because they think it's hip to do so. Either way, letting go causes confusion in the kids, not help in making their way into adulthood. Even if they are irritating or irritable, or just more withdrawn than they used to be, teens are seeking guidance.

Adults need to understand that it is very difficult to be a teenager nowadays. It takes a lot of understanding with so many problems like guns, drugs, AIDS, and gangs.
—Melissa, 14, Dallas, Texas

"I have this image of a kid groping through adolescence, kind of by himself" confides therapist Wagers, who sees a lot of parents out of touch with their kids. "The parents swarm around him, but don't actually talk to him, only to other people about him."

The mantra of therapists who work with adolescents and their families is "balance." Parents have to hold on, but not too tightly. They need to stay involved, even when their kids are ignoring them. Roland Montemayor, Ph.D., professor of psychology at Ohio State, finds it is not so different from learning how to deal with a two-year-old. You must stay within earshot, and be available whenever they falter or get themselves into trouble.

With a two-year-old, trouble means experimenting with mud pies or bopping a playmate; with a 14-year-old, it means experimenting with your car keys or sex. The task is the same—keep track of them and let them know what the rules are. Parents unfortunately taken up with their own midlife concerns may not embrace the task. God knows, it isn't easy. But it is vital.

Among parents who have gone through a real divorce, the emotional divorce that occurs between adolescents and their parents can heighten difficulty. It may reawaken feelings of sadness. Parents who don't have many interests outside the family are also vulnerable. Their kids are telling them to "Get a life!"—and that is exactly what they need to do.

DROPOUT PARENTS

As an adolescent reaches age 13, the time she is spending with parents is typically half that before age 10. "Teens come home and go into their bedrooms. They start to feel more comfortable by themselves than with siblings or parents around. They talk on the phone with friends, and their biggest worry usually has to do with a romantic interest," explains Reed Larson, Ph.D., who studies families and adolescents at the University of Illinois, Champaign-Urbana. Larson, coauthor of the recent book, *Divergent Realities: The Emotional Lives of Mothers, Fathers, and Adolescents*, studied 55 families who recorded their feelings and activities for one week, whenever prompted at random intervals by a beeper. He surveyed another 483 adolescents with the beeper method.

The families' reports revealed that a mutual withdrawal occurs. "When kids withdraw, parents get the message. They even feel intimidated. As a result they don't put in the extra effort to maintain contact with their kids," observes Larson. The kids feel abandoned, even though they're the ones retreating to their bedroom. The parents, in effect, cut their kids loose, just when they dip their toes in the waters of autonomy.

I don't think adults understand how complicated kids' minds are today, how much they think; they don't just accept something but wonder why it is.
—Adam, 14, Bethesda, Maryland

Separation is natural among humans as well as in the animal kingdom, Larson notes. Yet humans also need special care during this life transition—and suffer from reduced contact with parents and other adults. They still need to be taught how to do things, how to think about things, but above all they need to know that there is a safety net, a sense that their parents are paying attention and are going to jump in when things go wrong. The kids don't need the direct supervision they received at age two or eight, but they benefit emotionally and intellectually from positive contact with their parents.

Despite the tensions in family life, studies continue to confirm that the family remains one of the most effective vehicles to promote values, school success, even confidence in peer relationships. When it works, family functions as what Larson calls a "comfort zone," a place or a relationship that serves as a home base out of which to operate. Kids feel more secure, calm, and confident than those without a comfort zone. Similarly, Steinberg finds, the one common link among the many successful adolescents in his studies is that they all have positive relationships with their parents. Without positive relationships, the kids are subject to depression and likely to do poorly in school.

Parental withdrawal is a prime characteristic of families where adolescents get into trouble. It often catapults families into therapy. Wagers tells the story of a single parent who wasn't simply withdrawn, her head was in the sand: "I was seeing a mother and her 12-year-old son, who had depression and behavior problems. The mother called me up one time to say she had found all this marijuana paraphernalia in her son's room, in his pocket. She said she wasn't sure what it means. When I said 'it means that he's smoking pot,' she was very reluctant to agree. She didn't want to talk to her son about why he was getting into trouble or smoking pot. She wanted me to fix him." (Eventually, in therapy, the mother learned how to give her son a curfew and other rules, and to enforce them. He's doing much better.)

Teenagers know what is happening around them in school but adults hide things. Parents should shield their kids from some things but not so much that kids are afraid to go out into the world.
—Sarah, 17, Hanover, NH

Marital problems also enter into the distancing equation. Although the marital decline among teens' parents is part of the normal course of marriage, the adolescent can exacerbate the problem. "Here is a new person challenging you in ways that might make you irritable or insecure," explains Steinberg. "That can spill over into the marriage. The standard scenario involves the adolescent and the mother who have been home squabbling all afternoon. Well, the mom isn't exactly going to be in a terrific mood to greet her husband. It resembles the marital problems that occur when a couple first has a new baby." Trouble is, when the parents' marriage declines, so does the quality of the parenting—at a time when more parental energy is needed.

As if there are not enough psychological forces reducing contact between parents and adolescents today, social trends add to the problem, contends Roland Montemayor. Intensified work schedules, increased divorce and single parenthood, and poverty—often a result of divorce and single parenthood—decrease parent-child contact. A fourth of all teenagers live with one parent, usually their mother. Families have fewer ties to the community, so there are fewer other adults with whom teens have nurturing ties. The negative images of teenagers as violent delinquents may even intimidate parents.

ALONE AND ANGRY

Whatever the source, parental distancing doesn't make for happy kids. "The kids I work with at Ohio State are remarkably independent, yet they are resentful of it," says Montemayor. "There is a sense of not being connected somehow." Kids are angry about being left to themselves, being given independence without the kind of mentoring from their parents to learn how to use their independence.

I am insecure about my future. The main view toward people in my generation is that we are all slackers and it's kind of disturbing. We are actually trying to make something of ourselves.
—Jasmine, 16, Brooklyn, New York

Adult contact seems to be on teenagers' minds more than ever before. Sociologist Dale Blythe, Ph.D., is an adolescence researcher who directs Minneapolis' noted Search Institute, which specializes in studies of youth policy issues. He has surveyed teens in 30 communities across the country, and found that when you ask teens, they say that family is not the most important thing in their lives—peers and social activities are. Nevertheless a large proportion of them say that they want more time with adults—they want their attention and leadership. They want more respect from adults and more cues on how to make it in the adult world. What a shift from 25 years ago, when the watchword was "never trust anyone over 30"!

The Invention of Adolescence

Are Romeo and Juliet the Quintessential adolescents? On the yes side, they were rebelling against family traditions, in the throes of first love, prone to melodrama, and engaged in violent and risky behavior. But the truth is that there was no such thing as adolescence in Shakespeare's time (the 16th century). Young people the ages of Romeo and Juliet (around 13) were adults in the eyes of society—even though they were probably prepubescent.

Paradoxically, puberty came later in eras past while departure from parental supervision came earlier than it does today. Romeo and Juliet carried the weight of the world on their shoulders—although it was a far smaller world than today's teens inhabit.

Another way to look at it is that in centuries past, a sexually mature person was never treated as a "growing child." Today sexually mature folk spend perhaps six years—ages 12 to 18—living under the authority of their parents.

Since the mid-1800s, puberty—the advent of sexual maturation and the starting point of adolescence—has inched back one year for every 25 years elapsed. It now occurs on average six years earlier than it did in 1850—age 11 or 12 for girls; age 12 or 13 for boys. Today adolescents make up 17 percent of the U.S. population and about a third of them belong to racial or ethnic minorities.

It's still not clear exactly what triggers puberty, confides Jeanne Brooks-Gunn, Ph.D., of Columbia University Teachers College, an expert on adolescent development. "The onset of puberty has fallen probably due to better nutrition in the prenatal period as well as throughout childhood. Pubertal age—for girls, when their first period occurs—has been lower in the affluent than the nonaffluent classes throughout recorded history. Differences are still found in countries where starvation and malnutrition are common among the poor. In Western countries, no social-class differences are found." Although adolescence is a new phenomenon in the history of our species, thanks to a stable and abundant food supply, we've already hit its limits—it's not likely puberty onset will drop much below the age of 12.

If kids look like adults sooner than ever before, that doesn't mean they are. The brain begins to change when the body does, but it doesn't become a grown-up thinking organ as quickly as other systems of the body mature. The clash between physical maturity and mental immaturity not only throws parents a curve—they forget how to do their job, or even what it is—it catapults teens into some silly situations. They become intensely interested in romance, for example, only their idea of romance is absurdly simple, culminating in notes passed across the classroom: "Do you like me? Check yes or no."

Puberty isn't the only marker of adolescence. There's a slowly increasing capacity for abstract reasoning and relative thinking. Their new capacity for abstraction allows teens to think about big things—Death, Destruction, Nuclear War—subjects that depress them, especially since they lack the capacity to ameliorate them.

The idea that everything is relative suddenly makes every rule subject to debate. As time passes, teens attain the ability to make finer abstract distinctions. Which is to say, they become better at choosing their fights.

Teens also move toward autonomy. They want to be alone, they say, because they have a lot on their minds. Yet much of the autonomy hinges on the growing importance of social relationships. Evaluating the ups and downs of social situations indeed requires time alone. Family ties, however, remain more important than you might expect as teens increase identification with their peers.

Whatever else turns teens into the moody creatures they are, hormones have been given far too much credit, contends Brooks-Gunn. In fact, she points out, the flow of hormones that eventually shapes their bodies actually starts around age seven or eight. "Certain emotional states and problems increase between ages 11 and 14, at the time puberty takes place. These changes are probably due to the increased social and school demands, the multiple new events that youth confront, their own responses to puberty, and to a much lesser extent hormonal changes themselves."

The nutritional abundance that underlies a long adolescence also prompted the extension of education, which has created a problem entirely novel in the animal kingdom—physically mature creatures living with their parents, and for more years than sexually mature offspring ever have in the past. College-bound kids typically depend on their parents until at least age 21, a decade or more after hitting puberty.

Historically, children never lived at home during the teen years, points out Temple University's Laurence Steinberg. Either they were shipped out to apprenticeships or off to other relatives.

Among lower primates, physically mature beasts simply are not welcome in the family den; sexual competition makes cohabiting untenable. But for animals, physical maturity coincides with mental acuity, so their departure is not a rejection.

The formal study of adolescence began in the 1940s, just before James Dean changed our perception of it forever. There is a long-standing tradition of professional observers looking at adolescence as a pathology—and this one really did start with Freud. It continues still.

A 1988 study reported that although the under-18 population actually declined from 1980 to 1984, adolescent admissions to private psychiatric hospitals increased—450 percent! The study suggests a staggering cultural taste for applying mental health care to any problem life presents. It also hints at the negative feelings Americans have toward adolescence—we consider it a disease.

The study of adolescence has come with a context—a culture of, by, and for youth, arising in the postwar boom of the 1950s and epitomized by James Dean. Once the original badass depressive teenager from hell, Dean seems quaintly tame by today's standards. But the fear and loathing he set in motion among adults is a powerful legacy today's teens are still struggling to live down.—V.R.

> Many times teenagers are thought of as a problem that no one really wants to deal with. People are sometimes intimidated and become hostile because teenagers are willing to challenge their authority. It is looked at as being disrespectful. Teenagers are, many times, not treated like an asset and as innovative thinkers who will be the leaders of tomorrow. Adults have the power to teach the younger generation about the world and allow them to feel they have a voice in it.—**Zula, 16, Brooklyn, NY**

So it's up to parents to seek more contact with their kids—despite the conflict they'll encounter. "The role of parents is to socialize children, to help them become responsible adults, to teach them to do the right thing. Conflict is an inevitable part of it" says Montemayor. He notes that one of the biggest sources of conflict between parents and teens is time management. Teens have trouble committing to plans in advance. They want to keep their options wide open all the time. The only surefire way to reduce conflict is to withdraw from teenagers—an equally surefire way to harm them.

"In other countries parents don't shy away from conflict. In the United States we have this idea that things are going to be hunky-dory and that we are going to go bowling and have fun together. Most people in the world would find that a pretty fanciful idea. There is an inevitable tension between parents and adolescents, and there's nothing wrong with that."

I think there is going to be a lot of destruction and violence. There are all these peace treaties, but I don't think they are going to work out.

—Julia, 12, Albuquerque, NM

SILENCED SEX

Who can talk about teens without talking about sex? The topic of teenage sexuality, however, heightens parents' sense of powerlessness. Adults hesitate to acknowledge their own sexual experience in addressing the issue. They resolve the matter by pretending sex doesn't exist.

Sexuality was conspicuous by its absence in all the family interviews Steinberg, Montemayor, or Larson observed. Calling sex a hidden issue in adolescence verges on an oxymoron. Sprouting pubic hair and expanding busts aren't particularly subtle phenomena. But adolescent sexuality is only heightened by the silence.

> Doing the right thing and being good at what you're doing is important to me.
>
> As teenagers we have a lot of things on our back, a lot of people are looking for us to do many great things. We also take in a lot of things and we know a lot of things. I care about the environment because it's a place that we all have to live in, not just us but our families and children. Even though I'm 15, I still have to keep those things in mind because it's serious. As for my own future, I've had a good upbringing and I see all open doors.—**Semu, 15, New York City**

A postpubescent child introduces a third sexually mature person into the household, where once sex was a strictly private domain restricted to the older generation. It's difficult for everyone to get used to.

No matter how you slice it, sex can be an awkward topic. For parents, there's not only the feeling of powerlessness, there's discomfort. Most parents of adolescents aren't experiencing much sexual activity—neither the mechanics of sex nor its poetry—in this stage of the marriage (though this eventually improves).

The fact that fathers' marital satisfaction decreases when their kids start to date suggests the power of kids' sexuality, no matter how silenced, to distort parental behavior. Sex and marital therapist David Schnarch, Ph.D., points out that families, and the mythology of the

> I think Al Gore is a super environmentalist. With no ozone layer, the world is just going to melt. It's hard not to worry. The environment is really messed up and with no environment there will be no economy, no education, nothing. I hate it when people throw six-pack rings in the lake. We need to think about the environment because we need to get on with the rest of our lives. I don't think adults generally look to kids for opinions.—**Sam, 13, New York City**

culture, worship teen sexuality, mistakenly believing adolescence is the peak of human sexuality. Boys have more hard-ons than their dads, while the girls have less cellulite than their moms.

These kids may have the biological equipment, says Schnarch, but they don't yet know how to make love. Sex isn't just about orgasms, it is about intimacy. "All of our sex education is designed to raise kids to be healthy, normal adults. But we are confused about what we believe is sexually normal. Textbooks say that boys reach their sexual peak in late adolescence; girls, five to 10 years later. The adolescent believes it, parents believe it, schools believe it. In the hierarchy dictated by this narrow biological model of sexuality, the person with the best sex is the adolescent. On the one hand we are telling kids, 'we would like you to delay sexual involvement.' But when we teach a biological model of sexuality, we imply

---

The future sounds alright. It is probably going to be more modern and really scientific. Things will be run by computers and computers will do more for people.
—Emily, 13, New York City

---

to the kids 'we know you can't delay. We think these are the best years of your life.'"

Parents can help their children by letting them know that they understand sex and have valuable experience about decisions related to sex; that they know it isn't just a mechanical act; that they recognize that teens are going to figure things out on their own with or without guidance from their parents; and that they are willing to talk about it. But often, the experience or meaning of sex gets lost.

I asked a woman whose parents had handed her birth control pills at age 15 how she felt about it now, at age 30. "I wish sex had been a little more taboo than it was. I got into a lot more sexual acting out before I was 20, and that didn't go very well for me. Even though my parents talked about the health consequences of sex, they did not mention other consequences. Like what it does to your self-esteem when you get involved in a series of one-night stands. So I guess I wish they had been more holistic in

I don't feel any pressure about sex. It's a frequent topic of conversation, but we talk about other things, too—when I'm going to get my history paper done, movies, music. I listen to classical music a lot. I think about my maturity a lot, because I have recently had losses in my immediate family and it feels like I am maturing so fast. But then sometimes I feel so young compared to everything out there. I think adults have always felt that teens were more reckless.—Amanda, 16, New York City

their approach to sex. Not just to tell me about the pill when I was 15, but to understand the different issues I was struggling with. In every other aspect of my life, they were my best resource. But it turns out sex is a lot more complicated

Teenagers, like adults, are all different. One has a job that is hard, another has more money and more education, and one just gets by. It is unfair to look at all teens the same way. You have maturity in you, but you just don't want to show it because it's no fun. We've got problems, but not really big ones like my uncle who came over from China when he was 16, or going to war when you're 18. If teenagers make it through this era, adults will just bash the next generation of teenagers.—Mike, 14, Brooklyn, New York

than I thought it was when I was 15. At 30, sex is a lot better than it was when I was a teenager."

The distortions parents create about teen sexuality lead directly to events like the "Spur Posse," the gang of teenage football stars in Southern California who systematically harassed and raped girls, terrorizing the community in the late 80s. The boys' fathers actually appeared on talk shows—to brag about their sons'

Jackie Joyner-Kersee, the Olympic track star, is my hero because she has accomplished so much and she is one of the main female athletes.
—Kristy, 12, Woodbridge, New Jersey

conquests. "The fathers were reinforcing the boys' behavior. It was as if it were a reflection on their own sexuality," observes Schnarch.

By closing their eyes to teen sexual behavior, parents don't just disengage from their kids. They leave them high and dry about understanding anything

My hero is Queen Latifah. She is herself and doesn't try to be somebody else. My mother is also my hero because she raises me as well as she can and she is a single parent.
—Maria, 15, Bronx, New York

more than the cold mechanics of sex. Kids raised this way report feeling very alone when it gets down to making intimate decisions for the first time. They feel like they haven't been given any help in what turns out to be the bigger part of sex—the relationship part of it.

Returning to the authoritarian, insular family of Ward, June, Wally, and the Beaver is not the solution for teenagers any more than it is for their parents. But teenagers do need parents and other responsible adults actively involved in their lives, just as younger children do. Only when it comes to teenagers, the grown-ups have to tolerate a lot more ambiguity—about authority, safety, responsibility, and closeness—to sustain the connection. If they can learn to do that, a lot of young people will be able to avoid a whole lot of trouble.

Teenage Turning Point

Does adolescence herald the twilight of girls' self-esteem?

BRUCE BOWER

Youngsters often experience a decline in self-esteem as they enter their adolescent years, a time marked by the abrupt move from the relatively cloistered confines of elementary school to the more complex social and academic demands of junior high. Social scientists have documented this trend — often more pronounced among girls — over the past 20 years through questionnaires and interviews aimed at gauging how adolescents feel about themselves.

But a new survey of U.S. elementary and secondary students bears the worst news yet about plummeting self-esteem among teenage girls. The controversial findings, released in January by the American Association of University Women (AAUW), have refocused researchers' attention on long-standing questions about the meaning of such studies and their implications, if any, for educational reform and for male and female psychological development.

The concept of self-esteem itself remains vague, contends psychiatrist Philip Robson in the June 1990 HARVARD MEDICAL SCHOOL MENTAL HEALTH LETTER. Some researchers assess a person's "global" self-esteem with questions about general feelings of worth, goodness, health, attractiveness and social competence. Others focus on people's evaluations of themselves in specific situations. Robson, of Oxford University in England, notes that an individual might score high on one type of test but not on another, presumably because the measures reflect different aspects of self-esteem.

Moreover, he argues, high test scores may sometimes indicate conceit, narcissism or rigidity rather than healthy feelings of self-worth.

Despite the complexities involved in determining how people truly regard themselves, the AAUW survey suggests that adolescent girls experience genuine, substantial drops in self-esteem that far outpace those reported by boys. Girls also reported much less enthusiasm for math and science, less confidence in their academic abilities and fewer aspirations to professional careers.

The survey, conducted last fall by a private polling firm commissioned by AAUW, involved 2,400 girls and 600 boys from 36 public schools throughout the United States. Black and Hispanic students made up almost one-quarter of the sample. Participants, whose ages ranged from 9 to 16 (fourth through tenth grades), responded to written statements probing global self-esteem, such as "I like the way I look" and "I'm happy the way I am."

In a typical response pattern, 67 percent of the elementary school boys reported "always" feeling "happy the way I am," and 46 percent still felt that way by tenth grade. For girls, the figures dropped from 60 percent to 29 percent.

For both sexes, the sharpest declines in self-esteem occurred at the beginning of junior high.

Compared with the rest of the study sample, students with higher self-esteem liked math and science more, felt better about their schoolwork and grades, considered themselves more important and felt better about their family relationships, according to the survey.

Boys who reported doing poorly in math and science usually ascribed their performance to the topics' lack of usefulness, whereas girls who reported a lack of success in these areas often attributed the problem to personal failure.

Although the survey included too few boys to allow a racial breakdown for males, race did appear to play an important role in the strength of self-esteem among girls. White and Hispanic girls displayed sharp drops in all the measured areas of self-esteem — appearance, confidence, family relationships, school, talents and personal importance — as they grew older. In contrast, more than half the black girls reported high levels of self-confidence and personal importance in both elementary and high school, and most attributed this to strong family and community support, says psychologist Janie Victoria Ward of the University of Pennsylvania in Philadelphia, an adviser to the study. Their confidence in their academic abilities, however, dropped substantially as they passed through the school system, Ward says.

"Something is going on in the schools that threatens the self-esteem of girls in general," asserts psychologist Nancy Goldberger, another adviser to the survey. "A lot of girls come to doubt their own intelligence in school."

Goldberger, who teaches psychology at the Fielding Institute in Santa Barbara, Calif., calls for intensive, long-term studies to address how schools shortchange female students.

An AAUW pamphlet published last August argues that school-age girls represent the proverbial square peg attempting to fit into the round hole of most educational programs.

Starting early in life, societal pressures urge girls and boys to think and behave in contrasting ways that create gender-specific learning styles, according to the AAUW pamphlet. Schools, however, generally tailor instructional techniques to the learning style of boys, leaving girls with a tattered education and doubts about their academic abilities, the pamphlet contends.

This argument rests heavily on research directed by Harvard University psychologist Carol Gilligan. In her much-praised and much-criticized book, *In a Different Voice* (1982, Harvard University Press), Gilligan asserted that girls and boys generally follow divergent paths of moral development. She based her contention on several studies of Harvard undergraduates, men and women at different points in the life cycle, and women considering abortion.

In Gilligan's view, females respond to an inner moral voice emphasizing human connections and care, and they attempt to solve moral dilemmas by responding to the needs and situations of those

From *Science News*, March 23, 1991, pp. 184-186. © 1991 by Science Service, Inc. Reprinted with permission from *Science News*, the weekly newsmagazine of science.

affected by the problem. Males, on the other hand, focus on abstract principles such as justice and follow a moral code centered on the impartial application of rules of right and wrong.

Gilligan's most recent research, described in *Making Connections: The Relational Worlds of Adolescent Girls at Emma Willard School* (1990, Harvard University Press), draws on findings collected over a three-year period among 34 students at a private girls' school in Troy, N.Y. Gilligan and her co-workers argue that many girls, at least in this predominantly white, privileged sample, show an aggressive confidence in their identities and ideas around age 11, only to find their self-assurance withering by age 15 or 16.

During this period of increasing separation from parents, marked by a search for an independent identity and future career possibilities, girls feel torn between responding to others and caring for themselves, the Harvard researchers maintain. In addition, they say, adolescent girls encounter more pressure from parents and teachers to keep quiet and not make a fuss than do adolescent boys or younger girls.

The gender gap seen in academic achievement during early adolescence arises largely because a social and educational emphasis on career development and personal advancement clashes with girls' distinctive sense of connection to others, Gilligan's team asserts. The researchers maintain that girls often learn best and gain increased self-confidence through collaboration with other students and faculty, not through competition among individuals as practiced in most schools.

Boys, in contrast, often perform best on competitive tasks or in games with a strict set of prescribed rules, the investigators contend.

Some adolescence researchers argue that Gilligan paints too stark a contrast between the moral development of boys and girls. Others say Gilligan's ideas have an intuitive appeal, but her small studies lack a sound empirical foundation on which to build educational reforms. These researchers see Gilligan's work as a preliminary corrective for previous studies, based largely on male participants, that suggested the ability to reason from abstract principles represented the pinnacle of moral development.

Similarly, social scientists differ over the extent to which self-esteem dips during adolescence and the meaning of the AAUW survey data. In fact, some investigators question whether a significant gender gap in self-esteem exists at all.

Most surveys of teenagers' self-esteem, including the AAUW project, focus on

students and neglect school dropouts. This approach may lead to overestimates of self-esteem among boys, argues sociologist Naomi Gerstel of the University of Massachusetts in Amherst. More boys than girls drop out of school, and male dropouts may regard themselves in an especially poor light, Gerstel points out.

Furthermore, she says, since no one has examined the moral "voice" of boys in the intensive way Gilligan studied her group of girls, Gilligan's theory has yet to meet a scientifically rigorous test. Gilligan's ideas prove "problematic" when educators attempt to use them to formulate specific educational reforms, Gerstel writes in the Jan. 4 SCIENCE.

The self-esteem reports gathered in the AAUW survey fail to provide evidence for any particular need to change school instruction, contends psychologist Joseph Adelson of the University of Michigan in Ann Arbor. "It's been known for some time that girls report greater self-esteem declines in adolescence, but the reasons for those declines are unclear," he says. "It's inappropriate to take the correlations in this survey to politicized conclusions about educational reform."

In his view, gender differences in mathematics achievement remain particularly mysterious and probably stem from a number of as-yet-unspecified social or family influences (SN: 12/6/86, p.357). Preliminary studies directed by Carol S. Dweck, a psychologist at Columbia University in New York City, suggest that bright girls show a stronger tendency than bright boys to attribute their difficulty or confusion with a new concept — such as mathematics — to a lack of intelligence. Thus, when bright girls confront mathematics, initial confusion may trigger a feeling of helplessness, Dweck writes in *At The Threshold* (1990, S. Shirley Feldman and Glen R. Elliot, editors, Harvard University Press).

Many girls with considerable potential in mathematics may deal with this sense of helplessness by throwing their energies into already mastered verbal skills, Dweck suggests. Rather than indict their intelligence, both boys and girls who shrink from challenging new subjects may need to learn how to channel initial failures into a redoubled effort to master the material, she says.

Gender differences in reported well-being — an aspect of personal experience closely related to self-esteem — also prove tricky to study, Adelson observes. A statistical comparison of 93 independent studies, directed by psychologist Wendy Wood of Texas A&M University in College Station, serves as a case in point. In examining these studies, which focused on well-being and life satisfaction among adult men and women, Wood and her

colleagues found that women reported both greater happiness *and* more dissatisfaction and depression than men. Wood contends that societal influences groom women for an acute emotional responsiveness, especially with regard to intimate relationships, and that this helps explain why women report more intense emotional highs and lows than men.

"No clear advantage can be identified in the adaptiveness and desirability of [men's and women's] styles of emotional life," she and her colleagues write in the March 1989 PSYCHOLOGICAL BULLETIN.

Researchers have yet to conduct a similar statistical comparison of the literature on adolescent self-esteem and well-being. But according to Adelson, a persistent problem plagues the interpretation of all such studies. If females generally show more sensitivity to and awareness of emotions than males, they may more easily offer self-reports about disturbing feelings, creating a misimpression that large sex differences exist in self-esteem, he suggests.

Although this potential "response bias" muddies the research waters, psychologist Daniel Offer of Northwestern University in Evanston, Ill., cites several possible explanations for the tendency among early-adolescent girls to report more self-dissatisfaction than boys.

One theory holds that since girls experience the biological changes of puberty up to 18 months before boys, they may suffer earlier and more pronounced self-esteem problems related to sexual maturity. Several studies have found that early-maturing girls report the most dissatisfaction with their physical appearance, a particularly sensitive indicator of self-esteem among females. Social pressures to begin dating and to disengage emotionally from parents may create additional problems for early-maturing girls, Offer says.

Other research suggests that, unlike their male counterparts, adolescent girls often maintain close emotional ties to their mothers that interfere with the development of a sense of independence and self-confidence, Offer says. In addition, parents may interrupt and ignore girls more than boys as puberty progresses, according to observational studies of families, directed by psychologist John P. Hill of Virginia Commonwealth University in Richmond.

Despite these findings, the director of the most ambitious longitudinal study of adolescent self-esteem to date says her findings provide little support for the substantial gender gap outlined in the AAUW survey, which took a single-point-in-time "snapshot" of self-esteem.

During the 1970s, sociologist Roberta G. Simmons of the University of Pittsburgh and her co-workers charted the trajectory of self-esteem from grades 6 through 10 among more than 1,000 youngsters attending public schools in Milwaukee and Baltimore. Simmons discusses the research in *Moving Into Adolescence* (1987, Aldine de Gruyter).

Overall, adolescents reported a gradual increase in self-esteem as they got older, she says, but many girls entering junior high and high school did experience drops in feelings of confidence and self-satisfaction.

Simmons agrees with Gilligan that adolescent girls increasingly strive for intimacy with others. Large, impersonal junior high schools throw up a barrier to intimacy that initially undermines girls' self-esteem, Simmons asserts. As girls find a circle of friends and a social niche, their self-esteem gradually rebounds, only to drop again when they enter the even larger world of high school.

"We don't know if that last self-esteem drop [in high school] was temporary or permanent," Simmons points out.

As in the AAUW survey, Simmons' team found that black girls, as well as black boys, consistently reported positive and confident self-images.

But given the increased acceptance of women in a wide variety of occupations since the 1970s, Simmons expresses surprise at how much the self-esteem of girls lagged behind that of boys in the AAUW survey.

A new study of 128 youngsters progressing through junior high, described in the February JOURNAL OF YOUTH AND ADOLESCENCE, also contrasts with the AAUW findings. The two-year, longitudinal investigation reveals comparable levels of self-esteem among boys and girls, notes study director Barton J. Hirsch, a psychologist at Northwestern University. Hirsch and his colleagues used a global self-esteem measure much like the one in the AAUW survey.

The researchers gathered self-reports from boys and girls as the students neared the end of sixth grade, then repeated the process with the same youngsters at two points during seventh grade and at the end of eighth grade. Students lived in a midwestern city and came from poor or middle-class families. Black children made up about one-quarter of the sample.

In both sexes, about one in three youngsters reported strong self-esteem throughout junior high school, the researchers report. These individuals also did well in school, maintained rewarding friendships and frequently participated in social activities.

Another third of the sample displayed small increases in self-esteem, but their overall psychological adjustment and academic performance were no better than those of the group with consistently high self-esteem.

Chronically low self-esteem and school achievement dogged 13 percent of the students, who probably suffered from a long history of these problems, Hirsch says.

But the most unsettling findings came from the remaining 21 percent of the youngsters. This group — composed of roughly equal numbers of boys and girls — started out with high self-esteem, good grades and numerous friends, but their scores on these measures plunged dramatically during junior high, eventually reaching the level of the students with chronically low self-esteem.

The data offer no easy explanations for the steep declines seen among one in five study participants, Hirsch says. An examination of family life might uncover traumatic events that influenced the youngsters' confidence and motivation, but this remains speculative, he says.

One of the most comprehensive longitudinal studies of the relation between child development and family life (SN: 8/19/89, p. 117) suggests that particular parenting styles produce the most psycho-logically healthy teenagers. The findings indicate that parents who set clear standards for conduct and allow freedom within limits raise youngsters with the most academic, emotional and social competence.

Directed by psychologist Diana Baumrind of the University of California, Berkeley, the ongoing study has followed children from 124 families, most of them white and middle-class. At three points in the youngsters' lives — ages 3, 10 and 15 — investigators assessed parental styles and the children's behavior at home and school.

Baumrind assumes that self-esteem emerges from competence in various social and academic tasks, not vice versa. For that reason, she and her colleagues track achievement scores and trained observers' ratings of social and emotional adjustment, not children's self-reports of how they feel about themselves.

In fact, Baumrind remains unconvinced that girls experience lower self-esteem than boys upon entering adolescence. Her study finds that girls in elementary grades show a more caring and communal attitude toward others, while boys more often strive for dominance and control in social encounters. But by early adolescence, she maintains, such differences largely disappear.

The gender-gap debate, however, shows no signs of disappearing. In a research field characterized by more questions than answers, most investigators agree on one point. "Most kids come through the years from 10 to 20 without major problems and with an increasing sense of self-esteem," Simmons observes.

Yet that trend, too, remains unexplained. "Perhaps the steady increase in self-esteem noted in late adolescence results more from progressive indoctrination into the values of society than from increasing self-acceptance," says Robson. "We simply do not have the empirical data necessary to resolve this question."

Sports lift esteem in young athletes

Involvement in athletics also boosts student athletes' motivation.

Erin Burnette

Monitor staff

The payoff of playing Little League baseball doesn't only come in the form of stronger biceps and better hand-eye coordination. Participation in organized sports also boosts self-esteem and motivation among child athletes, psychologists' research has found.

Maureen Weiss, PhD, and her colleagues at the University of Oregon have conducted more than 60 studies on how participation in physical activity and sports affect youth social and psychological development. Her work in the early 1990s reveals an association between motivation, high self-esteem and sport participation.

"Physical activity and sports have tremendous potential to enhance children's self-esteem and motivation," said Weiss, a professor of sport and exercise psychology.

Her research has consistently demonstrated that self-esteem and perceptions of physical ability can predict achievement behavior, motivation and positive affect. For example, the research found that children who underestimated their abilities were less motivated and experienced more anxiety than those who estimated their capabilities accurately; that activity-specific self-perceptions predict achievement in that sport but not others; and that the positive and negative experiences in sports are directly related to self-esteem and motivation for future involvement.

Impact on schooling

Work by Ronald M. Jeziorski, EdD, an educational psychologist who consults for co-curricular programs in Santa Clara, Calif., supports the notion that youth who participate in sports earn higher grades and behave better in school and out. He is author of the book "The Importance of School Sports in American Education and Socialization," (University Press of America, 1994).

In one study, Jeziorski sought input from social workers, law enforcement officials and educators from throughout the United States to get their thoughts on the effects of school sports. He surveyed 18 professionals.

"Across the board, they all said that participants in sports earn better grades, behave better in the classroom, have fewer behavior problems outside the classroom, drop out significantly less, and attend school on a regular basis with fewer unexcused absences," Jeziorski said.

Jeziorski also relayed statistics that his colleague, Nicholas Zill of Rockville, Md., collected regarding nonparticipants in co-curricular programs. He found that nonparticipants are 57 percent more likely to drop out of school; 49 percent more likely to use drugs; 37 percent more likely to be teen parents; 35 percent more likely to smoke cigarettes; and 27 percent more likely to have been arrested, than co-curricular participants.

Life-skills teacher

Tara Scanlan, PhD, a researcher in sport psychology at the University of California, Los Angeles, (UCLA) says that sports can provide an achievement arena for youth, and that learning to achieve in that setting can teach children life skills such as how to communicate, commit and collaborate, if the coaches and parents are supportive. The life skills must be reinforced, however, so that they transfer to other settings, Scanlan said.

"We need to show them that what they have learned on the field applies in other areas of life. Learning how to work with peers and adults and the joy of mastering skills are just a few of the things that can be learned in that environment, if it's done right."

Structuring the team setting so children learn skills and helping them use those skills in other domains will also increase their confidence, she said.

"Youth need to understand why commitment will take them to the top of the talent domain so they will link what sports does for them to the rest of their lives," Scanlan said.

Scanlan now plans to conduct a study on whether youth sports participation has positive effects on adulthood.

What Is a Bad Kid?
Answers of Adolescents
and Their Mothers in
Three Cultures

David S. Crystal and
Harold W. Stevenson

University of Michigan

This study examined the behaviors and personality traits attributed to a "bad kid" by a cross-national sample of 204 American high-school students and 204 American mothers, 237 Chinese students and 224 Chinese mothers, and 157 Japanese students and 167 Japanese mothers. Correlates of students' responses were also examined, including the degree of valuing academics, level of academic achievement, level of psychological adjustment, and quality of social relationships. The behaviors most frequently associated with a bad kid were lack of self-control (American), acts against society (Chinese), and disruptions of interpersonal harmony (Japanese). In addition, American students mentioned substance abuse as a feature of a bad kid more often than did their Chinese and Japanese peers. Disturbances in interpersonal harmony received the highest frequency of response from Chinese and Japanese students and second highest frequency of response from American students. Adolescents and their mothers differed significantly in the frequency with which they mentioned the types of conduct attributed to a bad kid. Few associations were found between students' own characteristics and their descriptions of a bad kid.

Over the past 30 years, due, in large part, to the influence of the labelling theorists (e.g., Becker, 1964; Scheff, 1974), a growing number of social scientists have come to view deviance not as an objective quality but, rather, as a subjective definition made by a particular audience. From this perspective, a behavior is bad, wrong, or abnormal because it is defined that way by members of a particular society (Newman, 1976). Based on this premise, there is an increasing interest among psychologists and sociologists in identifying cross-cultural differences in perceptions of deviance and in understanding how these perceptions reflect the characteristics of the society or culture from which they derive.

One way of understanding the process by which cultural characteristics come to express themselves through perceptions of deviance may be seen in a paradigm put forth by LeVine (1973). According to the paradigm, the environment influences child rearing practices which, in turn, affect the nature of child and adult personality, as well as important facets of group life, including perceptions of good and bad. These latter products of culture may be seen as reflected in what Robin and Spires (1983) called the individual's "projective system" (p. 109) that guides a person's social and moral behavior. Because children and adults are socialized to be able to function within the existing cultural

Requests for reprints should be sent to David S. Crystal, Center for Human Growth and Development, 300 North Ingalls, 10th Level, University of Michigan, Ann Arbor, MI 48109-0406.

From the *Journal of Research on Adolescence*, Vol. 5, No. 1, 1995, pp. 71-91. © 1995 by Lawrence Erlbaum Associates, Inc. Reprinted by permission.

environment, looking at certain aspects of the projective system of children and adults, such as perceptions of deviance, may tell us important things about how adaptation within a specific culture takes place.

Cross-cultural studies on perceptions of deviance fall into two basic categories: those that examine expressions of psychological deviance such as mental illness (e.g., Hardy, Cull, & Campbell, 1987; Wilson & Young, 1988) and those that examine expressions of social deviance such as crime and juvenile delinquency (e.g., Newman, 1976; Rivers, Sarata, & Anagnostopulos, 1986). Although the literature contains numerous studies on perceptions of psychological deviance, we found relatively few investigations that examined cultural variations in the perception of social deviance and, of these, none that focused on adolescents.

This gap in the literature is surprising given that adolescents, who are in transition to adult society, should be a particularly rich source of information about perceptions of deviance. Some theories suggest that discrepancies that exist between the definitions of deviance of adolescent peer groups and those of adult society may explain, in part, the increase in antisocial behavior that occurs during the adolescent period (e.g., Sutherland, 1947). Even so, we have found no studies in which adolescents were directly asked what they consider to be deviant and none in which comparisons were made of the responses of adolescents and their parents or other adults.

We responded to this gap by exploring the concept of a "bad kid" among samples of high school students and their mothers in three cultures: American, Chinese, and Japanese. Our goals were threefold:

First, we wished to examine cross-cultural differences in perceptions of deviance as expressed in the image of a bad kid. As mentioned earlier, notions of *good* and *bad* represent fundamental aspects of culture that may be reflected in various projective systems. For example,

Funkhouser (1991) studied stereotypes of good and evil by asking college students in five countries to complete a questionnaire while imagining themselves to be, first, a very good person and, then, a very bad person. Ekstrand and Ekstrand (1986) had 9- to 13-year-old Swedish and Indian children and their parents describe what they regarded as good and bad behavior and the sanctions they expected for the latter. None of these studies focused primarily on adolescents and none of them directly compared American respondents with those from East Asian cultures.

We purposefully selected two East Asian cultures for comparison because of their widely diverse histories and cultural traditions and because other investigators have described distinctive attributes of what members of an East Asian society (i.e., Japan) considered a good child (White & LeVine, 1986). Because perceptions of deviance, like perceptions of normalcy, are assumed to be influenced by social values, the description of a bad kid was anticipated to be very different in Japan, Taiwan, and the United States. For example, the high value that Asian cultures traditionally place on education and academic achievement suggests that members of Japanese and Chinese societies would be likely to define a bad kid as someone who disrupts schoolwork and learning. The emphasis on group participation and social cooperation in Japan (e.g., Kojima, 1989; Reischauer, 1977) may also lead Japanese individuals to express more concern about disturbances in interpersonal and other social relationships than would their peers from an individualistic society such as the United States. Similarly, given the overriding importance that Asian cultures, especially the Chinese, place on maintaining order in society and in the family, individuals from these cultures would, to a greater degree than Americans, be expected to associate a bad kid with behavior that disrupts the social or-

der or damages family ties. Finally, the strongly individualistic nature of American culture (Bellah, Madsen, Sullivan, Swidler, & Tipton, 1985), in addition to the high incidence of aggressive and externalizing problem behaviors among adolescents in the United States (Weisz, Suwanlert, Chaiyasit, & Walter, 1987), implies that Americans may define a bad kid in terms of individual psychological characteristics, such as lack of self-control.

A second goal was to examine variables other than culture that might affect definitions of deviance. Perceptions of a bad kid are influenced not only by social values but also by the characteristics of the individuals themselves. We were interested in looking at three characteristics of heightened importance during the adolescent years: success in school, general adjustment, and social skills. For example, students within each culture who value academics or are successful in school may be more disturbed by a peer who disrupts activities at school than would students for whom school plays a less important role. Second, students who report good psychological adjustment may be more likely to consider behaviors related to lack of self-control as being characteristic of a bad kid than students who have less satisfactory adjustment. Third, adolescents who get along well with their peers may be more likely than those who are less adept at social relationships to see disturbances in interpersonal harmony as features of a bad kid.

A final goal was to gain a better understanding of the process by which cultural values and behavioral standards regarding deviance are transmitted to children in the different societies. To do this, we compared adolescents' ideas of a bad kid with those of their mothers. Given the emphasis on individualism in the United States, in contrast to the collectivistic orientation of East Asian cultures (e.g., Triandis, 1987) and the fact that parent-adolescent conflict appears to be less extreme and more subtle in Asian than in American families (Rohlen, 1983; White, 1993), we expected to find a greater degree of concordance in perceptions of deviance among Japanese and Chinese adolescents and mothers than among their American counterparts.

METHOD

Subjects

Data were collected in 1990 and 1991 in three large metropolitan areas: Minneapolis; Taipei, Taiwan; and Sendai, Japan. Respondents included 204 American eleventh-grade students and 204 American mothers, 237 Chinese students and 224 Chinese mothers, and 157 Japanese students and 167 Japanese mothers. Although the intent was to interview both students and their mothers, there were some cases in which students were interviewed but their mothers could not be interviewed and vice versa. In addition, some students and some mothers did not respond to the question about the bad kid. The students, who were selected to constitute a representative sample of children in each city, were part of a longitudinal study that was begun in 1980, when they were in first grade (see Stevenson, Stigler, & Lee, 1986, for a detailed description of sampling procedures and subject selection). The percentages of girls from Minneapolis, Taipei, and Sendai in the present samples were 55%, 49%, and 49%, respectively.

In Minneapolis, consent to participate in the study was obtained directly from the students themselves. In Taipei and Sendai, school authorities were responsible for giving consent. We first obtained permission from the school principal and then sought the cooperation of the teachers. After each teacher's permission was granted, participation from the students was obligatory and universal. Such procedures to obtain consent were those approved by the sponsoring agencies

and the relevant authorities in each city.

The families represented the full range of socioeconomic levels existing in each metropolitan area; however, the occupational and educational status of the families differed. Skilled workers in Japan (51%) and Taiwan (38%) accounted for the largest percentage of fathers' occupations. In the United States, semiprofessional (40%) was the most frequently indicated level of occupation among fathers. The fathers' average number of years in school was 15 in Minneapolis, 11 in Taipei, and 13 in Sendai. Occupational level of the mothers who worked was similar to that of their husbands, but their average number of years of education was lower: 14 in Minneapolis, 9 in Taipei, and 13 in Sendai.

Measures

We took great care in constructing the measures to ensure that the wording of the questions conveyed the same meaning in each language. Members of our research group included bilingual native speakers of Chinese, Japanese, and English. In contrast to the common procedure of translation and back translation, we devised all the items simultaneously in the three languages. Consensus on item selection and wording of the instruments was arrived at through further discussion with bilingual and trilingual colleagues in the United States, Taiwan, and Japan. We believe this process of simultaneous construction of the questions considerably reduced the inconsistencies in nuance that often arise when items are initially written in English and then translated into unrelated languages, such as Chinese and Japanese. Rather than trying to find appropriate words and questions in a second language after the questions have been constructed, simultaneous composition allows discussion of terms by psychologists

familiar with the languages before items are selected.

The items regarding a "bad kid" were part of a questionnaire that was given to students in all three locations.

Bad kid. In line with prior studies defining a good child (e.g., White & LeVine, 1986), we asked both students and their mothers the following question about a bad child: "Think of someone your (child's) age who you would consider to be a 'bad kid.' Describe what kind of person that would be." We also asked whether respondents were thinking of a boy, girl, or someone of no specific gender in answering the question about a bad kid.

It is not difficult to find equivalents for the phrase *bad kid* in Japanese and Chinese. We used the term *warui ko* in the Japanese version of the question, and *huai haizi* in the Chinese. The phrases are simple and straightforward and have approximately the same connotations in each language. For example, in a standard Japanese—English dictionary, examples of the word *warui* (bad) were given in sentences such as "He is a very bad boy—always up to mischief" (Kondo & Takano, 1986, p. 1897). Similarly, the Chinese word for bad—*huai*—was illustrated in a Chinese-English dictionary in the following way: "Bad elements held sway while good people were pushed around" (*Modern Chinese-English Dictionary*, 1988, p. 376).

We developed the coding scheme for the open-ended questions based on an analysis of the answers from subsamples of respondents in each culture. We were able to sort responses into 12 domains of behavior. We have concentrated our attention on the five major domains that appeared to us to be most likely to yield cross-cultural differences: *society, family, school, interpersonal harmony,* and *self-control.* In addition, two more major domains emerged in the analysis of the results: *substance abuse* and *crime.* (Examples of statements included in each domain are given later.) The seven major do-

TABLE 1
Means and Standard Deviations of Measurements of Students' Personal Characteristics

Measure	USA[e]		Taiwan[f]		Japan[g]	
	M	SD	M	SD	M	SD
Value of academics[a]	6.2	1.0	5.5	1.2	5.2	1.3
How important is it to you: (a) that you go to college? (b) that you get good grades? (c) to study hard to go to college? (d) to study hard to get good grades?						
Social relationships[b]	5.5	0.8	4.9	1.0	4.6	1.0
How would you rate yourself in comparison to other persons your age: (a) in getting along with other young people? (b) in working out everyday problems on your own? (c) in caring about others?						
Psychological adjustment[c]						
Stress: How often do you feel stressed (under pressure)?	3.7	1.0	3.4	1.2	2.9	1.3
Depression: How often do you feel depressed?	3.0	1.0	3.3	1.1	2.8	1.2
Aggression: In the past month, how often have you: (a) felt like hitting someone? (b) felt like destroying something (c) gotten into serious arguments or fights with other students? (d) felt angry at your teacher?	2.1	0.8	1.8	0.8	1.8	0.7
Achievement[d]	12.1	7.6	21.8	10.4	20.1	6.6

Note. All *df*s = (2,557–572), Fs = 6.93–75.10, ps < .001.

[a]Answers ranged from *not at all important* (1) to *very important* (7). Cronbach alphas ranged from .67 to .71. [b]Questions used 7-point scales ranging from *much below average* (1) to *much above average* (7). Cronbach alphas ranged from .65 to .74. [c]Students rated the frequency with which they experienced these feelings on 5-point scales ranging from *never* (1) to *almost every day* (5). Cronbach alphas for the aggression ratings ranged from .72 to .77. [d]The test of mathematics achievement (Stevenson, Chen, & Lee, 1993) contained 47 open-ended items covering a broad range of mathematical topics. The Cronbach alphas ranged from .92 to .95. [e]*n* = 190–199. [f]*n* = 221–228. [g]*n* = 147–154.

mains, including substance abuse and crime, accounted for 81% of American, 67% of Chinese, and 89% of Japanese students' responses. The remaining five domains dealt with *religion, sexual behavior, physical appearance, self-destructive behavior,* and *physical aggression.* None of these domains encompassed as many as 10% of the students' responses in each culture and yielded no significant cross-cultural differences. Five percent of American, 4% of Chinese, and 6% of Japanese students' responses were idiosyncratic and could not be categorized under one of the 12 domains.

The domains of behavior were coded according to a common scheme for the three languages and cultures. Responses were coded independently by two native speakers of each language. Each pair resolved any disagreements in coding through discussion between themselves and, if necessary, through group discussion among the coders from all three locations. The percentage of agreement among coders before resolution was 87% (United States), 87% (Taiwan), and 84% (Japan).

Respondents were allowed to give as many characteristics of a bad kid as they wished; however, we coded only the first six responses from each subject. Within the six responses, only one mention of each domain was counted, regardless of the number of examples given by a subject for a particular domain. Thus, we sought to determine the number of respondents in each culture who mentioned each domain, rather than the number of responses given by subjects within each of the domains.

Students also rated themselves on a number of variables, including the degree to which they valued academics, their social relationships, and their psychological adjustment (see Table 1).

RESULTS

Students' Responses

There was little concordance between the responses of the American and the Japanese or Chinese students or between the Chinese and Japanese students (see Table 2). Whereas interpersonal harmony predominated in the responses of the Japanese students, the responses of the American and Chinese students were much more evenly distributed across the five domains (see Figure 1). Consistent with the importance to adolescents of having satisfactory relations with their peers, the highest frequency of response of Chinese and Japanese students and the second highest of American students was interpersonal harmony. More than one third of the American students, however, also mentioned behaviors related to self-control, and more than one third of the Chinese students mentioned school and society. Additionally, American students noted substance abuse more frequently than Chinese and Japanese students, but Japanese students noted crime more frequently than did students in the other two groups. Cross-cultural differences in the percentages of students who mentioned a particular behavioral domain were evaluated by computing chi-square values. When they were found to be significant, a series of pairwise comparisons was conducted to identify possible sources of difference. Alpha levels for these pairwise tests were lowered to *p* < .016, according to the Bonferroni Correction (Neter, Wasserman, & Kutner, 1985).

Society-related behavior. Nearly one and a half times as many Chinese as American adolescents and three times as many Chinese as Japanese adolescents mentioned society-related conduct (i.e., "rebels against society," "makes trouble for society," and "is a member of a street gang") as characteristic of a bad kid. Because of the importance placed in Japan on identifying with the social world, we had anticipated that many more Japanese students would mention society-related behavior.

Family-related behavior. The family-related domain contained responses that referred to behavior such as being disrespectful of or disobedient toward one's parents, running away from home, or physically attacking family members. Contrary to our expectation, Chinese students were no more likely than American students to cite family-related behaviors as being a feature of their image of a bad kid. Both groups mentioned family-related behaviors more frequently than their Japanese peers.

School. Chinese and Japanese students were not more likely, as we had initially posited, than American students to mention behaviors related to school. In fact, nearly three times as many American as Japanese students mentioned misconduct dealing with school as characteristic of a bad kid.

Four major categories of response fell within the domain of school-related behaviors. Two— "skips school" and "having low motivation"—yielded no significant differences. The other two categories were "breaks rules" and teacher-related responses ("disrespectful to the teacher," "scolded by the teacher," and "badmouthing the teacher"). Among the 82 American, 92 Chinese, and 25 Japanese students giving school-related responses, more Japanese (28%) students mentioned breaking rules than did their Chinese (4%) or American (11%) peers, $\chi^2(1, N = 117) = 12.91$, $p < .05$ and $\chi^2(1, N = 107) = 4.37$, $p < .05$, respectively. Chinese (25%) and Japanese (12%) students were more likely, in turn, than American (2%) students to perceive disrespect for teachers as indicative of a bad kid, $\chi^2(1, N = 174) = 17.94$ $p < .05$ and $\chi^2(1, N = 107) = 3.93$, $p < .05$, respectively.

Interpersonal harmony. As anticipated, Japanese students were much more likely than American or Chinese students to view behaviors disruptive of interpersonal harmony ("hurting other people's feelings," "being argumentative and starting fights," "speaking badly of other people," and "not caring about others") as features of a bad kid.

Self-control. Responses that described a bad kid as "weak-willed," "goes to extremes," "childish," or "immature" were included in the do-

main of self-control. As anticipated, more American than Chinese or Japanese students associated a bad kid with problems in self-control.

Substance abuse. The domain of substance abuse primarily contained references to the use of drugs and alcohol. In the United States, the major type of substance abuse mentioned was drugs (81%), whereas in Taiwan and Japan it was alcohol (76% and 80%, respectively). American students were more likely than Chinese students, who, in turn were more likely than Japanese students, to perceive substance abuse as characterizing a bad kid.

Crime. Responses coded in the crime domain mentioned acts ranging from milder crimes, such as stealing and destruction of property, to serious crimes, such as rape and murder. Japanese students noted crime as a feature of a bad kid significantly more often than did Chinese students. There were no significant differences in the percentages of American and Asian students who mentioned crime.

To determine whether disparities within each culture in the socioeconomic status of the families might have had a significant effect on cross-cultural differences in adolescents' perceptions of a bad kid, log linear analyses were performed on the data. Each behavioral domain served as the dependent variable, with location and occupational level comprising the independent variables. No significant interactive or main effects of occupational level were found for any behavioral domain mentioned by the students in analyses involving either mothers' or fathers' occupation.

In summary, relative to their peers in the other two locations, American students emphasized problems with self-control, Chinese students emphasized disturbances of the social order, and Japanese students emphasized disruptions in interpersonal harmony in their descriptions of a bad kid. Students in the United States were as likely as Chinese and more likely than Japa-

TABLE 2
Percentages and Chi-Square Values for United States, Taiwan, and Japan for Analysis of Students' Responses Falling in Various Behavioral Domains

Domain	Percentage of Students			χ^2			
	U	T	J	U-T-J[ae]	U-T[bf]	U-J[cf]	T-J[df]
Society	29	40	14	29.63	7.28*	8.58	28.91
Family	17	24	5	25.01	ns	11.99	25.11
School	43	42	17	32.79	ns	28.77	25.92
Interpersonal harmony	53	50	84	53.19	ns	39.47	48.31
Self-control	38	24	24	13.00	9.44	9.00	ns
Substance abuse	62	40	12	8.90	19.60	89.16	36.54
Crime	10	8	19	10.80	11.5	11.5	9.75*

Note. All ps < .001, except where noted. U = United States. T = Taiwan. J = Japan.
[a]n = 563. [b]n = 411. [c]n = 340. [d]n = 375. [e]df = 2. [f]df = 1.
*p < .01.

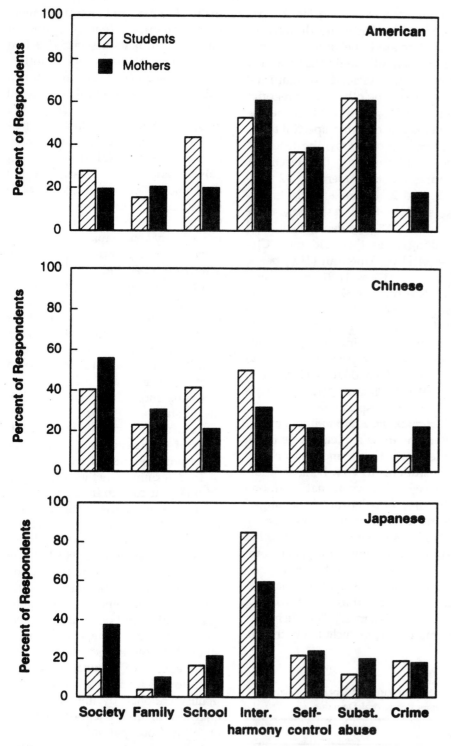

FIGURE 1 Mentions by students and mothers in each culture of the seven behavioral domains

nese students to mention school-related responses. In addition, American students noted substance abuse behaviors more frequently than did students in the other two locations. Japanese students mentioned crime significantly more often than Chinese students. For the most part, these emphases were in accord with the cultural orientations in each location.

Mothers' Responses

We next examined the mothers' impressions of a bad kid (see Figure 1 and Table 3). The most frequent re-sponses of American mothers fell into the domain of interpersonal harmony and self-control. Chinese mothers' responses were most frequently related to society. Japanese mothers gave primary emphasis to disruptions in interpersonal harmony. A relatively high proportion of mothers in the United States and Taiwan mentioned substance abuse. References to crime, however, were mentioned with similar frequencies across the three cultures.

Cross-cultural comparisons. With only two exceptions, cross-national differences in mothers' views of a bad kid were similar to those found for their children. First, the mothers in the three cultures displayed a surprising similarity in the low proportion of their responses that were related to school. Second, American mothers were as likely as Japanese, and twice as likely as Chinese mothers, to include disruptions of interpersonal harmony in their descriptions of a bad kid. In line with expectations, American mothers, like their children, tended to perceive lack of self-control as being characteristic of a bad kid more frequently than did their Chinese or Japanese counterparts. Also, Chinese mothers associated a bad kid with behaviors in the domains of society and family. In addition, American mothers were more likely than Chinese mothers, who, in turn, were more likely than Japanese mothers, to mention substance abuse in their descriptions of a bad kid. There were no significant differences in the percentages of mothers in the three cultures who perceived a bad kid as engaging in criminal behavior.

Log linear analyses were conducted to assess the possible influence of socioeconomic status on cross-cultural differences in mothers' perceptions of deviance. Results indicated that neither fathers' nor mothers' occupational level had any significant interactive or main effects on mothers' definitions of a bad kid.

TABLE 3
Chi-Square Values for United States, Taiwan, and Japan for Analysis of Frequency of
Mothers' Responses Falling in Various Behavioral Domains

Domain	Percentage of Mothers			χ^2			
	U	T	J	U–T–J[a,e]	U–T[b,f]	U–J[c,f]	T–J[d,f]
Society	19	56	37	57.46	57.38	14.33	12.01
Family	20	31	10	21.79	ns	6.61*	21.24
School	20	21	21	ns	ns	ns	ns
Interpersonal harmony	61	32	59	42.64	34.79	ns	27.82
Self-control	39	21	24	17.33	14.75	8.93*	ns
Substance abuse	61	40	20	61.37	17.78	60.50	16.86
Crime	18	22	18	ns	ns	ns	ns

Note. All ps < .001, except where noted. U = United States. T = Taiwan. J = Japan.
[a]$n = 562$. [b]$n = 407$. [c]$n = 356$. [d]$n = 361$. [e]$df = 2$. [f]$df = 1$.
*$p < .016$ (Bonferroni correction).

Comparison of Students and Mothers

We next examined the domains in which adolescents' ideas about a bad kid differed from those of the mothers. As can be seen in Table 4, culture played a major role in determining the nature of the differences. Among the three cultures, American students and mothers evidenced the highest degree of similarity in their perceptions of a bad kid. Only in the school-related domain did the frequency of responses differ between American mothers and students. Adolescents, more than mothers, viewed a bad kid as someone who disrupts activities in school. Chinese students were more likely than Chinese mothers to perceive a bad kid as disturbing school-related activities and interpersonal harmony. Chinese mothers, however, were more likely than students to cite behaviors related to society. Like their Chinese peers, adolescents in Japan referred to interpersonal harmony more often than did the mothers. In contrast, more Japanese mothers than students gave responses that fell in the domains of society and family. There were no significant differences in any of the three cultures in the percentages of responses of students and mothers that referred to substance abuse. Chinese mothers were, however, more likely than Chinese students to include the commission of crimes in their descriptions of a bad kid.

In addition to cross-generational group differences, we also compared the degree of within-family concordance in ideas about a bad kid across the three cultures (see Table 5). *Concordance* was defined as the number of agreements between adolescents and their mothers regarding a specific domain of bad kid behavior divided by the total number of adolescent-mother pairs in a particular culture. We then calculated T values to determine the significance of cross-cultural differences in the percentages of concordance.

Cross-national differences in the pattern of within-family concordance regarding notions of a bad kid were less consistent than those found in the cross-generational group comparisons. American and Chinese students and their mothers exhibited higher concordance in their view of a bad kid as disrupting school-related activities than did their Japanese counterparts. Adolescents and their mothers in the United States were more likely to agree that a bad kid lacked self-control than were their peers in Taiwan and Japan. Similarly, Chinese students and their mothers were in greater agreement than American and Japanese students and their mothers that disruptive behaviors related to family and society characterized a bad kid. In perceiving a bad kid as someone who disturbs interpersonal harmony, Japanese students and their mothers demonstrated a significantly higher degree of concordance than did their American and Chinese peers. Additionally, American students and their mothers demonstrated a much higher degree of concordance than their Chinese and Japanese counterparts in their mention of substance abuse as a feature of a bad kid. There were no significant cross-cultural differences in the degree of concordance with which students and their mothers described a bad kid as someone who commits a crime.

TABLE 4
Percentages and Chi-Square Values for Evaluating the Similarity of Students' and
Mothers' Responses Regarding Domains of Bad Kid Behavior

Domain	USA[a]			Taiwan[b]			Japan[c]		
	Percentage			Percentage			Percentage		
	Students	Mothers	χ^2	Students	Mothers	χ^2	Students	Mothers	χ^2
Society	28	19	ns	40	56	9.66*	15	37	19.80
Family	15	20	ns	23	31	ns	4	10	ns
School	44	20	24.29	41	21	19.69	16	21	ns
Interpersonal harmony	53	61	ns	50	32	13.95	85	59	23.52
Self-control	37	39	ns	23	21	ns	22	24	ns
Substance abuse	62	61	ns	40	40	ns	12	20	ns
Crime	10	18	ns	8	22	17.06	19	18	ns

Note. All ps < .001, except where noted.
[a]$n = 389$. [b]$n = 429$. [c]$n = 307$.
*$p < .01$.

In general, adolescents and mothers differed significantly in the frequency with which they mentioned behaviors falling under the five major behavioral domains, but within-family comparisons yielded even less concordance between students and their mothers. The domains in which significant discrepancies emerged were those that apparently were the most crucial to students in each of the cultures: school-related behavior in the United States and interpersonal harmony and society-related behavior in Taiwan and Japan. The direction of these differences—students emphasizing school and interpersonal harmony, mothers emphasizing society—suggests the broader, more conventional perspective of the mothers, in contrast to the more personal viewpoint of the students.

In terms of within-family concordance, American students and their mothers were in greater agreement that a bad kid lacked self-control, Chinese students and their mothers that a bad kid disrupted society and family, and Japanese students and their mothers that a bad kid disturbed interpersonal harmony, than were their counterparts in the other two cultures. In addition, American adolescents and their mothers exhibited a much greater degree of concordance regarding the mention of substance abuse than did their Chinese and Japanese peers. Generally, the domains in which cross-national

differences in within-family concordance were the greatest appeared to conform to the social values that are emphasized in each of the cultures.

Correlates of Student Mentions of Bad-Kid Behaviors

Finally, we sought to determine whether the personal characteristics of the adolescents themselves were related to ones they associated with a bad kid. To evaluate whether these characteristics were related to the likelihood that a student would mention behavior in a specific domain, we formed high and low groups on each of the six measures described in Table 1. Students were included in a high group if their ratings on the measures or mathematics test scores fell within the upper third of the students in their respective cultures. Students in the lower third constituted the low group.

We performed log linear analyses using location and one of the student characteristics as the independent variables and each behavioral domain as the dependent variable. To test for significant effects, factors in the model were systematically omitted over successive analyses, and differences in the -2 log likelihood statistics, which are distributed as chi-square values, were examined. We report these chi-square values in describing main and interaction effects.

There was little relation between the characteristics of the students and their descriptions of a bad kid. Only one main effect was significant. Students who held a high value for academics mentioned deviant behavior in school as characterizing a bad kid more often than did students who did not value academics (44% vs. 25%), $\chi^2(1, N = 384) = 8.36$, $p < .01$.

Gender Differences

Log linear analyses were also used to assess the effects of gender on the likelihood that students in different cultures would include a certain domain of behavior in their concept of a bad kid. Main effects of gender were found in the domains of school and family, $\chi^2(1, N = 563) = 7.59$, $p < .01$ and $\chi^2(1, N = 563) = 8.40$, $p < .01$. Girls were more likely than boys to view a bad kid as someone who disrupted school activities (41% vs. 29%) and damaged family ties (19% vs. 11%). No significant gender X country interactions emerged.

When asked whether they were thinking of a boy, girl, or someone of no specific gender in answering the question about the bad kid, the majority of students in all three countries reported that they were thinking of someone of no specific gender (see Figure 2). Furthermore, there were significantly more students in the United States and Taiwan who said they thought of a boy than those who said they thought of a girl, $\chi^2(1, N = 347)$ 22.82, $= p < .01$ and $\chi^2(1, N = 396) = 9.46$, $p < .01$, respectively. In contrast, Japanese students were far more likely than their American and Chinese peers to think of a girl, $\chi^2(1, N = 347) = 21.42$, $p < .001$ and $\chi^2(1, N = 396) = 22.40$, $p < .001$, respectively. Boys in all three countries more often thought of a bad kid as someone of their own gender than did girls (United States: 56% versus 35%, $\chi^2[1, N = 190] = 8.71$, $p < .01$; Taiwan: 49% versus 20%, $\chi^2[1, N = 239] = 22.08$, $p < .001$; Japan: 34% versus 7%, $\chi^2[1, N = 157] = 17.36$, $p < .001$). American (9% vs.

TABLE 5
Correlations of Mothers' and Their Children's Conceptions of Bad Kid Behavior
(Percentage of Pairs in Which Both Mother and Child Mentioned Some Item Falling
Within Each Domain)

Domain	Country			t		
	U^a	T^b	J^c	$U-T$	$U-J$	$T-J$
Society	.03	.21	.07	5.81	ns	4.06
Family	.04	.09	.01	2.11*	ns	4.82
School	.12	.11	.03	ns	3.23	3.10
Interpersonal harmony	.35	.17	.51	6.32	3.74	6.95
Self-control	.18	.04	.03	4.67	5.00	ns
Substance abuse	.41	.02	.02	10.26	10.26	ns
Crime	.02	.01	.03	ns	ns	ns

Note. U = United States. T = Taiwan. J = Japan. All *ps* < .001, except where noted.
$^a n = 182.$ $^b n = 204.$ $^c n = 146.$
*$p < .05$.

0%) and Japanese (33% vs. 8%), but not Chinese (9% vs 2%), girls thought of a girl significantly more often than did their male peers (United States: χ^2 [1, N = 190] = 7.98, p < .01; Japan, χ^2[1, N = 157] = 15.28, p <. 001).

DISCUSSION

When we began this study, we focused on five domains of behavior that we believed would lead to different definitions of a bad kid in American, Chinese, and Japanese cultures. Although our analyses yielded 12 different domains of behavior, 7 were sufficient to encompass the vast majority of the behaviors mentioned. Although there were differences in the degree to which these broad domains were represented among the three cultures, we also found commonalities across the cultures. For example, *disruptions in interpersonal harmony* was a dominant response in all three locations, reflecting the common pattern of adapting to the peer group and to the cultural demands faced by adolescents in all societies.

Interesting cross-cultural differences did emerge. Adolescents and mothers differed significantly in the frequency with which they mentioned behaviors falling under the five major behavioral domains. Students seemed to conceive of deviance from a more personal, circumscribed perspective, in contrast to the mothers, whose descriptions of a bad kid more consistently suggested broader, conventional concerns, a finding that agrees with that of Smetana (1988). In other words, students' perceptions of a bad kid tended to deviate more from expected cultural values than did those of the mothers, apparently reflecting the transitional nature of the socialization process that characterizes the adolescent period in the three societies (e.g., Chang, 1989; White, 1993).

Cross-cultural differences in the degree of within-family concordance

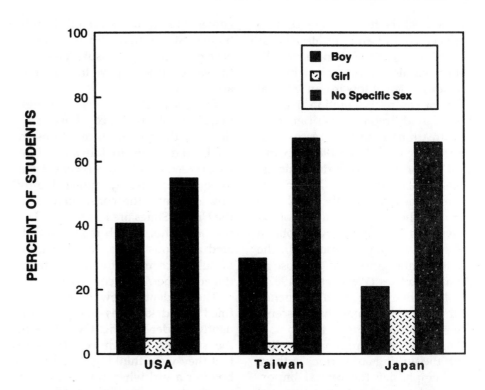

FIGURE 2 Percentages of students thinking of a boy, girl, or someone of no specific gender when describing a bad kid.

in perceptions of a bad kid were generally found in those domains that appear to represent the most prominent social values in each culture. American adolescents and their mothers exhibited higher concordance in the domain of self-control; Chinese adolescents and their mothers showed a greater level of agreement in the domains of society and family; and Japanese adolescents and their mothers were most likely to agree about the domain of interpersonal harmony. These results suggest that the nature of the socialization process by which perceptions of deviance are transmitted from mothers to children is basically similar in the three cultures. That is, in all three locations, the criteria that mothers deemed as being most important in defining an individual as bad were generally reflected in the responses of their adolescent children.

The concept of a bad kid found among American, Chinese, and Japanese high school students and their mothers, although generally

consistent with the social values espoused in the three cultures, did not necessarily accord with the actual prevalence of deviant behavior in each of the cultures. For example, a higher percentage of Chinese than American students mentioned society-related behavior, despite the fact that Taiwan has a much lower incidence of antisocial behavior than does the United States (Federal Bureau of Investigation, 1990; Ministry of the Interior, Republic of China, 1989). Similarly, a much larger percentage of Japanese than American students cited disruptions in interpersonal harmony in their descriptions of a bad kid, even though interstudent conflict in Japan is not more pervasive or serious than it is in the United States (Federal Bureau of Investigation, 1990; Headquarters of the Youth and Children Program, General Affairs Division, 1989).

The tendency of American students to define a bad kid in terms of lack of self-control is consonant with the work of Tropman (1986) who pointed out the fundamental conflict between control and permissiveness in American culture. A focus on self-control is also compatible with the greater tendency toward an internal locus of control orientation that has been found among American, relative to Chinese and Japanese, individuals (e.g., Chiu, 1986; Evans, 1981). In addition, American adolescents' descriptions of a bad kid as someone lacking in self-control concur with the higher frequency of externalizing and aggressive problem behaviors among adolescents in the United States compared to those in Asian countries (Weisz et al., 1987).

The remarkably high frequency with which Japanese adolescents mentioned behaviors in the domain of interpersonal harmony is in line with the writings of various authors who emphasize the central importance Japanese give to interpersonal consensus and cooperation (e.g., Kojima, 1989; Reischauer, 1977).

The importance of maintaining order and tranquility in the society and in family relationships is a cornerstone of Confucian philosophy upon which much of Chinese culture is based. This traditional emphasis is reflected in the frequent mention of society- and family-related behaviors among the Chinese respondents in our study. (The Chinese culture in Taiwan, it should be noted, tends to be more traditional in terms of customs and values than that in Hong Kong or Mainland China.)

In some cases, the students' responses departed greatly from what we expected on the basis of presumed cultural values. For example, students in the United States mentioned disruptive behaviors at school as characteristic of a bad kid more frequently than did students in Japan. One explanation is that American students place a higher value on school and academic achievement than do their counterparts in Japan, where education and learning are thought to be held in especially high esteem. In support of this explanation, we found that American

adolescents indicated significantly higher ratings than did their Japanese peers on our measure assessing the value students gave to academic achievement.

Of special interest was the high frequency of substance abuse, particularly drug-related, mentions in the United States. In Taiwan and Japan, possession of drugs is considered to be a serious felony, punishable by imprisonment; the consequences in the United States are less severe. The use of alcohol, which is not considered a serious crime, was the form of substance more frequently mentioned in the Asian countries.

The students' view of what defined a bad kid was not predominantly gender-specific: Over 50% of the students in each country said that they were thinking of neither a boy nor a girl when they answered the question about the bad kid. Nevertheless, when students did reply that they were thinking of a person of a specific gender, boys more than girls said that they were thinking of someone of their own gender. These findings are consistent with statistics showing that adolescent boys are more likely to engage in deviant behavior than are adolescent girls (Federal Bureau of Investigation, 1990).

Just as efforts to describe a good kid (White & LeVine, 1986) have yielded interesting insights into cultural differences, this exploratory study of the definitions of a bad kid given by adolescents and their mothers adds to our understanding of the socialization of cultural values in American and East Asian societies. These high school students' responses differed according to culture, as did those of their mothers; but adolescents and mothers were not always in agreement as to which behaviors defined a bad kid.

ACKNOWLEDGMENTS

This study was supported by National Science Foundation Grant MDR 89564683 to Harold W. Stevenson. The collection of the data in Taiwan was supported by National Science Council of R.O.C. Grants No. NSC 79-80-81-0301-H-006-08Y to Chen-Chin Hsu and Huei-Chen Ko.

We thank our colleagues, Shinying Lee and Kazuo Kato, and all the other people who have participated in this study. We are indebted to Yann-Yann Shieh, Kathy Kolb, Susan Fust, Heidi Schweingruber, and Etsuko Horikawa, to our research coordinators, and to the teachers and students for their cooperation. We also thank Chuansheng Chen for his helpful comments on the manuscript.

REFERENCES

Becker, H. (1964). *Outsiders*. Glencoe, IL: Free Press.

Bellah, R. N., Madsen, R., Sullivan, W. M., Swidler, A., & Tipton, S. M. (1985). *Habits of the heart: Individualism and commitment in American life*. Berkeley: University of California Press.

Chang, C. (1989). The growing generation in a changing Chinese society: Youth problems and strategies. *Bulletin of Educational Psychology, 22*, 243–254.

Chiu, L.-H. (1986). Locus of control in intellectual situations in American and Chinese schoolchildren. *International Journal of Psychology, 21*, 167–176.

Evans, H. M. (1981). Internal-external locus of control and work association: Research with Japanese and American students. *Journal of Cross-Cultural Psychology, 12*, 372–382.

Ekstrand, G., & Ekstrand, L. H. (1986). How children perceive parental norms and sanctions in two different cultures. *Educational and Psychological Interactions, 88*, p. 28.

Federal Bureau of Investigation. (1990). *Uniform crime reports for the United States*. Washington, DC: United States Government Printing Office.

Funkhouser, G. R. (1991). Cross-cultural similarities and differences in stereotypes of good and evil: A pilot study. *Journal of Social Psychology, 131*, 859–874.

Hardy, R. E., Cull, J. G., & Campbell, M. E. (1987). Perception of selected disabilities in the United States and Portugal: A cross-cultural comparison. *Journal of Human Behavior and Learning, 4*, 1–12.

Headquarters of the Youth and Children Program, General Affairs Division (1989) Seishonen hakusho, heisei gannenpan [Adolescent white paper, 1989]. Tokyo, Japan: Okurasho.

Kondo, I., & Takano, F. (Eds.). (1986). *Progressive Japanese-English dictionary.* Tokyo: Shogakkan.

Kojima, H. (1989). *Kosodate no dento o tazunete* [Inquiring into the tradition of childrearing]. Tokyo, Japan: Shinyosha.

LeVine, R. A. (1973). *Culture, behavior and personality.* Chicago: Aldine.

Modern Chinese-English Dictionary. (1988). Beijing, People's Republic of China: Foreign Language and Teaching Research Press.

Ministry of the Interior, Republic of China (1989). *Crime statistics.* Taipei, Taiwan: Ministry of the Interior.

Neter, J., Wasserman, W., & Kutner, M. (1985). *Applied linear statistical models.* Homewood, IL: Irwin.

Newman, G. (1976). *Comparative deviance: Perception and law in six cultures.* New York: Elsevier.

Reischauer, E. O. (1977). *The Japanese.* Cambridge, MA: Harvard University Press.

Rivers, P. C., Sarata, B. P., & Anagnostopulos, M. (1986). Perceptions of deviant stereotypes by alcoholism, mental health, and school personnel in New Zealand and the United States. *International Journal of the Addictions, 21,* 123–129.

Robin, M. W., & Spires, R. (1983). Drawing the line: Deviance in cross-cultural perspective. *International Journal of Group Tensions, 13,* 106–131.

Rohlen, T. (1983). *Japanese high schools.* Berkeley: University of California Press.

Scheff, T. S. (1974). The labelling theory of mental illness. *American Sociological Review, 39,* 444–452.

Smetana, J. G. (1988). Adolescents' and parents' conceptions of parental authority. *Child Development, 59,* 321–335.

Stevenson, H. W., Chen, C., & Lee, S. Y. (1993). Mathematics achievement Chinese, Japanese, and American children: Ten years later. *Science, 259,* 53–58.

Stevenson, H. W., Lee, S. Y., & Stigler, J. W. (1986). Mathematics achievement of Chinese, Japanese, and American children. *Science, 231,* 693–699.

Sutherland, E. (1947). *Principles of criminology.* Philadelphia, PA: Lippincott.

Triandis, H. C. (1987). Collectivism vs. individualism: A reconceptualization of a basic concept in cross-cultural social psychology. In C. Bagley & G. K. Verma (Eds.), *Personality, cognition and values: Cross-cultural perspectives of childhood and adolescence.* London: MacMillan.

Tropman, J. E. (1986). *Conflict in culture: Permissions versus controls and alcohol use in American society.* Lanham, MD: University Press of America.

Weisz, J. R., Suwanlert, S., Chaiyasit, W., & Walter, B. R. (1987). Over- and undercontrolled referral problems among children and adolescents from Thailand and the United States: The *wat* and *wai* of cultural differences. *Journal of Consulting and Clinical Psychology, 55,* 719–726.

White, M. (1993). *The material child: Coming of age in Japan and America.* New York: Free Press.

White, M. I., & LeVine, R. A. (1986). What is an *ii ko* (good child)? In H. Stevenson, H. Azuma, & K. Hakuta (Eds.), *Child development and education in Japan.* New York: Freeman.

Wilson, L. G., & Young, D. (1988). Diagnosis of severely ill inpatients in China: A collaborative project using the Structured Clinical Interview for DSM-III (SCID). *Journal of Nervous and Mental Disease, 176,* 585–592.

Received August 14, 1993
Revision received June 14, 1993
Accepted November 18, 1993

HIV Infected Youth Speaks About Needs for Support and Health Care

Wayne Davis is a 24-year-old, HIV positive youth from Oregon who became infected when he was 17. He currently lives in San Francisco and is the coordinator of the HIV Positive Youth Speakers Bureau, sponsored by Health Initiatives for Youth. He recently shared his personal experiences with the editor of Target 2000, stating that it sounded important to have the opportunity to let adolescent health care providers know about the needs of HIV infected youth. The following is his story.

Early Lessons in Life

I think in order to explain how I got where I am today, I have to go back a little earlier than when I actually tested positive for the virus. Most of my life from birth to the age of 9, I was with my mother and she was very abusive. Everyday she beat me. As she beat me she would say things like "this is your fault" and "if only you were a better child I wouldn't beat you like this. I would be a better mother if you were a better child." That taught me that things were my fault. It taught me guilt. It taught me to really feel bad about myself.

I had an uncle who was sexually abusive. He molested my brother and me. That taught me that my body wasn't mine and that other people had the right to do to me whatever they wanted to do. All of my messages growing up were very unhealthy. When I was 9, my mother left and joined the Hare Krishna's. Mental illness runs in my family, my grandmother was really strange and my mother is unstable mentally. She needed other people to run her life. She went through churches and different places to do this. When she joined the Hare Krishna's, I was in a foster home. She wrote us and said "some day you will understand but I have to leave." You know your mother is supposed to be there no matter what. It's a given. It's a very solid form of support. It's fundamental, regardless of how messed up she is, she is supposed to be there. So, her leaving taught me that I can't trust people, I can't trust my environment, I can't trust people to be there. That made me kind of bitter.

I started running away. I had run away before but I started running away to the streets. This was different because before I was running away from the beatings. When I went to the streets I found a real community. I found people who were willing to take care of me, be my friend, and treat me like I had decisions to make. That was really important to me. So I started to run away "to" things instead of "from" things. I started running away to my family on the streets.

Life on the Streets

There are few things that you can do on the streets to survive and being 9 years old there are even fewer things. You could rob people but I was too little. You could do burglaries but I got caught doing that. I couldn't deal drugs because I didn't have the heart for it. There was only one thing left that I could do. That was to sell myself. It made perfect sense to me because all I had known was hurt and that my body wasn't mine. All I had known was that I should feel bad about myself. That just fit right in. I started doing that and it's hard selling yourself on the streets. It really takes something out of you.

The only way that I could live with myself or the only way that I could deal with the pain that I was putting myself through was to do drugs. So I started shooting up speed when I was about 10, which for the first time in my life, I remember clearly I felt like I was in control. I felt that nobody could hurt me or do anything to me. No matter what anybody did I could deal with it. That was a really good feeling. It took foreign substances to make me feel like that but I didn't care. I felt like it and that's what was important. So, that was pretty much my life.

I would run away to the streets and stay gone from the juvenile system for anywhere from a couple of days to a couple of months. I would get caught and, since I was on probation for stealing, they would hold me for 8 days in juvenile hall and then place me into a foster home or group home. I would be there for all of about

3 hours and I would leave. I did that over and over again. All together I've been in 18 different group homes and 26 different foster homes. Finally they didn't have anywhere to send me. They ran out of places to put me so they committed me to the juvenile jail.

One Foster Home

I met a security guard at the juvenile jail who helped me to run away. He befriended me and treated me nice but while I was a runaway, he abused me. He pedophiled me. I remember at one point we were on the lake shooting at bottles and he turned to me and said, "what would stop me from raping you and killing you right now?" I remember I was thinking really hard about what I could say. I told him that I had called my sister and told her where I was and gave her his license plate number. He said, oh that's a good answer. I turned myself in to him and then went back to juvenile hall. They released me and I was back on the streets for awhile. I was about 14 then.

I was doing drugs for a while and I woke up one morning in a pair of shorts. I was in Portland, Oregon in the middle of winter which was really cold. I had the phone number of this security guard in my pocket so I called him up and he came and got me. I lived with him for about $1^{1}/_{2}$ years. I became a foster child of his and I received some really mixed messages from him. On the one hand, he was a real father figure which I had never had. He taught me how to hunt, how to fish, how to farm, and how to be what I felt was a man. On the other hand, at night time I was going to his room and he was having sex with me. It was really a mixed up time of my life. Then he started getting other foster children and ended up getting 6 or 7 other foster children ranging from the age of 9 to 14. I figured out that he was messing with them too and he kicked me out. So I went back to the streets. I felt so bad about myself because I knew what was going on in his home and I just did my best to block it out of my mind by using a lot of drugs.

Down and Out — With HIV

I had heard about HIV. What I was hearing was that if you get it you die and that older gay men get it. I figured out that there was a lot [of] attention that went along with HIV. I was hanging out with this guy who was HIV positive. He was young. He was 23 and he had access to money and to drugs. I did a pile of coke about the size of my fist for about a period of a day with him one time. At the end of it, I was coming down and feeling really bad. I looked at him and realized that he had my way out. I was hurting so bad that I just realized that he could help me out. He could stop my hurting. So I told him to give me his blood and he came over and he did.

So, October 16, 1988, I infected myself. It was strange because when I took the needle out of my arm, I didn't feel any different. For some reason I thought I would feel better. I thought something would change like some sparks would go off or I would become animated or feel better. I didn't. I was still here. I had been tested before that and I had tested negative. A couple days after this incident, I got really sick and went into the hospital. About 6 months later, I tested positive.

I remember when I tested, it was a confidential test. It was the type of place where you had to give a name. It didn't necessarily have to be yours. For some reason I gave them my real name. They called me back and told me to come in and get my results. So there was this woman from the Salvation Army Greenhouse named Margie who was really supportive of me. She is one of the few solid influences I had in my life. I asked her to go with me and she did. She had been diagnosed with cancer before. She had gone into remission and she knew what it was like to be told that you have a life threatening illness. She told me it was good idea to take somebody to hear what was being said because I wouldn't hear anything if I tested positive. She was right. She went in with me and we sat down and they told me that I tested positive to the HIV virus and all I could hear was mumbling and I was kind of just nodding my head. I think I was doing it at the right time.

For the next four years, all I did was get loaded. I don't really remember a lot about it. The things I do remember were really traumatic. I know I hurt a lot of people and myself a lot. I slept with a lot of people. Most of them I used condoms with and a lot of times I didn't. I didn't care. People were items, commodities, things. I was only a thing and that was as deep as people went.

A Move to San Francisco and to Medical Care

When I was 19, I ended up coming down to San Francisco because I was shot at in Portland. When I got here the drugs were better and so I decided to live here. Somebody from Portland told me to go to the Larkin Street Youth Center (see interview on page 4) and get myself "hooked up." I went to Larkin Street and talked with Mike Kennedy. I dressed up to go there. I was trying to show everybody how together I was. When I first meet people, I am really good at being presentable. Somehow or another they knew that I needed to be there. They hooked me up with medical care.

This was the first point in my whole life that I ever had solid medical care. It was a real strange adjustment.

There was a woman there named Susan Wayne, a nurse practitioner, who is really awesome. Every time she saw me, she was really supportive. She wasn't pushy, just supportive. She found the right balance with me. I started seeing her and developed a trust with her. So I started going in for my medical care. When I first started going I went when I was feeling really sick or when I had crabs or whatever. Slowly I went into this phase where I went every couple of weeks to check in. That was cool too. She gave me a little examination and then just sat down and talked with me a couple of minutes. It made me feel like I could be there and didn't have to have a reason. Then I started going when I needed to or just for regular check ups.

I realized during that time how much I was hurting myself. I was trying to find a way to not be hurting myself anymore. I had taken 175 Elavil to overdose and went into a coma. I just wanted to die. I realized that no matter what I tried I wasn't going to die and that I couldn't live the way I was living. So I decided that I needed to change my life. And that's what I did.

At Larkin Street, I was also hooked up with a case manager who was really helpful. When I went into the coma, the case manager was the first person I saw when I woke up. In a lot of ways I found a family. They all gave me the opportunity to try time and time again to help myself. They didn't try to push it on me. That was the key. It was like I picture myself in this room surrounded by doors. Every time a door opens up, it is an opportunity. I have to be looking at the door and get up. I have to have the motivation to walk over to the door, walk through it, and stay through it for the opportunities to happen. All the time I'm sitting there, all of these doors are opening and closing and people are crawling from the doors. It makes a combination of everything being set up at once for a person to be able to change in any direction. At the clinic, they just kept opening the doors. The opportunities empowered me and got me to the clinic when I was sick. More than once, people from the clinic came and got me and took me to where I needed to go — to the clinic or detox or wherever. There were opportunities for drug and alcohol abuse treatment and getting me to the hospital.

A New Life With Help From a Treatment Program

My case manager helped me check into a program called Walden House. It is a behavior modification program. I started learning the fundamental ways to deal with life that I had missed out on while growing up. Life is a rough thing to live in. If you miss out when you are young on how to deal with life, you have a really hard time. That's what they taught me. They taught me how to deal with life. Because I was leaving the streets, I switched my care from Larkin Street to the Cole Street Clinic. I saw the same nurse practitioner. That was really good because I had established a real trust with her.

Deciding What Is Important in Primary Care

I don't go to the Cole Street Clinic anymore. The nurse practitioner moved away and I was getting to the age anyway, where I decided to change my primary care. I found a nurse practitioner who isn't necessarily the most educated person on HIV but when I asked her about it she said that she was really willing to learn. She is a part of the UCSF hospital and they have special HIV services there. I really trust her so I decided this was the right choice.

When I went searching for health care providers, I decided that I wanted a nurse practitioner instead of a doctor. I have found in general, though this isn't always the case, but my experience is that the doctors think they really know everything. But HIV is something that nobody knows everything about. It is important for me to be in the driver's seat regarding what I'm going to do to take care of myself. There are so many different therapies, if I say I don't want to take AZT, I don't want some doctors telling me that I am going to die if I don't. I do a lot of research and need to be in control of my health. I need to work with the provider and have the provider work with me, instead of being told what to do. My experience has been that nurse practitioners are more education oriented and present me with options.

A Better Life

I've been in a relationship now for about 2 1/2 years. We're moving in together in about a month. She's negative. Sex is really hard to deal with in the relationship. If she isn't afraid, I am. If I'm not afraid, she's afraid. There are a lot of other issues to worry about, like what if I die. What if I get sick? So there is a lot more to deal with in this relationship besides the regular issues of being in a relationship. There are a lot of things that go along with one partner being HIV positive and one being negative.

Since I entered the treatment program I've been working with young people at risk. I've been trying to spread the word where I can. I go to schools to speak. I am the coordinator for the speakers bureau now, which is really a big step for me. My life is about healing people, healing myself, and about teaching people some of the things that I've learned along the way. Today I know that I don't have to hurt myself. I know that I don't have to let anybody touch me that I don't want to. I don't have to lie to somebody or do what it was that I used to do just to survive. Today I know that there is a different way. And that's pretty much my story.

PSYCHOTRENDS

Taking Stock of Tomorrow's Family and Sexuality

Where are we going and what kind of people are we becoming? Herewith, a road map to the defining trends in sexuality, family, and relationships for the coming millenium as charted by the former chair of Harvard's psychiatry department. From the still-rollicking sexual revolution to the painful battle for sexual equality to the reorganization of the family, America is in for some rather interesting times ahead.

Shervert H. Frazier, M.D.

Has the sexual revolution been side-tracked by AIDS, and the return to traditional values we keep hearing about? In a word, no. The forces that originally fueled the revolution are all still in place and, if anything, are intensifying: mobility, democratization, urbanization, women in the workplace, birth control, abortion and other reproductive interventions, and media proliferation of sexual images, ideas, and variation.

Sexuality has moved for many citizens from church- and state-regulated behavior to a medical and self-regulated behavior. Population pressures and other economic factors continue to diminish the size of the American family. Marriage is in sharp decline, cohabitation is growing, traditional families are on the endangered list, and the single-person household is a wave of the future.

AIDS has generated a great deal of heat in the media but appears to have done little, so far, to turn down the heat in the bedroom. It is true that in some surveys people *claimed* to have made drastic changes in behavior—but most telling are the statistics relating to marriage, divorce, cohabitation, teen sex, out-of-wedlock births, sexually transmitted diseases (STDs), contraception,

and adultery. These are far more revealing of what we *do* than what we *say* we do. And those tell a tale of what has been called a "postmarital society" in continued pursuit of sexual individuality and freedom.

Studies reveal women are more sexual now than at any time in the century.

Arguably there are, due to AIDS, fewer visible sexual "excesses" today than there were in the late 1960s and into the 1970s, but those excesses (such as sex clubs, bathhouses, backrooms, swinging singles, group sex, public sex acts, etc.) were never truly reflective of norms and were, in any case, greatly inflated in the media. Meanwhile, quietly and without fanfare, the public, even in the face of the AIDS threat, has continued to expand its interest in sex and in *increased*, rather than decreased, sexual expression.

Numerous studies reveal that women are more sexual now than at any time in the century. Whereas sex counselors used to deal with men's complaints about their wives' lack of "receptivity," it is now more often the women complaining about the men. And women, in this "postfeminist"

era, are doing things they never used to believe were "proper." Fellatio, for example, was seldom practiced (or admitted to) when Kinsey conducted his famous sex research several decades ago. Since that time, according to studies at UCLA and elsewhere, this activity has gained acceptance among women, with some researchers reporting that nearly all young women now practice fellatio.

Women's images of themselves have also changed dramatically in the past two decades, due, in large part, to their movement into the workplace and roles previously filled exclusively by men. As Lilian Rubin, psychologist at the University of California Institute for the Study of Social Change and author of *Intimate Strangers*, puts it, "Women feel empowered sexually in a way they never did in the past."

Meanwhile, the singles scene, far from fading away (the media just lost its fixation on this subject), continues to grow. James Bennett, writing in *The New Republic*, characterizes this growing population of no-reproducers thusly: "Single adults in America display a remarkable tendency to multiply without being fruitful."

Their libidos are the target of million-dollar advertising budgets and entrepreneurial pursuits that seek to put those sex drives on line in the information age. From video dating to computer coupling to erotic faxing, it's now "love at first

From *Psychology Today*, January/February 1994, pp. 32-37, 64, 66. Excerpted from *Psychotrends: What Kind of People Are We Becoming?* by Shervert H. Frazier, M.D. © 1994 by Shervert H. Frazier, M.D. Reprinted by permission of Simon & Schuster, Inc.

byte," as one commentator put it. One thing is certain: the computer is doing as much today to promote the sexual revolution as the automobile did at the dawn of that revolution.

Political ideologies, buttressed by economic adversities, *can* temporarily retard the sexual revolution, as can sexually transmitted diseases. But ultimately the forces propelling this revolution are unstoppable. And ironically, AIDS itself is probably doing more to promote than impede this movement. It has forced the nation to confront a number of sexual issues with greater frankness than ever before. While some conservatives and many religious groups have argued for abstinence as the only moral response to AIDS, others have lobbied for wider dissemination of sexual information, beginning in grade schools. A number of school districts are now making condoms available to students—a development that would have been unthinkable before the outbreak of AIDS.

Despite all these gains (or losses, depending upon your outlook) the revolution is far from over. The openness that it has fostered is healthy, but Americans are still ignorant about many aspects of human sexuality. Sexual research is needed to help us deal with teen sexuality and pregnancies, AIDS, and a number of emotional issues related to sexuality. Suffice it to say for now that there is still plenty of room for the sexual revolution to proceed—and its greatest benefits have yet to be realized.

THE REVOLUTION AND RELATIONSHIPS

The idea that the Sexual Revolution is at odds with romance (not to mention tradition) is one that is widely held, even by some of those who endorse many of the revolution's apparent objectives. But there is nothing in our findings to indicate that romance and the sexual revolution are inimical—unless one's defense of romance disguises an agenda of traditional male dominance and the courtly illusion of intimacy and communication between the sexes.

The trend now, as we shall see, is away from illusion and toward—in transition, at least—a sometimes painful reality in which the sexes are finally making an honest effort to *understand* one another.

But to some, it may seem that the sexes are farther apart today than they

ever have been. The real gender gap, they say, is a communications gap so cavernous that only the most intrepid or foolhardy dare try to bridge it. Many look back at the Anita Hill affair and say that was the open declaration of war between the sexes.

The mistake many make, however, is saying that there has been a *recent* breakdown in those communications, hence all this new discontent. This conclusion usually goes unchallenged, but there is nothing in the data we have seen from past decades to indicate that sexual- and gender-related communication were ever better than they are today. On the contrary, a more thoughtful analysis makes it very clear they have always been *worse*.

What has changed is our *consciousness* about this issue. Problems in communication between the sexes have been masked for decades by a rigid social code that strictly prescribes other behavior. Communication between the sexes has long been preprogrammed by this code to produce an exchange that has been as superficial as it is oppressive. As this process begins to be exposed by its own inadequacies in a rapidly changing world, we suddenly discover that we have a problem. But, of course, that problem was there for a long time, and the discovery does not mean a decline in communication between the sexes but, rather, provides us with the potential for better relationships in the long run.

Thus what we call a "breakdown" in communications might more aptly be called a *breakthrough*.

Seymour Parker, of the University of Utah, demonstrated that men who are the most mannerly with women, those who adhere most strictly to the "code" discussed above, are those who most firmly believe, consciously or unconsciously, that women are "both physically and psychologically weaker (i.e., less capable) than men." What has long passed for male "respect" toward women in our society is, arguably, *disrespect*.

Yet what has been learned can be unlearned—especially if women force the issue, which is precisely what is happening now. Women's views of themselves are changing and that, more than anything, is working to eliminate many of the stereotypes that supported the image of women as weak and inferior. Women, far from letting men continue to dictate to them, are making it clear they want more *real* respect from men and will accept

nothing less. They want a genuine dialogue; they want men to recognize that they speak with a distinct and equal voice, not one that is merely ancillary to the male voice.

The sexual revolution made possible a serious inquiry into the ways that men and women are alike and the ways that each is unique. This revolutionary development promises to narrow the gender gap as nothing else can, for only by understanding the differences that make communication so complex do we stand any chance of mastering those complexities.

SUBTRENDS

Greater Equality Between the Sexes

Despite talk in the late 1980s and early 1990s of the decline of feminism and declarations that women, as a social and political force, are waning, equality between the sexes is closer to becoming a reality than ever before. Women command a greater workforce and wield greater political power than they have ever done. They are assuming positions in both public and private sectors that their mothers and grandmothers believed were unattainable (and their fathers and grandfathers thought were inappropriate) for women. Nonetheless, much remains to be achieved before women attain complete equality—but movement in that direction will continue at a pace that will surprise many over the next two decades.

Women voters, for example, who have long outnumbered male voters, are collectively a sleeping giant whose slumber many say was abruptly interrupted during the Clarence Thomas–Anita Hill hearings in 1991. The spectacle of a political "boy's club" raking the dignified Hill over the coals of sexual harassment galvanized the entire nation for days.

On another front, even though women have a long way to go to match men in terms of equal pay for equal work, as well as in equal opportunity, there is a definite *research* trend that shows women can match men in the skills needed to succeed in business. This growing body of data will make it more difficult for businesses to check the rise of women into the upper echelons of management and gradually help to change the corporate consciousness that still heavily favors male employees.

As for feminism, many a conservative wrote its obituary in the 1980s, only to find it risen from the dead in the 1990s. Actually, its demise was always imaginary. Movements make headway only in a context of dissatisfaction. And, clearly, there is still plenty for women to be dissatisfied about, particularly in the wake of a decade that tried to stifle meaningful change.

The "new feminism," as some call it, is less doctrinaire than the old, less extreme in the sense that it no longer has to be outrageous in order to call attention to itself. The movement today is less introspective, more goal oriented and pragmatic. Demands for liberation are superseded—and subsumed—by a well-organized quest for power. Women no longer want to burn bras, they want to manufacture and market them.

The New Masculinity

To say that the men's movement today is confused is to understate mercifully. Many men say they want to be more "sensitive" but also "less emasculated," "more open," yet "less vulnerable." While the early flux of this movement is often so extreme that it cannot but evoke guffaws, there is, nonetheless, something in it that commands some respect—for, in contrast with earlier generations of males, this one is making a real effort to examine and redefine itself. The movement, in a word, is *real*.

Innumerable studies and surveys find men dissatisfied with themselves and their roles in society. Part of this, undoubtedly, is the result of the displacement men are experiencing in a culture where *women* are so successfully transforming themselves. There is evidence, too, that men are dissatisfied because their own fathers were so unsuccessful in their emotional lives and were thus unable to impart to their sons a sense of love, belonging, and security that an increasing number of men say they sorely miss.

The trend has nothing to do with beating drums or becoming a "warrior." It relates to the human desire for connection, and this, in the long run, can only bode well for communications between humans in general and between the sexes in particular. Many psychologists believe men, in the next two decades, will be less emotionally closed than at any time in American history.

More (and Better) Senior Sex

People used to talk about sex after 40 as if it were some kind of novelty. Now it's sex after 60 and it's considered not only commonplace but healthy.

Some fear that expectations among the aged may outrun physiological ability and that exaggerated hopes, in some cases, will lead to new frustrations—or that improved health into old age will put pressure on seniors to remain sexually active beyond any "decent" desire to do so.

But most seem to welcome the trend toward extended sexuality. In fact, the desire for sex in later decades of life is *heightened,* studies suggest, by society's growing awareness and acceptance of sexual activity in later life.

Diversity of Sexual Expression

As sex shifts from its traditional reproductive role to one that is psychological, it increasingly serves the needs of the individual. In this context, forms of sexual expression that were previously proscribed are now tolerated and are, in some cases increasingly viewed as no more nor less healthy than long-accepted forms of sexual behavior. Homosexuality, for example, has attained a level of acceptance unprecedented in our national history.

More Contraception, Less Abortion

Though abortion will remain legal under varying conditions in most, if not all, states, its use will continue to decline over the next two decades as more—and better-contraceptives become available. After a period of more than two decades in which drug companies shied away from contraceptive research, interest in this field is again growing. AIDS, a changed political climate, and renewed fears about the population explosion are all contributing to this change.

Additionally, scientific advances now point the way to safer, more effective, more convenient contraceptives. A male contraceptive that will be relatively side-effect free is finally within reach and should be achieved within the next decade, certainly the next two decades. Even more revolutionary in concept and probable impact is a vaccine, already tested in animals, that some predict will be available within 10 years—a vaccine that safely stops ovum maturation and thus makes conception impossible.

Religion and Sex: A More Forgiving Attitude

Just a couple of decades ago mainstream religion was monolithic in its condemnation of sex outside of marriage. Today the situation is quite different as major denominations across the land struggle with issues they previously wouldn't have touched, issues related to

adultery, premarital sex, homosexuality, and so on.

A Special Committee on Human Sexuality, convened by the General Assembly of the Presbyterian Church (USA), for example, surprised many when it issued a report highly critical of the traditional "patriarchal structure of sexual relations," a structure the committee believes contributes, because of its repressiveness, to the proliferation of pornography and sexual violence.

All this will surely pale alongside the brave new world of virtual reality.

The same sort of thing has been happening in most other major denominations. It is safe to say that major changes are coming. Mainstream religion is beginning to perceive that the sexual revolution must be acknowledged and, to a significant degree, accommodated with new policies if these denominations are to remain in touch with present-day realities.

Expanding Sexual Entertainment

The use of sex to sell products, as well as to entertain, is increasing and can be expected to do so. The concept that "sex sells" is so well established that we need not belabor the point here. The explicitness of sexual advertising, however, may be curbed by recent research finding that highly explicit sexual content is so diverting that the viewer or reader tends to overlook the product entirely.

Sexual stereotyping will also be less prevalent in advertising in years to come. All this means, however, is that women will not be singled out as sex objects; they'll have plenty of male company, as is already the case. The female "bimbo" is now joined by the male "himbo" in ever-increasing numbers. Sexist advertising is still prevalent (e.g., male-oriented beer commercials) but should diminish as women gain in social and political power.

There's no doubt that films and TV have become more sexually permissive in the last two decades and are likely to continue in that direction for some time to come. But all this will surely pale alongside the brave (or brazen) new world of "cybersex" and virtual reality, the first erotic emanations of which may well be experienced by Americans in the coming two decades. Virtual reality aims to be just that—artificial, electronically induced experiences that are virtually indistinguishable from the real thing.

The sexual revolution, far from over, is in for some new, high-tech curves.

FROM BIOLOGY TO PSYCHOLOGY: THE NEW FAMILY OF THE MIND

Despite recent pronouncements that the traditional family is making a comeback, the evidence suggests that over the next two decades the nuclear family will share the same future as nuclear arms: there will be fewer of them, but those that remain will be better cared for.

Our longing for sources of nurturance has led us to redefine the family.

Demographers now believe that the number of families consisting of married couples with children will dwindle by yet another 12 percent by the year 2000. Meanwhile, single-parent households will continue to increase (up 41 percent over the past decade.) And household size will continue to decline (2.63 people in 1990 versus 3.14 in 1970). The number of households maintained by women, with no males present, has increased 300 percent since 1950 and will continue to rise into the 21st century.

Particularly alarming to some is the fact that an increasing number of people are choosing *never* to marry. And, throughout the developed world, the one-person household is now the fastest growing household category. To the traditionalists, this trend seems insidious—more than 25 percent of all households in the United States now consist of just one person.

There can be no doubt: the nuclear family has been vastly diminished, and it will continue to decline for some years, but at a more gradual pace. Indeed, there is a good chance that it will enjoy more stability in the next two decades than it did in the last two. Many of the very forces that were said to be weakening the traditional family may now make it stronger, though not more prevalent. Developing social changes have made traditional marriage more elective today, so that those who choose it may, increasingly, some psychologists believe, represent a subpopulation better suited to the situa-

tion and thus more likely to make a go of it.

As we try to understand new forms of family, we need to realize that the "traditional" family is not particularly traditional. Neither is it necessarily the healthiest form of family. The nuclear family has existed for only a brief moment in human history. Moreover, most people don't realize that no sooner had the nuclear family form peaked around the turn of the last century than erosion set in, which has continued ever since. For the past hundred years, reality has chipped away at this social icon, with increasing divorce and the movement of more women into the labor force. Yet our need for nurturance, security, and connectedness continues and, if anything, grows more acute as our illusions about the traditional family dissipate.

Our longing for more satisfying sources of nurturance has led us to virtually redefine the family, in terms of behavior, language, and law. These dramatic changes will intensify over the next two decades. The politics of family will be entirely transformed in that period. The process will not be without interruptions or setbacks. Some lower-court rulings may be overturned by a conservative U.S. Supreme Court, the traditional family will be revived in the headline from time to time, but the economic and psychological forces that for decades have been shaping these changes toward a more diverse family will continue to do so.

SUBTRENDS

Deceptively Declining Divorce Rate

The "good news" is largely illusory. Our prodigious national divorce rate, which more than doubled in one recent 10-year period, now shows signs of stabilization or even decline. Still, 50 percent of all marriages will break up in the next several years. And the leveling of the divorce rate is not due to stronger marriage but to *less* marriage. More people are skipping marriage altogether and are cohabiting instead.

The slight dip in the divorce rate in recent years has caused some prognosticators to predict that younger people, particularly those who've experienced the pain of growing up in broken homes, are increasingly committed to making marriage stick. Others, more persuasively, predict the opposite, that the present lull precedes a storm in which the divorce rate will soar to 60 percent or higher.

Increasing Cohabitation

The rate of cohabitation—living together without legal marriage—has been growing since 1970 and will accelerate in the next two decades. There were under half a million cohabiting couples in 1970; today there are more than 2.5. The trend for the postindustrial world is very clear: less marriage, more cohabitation, easier and—if Sweden is any indication—less stressful separation. Those who divorce will be less likely to remarry, more likely to cohabit. And in the United States, cohabitation will increasingly gather about it both the cultural acceptance and the legal protection now afforded marriage.

We need to realize the "traditional family" is not particularly traditional.

More Single-Parent Families and Planned Single Parenthood

The United States has one of the highest proportions of children growing up in single-parent families. More than one in five births in the United States is outside of marriage—and three quarters of those births are to women who are not in consensual unions.

What is significant about the single-parent trend is the finding that many single women with children now *prefer* to remain single. The rush to the altar of unwed mothers, so much a part of American life in earlier decades, is now, if anything, a slow and grudging shuffle. The stigma of single parenthood is largely a thing of the past—and the economic realities, unsatisfactory though they are, sometimes favor single parenthood. In any case, women have more choices today than they had even 10 years ago; they are choosing the psychological freedom of single parenthood over the financial security (increasingly illusory, in any event) of marriage.

More Couples Childless by Choice

In the topsy-turvy 1990s, with more single people wanting children, it shouldn't surprise us that more married couples *don't* want children. What the trend really comes down to is increased freedom of choice. One reason for increasing childlessness among couples has to do with the aging of the population, but many of the reasons are more purely psychological.

With a strong trend toward later marriage, many couples feel they are "too old" to have children. Others admit they like the economic advantages and relative freedom of being childless. Often both have careers they do not want to jeopardize by having children. In addition, a growing number of couples cite the need for lower population density, crime rates, and environmental concerns as reasons for not wanting children. The old idea that "there must be something wrong with them" if a couple does not reproduce is fast waning.

The One-Person Household

This is the fastest growing household category in the Western world. It has grown in the United States from about 10 percent in the 1950s to more than 25 percent of all households today. This is a trend that still has a long way to go. In Sweden, nearly *40 percent* of all households are now single person.

"Mr. Mom" a Reality at Last?

When women began pouring into the work force in the late 1970s, expectations were high that a real equality of the sexes was at hand and that men, at last, would begin to shoulder more of the household duties, including spending more time at home taking care of the kids. Many women now regard the concept of "Mr. Mom" as a cruel hoax; but, in fact, Mr. Mom *is* slowly emerging.

Men *are* showing more interest in the home and in parenting. Surveys make clear there is a continuing trend in that direction. Granted, part of the impetus for this is not so much a love of domestic work as it is a distaste for work outside the home. But there is also, among many men, a genuine desire to play a larger role in the lives of their children. These men say they feel "cheated" by having to work outside the home so much, cheated of the experience of seeing their children grow up.

As the trend toward more equal pay for women creeps along, gender roles in the home can be expected to undergo further change. Men will feel less pressure to take on more work and will feel more freedom to spend increased time with their families.

More Interracial Families

There are now about 600,000 interracial marriages annually in the United States, a third of these are black-white, nearly triple the number in 1970, when 40 percent of the white population was of the opinion that such marriages should be illegal. Today 20 percent hold that belief. There is every reason to expect that both the acceptance of and the number of interracial unions will continue to increase into the foreseeable future.

Recognition of Same-Sex Families

Family formation by gay and lesbian couples, with or without children, is often referenced by the media as a leading-edge signifier of just how far society has moved in the direction of diversity and individual choice in the family realm. The number of same-sex couples has steadily increased and now stands at 1.6 million such couples. There are an estimated 2 million gay parents in the United States.

And while most of these children were had in heterosexual relationships or marriages prior to "coming out," a significant number of gay and lesbian couples are having children through adoption, cooperative parenting arrangements, and artificial insemination. Within the next two decades, gays and lesbians will not only win the right to marry but will, like newly arrived immigrants, be some of the strongest proponents of traditional family values.

The Rise of Fictive Kinships

Multiadult households, typically consisting of unrelated singles, have been increasing in number for some years and are expected to continue to do so in coming years. For many, "roommates" are increasingly permanent fixtures in daily life.

In fact housemates are becoming what some sociologists and psychologists call "fictive kin." Whole "fictive families" are being generated in many of these situations, with some housemates even assigning roles ("brother," "sister," "cousin," "aunt," "mom," "dad," and so on) to one another. Fictive families are springing up among young people, old people, disabled people, homeless people, and may well define one of the ultimate evolutions of the family concept, maximizing, as they do, the opportunities for fulfillment of specific social and economic needs outside the constraints of biological relatedness.

THE BREAKUP OF THE NUCLEAR FAMILY

It's hard to tell how many times we've heard even well-informed health professionals blithely opine that "the breakup of the family is at the root of most of our problems." The *facts* disagree with this conclusion. Most of the social problems attributed to the dissolution of the "traditional" family (which, in reality, is *not* so traditional) are the product of other forces. Indeed, as we have seen, the nuclear family has itself created a number of economic, social, and psychological problems. To try to perpetuate a manifestly transient social institution beyond its usefulness is folly.

What *can* we do to save the nuclear family? Very little.

What *should* we do? Very little. Our concern should not be the maintenance of the nuclear family as a *moral* unit (which seems to be one of the priorities of the more ardent conservative "family values" forces), encompassing the special interests and values of a minority, but, rather, the strengthening of those social contracts that ensure the health, well-being, and freedom of individuals.

Who Stole Fertility?

CONTRARY TO POPULAR BELIEF, THERE IS NO INFERTILITY CRISIS SWEEPING THE NATION. WE'VE JUST LOST ALL CONCEPTION OF WHAT IT TAKES TO CONCEIVE. REPRODUCTIVE TECHNOLOGY HAS MADE US IMPATIENT WITH NATURE. SO FOR INCREASING NUMBERS OF COUPLES THE CREATION OF A NEW HUMAN BEING HAS BECOME A STRANGELY DEHUMANIZING PROCESS.

VIRGINIA RUTTER

My great-aunt Emily and great-uncle Harry never had kids, and nobody in our family talked about it. Growing up, I knew not to ask. It would have been impolite, as crass as asking about their income or their weight. The message was clear: If they didn't have kids, they couldn't have them, and talking about it would only be humiliating.

How times have changed. Today, a couple's reproductive prospects—or lack of them—are not only apt to be a conversation topic at your average dinner party, they're the subject of countless news stories illustrating our nationwide infertility "crisis."

In an infertility cover story last year, *Newsweek* reported that more than 3 million American couples would seek procreative help in 1995. Diagnostic tests, hormone treatments, fertility drugs, and assisted-reproduction techniques with names like in vitro fertilization (IVF), gamete intra-fallopian transfers (GIFT), intrauterine insemination (IUI), zygote intrafallopian transfer (ZIFT), intracytoplasmic sperm injection (ICSI)—to name the top five procedures—have

become as much a part of the reproductive process as the more poetic aspects of family making. While some of those 3 million–plus couples were legitimate candidates for the host of high-tech options now available to them, most wound up needing only low-tech assistance, such as boxer shorts instead of briefs.

Earlier this year, in a four-part series, the *New York Times* reported on the fertility industry's growth and the increased competition among clinics.

And that's how an infertility crisis is created and perpetuated. For contrary to popular belief, infertility rates are not on the rise. Creighton University sociologist Shirley Scritchfield, Ph.D., says that American infertility rates have not increased during the past three decades: In 1965, the infertility rate for the entire U.S. population was around 13.3 percent; in 1988, it was 13.7 percent. According to the U.S. Office of Technology Assessment, infertility rates for married women have actually *decreased* from 11.2 percent in 1965 to a little less than eight percent in 1988. These rates even include the "subfecund,"

the term used to describe people who have babies, just not as many as they want as quickly as they want. This means that more than 90 percent of couples have as many babies—or more than as many babies—as they want.

LETTING NATURE TAKE ITS COURSE

Rather than an infertility crisis, what we have is a society that's allowed technology to displace biology in the reproductive process, in effect dehumanizing the most human of events. At the very least, this means stress replaces spontaneity as women become tied to thermometers—constantly checking to see when they're ovulating—while men stand by waiting to give command performances. At the most, it involves women and men subjecting themselves to invasive procedures with high price tags. Whatever happened to love and romance and the idea of letting nature take its course? Instead, we seem to have embraced the idea that science, not sex, provides the best chance for producing biological children. Technicians have stolen human reproduction. And

Reprinted with permission from *Psychology Today*, March/April 1996, pp. 46-49, 65-69. © 1996 by Sussex Publishers, Inc.

there are some 300 fertility clinics—with annual revenues of $2 billion—to prove it.

Infertility has become big business, one that's virtually exempt from government regulation. And it's not for the faint of heart—or pocketbook (see "Bucks for Babies"). But all the hype has made us lose sight of what it really takes to make a baby. Conception takes time. Infertility is classically defined as the inability to conceive or carry a baby to term after one year of unprotected sex two to three times a week. On average, it takes less time for younger (in their 20s) would-be parents than older (in their 30s) ones; as couples move through their 30s, experts suggest staying on the course for two years. But even couples in their reproductive prime—mid- to late 20s—need around eight months of sex two to three times a week to make a baby. (Last December, the New England Journal of Medicine reported that healthy women are most fertile, and therefore most likely to conceive, when they have intercourse during the six-day period leading up to ovulation.)

The correlation between how often a couple has sex and the speed with which they succeed in conceiving may seem obvious. But psychologist and University of Rochester Medical School professor Susan McDaniel, Ph.D., says she counseled one infertile couple for six months

The confidence we have in preventing pregnancies has given us a false sense of control over our fertility.

before discovering they had only been having sex once or twice a month!

Of course, these days the one thing many prospective parents feel they don't have is time. During the baby boom, couples began having children at about age 20. But by 1980—when women were in the workforce in record numbers and putting off motherhood—10.5 percent of first births were to women age 30 and older. By 1990, 18 percent of first births were to women age 30 and up. Because more would-be parents are older and hear their biological clocks ticking, they're more likely to become impatient when they don't conceive instantly. But how much of a factor is age in the conception game? Men have fewer age-related fertility problems than women do. The quality of their sperm may diminish with age; when they reach their 50s, men may experience low sperm motility (slow-moving sperm are less likely to inseminate).

After about age 37, women's eggs tend to show their age and may disintegrate more easily. This makes it increasingly difficult for women to conceive or maintain a pregnancy. That's not to say there's anything unusual about a 40-year-old woman having a baby, however. Older women have been having children for eons—just not their first ones. In many cultures, the average age of a last child is around age 40.

Some older women may even be as fertile as their younger sisters. A 40-year old woman who has been taking birth control pills for a good part of her reproductive life—thus inhibiting the release of an egg each month—may actually benefit from having conserved her eggs, says Monica Jarrett, Ph.D., a professor of nursing at the University of Washington. She may even have a slight edge over a 40-year-old mother with one or two children trying to conceive.

"Focusing on aging as the primary source of infertility is a distraction." says Scritchfield. "Age becomes a factor when women have unknowingly always been infertile. These are women who, even if they'd tried to get pregnant at age 20 or 27, would have had difficulty despite the best technology."

GENDER POLITICS AND INFERTILITY

Some feminists suggest all this talk of infertility is part of a backlash, an effort

ho Is Infertile?

Although infertility rates are not on the rise overall, Creighton University sociologist Shirley Scritchfield, Ph.D., points out that they are rising among some subgroups of the population: all young women between the ages of 20 and 24 and women of color. She says this is due to an increase in sexually transmitted diseases (STDs) among the young. STDs, including chlamydia, gonorrhea, and genital warts, can permanently harm reproductive organs. Pelvic inflammatory disease, which women can develop as a consequence of other STDs, is perhaps most responsible for infertility in young women, in part because it—as well as other STDs—often goes undetected.

With few records having been kept, it's difficult to determine whether male infertility is on the rise. A 1992 study by

Norwegian scientists looked at semen quality over the past 50 years by pooling the evidence available from earlier research. They concluded that, in general, sperm counts had decreased.

Rebecca Sokol, M.D., professor of medicine and obstetrics/gynecology at the University of Southern California, says that while the Norwegian study reports a significant reduction in sperm counts over half a century, the reductions are not "clinically significant." That is, if sperm counts have decreased over time—and many scientists do not agree that they have—they've simply gone from a very high count to moderate levels.

"We're exposed to higher levels of estrogens than ever before; we inject cows and other animals with estrogens and estrogen-like hormones to keep them healthy. There isn't any data that directly proves this alters sperm counts, but we know an increase in estrogens in men is toxic to sperm. The theory is that in some way, this low-grade constant exposure to estrogen is ultimately altering sperm."

to drive women out of the boardroom and back into the nursery. While there may be some truth to this, it's only part of the story. The fertility furor is also a result of increasing expectations of control over nature by ordinary men and women.

Ironically, the growing intolerance for the natural course of conception stems from technological advances in contraception. Birth control is more reliable than ever. The confidence we have in preventing pregnancies has given us a false sense of control over our fertility. "People have the idea that if they can prevent conception, then they should also be able to conceive when they want to," says McDaniel.

This illusory sense of control, says Judith Daniluk, Ph.D., a University of British Columbia psychologist and fertility researcher, weighs most heavily on women. "Women are told that if they miss taking even one birth control pill, they risk becoming pregnant. This translates into feeling extremely responsible when it comes to getting pregnant, too."

If we've let technicians steal fertility from us, perhaps it's because it was up for grabs. Until recently, infertility was considered a woman's problem rather than a couple's problem. In the 1950s, physicians and psychologists believed that women whose infertility couldn't be explained were "suppressing" their true femininity. Of course, in those days men were rarely evaluated; the limited technology available focused mostly on women.

When a couple steps into the infertility arena today, both partners receive

An overestimation of success rates by the technofertility industry hooks couples in.

full evaluations—in theory. In practice, however, this doesn't always happen because technology is such that even a few sperm from an infertile man are enough for high-tech fertilization. About 40 percent of infertility is the result of "female factors"—problems with hormones, eggs, or reproductive organs. Another 40 percent is explained by "male factors"— problems with low sperm count or slow-moving sperm. The remaining 20 percent is unexplained or due to factors in both partners. There may be an immune problem, where the sperm and egg are "allergic" to each other. Advances— such as ICSI, a way of injecting a single sperm into an egg during IVF—have been made to get around this immune system clash. Advances have also been made in understanding male infertility, including treatments for low sperm motility that involve extracting sperm directly from the testes. But the bulk of fertility treatments still focus on women.

Women also tend to "carry" the issue for a couple, says McDaniel. "As much as men are invested in having children, they don't have to think about it, or perhaps be as conscious of it—because women are so focused on the problem. It makes

sense, then, that when it comes to an infertility workup, men will often be the ones to put on the brakes. If both partners were running headlong onto the conveyor belt of technology, there'd be a mess. So what happens—largely because of sex roles—is women become advocates of the process, and men, who may be more ambivalent, question it and wonder whether it's time to stop."

Women will go so far as to protect their partner from the diagnostic process, as well as treatment, observes Daniluk. She says they'll even shield their partner from blame when he's the infertile one.

COMPELLED TO PRODUCE

Regardless of its cause, infertility is a profound blow to people's sense of self, who they are, and who they think they should be. To understand just how devastating infertility is, it helps to know why we want babies in the first place.

"The most essential thing the human animal does is reproduce," insists anthropologist Helen Fisher, Ph.D., author of *Anatomy of Love*. Citing survival of the species as the reason why our drive to reproduce is so strong, Fisher says it's not surprising that couples will go to great emotional and financial lengths to conceive. "The costs of reproducing have always been great. The time-consuming and costly procedures a modern couple uses to pursue their reproductive ends may never be as costly as it was on the grasslands of Africa, when women regularly died in childbirth."

Fisher says men, too, feel obliged to plant their seed or die out, so they'll work very hard to sire and raise their own kids.

 *ucks for Babies*

The fertility industry may boast of its dedication to bringing healthy babies into the world, but in reality, it appears to be interested in producing only *wealthy* ones.

A thorough fertility workup to diagnose the source of a couple's problem can take up to two months and cost from $3,000 to $8,000. That's just for starters. For a simple procedure, like hormone shots to stimulate egg production, it's $2,300 per cycle. Expect to pay $10,000 for one round of in vitro fertilization (IVF). About 30,000 women a year attempt pregnancy via IVF. Intracytoplasmic sperm injection, where doctors inject a single sperm into an egg, adds $1,000 to the price of IVF. A procedure requiring an egg donor (in demand among older mothers) runs from $8,500 to $16,000—per cycle. A varicocelectomy, to correct varicose veins around the testicles, costs $3,500. Few health plans include coverage for fertility treatment. Even when insurance does kick in, it doesn't cover all of the direct costs, to say nothing of the many indirect costs, including lost income from missed work and child care expenses.

They aren't exempt from social pressures either. "Male sexuality has always been tied to potency," says William Doherty, Ph.D., a professor of family social science at the University of Minnesota. "The slang term for male infertility is 'shooting blanks.' After all, what good is a man if he can't reproduce? That's probably why we've blamed women for infertility for millennia. It's too humiliating for men."

Animal instincts may provide the primal motivation for having kids. But notions of masculinity and femininity are another big influence. Infertility taps into our deepest anxieties about what it is to be a man or a woman, a core part of our identity. McDaniel says many of the infertile women she sees speak of feeling incomplete. They also talk about a loss of self-confidence and a sense of helplessness and isolation. Women still get the message that much of their femaleness is derived from motherhood—more so than men are taught their maleness is tied to fatherhood. Losing the dream of motherhood may fill a woman with such grief that she'll consciously avoid the places kids populate. It's a loss that can be difficult to share because it's the death of something that never was.

Infertile men also experience a loss, says McDaniel. They, too, may insulate themselves from the world of kids. They may be even less likely than women, says Doherty, to talk about their sad feelings. "Men feel if they're not able to pass on their seed, they're not living up to what's expected of them as men," says Andrew McCullough, M.D., director of the Male Sexual Health and Fertility Clinic at New York University Medical Center.

Parental expectations are yet another powerful reason people feel the procreational pull. "When it comes to having kids," says McDaniel, "there can be a lot of familial pressure. If you don't have them, everybody wonders why."

Technofertility Takes Over

With all of these pressures to produce, is it any wonder couples get caught up in the technofertility maze? Seduced by well-meaning doctors who hold out hope and the availability of all kinds of treatments, two vulnerable people—alone—are left to decide how much reproductive assistance they will or won't accept. There are no guidelines.

It wasn't until about their seventh year of fertility treatments that a physician finally sat Steve and Lori down and told them that their chances of having a baby were slim, given their ages—37 and 32—and their efforts until that point. Steve had had a varicocele, a twisting of veins in the testicles, and Lori had had various explorations of her ovaries by endoscopy in search of ovarian cysts, plus two failed IVFs.

"It turned out that my wife's gynecologist wasn't really competent to tell us about fertility treatments," Steve says. "It ended up being like going to the Motor Vehicle Bureau. First, they tell you to take care of one thing, but it turns out you need to take care of something else. Then they tell you to go do a third thing. You wind up moving from place to place with no particular plan. It's rare that you get a doctor who explains in plain English what's going on and helps you evaluate your choices. Instead of talking with Lori and me and asking us what was in our hearts, they were saying, 'Okay, you want a baby, how can we make one for you?'"

Even as they went through test after test, procedure after procedure, it seemed at least semicomical to them: drives at the crack of dawn to a distant clinic, painful shots Steve was obliged to administer to Lori, even a "hamster penetration" test that involved Steve producing a sperm sample to see whether his sperm could penetrate a hamster's egg. All of it was very difficult to resist. "I think it was partly the adventure that kept us going," Steve says. "Once you commit and say you're going to give it a go, you don't want to stop midstream. There's always the chance that it might work. I mean, medicine is fantastic; you take some pills, stick some stuff in you, and maybe you get a baby."

Fertility treatments are so technically focused, says McDaniel, that people's feelings get left behind. She advocates a more human "biopsychosocial" approach. "Couples' emotional needs should dictate the pacing and decision making as they move up the pyramid of technological possibilities. But in some, maybe even most clinics, little or no attention is paid to the process, only the possible product. As a result, the patients suffer."

Even under normal circumstances, conception is immaculate—it tends to clean all else out of the mind. Whenever people begin to plan a family, says McDaniel, their worldview narrows. But with technofertility, a couple's worldview can narrow to the exclusion of all else. Because the outcome is the entire focus, fertility treatments intensify our instincts to give birth and nurture a baby. So the very technology that disregards couples' emotions also heightens their desire to nurture. For women, especially, maternal instincts are intensified by all-consuming fertility treatments that leave little time for anything else and cause women to define themselves solely as mothers.

Indeed, as soon as prospective parents seek help, statistics and biology become the focus. Before long, they're up on the latest research and talking in terms of "control groups," "statistical significance," and "replication." The walls of fertility clinics are plastered with pictures of newborns, and staffers and customers alike speak endlessly about "take-home baby rates," the bottom line when it comes to success. But take-home baby rates are more than numbers. They represent people's hopes for a family.

As a result, couples undergoing intensive fertility treatments lose their wide-angle perspective on life. They may fall behind in their careers and cut themselves off from friends and family, all in the narcissistic pursuit of cloning their genes. Technology may provide us with the illusion that it's helping us control our reproductive fate, but in reality, it just adds to the narcissism. "The higher tech the treatment, the more inwardly focused couples become," says Doherty.

"Biological connections are so strongly emphasized in our culture that it's hard not to become self-absorbed," Steve explains. "You even see it in the adoption process. Couples are often concerned that the kids they adopt have similar characteristics to their own. But the truth is, kids are kids." (Steve and Lori have since adopted a baby.)

An overestimation of success rates by the technofertility industry hooks couples in and fuels the narcissism. Fertility clinics typically report about a 25 percent success rate. But this rate is usually calculated after clinics have screened out the

How Couples Cope with Infertility

In general, couples without children are more likely to split up than partners with children, reports demographer Diane Lye, Ph.D., a professor of sociology at the University of Washington. What about mates who can't have kids, or who want them but encounter difficulties? Researchers don't know about the ones who don't seek fertility treatment—and who tend to be poor. But Lauri Pasch, Ph.D., a psychologist and fertility researcher at the University of California at San Francisco, did study 50 couples who, on average, had been trying to get pregnant for two years. She says infertile couples going for fertility treatment tend to have higher rates of marital satisfaction than the rest of the population.

"Most couples who seek fertility treatment are committed enough to their relationship that they will go through pain and suffering to have a child together," says Pasch. And if they have the skills to address their problem, their relationships tend to become stronger—even if they never have a baby."

So what kind of skills does a couple confronting infertility need? Mates with matching coping styles do best, says Pasch, who points out that infertility, like other major stressors, tends to bring out people's natural ways of coping. "Couples who have similar ways of living with problems and relieving their distress are better off than those with different styles," says Pasch. "Both might be support seekers, or both might be private and keep to themselves. So long as they both go about things in the same way."

Pasch finds that spouses who rely on emotional expression can do harm to their relationship. That's because they tend to let their feelings out *at* their partner rather than sharing them *with* him or her. (So much for the old saw that talking things out always makes them better.) "In this destructive communication pattern, one person eventually demands and one withdraws," says Pasch. "One member of the couple pressures for change, while the other one withdraws, refusing to discuss the problem."

Though which partner demands and which one withdraws can shift, typically women are the ones who demand more, and men are the ones who withdraw. In the case of an infertile couple, the woman may get alarmed sooner than her husband about not being able to have children. But they may switch roles, and she may become more resigned to it while he becomes more concerned and wants to start treatment. Either way, the couple is at odds.

Tammy and Dan, the parents of two children—the products of five IVFs and eight years of fertility treatments—were just such a couple. "I was the leader, taking care of everything," says Tammy. Her daily routine included being at the fertility clinic at 6:30 every morning for blood tests, and returning every afternoon for more exams. Once she became pregnant, she had to stay in bed practically from the day she conceived until the day her children were born.

"When you're trying to get pregnant, it becomes your whole focus. Everything you do is planned around it. You are told what to do every day, and you can't do very much. Then, all of a sudden, you realize you have focused your whole life on getting pregnant and not on your relationship. After our second child was born, and we didn't have a crisis to deal with every day, it was difficult being normal."

The emotional climate becomes even more difficult when one partner chooses to withdraw from the entire fertility process. Psychologist Susan McDaniel, Ph.D., of the University of Rochester School of Medicine, saw one couple where the wife underwent extensive tests to see whether she was infertile. Her husband, meanwhile, could never seem to make it to the urologist to be tested. He couldn't tolerate the idea that his sperm count might be low. Of course, his wife was furious. She had gone through painful and stressful—not to mention expensive—workups. When her husband finally went to the urologist, he couldn't produce a sperm sample. When he finally did, it turned out he was the infertile one. Both partners had trouble understanding what the prospect of infertility was like for the other one. Eventually, they decided to get a divorce.

most hopeless cases. The true rate—which counts everyone who has sought reproductive help and which considers live births rather than pregnancies as success—is closer to half, Scritchfield says. "Unfortunately, this isn't what the public hears. If we were really concerned about infertility, we would be working on preventive measures. That's not addressed by biomedical entrepreneurs because they don't deal with people, just body parts."

Yet technofertility can create such stress in a couple that it can come close to undoing their relationship—the raison d'être for baby making. McDaniel remembers one couple who were at complete odds, having come to see her a year after having undergone five years of unsuccessful fertility treatments. The woman still hoped technology could help them, but the man felt his wife had gone too far; the procedures were invasive and the lack of results too painful. Attempting to protect both of them from any more disappointment, he insisted they stop.

The husband questioned why they'd ever gotten involved in the first place, and the wife felt unsupported by his reaction. No one at the fertility clinic had helped them work through any of their reactions. In therapy with McDaniel, they ultimately admitted to themselves—and to each other—what their expectations had been and the anxiety and grief they felt over the loss of an easy pregnancy. Then they decided to adopt.

Given the single-mindedness of baby making, adding infertility and technology to the mix creates the perfect recipe for obsession. But it's an obsession only for the rich. Which means having a baby becomes a luxury that many truly infertile couples, who might otherwise make wonderful parents, will never be able to afford.

Is There Love After Baby?

Why the passage to parenthood rocks even the best of couples today: A cautionary tale.

Carolyn Pape Cowan, Ph.D., and Philip A. Cowan, Ph.D.

Carolyn Pape Cowan, Ph.D., and Philip A. Cowan, Ph.D., are co-directors of the Becoming a Family Project at the University of California at Berkeley. Carolyn codirects the Schoolchildren and Their Families Project and is the co-editor of Fatherhood Today: Men's Changing Roles in the Family. *Philip is the author of* Piaget: With Feeling, *and co-editor of* Family Transitions: Advances in Family Research, Vol. 2. *They are the parents of three grown children.*

Babies are getting a lot of bad press these days. Newspapers and magazine articles warn that the cost of raising a child from birth to adulthood is now hundreds of thousands of dollars. Television news recounts tragic stories of mothers who have harmed their babies while suffering from severe postpartum depression. Health professionals caution that child abuse has become a problem throughout our nation. Several books on how to "survive" parenthood suggest that parents must struggle to keep their marriage alive once they become parents. In fact, according to recent demographic studies, more than 40 percent of children born to two parents can expect to live in a single-parent family by the time they are 18. The once-happy endings to family beginnings are clouded with strain, violence, disenchantment, and divorce.

What is so difficult about becoming a family today? What does it mean that some couples are choosing to remain "child-free" because they fear that a child might threaten their well-established careers or disturb the intimacy of their marriage? Is keeping a family together harder than it used to be?

Over the last three decades, sociologists, psychologists, and psychiatrists have begun to search for the answers. Results of the most recent studies, including our own, show that partners who become parents describe:

• an ideology of more equal work and family roles than their mothers and fathers had;

• actual role arrangements in which husbands and wives are sharing family work and care of the baby less than either of them expected;

• more conflict and disagreement after the baby is born than they had reported before;

• and increasing disenchantment with their overall relationship as a couple.

To add to these disquieting trends, studies of emotional distress in new parents suggest that women and possibly men are more vulnerable to depression in the early months after having a child. Finally, in the United States close to 50 percent of couples who marry will ultimately divorce.

We believe that children are getting an unfair share of the blame for their parents' distress. Based on 15 years of research that includes a three-year pilot study, a 10-year study following 72 expectant couples and 24 couples without children, and ongoing work with couples in distress, we are convinced that the seeds of new parents' individual and marital problems are sown long before baby arrives. Becoming parents does not so much raise new problems as bring old unresolved issues to the surface.

Our concern about the high incidence of marital distress and divorce among the parents of young children led us to study systematically what happens to partners when they become parents. Rather than simply add to the mounting documentation of family problems, we created and evaluated a new preventive program, the Becoming a Family Project, in which mental-health professionals worked with couples during their transition to parenthood, trying to help them get off to a healthy start. Then we followed the families as the first children progressed from infancy through the first year of elementary school.

What we have learned is more trou-

From *Psychology Today*, July/August 1992, pp. 59-63, 78-79. Excerpted from *When Partners Become Parents: The Big Life Change for Couples* by Carolyn Pape Cowan and Philip A. Cowan. © 1992 by Basic Books, Inc. Reprinted by permission of Basic Books, Inc., a division of HarperCollins Publishers, Inc.

bling than surprising. The majority of husbands and wives become more disenchanted with their couple relationship as they make the transition to parenthood. Most new mothers struggle with the question whether and when to return to work. For those who do go back, the impact on their families depends both on what mothers do at work and what fathers do at home. The more unhappy parents feel about their marriage, the more anger and competitiveness and the less warmth and responsiveness we observe in the family during the preschool period—between the parents as a couple and between each parent and the child. The children of parents with more tension during the preschool years have a harder time adjusting to the challenges of kindergarten.

For couples who thought having a baby was going to bring them closer together, the first few months are especially confusing and disappointing.

On the positive side, becoming a family provides a challenge that for some men and women leads to growth—as individuals, as couples, as parents. For couples who work to maintain or improve the quality of their marriage, having a baby can lead to a revitalized relationship. Couples with more satisfying marriages work together more effectively with their children in the preschool period, and their children tend to have an easier time adapting to the academic and social demands of elementary school. What is news is that the relationship *between* the parents seems to act as a crucible in which their relationships with their children take place.

The transition to parenthood is stressful even for well-functioning couples. In addition to distinctive inner changes, men's and women's roles change in very different ways when partners become parents. It seems to come as a great surprise to most of them that changes in some of their major roles affect their feelings about their overall

relationship. Both partners have to make major adjustments of time and energy as individuals at a time when they are getting less sleep and fewer opportunities to be together. They have less patience with things that didn't seem annoying before. Their frustration often focuses on each other. For couples who thought that having a baby was going to bring them closer together, this is especially confusing and disappointing.

Why does becoming a parent have such a powerful impact on a marriage? We have learned that one of the most difficult aspects of becoming a family is that so much of what happens is unexpected. Helping couples anticipate how they might handle the potentially stressful aspects of becoming a family can leave them feeling less vulnerable, less likely to blame each other for the hard parts, and more likely to decide that they can work it out before their distress permeates all of the relationships in the family.

But when things start to feel shaky, few husbands and wives know how to tell anyone, especially each other, that they feel disappointed or frightened. "This is supposed to be the best time of our lives; what's the matter with me?" a wife might say through her tears. They can't see that some of their tension may be attributable to the conflicting demands of the very complex stage of life, not simply to a suddenly stubborn, selfish, or unresponsive spouse.

Becoming a family today is more difficult than it used to be. Small nuclear families live more isolated lives in crowded cities, often feeling cut off from extended family and friends. Mothers of young children are entering the work force earlier; they are caught between traditional and modern conceptions of how they should be living their lives. Men and women are having a difficult time regaining their balance after having babies, in part because radical shifts in the circumstances surrounding family life in America demand new arrangements to accommodate the increasing demands on parents of young children. But new social arrangements and roles have simply not kept pace with the changes, leaving couples on their own to manage the demands of work and family.

News media accounts imply that as mothers have taken on more of a role in the world of paid work, fathers have taken on a comparable load of family work. But this has just not happened. It is not simply that men's and women's

roles are unequal that seems to be causing distress for couples, but rather that they are so clearly discrepant from what both spouses expected them to be. Women's work roles have changed, but their family roles have not. Well-intentioned and confused husbands feel guilty while their overburdened wives feel angry. It does not take much imagination to see how these emotions can fuel the fires of marital conflict.

Separate (Time)Tables

As they bring their first baby home from the hospital, new mothers and fathers find themselves crossing the great divide. After months of anticipation, their transition from couple to family becomes a reality. Entering this unfamiliar territory, men and women find themselves on different timetables and different trails of a journey they envisioned completing together.

Let's focus on the view from the inside, as men and women experience the shifting sense of self that comes with first-time parenthood. In order to understand how parents integrate Mother or Father as central components of their identity, we give couples a simple pie chart and ask them to think about the various aspects of their lives (worker, friend, daughter, father, so on) and mark off how large each portion feels, not how much time they spend "being it." The size of each piece of the pie reflects their psychologic involvement or investment in that aspect of themselves.

Almost all show pieces that represent parent, worker or student, and partner or lover. The most vivid identity changes during the transition to parenthood take place between pregnancy and six months postpartum. The part of the self that women call Mother takes up 10 percent of their pictures of themselves in late pregnancy. It then leaps to 34 percent six months after birth, and stays there through the second year of parenthood. For some women, the psychological investment in motherhood is much greater than the average.

Most of the husbands we interviewed took on the identity of parent more slowly than their wives did. During pregnancy, Father takes half as much of men's pie as their wives' Mother sections do, and when their children are 18 months old, husbands identity as parent is still less than one third as large as their wives'. We find that the larger the difference between husbands and wives in the size of their parent piece of the pie when their babies are six months old, the less satisfied both spouses are with the marriage, and the more their satisfaction declines over the next year.

The Big Squeeze

Men's and women's sense of themselves as parents is certainly expected to increase once they have had a baby. What comes as a surprise is that other central aspects of the self are getting short shrift as their parent piece of the pie expands. The greatest surprise—for us and for the couples—is what gets squeezed as new parents' identities shift. Women apportion 34 percent to the Partner or Lover aspect of themselves in pregnancy, 22 percent at six months after the birth, and 21 percent when their children are 18 months. Men's sense of themselves as Partner or Lover also shows a decline—from 35 percent to 30 percent to 25 percent over the two-year transition period.

The size of the Partner piece of the pie is connected to how new parents feel about themselves: A larger psychological investment in their relationship seems to be good for both of them. Six months after the birth of their first child, both men and women with larger Partner/Lover pieces have higher self-esteem and less parenting stress. This could mean that when parents resist the tendency to ignore their relationship as a couple, they feel better about themselves and less stressed as parents. Or that when they feel better about themselves they are more likely to stay moderately involved in their relationship.

At our 18-month follow-up, Stephanie and Art talk about the consequences for their marriage of trying to balance—within them and between them—the pulls among the Parent, Worker, and Partner aspects.

Stephanie: We're managing Linda really well. But with Art's promotion from teacher to principal and my going back to work and feeling guilty about being away from Linda, we don't get much time for *us*. I try to make time for the two of us at home, but there's no point in making time to be with somebody if he doesn't want to be with you. Sometimes when we finally get everything done and Linda is asleep, I want to sit down and talk, but Art says this is a perfect opportunity to get some prepara-

tion done for one of his teachers' meetings. Or he starts to fix one of Linda's toys—things that apparently are more important to him than spending time with me.

Art: That does happen. But Stephanie's wrong when she says that those things are more important to me than she is. The end of the day is just not my best time to start a deep conversation. I keep asking her to get a sitter so we can go out for a quiet dinner, but she always finds a reason not to. It's like being turned down for a date week after week.

Stephanie: Art, you know I'd love to go out with you. I just don't think we can leave Linda so often.

Stephanie and Art are looking at the problem from their separate vantage points. Art is very devoted to fatherhood, but is more psychologically invested in his relationship with Stephanie than with Linda. In his struggle to hold onto himself as Partner, he makes the reasonable request that he and Stephanie spend some time alone so they can nurture their relationship as a couple. Stephanie struggles with other parts of her shifting sense of self. Although Art knows that Stephanie spends a great deal of time with Linda when she gets home from work, he does not understand that juggling her increasing involvement as Mother while trying to maintain her investment as Worker is creating a great deal of internal pressure for her. The Partner/Lover part of Stephanie is getting squeezed not only by time demands but also by the psychological reshuffling that is taking place inside her. Art knows only that Stephanie is not responding to his needs, and to him her behavior seems unreasonable, insensitive, and rejecting.

Stephanie knows that Art's view of himself has changed as he has become a parent, but she is unaware of the fact that it has not changed in the same way or to the same degree as hers. In fact, typical of the men in our study, Art's psychological investment in their relationship as couple has declined slightly since Linda was born, but his Worker identity has not changed much. He is proud and pleased to be a father, but these feelings are not crowding out his sense of himself as a Partner/Lover. All Stephanie knows is that Art is repeatedly asking her to go out to dinner and ignoring her inner turmoil. To her, his behavior seems unreasonable, insensitive, and rejecting.

It might have been tempting to con-

clude that it is natural for psychological involvement in one's identity as Partner or Lover to wane over time—but the patterns of the childless couples refute that. The internal changes in each of the new parents begin to have an impact on their relationship as a couple. When women add Mother to their identity, *both* Worker and Partner/Lover get squeezed. As some parts of identity grow larger, there is less "room" for others. The challenge, then, is how to allow Parent a central place in one's identity without abandoning or neglecting Partner. We find that couples who manage to do this feel better about themselves as individuals and as couples.

Who Does What?

How do new parents' internal shifts in identity, and their separate timetables, play out in their marriage? We find that "who does what?" issues are central not only in how husbands and wives feel about themselves, but in how they feel about their marriage. Second, there are alternations in the emotional fabric of the couple's relationship; how caring and intimacy get expressed and how couples manage their conflict and disagreement have a direct effect on their marital satisfaction.

Husbands and wives, different to begin with, become even more separate and distinct in their years after their first child is born. An increasing specialization of family roles and emotional distance between partners-become-parents combine to affect their satisfaction with the relationship.

Behind today's ideology of the egalitarian couple lies a much more traditional reality. Although more than half of mothers with children under five have entered the labor force and contemporary fathers have been taking a small but significantly greater role in cooking, cleaning, and looking after their children than fathers used to do, women continue to carry the overwhelming responsibility for managing the household and caring for the children. Women have the primary responsibility for family work even when both partners are employed full time.

Couples whose division of household and family tasks was not equitable when they began our study tended to predict that it would be after the baby was born. They never expected to split baby care 50-50 but to work as a team in rearing their children. Once the babies are born, however, the women do more of the housework than before they became mothers, and the men do much less of the care of the baby than they or their wives predicted they would. After children appear, a couple's role arrangements—and how both husband and wife feel about them—become entwined with their intimacy.

Ideology vs Reality

In both expectant and childless couples, spouses divide up the overall burden of family tasks fairly equitably. But new parents begin to divide up these tasks in more gender-stereotyped ways. Instead of both partners performing some of each task, he tends to take on a few specific household responsibilities and she tends to do most of the others. His and her overall responsibility for maintaining the household may not shift significantly after having a baby, but it feels more traditional because each has become more specialized.

In the last trimester of pregnancy, men and women predict that the mothers will be responsible for more of the baby care tasks than the father. Nine months later, when the babies are six months old, a majority describe their arrangements as even more Mother's and less Father's responsibility than either had predicted. Among parents of six-month-old babies, mothers are shouldering more of the baby care than either parent predicted on eight of 12 items on our questionnaire: deciding about meals, managing mealtime, diapering, bathing, taking the baby out, playing with the baby, arranging for baby sitters, and dealing with the pediatrician. On four items, women and men predicted that mothers would do more and their expectations proved to be on the mark: responding to baby's cries, getting up in the middle of the night, doing the child's laundry, and choosing the baby's toys.

From this we contend that the ideology of the new egalitarian couple is way ahead of the reality. The fallout from their unmet expectations seems to convert both spouses' surprise and disappointment into tension between them.

Jackson and Tanya talked a lot about their commitment to raising Kevin together. Three months later, when the baby was six months old, Tanya explained that Jackson had begun to do more housework than ever before but

that he wasn't available for Kevin nearly as much as she would have liked.

Tanya: He wasn't being a chauvinist or anything, expecting me to do everything and him nothing. He just didn't *volunteer* to do things that obviously needed doing, so I had to put down some ground rules. Like if I'm in a bad mood, I may just yell: "I work eight hours just like you. This is half your house and half your child, too. You've got to do your share!" Jackson never changed the kitty litter box once in four years, but he changes it now, so we've made great progress. I just didn't expect it to take so much work. We planned this child together and we went through Lamaze together, and Jackson stayed home for the first two weeks. But then—wham—the partnership was over.

Tanya underscores a theme we hear over and over: The tension between new parents about the father's involvement in the family threatens the intimacy between them.

The fact that mothers are doing most of the primary child care in the first months of parenthood is hardly news. What we are demonstrating is that the couples' arrangements for taking care of their infants are *less equitable* than they expected them to be. They are amazed they became so traditional so fast.

It's not just that couples are startled by how the division of labor falls along gender lines, but they describe the change as if it were a mysterious virus they picked up while in the hospital having their baby. They don't seem to view their arrangements as *choices* they have made.

Husbands' and wives' descriptions of their division of labor are quite similar but they do shade things differently: Each claims to be doing more than the other gives him or her credit for. The feeling of not being appreciated for the endless amount of work each partner actually does undoubtedly increases the tension between them. Compared with the childless couples, new parents' overall satisfaction with their role arrangements (household tasks plus decision making plus child care) declined significantly—most dramatically between pregnancy and six months after baby's birth.

Parents who had been in one of our couples groups maintained their satisfaction with the division of household and family tasks. This trend is particularly true for women. Since the actual role arrangement in the group and non-

group participants were very similar, we can see that men's and women's satisfactions with who does what is, at least in part, a matter of perspective.

Some men and women are happy with traditional arrangements. Most of the men in our study, however, wanted desperately to have a central role in their child's life.

Is There Sex after Parenthood?

Most new parents feel some disenchantment in their marriage. It is tempting to blame this on two related facts reported by every couple. First, after having a baby, *time* becomes their most precious commodity. Second, even if a couple can eke out a little time together, the effort seems to require a major mobilization of forces. They feel none of the spontaneity that kept their relationship alive when they were a twosome.

We asked husbands and wives what they do to show their partners that they care. It soon became clear that different things feel caring to different people: bringing flowers or special surprises,

The division of workload in the family wins hands down as the issue most likely to cause conflict in the first two years.

being a good listener, touching in certain ways, picking up the cleaning without being asked.

New parents describe fewer examples of caring after having a baby compared to before, but as we keep finding in each domain of family life, men's and women's changes occur at different times. Between the babies' six- and 18-month birthdays, wives and husbands report that the women are doing fewer caring things for their husbands than the year before. In the parents' natural preoccupation with caring for baby, they seem less able to care for each other.

Both husbands and wives also report a negative change in their sexual relationship after having a baby. The frequency of lovemaking declines for almost all couples in the early months of parenthood.

There are both physical and psychological deterrents to pleasurable sex for new parents. Probably the greatest interference with what happens in the bedroom comes from what happens between the partners outside the bedroom. Martin and Sandi, for example, tell us that making love has become problematic since Ellen's birth. To give an example of a recent disappointment, Martin explains that he had had an extremely stressful day at work. Sandi greeted him with a "tirade" about Ellen's fussy day, the plumber failing to come, and the baby-sitter's latest illness. Dinnertime was tense, and they spent the rest of the evening in different rooms. When they got into bed they watched TV for a few minutes, and then Martin reached out to touch Sandi. She pulled away, feeling guilty that she was not ready to make love.

Like so many couples, they were disregarding the tensions that had been building up over the previous hours. They had never had a chance to talk in anything like a collaborative or intimate way. This is the first step of the common scenario for one or both partners to feel "not in the mood."

Ninety-two percent of the men and women in our study who became parents described more conflict after having their baby than before they became parents. The division of workload in the family wins hands down as the issue most likely to cause conflict in the first two years. Women feel the impact of the transition more strongly during the first six months after birth, and their husbands feel it more strongly in the following year.

Why does satisfaction with marriage go down? It begins, we think, with the issue of men's and women's roles. The new ideology of egalitarian relationships between men and women has made some inroads on the work front. Most couples, however, are not prepared for the strain of creating more egalitarian relationships at home, and it is this strain that leads men and women to feel more negatively about their partners and the state of their marriage.

Men's increasing involvement in the preparation for the *day* of the baby's birth leads both spouses to expect that he will be involved in what follows—the ongoing daily care and rearing of the children. How ironic that the recent widespread participation of fathers in the births of their babies has become a source of new parents' disappointment when the men do not stay involved in their babies' early care.

The transition to parenthood heightens the differences between men and women, which leads to more conflict between them. This, in turn, threaten the equilibrium of their marriage.

Needed: Couples Groups

Family making is a joint endeavor, not just during pregnancy, but in the years to come. Men simply have little access to settings in which they can share their experiences about intimate family matters. Given how stressful family life is for so many couples, we feel it is important to help them understand how their increasing differences during this transition may be generating more distance between them. Most couples must rebalance of the relationship.

Our results show that when sensitive group leaders help men and women focus on what is happening to them as individuals and as a couple during their transition to parenthood, it buffers them from turning their strain into dissatisfaction with each other. Why intervene with couples in *groups*? We find that a group setting provides the kind of support that contemporary couples often lack.

Groups of people going through similar life experiences help participants "normalize" some of their strain and adjustment difficulties; they discover that the strain they are experiencing is expectable at this stage of life. This can strengthen the bond between husbands and wives and undercut their tendency to blame each other for their distress.

Group discussions, by encouraging partners to keep a focus on their couple relationship, help the women maintain their identity as Partner/Lover while they are taking on Motherhood and returning to their jobs and careers. Fathers become painfully aware of what it takes to manage a demanding job and the day-to-day care of a household with baby.

The modern journey to parenthood, exciting and fulfilling as it is, is beset with many roadblocks. Most couples experience stress in the early years of family life. Most men and women need to muster all the strength and skills they have to make this journey. Almost all of the parents in our studies say that the joyful parts outweigh the difficult ones. They also say that the lessons they learn along the way are powerful and well worth the effort.

Why They Stay: A Saga of Spouse Abuse

Whatever else American culture envisions of petite blondes, it doesn't expect them to end up as social revolutionaries. But just that turn of fate has brought Sarah Buel to Williamsburg, Virginia, from suburban Boston, where she is assistant district attorney of Norfolk County. To a gathering of judges, lawyers, probation and police officers, victim advocates, and others, she has come to press an idea that meets persistent resistance—to explain why and, perhaps more importantly, precisely how domestic violence should be handled, namely as the serious crime that it is, an assault with devastating effects against individuals, families, and communities, now and for generations to come.

Hara Estroff Marano

Hara Estroff Marano is an author living in Brooklyn Heights, NY. She is currently Editor at Large of *Psychology Today,* contributor to many national publications, and working on a book about the social development of children.

Buel, 41, a speed talker—there is, after all, so much to say—tells them what Los Angeles prosecutors failed to explain in the O. J. Simpson case: how batterers cannily dodge responsibility for their own actions, as if other people sneak into their brains and ball their fingers into fists; how they are deft at shifting the blame to others, especially their mates; how they watch and stalk partners, even those under the protection of the court, and especially those who have separated or divorced. Instead of holding up Simpson as the poster boy for domestic violence, the California trial let him get away with doing what batterers almost always do—put on a great public face and portray themselves as victims.

The judges and cops and court officers pay attention to Buel because domestic violence is a daily hassle that takes a lot out of them. And if there's one thing Buel knows, it's how batterers manipulate the law enforcement system. They listen because Buel has that most unassailable credential, an honors degree from Harvard Law School. But mostly they listen because Buel has been on the receiving end of a fist.

"Sometimes I hate talking about it," she confides. "I just want people to see me as the best trial lawyer." But, as Deborah D. Tucker says, "she grabs them by the heart." Tucker, head of the Texas Council on Family Violence and chairman of the national committee that pushed the Violence Against Women Act into the 1994 Omnibus Crime Bill, explains: "She gets people to feel what they need to feel to be vulnerable to the message that domestic violence is not we/they. Any of us can become victimized. It's not about the woman. It's about the culture."

Certainly Buel never had any intention of speaking publicly about her own abuse. It started accidentally. She was in a court hallway with some police officers on a domestic violence case. "See, a smart woman like you would never let this happen," the chief said, gesturing her way. And in an instant Buel made a decision that changed her life irrevocably, and the lives of many others. "Well, it did happen," she told him, challenging his blame-the-victim tone. He invited her to train his force on handling domestic violence. **"It changed things completely. I decided I had an obligation to speak up. It's a powerful tool."**

It has made her a star, says psychologist David Adams, Ed.D. By speaking from her own experience, Buel reminds people that law can be a synonym for justice. In conferences

From *Psychology Today,* May/June 1996, pp. 56-60, 62, 66, 68, 70, 74, 76, 78. © 1996 by Hara Estroff Marano. Reprinted by permission.

and in courts, she has gotten even the most cynical judges to listen to battered women—instead of blaming them. "I am amazed at how often people are sympathetic as long as the victim closely resembles Betty Crocker. I worry about the woman who comes into court who doesn't look so pretty. Maybe she has a tattoo or dreadlocks. I want judges to stop wondering, 'What did she do to provoke him?' " Sarah Buel is arguably the country's sharpest weapon against domestic violence.

Buel finishes her talk, and in the split second before the audience jumps to its feet cheering, you can hear people gasp "Whew!" Not because they're tired of sitting, but because in her soft but hurried tones, the prosecution of batterers takes on a passionate, even optimistic, urgency. It's possible, she feels, to end domestic violence, although not by prosecution alone. Buel does not dwell on herself as victim but transmutes her own experience into an aria of hope, a recipe for change, "so that any woman living in despair knows there's help."

Not like she knew. She herself **was clueless.**

One of five children, Buel was born in Chicago but moved endlessly with her family from the age of four. Her father, an auto mechanic fond of drink, always felt success lay elsewhere. Her mother, a Holocaust refugee who fled Austria as a child, went along selflessly—"she didn't know how to speak up," says Buel, which fueled her own desire to do so.

In the seventh grade, Buel was put on a secretarial track. "I was told I wasn't smart enough. So I refused to learn how to type." When she was 14, her parents ·divorced. Rather than choose which one to live with (her siblings split evenly), Buel headed for New York.

She went to school—at first—while working as a governess. For the first time, she saw television and while watching Perry Mason decided "this is what I want to do." The next year Buel bounced around to four different schools and families, including her

mother's. "I went home for three months, but it was too different," she recalls.

Buel eventually went back to New York, where she had relatives, and began a very erratic course through high school, cutting class and shoplifting with a cousin. By the time she was 22, Buel was an abused woman. It came completely out of the blue. She was listening to a song on the radio, "Jeremiah Was a Bullfrog." "I bet that makes you think of Jeremy [a boyfriend of hers way back when she was 15]," her partner said. Actually what she was thinking was how stupid the song was. "Admit it," he insisted, "it does, doesn't it?" No, she said, it doesn't. He accused her of lying—and slapped her across the face.

The verbal and psychological abuse proved more damaging than the physical abuse. There was endless criticism. "He always said I looked frumpy and dumpy. He was enraged if I bought the *New York Times.*" He read the tabloid *Daily News.* " 'Isn't it good enough for you?' he demanded. He was extremely jealous. If I so much as commented on, say, a man's coat, he'd accuse me of wanting an affair and flirting. If I wanted to take courses, he insisted the only reason was to flirt with other men. I didn't cook like his mother, clean like his mother. By the time I left I thought, 'The only thing I do well is, I'm a good mother.' "

Suddenly, Buel is surprised to find herself revealing this much personal detail. "I never tell other women the details of my own abuse. They'll measure. Was theirs more or less?"

In 1993 and 1994, a coveted Bunting fellowship from Radcliffe College allowed Buel to work only part time as a public prosecutor. Now, in between court appearances, she crisscrosses the country, finally able to accept invitations to train judges and address gatherings such as this, a first-ever assembly of Virginians Against Domestic Violence. She has visited 49 states. She has testified before Congress. She was even asked to introduce the president of the United States at a press conference last spring, when the federal government set up a new Violence Against Women Office.

But no matter who she talks to or what she says about domestic violence, "it always comes down to one thing,"

says Buel. "They all ask the same question: Why do they [the women] stay."

First she points out that there are half as many shelters for battered women as there are for stray animals—about 1,800—and most do not accept children. For every two women sheltered, five are turned away. For every two children sheltered, eight are turned away.

A Texas study shows that 75 percent of victims calling domestic violence hotlines had left at least five times. Buel herself first went to the Legal Aid Society. There was a three-year wait for help. They never informed her about safety, never told her about alternatives. She did see a counselor at a family center, but her partner wouldn't go; he would only drive her.

Buel left her abuser and got a job in a shoe factory. But the wage was so low she couldn't pay the rent and a babysitter. "I went back because he said he was sorry, it'll never happen again. When I realized it wasn't true, I left again. I told him I was packing to go to my brother's wedding. I took a bus to New Hampshire, where my mother lived. That didn't work out—she was living on a remote farm, I had no car, and my son was allergic to many of the animals—but I never went back. So 18 years ago I stood on a welfare line with three kids, my own son and two foster children I was raising. But you can't live on that amount of money. We trade our safety for poverty. We go back because we don't know what else to do."

Batterers are expert at portraying themselves as the injured party. The first time her batterer threw her against a wall, Buel's son screamed, "Don't hurt my mom." Then the batterer shouted, "See, you're turning the kid against me."

"I used to think, 'Why me? I must have done something terrible.' Women come to think it was their fault. They feel guilty for not doing a good enough job as a mom because they are unable to protect themselves, or their children."

A major obstacle to leaving, says Buel, is battered women's fear of losing their children or of being unable to protect them. "A Massachusetts study documented that in 70 percent of cases where fathers attempted to get custody of their children, they did so successfully. So when the abuser says to her, 'Sure, you can leave, but I've got the money to hire a good lawyer and I'll get the kids,' he may be right.

"We go back because we think we'll figure out a way to stop the violence, the magic secret everybody else seems to know. We don't want to believe that our marriage or relationship failed because we weren't willing to try just a little harder. I felt deeply ashamed, that it must be my fault. I never heard anyone else talking about it. I assumed I was the only one it was happening to."

One of the biggest reasons women stay, says Buel, is that they are most vulnerable when they leave. That's when abusers desperately escalate tactics of control. More domestic abuse victims are killed when fleeing than at any other time.

Buel has a crystal-clear memory of a Saturday morning at the laundromat with her young son, in the small New Hampshire town where she had fled, safely, she thought, far from her abuser. "I saw my ex-partner, coming in the door. There were people over by the counter and I yelled to them to call the police, but my ex-partner said, 'No, this is my woman. We've just had a little fight and I've come to pick her up. Nobody needs to get involved.' I still had bruises on the side of my face, and I said, 'No, this is the person who did this to me, you need to call the police.' But he said, 'No, this is my woman. Nobody needs to get involved.' Nobody moved. And I thought, as long as I live I want to remember what it feels like to be terrified for my life while nobody even bothers to pick up the phone."

It's time, Buel sighs, to stop asking why they stay and start asking what they need to feel safe. "I'm obsessed with safety now," she confides. "More important than prosecution, more important than anything, is a safety plan, an action plan detailing how to stay alive." And so a first encounter with a victim requires a verbal walk-through of what she'll need to feel safe at her place of work, at home, on the streets, and suggestions about what she'll need for leaving—birth certificates, legal papers, bank accounts—and for dealing with the abuser.

Buel entered Harvard Law in 1987. "I would love to have gone sooner but I had no idea how to get there. I didn't know you had to go to college to go to law school." She imagined you first had to work long enough as a legal secretary. In 1977, after two months on welfare, Buel entered a federally funded job-training program that, despite her awful typing, landed her in a legal services office. Eventually, she became a paralegal aide and began helping domestic violence victims.

In 1980, she started seven years of undergraduate study, first at Columbia University on scholarship, which necessitated "nine horrible months" in a drug-ridden building in New York while on welfare, so that instead of working nights she could spend them with her son. Ultimately she returned to New England and, two nights a week, attended Harvard Extension School, a vastly different world from Harvard Yard. She did well.

Days were spent working as a women's advocate in federal legal services offices, first in New Hampshire, then in grimy Lowell, Massachusetts. Buel started shelters and hotlines for battered women. She helped draft an abuse prevention law. She dreamed about being a voice for the women she represented.

She learned to write. She took classes in public speaking. Toward the end of her undergraduate studies, her bosses asked her where she wanted to go to law school. "Harvard," she replied, "because they're rich and they'll give me money." The lawyers laughed and told her that wasn't how it worked: "They do the choosing, not you." They took pains to point out she just wasn't Harvard material. "You're a single mother. You've been on welfare. You're too old."

Angry and humiliated, Buel began a private campaign that typifies her fierce determination. In the dark after classes, she drove around the law school, shouting at it: "You're going to let me in." Soon she got braver and stopped the car to go inside and look around. Then she had to see what it was like to sit in a classroom. She decided if she ever got accepted, she'd choose one of the orange-colored

lockers, because her son was a fan of the Syracuse Orangemen.

Harvard Law not only accepted Buel but gave her a full scholarship. Once there, she was surprised there was nothing in the criminal-law syllabus about family violence—this despite the fact that women are more likely to be the victim of a crime in their own home, at the hands of someone they know, than on the streets. Buel mentioned the oversight to her professor. He told her to take over the class for one hour one day. She thought she'd be educating movers and shakers for the future. "I was amazed when, during the next six weeks, no less than 16 classmates came up to me either because they were in violent relationships or their parents or friends were."

When Boston-area colleagues requested help on an advocacy program for battered women and she couldn't do it alone, Buel put an ad in the student newspaper; 78 volunteers showed up for the first meeting. By year's end there were 215. She started a pro bono legal counseling program. The Battered Women's Advocacy Project is now the largest student program at Harvard Law; a quarter of the participants are men.

In 1990, at age 36, Buel graduated, cum laude. She sent a copy of her transcript to her old junior-high teacher with a note suggesting that she not judge the future of 12-year-old girls.

At first Buel thought it would be enough to become a prosecutor and make sure that batterers are held accountable for assaulting others. But she has come to see it differently. "That's not enough. My role is not just to make women safe but to see that they are financially empowered and that they have a life plan." So every morning, from 8:30 to 9:15, before court convenes, she sees that all women there on domestic issues are briefed, given a complete list of resources, training options, and more. "We surveyed battered women. We asked them what they needed to know. I wanted everyone to listen to them. Usually no one ever does. Most people tell them what to do. 'Leave him.' 'Do this.' 'Do that.' You can't tell women to leave until you give them—with their children—a place to go, the knowledge how and the resources to get by on their own, and the safety to do so. It's all about options."

What's more, Buel now sees domestic violence as just one arc of a much bigger cycle, intimately connected to all violence, and that it takes a whole coordinated community effort to stop it, requiring the participation of much more than attorneys and judges. It takes everyone; even the locksmith, so that when a woman suddenly needs her locks changed, the call will be heeded.

Rather than drive her own career narrowly forward, Buel has instead broadened her approach, venturing into places few lawyers ever go. She regularly attends community council meetings in Germantown, a dreary outpost of public housing in Quincy, known for its high crime rate. The council—Head Start teachers, the parish priest, two cops who requested duty in the projects, a few community members—celebrates mundane triumphs. A parents dinner at Head Start. A potluck supper at the church.

Buel is absolutely certain that this is the real answer to crime. It is the prevailing fallacy to assume that big problems require big solutions. First a community has to knit itself together—and from the sound of things the best way is on its stomach. "People here hear that some things are unacceptable," says one. A cop reports, remarkably, there has not been a single incident in a month.

Buel tells the assembled that emergency housing funds are available for battered women whose husbands are not paying support. "This is how I get the dirt on what's going on," she tells me. "These officers will call me when there's a domestic violence problem but the woman isn't ready to enter the legal system. At least we can keep on eye on her, and the children, to make sure she's safe."

Buel is particularly concerned about the children. She knows that children who witness violence become violent themselves. "Some take on the role of killing their mother's batterer," says Buel, who notes that 63 percent of males between ages 11 and 20 who are doing time for homicide have killed their mother's batterer. "We adults have abdicated the role of making the home safe."

Children who witness violence may commit suicide as adolescents, says Buel,

pointing to soaring suicide rates among teenagers. Or grow up to soothe the pain with drugs. Or run away from home. A University of Washington study demonstrates that the vast majority of runaway and pregnant teenagers grew up in violent households.

BECAUSE SHE CARES SO MUCH

about the kids, in 1992 Buel started the What Is Your Dream Project in an adolescent center in Chelsea, a depressed community. It grew out of her frustration about pregnant teens, the group at highest risk for domestic violence. "Most of them have no person in their life talking to them about the future. That made me angry. That's how I was stereotyped. There was no assumption I'd be college-bound." The program trains at-risk teens to champion younger kids, telling them about educational and job options, about grants for beautician school or training as electricians or computer technicians, for example. "It was a powerful force for me to name going to law school as a dream. It focused my life," Buel recalls.

For her unusually diversified approach to domestic violence, Buel gives full credit to William Delahunt, her boss, the district attorney. "He has allowed me to challenge the conventional notion of what our job is."

"My boss gets complaints about me all the time," Buel says proudly. There was the batterer who, despite divorce and remarriage, was thought to be the source of menacing gifts anonymously sent to his ex-wife—a gun box for Christmas, a bullet box for Valentine's Day, followed by the deeds to burial plots for her and her new husband. The woman repeatedly hauled her ex into court for violating a restraining order; one lawyer after another got him off. "Finally I got him for harassing her in the parking garage where she was going to college; of course he denied it. The lawyer contended she was making up all the stories. But a detective found a videotape from the garage, which corroborated her charge. In the appeals court, his lawyer, a big guy, leaned into my face and hissed, 'You may be a good little advocate for your cause, but you're a terrible lawyer.'" She won the appeal.

Because the students asked for one, Buel teaches a class on domestic violence

to 43 students at Boston College Law School. Over a third of them are males.

And she lectures widely to the medical profession. "Doctors see abused women all the time and don't know it," she says. She is especially interested in reaching family doctors and obstetrician/gynecologists, because in over a third of instances, abuse occurs during pregnancy—as it did for her. It is the primary time for the onset of violence. Her goal is to see that all doctors routinely ask every woman at every visit whether she has been hit or threatened since her last visit, explain that they are now routinely asking the question, state that no woman deserves to be abused, and then provide information and referral if she has. This simple question, by exposing abuse to plain daylight, brilliantly erases some of its shame. It is only when shame is gone that abused women can ask for help.

YOU COULD SAY THAT 1994

was the best of times and the worst of times for domestic violence. Spouse abuse was "discovered" by Congress, which passed the Violence Against Women Act. Among its provisions are federal standards that permit enforcement of restraining orders across state lines, the single most important weapon women have to keep abusers from threatening or attacking them or their children.

And spouse abuse was "discovered" by the public at large after O. J. Simpson was arrested for the murder of ex-wife Nicole Brown Simpson and her friend Ronald Goldman. Clear evidence quickly emerged that O. J. Simpson had beaten his wife in the past. To those who know about domestic violence, Simpson fit a well-established pattern—when his partner got serious about leaving him for good, he began a campaign of terror. He began stalking her. He followed her movements. He peeked in her windows. He wouldn't, couldn't, let go.

Despite his ultimate acquittal, O. J., nevertheless, was the answer to some people's prayers. Like Deborah Tucker's. One of those whip-smart, wise-crackin', well-coifed dynamos that Texas seems to breed, who have you howling on the floor while they're stripping your political illusions, Tucker not only heads Texas's Council on Family Violence, she runs the new national Domestic Violence Hotline (1-800-799-SAFE). If the world of action against domestic violence has an axis on which it turns, Tucker is its south pole to Sarah Buel's north.

"Many people worked awfully hard for 20 years to see that violence against women was taken seriously and recognized as a crime. We had seen a law passed, established 1,800 organizations around the country providing services to battered women. We had built an infrastructure to respond to domestic violence and educate about it. Now all that was needed was visibility for the cause. Many of us talked among ourselves that that would happen only when a famous person killed his wife." Of course, no one imagined that person would be black, opening the racial divide. Tucker is now more cautious about what she wishes for.

O. J.'s arrest, says Tucker, "put domestic violence on the map. O. J. and Nicole were wealthy. They were visible. We tend to accept domestic violence in invisible people. We were at a juncture where something like that needed to happen. Social change is slow.

"The murder created a vehicle for common discourse about spouse abuse. The trial was a fiasco. The prosecutor never educated the public about stalking or about patterns of domestic violence. O. J. had followed Nicole and watched her. Everywhere I went, people asked: 'Why would he do that? He was divorced; he even had a girlfriend.' It was a chance to discuss tactics of power and control that do not stop with divorce, a chance to point out that women are in more danger when they leave—though everyone always asks why they stay."

If the Los Angeles D.A.s did little to explain, that is not the case with Buel. She has talked almost nonstop since.

In her travels, Buel has observed firsthand that many jurisdictions have figured out how to reduce violence against women. She sees her mission as spreading the word about them. Buel's considerable charisma stems in no small measure from her conviction that the solutions are out there, if only everyone knew about them. "People are always surprised at my optimism," she says.

"There's no one solution," she insists. "You need a message from the whole community. People point to the policy of mandatory arrest of all batterers in Duluth, Minnesota. But Duluth also has billboards that warn, 'Never hit a child.'" Buel's list of what works includes:

- **the end of silence about spouse abuse.**
- **probation officers sensitive to the safety needs of victims and serious monitoring of offenders.**
- **mandatory group treatment programs for batterers. Programs must last at least a year, hold them alone accountable, and teach them to respect women.**
- **sanctions for failure to comply with probation or restraining orders.**
- **the use of advocates to follow cases.**
- **training cops in how to investigate and gather complete evidence when answering domestic violence calls.**

Buel waves an investigation checklist she got from police in San Diego. If information gathering is done correctly, prosecution can proceed even when the victim refuses to press charges or come to court as a witness. "When a woman refuses to testify, she's not 'failing to cooperate,'" she says. "She's terrified. She's making the statement, 'I want to stay alive.'"

I ask Buel about her working relationships with judges. "In Massachusetts, I'm characterized as too harsh. I simply ask for some mechanism of accountability. Judges here are appointed for life without mandatory training. Many come from the big law firms that represent the batterers. Some do a great job. Others lose sight of the victims and children."

Discrimination against women through the law infuriates Buel. A recent study shows that a batterer who kills his wife typically gets a jail term of two to four years. But a woman who kills her abuser gets 14 to 18 years.

Of course, a great deal of domestic violence never finds its way into the criminal justice system; it's handled by private psychotherapists. "No one wants her husband arrested," especially women from the upper income strata, says Buel. She regrets that she is rarely invited to speak to the mental health community.

"Unfortunately," she charges, "most therapists, including family counselors, have little training in domestic violence. They are often conned by the stories of the batterers, experts at shifting blame. Without realizing it, therapists often put women at greater risk of abuse. There is nothing victims can disclose to them for which there will not be later retaliation. At the very least, therapists don't think in terms of safety plans for the victims.

"Batterers are extraordinarily talented in sucking in therapists, the community, even their wives' families. Their whole M.O. is manipulation. They'll get the priest to testify that they're family-loving men, but the priest isn't there during the abuse. They are notorious liars; they'll say whatever makes them look good. Even if the woman gets a restraining order barring her partner from having any contact with her, these guys will make calls or send flowers. They're not really showing love, just proving they can get around the system, showing who's boss." In the toxic world of domestic violence, simply receiving an unsigned birthday card can be a deadly threat.

Yet domestic violence thrives in the best of zip codes, including the bedroom communities for Boston's medical chiefs. "Two of the worst cases I ever prosecuted involved doctors," says Buel, who finds that domestic violence is increasing in severity among wealthier families. "There's a much greater use of weapons. Ten years ago you would never have heard of a computer executive putting a gun to his wife's head."

BECAUSE TOO MANY VICTIMS stay with their batterers, Buel has begun to radically shift her approach to ending violence. "I'm learning new ways to compromise, reaching out to defense attorneys." In this she is crossing a divide most feminist lawyers shun. The defense attorneys, after all, represent batterers, "because they have the money." But they also have some power over their clients. "Some defense attorneys are willing to change their practices, to agree to take on batterers only if they go to a treatment program and stick with it."

This braving of the breach gives the lie to any suggestion that Buel is motivated by vindictiveness. She rolls her huge eyes at characterizations of activists as man haters. Or as do-gooders blind to the "fact" that people don't change.

There are men in her life. First and foremost is her son; he's away—but not too far away—at college. And there is a serious relationship. "He works in another domain, so there's no sense of competition. He is very emotionally supportive and respects the work I do. I had pretty much given up. Most men say I'm too intimidating."

Not David Adams, who runs the first and arguably best counseling program set up in the United States for men who batter. "It's taken someone like her to move the system forward. Only recently have the courts begun to hear women's concerns; they're more attuned to men's perspectives and complaints. She's a tremendous leader widely respected in the criminal justice system. She's become the conscience of the system, always looking at ways victims can be helped and perpetrators held accountable."

Holding men accountable for their violence is a full-time job for Adams, who sees 300 abusers a week at his Cambridge-based Emerge program. "These guys constantly minimize their own behavior. They'll say, 'She provoked me; if she'd only just shut up or respect me more.'" Excuse number two is "I lost control. I just snapped." Observes Adams: "But their 'snapping' is awfully selective; they snap only with the victim, not with their boss or other people."

Battering, Adams insists, "is primarily an instrument of control. It's not anger, though abusers always claim they're impulsive. It is purposeful, though from the outside it looks as if it's irrational behavior. And there's a logic to it; it enforces social rules. It is a learned behavior that's self-reinforcing—batterers get what they want through violence—and socially reinforced through beliefs about women as the social and sexual caretakers of men." He finds it takes at least nine months in the program just to puncture men's denial.

Returning to Boston from Williamsburg, Buel attends back-to-back meetings. First is the board session of a foundation that funds battered-women's shelters. Next comes the Domestic Violence Council, a regional group of private and public attorneys who share information and strategies. Buel started the council in law school. It has grown exponentially since, and now meets at one of Boston's prestige law firms. Discussions this day focus on:

• Lawyers' safety. Being the barrier between a woman and her batterer sometimes leads to threats, or worse; victims and their attorneys have been murdered—even in the courthouse. A lawyer reports that her tires were punctured.

• A new cultural trend toward what look like organizations for the preservation of fatherhood. Masquerading as involved fathers, members are often batterers who use their kids as a way of stalking or threatening ex-partners. A law student assigned to check out one group's roster reports that 86 percent of the men have restraining orders against them.

• Monitoring the courts. For two years, practicing and student attorneys have been trained to evaluate how the state's judges handle domestic violence cases. Now they're assembling a committee to meet with those doing a bad job—those who, say, don't ask about kids or weapons when considering requests for restraining orders—and inform them how to do better.

The day has no end. Dinner isn't simply a meal, it's an opportunity to give support and advice to two Harvard Law grads who have formed the fledgling Women's Rights Network. Where should they go for funding? Does she know a defense attorney in Edmonton (Canada) for the international information they are putting together on domestic violence?

And Buel whips out some formidable pieces of paper, legal-pad sheets neatly filled with the names and phone numbers of people—73 per side—whose calls she must return. There were, I think, four of them, neatly written, neatly folded, representing two or three days' worth of calls to her office and her home. She keeps her number listed so women in trouble can find her. Somewhere on the list is an Edmonton attorney.

The two young women complain that despite its own budget surplus, Harvard Law has cut funding for law clinics, needed now more than ever as the public sector cuts back. "They'll no doubt use the money to put in more rosewood desks," they scoff.

But all three know it is the very credibility a Harvard Law degree bestows that compels the attention of so many others. And that, says Buel, "also pisses me off. People who wouldn't pay attention to me before suddenly hang on every word."

That seventh-grade teacher, I am certain, the one who almost derailed her for good, is never far from Buel's mind.

Development during Middle and Late Adulthood

• **Middle Adulthood** (Articles 40–42)
• **Late Adulthood** (Articles 43–47)

There is a gradual slowing of the rate of mitosis of cells of all the organ systems with age (except the neurons, which do not undergo mitosis after birth). This gradual slowing of mitosis translates into a slowed rate of repair of cells of all the organs. By the thirties, signs of aging can be seen in skin, skeleton, vision, hearing, smell, taste, balance, coordination, heart, blood vessels, lungs, liver, kidneys, digestive tract, immune response, endocrine functioning and ability to reproduce. To some extent, moderate use of any body part (as opposed to disuse or misuse) helps it retain its strength, stamina, and reparability. However, by middle and late adulthood, persons become increasingly aware of the aging effects of their organ systems on their total physical fitness. A loss of height occurs as spinal disks and connective tissues diminish and settle. Demineralization, especially loss of calcium, causes weakening of bones. Muscles atrophy, and the showing of cardiovascular and respiratory responses create a loss of stamina for exercise. All of this may seem cruel, but it occurs very gradually and need not adversely affect one's enjoyment of life.

Healthful aging, at least in part, seems to be genetically preprogrammed. The females of many species, including humans, outlive the males. The sex hormones of females may protect them from some early aging effects. Males, in particular, experience earlier declines in their cardiovascular systems. Diet and exercise can ward off many of the deleterious effects of aging. A reduction in saturated fat intake coupled with regular aerobic exercise contributes to less bone demineralization, less plaquing up of arteries, stronger muscles (including heart and lung muscles), and a general increase in stamina and vitality. An adequate intake of complex carbohydrates, fibrous foods, fresh fruits, fresh vegetables, and water also enhances good health.

Cognitive abilities do not appreciably decline with age in healthy adults. Research suggests that the speed with which the brain carries out problems involving abstract (fluid) reasoning may slow, but not cease. Complex problems may simply require more time to solve with age. On the other hand, research suggests that the memory banks of older people may have more knowledge crystallized (accumulated and stored). One's ken (range of knowledge) and practical skills (common sense) grow with age and experience. Older human beings become more expert at the tasks they frequently do. The first article included in the middle adulthood section of this unit examines the speculation about sex differences in the cognitive abilities of adults. Are women better at emotional and linguistic types of reasoning? If so, is their superiority due to brain differences, or does it reflect dissimilar experiences from men? Conversely, men seem to be better at spatial orientating ability. Is this superiority a result of nature or nurture? The research suggests that there are subtle but real differences in adults' cognitive styles related to their sex, which may be due to brain differences.

Erik Erikson, the psychosocial personality theorist, defined the passage into middle adulthood as a growing concern for generativity. Humans who feel productive with their skills and abilities and who help guide the next generation into similar skill usage achieve a sense of generativity. Persons who do not generate often feel that their lives are stagnating. The second article included in this section discusses the question of how bad stress is for adults attempting to achieve generativity. The research suggests that a person may outwardly believe that his or her stress is unimportant, but inwardly (physiologically) may respond as if his or her life were on the line. The author suggests several proactive ways to alleviate dangerous stress responses and several active ways to stop it before it does too much damage.

The third article takes on many other myths about midlife changes: midlife crisis, career doldrums, marital unhappiness. The author contends that middle age may be the very best time of life. Many people turn inward, take better care of themselves, and please themselves rather than the outside world.

Erik Erikson suggested that the most important psychological conflict of late adulthood is achieving a sense of ego integrity. This is fostered by self-respect, self-esteem, love of others, and a sense that one's life has order and meaning. The articles in the subsection on aging reflect Erikson's concern with experiencing ego integrity rather than despair. The first article "Learning to Love (Gulp!)

The second article in the aging section of this unit describes the aging brain from a new perspective such as imaging techniques like positron emission tomography (PET scans) and magnetic resonance imaging (MRI). Data from healthy seniors in their 80s and 90s reveal that loss of brain tissue is modest and largely confined to selective areas. Intellectual functioning can continue to be robust and may even continue to grow in areas such as vocabulary and overall knowledge.

The third article in this section looks at grandparents and the possibilities for their keeping up with grandchildren and great-grandchildren in areas such as computer skills. The authors describe other educational curricula as well which benefit grandparent development and impact positively on family life.

The fourth and fifth articles in this section take a kinder, gentler view of some of the very real challenges faced by old people. In "Ageing with Attitude," the writer discusses job discrimination, housing discrimination, and poverty. She suggests a way forward from prejudice against the aged to societal programs like Pro Vida (For Life). Robert Sapolsky's essay on the patterns of life ends this section and this anthology. He takes a positive view of dying, death, and bereavement. He finds solace in experiencing the human life span as a cycle complete with predictable patterns and stages.

Looking Ahead: Challenge Questions

Do men's and women's brains function differently? Why?

Is stress worse for you than you think? How?

Midlife: What are the positive and satisfying aspects?

In what ways can loving growing old make the passage through old age a jubilee?

How can grandparents join the computer generation?

How should we prepare for 1999, the International Year of Aging?

Why is there solace to be found in predictable patterns of living and dying?

Growing Old" advocates conscious enjoyment of the aging process. Rather than spending billions of dollars on plastic surgery and fountain-of-youth elixirs, the author recommends improving the quality of life for aging people. Fear of memory loss can cause memory loss; but belief in the wisdom of old age can reveal sage insights into the meanings of life with its ebb and flow.

Man's World, Woman's World? Brain Studies Point to Differences

Gina Kolata

Dr. Ronald Munson, a philosopher of science at the University of Missouri, was elated when Good Housekeeping magazine considered publishing an excerpt from the latest of the novels he writes on the side. The magazine eventually decided not to publish the piece, but Dr. Munson was much consoled by a letter from an editor telling him that she liked the book, which is written from a woman's point of view, and could hardly believe a man had written it.

New scanner finds more evidence of how the sexes differ in brain functions.

It is a popular motion: that men and women are so intrinsically different that they literally live in different worlds, unable to understand each other's perspectives fully. There is a male brain and a female brain, a male way of thinking and a female way. But only now are scientists in a position to address whether the notion is true.

The question of brain differences between the sexes is a sensitive and controversial field of inquiry. It has been smirched by unjustifiable interpretations of data, including claims that women are less intelligent because their brains are smaller than those of men. It has been sullied by overinterpretations of data, like the claims that women are genetically less able to do everyday mathematics

because men, on average, are slightly better at mentally rotating three dimensional objects in space.

But over the years, with a large body of animal studies and studies of humans that include psychological tests, anatomical studies, and increasingly, brain scans, researchers are consistently finding that the brains of the two sexes are subtly but significantly different.

Now, researchers have a new non-invasive method, functional magnetic resonance imaging, for studying the live human brain at work. With it, one group recently detected certain apparent differences in the way men's and women's brains function while they are thinking. While stressing extreme caution in drawing conclusions from the data, scientists say nonetheless that the groundwork was being laid for determining what the differences really mean.

"What it means is that we finally have the tools at hand to begin answering these questions," said Dr. Sally Shaywitz, a behavioral scientist at the Yale University School of Medicine. But she cautioned: "We have to be very, very careful. It behooves us to understand that we've just begun."

The most striking evidence that the brains of men and women function differently came from a recent study by Dr. Shaywitz and her husband, Dr. Bennett A. Shaywitz, a neurologist, who is also at the Yale medical school. The Shaywitzes and their colleagues used functional magnetic resonance imaging to watch brains in action as 19 men and 19

women read nonsense words and determined whether they rhymed.

In a paper, published in the Feb. 16 issue of Nature, the Shaywitzes reported that the subjects did equally well at the task, but the men and women used different areas of their brains. The men used just a small area on the left side of the brain, next to Broca's area, which is near the temple. Broca's area has long been thought to be associated with speech. The women used this area as well as an area on the right side of the brain. This was the first clear evidence that men and women can use their brains differently while they are thinking.

Another recent study, by Dr. Ruben C. Gur, the director of the brain behavior laboratory at the University of Pennsylvania School of Medicine, and his colleagues, used magnetic resonance imaging to look at the metabolic activity of the brains of 37 young men and 24 young women when they were at rest, not consciously thinking of anything.

In the study, published in the Jan. 27 issue of the journal Science, the investigators found that for the most part, the brains of men and women at rest were indistinguishable from each other. But there was one difference, found in a brain structure called the limbic system that regulates emotions. Men, on average, had higher brain activity in the more ancient and primitive regions of the limbic system, the parts that are more involved with action. Women, on average, had more activity in the newer and more complex parts of the limbic system, which are involved in symbolic actions.

Men have larger brains; women have more neurons.

Dr. Gur explained the distinction: "If a dog is angry and jumps and bites, that's an action. If he is angry and bares his fangs and growls, that's more symbolic."

Dr. Sandra Witelson, a neuroscientist at McMaster University in Hamilton, Ontario, has focused on brain anatomy, studying people with terminal cancers that do not involve the brain. The patients have agreed to participate in neurological and psychological tests and then to allow Dr. Witelson and her colleagues to examine their brains after they die, to look for relationships between brain structures and functions. So far she has studied 90 brains.

Several years ago, Dr. Witelson reported that women have a larger corpus callosum, the tangle of fibers that run down the center of the brain and enable the two hemispheres to communicate. In addition, she said, she found that a region in the right side of the brain that corresponds to the region women used in the reading study by the Shaywitzes was larger in women than in men.

Most recently, Dr. Witelson discovered, by painstakingly counting brain cells, that although men have larger brains than women, women have about 11 percent more neurons. These extra nerve cells are densely packed in two of the six layers of the cerebral cortex, the outer shell of the brain, in areas at the level of the temple, behind the eye. These are regions used for understanding language and for recognizing melodies and the tones in speech. Although the sample was small, five men and four women, "the results are very, very clear," Dr. Witelson said.

Going along with the studies of brain anatomy and activity are a large body of psychological studies showing that men and women have different mental abilities. Psychologists have consistently shown that men, on average, are slightly better than women at spatial tasks, like visualizing figures rotated in three dimensions, and women, on average, are slightly better at verbal tasks.

Dr. Gur and his colleagues recently looked at how well men and women can distinguish emotions on someone else's face. Both men and women were equally adept at noticing when someone else was happy, Dr. Gur found. And women had no trouble telling if a man or a woman was sad. But men were different. They were as sensitive as women in deciding if a man's face was sad—giving correct responses 90 percent of the time. But they were correct about 70 percent of the time in deciding if women were sad; the women were correct 90 percent of the time.

"A woman's face had to be really sad for men to see it," Dr. Gur said. "The subtle expressions went right by them."

Studies in laboratory animals also find differences between male and female brains. In rats, for example, male brains are three to seven times larger than female brains in a specific area, the preoptic nucleus, and this difference is controlled by sex hormones that bathe rats when they are fetuses.

"The potential existence of structural sex differences in human brains is almost predicted from the work in other animals," said Dr. Roger Gorski, a professor of anatomy and cell biology at the University of California in Los Angeles. "I think it's a really fundamental concept and I'm sure, without proof, that it applies to our brains."

But the question is, if there are these differences, what do they mean?

Dr. Gorski and others are wary about drawing conclusions. "What happens is that people overinterpret these things," Dr. Gorski said. "The brain is very complicated, and even in animals that we've studied for many years, we don't really know the function of many brain areas."

This is exemplified, Dr. Gorski said, in his own work on differences in rat brains. Fifteen years ago, he and his colleagues discovered that males have a comparatively huge preoptic nucleus and that the area in females is tiny. But Dr. Gorski added: "We've been studying this nucleus for 15 years, and we still don't know what it does. The most likely explanation is that it has to do with sexual behavior, but it is very, very difficult to study. These regions are very small and they are interconnected with other things." Moreover, he said, "nothing like it has been shown in humans."

And, with the exception of the work by the Shaywitzes, all other findings of differences in the brains or mental abilities of men and women have also found that there is an amazing degree of overlap. "There is so much overlap that if you take any individual man and woman, they might show differences in the opposite direction" from the statistical findings, Dr. Gorski said.

Dr. Munson, the philosopher of science, said that with the findings so far, "we still can't tell whether the experiences are different" when men and women think. "All we can tell is that the brain processes are different," he said, adding that "there is no Archimedean point on which you can stand, outside of experience, and say the two are the same. It reminds me of the people who show what the world looks like through a multiplicity of lenses and say, 'This is what the fly sees.' " But, Dr. Munson added, "We don't know what the fly sees." All we know, he explained, is what we see looking through those lenses.

Some researchers, however, say that the science is at least showing the way to answering the ancient mind-body problem, as applied to the cognitive worlds of men and women.

Dr. Norman Krasnegor, who directs the human learning and behavior branch at the National Institute of Child Health and Human Development, said the difference that science made was that when philosophers talked about mind, they "always were saying, 'We've got this black box.' " But now, he said, "we don't have a black box; now we are beginning to get to its operations."

Dr. Gur said science was the best hope for discovering whether men and women inhabited different worlds. It is not possible to answer that question simply by asking people to describe what they perceive, Dr. Gur said, because "when you talk and ask questions, you are talking to the very small portion of the brain that is capable of talking." If investigators ask people to tell them what they are thinking, "that may or may not be closely related to what was taking place" in the brain, Dr. Gur said.

On the other hand, he said, scientists have discovered that what primates perceived depends on how their brains function. Some neurons fire only in response to lines that are oriented at particular angles, while others seem to recognize faces. The world may well be what the philosopher Descartes said it was, an embodiment of the workings of the human mind, Dr. Gur said. "Descartes said that we are creating our world," he said. "But there is a world out there that we can't know."

Dr. Gur said that at this point he would hesitate to baldly proclaim that men and women inhabit different worlds. "I'd say that science might be leading us in that direction," he said, but before he commits himself he would like to see more

definite differences in the way men's and women's brains function and to know more about what the differences mean.

Dr. Witelson cautioned that "at this point, it is a very big leap to go from any of the structural or organizational differences that were demonstrated to the cognitive differences that were demonstrated." She explained that "all you have is two sets of differences, and whether one is the basis of the other has not been shown." But she added, "One can speculate."

Dr. Witelson emphasized that in speculating she was "making a very big leap," but she noted that "we all live in our different worlds and our worlds depend on our brains.

"And," she said, "if these sex differences in the brain, with 'if' in big capital letters, do have cognitive consequences, and it would be hard to believe there would be none, then it is possible that there is a genuine difference in the kinds of things that men and women perceive and how these things are integrated. To that extent it may be possible that in some respects there is less of an easy cognitive or emotional communication between the sexes as a group because our brains may be wired differently."

The Shaywitzes said they were reluctant even to speculate from the data at hand. But, they said, they think that the deep philosophical questions about the perceptual worlds of men and women can eventually be resolved by science.

"It is a truism that men and women are different," Dr. Bennett Shaywitz said. "What I think we can do now is to take what is essentially folklore and place it in the context of science. There is a real scientific method available to answer some of these questions."

Dr. Sally Shaywitz added: "I think we've taken a qualitative leap forward in our ability to ask questions." But, she said, "the field is simply too young to have provided more than a very intriguing appetizer."

Approaches to Understanding Male-Female Brain Differences

Studies of differences in perception or behavior can suggest how male and female thinking may diverge; studies of structural or metabolic differences can suggest why. But only now are differences in brain organization being studied.

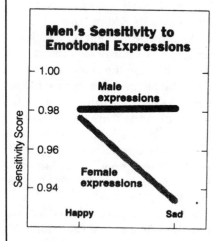

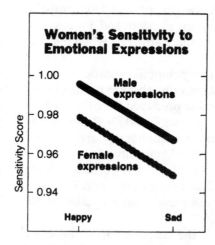

A study compared how well men and women recognized emotions in photos of actors portraying happiness and sadness. Men were equally sensitive to a range of happy and sad faces in men but far less sensitive to sadness in women's faces.

The women in the study were generally more sensitive to happy faces than to sad ones. They were also better able to recognize sadness in a man's face. For both sexes, sensitivity scores reflected the percent of the time the emotion was correctly identified.

STRESS

IT'S WORSE THAN YOU THINK

Psychological stress doesn't just put your head in a vise. New studies document exactly how it tears away at every body system—including your brain. But get this: The experience of stress in the past magnifies your reactivity to stress in the future. So take a nice deep breath and find a stress-stopping routine this instant.

John Carpi

JOHN CARPI writes on health, medicine, and the environment for a variety of publications. His articles have appeared in magazines as diverse as *Scientific American, Parenting,* and *Earth,* as well as in dozens of daily newspapers in the United States and abroad. He was the founding editor and later Editor-in-Chief of a *New York Times* medical news service. He teaches writing at New York University's graduate program in Science and Environmental Reporting. Between deadlines, Carpi is usually covering meetings around the world. The week he turned in his article on stress, he left town—on his honeymoon.

Technologic advances have expanded the business day. Leisure time has shrunk. Bathing-suited business men walk beaches on Sundays with cellular phones stuck to their ears, planning the next morning's meetings. Laptop computers find their way on vacations. The family icons of the 1990s are working couples picking up their children on their way home to dinners prepared by caterers or fast food chefs. Grieving time has shrunk. The divorce rate hovers near its highest in history. The concept of job security has gone the way of the dirigible. Yet there is no time to pick up the pieces. "Just snap out of it," yells the therapist as he slaps his patient in a newspaper cartoon. The caption: Time-saving single-visit psychotherapy.

Stress has become so endemic it is worn like a badge of courage. The business of stress reduction, from workshops to relaxation tapes to light and sound headsets, is booming. If ours is a culture without deep intimacy, then our relationship with stress is the exception.

Yet not even this familiarity can cushion the findings of the latest research: The effects of stress are even more profound than imagined. It penetrates to the core of our being. Stress is not something that just grips us and, with time or effort, then lets go. It changes us in the process. It alters our bodies—and our brains.

We may respond to stress as we do an allergy. That is, we can become sensitized, or acutely sensitive, to stress. Once that happens, even the merest intimation of stress can trigger a cascade of chemical reactions in brain and body that assault us from within. Stress is the psychological equivalent of ragweed. Once the body becomes sensitized to pollen or ragweed, it takes only the slightest bloom in spring or fall to set off the biochemical alarm that results in runny noses, watery eyes, and the general misery of hay fever. But while only some of us are genetically programed to be plagued with hay fever, all of us have the capacity to become sensitized to stress.

Stress sensitization is uncharitably subversive. While the chemical signaling systems of body and brain are running amok in a person sensitized to stress, that person's perception of stress remains unchanged. It's as if the brain, aware that the burner on the stove is cool, still signals the body to jerk its hand away. "What happens is that sensitization leads the brain to re-circuit itself in response to stress," says psychologist Michael Meaney, Ph.D., of McGill University. "We know that what we are encountering may be a normal, everyday episode of stress, but the brain is signaling the body to respond inappropriately." We may not think we are getting worked up over running late for an appointment, but our brain is treating it as though our life were on the line.

Because some stress is absolutely necessary in living creatures, everyone has a built-in gauge that controls our reaction to it. It's a kind of biological thermostat that keeps the body from launching an all-out response literally over spilled milk. Sensitization, however, lowers the thermostat's set point, says psychologist Jonathan C. Smith, Ph.D., founder and director of the Stress Institute at Roosevelt University in Chicago. As a result, the body response typically reserved for life-threatening events is turned on by life's mundane aggravations. In this hothouse of hyperreactivity, biochemicals unleashed by stress may boil over at the most trivial of events, like our missing a train or being shunted to voice mail.

"Years of research has told us that people do become sensitized to stress and that this sensitization actually alters physical patterns in the brain," says Seymour Levine, Ph.D., of the University of Delaware. "That means that once sensitized, the body just does not respond to stress the same way in the future. We may produce too many excitatory chemicals or too few calming ones; either way we are responding inappropriately."

The revelation that stress itself alters our ability to cope with stress has produced yet another remarkable finding: Sensitization to stress may occur before we are old enough to prevent it ourselves. New studies suggest that animals from rodents to monkeys to humans may experience still undetermined developmental periods during which exposure to stress is more damaging than in later years. "For example, we have known that losing a parent when you are young is harder to get over than if your parent dies when you are an adult," says Jean King, Ph.D., of the University of Massachusetts Medical School. "What we now believe is that a stress of that magnitude occurring when you are young may permanently rewire the brain's circuitry, throwing the system askew and leaving it less able to handle normal, everyday stress."

It is the stew of chemicals released by such provocations that ultimately explains the noose stress ties between mind and body. "This new paradigm of stress demonstrates that there is a link between psychological events and physical eruptions, between mind and body," King says. "The psychological events that are most deleterious probably occur during infancy and childhood—an unstable home environment, living with an alcoholic parent, or any other number of extended crises." The new paradigm also firmly ties everyday psychological stress to such suspect complaints as ulcers, headaches, and fatigue.

The new blueprint of how we respond to stress also may explain why people have different tolerances for stress. In the past stress tolerance may have been chalked up to mental fortitude: "He's a rock," or "She's really bearing up under pressure." Now it's clear that our ability to withstand stress has less to do with whether we are strong-willed than with how much and what kind of stress we encountered in the past.

Whether we end up stressed-out executives or laid-back surfers, we all start out with the same biological machinery for responding to stress. Stress activates primitive

Stress does not just grip us and let go. It changes us. It alters our bodies—and our brains.

regions of the brain, the same areas that control eating, aggression, and immune response. It switches on nerve circuits that ignite the body's fight-or-flight response as if there were a life-threatening danger.

From this evidence researchers have concluded that the stress response is "wired" into the brain, that we inherit the same ancient reactions that jump-started hunter-gatherers to escape a charging saber-tooth tiger without having to give their actions time-consuming thought. Only this same life-or-death reaction is now called into play largely by non–life-threatening situations. Studies have found the same fight-or-flight circuits all working overtime in response to such varied stressors as extreme exercise, the death of a loved one, an approaching deadline.

One conclusion from the evidence is that we may be victims of evolution, saddled with a stress response system that's better suited to a life filled with occasional life-threatening events than one filled with everyday irritations like failing a test or blowing a sales call. Unfortunately, when stresses become routine, the constant biochemical pounding takes its toll on the body; the system starts to wear out at an accelerated rate.

By responding to the stress of everyday life with the same surge of biochemicals released during major threats, the body is slowly killing itself. The biochemical onslaught chips away at the immune system, opening the way to cancer, infection, and disease. Hormones unleashed by stress eat at the digestive tract and lungs, promoting ulcers and asthma. Or they may weaken the heart, leading to strokes and heart disease. "Chronic stress is like slow poison," King observes. "It is a fact of modern life that even people who are not sensitized to stress are adversely affected by everything that can go wrong in the day."

If stress has a central command post, it is the hypothalamus, a primitive area of the brain located near where the spine runs into the skull. By way of a dazzling array of hormonals signals, the hypothalamus is closely connected

with the nearby pituitary gland and the distant adrenal glands, perched atop the kidneys. The so-called hypothalamic-pituitary axis (HPA) has a virtual monopoly on basic body functions. It regulates blood pressure, heart rate, body temperature, sleep patterns, hunger and thirst, and reproductive functions, among many other activities.

About the size of a grape, the hypothalamus does its work by releasing two types of signaling hormones; those that stimulate glands to release other hormones and those that inhibit the glands from performing their job. Among the best known of these hormones are follicle-stimulating and luteinizing hormones, which, dispatched on a strict schedule from the pituitary, begin the monthly process that prepares women for pregnancy or menstruation.

Like a cherry attached by its stem, the pituitary gland hangs off the hypothalamus, waiting to receive instructions on which of its many hormones to release and in what quantity. In hormonal terms it is the little gland that could. The pituitary releases substances that regulate growth, sex, skin color, bone length, and muscle strength. It also releases adrenocorticotropin, a hormone that activates the third part of the body's stress system, the adrenal glands.

When stress sets off the usual ferocious communication between the hypothalamus and the pituitary, the buck stops at the adrenal glands. They manufacture and release the true stress hormones—dopamine, epinephrine (also known as adrenaline), norepinephrine (noradrenaline), and especially cortisol. So responsive to the adrenal hormones are basic body functions like blood flow and breathing that even minute changes in levels of these substances can significantly affect health.

Slight overproduction of dopamine can constrict blood vessels and raise blood pressure; a shift in epinephrine could precipitate diabetes, or asthma, by constricting tiny airways in the lungs. If the adrenal gland slacks off on cortisol production the result may be obesity, heart disease, or osteoporosis; too much of the hormone can cause women to take on masculine traits like hair growth and muscle development and lead to one of the greatest fears of all for aging men—baldness. High levels of cortisol also may kill off brain cells crucial for memory.

The adrenal gland is also home of the granddaddy of all stress reactions, the fight-or-flight response. Sensing impending danger the hypothalamus presses out cortisol-releasing factor, a hormone that prompts the pituitary gland to release adrenocorticotropin (ACTH). Carried in the bloodstream to the adrenal glands, ACTH triggers production of cortisol and epinephrine. The end result of this hormonal relay is a sudden surge in blood sugar, heart rate, and blood pressure—everything the body needs to flee or confront the imminent danger.

The problem is, what we call the stress system is actually responsible for coordinating much more than just our response to stress. "Initiating a response to stress is just one of many things the system controls," says Jean King. "These hormones are carefully regulated substances that direct everything from the immune system to the cardiovascular system to our behavioral system."

For example, cortisol directly impacts storage of short-term memory in the hippocampus. The stress hormones dopamine and epinephrine are also neurotransmitters widely active in enabling communication among brain cells. Directly and indirectly, they act on numerous neural networks in the brain and throw off levels of other neurotransmitters. Stress, it's now known, alters serotonin pathways. And through effects on serotonin, stress is now linked with depression on one hand, aggression on the other.

The developing picture of the biochemistry of stress in some ways takes the heat off psychology. "We used to say that physical manifestations of stress were psychological defense mechanisms employed as a way to shield the person from revisiting a particularly troubling event in their past," says Roosevelt's Smith. "What is far more likely is that the same chemicals being released in response to stress are triggering physical reactions throughout the body."

A torrent of new studies catalogue how even a little stress can have wide-ranging effects on the body. Researchers have recently found that:

• Epinephrine, released by the adrenal glands in response to stress, instigates potentially damaging changes in blood cells. Epinephrine triggers blood platelets, the cells responsible for repairing blood vessels, to secrete large quantities of a substance called ATP. In large amounts, ATP can trigger a heart attack or stroke by causing blood vessels to rapidly narrow, thus cutting off blood flow, says Thomas Pickering, M.D., a cardiologist at the New York Hospital-Cornell Medical Center.

• Other substances released in the stress response impair the body's ability to fight infections. In one study, researchers tracked the neurohormones of parachute jumpers. They found an 84 percent surge in nerve growth factor (NGF) among young Italian soldiers attempting their first jump, compared with nonjumpers. Up to six hours after they hit ground, the jumpers' NGF levels were 107 percent higher than in nonjumping soldiers. Released by the pituitary gland as part of the stress response, NGF is attracted like a magnet to disease-fighting cells, where it hinders their ability to ward off infections. An immune system thus suppressed can raise susceptibility to colds—or raise the risk of cancer.

• Cortisol activation can similarly damage the immune system. Sheldon Cohen, Ph.D., professor of psychology at Carnegie Mellon University, gave 400 people a questionnaire designed to quantify the amount of stress they were under. He then exposed them to nose drops containing cold viruses. About 90 percent of the stressed subjects (versus 74 percent of those not under stress) caught a cold. He found they had elevated levels of corticotrophin-releasing factor (CRF). "We know that CRF interferes with the immune system," Cohen says. "That is likely the physical expla-

nation why people under stress are more likely to catch a cold."

• Stress hormones are also implicated in rheumatoid arthritis. The hormone prolactin, released by the pituitary gland in response to stress, triggers cells that cause swelling in joints. In a study of 100 people with rheumatoid arthritis, Kathleen S. Matt, Ph.D., and colleagues at Arizona State University found that levels of prolactin were twice as high among those reporting high degrees of interpersonal stress than among those not stressed. Other studies have shown that prolactin migrates to joints, where it initiates a cascade of events leading to swelling, pain, tenderness. "This is clearly what people mean when they say stress is worsening their arthritis," Matt says. "Here we have the hormone released during stress implicated in the very thing that causes arthritis pain, swollen joints."

• After being released by the pituitary gland, the stress hormone ACTH can impede production of the body's natural pain relievers, endorphins, leading to a general feeling of discomfort and heightened pain after injury. High levels of ACTH also trigger excess serotonin, now linked to bursts of violent behavior.

By charting the pathways stress hormones take throughout the body, biological cartographers are doing more than mapping the links between stress and disease. Having caught cascades of biochemicals in flagrante delicto, researchers are diagraming the exact lines of communication between mind and body. Ultimately, they will force us to erase the dividing line between what is biological and what is psychological.

Important as they are, elucidating the neurohormones released during stress and relating them to body systems is not even the whole story. If that were all there was to how stress works, you would expect any physical reaction to occur immediately, since these hormones typically remain elevated for only a short time. And you would expect everyone to show some physical reaction. Certainly, not all people suffer a heart attack or asthma attack when they get upset. Some seem able to take stress in their stride, while others routinely are hobbled.

In studies only recently completed, Lawrence Brass, M.D., associate professor of neurology at Yale Medical School, found that severe stress is one of the most potent risk factors for stroke—more so than high blood pressure—even 50 years after the initial trauma. Brass studied 556 veterans of World War II and found that the rate of stroke among those who had been prisoners of war was eight times higher than among those veterans who had not been captured.

Stress is like an allergy; once we're sensitized, just a touch triggers a blitz from within.

● ● ●

"If you counter stress after it hits, that's too late. You must be proactive, not reactive."

● ● ●

The findings at first confused Brass. After all, the stress hormones that cause heart disease and stroke are elevated only for a few hours after a stressful event. "I began to realize we would have to take our understanding of stress farther when I began to see that in some people stress can cause disease years after the initial event," he says. He concluded that the immediate effect of the war trauma on the stress response system had to have been permanent. "The stress of being a POW was so severe it changed the way these folks responded to stress in the future—it sensitized them."

Their neurohormonal system was kicked off-kilter. Instead of churning out the normal amount of hormones in the face of stress, their systems were now so dysregulated that at the slightest provocation, they either pumped out too much of some chemicals needed or not enough of others. "Years of this kind of hormonal assault may have weakened their cardiovascular systems and led to the strokes," Brass says.

Brass was unable to document actual changes in the neurohormonal system. But another study, of child abuse victims, reported last June at the meeting of the American Psychiatric Association, provides some of the earliest proof that stress can physically alter people. With magnetic resonance imaging, researchers took pictures of the brains of 38 women, 20 with a documented history of sexual abuse, 18 without. Among those women sexually abused as children, the researchers discovered, the hippocampus is actually smaller than normal. A tiny seahorse-shaped structure in the middle of the brain, the hippocampus is partially responsible for storing short-term memory. It is activated by some of the same neurohormones released during stress. "What we are seeing," says Murray Stein, Ph.D., of the University of California at San Diego, "is evidence that psychological stress can change the brain's makeup."

If stress sensitization begins with a major trauma and results in wholesale neurochemical and neuroanatomical changes, there should be other examples of its ravages. Perhaps, but they won't be easy to find, says UMass's King. "Most kids who suffer a trauma are not brought to the doctor," she says. "They get through the problem, go on with their lives, and wind up in our offices years later, suffering from depression or heart disease. And unless we were able measure amounts of hormones released before the initial exposure to stress, we wouldn't know if the levels were elevated." So researchers are looking at laboratory animals.

Even the lowly rat appears to become sensitized to stress. One study at UMass found that rats repeatedly stressed by exposure to life-threatening cold and being deprived of maternal contact immediately after birth became hyperresponsive to stress. "Rats stressed from birth had a blunted release of ACTH in response to later stress," reports King. Then she reexposed them to cold after the age of 14 days, when their hypothalamic-pituitary axis matures. "Without enough ACTH, the rats were less able to mount a fight-or-flight response. The trauma of the early stress seems to have altered their response system."

"Hormonal changes from stress sensitization are quite clear in animals," notes Delaware's Levine. His own studies of monkeys document permanent changes in cortisol output in response to stress among monkeys subjected to early psychological trauma. "What's interesting are the fine variations in the changes depending on the type and time of the trauma," Levine says.

For instance, monkeys separated from their mothers for a mere 15 minutes a day during the first few months of life develop a stress response system that is slightly muted, compared with monkeys reared normally. But if the monkeys are separated from their mothers for a full three hours a day during the first few months, their later response to stress is hyperreactive. These sensitized monkeys literally run around the cage or cower in a corner in the presence of other nonthreatening animals.

"At first this may appear contradictory, but actually it is logical," Levine explains. "Being separated from their mothers for a few minutes a day is stressful, but not traumatic. It is not life-threatening, and so the animals did not have to develop a different set of mechanisms to get through that time. The muting of their stress response can be seen as a kind of defense against this daily intrusion," as if the monkeys are telling themselves "why get all worked up over this when I know it soon will be over."

"On the other hand, being separated from their mother for three hours a day is very traumatic," observes Levine. "Anything can happen during that time, so the monkeys must develop a heightened sense of awareness to protect themselves. This need may permanently alter their response so it is hyperresponsive all the time."

Is the same true for us? "We do know that sensitization happens, but we don't know what kind of stress it takes or when the stress must take place in order to produce the changes. There are a lot of variables in humans that are very difficult to control for, like the emotional environment in the home, genetic susceptibilities, and more. Some factors may cancel out the effects of an early trauma. We don't know."

The most likely truth about stress sensitization is that it is not a simple alteration in the amount of any single stress hormone. "It takes finely-tuned amounts of many neurohormones for the hypothalamic-pituitary axis to remain in balance," says Georgia Witkin, Ph.D., director of the Stress Program at Mt. Sinai Medical Center in New York. "No one thing is going to explain stress because there is not just one chemical reaction to stress. And it also does not mean that everyone who loses a parent or is the victim of a violent crime will suffer from stress the rest of his life. There are things about individuals—genetic susceptibilities, pre-existing medical conditions, the environment they were brought up in, any alteration that may have taken place in their HPA axis—that must all be factored in.

"But the first pieces of the puzzle are being put into place. Looking at stress as a chemical reaction and realizing that this reaction, if strong enough, can change how we react in the future, offers the possibility of explaining many things we have witnessed regarding stress. For instance, the reactions we see in rats that are exposed to early trauma may give us a biological perspective on the phenomenon of learned helplessness. Perhaps what we call learned helplessness is biologically-programmed helplessness. If these animals become physically unable to respond to stress because trauma has altered their biology, we can't really call that learned behavior."

If this new picture of stress is not yet quite in full focus, that's because it requires the melding of disciplines ranging from genetics to psychology to medicine, and demands a new theory of mind/body interactions. But it holds the promise of entirely new strategies to combat stress.

Roosevelt's Smith envisions the day when "we may be able to develop drugs that can retune the entire neurochemical system. I think it's going to take years more research to better understand how an early trauma actually alters the neurochemical system. What is the mechanism by which psychological stress changes the way the brain communicates with the body? Does the same stress cause the same changes all the time? When are the developmental periods during which stress may be most harmful? As we continue to unveil the complex interactions between the mind and body, we may be able to isolate these reactions. That raises the possibility we can develop drugs to change them."

For now, says UMass's Jean King, "we have to remember that the reason some people deal poorly with current events is because of a past trauma. We must remember that there are physical reactions in our bodies when we are under stress and the extent to which we endure these reactions may be dictated by our past. Telling someone to 'just take it easy' is of no help. We are still a long way from knowing just what to say, but we are getting there."

A Smorgasbord of Stress-Stoppers

The future may hold specific ways of desensitizing brain and body so that they do not automatically hyperrespond to minor provocations. But for now, recognition of stress sensitization requires one all-important change in the way most of us approach de-stressing.

"If you wait until you're feeling stressed before you employ some technique for managing stress," contends psychologist Robert Epstein, Ph.D., "it's already too late. You need to have a bag of tricks that you can deploy proactively. If you turn to them throughout the day, that changes your threshold of stress tolerance."

Epstein, director emeritus of the Cambridge Center for Behavioral Studies and a researcher at San Diego State University, insists that "it's more important than ever to learn as many antistress techniques as possible, as young as possible."

"What we can now get out of the notion of sensitization is that people being treated for stress need individualized therapies," adds Saki F. Santorelli, Ed.D., associate director of the Stress Reduction Clinic at the University of Massachusetts Medical Center. "If we are saying that everyone responds to stress differently because of past experiences, then as therapists we need to be flexible and allow each person to focus on the part of therapy that works best for them. The only way to find that out is by trying different stress-reduction techniques."

There is no one-size-fits-all way to reduce stress. For example, "study upon study has shown that simple relaxation does not work in many people," says Rachel Yehuda, Ph.D., of Mt. Sinai Medical Center in New York. "Telling someone who has been sensitized to stress to just relax is like telling an insomniac to just fall asleep."

"What you don't want to do is resort to quick fixes that have no staying power," says Santorelli. "Smoking cigarettes, drinking alcohol, bringing on food; these are sure-fire stress failures. They may give the impression that they are relieving tension, but they will not work over time and sooner or later you will be right back where you started." He also advises those who feel stressed to avoid coffee and high-fat foods. "Caffeine is a stimulant and foods high in fat make the body work overtime to digest them, so both will probably add to your level of stress."

Mindfulness Meditation

At Santorelli's clinic, patients are taught mindfulness meditation, which comes out of the Buddhist tradition. Practitioners set aside 20 to 40 minutes a day when they focus on calming and becoming aware of their bodies with the aim of catching them—and interrupting them—in the act of hyperresponding to stress. "But the meditation really becomes a way of life. Once you begin practicing you realize that whenever you start feeling stressed during the day you are able to retrieve the feelings of relaxation you get during deep meditation. It becomes a way to take a few breaths and settle down just when you feel like you are beginning to explode."

Other forms of meditation use other devices to bring on moments of quiet contemplation, but all are designed to get you to focus on your body. "The most important thing is becoming aware of your body so you can sense when you are getting stressed. Meditation is an excellent way to do that" says Santorelli. "But it's not for everyone."

Biofeedback

If meditation is not for you, maybe biofeedback is. There are three main forms of it: electromyography (EMG), galvanic skin response (GSR), and electroencephalography (EEG). By attaching electrodes to a body system that readily reacts to stress—muscles, skin, and brain waves, respectively—you can monitor your actual stress level and learn to control, even reduce it. Modern biofeedback devices give off some signal—a blinking light, a bell—that announces a high level of tension. You concentrate on slowing the blinking light or bell.

Studies have found that each form of biofeedback works best for specific stress-related problems. EMG biofeedback, for example, reduces tension headaches; it allows people to focus and relax the muscles in the forehead that cause head pain. GSR seems to work best for stress-induced migraines, which tend to coincide with a rise in body temperature. EEG biofeedback leads to the deepest relaxation states.

What Calms You

But you don't have to meditate or go to a biofeedback clinic to avoid stress. "I meditate regularly, but when I am feeling unusually stressed I practice yoga or go exercise or tend to my garden, or I hang out with family or even just read and write," Santorelli says. "You have to become aware of what calms you best."

For Jean King, Ph.D., of the UMass Medical School, listening to music, going for a walk, or exercising always seems to put her mind at ease. "I love the water, so if I'm having a rough day I just go and look at it. I don't even have to go in, all I have to do is be near it."

Boston University biologist Eric Widmaier, Ph.D., confides that he used to combat stress by running and exercising. "But I've changed to a more thoughtful approach." He is an advocate of "internal conversations" in which he asks himself, "am I doing the right thing?" But the most important technique, he says, is "to learn to say no. People are constantly pushing at us by asking for favors."

Relaxation Response

One of the best-studied stress-relievers is the relaxation response, first described by Harvard's Herbert Benson, M.D., more than 20 years ago. Its great advantage is that it requires no special posture or place. Say you're stuck in traffic when you're expected at a meeting. Or you're having trouble falling asleep because your mind keeps replaying some awkward situation.

• Sit or recline comfortably. Close your eyes if you can, and relax your muscles.

• Breathe deeply. To make sure that you are breathing deeply, place one hand on your abdomen, the other on your chest. Breath in slowly through your nose, and as you do you should feel your abdomen (not your chest) rise.

• Slowly exhale. As you do, focus on your breathing. Some people do better if they silently repeat the word *one* as they exhale; it helps clear the mind.

• If thoughts intrude, do not dwell on them; allow them to pass on and return to focusing on your breathing.

Although you can turn to this exercise any time you feel stressed, doing it regularly for 10 to 20 minutes at least once a day can put you in a generally calm mode that can see you through otherwise stressful situations.

Cleansing Breath

Epstein, who has searched the world literature for techniques people have claimed valuable for coping, focuses on those that are simple and powerful. He calls them "gems," devices that work through differing means, can be learned in minutes, can be done anytime, anywhere, and have a pronounced physiologic effect. At the top of his list is the quickest of all—a cleansing breath.

Take a huge breath in. Hold it for three to four seconds. Then let it out v-e-r-y s-l-o-w-l-y. As you blow out, blow out all the tension in your body.

Relaxing Postures

"The research literature demonstrates that sitting in certain positions, all by itself, has a pronounced effect," says Epstein. Sit anywhere. Relax your shoulders so that they are comfortably rounded. Allow your arms to drop by your sides. Rest your hands, palm side up, on top of your thighs. With your knees comfortably bent, extend your legs and allow your feet, supported on the heels, to fall gently outward. Let your jaw drop. Close your eyes and breathe deeply for a minute or two.

Passive Stretches

It's possible to relax muscles without effort; gravity can do it all. Start with your neck and let your head fall forward to the right. Breathe in and out normally. With every breath out, allow your head to fall more. Do the same for shoulders, arms, back.

Imagery

Find a comfortable posture and close your eyes. Imagine the most relaxed place you've ever been. We all have a place like this and can call it to mind anywhere, any time. For everyone it is different. It may be a lake. It may be a mountain. It may be a cottage at the beach. Are you there?

Five—Count 'Em, Five—Tricks

Since you can never have too many tricks in your little bag, here are some "proven stress-busters" from Paul Rosch, M.D., president of the American Institute of Stress:

• Curl your toes against the soles of your feet as hard as you can for 15 seconds, then relax them. Progressively tense and relax the muscles in your legs, stomach, back, shoulders, neck.

• Visualize lying on a beach, listening to waves coming in and feeling the warm sun and gentle breezes on your back. Or, if you prefer, imagine an erotic fantasy or picture yourself in whatever situation makes you happiest.

• Set aside 20 to 30 minutes a day to do anything you want—even nothing.

• Take a brisk walk.

• Keep a Walkman handy and loaded with relaxing, enjoyable music.

"Beating stress is a matter of removing yourself from the situation and taking a few breaths," says Rosch. "If I find myself getting stressed I ask myself 'is this going to matter to me in five years?' Usually the answer is no. If so, why get worked up over it?"

The Power of Understanding

Simply knowing about stress sensitization seems to help some. "We tell patients about stress sensitization and I see a change in them," Yehuda says. "We explain that they have inappropriate reactions to stress because something has gone wrong with control mechanisms in the brain. It is like a light goes on and they can see:'Oh, so that may be the problem.' They do the same meditation and therapy but they are aware of the basis of their problem. There is something for them to focus on. There is a reason for them to say 'I'm not crazy. This is something real.'"

(Continued)

So You Think This Is the "Age of Stress"?

Quick, which would you rather be: late to work or lunch for a lion?
The stress response we have today is out of synch with current
needs. But it once was a Jurassic perk.

Eric P. Widmaier, Ph.D.

Nowadays, we are bombarded with what might be called the mythology of stress, which suggests that our psychological and physiological well-being is constantly threatened by degrees of stress unparalleled in history. Nothing could be farther from the truth.

What are some of these real or perceived stressors with which we continually do battle? Coping with rush-hour traffic, job and financial difficulties, troubled relationships, and family problems are just a few of hundreds of stressful stimuli that can be identified.

Anxiety over personal problems (will I be able to pay the rent this month?), or more global concerns (will there be another war?) is another type of stress that we all encounter much too often.

Nonetheless, anxiety and these other stressors are not immediate threats to survival, even if they do raise our blood pressure a bit now and then. Of greater concern is that the internal defense mechanisms of the body respond to these types of psychological stimuli in the same way as they would respond to life-threatening ones.

Why is this unfortunate? Because over the long haul, excess release of potent stress-fighting factors like the adrenal-gland hormones cortisol and epinephrine (also known as adrenaline) can suppress the immune system, cause ulcers, produce muscle atrophy, elevate blood sugar, place excessive demands on the heart, and eventually lead to the death of certain brain cells.

A person in the midst of a divorce does not require the hormonal, neuronal, and metabolic responses of someone who falls through thin ice on a wintery pond—yet in both cases the same internal changes are occurring.

Why do emotionally stressful events elicit the same chemical changes in our bodies as do events that are actual threats to survival? The answer may lie in a comparison of stress as we know it today and stress as it must have been when vertebrate animals were first evolving.

Are we really any more "stressed out" than our prehistoric ancestors? Presumably not, since the defense mechanisms that developed in mammals like ourselves did so very early in the evolution of life. We even see similar biological responses to stress in non-mammalian vertebrates like birds and reptiles.

These defenses consist of hormonal and neuronal signals that increase breathing, accelerate heart rate, increase blood pressure, increase the liver's ability to pump sugar into the bloodstream, and open up blood vessels in the large muscles to maximize the delivery of nutrients and oxygen.

The net effect is an animal that has lots of fuel in its blood, a more forceful heart to pump the blood around, plenty of oxygen, and efficient muscles. For an antelope in the wild that has spotted a nearby lion, these changes are exactly what the antelope needs to avoid becoming a meal.

Not surprisingly, then, animals evolved internal mechanisms to combat the stresses of infection, starvation, dehydration and pain, to name a few. Cortisol breaks down bone, muscle, fat, and other body tissues to provide material for the liver to convert into sugar. This sugar, essentially formed by the body's own self-digestion, can supply the needs of the heart and brain during a crisis. The natural pain-killer endorphin developed to combat severe pain.

Picture the antelope being attacked by the lion, but escaping to live another day. Its endorphin would allow the animal to cope with the pain of its wound, if only temporarily, and continue with the herd. Other hormones enable the kidney to retain more water than normal during periods of drought and dehydration.

All of these varied measures are short-term responses to very different types of stress. But they act in a concerted way to give an organism a fighting chance to get back on its feet.

Imagining the types of stress our paleolithic forebears must have encountered makes our daily aggravations seem much less overwhelming. Prior to the advent of agriculture, the typical cave-dweller would rarely have had the luxury of a steady and nutritious diet. On the contrary, malnutrition, vitamin and mineral deficiencies, even starvation would have been extremely common in the winter months, and sporadic dehydration from lack of clean or available water may have been common in the summer.

Hypothermia was a constant threat in the winter, especially in northern climes during the many ice ages. Injuries and infections that resulted from untreated minor wounds or parasite invasion would not only have been physiologically stressful but often lethal. Anthropological data suggest that our ancestors suffered many of the same maladies that continue to plague us today (arthritis, back problems, tooth decay, osteoporosis, to name a few).

However, as stressful as those conditions are for modern man, they would have been far more stressful at a time when no medical treatment of any kind was available.

What about the other type of stress that is not life-threatening, but is *perceived* to be of potential danger? When the antelope spotted the lion, there are not yet physical damage to the antelope's body. Nonetheless, the hormonal systems responded as if the damage was already done, in *anticipation* of impending doom. If the crisis were luckily averted, a complex system of hormonal feedback loops would apply a brake on the stress response to prevent unabated secretion of cortisol and other stress hormones.

Our prehistoric ancestors did not need to negotiate city traffic and deal with short-tempered bosses, but they had their share of psychological stress that produced no actual physical bodily insult.

Not knowing when (or *if*) your next meal will come would have been (and for much of the world's population continues to be) a chronic source of anxiety. Each empty-handed trip back to the cave would have increased the tribe's fears for the next day.

For that matter, obtaining a meal might have meant coping with the terror of chasing down a herd of animals much faster and larger than oneself, using a puny flint arrowhead tied to a stick.

Prehistoric man also differed in one profound way from modern man. Although an awareness of the cycles of nature and physical principles like gravity would likely have been present in even our most primitive ancestors, an *understanding* of the forces of nature would have completely eluded them.

Having no understanding of science meant having no sense of control over one's environment. Ancient man appears to have worried endlessly about celestial "beings" (sun gods, moon gods, etc.), and we know that until relatively recent times it was common for people to assign human traits to these deities.

This would have implied that it was within the realm of possibility for, say, the sun god to feel angry or neglected one day, thus deciding not to rise and plunging the world into darkness and chaos. Imagine going to sleep each night fretting that you may have failed to properly perform a certain worshipful ritual and that as a consequence your entire tribe or family might be forever doomed to darkness and misery.

From both a physical and psychological vantage point, our ancestors lived a much more stressful existence that we do today. The mechanisms that evolved to combat the deleterious effects of those stressors are still intact and usually serve us well.

However, we clearly make things worse for ourselves. Take compulsive exercisers. These people can actually become addicted to strenuous exercise, because this behavior imposes a severe stress on metabolism and results in the steady release of endorphin. Responsible for "runner's high," this pain-killer is similar to morphine in its addictive capabilities.

Extreme exercise also releases cortisol, which though useful in maintaining circulatory and respiratory function, can lead to immunosuppression, bone loss, hypertension, and death of brain cells. In yet another scenario, meeting a deadline at work is a source of pressure, but is not life-threatening, and yet it contributes to ill health by invoking an unnecessary release of stress hormones.

Are we stressed in today's society? Of course we are. But the important thing to remember is that all animals, including ourselves, are confronted with innumerable types of stress and always have been. We should ignore the incessant mantra of ours being the Age of Stress and put things in a more historical and evolutionary perspective.

Given the choice, who wouldn't prefer the aggravation of two working parents getting their kids off to day care or school on time to the dread of being eaten in one's sleep by a lion?

Far from being the slough of despond it is considered, middle age
may be the very best time of life, researchers say—the "it" we work toward

MIDLIFE MYTHS

WINIFRED GALLAGHER

Winifred Gallagher ("Midlife Myths") is a senior editor of American Health. *Her latest book [is]* The Power of Place: How Our Surroundings Shape Our Thoughts, Emotions, and Actions.

According to the picture of human development drawn by traditional scientific literature, after a busy childhood and adolescence young adults launch their careers and social lives and then stride into a black box, from which they hobble some forty years later to face a darkly eventful senescence. According to popular literature, what takes place inside the box is an anticlimactic, unsatisfying, and even traumatic march over the hill and toward the grave—or, worse, the nursing home. This scenario complements the anecdotes that often figure in conversations about middle age: that friend of a friend whose lifetime investment in career and family went up in the flames of a passion for the au pair, or that second cousin rumored to have gone off the deep end during the "change of life" when the kids left for college.

So entrenched is the idea that middle age is bad or boring or both that the almost 80 million members of the graying Baby Boom generation won't use the term except in referring to Ozzie and Harriet Nelson or Ward and June Cleaver. "We have a problem here, and it's called denial," the television producer Stan Rogow, whose 1992 series *Middle Ages* was a critical success, recently told *Newsweek*. He blames the show's title for its commercial failure: "'Middle age' is this horrible-sounding thing you've heard throughout your life and hated." The denial he describes frustrates the efforts of researchers who are conducting the first comprehensive, multidisciplinary studies of middle age. They are finding that it is not just an aging process but life's peak experience.

The study of development concentrates mostly on life's early stages, when behavioral and physiological growth and change are simultaneous. In the 1960s the new discipline of gerontology revealed that as people lived much further into old age, a reverse synchrony obtained toward life's end. Looking back from studies of the elderly and, to a lesser extent, forward from studies of the young, researchers began to suspect that middle age might be not simply a long interval during which things are worse than they are in youth and better than they are in old age but a developmental process in its own right—albeit one not particularly tied to changes in the body. Common perceptions of middle age are that it occurs from roughly forty to sixty; in the future, increased longevity and better health may push back the period of middle age even further. The scientists and scholars exploring this part of life, which is probably better described experientially than chronologically—the very concept of middle age itself is something of a cultural artifact, with social and economic components—range from the medically, sociologically, and psychologically oriented John D. and Catherine T. MacArthur Foundation Research Network on Successful Midlife Development (MIDMAC), administered from Vero Beach, Florida, to the psychoanalytically and spiritually grounded C. G. Jung Foundation's Center for Midlife Development in New York City.

Although there are plenty of exceptions, "the data show that middle age is the very best time in life," says Ronald Kessler, a sociologist and MIDMAC fellow who is a program director in the survey research center of the University of Michigan's Institute for Social Research. "When looking at the total U.S. population, the best year is fifty. You don't have to deal with the aches and pains of old age or the anxieties of youth: Is anyone going to love me? Will I ever get my career off the ground? Rates of general distress are low—the incidences of depression and anxiety fall at about thirty-five and don't climb again until the late sixties. You're healthy. You're productive. You have enough money to do some of the things you like to do. You've come to terms with your relationships, and the chance of divorce is very low. Midlife is the 'it' you've been working toward. You can turn your attention toward being rather than becoming."

Whereas Kessler's picture of middle age is drawn from facts and figures, the image in most Americans' minds is based on myths, derived not from the ordinary experiences of most people but from the unusual experiences of a few. Although these make for livelier reading and conversation, they generate an unnecessarily gloomy attitude about the middle years which limits people's horizons, according to Margie Lachman, a psychologist, a MIDMAC fellow, and the director of the Life-span Developmental Psychology Laboratory at Brandeis University. When Lachman asked young adults what it means to be middle-aged, they gave such answers as "You think more

The overwhelming majority of people, surveys show, accomplish the task of coming to terms with the realities of middle age through a long, gentle process—not an acute, painful crisis.

about the past than the future" and "You worry about money for health care." They also assumed that the stress experienced in middle age came from the desire to be young again. Older subjects Lachman surveyed, who knew better, attributed stress to coping with the many demands of the busiest time in life. And whereas the older group saw their lives as generally stable, the younger expected to experience a lot of change—and a crisis—in midlife. "The images and beliefs we have about middle age are the guideposts for our planning, evaluation, and goal-setting," Lachman says. "Are they accurate? Or negative self-fulfilling prophesies?"

Gilbert Brim, a pioneer in the study of social development through the life-span and the director of MIDMAC, agrees. "Passed on from generation to generation," he says, "widely shared cultural beliefs and untested theories about middle age put forward in the media continue to be played out in society. But they're likely to be wrong. There are probably as many myths about midlife now as there were about aging thirty years ago, before the advent of gerontology. The time has come to rid ourselves of these obsolete ideas."

The Inexorable Midlife Crisis?

MOST YOUNGER ADULTS ANTICIPATE THAT BEtween their late thirties and their early fifties a day will come when they suddenly realize that they have squandered their lives and betrayed their dreams. They will collapse into a poorly defined state that used to be called a nervous breakdown. Escape from this black hole will mean either embracing an un-American philosophy of eschatological resignation or starting over—jaded stockbrokers off to help Mother Teresa, phlegmatic spouses off to the StairMaster and the singles scene. In short, they will have a midlife crisis.

If youth's theme is potential, midlife's is reality: childhood fantasies are past, the fond remembrances of age are yet to be, and the focus is on coming to terms with the finite resources of the here and now. The overwhelming majority of people, surveys show, accomplish this devel-

opmental task, as psychologists put it, through a long, gentle process—not an acute, painful crisis. Over time the college belle or the high school athlete leans less on physical assets, the middle manager's horizons broaden beyond the corner office, and men and women fortunate enough to have significant others regard the rigors of courtship with indulgent smiles. In relying on brains and skill more than beauty and brawn, diffusing competitive urges to include the tennis court or a community fund-raising project, and valuing long-term friendship and domestic pleasures over iffy ecstasies, these people have not betrayed their youthful goals but traded them in for more practical ones that bring previously unsuspected satisfaction. Ronald Kessler says, "The question to ask the middle-aged person isn't just What has happened to you? but also How has your experience changed your thinking?"

The middle-aged tend to be guided not by blinding revelations associated with emotional crisis but by slowly dawning adaptive insights into the self and others, which Kessler calls "psychological turning points." Early in midlife these usually involve a recognition of limitations: the local politician realizes that she'll never make it to the U.S. Senate, and the high school English teacher accepts that he's not going to be a famous man of letters. In the middle period of middle age the transitions usually concern what Kessler calls a redirection of goals: "You say to yourself, 'I'm killing myself at work, but the thing that really satisfies me is my family. I'm not going to change jobs, but from now on I'm going to focus more on home, and career will mean something different to me.'" In later middle age, turning points, especially for women, often involve a recognition of strength—"just the opposite of what you'd suppose," Kessler says. "The shy violet, for example, finds herself chairing a committee." These soundings taken and adjustments made prompt not dramatic departures from one's life course but gentle twists and curves.

"Mastery experiences," the more robust versions of which figure in Outward Bound–type adventure vacations, can be catalysts for middle-aged people in their ordinary settings as well. One of Kessler's subjects finally got his college diploma at fifty-eight, observing that he

"Mastery experiences," the more robust versions of which figure in Outward Bound–type vacations, can be catalysts for middle-aged people in their ordinary settings as well.

had thereby "resolved a lot of things and completed something important"; in almost the same language, a man of fifty said that he had "done something important" when he became proficient enough in his hobby of electronics to tutor others. Overcoming her lifelong fear of water, one woman learned to swim at the age of forty-five. "One day her family went to the pool, and she just jumped in," Kessler says. "This was a very powerful experience for her, not because she wanted to be a lifeguard but because she had mastered her anxiety as well as a new skill."

Even an apparently negative turning point can have benefits. Quite a few of Kessler's subjects, when asked if they had realized a dream in the past year, said yes, "but quite a few said they had given up on one," he says. "When the folks who have dreamed for years about a big summer house where all the kids would flock finally accept that they don't have the money and the kids have other plans, they release a lot of tension. This kind of surrender is very productive, because dreams that run counter to reality waste a lot of energy."

Although all people make psychological transitions and adjustments in the course of middle age, relatively few experience these as catastrophic. In surveys 10 to 12 percent of respondents report that they have had a midlife crisis, Kessler says. "What they often mean is that the kind of disaster that can happen at other times in life—divorce, or being fired, or a serious illness—happened to them during their middle years." An unusual convergence of such unhappy events can push even a hardy middle-aged person into a state of emotional emergency. "First you notice that your hair is falling out," Gilbert Brim says. "Then you go to the office and learn you didn't get that raise, and when you get home, your wife says she's leaving." But most of those who have a true psychological crisis in middle age—according to MIDMAC, about five percent of the population—have in fact experienced internal upheavals throughout their lives. "They see the world in those terms," says David Featherman, a MIDMAC fellow and the president of the Social Science Research Council, in New York City. "They aren't particularly good at absorbing or rebounding from life's shocks."

People prone to midlife crisis score low on tests of introspection, or reflecting on one's self and on life, and high in denial, or coping with trouble by not thinking about it. "Take the guy who still thinks he's a great athlete," Kessler says. "Somehow he hasn't let reality intrude on his boyhood fantasy. But one day something forces him to wake up. Maybe he's at a family reunion playing ball with his twelve-year-old nephew and he can't make his shots. Suddenly he's an old man, a failure." Heading for the same kind of shock are the people banking on the big promotion that their colleagues know will never happen, along with those who believe that hair transplants and breast implants mean eternal youth. "Such individuals have to work hard to maintain their illusions," Kessler says. "They spend a lot of energy on the cogni-

tive effort of self-delusion, until reality finally intervenes." Because most middle-aged people have grown skilled at monitoring changes in reality—the jump shot isn't what it used to be, the figure has changed for good—they are spared the abrupt, traumatic run-ins with reality that result in a psychic emergency.

Midlife crises are an affliction of the relatively affluent: rosy illusions are easier to maintain when a person is already somewhat shielded from reality. Just as childhood is often constricted among the poor, who early in life face adult realities and burdens, so middle age may be eclipsed by a premature old age brought on by poverty and poor health. Among working-class people, for whom strength and stamina mean earning power, middle age may begin at thirty-five rather than the forty-five often cited in studies by respondents drawn from the sedentary middle class. Because any fanciful notions that poor and blue-collar people might have are rigorously tested by daily life, Kessler says, they rarely dwell in fantasy. "In terms of career, factory workers are likelier to be wherever they're going to be at thirty than executives," he says. "In terms of mental health, being disappointed at what *is* is a better kind of problem to have than being anxious about what will be. Once you know the reality, you can say, 'I can't afford to buy a boat, so I'll rent one for vacations.' Being up in the air is the big problem."

Despite the lurid tales of fifty-year-olds who run off with their twenty-five-year-old secretaries, such events are relatively rare in real-life midlife. Most couples who divorce break up in the first six or eight years of matrimony, and by midlife the majority report being more or less content. "The family-demography side of the midlife crisis just isn't there," says Larry Bumpass, a MIDMAC fellow and a professor of sociology at the University of Wisconsin at Madison, who directs the federally funded National Survey of Families and Households, the largest demographic study of its kind. "After ten or fifteen years together, the probability that a couple will split up is low. I've looked at the data every way possible to see if there's even a blip in the divorce rate when the children leave home, but that's just folklore too."

Even the nature of the difficulties most commonly reported suggests that the majority of the middle-aged operate from a position of strength. "The problems mentioned usually concern not the self but someone else—a child or parent," Kessler says. "Part of the reason for this outward focus is that the middle-aged person has secured his or her own situation and can afford to pay attention to others. Compared with the issues that arise in youth and old age, for most people the management-type problems that crop up in midlife aren't nearly as emotionally devastating."

Carl Jung divided life into halves—the first devoted to forming the ego and getting established in the world, the second to finding a larger meaning for all that effort. He then took the unorthodox step of paying more attention to the second. When shifting from one stage to the other, Jung observed, people experience an external loss of some kind—physical prowess or upward mobility or a relationship. When they treat this loss as a signal that it's time to develop new dimensions, Jung thought, transformation is in store. However, he predicted stagnation or even a breakdown if the loss is met with denial, fear, or a sense of defeat. Aryeh Maidenbaum, the executive director of the C. G. Jung Foundation's Center for Midlife Development, offers the Jungian rule of thumb for midlife crises: "The greater the disparity between the outer and inner person, the greater the chance for trouble. The most important inner need people have is to be seen for who they are. If that's what's happening at midlife, there's no crisis."

The Change for the Worse

IF THERE'S ONE ISSUE REGARDING WHICH MISINFORmation feeds mounting hysteria about middle age, it's menopause. After finishing any of a number of recent books and articles, a reader might conclude that for a few years a middle-aged woman might as well choose between sobbing alone and riding around on a broom. One of the few people who have gleaned their own hard data on the subject is Karen Matthews, a professor of psychiatry, epidemiology, and psychology at the University of Pittsburgh School of Medicine, who has conducted a longitudinal survey of the psychological and physical changes experienced by 500 women passing through menopause. "The fact is that most women do very well in the menopausal transition," she says, refuting the popular image of women who are invariably depressed, extremely unpleasant, or both. "There are some common physical symptoms that aren't fun, notably hot flashes, but only a minority of women—about ten percent—have a tough time psychologically."

Matthews has identified the characteristics of those who experience few problems in menopause and those who experience many. "The women who do well respond to the menopause with action," she says. "That may not be their direct intention, but they end up coping with the stressor by making positive changes. Those who, say, step up their exercise regimen don't even show the biological changes, such as the adverse shifts in lipids implicated in coronary disease, that others do. These 'active copers' say, 'Hey, I look a little different, feel a little less energetic. Why don't I . . .'"

Try hormone-replacement therapy? In evaluating its effects on physical health, women and doctors must juggle evidence suggesting that while HRT cuts the number of hot flashes by about half and reduces vulnerability to osteoporosis and perhaps coronary disease, it may raise the risk of breast cancer and, if estrogen is taken without progestin, uterine cancer. The National Institutes of Health is now conducting a badly needed controlled long-term clinical trial of large numbers of women on HRT which should provide some answers. Meanwhile, some doctors, confronted with incomplete data, tell women that the decision is up to them. Considering the threat of os-

teoporosis and of coronary disease, which is the leading cause of death for women over fifty, many other doctors recommend HRT to those whose risk of breast cancer is low. Still others regard its widespread use with dismay. Their concerns range from the fact that only one in three women is vulnerable to osteoporosis to a flaw in the argument that hormones can prevent heart disease. In part because doctors are cautious about prescribing HRT for women with illnesses such as hypertension and diabetes, the population that takes it is healthier to begin with—a built-in selection bias that skews studies of the therapy's effects. Among HRT's vocal critics are the doctors Sonja and John McKinlay, epidemiologists at the New England Research Institute, in Watertown, Massachusetts. "HRT is inappropriate for the vast majority of women, who shouldn't use it," John McKinlay says. "Yet the pharmaceutical industry's goal is to have every post-menopausal woman on it until death." Having surveyed the literature on menopause and HRT, Alice Rossi, a MIDMAC fellow and an emeritus professor of sociology at the University of Massachusetts at Amherst, says, "I wish we had a better scientific foundation for deciding if it's appropriate for women to take hormones for decades. At this point there's no strong evidence for a pro or anti position."

Although the process of weighing HRT's effects on physical health continues, Matthews has determined that as far as behavioral effects are concerned, HRT is "not the most important factor in most women's psychological well-being during menopause." For that matter, she says, women who do and don't use HRT may report differing experiences because they are different types of people to begin with. In Matthews's study the typical user was not only better educated and healthier but also likely to be a hard-driving "Type A" person, less content with the status quo. "These women are up on the literature," Matthews says, "more aware of HRT, and more interested in seeking treatment."

If active copers, whether or not they take hormones, fare best during menopause, Matthews says, the women likely to have the worst time have two disparate things in common: HRT and a low regard for themselves. "Women who have poor self-esteem but don't use hormones don't have a hard time," she says. One hypothesis is that reproductive hormones, particularly progesterone, cause some women to become dysphoric, or moody; if a woman who has this adverse reaction to HRT also has a poor self-image, she is likely to be more upset by a stressor such as a menopausal symptom than a woman with a sturdier ego.

"The idea that most women have a hard time psychologically is the major myth our data have dispelled," Matthews says. "Eighty percent of our subjects thought they were going to become depressed and irritable at menopause, but only ten percent did. Those who had a rough time had showed signs long before of being anxious, depressed, or pessimistic. Menopause makes women with that pre-existing set of characteristics, which are not age-related, more emotionally vulnerable."

Much of the dark mythology of menopause derives not from the thing itself but from simultaneous aspects of the aging process. "It's the physical manifestation of aging—and a woman's reaction to it—that's critical in predicting whether the years from forty-five to fifty-five will be difficult or not," Alice Rossi says. "Society's image of an attractive woman is ten years younger than that of an attractive man. Graying at the temples and filling out a bit can be attractive in a man—look at Clinton and Gore. But their wives are still trying to look twenty-eight." Rossi isn't necessarily advocating the grin-and-bear-it attitude toward aging favored by Barbara Bush. Seeming ten years younger than you are can be a good thing, she says, if it means a concern for good health and well-being, rather than an obsession with youth.

Matthews considers a lot of the anxiety expressed by women about menopause to be unnecessary. In response to the often-heard complaint that there has been no good research on the subject, she points to several major long-term investigations—including hers, one by Sonja and John McKinlay, and one conducted in Sweden—that independently show that the majority of women have no serious problems making the transition.

In discussing a recent bestseller on the subject, Gail Sheehy's *The Silent Passage*, she says, "Ms. Sheehy interviewed me at length, but the experience of menopause she describes in her book is not the one that emerges as typical in the three major studies. Some women have a very difficult menopause, and Ms. Sheehy feels there's a message there. We need to figure out why some women do have problems, so that we can help. "There has been no generation of women like this one. They're better educated. They're healthier to the point that they now live half their adult lives after the menopause. For them, the menopausal transition is best characterized as a time of optimism. It's a bridge—an opportunity for women to think about what they want to do next."

Despite persistent rumors, there's probably no such thing as male menopause. Men simply don't experience a midlife biological change equivalent to the one women undergo. Whereas nature is responsible for that inequity, culture is at the bottom of a far more destructive one. For a research project, John McKinlay videotaped visits to doctors' offices made by patients matched for every variable but gender. The films showed that a man and a woman who complained of the same symptoms were often treated very differently: men were twice as likely to be referred to a medical specialist, and women were much likelier to be referred to a psychotherapist; men were urged toward health-enhancing behavior such as dieting and exercise, but women rarely were. ("This is particularly unfortunate where smoking is concerned," McKinlay says, "because the health benefits for women who give it up may be greater than those for men.") He concludes that the gender-related disparities apparent in much medical literature may reflect what doctors see more than actual physiological differences. Accordingly,

Many studies show that satisfaction with the marital relationship climbs again after couples weather the labor-intensive period of launching careers and babies.

he suspects that when middle-aged men complain of bad moods and decreased libido and energy, most doctors see a need for behavioral change. When women report the same symptoms, many doctors attribute them to menopause and prescribe hormones. "Don't forget that most women get their primary health care from a gynecologist," McKinlay says, "which would be like most men getting theirs from a urologist."

Among endocrinologists outside the United States there is more support for the notion of a male climacteric, in which older men's lower testosterone levels cause decreased fertility, increased body fat, bone loss, and skin-tone changes, along with the same behavioral symptoms that are often attributed to female menopause. While allowing that a small percentage of older men suffer from an endocrinological problem and can benefit from hormone-replacement therapy, McKinlay insists that there is no evidence that the majority would benefit. For that matter, he says, testosterone has little effect on the sexuality of those over fifty or fifty-five, and taking it as a supplement may in fact increase the risk of prostate cancer. Having conducted a study of the sex lives of 1,700 men aged forty to seventy which is considered by many to be the best information on the subject, he says, "There's no physiological, endocrinological, psychological, or clinical basis for a male menopause. Whether or not people believe in it has nothing to do with whether it exists, only with whether the pharmaceutical industry can persuade them that it does. In ten years male climacteric clinics will sprout up to treat a condition that may or may not exist—but, of course, they'll make money."

McKinlay's major reservation about most of the existing research on the effects of reproductive hormones is that it has been conducted with "small, atypical" samples of people who are seeking treatment in the health-care system. "What's talked about in the literature—both professional and popular—is the experience of *patients*," he says, "not healthy people, about whom we know very little."

The Best Years of Your Life Are Over

MANY PEOPLE HAVE A MEMORY FROM ADOLEScence of gazing around a gathering of adults, no longer in the green days of their youth yet dressed to kill and living it up, and thinking the equivalent of "How valiant they are to make an effort at their age." Because Hollywood and Madison Avenue project this same juvenile notion, many of the middle-aged are surprised and relieved to find that their lives aren't nearly so dreary as they expected. After analyzing decades of social research for his 1992 book *Ambition*, Gilbert Brim found that a person's zest for and satisfaction with life don't depend on youth—or on status, sexuality, health, money, or any of the other things one might expect. "What people really want out of life are action and challenge—to be in the ballgame," he says. "To feel satisfied, we must be able to tackle a task that's hard enough to test us, but not so difficult that we'll repeatedly fail. We want to work hard, then succeed."

This maxim has a special resonance for today's middle-aged, career-oriented middle class, often portrayed as beleaguered victims of "role strain" or burnt-out cases operating on automatic pilot. In fact, Brim says, most are instinctively seeking the level of "just manageable difficulty"—an optimum degree of effort that taps about 80 percent of a person's capacity and generates that satisfied, job-well-done feeling. Pushing beyond that level for prolonged periods leaves people stressed and anxious; falling below it leaves them bored. Because what is just manageable at forty might not be at sixty, people rearrange their lives, often unconsciously, to balance capacities and challenges. When one does well at something, one ups the ante; when one fails, one lowers the sights a bit or even switches arenas. Brim draws an illustration from a study of AT&T executives: over time the most successful grew more work-oriented; the others began to turn more to their families and social lives—educating the children or lowering the golf handicap—for feelings of accomplishment. The key point, he says, is that neither group was more satisfied than the other. "This intuitive process by which we constantly reset our goals in response to our gains and losses is one of the most overlooked aspects of adult development."

One way in which the middle-aged are particularly skilled in adjusting their goals is in choosing which Joneses to keep up with. "Our mental health is very much affected by our estimation of how we're doing in terms of the people around us," says Carol Ryff, a psychologist and a MIDMAC fellow who is the associate director of the Institute on Aging and Adult Life, at the University of Wisconsin at Madison. "We all make these important measurements, even though we're often barely conscious of doing so." Whereas the young person launching a career might try to outdo Maurizio Pollini or Donna Karan, the savvy middle-aged one knows that holding to this standard beyond a certain point ensures misery—or a genuine

midlife crisis. Particularly when faced with a difficult situation, the mature person makes a "downward comparison" that puts his own problems in a different perspective and helps him soldier on. Thus the executive who has just been laid off compares his finances not with the Rockefellers' but with those of the couple across the street who are both on unemployment, and reminds himself that at least his wife's position is secure. "The better your mental health, the less often you measure yourself against people who make you feel crummy," Ryff says. "In midlife you begin to say, 'Well, so I'm not in the same category as the Nobelists. That's just not an expectation I'm going to drag around anymore.'"

By middle age most people destined for success have achieved it, which erects some special hurdles in the just-manageable course of life. "Winning is not simply the opposite of losing," Brim says. "It creates its own disruptions." If a person becomes psychologically trapped by the need to do better, go higher, and make more, for example, he can end up operating at 90 to 100 percent of his capacity—a level at which stress makes life very uncomfortable. At this level, too, Brim says, he will begin to lose more than he wins. Burdened with more roles than he can handle, or promoted beyond the level of just-manageable difficulty, he may end up "held together by a thin paste of alcohol, saunas, and antibiotics." Brim says that because our society does not supply many ways to step down gracefully, it "pays the price in burnout and incompetence in high places."

Even those who can sustain Hollywood-style success must do some internal retooling in order to maintain the charge of the just-manageable mode. To keep life interesting, Brim says, the people who handle winning best don't merely raise the challenge in the same area but go into a new one—a sport, a hobby, a community project—where they again find a lot of room for moving up. "Certain professional athletes are good examples," he says. "Because they know that their peak will be short-lived, at a certain point they diversify their aspirations to include family, business interests, and volunteer activities."

So skilled are most people at maintaining a just-manageable life through the years that Brim finds no appreciable differences in the sense of well-being reported by different age groups. Indeed, he says, despite the insistent propaganda to the contrary, "except for concerns about health, most research shows that older people are as happy as younger ones."

Midlife Romance: The Bloom Is Off the Rose

IF MIDDLE AGE IS SEEN AS A DULL BUSINESS, ITS RELAtionships are imagined to be the dreariest part. In the course of studying beliefs about and images of midlife, Margie Lachman compared the experiences of a group of Boston-area people aged eighteen to eighty-five, and found no evidence that the middle-aged are less loving. In fact, steady levels of intimacy and affection were two of the few constants she tracked. Largely because married people make up the majority of the middle-aged—about 75 percent—most of the data about life relationships concern them. Then too, less is known about other bonds because until the mid-seventies studies of midlife focused on the experience of white middle-class heterosexual men. Although there is still very little information about gay midlife, some data are emerging about how single people in general fare socially during middle age.

It's about time, according to Alice Rossi. "Considering the longer life-span, a person may be without a partner at many points in life," she points out. "We not only marry later today but often have intervals between relationships, and perhaps lengthy spells as widows and widowers." She thinks that the stereotype of the aging spinster who is unfulfilled without a man is heading into the realm of midlife mythology. "There's recent evidence that single women have better mental and physical health and social lives than single men," she says. "Rather than being all alone, they have friends and close family ties, not only with parents but also with young nieces and nephews, with whom they may enjoy special relationships."

As for the married, many studies show that satisfaction with the relationship is lower throughout the child-rearing years that it had been, but climbs again after couples weather the labor-intensive period of launching careers and babies. In Lachman's Boston survey, reports of stress related to marriage decreased steadily from youth through old age. Although divorce and death may account for some of that decline, she says, "people may in fact grow more skilled in handling their relationships." Observing that by midlife couples have fewer fights and more closeness, Ron Kessler says, "Once they get the little kids out of their hair, husbands and wives catch their breath, look at each other, and ask, 'What are we going to talk about now? What was it all about twenty years ago?'"

In his study of sexuality John McKinlay found that only two percent of the 1,700 middle-aged and older men reported having more than one current sexual partner. This figure, vastly lower than the usual guesstimates, challenges the stereotype of the bored middle-aged philanderer. Moreover, although McKinlay recorded steady declines in the men's sexual activity, from lusty thoughts to erections, he found no decrease in their sexual satisfaction—a phenomenon Gilbert Brim calls "a triumph of the adaptation of aspirations to realities." Equivalent data about women have not been gathered, but McKinlay's findings complement other surveys that show that aging has little impact on people's enjoyment of sex.

People and their doctors, McKinlay says, should distinguish between sexual problems caused by aging and those caused by things that often get lumped with it, such as poor health, weight gain, lack of exercise, and the use of nicotine or too much alcohol. Compared with a healthy nonsmoking peer, for example, a smoker who has heart disease has a sevenfold greater risk of impotence.

Psychological fitness, too, plays a vital role. A man may think his primary problem is impotence caused by age when in fact his sexual trouble is a symptom of a very treatable depression. "We must not resort to biological reductionism, which is what women have been struggling against," McKinlay says.

Widely publicized conclusions drawn from the sex lives of the ill—that a vigorous sex life is not a reasonable expectation in middle age, for instance—may cast their pall on the well. "When I hear a healthy fifty-year-old man say, 'That sexy stuff is for kids,' I feel sorry for him," McKinlay says. "Only five percent of the women in our institute's long-term study of menopause reported suffering from vaginal dryness, but women are told it's a very common problem after a certain age." Contrary to the stereotype of the asexual older woman, he says, some women feel liberated by menopause and the end of birth control. If older women have a problem with their sex lives, according to McKinlay, it may be that their husbands aren't in good health. His prescription for a vital midlife: "If I were feeling troubled about aging, I'd look first at the behavioral modifications I could make—diet, exercise, alcohol-monitoring, and so on. If they didn't work, then I'd think about treatments."

Having edited a book about sexuality through the course of life, Alice Rossi observes that although the mature expression of eroticism remains poorly understood by science, let alone by our youth-oriented culture, middle-aged people are likely to expand their definition of sex to include sensual, not just reproductive, acts. "If the message we get from society is that we have to keep on acting as we did at thirty," she says, "a lot of us are going to feel that we have a sexual disorder at some point." After a certain age, for example, men in particular may require physical stimulation to feel aroused. An awareness of this normal tendency, Rossi says, added to modern women's generally greater assertiveness, lays the groundwork for a new kind of relationship for older couples—one in which women have a more active role. "If the middle-aged don't feel pressured to conform to a youthful stereotype," she says, "I think we can predict some good things for their sex lives."

The Empty Nest and the Sandwich Generation

WHEN THE ROLE OF FAMILY IN THE EXPERIENCE of middle age is mentioned, one of two scenarios usually comes to mind. In the better established, the abandoned mother waves a tearful good-bye to her last chick and dully goes through the motions of life in the "empty nest." According to Larry Bumpass's demographic survey, however, the nest may be anything but empty: expensive housing and a weak economy and job market mean that the young delay their own marriages and are likelier to return home after a brief foray outside.

The more contemporary midlife family myth concerns the plight of the "sandwich generation": in a recent *Doonesbury* cartoon starring a professional couple, the forty-something husband tells his wife, busy juggling the needs of her children and their grandmother, "Don't die. Everyone's counting on you." Women's entry into the job market has focused much attention on a purported host of adults who make the circuit from the day-care center to Gramps's place to the office with nary a moment for themselves. "It's true that there's a lot going on in your life in middle age and you have little time for leisure," Margie Lachman says. "Fortunately, you're also at your peak in terms of competence, control, the ability to handle stress, and sense of responsibility. You're *equipped* for overload." According to Carol Ryff, people busy with both careers and relationships enjoy not only greater financial security and intellectual and social stimulation but also a psychological benefit. The eminent behavioral scientist Bernice Neugarten thinks that the hallmark of healthy middle age is "complexity," or a feeling of being in control of a crowded life and involved in the world at the same time. Ryff found in the course of one of her studies that this quality was most marked among the first generation to combine family and career. "It seems," she says, "that all the role-juggling that middle-aged people complain about actually makes them feel more engaged in life."

Rossi is dubious that the sandwich-generation problem is either new or widespread. "This phenomenon is a lot like the supposed midlife crisis," she says. "There are people who think that spending two hours a week with Mother is a big deal. But the fact is that very few men or women are caring both for little children and for elderly parents." One reason for this is that the "old old" who need considerable care are still a small group, and few of them are a daily drain on their children. Then, too, as Bumpass says, "over the past several decades the elderly have increasingly lived independently. They're economically more able to do so, and both sides prefer things that way." According to research conducted by Glenna Spitze, of the State University of New York at Albany, close involvement by the middle-aged with their parents—usually with a mother who has already cared for and buried her own husband—is likeliest to occur when the middle-aged person's children are older and need less attention. "For that matter," Rossi says, "rather than being a drain, the children are likely to be a comfort and help. It's important to remember that intimacy with children, which bottoms out from ages fifteen to nineteen, climbs steeply through the twenties and thirties. One of the things to look forward to in midlife is the continuity and shared interests that will come as your children in turn become parents."

To the list of underestimated family pleasures Ryff adds the satisfaction that parents take in knowing that grown-up children have turned out all right. She found that adult offspring are a vital if underrecognized element in middle-aged well-being, and that adjusting to how well or poorly they have matured is another of midlife's important developmental tasks. After studying 215 parents, Ryff found that their adult children's level of psychological adjustment was a major predictor for almost all aspects of both fathers' and mothers' mental health—although mothers took more credit for it. "The literature on parenting includes very little on what *parents* get out of it," she says, "or on how it affects their self-image, especially when the kids are older. Parenting never ends."

At Last, the Reward: Wisdom

LONG ON THE PROCESS OF BECOMING, THE LITERature of human development remains short on the business of being. That adults don't grow and change in the predictable, simultaneously physiological and behavioral fashion that children do partly explains why. So tidy is early development by comparison that it's even possible to link certain ages to certain behavioral stages, such as the "terrible twos" and the "temperamental teens." Although Gail Sheehy's bestseller *Passages* (described by Gilbert Brim as focused on "selected case studies that illustrate a theory that has no broad empirical support") advanced an adult model of such "age-stage" development, research continues to show that the ways in which adults evolve are not universal, not likely to occur in clear-cut stages, and not tied to particular ages. So poorly do the middle-aged fit into developmental patterns, in fact, that the huge National Survey of Families and Households revealed that of more than forty projected "typical midlife events," none was likely to happen at a certain, predictable age.

Biologically oriented behavioral scientists argue that at the individual level certain basic tendencies evident at birth or shortly after are the immutable building blocks of personality. The aversion to novel stimuli which becomes shyness, denoted by a low score in extroversion, is one such element. Some claim, moreover, that anyone can be defined even in early childhood in terms of how high or low he or she scores in tests that measure the "big five"

Most middle-aged adults benefit from knocking about in the world. When they go down a blind alley, they soon recognize the mistake, and save themselves much time and energy.

traits: neuroticism, extroversion, openness, agreeableness, and conscientiousness. This largely biological programming, trait theorists believe, means that personality is set in concrete around the time that physical development ceases. Afterward one may grow in terms of changing attitudes, skills, interests, and relationships, but only in ways consistent with one's big-five template.

Environment-minded researchers, including the MIDMAC team, take the influence of things like attitudes, interests, and relationships more seriously. They're working on a different, flexible model of adult development, based not on genes but on experience. Brim and his colleagues don't dispute that someone born shy or dutiful may very well stay that way, but they stress that whether he or she is raised in a sociable or a reclusive family, has a happy or an unhappy marriage, gets an exciting or a dull job, and has good or poor health will have considerable impact on identity. Bringing up reports of "aberrant outcomes"—people who early in life seem destined for success or failure yet somehow turn out the other way—Brim observes that adult change is shaped not just by the characteristics a person brings to bear on life but also by what life brings to bear on him or her, from family feuds to fatal attractions, religious experiences to traffic accidents. Accordingly, the MIDMAC group and others interested in tracking adult development focus on the ways in which, as a result of the depth and variety of their experience, their subjects' goals and values alter over time.

To illustrate experiential midlife development, Ron Kessler points to ways in which people are shaped by the influence of the workplace. "During early life you're socially segregated—all your school companions are also eight- or twelve-year-olds from the same neighborhood," he says. "Then comes adulthood, and suddenly you're working alongside different kinds of people of different ages. You can look around and say to yourself, 'In twenty years, if I act like him, I could have a heart attack, or end up divorced.' Or 'Sure, she makes a lot of money, but do I really want to work sixty hours a week?'"

Most middle-aged adults benefit from knocking about in the world, a process that greatly increases their efficiency in managing life. When they go down a blind alley, they soon recognize the mistake, and save themselves much time and energy. "Because they have all this material to plot trajectories with, the middle-aged are equipped to do an enormous amount of internal reshuffling," Kessler says. "Unlike younger people, they don't have to test everything themselves in the real world. Adults who learn from their mistakes change and grow, and those who don't, don't." Kessler describes a bright corporate lawyer who remains developmentally stalled in the "becoming" phase appropriate to youth: "He goes around saying '*This* is being a lawyer? I'd rather be a kid *wanting* to be a lawyer.'"

Perhaps the best refutation of the myths that adults don't develop and that adults do develop but only in rigid stages is a new body of research on the genesis of a psychological and cognitive capacity that scientists can only call wisdom. As is often the case in science, this inquiry began with the investigation of a mistaken premise. Assuming that the formalistic SAT-type process was the human norm in solving problems, those studying the effects of aging concluded that older people suffer a cognitive deficit, because they do worse than the young on such tests. The more researchers explored this apparently biological decline, however, the more they had to consider another possibility: people of different ages may perceive the same problem differently.

Any adult who has debated with a bright adolescent about, say, the likelihood that the world's nations will erase their boundaries and create a passportless global citizenry knows that there are two types of intelligence: the abstract, objective, Platonic-dualism sort that peaks early, and the practical, subjective type, born of shirtsleeves experience, which comes later. When asked the way to Rome, the young trace the most direct route very quickly, while their elders ponder: "Why Rome? Is this trip really a good idea? At what time of year? For business or pleasure? Alone or with others?"

The pre-eminent wisdom researcher is Paul Baltes, a MIDMAC fellow and a co-director of the Max Planck Institute for Human Development and Education, in Berlin. Baltes conducts studies of "whether living long can produce a higher level of mental functioning." The cognitive mechanics of the brain—the speed and accuracy with which we process information—are biological and subject to decline, he finds. But the brain's pragmatics—our knowledge and skill in using information—are not. When Baltes's subjects take the intellectual equivalent of a medical stress test, the young do in two seconds what the older do, with many more mistakes, in eight. But, Baltes says, unlike other species, ours can compensate for biological deficits. "If people have hearing problems, society develops hearing aids, and if I train an older subject in test-taking skills, he'll outperform an untutored younger person. By providing knowledge and strategies for using it, culture outwits biology. In all the areas of functioning in which age means more access to information, older people may be better off than young ones." In short, the middle-aged may be slower but they're smarter.

Beyond the commonsensical savvy acquired through daily experience lies a rarefied ability to deal with the fundamental problems of the human condition: matters ambiguous and existential, complex and conflicted, which call for the wisdom of Solomon. Using literary analysis, Baltes finds evidence in all cultures of people equipped to deal with these difficult issues, and he has devised several ways to test for the presence of this ability. In one type of study, subjects read vignettes of difficult situations—for example, a person pondering how to respond to a friend who has decided to commit suicide—and then "think aloud" through their decision-making process to a resolution of the problem. In another type, people with many contacts in the world of high achievers are asked to nominate those they consider especially wise; researchers then monitor how these candidates think about difficult problems. Both forms of testing allow Baltes to score subjects on his "wisdom criteria," which include great factual and procedural knowledge, the capacity to cope with uncertainty, and the ability to frame an event in its larger context. "Those who have these attributes are the people we call wise," he says, "and they are easily recognized. People who are said to have this quality do score higher than others."

To sense the difference between the wise and the hoi polloi, one might imagine a successful fifty-year-old urban lawyer who announces that she is going to quit her job, move to the country, and start a mail-order seed and bulb business. Most listeners will think, if not say, something like "What a crazy idea." But there might be someone who says, "Wait. What are the circumstances? Maybe this lawyer feels that her life has grown sterile. Maybe she has some solid plans for this change. Let's talk some more." According to Baltes's statistics, this wise person is probably neither young nor very old but somewhere between the ages of forty and seventy. "The highest grades we record occur somewhere around sixty," he says. "Wisdom peaks in midlife or later."

While intelligence is essential to wisdom, certain personal qualities predict with greater accuracy who will be wise. Thoreau observed, "It is a characteristic of wisdom not to do desperate things," and Baltes agrees. "Modulation and balance are crucial elements," he says, "because wisdom has no extremes. You can't be passionate or dogmatic and wise at the same time." Just as the Lao-tzus and Lincolns among us are likely to be reasonable and

open-minded, they are not likely to be motivated by selfish concerns, at least not markedly so: Machiavelli was clever but not wise.

"At some point in middle age," says David Featherman, of the Social Science Research Council, "we're inclined to become more tolerant of the uncertain, the complex, and the impossible, and even to learn to dismiss some problems as unsolvable or not worth our effort. Perhaps most important, we grow more interested in how our solutions affect others. Along with being good at figuring out what to do in real-life situations themselves, the wise are skilled in advising others—in sharing their wisdom. Unfortunately, Americans' Lone Ranger mentality about solving everything on our own means we don't always profit from this resource." The concern for others that is a hallmark of wisdom seems to augur well for those who have it as well as for its beneficiaries. The evolutionary neurobiologist Paul D. MacLean once observed, "We become nicer mammals as we age." Featherman points out that the benignity integral to wisdom seems characteristic of people who enjoy a happy, healthy old age.

In a youth-obsessed culture the suggestion that at least one element of character emerges only in middle age is both appealing and iconoclastic. "Wisdom doesn't happen at the age of six, or eighteen," Featherman says. "It may take a long time for all of its components to be in place. The timing of its emergence means that in maturity we get a new start—a new way of understanding life that's more apt to benefit others. It may turn out that caring about people is the capstone of the process of living."

Learning to *Love* (GULP!) Growing *Old*

Fear of aging speeds the very decline we dread most. And it ultimately robs our life of any meaning. No wonder there's an attitude shift in the making.

Jere Daniel

Jere Daniel is a free-lance writer specializing in health and human behavior. His articles have appeared in publications as diverse as The New York Times Magazine, American Health, *and* Family Circle. *He has pioneered corporate communications on health and produced a newsletter for America's leading companies. He is also the author of numerous television and radio scripts. He resides in Brooklyn Heights, New York.*

Technically, they are all still baby boomers. But on the cusp of 50, much to their surprise, having come late into maturity, they can suddenly envision themselves becoming obsolete, just as their fathers, mothers, grandparents, uncles, and aunts did when they crossed the age-65 barrier, the moment society now defines as the border line between maturity and old age.

Although they may be unprepared psychologically, they are certainly fortified demographically to notice the problems their elders now face—isolation, loneliness, lack of respect, and above all, virtual disenfranchisement from the society they built. The number of people reaching the increasingly mythic retirement age of 65 has zoomed from about seven and a half million in the 1930s (when Social Security legislation decreed 65 as the age of obsolescence) to 34 million today. By the turn of the century, that figure will be 61.4 million.

If the boomers' luck holds out, they will be spared what amounts to the psychological torture of uselessness and burdensomeness that every graying generation this century has faced before them. For there is an attitude shift in the wind. In an irony that boomers will no doubt appreciate (as

rebellion is an act usually reserved for the young), a revolution in attitude about age is coming largely from a corner of the population that has traditionally been content to enjoy the status quo—a cultural elite whose median age is surely over 65.

A small but growing gaggle of experts (themselves mostly elders)—a diverse lot of gerontologists, physicians, psychologists, sociologists, anthropologists, philosophers, ethicists, cultural observers, and spiritual leaders—are the vanguard of a movement to change the way society looks at and deals with growing old. They seek to have us stop viewing old age as a problem—as an incurable disease, if you will—to be "solved" by spending billions of dollars on plastic surgery in an attempt to mask visible signs of aging, other billions on medical research to extend the life span itself,

⁶We pretend that old age can be turned into an endless middle age, thereby giving people a false road map to the future.⁷

and billions more on nursing and retirement homes as a way to isolate those who fail at the quest to deny aging.

Separately and together, this cultural elite is exploring ways to move us and our social institutions toward a new concept of aging, one they call "conscious aging." They want us to be aware of and accept what aging actually is—a notice that life has not only a beginning and a middle but an end—and to eliminate the denial that now prevents us from anticipating, fruitfully using, and even appreciating what are lost to euphemism as "the golden years."

"Conscious aging is a new way of looking at and experiencing aging that moves beyond our cultural obsession with youth toward a respect and need for the wisdom of age," explains Stephan Rechtschaffen, M.D., a holistic physician who directs the Omega Institute, a kind of New Age think tank that is a driving force in this attitude shift. He would have us:

• Recognize and accept the aging process and all that goes with it as a reality, a natural part of the life cycle; it happens to us all. The goal is to change the prevailing view of aging as something to be feared and the aged as worthless.

• Reverse our societal attitude of aging as an affliction, and instead of spending billions on walling off the aging, spend more to improve the quality of life among the aged.

Our denial of aging has its costs. Rechtschaffen is adamant that it is not merely our elders who suffer. Quoting the late psychoanalyst Erik Erikson, he says, "Lacking a culturally viable ideal of old age, our civilization does not really harbor a concept of the whole of life."

We now live, and die, psychologically and spiritually incomplete. It may be a troubling sense of incompleteness that most stirs an appreciation for age among the baby boomers, so unfamiliar is any sense of incompleteness to the generation that invented the possibility of and has prided itself on "having it all."

Next month, a group of these thinkers will gather at an open-to-the-public conference under the auspices of the Omega Institute. Participants range from Sherwin Nuland, M.D., surgeon-author of the surprise best-seller *How We Die*, to Betty Friedan, who has dissected American attitudes toward aging in her latest book, *Fountain of Youth*, to spiritualist Ram Dass, Columbia University gerontologist Renee Solomon, Ph.D., and Dean Ornish, M.D., director of the University of California's Preventive Medicine Research Institute.

Until now, the conventional wisdom has been that only the aged, or those approaching its border, worry about its consequences: rejection, isolation, loneliness, and mandated obsolescence. Only they care about how they can give purpose to this final stage of their lives.

Sherwin Nuland has clear new evidence to the contrary. His book, *How We Die*, paints a shimmeringly lucid and remarkably unsentimental picture of death—the process and its meaning to the dying and to those around them. The biggest group of readers of this best-seller? Not the elderly, as most observers, and even the author himself, had anticipated. It's the baby boomers. Curiosity about age and death is booming among the boomers.

"The baby boomers, who started out rejecting the wisdom and experience of anyone over 30, are buying my book in droves," Nuland told *Psychology Today*. "To young people, death is an abstract concept. But face-to-face with aging parents and illnesses like cancer and strokes among themselves, newly graying baby boomers stare into their own mortality totally unprepared. Now this best-educated of all our generations wants information and doesn't want to turn away from what it's been trying to escape—the effects of getting old."

We fear and deny aging, the Omega experts emphasize, because we fear and deny death. "In our denial of death and the aging of the body, we have rejected the wisdom of the aged, and in doing so have robbed old age of its meaning and youth of its direction," Rechtschaffen asserts. We pretend that old age can be turned into a kind of endless middle age, thereby giving young people a false road map to the future, one that does not show them how to plan for their whole life, gain insight into themselves, or to develop spiritually.

The signs of denial and anxiety over aging permeate every aspect of our lives. We have no role models for growing old gracefully, only for postponing it. For example:

• The vast dependence on plastic surgery specifically to hide the visual signs of aging is arguably the sharpest index of our anxiety. In just two decades, from the 1960s to the 1980s, the number of rhytidectomies, wrinkle-removing face-lifts, rose from 60,000 to an estimated 2 million a year at an annual cost of $10 billion.

• The negative view of aging is disastrously reinforced by the media. Articles and advertising never show a mature model, even in displaying fashions designed for women over 50. A *Newsweek* cover of a sweating, gray-haired young man bears the cover line, "Oh God...I'm really turning 50." Nursing home ads ask: "What shall we do about Mother?" By some sleight of mind, we not only come to accept these images, we come to expect them as truths.

We denigrate aging, Friedan persuasively notes, by universally equating it with second childhood, "so negatively stereotyped that getting old has become something to dread and feel threatened by." A series of studies by psychologists Ellen Langer, Ph.D. of Harvard and University of Pennsylvania President Judith Rodin, Ph.D. (then at Yale) suggests how we grow to revile our aging selves.

Influenced by the fairy tales we hear as children, and what we see on television and hear in everyday life, we develop negative stereotypes about aging by the time we are six years old, the same age we develop negative stereotypes about race and sex. These stereotypes persist as we grow up, completely unaware that we even acquired them or granted them our unconditional acceptance. With our understanding of the subject forever frozen, we grow into old age assuming the stereotypes to be true. And we live down to them.

If there is a single myth about aging that most symbolizes our dread, it is the assumption that our memory will inevitably decline in old age. In a stunning new study, psychologist Langer has demonstrated that it is our own psychology—the near-universal expectation of memory loss—that actually brings that fate upon us. The lesson to be learned is an extraordinary one: Fear of aging is the single most powerful agent creating exactly what we fear.

The negative stereotypes acquired in childhood parade across the adult life span as expectations. As people age, Langer finds, low expectations lead to "decreased effort, less use of adaptive strategies, avoidance of challenging situations, and failure to seek medical attention for disease-related symptoms."

In her newest study, Langer and Harvard colleague Rebecca Levy, Ph.D., confirm the effect of these negative stereotypes on aging Americans. Using standard psychological measurements of memory, the researchers studied two populations of people who hold their elders in high esteem—elderly mainland Chinese and older, deaf Americans—and compared them to a group of elderly mainstream Americans. In addition, the researchers compared memory retention in the elderly with younger people in all three groups.

Not only did the mainland Chinese and American deaf far outperform the mainstream Americans on four psychological memory tests, but the oldest in these two groups, especially the Chinese, performed almost as well as the youngest. Their performance was so strong even the researchers were surprised. They conclude that the results can be explained entirely by the fact that the Chinese have the most positive, active, and "internal" image of aging across the three cultures studied.

What is particularly striking about the Langer–Levy study is that it meticulously tracks how our fears, which are so culturally constructed, become self-fulfilling prophecies. "The social, psychological component of memory retention may be even stronger than we believed."

Just as our fear of memory loss can create actual memory decline, the dread of aging may be taking its toll on many other body systems.

The current collective view of aging is so relentlessly negative that neither our social institutions nor the aging themselves believe what worldwide research points to—that those of us alive today may be aging better than our parents.

A landmark, 15-year longitudinal study of older people, begun in 1970 by Alvar Svanborg in the industrial city of Gothenburg, Sweden, showed no measur-able decline in many body functions until after age 70, and very little decline by 81. Cognitive abilities were intact to at least age 75, and still intact in almost all who had reached 81, although speed at rote memory declined. "The vitality of old people in Sweden today, among the longest-lived people in the world, seems to be greater than it was only five or 10 years ago," Svanborg asserts.

American studies of healthy people aging in their own communities, as opposed to those shunted off to institutions, failed to show evidence of decline in intelligence, cognitive skills, and even memory that had appeared in all previous cross-sectional studies of aging. The combined thrust of the studies of "normal aging" is inescapable. Physical and mental decline is not inevitable. Belief that it is accelerates whatever decline occurs.

Still, we continue to mythologize and denigrate aging because we devalue death itself. "We refuse even to admit that we die of old age," says Nuland, a retired Yale surgeon, whose book embodies the proposition that death is a normal stage in the life cycle. This refusal is perpetuated by the medical profession and the law. "I cannot write 'Old Age' on a death certificate even though people over 70 die because they're over 70," he says.

"An octogenarian who dies of myocardial infarction is not simply a weather-beaten senior citizen with heart disease—he is the victim of an insidious progression that involves all of him, and that progression is called aging," Nuland says. He deplores the prevailing view of aging as a disease that can be cured and the biomedical search for a fountain of youth.

"Though biomedical science has vastly increased mankind's average life expectancy (78.6 years for American women, 71.6 for men), the maximum (114 years) has not changed in verifiable recorded history. Even the home-cultured yogurt of the Caucasus cannot vanquish nature," Nuland says. "Trying to add a few more years to the human life span is meaningless and wasteful."

The promise of an extended life span simply adds unnecessary stress to the ability to accept aging. "An extended life span without extended awareness of the possibilities of a productive old age means we aren't sure we're living longer. Maybe we're just dying longer," says Rabbi Zalman Schachter-Shalomi, founder of a pioneering Spiritual Eldering Project at Philadelphia's B'nai Or Religious Fellowship. Schachter-Shalomi is the recipient of the first annual Conscious Aging Award by the Omega Institute. In place of fear of death we'd be better off with a belief in the possibilities of life, as long as it is lived.

"If age itself is defined as a 'problem,' then those over 65 who can no longer 'pass' as young are its carriers and must be quarantined lest they contaminate, in mind or body, the rest of society," Friedan asserts. So we banish the elderly from our midst and wall them off in nursing homes. We encourage them to isolate themselves in retirement homes and communities, in San Diego condos and Miami Beach hotels.

But isolating ourselves into ageist groups only sets the stage for a class warfare that is bound to get louder and more violent. Younger generations grow to resent the older, and vice versa. And so, says Nuland, the elderly grow demanding and greedy for health and custodial care while the rest of the population bemoans the financial drain the aged make on society, all the while feeling guilty for the situation.

With the old now successfully segregated out, Americans are in no position to exploit the benefits of age—or even to recognize or acknowledge that there are any. Which brings us to the special brand of intelligence called wisdom.

Sure, we have our "elder" statesmen, but the titles are honorary, often conferred with an underlying tinge of humor. They signify reverence for past accomplishments more than real respect for the wisdom that only elders have to contribute. Wisdom remains a very special commodity, a great natural resource that is undervalued—and almost totally untapped in doing what it's meant for: guiding the young. And there's only one way to get it.

It is not easy to talk about wisdom without lapsing into platitudes and vagueness, so a team of European researchers—no surprise there—has taken on the challenge to isolate the features of wisdom in clinical detail. From their ongoing studies of the aging mind, psychologists Paul B. Baltes and Ursula M. Staudinger, both of the Max Planck Institute for Human Development in Berlin, define wisdom:

• It's an expertise that wraps information in the human context of life and relates it to generational and historical flow.

• It is factual and procedural knowledge about the world and human affairs.

• It mingles insight and judgment involving complex and uncertain matters of the human condition; there is an appreciation for and understanding of the uncertainties of life.

• It involves a fine-tuned coordination of cognition, motivation, and emotion, knowledge about the self and other people and society.

• It carries knowledge about strategies to manage the peaks and valleys of life.

• It integrates past, present, and future.

A product of cultural and knowledge-based factors, rather than biologically based mechanics of the mind, wisdom accumulates with time—but only among those who remain open to new experiences. If we must insist on outwitting the constraints of biology, then wisdom—and not the scalpel—is our thing.

It may be that we ignore wisdom because, especially over the lifetime of the boomers, we have come to overvalue, say, rocket science. The technological advancement of modern society has bred in us an infatuation with the data we have accumulated. "We've traded information for wisdom," Rechtschaffen offers.

We have confounded the accumulation of data with its application, or even an understanding of it. Wisdom, on the other hand, always puts information back in the context of human life.

Sherwin Nuland is a man forced by the exigencies of his profession to look time squarely in the eye. Old age, he says, is a "time to become contemplative, to recognize our value to people younger than ourselves." Now in his sixties, Nuland stopped operating when "I realized I was no longer as nimble as a 45-year-old. But I expect to continue contributing my knowledge and experience as long as possible." Unfortunately, he says, "the younger generation doesn't always accept it, from me or others. They see their elders as crotchety and selfish, their maturity and wisdom of no use—outdated. Age warfare continues."

Perhaps we don't recognize the wisdom of aging because our anxiety about the future—of the world, of ourselves—has overwhelmed our respect for history. We live, Rechtschaffen says, with only a linear sense of time. We push inexorably toward the future; the past is nothing. In other eras, we lived by a more circular sense of time, which allowed for a father's, even a grandfather's, experience to guide us. There was an intuitive apprehension—wisdom, if you will—that the way to deal with the future rests in an understanding of the past. Even today, many indigenous tribal societies and Eastern cultures live by a circular sense of time.

The baby boomers have made it successfully, albeit noisily, through the first two-thirds of their lives, having rejected—indeed defying—the teachings of their elders. But the prospect of making it through the next third satisfied with their accomplishments and their selves requires they find inner meaning in their lives.

To give their lives purpose, they might turn from what Nuland calls "the hurly-burly of getting and spending" to a more contemplative life. And they might pay more attention to those who have already crossed the border into old age, to value their experience; to embrace their elders is to embrace their future selves. Perhaps, most of all, they might begin to think of their own death. After all, to be fully alive includes being fully aware of dying.

So long as we lock ourselves into an obsession with the youth culture, we can only develop age rage and dehumanize ourselves, says Betty Friedan. Those who give up their denial of age, who age consciously, "grow and become aware of new capacities they develop while aging....[They] become more authentically themselves."

Studies Suggest Older Minds Are Stronger Than Expected

DANIEL GOLEMAN

The conventional image of the aging brain is that people lose neurons the way balding men lose hair. Brain cells are supposed to start falling away around the age of 20, with everything downhill from there. Some people go bald, or senile, early. Some lucky and unusual ones keep their hair, or their wits, about them into their 90's and beyond.

Science has precious little good news about hair loss, but new findings on the death of brain cells suggest that minoxidil for the mind is unnecessary. Data from men and women who continue to flourish into their 80's and 90's show that in a healthy brain, any loss of brain cells is relatively modest and largely confined to specific areas, leaving others robust. In fact, about 1 of every 10 people continues to increase in mental abilities like vocabulary through those decades.

New imaging techniques, like the PET scan and magnetic resonance imaging, or M.R.I., have shown that the brain does gradually shrink in life's later decades, just not as much as had been thought. Furthermore, the shrinkage of a healthy brain does not seem to result in any great loss of mental ability.

"We used to think that you lost brain cells every day of your life everywhere in the brain," said Dr. Marilyn Albert, a psychologist at Massachusetts General Hospital in Boston. "That's just not so—you do have some loss with healthy aging, but not so dramatic, and in very selective brain areas."

The new imaging techniques have also enabled neuroscientists to discover a flaw in many earlier studies of the aging brain: they included findings from people in the early stages of Alzheimer's disease. Now, both by scanning the brain and by more carefully screening to measure cognitive function, most people with Alzheimer's are excluded from such studies.

Researchers measure brain shrinkage by keeping track of the fjord-like spaces that crease the wrinkled surface layer of the cerebral cortex, the topmost layer that is critical for thought. These tiny crevasses are called ventricles and sulci, and the amount of space in them gradually increases with age, reflecting a loss in the overall mass of the brain.

From age 20 to 70, the average brain loses about 10 percent of its mass, said Dr. Stanley Rapoport, chief of the neuroscience laboratory at the National Institute on Aging in Bethesda, Md.

But that loss "seems related only to subtle differences in cognitive abilities," Dr. Rapoport said. "We think the brain's integrity is maintained because the massive redundancy of interconnection among neurons means that even if you lose some, the brain can often compensate."

Compensation is precisely what studies of the "successful" elderly show. When neuroscientists weed out people with cognitive decline that is a sure sign of illness, the shrinkage is still there, but performance on mental tests is good. And what analyses of healthy old brains show is that old people may use different parts of the brain from young people to accomplish the same task. In some ways a healthy old brain is like a pitcher whose fastball has faded but who can still strike a batter out with other pitches.

Some of the data come from autopsies of 25 men and women from 71 to 95 years old who had volunteered to be part of a control group in a 16-year study of Alzheimer's disease. Dr. John Morris, a neurologist at Washington University in St. Louis who did the study, said the brains of the mentally alert group showed some of the tangles that, more than shrinkage, seem to be the main problem in Alzheimer's disease. But these tangles were in the hippocampus, a structure involved in memory, rather than the centrally important cerebral cortex.

Dr. Morris said his data, which will be published next month in the journal Neurology, suggest "there may be a pool of people who not only have no important cognitive declines, but no brain changes of consequence for mental function, even into their 80's and 90's." Changes in the hippocampus may only slow the rate of retrieval from memory, he said, but not diminish its accuracy.

Similar findings have been made by Dr. Brad Hyman of Massachusetts General Hospital. "We've found no appreciable neuronal loss in people from their 60's to 90's who had retained their mental clarity until they died," said Dr. Hyman, who studied two specific regions of the cortex. "The dire picture we've had of huge cell losses is wrong for a healthy person whose brain remains structurally intact into old age."

Apart from a reduction in the number of brain cells, another aspect of aging in the healthy brain seems to be a drop in the connections between them. Dr. Albert at Massachusetts General said her studies of brain tissue had uncovered specific structures deep in the brain that did show more neuronal loss, even with healthy aging. These include areas important for memory like the basal forebrain.

But, Dr. Albert said, "It's important for mental abilities that most of the neurons in the cortex are re-

tained—they store information once you've learned it."

Some of the most intriguing evidence for the resourcefulness of the aging brain comes from PET scans of the brain at rest and while engaged in mental tasks. In one study using PET scans that compared people in their 20's with those 60 to 75, Dr. Cheryl L. Grady, a neuroscientist at the National Institute on Aging, found that the younger people were indeed quicker and more accurate in recognizing faces, and used more diverse areas of their brains during the task, than did the older people.

But in similar studies at the institute comparing people from 20 to 40 with those 55 and older, the older group was able to recognize the faces with about the same accuracy, though they needed more time to do so than the younger group, Dr. Rapoport said. Images of the brains of the older group showed less activity in visual areas of the brain, but more activity in the prefrontal cortex, suggesting increased mental effort.

Dr. Rapoport said that in older people there seemed to be some loss of circuits involved in visual memory. "So the brain has to recruit other circuits to get the task done," he said.

But recruit it does. The prefrontal cortex, which is the brain's executive area for intellectual activity, appears especially crucial in compensating for areas that no longer function so well in mental tasks.

All is not rosy. The number of people who do end up with Alzheimer's disease and fall into senility is still quite large.

"There are three very different groups among the elderly," said Dr. Guy McKhann, director of the Zanville and Krieger Mind Brain Institute at the Johns Hopkins Medical School. "One does remarkably well, aging very successfully into their 80's and 90's. The second group slides a bit, having some problems with memory and recall, but the problems are typically more aggravating than they are real."

Dr. McKhann said that the third group, which largely consists of people with Alzheimer's disease, suffers inexorable losses in mental function leading to senility. That group accounts for about 15 percent of those in their 70's and 30 percent to 40 percent of those in their 80's.

But for those without disease, the brain can withstand aging remarkably well. "Some people stay very good at intellectual tasks all their lives," said Dr. Judith Saxton, a neuropsychologist at the University of Pittsburgh Medical Center, who is analyzing data from a two-year follow-up of more than 700 men and women from 65 to 92.

"Their overall knowledge and vocabulary continues to grow as they age, even though their speed of retrieval slows a bit," Dr. Saxton added. "I'd guess up to 10 percent of people above 70 fall in this range." The question that interests many people who are headed toward 70, as well as some new and unconventional researchers, is how and why one ends up in the 10 percent. Is a person's neurological fate predetermined? Or is their something that can be done to stay healthy and mentally alert?

Grandparent Development and Influence

Robert Strom and Shirley Strom

Robert Strom is Professor of Lifespan Developmental Psychology, Division of Psychology in Education, Arizona State University, Tempe, Arizona 85287-0611. Shirley Strom is Research Coordinator, Office of Parent Development International Division of Psychology in Education, Arizona State University, Tempe, Arizona 85287-0611.

ABSTRACT

The educational needs of grandparents have been overlooked. They deserve access to a curriculum that can help them adjust to their changing role and illustrates how to build satisfying family relationships. The nation's first educational program developed for grandparents is described in terms of underlying assumptions, measures to assess learning needs, elements of curriculum, and procedures for instruction. Fieldtest evidence regarding the effectiveness of this approach to strengthening families is presented along with implications for the future.

A strong family is one that includes mutually satisfying relationships and the capacity of members to meet each other's needs (Stinnett & DeFrain, 1985). Most efforts to strengthen families involve classes which help parents acquire effective methods of guidance and set reasonable expectations for children. A similar approach could provide greater success for 55 million grandparents in the United States. Observers agree that grandparents have the potential to make a more significant contribution to their families and society should do whatever is necessary to ensure this possibility (Bengston & Robertson, 1985; Elkind, 1990; Kornhaber, 1986). The status of grandparents can be enhanced by (1) better understanding of how family relationships are influenced by technological change, (2) widespread recognition of the need to establish educational expectations for grandparents, and (3) the development of practical curriculum to help them adjust to their emerging role.

FAMILY RELATIONSHIPS AND TECHNOLOGICAL CHANGE

Learning in a past-oriented society. When the older people of today were children, the world was changing less rapidly. Because there was a slower rate of progress, the past dominated the present. Consequently, youngsters learned mostly from adults. In those days a father might reasonably say to his son: "Let me tell you about life and what to expect. I will give you the benefit of my experience. Now, when I was your age . . ." In this type of society the father's advice would be relevant since he had already confronted most of the situations his son would face. Given the slow pace of change, children could see their future as they observed the day-to-day activities of parents and grandparents.

There are still some past-oriented societies in the world today, places where adults remain the only important source of a child's education. On the island of Bali in Indonesia, parents can be observed passing on their woodcarving and painting skills to sons and daughters who expect to earn a living in much the same way. Similarly, aboriginal tribes in Australia are determined to perpetuate their traditional community. Amish people in the United States maintain a pattern of living that closely resembles the priorities and routine of their forefathers. For children growing up in each of these static environments, the future seems essentially a repetition of the past. When life is so free of uncertainty, so predictable, it appears justified to teach boys and girls that they should adopt the lifestyle of their elders. Therefore, in every slow-changing culture, grandparents are viewed as experts, as authorities, as models for all age groups. The role expected of children is to be listeners and observers, to be seen but not heard (Strom & Strom, 1987).

Learning in a present-oriented society. When technology is introduced and accelerated in a society, there is a corresponding increase in the pace of social change. Long-standing customs and traditions are permanently modified. Successive generations of grandparents, parents and children come to have less in common. Children today have many experiences that were not part of their parents' upbringing. This means there are some

This paper was presented to the Japan Society for the Promotion of Science in Tokyo, Japan on July 1, 1991.

things adults are too old to know simply because we are not growing up at the present time. It is a reversal of the traditional comment to children that "You're too young to understand." Boys and girls now encounter certain conditions which are unique in history to their age group. Access to drugs, life in a single parent family, computer involvement and global awareness are common among children. They are exposed to day care, racially integrated schools, and the fear of life-threatening sexually-transmitted diseases. Adults cannot remember most of these situations because we never experienced them.

The memory of childhood as a basis for offering advice ("When I was your age . . .") becomes less credible as the pace of social change quickens. Because of the gap between experiences of adults and children, there is a tendency to seek advice mostly from peers. An increasing number of people feel that the only persons who can understand them are those at the same stage of life as themselves or who share similar challenges. Unfortunately, when people are limited to their peers for extended conversations, they are less inclined to develop the communication skills needed for successful interaction with other generations.

A peer orientation undermines cultural continuity as it divides the population into special interest groups. Because a rapidly changing society assigns greater importance to the present than the past, older people cease to be seen as models for everyone. Each generation chooses to identify with famous people of their own or next higher age group. Therefore, respect for the elderly declines. Older adults are no longer regarded as experts about much of anything except aging (Strom, Bernard & Strom, 1989).

Learning in a future-oriented society. The phase of civilization we are entering is referred to as the Information Age. Within this context schooling for children begins earlier, continues longer, and includes a vast amount of knowledge which was unavailable to previous generations of students. Given these conditions, children are bound to view the world from a different vantage and therefore should be seen by adults as an important source of learning. Certainly intergenerational dialogue is necessary to shape the future in a democratic society. Unless such contacts are sustained and mutually beneficial, the future could bring conflict as low birth rates provide fewer working age taxpayers to meet the needs of a growing elderly population. Some social scientists expect relationships between the young and older populations to replace the relationship between races as the dominant domestic conflict in the next half century (Toffler, 1990).

Intergenerational relationships are valuable because they offer a broader orientation than can be gained from any peer group. Until recently, it was supposed that aging is accompanied by a sense of perspective. This assumption still makes sense in slow-changing cultures. But, in technological societies the attainment of perspective requires something more than getting older. Becoming aware of how age groups other than our own see things and feel about the world is necessary for a broad perspective and responding to the needs of others. Unless the viewpoints of younger generations are taken into account, perspective tends to diminish rather than grow as people age (Strom & Strom, 1985, 1991).

ESTABLISHING EDUCATIONAL EXPECTATIONS FOR GRANDPARENTS

Our efforts to help grandparents began by offering a free course for them at senior citizen centers and churches in metropolitan Phoenix. The 400 people who enrolled in these classes were told they would learn something of what it is like for children to be growing up in the contemporary society and how parents view their task of raising children at the present time. In return, the participants agreed to share their experience as grandparents. This format was chosen because the literature on family relations revealed a patronizing attitude toward grandparents instead of educational programs to help them grow. Previous investigators had not made an effort to identify grandparent learning needs so there were no educational solutions. The following assumptions emerged from our preliminary research and guide the continuing project (Strom & Strom, 1989).

Grandparent responsibilities can be more clearly defined. Mothers and fathers have access to parenting courses that help them maintain competence in their changing role but similar opportunities are unavailable to grandparents. Instead, they are left alone to wonder: What are my rights and my responsibilities as a grandparent? How can I continue to be a favorable influence as my grandchild gets older? How well am I doing as a grandparent? These kinds of questions are likely to persist until there are commonly known guidelines for setting goals and self-evaluation. Many grandparents have difficulty defining their role and understanding how they could make a greater contribution. As a result the responsibility for raising youngsters has become disproportionate in many families with grandparents assuming less obligation than is in everyone's best interest.

Grandparents can learn to improve their influence. Mothers and fathers who can count on grandparents to share the load for caregiving and guidance less often seek support outside the family. The success of grandparents requires being aware of the parenting goals of sons and daughters and acting as a partner in reinforcing these goals. However, even though research indicates that people remain capable of adopting new attitudes and skills during middle and later life, grandparent development has not received priority in adult education. This missing element lessens the possibility of a meaningful life for many grandmothers and grandfathers.

The concept of life-long learning should include a concern for curriculum development. This means society has to reconsider its view that continuous learning is essential only for young people. The myth that aging is accompanied by wisdom has misled many older adults to underestimate their need for further education. When grandparents are mentally active, they remain a source of advice. Everyone at every age has a responsibility to keep growing in order to achieve their potential.

A practical grandparent program should be widely available. Older men and women have been led to believe that learning in later life should consist of whatever topics they find interesting without any societal expectations as there are for younger learners. But as people continue to age, they should also continue to grow—and not just in terms of acquiring leisure-oriented skills. Some of education in later life should emphasize obligations and roles, just as curriculum does for younger age groups. Senior citizens are the only population without any defined educational needs or cooperatively planned curricula. Since the size of this group is expected to grow faster than any other age segment, it seems reasonable to provide them educational opportunities which can help strengthen their families.

Society should set higher expectations for grandparents. By themselves grandparents may be unable to generate the motivation necessary to stimulate educational commitment within their peer group. This is a difficult task because so many people think of retirement as a time when they can withdraw from active community responsibility. Peers reinforce the perception that being carefree and without obligation is an acceptable goal in later life. The problem is compounded by age segregation. When older adults are limited to one another for most of their interaction, they establish standards which may not be in accord with what the society as a whole believes is best.

In order to favorably revise existing norms for older adults in terms of greater learning and more significant contributions to the family, younger age groups must raise their expectations and make these known. The talent and potential contribution of seniors could enrich the lives of everyone. Accordingly, we should expect them to demonstrate a commitment to personal growth, concern themselves about others through volunteering, and support the schools to ensure a better future for children. If educational expectations are not established for older adults, they will experience less influence and lower self-esteem.

The benefits of grandparent education can be assessed. Popular support can be expected for programs that help grandparents enlarge the scope of their influence, improve their ability to communicate with loved ones, become more self confident, and experience greater respect in the family. These benefits would be even more credible if the sources confirming them included other persons than just the participating grandparents. By comparing the results from three generational versions of the authors' Grandparent Strengths and Needs Inventory, the merits of various educational approaches to family development can be determined. This inventory also enables educators to adapt curriculum in a way that honors group and individual differences (Strom & Strom, 1990; Strom, Strom, & Collinsworth, 1991).

GOALS FOR GRANDPARENT DEVELOPMENT

There are six fundamental aspects of the grandparent experience that we try to influence in our program. Each of them have implications for child and adult development. The goals we pursue are to:

Increase the satisfaction of being a grandparent. It would seem that the longer lifespan today gives grandparents more years to influence their grandchildren. But the actual consequence depends on whether or not a relationship is mutually satisfying. When family members avoid sharing their feelings, or they experience insufficient satisfaction with one another, the relationship is in jeopardy. Grandmothers and grandfathers who enjoy their role are more able to cope with difficulties.

Improve how well grandparents perform their role. The efforts of grandparents to guide grandchildren depend on how self-confident they feel in their family role. Those who seek to support the parenting goals of their sons and daughters will continue to teach grandchildren. These persons realize that it is unreasonable to expect parents to be exclusively responsible for the care and guidance of grandchildren. By being active contributors in the family, they are seen as a valuable and long-term source of influence.

Enlarge the scope of guidance expected of grandparents. There is abundant evidence that, by itself, academic learning is an insufficient preparation for success in life. It follows that grandparents should help grandchildren acquire some of the out of school lessons they need. By defining the aspects of growth that should be obtained at home, it is possible to improve a child's total education and establish a helpful role for grandparents.

Decrease the difficulties of being a grandparent. Grandparents encounter some difficulty in getting along with sons, daughters, in-laws, and grandchildren. The manner in which these problems are handled is a sign of personal effectiveness. Every grandmother and grandfather should have access to education which focuses on their changing role. When grandparents are aware of the childrearing strategies of their sons and daughters and they know the predictable difficulties to expect as grandchildren get older, they can prepare themselves by obtaining the skills necessary for continued success.

Reduce the frustrations experienced by grandparents. Some frustration is to be expected. But grandparents vary in the frequency with which they sense frustration. One way to reduce their discontent is by understanding why certain child behaviors occur and why some of them should be allowed to continue. When the expectations of grandparents are consistent with a child's developmental needs, the tendency is to encourage normative behavior and offer support for a favorable self concept.

Reduce the family information needs of grandparents. Grandparents need accurate perceptions about their grandchild's abilities and their social relationships. Besides the information which teachers and parents provide for them, grandparents should listen to grandchildren themselves to learn about their hopes, fears, goals and concerns. If educational programs for grandparents can regularly include access to the views of people who are the same age as grandchildren, it is easier to understand how family members resemble and differ from their peers.

ELEMENTS OF CURRICULUM AND INSTRUCTION

The learning activities that grandparents consider appealing deserve priority in planning educational programs for them. Just as young students need a variety of teaching methods, older men and women can also benefit from a wide range of instructional techniques. The two courses we have developed on "Becoming A Better Grandparent" and "Achieving Grandparent Potential" follow the same format of focusing on all three generations. Some of the lessons concerning grandparents involve keeping up with the times, giving and seeking advice, communicating from a distance, growing as a couple, and learning in later life. Lessons about the middle generation call for recognizing indicators of parental success, helping single and blended families, developing values and morals, building child self-esteem, and watching television together. The lessons on grandchildren emphasize getting along with others, sharing fears and worries, understanding children's thinking, deciding about sex and drugs, and encouraging the college student. All twenty-four lessons consist of the same instructional elements. In turn, each of these elements deserve a brief explanation.

Discussion and brainstorming. Grandparents meet in small groups to consider agenda from their guidebook that encourages their expression of ideas, concerns, mistakes, goals and solutions (Strom & Strom, 1991a, 1991c). During these discussions the participants inform, challenge, and reassure each other. They quickly discover there is much to gain from sharing feelings and thoughts. Conversations with emotionally supportive peers cause men and women to feel less alone, help them organize their thinking, and increase awareness of the possibilities for becoming a better grandparent. Creative thinking is practiced during each discussion when the group shifts to consideration of a brainstorming task.

Problem solving. The next activity invites grandparents to consider how they might handle a particular problem if they had to cope with it. A family incident is described which offers everyone the same information including several possible solutions. Grandparents like to reflect and then discuss pros and cons they see for each of the given choices. It is stimulating to think of additional options and to identify relevant information that may be missing. Everyone has an opportunity to share their reasoning about the advice they consider to be best. This scenario approach broadens the range of solutions individuals see and discourages premature judgment. Later, in their home, grandparents present the scenarios to relatives and find out their viewpoint.

Grandparent principles. Several written principles accompany each unit. Grandparents rely on these practical guidelines for review, reflection, and personal application. Participants benefit from reading the companion volume of viewpoints which match each lesson in the guidebook (Strom & Strom, 1991b, 1991d). These essays, from which the principles are drawn, offer insights, observations and suggestions for making the grandparent experience more satisfying. In addition, local resource persons can enrich the learning by acquainting grandparents with the way problems are handled in their own community. Because each individual represents a unique family, grandparents must decide for themselves which principles are most appropriate in their present situation, the ones to apply immediately, and those that can be deferred until a later time.

Self-evaluation and observation. Personal growth requires self-examination. Grandparents are encouraged to practice this important skill as part of their homework. Each homework assignment consists of several multiple-choice questions that give participants a chance to state their feelings about issues such as family relationships, communication problems, and expectations of children. The anonymous homework is submitted at the beginning of each class. After responses are tallied for each item, the previously unknown norms of perception and behavior are announced to the class. This helps individuals know how their experience as grandparents resemble and differ from peers.

Intergenerational conversations. Grandparents should strive to know each grandchild as an individual. The way to achieve this goal is through interaction with the particular grandchild. However, most grandmothers and grandfathers admit that they sometimes have difficulty keeping a conversation going with youngsters. This is why they appreciate questions focusing on realms of experience that the generations commonly encounter, topics that transcend age. Every lesson includes a set of questions dealing with topics of mutual concern such as music, health, school, money, fears, friends, and careers. These questions facilitate the dialogue that we expect grandparents to initiate face to face or by phone. Most of the inquiries fit all grandchildren while some are more appropriate for teenagers. A portion of each class session is devoted to hearing grandparents comment about the insights they have acquired through intergenerational interviews.

Grandparents also need to know something about the norms of their grandchild's age group. It is unreasonable to suppose that all the information we need about the orientation of relatives will be provided by them alone. In a society where peers have considerable influence it is wise to find out how people in a grandchild's age group think and feel. This improves our understanding of how loved ones resemble and differ from their peers. One approach we use is to videotape interviews with children and parents who express their views on topics like peer pressure, school stress, and family conflict. This method reflects our belief that the broad perspective of life each of us ought to acquire emerges only when the thoughts and feelings of other age groups are taken into account.

EVALUATING GRANDPARENT SUCCESS

The effectiveness of grandparent education has been confirmed by research. In one study 800 people representing three generations evaluated the attitudes and behavior of grandparents before and after their participation in the "Becoming A Better Grandparent" course. At the end of the program grandparents reported that they had made significant improvements. This progress was corroborated by inventory scores of the parents and grandchildren (Strom & Strom, 1990). Specifically, grandparents benefit from the mentally stimulating experience by understanding how their role is changing, acquiring a broader perspective, learning new attitudes, gaining greater confidence and self-esteem, improving communication skills, and strengthening family relationships (Strom & Strom, 1985, 1989; Strom, Strom & Collinsworth, 1990).

These feelings expressed by the grandparents show the importance of the program for them: "I realized that I must keep on growing in order to understand other family members and be seen by them as a positive influence." "Now I understand my privileges as a grandparent as well as the duties I owe my grandchildren." "I found that helping my son and daughter achieve their parenting goals has upgraded my status to that of a valued partner." "I feel so much better about myself as a grandmother and more optimistic about my grandchildren."

Sons and daughters also identified some important benefits of grandparent education: "My parents seem more willing to share their feelings with us and they are more supportive of the way we are bringing up our children." "Taking this class has really helped my mom think about her role in my child's life. She is working hard to get to know my children as individuals." "My Dad has realized that listening and learning from his grandchildren is the key to being respected by them." "My mother has always been kind and loving to all of us but now she is more interesting to be around. It's fun to hear what she is learning."

It would be pleasing to report a balance in the proportion of men and women who seek to improve themselves through grandparent education. However, just as mothers significantly outnumber fathers in parenting classes, grandmothers are over represented in classes for grandparent development. Usually three out of four students in our courses are grandmothers. Does this ratio indicate that grandmothers need more guidance than grandfathers? On the contrary, it suggests grandmothers are more motivated to keep growing in this aspect of life. This conclusion was reached after comparing the influence of 155 grandmothers and 55 grandfathers who had just completed the program. Assessments were made to determine how each gender was perceived by themselves, their sons, daughters and grandchildren. Although the grandmothers reported having less formal education than grandfathers, they were seen as more successful grandparents in the estimate of all three generations (Strom & Strom, 1989).

In this study grandparents, parents and grandchildren portrayed grandmothers as emotionally closer to grandchildren, better informed about family affairs, and more willing to commit themselves to helping others. They were better at seeing the positive side of situations, learning from other family members, and making their feelings known. Grandmothers were credited with knowing more than grandfathers about the fears and concerns of grandchildren and spending more time with them. They were regarded as more effective in teaching grandchildren how to show trust, get along with others, and handle arguments. Grandmothers were viewed as better at passing on family history and cultural traditions, and more willing to accept help from grandchildren.

Strengths of grandfathers were recognized too. They saw themselves as having less difficulty than grandmothers in giving advice to sons and daughters, and were less frustrated by televiewing and listening habits of grandchildren. Parents observed grandfathers as being more satisfied than grandmothers when grandchildren asked for advice. Grandchildren felt their outlook on life was appreciated more by grandfathers.

Perhaps it is unfair to compare grandfathers with grandmothers. Consider the more positive results that emerge when the emphasis is on identifying change in grandfather attitudes and behaviors after instruction. The grandfathers in this study felt they made improvement in terms of satisfaction with their role, success in carrying out their obligations, effectiveness in teaching, overcoming difficulties, coping with frustrations, and

becoming more informed. Parents and grandchildren confirmed these gains had occurred. By joining grandmothers as participants in family-oriented education, grandfathers have proven they can learn to build more successful relationships with their spouse, children and grandchildren. Toward this goal grandfathers are urged to grow along with their partner and be actively involved in strengthening the family (Strom & Strom, 1989).

CONCLUSION

As we contemplate the future it is important to bear in mind that the baby-boomers, those persons born between 1946–1964, will become the largest group of older adults in history. This population of 77 million people is going to be better educated, healthier, and live longer than preceding generations. If the preparation they receive for retirement focuses only on financial and leisure readiness, a lifestyle of strictly recreation could become the norm. On the other hand, if getting ready for leisure activities is joined by an emphasis on continued responsibility as family members, then baby-boomers can make an enormous contribution to society. This possibility is supported by the emerging concept of grandparent education (Strom & Strom, 1991e).

REFERENCES

Bengston, V., & Robertson, J. (1985). *Grandparenthood*. Beverly Hills, CA: Sage Publications.

Elkind, D. (1990). *Grandparenting*. Glenview, IL: Scott, Foresman.

Kornhaber, A. (1986). *Between parents and grandparents*. New York: St. Martin's Press.

Stinnet, N., & DeFrain, J. (1985). *Secrets of strong families*. Boston: Little, Brown.

Strom, R., Bernard, H., & Strom, S. (1989). *Human development and learning*. New York: Human Sciences Press.

Strom, R., & Strom, S. (1985). Becoming a better grandparent. In *Growing together: An intergenerational sourcebook*, K. Struntz & S. Reville (eds.). Washington, DC: American Association of Retired Persons and Elvirita Lewis Foundation, pp. 57–60.

Strom, R., & Strom, S. (1987). Preparing grandparents for a new role. *The Journal of Applied Gerontology*, 6(4), 476–486.

Strom, R., & Strom, S. (1989). *Grandparent development*. Washington, DC: American Association of Retired Persons Andrus Foundation.

Strom, R., & Strom, S. (1990). Raising expectations for grandparents: A three-generational study. *International Journal of Aging and Human Development*, 31(3), 161–167.

Strom, R., & Strom, S. (1991a). *Achieving grandparent potential: A guidebook for building intergenerational relationships*. Newbury Park, CA: Sage Publications.

Strom, R., & Strom, S. (1991b). *Achieving grandparent potential: Viewpoints on building intergenerational relationships*. Newbury Park, CA: Sage Publications.

Strom, R., & Strom, S. (1991c). *Becoming a better grandparent: A guidebook for strengthening the family*. Newbury Park, CA: Sage Publications.

Strom, R., & Strom, S. (1991d). *Becoming a better grandparent: Viewpoints on strengthening the family*. Newbury Park, CA: Sage Publications.

Strom R., & Strom, S. (1991e). *Grandparent education: A guide for leaders*. Newbury Park, CA: Sage Publications.

Strom, R., Strom, S., & Collinsworth, P. (1990). Improving grandparent success. *The Journal of Applied Gerontology*, 9(4), 480–492.

Strom, R., Strom, S., & Collinsworth, P. (1991). The Grandparent Strengths and Needs Inventory: Development and factorial validation. *Educational and Psychological Measurement*, 51(4).

Toffler, A. (1990). *Powershift*. New York: Bantam Books.

Ageing
with attitude

Human beings are living longer and longer. At the same time, prejudice against older people is getting stronger. Where will this lead us? *Nikki van der Gaag* **explores the paradox and suggests a way forward.**

'Will you still need me, will you still feed me/When I'm 64?' The Beatles' song may be old itself, but it lies at the heart of what most of us fear about ageing—not death, but neglect; not the added years but lack of love, lack of respect.

We wake up on the morning of our 60th or 65th birthdays, and suddenly we are 'old age pensioners' and 'senior citizens'. We don't feel any different from the day or the month or the year before, but we are now officially 'old'. Suddenly we are no longer part of the workforce, no longer 'productive'.

And many people, both young and old, feed this feeling of uselessness by saying, "I've done my bit, I deserve a rest'. So they 'rest'. And the myth of old people as 'past it' is perpetuated from generation to generation.

It is a dangerous myth, not just for our own self-respect as we grow older, but also for a world with an ever-growing population and shrinking resources. If the 'old' do not participate in society, it is society's loss as well as their own.

'Ageing,' says Alex Kalache, Head of the Programme on Ageing at the London School of Hygiene and Tropical Medicine, 'is the number one problem in the world. And if it is not addressed *now*, there will be serious consequences.'[1]

It is the 'number one problem' because the numbers of people over 60 – and particularly those over 80 – are growing fast. In 1959 there were 200 million people over 60 in the world, accounting for eight per cent of the total population. By 2025 there will be 1.2 billion – 14 per cent of the total. Contrary to popular myth, by early in the next century three-quarters of these will live in the Third World.[2]

And it is in developing countries that the growth is greatest and the problems are most acute. Their elderly populations are growing at many times the rate of those in the North. For example, over the next 50 years the numbers of those over 60 in Britain will increase by 23 per cent and by 100 per cent in the US – but by 201 per cent in Bangladesh and 300 per cent in Brazil.[3]

Where Britain and the US, Australia and Canada have had 100 years to deal with increased longevity, China or Brazil have only 20 or 30 years to deal with the same rate of growth – and fewer resources with which to do so. And even countries which have had an older population for longer are struggling for positive ways of responding.

They are not helped by the fact that 'age' is a relative concept. Each one of us will

> **In Vilcabamba, you may not be considered 'old' until you are 90. In Potosi, you might be 'old' at 30**

know people in their sixties who regard themselves as 'old' – and are therefore seen as 'old' by everyone else. We will also know and people in their seventies, eighties or even nineties who remain very much part of society and who are mentally if not physically agile.

'Old' also varies from country to country and place to place. The Vilcabamba Valley in Ecuador, for example, is known locally as the *Valle de la Ancianidad* (Valley of Old Age) or the *Isla de Imunidad* (Island of Immunity). It is one of three places in the world where many people live to be over 100 – the others are in the Georgian Republic and in Pakistan. No-one really knows why, but a number of factors have been suggested, including the altitude, a mainly vegetable diet with little fat, reasonable work conditions, comparatively little stress, the beneficial effects of the *huilco* tree which recycles air – and the relative isolation of the valley.

Further down in South America, in Potosi in Bolivia, life expectancy is at the other extreme – people don't expect to live beyond their 40th birthday. Mining is the main occupation. The miners and their families suffer from harsh conditions, poverty, overwork, accidents, silicosis and other forms of lung poisoning.[4]

In Vilcabamba, you may not be considered 'old' until you are 90. In Potosi, you might be 'old' at 30.

So if we can't even really generalize about the meaning of 'old', can we say that there is an 'ageing crisis'? Under current conditions and in the light of today's population predictions, I think the answer must be 'yes'. As more and more people live longer and their numbers increase both in actual numbers and relative to the general population, there will be fewer people to care for them if and when they need it. The dependency ratio, as it is called, is also affected by the increasing financial pressures put on families, particularly in the Third World. More and more women everywhere are working. Because women form the vast majority of carers, this also affects the numbers of people able to support elderly members of the family. As governments squeeze pensions and health systems in an attempt to keep taxes low or to conform to the 'structural adjustment' policies imposed by the International Monetary Fund, it is old people who are likely to suffer most.

But this need not be. As Simone de Beauvoir said: 'The meaning or lack of meaning that old age takes on in any given society puts that whole society to the test.'

If so, governments and international agencies have failed that test – neither seriously addressing the issue nor seeing the need to invest major resources in it. For example, one of the main reasons that people in Africa or Asia or South America cite for having large numbers of children is to 'provide security' in old age. If people

From *New Internationalist*, February 1995, pp. 7-10. © 1995 by New Internationalist Publications, Ltd. Reprinted by permission.

knew that they could remain independent and yet be supported in their old age, then they would not feel the need to have so many children. Nor would they fear the isolation from society that arises from not having children. And yet, time after time, support for old people is ignored in discussions on population.

As it is 'old' people – both in the North and the South – have been increasingly

In almost every culture, financial independence gives older people respect from others and consequently more dignity

isolated from the rest of society in retirement homes which were seen as the model of how to deal with old age. People's need for health care increases as they grow older, and the seriously-disabled minority need special care and attention. But many people who do not have serious physical or mental disabilities have nonetheless been shut away in unsuitable homes, cut off from the rest of the world.

Today a growing number of governments are promoting another model which ostensibly helps people to live more independently: 'care in the community', as it is often known. What it usually means is 'care in the family' and in most cases it does not spring from a philosophical belief that families care best for their own but rather from the need to find a cheap solution to the problem of caring for the old.

In Muslim countries, putting the aged into old people's homes has always been anathema. King Hassan II has said that: 'If an old-age home were built in Morocco, I believe it would mean the country no longer existed. Moreover, I would be the first to burn it, in an act of auto-da-fé.'[5]

This is all very well, but it puts the burden of caring very much back into the family – usually the women. While families can in some cases provide the support needed, the breakdown of the extended family and the squeezing of household resources have often led to neglect of, rather than succour for the elderly. When resources are stretched, the old are likely to be the ones who go without.

It is precisely for this reason that in most of the world, 'old' people continue to work until they die. They have no choice. They need to earn an income – of sorts – or they don't eat. In Malawi, for example, a recent survey showed that 85 per cent of men over 65 were still part of the 'labour force'. In Liberia it was 70 per cent and in Guatemala, 63 per cent.[6] Indeed, people may even have to work harder as they get older, taking on

the manual labour that younger people do not want to do. Many have to uproot themselves – old women who outlive their husbands are forced to leave their villages to seek work in the cities. In most Third World countries, older people figure as part of the huge informal economy, selling vegetables on the streets or recycling garbage.

In almost every culture, financial independence gives older people more respect from others and consequently more dignity. Yet 'old' people are not considered to be officially productive because they are not usually earning an official wage.

All over the world older people, particularly women, are looking after grandchildren so that their daughters or sons can work. In parts of Africa particularly stricken by the AIDS epidemic, the young and sexually active have nearly all died, leaving the oldest generation to care for the youngest. And in Asia migration to the cities produces the same result.

Unpaid childcare, housework and people-maintenance is the work that makes the world go round. But in a world increasingly based on a cash economy this kind of work is not regarded as 'real work' and the size of their pay packet has become the only measure of a person's worth.

This is illustrated in a classic manner by the World Bank's recent report entitled: *Averting the Old Age crisis: policies to protect the old and promote growth*. This report pretty much ignored the informal economy and advocated a 'three-pillar approach' to financing the old which is based entirely on pensions. But even according to the World Bank, an estimated 60 per cent of the world's labour force and 70 per cent of old people, are part of the informal economy – they have no pension plan and are unlikely to be able to save.

Kasturi Sen, a specialist on ageing and policy issues, has quite a different strategy. She calls it the 'life-cycle approach'. The circumstances that people find themselves in when they are older, she says, is simply a continuation of the situation that they have been in throughout their lives. If you are poor, overworked and in ill-health when you are young, these conditions are likely to be the same or worse when you are old.

She argues that in order to improve the quality of peoples' lives – and especially the lives of women, who in most societies live longer – policies should aim at improving education in earlier life, helping people to move in and out of the labour market, and enabling women to take out financial credit and buy land. Better nutrition and access to contraception would improve health. These things, she says, would do more than anything else to 'reduce the possibilities of acute vulnerability in later stages of life'.[7]

In other words, the 'problem' of the elderly is something which concerns us not only in old age but in youth and middle age as well.

This is also one of the key messages of activist groups on ageing issues like the Gray Panthers. Started in the US in 1970 to oppose the war in Vietnam, they have become a worldwide network active on health care, housing, discrimination and work. Maggie Kuhn, one of the founders, is now in her eighties, but as feisty as ever. She spoke to Betty Friedan about the importance of old and young working together: 'Our philosophy was using gray power with the young for issues on the cutting edge of social change. I think we've established the fact that old age is a triumph. What we've done is establish the intergenerational bond necessary for real social change, the continuity of life. The old and the young need each other. We're opposed to the segregation of old people...

'The meaning or lack of meaning that old age takes on in any given society puts that whole society to the test'

Older people have so much to give to society...'[8]

The recognition that older people have valuable contributions to make is slowly permeating the thinking of development activists. Mark Gorman of HelpAge International recognizes that in recent years there has been 'a growing focus on the involvement of older people as active participants in development'.[9]

In Colombia, older people who are part of *Pro Vida* (For Life) have set up the city's first recycling scheme. In Kenya, a group of middle-aged women got together to tackle the problem of earning income in their later years. They set up schemes for clean water and a successful poultry-keeping project. They called themselves *Itambya Yaa Aka Kichakasimba* (women of Kichakasimba take a step ahead).[10]

In Argentina old people have been leading a militant grassroots campaign since the pension cuts of 1992. They held a 24-hour-a-day vigil in the Plaza de Mayo in Buenos Aires, enduring great cold and hardship until they were finally expelled by the police two months later. After that they began a vigil and protest every Thursday outside Parliament. Occasionally they stopped traffic, occupied government buildings and even scuffled with police and government officials in the streets of the capital.

On many occasions protesters were arrested but sometimes armed riot police withdrew before them, unable to frighten and unwilling to club down these dignified grandmothers. On 2 March 1994 thousands of elderly people converged on the centre of the capital to mark 100 weeks of these dramatic protests.[6]

Finally the Argentinian Government realized that they could not discredit the protesters. They raised pensions for the oldest, agreed to pay some of the money owed to the poorest and promised a reform of the pension system. But they failed to restore the cuts. So the old people took to the law. As of today, 350,000 court cases have been lodged with the High Court. Around 100,000 have already been won and the 'old people's' protest threatens to throw the whole economic policy of the Argentinian Government off course.

We too can push for change in policy and in attitudes – including our own. We can plan for our old age like the women of Kichakasimba. And we can work together, young, middle-aged and old, to ensure that everyone has enough to provide them with a satisfying and dignified life.

1999 will be the International Year of Ageing. Let us use the four years between now and then to take up the challenge of David Pitt, a non-retired 'retired person' who volunteers here at the *New Internationalist*:

'Let us direct our energies against those responsible for the poverty... and for declining health services. Let us also do what we can to support those living in other countries where care for the aged is a matter of gross neglect. Let us band together and be willful and cantankerous and obstreperous. Above all, let us never apologize for growing old.'

1 Quotes from Alex Kalache taken from an interview by Nikki van der Gaag. 2 MSJ Pathy (Ed.) 'Ageing in Developing Countries' by Alex Kalache in *Principles and Practices of Geriatric Medicine*, John Wiley 1991. 3 Kasturi Sen *Ageing – Debates on demographic transition and social policy*, Zed Press 1994. 4 Ken Tout *Ageing in Developing Countries*, Oxford University Press 1989. 5 Jeannine Jacquemin *Elderly Women and the Family* Soroptomist International. 6 Suzanne S Paul and James A Paul *Humanity Comes of Age*, WCC Publications 1994. 7 Kasturi Sen *Women in later life: health, security and poverty*, International Health Exchange, April 1994. 8 Betty Friedan *The Fountain of Age*, Vintage 1993. 9 Mark Gorman from a discussion with Nikki van der Gaag 10 United Nations *The World Aging Situation* 1991.

The Solace of Patterns

The strange attractors that define life's stages give shape even to grief

ROBERT M. SAPOLSKY

Robert M. Sapolsky is a MacArthur Fellow and a professor of biological sciences and neuroscience at Stanford University. His most recent book, Why Zebras Don't Get Ulcers: A Guide to Stress, Stress-Related Diseases, *and Coping, is published by W. H. Freeman and Company.*

A SHORT TIME AGO MY FATHER died, having spent far too many of his last years in pain and degeneration. Although I had expected his death and tried to prepare myself for it, when the time came it naturally turned out that you really can't prepare. A week afterward I found myself back at work, bludgeoned by emotions that swirled around a numb core of unreality—a feeling of disconnection from the events that had just taken place on the other side of the continent, of disbelief that it was really him frozen in that nightmare of stillness. The members of my laboratory were solicitous. One, a medical student, asked me how I was doing, and I replied, "Well, today it seems as if I must have imagined it all." "That makes sense," she said. "Don't forget about DABDA."

DABDA. In 1969 the psychiatrist Elisabeth Kübler-Ross published a landmark book, *On Death and Dying*. Drawing on her research with terminally ill people and their families, she described the process whereby people mourn the death of others and, when impending, of themselves. Most of us, she observed, go through a fairly well defined sequence of stages. First we deny the death is happening. Then we become angry at the unfairness of it all. We pass through a stage of irrational bargaining, with the doctors, with God: *Just let this not be fatal and I will change my ways. Please, just wait until Christmas.* There follows a stage of depression and, if one is fortunate, the final chapter, serene acceptance. The sequence is not ironclad; indi-

viduals may skip certain stages, experience them out of order or regress to earlier ones. DABDA, moreover, is generally thought to give a better description of one's own preparation for dying than of one's mourning the demise of someone else. Nevertheless, there is a broadly recognized consistency in the overall pattern of mourning: denial, anger, bargaining, depression, acceptance. I was stuck at stage one, right on schedule.

Brevity is the soul of DABDA. A few years ago I saw that point brilliantly dramatized on television—on, of all programs, *The Simpsons*. It was the episode in which Homer, the father, accidentally eats a poisonous fish and is told he has twenty-four hours to live. There ensues a thirty-second sequence in which the cartoon character races through the death and dying stages, something like this: "No way! I'm not dying." He ponders a second, then grabs the doctor by the neck. "Why you little. . . ." He trembles in fear, then pleads, "Doc, get me outta this! I'll make it worth your while." Finally he composes himself and says, "Well, we all gotta go sometime." I thought it was hilarious. Homer substituted fear for depression and got it on the other side of anger. Even so, here was a cartoon suitable to be watched happily by children, and the writers had sneaked in a parody of Kübler-Ross.

But for sheer conciseness, of course, Homer Simpson's vignette has nothing on DABDA. That's why medical students, my laboratory colleague included, memorize the acronym along with hundreds of other mnemonic devices in preparation for their national board examinations. What strikes me now is the power of those letters to encapsulate human experience. My father, by dint of having been human, was unique; thus was my relationship to him, and thus must be my grieving. And yet I come up with something reducible to a medical school acronym. Poems, paintings, symphonies by the most creative artists who ever lived have been born out of mourning; yet, on some level, they all sprang from the pattern invoked by two

pedestrian syllables of pseudo-English. We cry, we rage, we demand that the oceans' waves stop, that the planets halt their movements in the sky, all because the earth will no longer be graced by the one who sang lullabies as no one else could; yet that, too, is reducible to DABDA. Why should grief be so stereotypical?

SCIENTISTS WHO STUDY HUMAN THOUGHT and behavior have discerned many stereotyped, structured stages through which all of us move at various times. Some of the sequences are obvious, their logic a quick study. It is no surprise that infants learn to crawl before they take their first tentative steps, and only later learn to run. Other sequences are more subtle. Freudians claim that in normal development the child undergoes the invariant transition from a so-called oral stage to an anal stage to a genital stage, and they attribute various aspects of psychological dysfunction in the adult to an earlier failure to move successfully from one stage to the next.

Similarly, the Swiss psychologist Jean Piaget mapped stages of cognitive development. For example, he noted, there is a stage at which children begin to grasp the concept of object permanence: Before that developmental transition, a toy does not exist once it is removed from the child's sight. Afterward, the toy exists—and the child will look for it—even when it is no longer visible. Only at a reliably later stage do children begin to grasp concepts such as the conservation of volume—that two pitchers of different shapes can hold the same quantity of liquid. The same developmental patterns occur across numerous cultures, and so the sequence seems to describe the universal way that human beings learn to comprehend a cognitively complex world.

The American psychologist Lawrence Kohlberg mapped the stereotyped stages people undergo in developing morally. At one early stage of life, moral decisions are based on rules and on the motivation to avoid punishment: actions considered for their effects on oneself. Only at a later stage are decisions made on the basis of a respect for the community: actions considered for their effects on others. Later still, and far more rarely, some people develop a morality driven by a set of their own internalized standards, derived from a sense of what is right and what is wrong for all possible communities. The pattern is progressive: people who now act out of conscience invariably, at some earlier stage of life, believed that you don't do bad things because you might get caught.

The American psychoanalyst Erik Erikson discerned a sequence of psychosocial development, framing it as crises that a person resolves or fails to resolve at each stage. For infants, the issue is whether one attains a basic attitude of trust toward the world; for adolescents, it is identity versus identity confusion; for young adults, intimacy versus isolation; for adults, generativity versus stagnation; and for the aged, peaceful acceptance and integrity versus despair. Erikson's pioneering insight that one's later years represent a series of transitions that must be successfully negotiated is reflected in a quip by the geriatrician Walter M. Bortz II of Stanford University Medical School. Asked whether he was interested in curing aging, Bortz responded, "No, I'm not interested in arrested development."

Those are some of the patterns we all are reported or theorized to have in common, across many settings and cultures. I think such conceptualizations are often legitimate, not just artificial structures that scientists impose on inchoate reality. Why should we share such patterning? It is certainly not for lack of alternatives. As living beings, we represent complex, organized systems—an eddy in the random entropy of the universe. When all the possibilities are taken into account, it is supremely unlikely for elements to assemble themselves into molecules, for molecules to form cells, for vast assemblages of cells to form us. How much more unlikely, it seems, that such complex organisms conform to such relatively simple patterns of behavior, of development, of thought.

ONE WAY OF COMING TO GRIPS WITH the properties of complex systems is through a field of mathematics devoted to the study of so-called cellular automata. The best way of explaining its style of analysis is by example. Imagine a long row of boxes—some black, some white—arranged to form some initial pattern, a starting stage. The row of boxes is to give rise to a second row, just below the first. The way that takes place in a cellular automaton is that each box in the first row is subjected to a set of reproduction rules. For example, one rule might stipulate that a black box in the first row gives rise to a black box immediately below it in the next row, only if exactly one of its two nearest neighbors is black. Other rules

MOST COMPLEX PATTERNS collapse into extinction. Only a few combinations beat the odds.

might apply to a black box flanked by two white boxes or two black boxes. Once the set of rules is applied to each box in the first row, a second row of black and white boxes is generated; then the rules are applied again to each box in the second row to generate a third row and so on.

Metaphorically, each row represents one generation, one tick of a clock. A properly programmed computer could track any possible combination of colored boxes, following any conceivable set of reproduction rules, down through the generations. In the vast majority of cases, somewhere down the line it would end up with a row of boxes all the same color. After that, the single color would repeat itself forever. In other words, the line would go extinct.

Return now to my earlier question: How can it be, in this entropic world, that we human beings share so many stable patterns—one nose; two eyes; a reliable lag time before we learn object permanence; happier adulthoods if we become confident about our identities as adolescents; a tendency to find it hard to believe in tragedy when it strikes? What keeps us from following an almost infinite number of alternative developmental paths? The studies of cellular automata provide a hint.

Not all complex patterns, it turns out, eventually collapse into extinction. A few combinations of starting states and reproduction rules beat the odds and settle down into mature stable patterns that continue down through the generations forever. In general, it is impossible to predict whether a given starting state will survive, let alone which pattern it will generate after, say, n generations. The only way to tell is to crank it through the computer and see. It has been shown, however, that a surprisingly small number of such mature patterns are possible.

A similar tendency in living systems has long been known to evolutionary biologists. They call it convergence. Among the staggering number of species on this planet, there are only a few handfuls of solutions to the problem of how to locomote, how to conserve fluids in a hot environment, how to store and mobilize energy. And among the staggering variety of humans, it may be a convergent feature of our complexity that there are a small number of ways in which we grow through life or mourn its inevitabilities.

IN AN ENTROPIC WORLD, WE CAN TAKE a common comfort from our common patterns, and there is often consolation in

attributing such patterns to forces larger than ourselves. As an atheist, I have long taken an almost religious solace from a story by the Argentine minimalist Jorge Luis Borges. In his famous short story, *The Library of Babel,* Borges describes the world as a library filled with an unimaginably vast number of books, each with the same number of pages and the same number of letters on each page. The library contains a single copy of every possible book, every possible permutation of letters. People spend their lives sorting through this ocean of gibberish for the incalculably rare books whose random arrays of letters form something meaningful, searching above all else for the single book (which must exist) that explains everything. And of course, given the completeness of the library, in addition to that perfect book, there must also be one that convincingly disproves the conclusions put forth in it, and yet another book that refutes the malicious solipsisms of the second book, plus hundreds of thousands of books that differ from any of those three by a single letter or a comma.

The narrator writes in his old age, in an isolation brought about by the suicides of people who have been driven to despair by the futility of wandering through the library. In this parable of the search for meaning amid entropy, Borges concludes:

Those who judge [the library to be finite] postulate that in remote places the corridors and stairways and hexagons can conceivably come to an end—which is absurd. Those who imagine it to be without limit forget that the possible number of books does have such a limit. I venture to suggest this solution to the ancient problem: *The library is unlimited and cyclical.* If an eternal traveler were to cross it in any direction, after centuries he would see that the same volumes were repeated in the same disorder (which, thus repeated, would be an order: the Order). My solitude is gladdened by this elegant hope.

IT APPEARS THAT AMID THE ORDER WITH which we mature and decline, there is an order to our mourning. And my own recent solitude is gladdened by that elegant hope, in at least two ways. One is inward-looking. This stereotypy, this ordering, brings the promise of solace in the predicted final stage: if one is fortunate, DABDA ends in *A*.

Another hope looks outward, to a world whose tragedies are inexorably delivered from its remotest corners to our nightly news. Look at the image of a survivor of some carnage and, knowing nothing of her language, culture, beliefs or circumstances, you can still recognize in the fixed action patterns of her facial muscles the unmistakable lineaments of grief. That instant recognition, the universal predictability of certain aspects of human beings, whether in a facial expression or in the stages of mourning, is an emblem of our kinship and an imperative of empathy.

Index

Credits/Acknowledgments

Cover design by Charles Vitelli

1. Genetic and Prenatal Influences on Development
Facing overview—UNICEF photo "Mother and Child" by Oskar Kokoschka.

2. Development during Infancy and Early Childhood
Facing overview—Photo by Leslie Holmes Lawlor.

3. Development during Childhood: Cognition and Schooling.
Facing overview—Photo by Cheryl Greenleaf. 94—Illustration by John Michael Yanson.

4. Development during Childhood: Family and Culture
Facing overview—New York Times Pictures photo by Steve Miller.

5. Development during Adolescence and Young Adulthood
Facing overview—Photo by Louis P. Raucci.

6. Development during Middle and Late Adulthood
Facing overview—Photo by Addie Raucci.

ANNUAL EDITIONS **ARTICLE REVIEW FORM**

■ NAME: _____ DATE: _____

■ TITLE AND NUMBER OF ARTICLE: _____

■ BRIEFLY STATE THE MAIN IDEA OF THIS ARTICLE: _____

_____

■ LIST THREE IMPORTANT FACTS THAT THE AUTHOR USES TO SUPPORT THE MAIN IDEA:

_____

_____

_____

_____

_____

■ WHAT INFORMATION OR IDEAS DISCUSSED IN THIS ARTICLE ARE ALSO DISCUSSED IN YOUR
TEXTBOOK OR OTHER READINGS THAT YOU HAVE DONE? LIST THE TEXTBOOK CHAPTERS AND
PAGE NUMBERS:

_____

_____

_____

_____

_____

■ LIST ANY EXAMPLES OF BIAS OR FAULTY REASONING THAT YOU FOUND IN THE ARTICLE:

_____

_____

_____

_____

■ LIST ANY NEW TERMS/CONCEPTS THAT WERE DISCUSSED IN THE ARTICLE, AND WRITE A SHORT
DEFINITION:

_____

_____

_____

_____

We Want Your Advice

ANNUAL EDITIONS revisions depend on two major opinion sources: one is our Advisory Board, listed in the front of this volume, which works with us in scanning the thousands of articles published in the public press each year; the other is you—the person actually using the book. Please help us and the users of the next edition by completing the prepaid article rating form on this page and returning it to us. Thank you for your help!

ANNUAL EDITIONS: HUMAN DEVELOPMENT 97/98
Article Rating Form

Here is an opportunity for you to have direct input into the next revision of this volume. We would like you to rate each of the 47 articles listed below, using the following scale:

1. **Excellent: should definitely be retained**
2. **Above average: should probably be retained**
3. **Below average: should probably be deleted**
4. **Poor: should definitely be deleted**

Your ratings will play a vital part in the next revision. So please mail this prepaid form to us just as soon as you complete it.
Thanks for your help!

Rating	Article	Rating	Article
	1. Unraveling the Mystery of Life		25. Children Who Witness Domestic Violence: The Invisible Victims
	2. Biologists Find Key Genes That Shape Patterning of Embryos		26. The Lasting Effects of Child Maltreatment
	3. Choosing a Perfect Child		27. Alienation and the Four Worlds of Childhood
	4. The Role of Lifestyle in Preventing Low Birth Weight		28. WAAAH!! Why Kids Have a Lot to Cry About
	5. Cocaine-Exposed Infants: Myths and Misunderstandings		29. The Miracle of Resiliency
	6. Sperm under Siege		30. TV Violence: Myth and Reality
	7. How Breast Milk Protects Newborns		31. Adolescence: Whose Hell Is It?
	8. The Amazing Minds of Infants		32. Teenage Turning Point
	9. The Realistic View of Biology and Behavior		33. Sports Lift Esteem in Young Athletes
	10. Case Studies of Environmental Risks to Children		34. What Is a Bad Kid? Answers of Adolescents and Their Mothers in Three Cultures
	11. Your Child's Brain		35. HIV Infected Youth Speaks about Needs for Support and Health Care
	12. Changing Demographics: Past and Future Demands for Early Childhood Programs		36. Psychotrends: Taking Stock of Tomorrow's Family and Sexuality
	13. Assertiveness vs. Aggressiveness: What's the Difference?		37. Who Stole Fertility?
	14. It's Magical! It's Malleable! It's . . . Memory		38. Is There Love after Baby?
	15. DNA-Environment Mix Forms Intellectual Fate		39. Why They Stay: A Saga of Spouse Abuse
	16. Malnutrition, Poverty, and Intellectual Development		40. Man's World, Woman's World? Brain Studies Point to Differences
	17. Life in Overdrive		41. Stress: It's Worse Than You Think
	18. The EQ Factor		42. Midlife Myths
	19. Bell, Book, and Scandal		43. Learning to Love (Gulp!) Growing Old
	20. The Role of Schools in Sustaining Early Childhood Program Benefits		44. Studies Suggest Older Minds Are Stronger than Expected
	21. Fears in the Classroom: Psychological Issues and Pedagogical Implications		45. Grandparent Development and Influence
	22. Your Loving Touch		46. Ageing with Attitude
	23. Fathers' Time		47. The Solace of Patterns
	24. Sibling Connections		

(Continued on next page)

ABOUT YOU

Name _____ Date _____

Are you a teacher? ❏ Or a student? ❏

Your school name _____

Department _____

Address _____

City _____ State _____ Zip _____

School telephone # _____

YOUR COMMENTS ARE IMPORTANT TO US!

Please fill in the following information:

For which course did you use this book? _____

Did you use a text with this *ANNUAL EDITION*? ❏ yes ❏ no

What was the title of the text? _____

What are your general reactions to the *Annual Editions* concept?

Have you read any particular articles recently that you think should be included in the next edition?

Are there any articles you feel should be replaced in the next edition? Why?

Are there other areas that you feel would utilize an *ANNUAL EDITION?*

May we contact you for editorial input?

May we quote you from above?

ANNUAL EDITIONS: HUMAN DEVELOPMENT 97/98

BUSINESS REPLY MAIL

First Class   Permit No. 84   Guilford, CT

Postage will be paid by addressee

Dushkin Publishing Group/
Brown & Benchmark Publishers
Sluice Dock
Guilford, Connecticut 06437